PENGUIN BOOKS

EMERSON AMONG THE ECCENTRICS

Carlos Baker was a distinguished scholar and literary critic at Princeton University for more than forty years. In addition to novels, short stories, and poetry, he is the author of the land-mark biography *Ernest Hemingway: A Life Story*, which was translated into twelve languages, and the editor of *Ernest Hemingway: Selected Letters, 1917–1961*. *Emerson Among the Eccentrics* was completed just before his death in 1987.

Also by Carlos Baker

CRITICISM

Shelley's Major Poetry: The Fabric of a Vision
Hemingway: The Writer as Artist
The Echoing Green:
  Romanticism, Modernism, and the Phenomena
  of Transference in Poetry

BIOGRAPHY

Hemingway: A Short Critical Biography
Ernest Hemingway: A Life Story

FICTION

A Friend in Power
The Land of Rumbelow
The Gay Head Conspiracy
The Talismans and Other Stories

POETRY

Shadows in Stone
A Year and a Day

EMERSON AMONG THE ECCENTRICS

A Group Portrait

Carlos Baker

Introduction and Epilogue by James R. Mellow

PENGUIN BOOKS

PENGUIN BOOKS
Published by the Penguin Group
Penguin Putnam Inc., 375 Hudson Street,
New York, New York 10014, U.S.A.
Penguin Books Ltd, 27 Wrights Lane,
London W8 5TZ, England
Penguin Books Australia Ltd, Ringwood,
Victoria, Australia
Penguin Books Canada Ltd, 10 Alcorn Avenue,
Toronto, Ontario, Canada M4V 3B2
Penguin Books (N.Z.) Ltd, 182–190 Wairau Road,
Auckland 10, New Zealand

Penguin Books Ltd, Registered Offices:
Harmondsworth, Middlesex, England

First published in the United States of America by Viking Penguin,
a division of Penguin Books USA Inc. 1996
Published in Penguin Books 1997

10 9 8 7 6 5 4 3 2

THE LIBRARY OF CONGRESS HAS CATALOGUED THE HARDCOVER AS FOLLOWS:
Baker, Carlos, 1909–1987.
Emerson among the eccentrics / by Carlos Baker.
p.   cm.
Includes bibliographical references and index.
ISBN 0-670-86675-X (hc.)
ISBN 0 14 02.6029 3 (pbk.)
1. Emerson, Ralph Waldo, 1803–1882—Friends and associates.   2. Eccentrics and
eccentricities—United States—Biography.   3. Emerson, Ralph Waldo, 1803–1882—Contemporaries.
4. United States—Intellectual life—19th century.   5. Authors, American—19th century—Biography.
I. Title.
PS1633.B34 1996
814'.3—dc20
[b]   95–34146

Printed in the United States of America
Set in Bulmer
Designed by Brian Mulligan

CONTENTS

Part Two: THE FORTIES

Part Three: THE FIFTIES

Part Four: THE SIXTIES

Part Five: THE SEVENTIES

ACKNOWLEDGMENTS

Since Carlos Baker is not here to thank the myriad persons who assisted him in research for this volume, I can only thank those who helped me in various ways to bring the manuscript to press.

I give sincere thanks to James R. Mellow and to Donald Fehr of Viking for their loyal support of this project. My mother, Dorothy S. Baker; my sister, Diane Wagner; my brother, Brian Baker; and Samuel W. Lambert III, Esq., have been helpful throughout. Carlos Baker wished to thank Professor Janet Martin and Colonel Lawrence Spellman.

Archivists Marcia E. Moss, Joyce Woodsman, and Leslie Wilson are also due special thanks for their kind and learned assistance at the Concord Free Public Library.

For help of various kinds I thank Stephen and Michael Carter, Carl F. Hovde, Mary Mygatt, Edward Marks, Margery B. Lesnak, Nancy Craig Simmons, and Leslie A. Morris.

My daughter Catherine E. Carter has provided valuable help in editorial and procedural matters. My husband, Paul D. Carter, has offered total support in research, organization, editorial, and proofreading functions, for which I am profoundly grateful.

—Elizabeth B. Carter

INTRODUCTION

IN THE MORNING OF THE REPUBLIC, CONCORD STILL HELD its honored place as the spot where once, in Ralph Waldo Emerson's rousing lines, "the embattled farmers stood / And fired the shot heard round the world." Its more enduring fame, however, would derive from the extraordinary congregation of individuals who settled and visited there during the eventful span of the nineteenth century. Emerson, undoubtedly, was the town's foremost citizen, but certainly Henry Thoreau, Nathaniel Hawthorne, and Amos Bronson Alcott figured prominently among the writers, poets, teachers, and Transcendentalists who made Concord a mecca for American intellectuals. Margaret Fuller, Elizabeth Palmer Peabody, Walt Whitman, even the militant abolitionist John Brown were also drawn there in the course of their careers.

It was typical of Emerson's probity that he recognized that in the nineteenth century the subject of a biography could be charged with complicity in the writing of his life. "I have the feeling that every man's biography is at his own expense," Emerson claimed. "He furnishes not only the facts, but the report. I mean that all biography is autobiography. It is only what he tells himself that comes to be known and believed." This was certainly more true of Emerson than of many another man of his time. His voluminous journals, his wide-ranging friendships, his extensive correspondence—to say nothing of his published writings and lectures—were hostages to biography. We can probably excuse him for not knowing that the general relaxation of American morals and the investigative skills of later biographers would give the biographical tribe access not only to the civilities of the parlor but to the guilty secrets of bedrooms, motels, and backrooms and boardrooms. It says something about Emerson's character that he was too high-minded for the latter approach in his own lifetime—and still is in ours. "His ideas of friendship, as of love," said his contemporary and friend, Oliver Wendell Holmes, "seem almost too exalted for our earthly conditions." Yet Holmes was not so privy to Emerson's views as was Margaret Fuller, to whom Emerson, during one of their September talks in the Concord woods, confided that "Love was only phenomenal, a contrivance of nature. . . ." A startling idea that may have meant only that Margaret Fuller had been pursuing the subject too ardently.

Emerson was one of the most interesting American minds of his century—not only at home but abroad. His English admirers included Thomas Carlyle, with whom he had a lengthy correspondence, and George Eliot, with whom he shared a fondness for Rousseau's *Confessions*. In Paris, as early as the 1840s, an Emerson cell had been established at the Collège de France by such illustrious professors as the exiled Polish patriot Adam Mickiewicz and the social historian Jules Michelet. The radical, bluestocking Comtesse d'Agoult, writing under the pseudonym of Daniel Stern, considered Emerson the personification of American genius. In Concord, Emerson's parlor became an obligatory stop for traveling Europeans like the Swedish novelist Fredrika Bremer and the controversial English abolitionist Harriet Martineau.

When, in the early 1970s, Carlos Baker began work on *Emerson Among the Eccentrics* he set down some notes on his intentions:

> To write what will amount to a new biography of Emerson, developed by reference to some of his leading friendships, chiefly but not exclusively literary. These will include Alcott, Edward Thompson Taylor, Jones Very, Margaret Fuller, Thoreau, Hawthorne, Theodore Parker, Walt Whitman, Mary Moody Emerson, Charles Newcomb and Ellery Channing. Through [Emerson's] connections with these, it should be possible to watch the unfolding of his religious, literary, and political ideas, his changing views of nature, man and God; to show how his friends reflected, contradicted, partly diverged from, or zealously mis-

represented his philosophical and ethical teachings; to use their views to throw light on his, and his to throw light on them in a program of spiritual ecology, complicated by the fact that he both half-created the climate of opinion by which he was nurtured, while partly adapting his opinions to the ideological environment which local and national events thrust upon him.

As a group biography, then, it would comprise a network of relationships that would flesh out an age as well as the man. By concentrating on Emerson's letters and journals as well as the writings of his contemporaries, it was Baker's "aim and hope" to bring Emerson "to life in his quotidian relationships; young man and old, husband, father, son, and brother; preacher, lecturer, editor, clubman; farmer, householder, host and guest." That Baker has done, admirably; the Emerson book is the masterwork of his last years, one more book in the rediscovery of the American past for which a reader should be grateful. The extensive quotations from the journals and letters of the period give voice once again to nineteenth-century thought and discourse in a compelling way.

Baker, understandably, was best known for his landmark biography of Hemingway, *Ernest Hemingway: A Life Story*, first published in 1969 and subsequently translated into twelve languages. As a professor at Princeton, he was appreciated for his courses in the English Romantics and in modern American Literature. He had a reputation, too, as a novelist, short-story writer, and poet. As early as 1934, he had become interested in the writers of the American Renaissance, having published an article on Emerson and the mad poet Jones Very in the *New England Quarterly*. His Emerson project, however, was put aside while he undertook the major task of editing the Hemingway letters (*Ernest Hemingway: Selected Letters, 1917–1961*; published in 1981). It was only later that he was able to take up the Emerson book again, which he worked on until 1986, some months before his death from cancer in April 1987. He had completed most of the book, with the exception of an introduction in which he had intended to discuss, appropriately for a group biography, Emerson's philosophy of friendship. (He left a handful of notes and ideas on the subject.) He had also intended to write an epilogue to be entitled "Exeunt Omnes," presumably a summary closure to the lives of the remaining cast of characters with whom he had been dealing. It was one of

Baker's regrets at the end of his life that his Emerson book might not be published. His daughter, Elizabeth Carter, wisely recognized that the book was virtually complete as it stood. She has updated her father's extensive notes and citations for publication. At her request, I agreed to provide a brief introduction and an epilogue. I have made no attempt to match Carlos's style or his intentions. The book is very much as Carlos Baker wrote it.

A biography that begins when its principal subject is twenty-seven is unusual. By the early 1830s—the decade with which Baker's biography begins—Emerson (1803–1882) had lost his first wife, Ellen, who died of tuberculosis after sixteen months of marriage. (Emerson regularly walked from Boston to a Roxbury cemetery to visit her grave.) Two of his brothers had only recently been confined in the McLean Asylum in Charlestown. He was responsible for the partial support of his widowed mother. (His minister-father had died when Emerson was only a few days short of his eighth birthday.) At the age that we meet him, he is suffering through a crisis of faith and will shortly give up his pastorate in the Second Church of Boston. Yet, paradoxically, he is a man and a philosopher on the verge of his public life.

Baker's study adds immeasurably to a more intimate portrait of the Sage of Concord than the steel engraving many of us remember from earlier high school and college texts. And his "philosophy of friendship," as Baker refers to it, was hardly the sentimental or spiritual approach that Holmes considered. In his essay "Friendship," Emerson reported that the friend, among other virtues, should also serve an adversarial role, should be "for ever a sort of beautiful enemy, untamable, devoutly revered, and not a trivial conveniency to be soon outgrown and cast aside." Emerson relished the opportunity of meeting other minds and opinions. But he could also rail against the "devastators of the day" who cornered him in his study and used up his time. Among Baker's notes for the introduction one finds quotes that reveal Emerson's ambivalence on the subject, particularly after a siege of visitors. "A barn chamber with a salad or a potato would seem to be the needful regimen for weeks and moons of a hermit so dangerously favored by the Social Gods," he complains in a letter to Margaret Fuller. Oddly, he took the same nutritional approach when stressing the opposite point of view. "To live in a field of pumpkins, yet eat no pie!" he writes in a queer entry in his journal during harvest season. One needs to know that pie was Emerson's indispensable choice for breakfast and that the neighbors in the pumpkin patch of Concord included the likes of Thoreau, Alcott, and the usually taciturn Hawthorne. It is the down-to-earth Emerson that one becomes acquainted with in Baker's pages.

Emerson Among the Eccentrics is an invaluable book, relaxed and spirited in style, a joy to read with its insights on national character and national ambition during a period of American life that still needs study and reappraisal. It alters one's sense of Emerson the man; it revives one's appreciation of Emerson the observer and thinker. And it confirms what seems to me the mission of any biographer: to make readers aware that a country that loses touch with its past—its cultural as well as its historic past—is a country that has lost touch with itself.

—James R. Mellow
Folly Cove, July 1995

Part One

THE

THIRTIES

Chapter One

THE
BROTHERS

BY THE TIME OF HER DEATH AT AGE EIGHTY-FIVE IN THE fall of 1853, Ruth Haskins Emerson had long been the gentle matriarch of the branch of the family into which she had married in 1796. Having outlived her husband, the Reverend William Emerson, by more than forty years, she had assiduously raised five of the eight children that she had borne to him. Phebe, John Clarke, and Mary Caroline all died in childhood, and their father lived only to the age of forty-two. By 1814, the family consisted of the small and energetic widow and her five sons, ranging in age from thirteen to six. The five brothers were named William, Ralph Waldo, Edward, Robert Bulkeley, and Charles. "She kept her family together," wrote Ralph Waldo after her death, "and at once adopted the only means open to her by receiving boarders into her house." By the early 1830s, with "the assistance of some excellent friends," all but one of the boys had been graduated from Harvard College. As Waldo added, "Her children as they grew up had abundant reason to thank her prudence which secured to them an education. . . I remember being struck with the comment of a lady . . . when some debate arose about my Mother's 'thrift' in her time: 'Ah, but she secured the essentials. She got the children educated.' "

In spite of a paternal ancestry in which clergymen had predominated for seven generations, Waldo was the only son who chose that profession, and even he did not stay with it for long. The eldest boy, William, studied theology at Göttingen for a short time in the middle 1820s, but soon dropped his plans in favor of the law. Both Edward and Charles followed his example as if they hoped, after the penury of their boyhood, to succeed in a profession that promised higher monetary rewards than they could have earned through preaching. Or teaching, though William and Waldo, Edward and Charles all served as schoolmasters during or after their college years in order to help support their quietly heroic mother and to minimize their gradually mounting debts.

Apart from the genteel poverty from which they were seeking to emerge, two darker shadows overhung the fortunes of the five brothers. One was tuberculosis, which had killed John Clarke at the eight of eight and hastened, if it did not immediately cause, the father's death in what might have been his prime. Doctors had urged Edward to take a recuperative voyage as early as 1822, and Waldo had been obliged to spend the winter of 1826–27 in South Carolina and Florida in an attempt, luckily successful, to stave off the incursions of the same disease. His young wife, Ellen Tucker, was to die of tuberculosis in 1831 after only a year and a half of marriage, and the health of both Edward and Charles was always precarious owing to persistent weakness of the lungs.

The other shadow was that of mental illness. One March day in 1833, Waldo's *cicerone* conducted him through the Spedale dei Pazzi, the insane asylum of Palermo. "I did not know where I was going," he wrote in his travel diary, "or should not have visited it. I could not help them and have seen enough of their sad malady without coming to Sicily." Behind his journal entry lay his memories of the McLean Asylum, an American Spedale dei Pazzi in Charlestown, Massachusetts, where two of his brothers had been confined some five years earlier, and one of the two even more recently.

Bulkeley, the fourth of the living sons, was mentally retarded and emotionally unstable. From late adolescence he had been boarded out sporadically, and he divided his time between simple labors on the farmstead of Israel Putnam in Chelmsford, the village where Waldo had taught school in the fall of 1825, and frequent and often prolonged visits to McLean. In a letter sent from Chelmsford in December 1825, Waldo had written, "Bulkeley is perfectly deranged and has been ever since I have been here"—a matter of three months. Poor Bulkeley was seldom better than "pretty well," with periods of relative calm between outbursts of dementia. He had a loud voice and was of course eager to be recognized as more nearly normal than he ever could be-

come. Easily irritated, notably garrulous, he sometimes displayed a sly ingenuity characteristic of his disease. In the spring of 1827 he escaped his caretaker for a two-week ramble that led him to Mount Vernon, New Hampshire.
There he made door-to-door calls bearing a roughly written paper that said
he was organizing a singing school. He had lined up some fifteen gullible
subscribers before the village fathers found him out and sent him back to
Chelmsford.

All the Emerson brothers were fiercely determined to make their way in
the world. Following his return from Europe, William established himself in
New York, studying law at the Wall Street offices of Ketchum and Fessenden
and living in garret rooms upstairs. "How dare you work so hard?" wrote
Waldo. "Have you forgotten that all the Emersons overdo themselves? Dont
you die of the leprosy of your race—ill weaved ambition. Pah how it smells,
I'll none of it. Why here am I lounging on a system for these many months
writing something less than a sermon a month for my main business,—all the
rest of the time being devoted to needful recreation after such unparalleled ex-
ertions. And the consequence is—I begin to mend, and am said to look less
like a monument and more like a man. I cant persuade that wilful brother Edward of mine to use the same sovereign nostrum."

The handsome, fair-haired, blue-eyed Edward, two years younger than
Waldo, had begun the study of law in the Boston firm of the renowned Daniel
Webster. But the perilous state of his health sent him abroad between the Oc-
tobers of 1825–26, and he had been home only a year and a half when he suffered a severe nervous breakdown. Toward the end of May 1828, a month
after Waldo had warned William not to overdo, Edward was seized with faint-
ing fits that obliged him to abandon his legal work in Boston. A month later
he became "violently" deranged, requiring physical restraint, and his distraught brother Waldo carried him to McLean Asylum, where Bulkeley was
already a patient. The two young men shared their limbo until late July, when
Waldo conducted Bulkeley back to Chelmsford. But Edward was obliged to
stay on through the whole summer and fall. Waldo looked in on him as often
as possible, and wrote in his journal of "the constitutional calamity of my
family which in its falling upon Edward has buried at once so many towering
hopes."

He had few such fears about himself. Providence, he thought, had tem-
pered his intellectual frame with "much mixture of *silliness.*" Where Edward

"lived and acted and spoke," as he was now doing, "with preternatural energy," Waldo called his own manner sluggish and his speech "embarrassed and ragged." Edward "had always great power of face"; Waldo believed (falsely) that he had none. Such built-in imperfections kept him, he felt, from the kind of illness that had stricken his too-energetic brother. Yet it was he who had taken charge in the face of calamity. "We are devising how he shall leave Charlestown," he wrote on November 10, 1828. Edward's illness had lasted a full six months before he was released in Waldo's care.

For Edward the whole affair had been like a tragic fall from high estate— Edward, so handsome, so poised, who walked always with a "military carriage," and had led his class of 1824 at Harvard with his eloquence, his surging ambition, and his marked executive ability, easily convincing others of what Waldo called his "rich inherent worth." Members of the family knew also of Edward's "unsleeping goading conscience that never let him spare himself."

"I do not know that there is any chance of rescuing Edward from the Law nor do I know that it were desireable [sic]," wrote Waldo in the following January. "If his talents look any way, it is that way. And his health certainly appears more firmly established than any one cd. have believed possible a year ago." This suggests what may have been true, that the onset of Edward's breakdown had been visible for some months before the actual derangement set in. Along with Charles, he was present at Emerson's ordination in March 1829, and in October he was admitted to the bar. But his tentative plan of "taking a chair" in the law firm of Samual Hoar, one of Concord's leading citizens, was soon abandoned, and in November he joined William in New York.

Evidently fearing a recurrence of the breakdown, Waldo urged William to let Edward work only "with lounging moderation," and sent along what money he could spare to keep Edward's purse from becoming "windy." Except for a brief holiday with his family in the fall of 1830, Edward stayed on with William until December, when a severe cold settled in his chest. On the twelfth he took ship for St. Croix in the Caribbean, hoping that the milder climate would ease his ailments.

It was a rough time for Waldo—the "theolog brother," as Edward once called him. His young wife, Ellen, grew steadily weaker, and Bulkeley had reentered McLean late in September for an extended stay—"a longer illness," wrote Waldo, "than any for years." Nor was there much to celebrate in Edward's early letters from the West Indies, their tone suggesting a sluggish convalescence. "Edward writes always sadly," said Waldo. He seemed to have made no move to find employment, which would have helped to take his mind off his woes, besides relieving Waldo, who was paying Bulkeley's bills at McLean, as well as supporting his wife, his mother, and his youngest brother, Charles.

Ellen's death on the morning of February 8, 1831, was an immense blow to her husband. As she lay dying she told him that "she should do me more good by going than by staying"—a remark that he recorded and long remembered. His private grief was spread upon the pages of his journal. Five days after her death he wrote, "O willingly, my wife, I would lie down in your tomb. . . . Dear Ellen (for that is your name in heaven) shall we not be united even now more and more, as I more steadfastly persist in the love of truth and virtue which you loved?" Presently also there were shards of poetry:

In yonder ground thy limbs are laid
Under the snow
And earth has no spot so dear above
As that below. . . .

Her delicate ghost continued to haunt the house in Chardon Street to which he had brought her as a bride in the fall of 1829. She had been dead for a month when he complained, like so many thousands of bereaved before and since, that "the common things go on and she is not here."

His cousin David Haskins recalled long afterward that Waldo "walked out regularly in the early morning" to visit Ellen's tomb in Roxbury. Although he continued to insist that all his thoughts of her were happy, he once said that the grave was "pleasanter to me than the house," because she lay there. His memories kept turning back "to her beautiful character for a charm that I might seek in vain thro the world." The dead, said his journal for April 4, "do not return and sometimes we are negligent of their image. Not of yours Ellen—I know too well who is gone from me."

If his own life now seemed to him of "little worth," his faith in personal immortality stayed strong. Once he paraphrased the words of King David from 2 Samuel 12:23: "I shall go to her but she shall not return to me." Trying to comprehend the meaning of death, he wrote Edward that the ethical truths that had allured him all his life were being only "slowly disclosed." When Ellen's sister Margaret lay gravely ill with the same dread disease, he wrote that "every star that sinks on this rises in the other firmament and makes the vision of that more full of glory and delight." A month later in a letter to Edward he reaffirmed his belief in the transcendental consolations: "High over all calamities, high over all fears, let the constant soul linked by philosophy and faith to the First Cause, calmly pursue her own appointed and glorious path." Calm, delight, and glory must exist in that other firmament, though on board what he once called "this sickening planet" they were notably rare.

With his brother Charles he made a two-week journey into northern Vermont in June 1831. The flowering landscapes reminded him of rides through similar country with Ellen and her mother in the summer of 1829. His "bitter sweet" memories were accordingly far more active than they would have been had he "staid at home." Travel among the Green Mountains and along the shores of Lake Champlain was, he said, a "sad recreation," since he found Ellen "nowhere and yet everywhere." The burial motif was still much in his mind.

> O pleasant pleasant in my eye
> The grave is become
> And with all this green majesty
> 'Twill be a sweeter home.

These lines, set down in his journal at Burlington that June, were reflected in another entry six months later: "I do not fear death. . . . Following my own thoughts, especially as sometimes they have moved me in the country (as in the Gulf Road in Vermont) I should lie down in the lap of earth as trustingly as ever on my bed." Back in Boston he declined an invitation to write the Phi Beta Kappa poem for the coming Harvard commencement on the grounds that he could not summon up the necessary powers except for a dirge, which would hardly have suited the occasion.

By May 1831, shortly before Waldo's trip to Vermont, Edward's Caribbean luck had taken a turn for the better. Having moved from St. Croix to San Juan, Puerto Rico, he fell in with the American consul, a wealthy merchant and entrepreneur named Sidney Mason, and there seemed to be some cause for hope that he could secure gainful employment. Waldo continued to keep his fingers crossed. "We must never be sanguine again," he told his brother William. He advised Edward to "keep your tranquil temper as the apple of your eye and if it comes, as I hope, from a spirit of boundless *trust,* come life, come death, come eternity, this shall be armour and preparation." It was the "theolog brother" talking to one who had come, as he hoped, through a very dark time.

Waldo was doing his best to follow the same advice. In July he wrote another poem to Ellen:

And as the delicate Snow
That latest fell the thieving wind first takes
So thou dear wife must go
As frail, as spotless as those newfal'n flakes. . . .

But the snow-maiden imagery, so apposite because she had died in winter, did not appear in his direct address to her on the still-persistent theme of immortality: "When I think of you sweet friend, wife, angel, Ellen on whom the spirit of knowledge and the spirit of hope were poured in equal fulness. . . I am sure we have not said everlasting farewells."

"I rejoice to hear of yr mending health," he had told Edward in June. ". . . Mother is very well. Things go kindly with us, yet it is hard to be happy. Who is? not one." In the fall of the year came news that William had been appointed "Counsellor of the Supreme Court of New York," a significant proof that his years of overwork were beginning to pay off. Waldo also rejoiced over a letter from Edward that included one "happy and happy making line" hinting at a marked improvement in his sense of well-being. But Edward's purse was still "windy" enough to need refilling, which he partly accomplished by selling to a Spanish soldier his new blue frock coat with metal buttons over which his mother had labored long in Chardon Street. "She is not flattered at all," wrote Waldo to William, "by the new destination of her needlework."

Now, unhappily, it was Charles's turn—Charles, the gifted, the animated, the easily companionable brother. Waldo had once admiringly called him a "honey catcher of pleasure, favor, and honour" who did not have to pay for his attainments, like Edward, "with life and limb." "I wish Charles was stouter," wrote Waldo late in September. This youngest member of the tribe, aged twenty-three, was "in body like a wilted apple," even though in spirit he remained as saucily sardonic as ever. Presently he came down with a severe cold and a hacking cough, always a danger signal in the family, and particularly so in one whose frame was so frail. Blisters, leeches, and bloodletting relieved his pleurisy, but left him so weak that he resolved to join Edward in the tropics. On December 7, almost exactly the first anniversary of his brother's departure, he hastily set sail for San Juan. Waldo could not shed his gloom. "Who would have thot," he had asked William, "that Edward and Charles on whom we put so much fond pride shd. be the first to fail whilst Ellen, my rose, is gone."

Charles spent nearly five months with Edward in Puerto Rico. Down there, he said, one's feet were never cold, one seldom needed a pocket handkerchief, and it was always easy to get out of bed: "Every morning I am up, like Bunker-Hill monument, to meet the sun in his coming." He told of riding his pony out to Santa Barbara where Mason owned a plantation of which Charles was then the sole occupant. The views from the tops of the nearby hills reminded him of the meadows beside the Connecticut River "as seen from Mt. Holyoke at the close of summer."

To Waldo in the iron grip of a Boston winter it must have seemed that history was repeating itself. As he had played a kind of poor man's golf by propelling green oranges with his stick along the beach at St. Augustine in 1827, so now, five years later, Charles reported that he and Edward were taking evening strolls along the San Juan shore, "battening (would I might say fattening) on the fresh and fragrant air." Edward was working ten hours a day in Mason's countinghouse, where Charles set up a table and chair in one corner for use as a study. When he came back to Boston in May 1832, his collection of tropical seashells fascinated Waldo with their forms and colors. But he brought also some news that cheered the whole family: Edward was "turning merchant in earnest—sending [out] hogsheads of sugar" and other comestibles for export to American markets.

Refreshed by his sojourn in San Juan, Charles must have noticed the signs of strain in the face and figure of his brother Waldo. Still suffering from the loss of Ellen, as well as from worry over the welfare of his three younger brothers, Waldo was moving into a period fraught with momentous personal decisions. On her deathbed Ellen had said that she could do him "more good by going than by staying." One possible corollary of this somewhat enigmatic statement had become visible by the spring of 1831. On the eve of his twenty-eighth birthday, Waldo wrote William: "It seems that Ellen is to continue to benefit her husband whenever hereafter the estate shall be settled. . . . I please myself that Ellen's work of mercy is not done on earth, but she shall continue to help Edward and B[ulkeley] and Charles." Within a month, Pliny Cutler, executor of Ellen's father's estate, confirmed in lengthy legalese that Waldo's claim to Ellen's share was under serious consideration. "I may have legal rights," said Waldo, "which I shall not choose to enforce." He meant that he had no wish to deprive Ellen's mother and her sister Margaret of their rightful inheritance, and he added, quite truthfully, that they were his "living monument" to Ellen.

An associated problem was the claim of the other sister, Paulina, wife of Captain Joshua Nash. Nash was inclined to dispute Waldo's expectations. The litigation dragged on through the winter of 1831–32. In March Waldo heard an ugly rumor that he had "refused all compromise" with the other potential heirs. The truth, he wrote to William, was that he had made no legal moves without full consultation with Margaret and her mother and that the Massachusetts Supreme Court in Chancery was empowered to rule in due course on the distribution of the estate. If Captain Nash thought otherwise, he had "certainly had opportunity to know better." The dirty rumor about his alleged intransigence may have stirred Waldo to a curious action only three days after his letter to William.

On March 29 he wrote in his journal, "I visited Ellen's tomb and opened the coffin." Nothing in the context of this bare entry offers a clue to his motivation. Perhaps he yielded to an impulse, whether morbid or scientifically exploratory, to discover what the past thirteen months had wrought upon the face and form of this child bride whom he still so greatly loved. Or he may have supposed that her saintliness in life might conceivably have preserved her intact in death, as in the legends of the hagiographers. Or he could have been wishing, in his macabre vis-à-vis, to pray for their spiritual reunion in the world beyond. What met his eyes inside the open coffin he never said. Yet his memories of Ellen were closely associated with his ministry at the Second Church of Boston. He assumed his pastorate soon after their engagement. With her death a light had gone out both in his personal life and his professional life in the pulpit. He had even begun to think seriously of resigning his post. Perhaps he chose this occasion to pray in her presumed presence for guidance in this epochal decision.

Some days later he quoted an old Italian proverb which held that "working in your calling is half praying." But what was his true calling? Could his goals be realized outside the ministry? For months he had been agonizing over such questions. "It is the best part of the man, I sometimes think," he had written in January, "that revolts most against his being the minister. His good revolts from official goodness. . . . We . . . fall into institutions already made and have to accommodate ourselves to them to be useful at all, and this accommodation is, I say, a loss of so much integrity and . . . power." Early in June he returned to the theme during what he called "a week of moral excitement." To be a good minister one ought perhaps to leave the ministry. "The profession is antiquated. In an altered age, we worship in the dead forms of our forefathers. Were not a Socratic paganism better than an effete superannuated Christianity?"

The challenge to orthodox beliefs and customs implicit in these journal entries had now come to focus in his determination to raise up as a test case the ordinance of the Last Supper. In the Gospel according to Luke, Jesus asked his disciples to eat the bread and drink the wine "in remembrance of me." The crucial question was whether he meant the injunction to apply only to his disciples so long as they lived, or whether he was looking "beyond the living generation" with the intent to "impose a memorial feast" upon the whole future world. Waldo favored the first possibility: "I think Jesus did not mean to institute a perpetual celebration." He was already working out a sermon on the subject. Now in June, taking his courage in his hands as if it were a shield to guard his moral integrity, he addressed a letter to the Committee of the Second Church in which he notified them of an alteration in his views concerning the ordinance. The communication was noted in the church records for June 16 and would eventually lead to a parting of the ways between the minister and his congregation.

While the church building was undergoing repairs in July, he made another trip with his brother Charles, this time to Maine and New Hampshire. Charles left him brooding in Conway, New Hampshire. "Here among the mountains," wrote Waldo, "the pinions of thought should be strong and one should see the errors of men from a calmer height of love and wisdom."

Presently he recorded his wish to become "the vehicle of that divine principle that lurks within and of which life has afforded only glimpses enough to assure me of its being." The epitome of his thought was simple and profound: "God is, and we in him." He had found a supporting pagan text in Ovid's *Fasti*: "There is a god within us. It is when he stirs us that our bosom warms."

"I can only do my work well," he told his Aunt Mary in August, "by abjuring the opinions and customs of all others and adhering strictly to the divine plan a few dim inches of whose outline I faintly discern in my breast." Dim as it was, he thought he saw the light. "The true doctrine," he wrote in September, is that ". . . Christianity aims to form in a man a critical conscience." Once that was developed—and this was presumably a continuing process— the man would become "the only and absolute judge of every particular form that the established religion presents to him." It was his own critical conscience that had persuaded him to oppose, for himself if not for others, the received doctrine of the Eucharist as a "perpetual celebration." He said flatly that he was not "prepared to eat or drink religiously."

When at last he preached his convictions on September 9, all the pews in the church were filled, and his brother Charles's word for the closely reasoned sermon was "noble." A clear majority among his parishioners were disinclined to let him go, and the Committee deliberated for more than forty days before deciding to grant his "dismission." Charles, watching his brother closely, thought that "Waldo looks very sad. He would have been glad to have been well these last few months."

The spiritual ordeal precipitated by his "hour of decision" in June had in fact led to serious physical consequences. On his return from New Hampshire late in July he had fallen ill with a colonic disorder, possibly dietary though more likely psychosomatic in origin. "A stomach ache will make a man as contemptible as a palsy," he wrote in mid-August. "Under the diarrhoea have I suffered now one fortnight and weak am as a reed." He added an ironic footnote: "When one of these days I see this body going to ruin like an old cottage I will remember that after the ruin the resurrection is sure."

Two events of that month helped to raise his sagging spirits. One was a visit from William, who came north to celebrate his engagement to Susan Haven of Portsmouth, New Hampshire. The other, at least equally heartening, was the arrival of Edward from Puerto Rico. He planned to spend a

month but stayed for two, surprising the family with every evidence of good
health and "fine spirits." When he sailed back to San Juan on October 6, he
formalized his sense of separation from his brothers in a lyric he called "A
Last Farewell: Lines Written While Sailing out of Boston Harbor for the West
Indies." It said in part:

> Farewell my brothers true
> My betters yet my peers,
> How desert without you
> My few and evil years!
> But though aye one in heart,
> Together sad or gay,
> Rude ocean doth us part,
> We separate today,
> Far away, far away.

Waldo's illness continued, with partial recoveries followed by relapses,
throughout the fall season. Even as he preached his "noble" sermon on the
Last Supper he was slowly recuperating from a new bout with his "tedious
complaint," and his tall body, under the loose and flapping clothes, was emaciated. At the same time he was fiercely determined to stick to his decision to
resign his pastorate. In October he set down in his journal an imaginary colloquy between his critical conscience and an orthodox respondent:

> [Question:] Why must I obey Christ?
> [Answer:] Because God sent him.
> [Q:] But how do I know God sent him?
> [A:] Because your own heart teaches the same thing he taught.
> [Q:] Why then shall I not go to my own heart at first?

A week later, in some journal verses, he declared once again for spiritual
independence:

> I will not see with others' eyes . . .
> I dare attempt to lay out my own road . . .
> Henceforth, please God, forever I forego

The yoke of men's opinions. I will be
Lighthearted as a bird and live with God.
I find him in the bottom of my heart.

He was now ready to assert that "the severing of our strained cord that bound me to the church is a mutual relief. . . . I walk firmly toward a peace and a freedom which I plainly see before me albeit afar."

Just before Thanksgiving came a resurgence of former sorrows. The death of Ellen's sister Margaret on November 24 brought home with fresh intensity the remembrance of his earlier bereavement. "Farewell to thee for a little time my kind and sympathizing sister," he wrote in his journal. "Go rejoice with Ellen, so lately lost, in God's free and glorious universe. Tell her if she needs to be told how dearly she is remembered, how dearly valued. Rejoice together that you are free of your painful corporeal imprisonment."

He was still trying to throw off the depressive symptoms occasioned by his long illness. Once, at least, his ironic humor came briefly to his rescue, as it had done in August. On November 19 he wrote to William: "I have wire-drawn to an infinitesimal ductility all the sympathies of men women and children, for there is a limit beyond which peoples interest in other peoples bowels cannot go." But neither wry humor nor sober joy in the contemplation of a glorious afterlife could solve his recurrent problem. "Waldo is sick again," Charles reported, "—very much dispirited—and talking of the South, the West Indies and other projects. . . ."

By December 10, Waldo had made up his mind. "I proposed to make a modest trip to the West Indies and spend the winter with Edward but in a few hours the dream changed into a purpureal vision of Naples and Italy and that is the rage of yesterday and today in Chardon St. A vessel sails this week for Sicily and at this moment it seems quite possible I shall embark in it—the brig Jasper." As of this date his term for himself was candid and exact: "A wasted peevish invalid." The months since Ellen's death had not been easy. Now, through his own decision, he had lost his church and, it seemed, his profession as well.

Luckily, he still had his brothers. One of Ellen's nicknames for him had been "Grampa," partly because he was eight years her senior, and partly because the serious maturity of his behavior must sometimes have struck her as that of a man well past his actual age of twenty-six. Before and during his marriage and since Ellen's premature death, something of the same attitude had mingled with his regard and affection for his brothers. With what amounted to an almost paternal solicitude he had watched over Bulkeley and Edward in the dark time of their derangements, repeatedly warned William and Edward against overwork, and remained alert to the vicissitudes in Charles's health and welfare. In some ways he seems to have thought of himself as keeper, not only of their revered mother, now in her mid-sixties, but also of the home fires—a man gregarious of brotherhood and eager to perpetuate the kind of camaraderie that all the boys had known in their youth. Near the end of 1832, harassed by his stubborn affliction, he could yet cry out: "Give me my household gods against the world. William and Edward and Charles." Conscientious to a fault, ever vigilant, always considerate, Waldo was now in many respects the spiritual head of the family.

But a change was imminent for them all. "We may break up and disperse at any moment," wrote Charles on the eve of Waldo's departure. By Christmas Day of 1832, when Waldo sailed out of Boston harbor bound for Malta, the dispersal was complete. Mrs. Emerson was to stay with her sister Mary Ladd in the village of Newton. William was in New York, Waldo at sea, Edward back in his counting room in San Juan, Bulkeley in Chelmsford, and Charles in Boston. Even the chattels from Chardon Street were, as Waldo said, dispersed "to the four winds by that domestic crack of doom and type of all forlornness, an auction."

Chapter Two

AUNT MARY

IN 1822, A YEAR OUT OF COLLEGE, EMERSON PRAISED THE Arabian "Bedoween" for having preserved over the centuries "his savage Ishmaelitish independence." In ten years' time his views had come to resemble those of a latter-day Ishmaelite. He shrugged off the yoke of men's opinions, and told his Aunt Mary that he could do his work well only by "abjuring" the customs that others kept. His frequent correspondent, Mary Moody Emerson, the sister of his father, was not only the most notably eccentric of all his relatives, but also so fiercely independent that she might have laid claim to Ishmaelitish qualities of her own. Her nephew delighted in "the wild freedom of MME's genius" and all through his youth profited by "the fire of her piety, her zeal for learning, her brilliant expression," and the always "unsparing criticism" by which she sought to keep her five nephews in line. Both then and afterward she stood out in Emerson's mind as the epitome of the nonconformist.

Born at the Manse in Concord in 1774, she had lost her father when young and was raised by various relatives in Malden, Newburyport, and later at a farm called Elm Vale in Waterford, Maine. She had been present in Boston at the time of her brother's early death, and had vigorously assumed the role of adviser to the Emerson boys: "the kind aunt," Emerson called her, "whose cares instructed my youth." "Never any gave higher counsels," he wrote later on, "nor played with all the household incidents with more wit and humour." She was already close to thirty when Emerson was born and in those days was rather comely. Her silhouette shows a pleasant profile with a well-formed head and graceful neck. Small in stature, standing only four feet three, she wore her blond hair cut short under a kind of mobcap that gave her the appearance of a diminutive nun. When Emerson versified a passage from one of her "Almanacks," as she called her journals, he gave it the title "The Nun's Aspiration." One couplet said:

> I tire of shams, I rush to be:
> I pass with yonder comet free . . .

She said repeatedly that her nephews were "born to be educated." In a letter to Emerson's mother she wrote: "Oh Ruthy, may you have grace to leave nothing undone to forming those children to *faith in a Redeemer, to humility, to honesty,* and disinterestedness." Kind as she was to the growing brood, taking occasional charge of Bulkeley, harboring Charles on her farm in Maine, she refused to temper her criticisms. Emerson was nineteen when she wrote him, perhaps prophetically, that "like Cicero perhaps, your poetry will not be valued because your prose is so much better." In another letter she asked, "What has done the most injury to men and women since the allegory of Adam?" and answered her question, "Sexual influence." He later recalled that in his childhood she had written the prayers for the family devotions, to be read aloud morning and evening by the two older boys. Years after the fact, his ears still rang with Aunt Mary's "prophetic and apocalyptic ejaculations." The depth of her religious sentiment, he wrote in 1837, "imbuing all her genius . . . was itself a culture, an education."

Certain of her ideas left their mark on his developing religious attitudes. In 1832 she told him that "the relation between you and your Creator, if you have one, remains paramount." The only true philosophy must be "the divine personal agency, as of your own consciousness." She believed, as he did, that human beings could "reach perfection by their own free agency and divine help." Emerson's limited view of the place of Jesus in the hierarchy seems to have owed some part of its origin to his aunt's opinions. She called herself an Arian, embracing the opinion of the fourth-century heretic who denied that Christ was consubstantial with God. "I had too proud a spirit, too elate," said one of her almanack entries, ". . . ever to have that affinity to Jesus which his better holier ones have." Emerson commented: "No aristocrat, no porphyrogenet, can begin to compare with the self-respect of the saint. M.M.E in her vision of her place in heaven looks very coolly at her 'Divine Master.' "

When Waldo gave up his ministry in 1832, she said that he had never loved holy offices and that it was well that he had left them. Yet she was deeply troubled by his latitudinarianism, and complained to his brother Charles that Waldo seemed to have "no fixed faith in a personal God." His recent letters struck her as "confused and dark—a mixture of heathen greatness . . . pantheism, Swedenborgianism, hypotheses of nature, and German rationalism." Emerson's wry rejoinder was that "Aunt Mary wished everybody to be a Calvinist except herself."

His most revealing commentary on the contradictions in her character came in 1841. The key to her life, he suggested, lay in "the conflict of the new and the old ideas in New England. The heir of whatever was rich and profound in thought and emotion in the old religion . . . she strangely united to this passionate piety the fatal gift of penetration . . . and was thus a religious skeptic. She held on with both hands to the faith of the past generation as to the palladium [the image of Pallas Athena, the Athenian goddess-protectress] of all that was good and hopeful in the physical and metaphysical worlds, and in all companies . . . extolled and poetised this beloved Calvinism. Yet all the time she doubted and denied it, and could not tell whether to be more glad or sorry to find that [her beloved nephews] were irremediably born to the adoption and furtherance of the new ideas."

Their correspondence continued with rare intermissions from his college days through the early 1830s. She sometimes complained of his "sneaky short letters" and he responded that it was often harder to extract words from her than from those "weird-women" in Thomas Gray's Norse translation, "The Descent of Odin," where the prophet moans, "Now my weary lips I close; / Leave me, leave me to repose." The phrase "weird-women" does not appear in the original and might have been Emerson's adaptation from the "weird sisters" in the first act of *Macbeth*. But Aunt Mary took umbrage: "Pardon the whim . . . to ask you not to compare me to any weird women. I who live so as to try never to offend by one singular word . . . pray you spare my age and vocation." But he had already made an exotic anagram of her name, Tnamurya, as if she might belong to Norse or some other heathen mythology, and recorded her boast that she possessed an eye like a needle that enabled her to read the characters of others. This disturbed whoever thought that "she knew them too well." For her part, she was offended "by the irritating phlegm" of her companions and made no attempt to conceal her impatience with them. "She could keep step with no human being," said Emerson. She gloried in her own uniqueness: "I have from lonely youth laughed at what others cry." In April 1835, writing to his fiancée, Lydia, Emerson explained that though Aunt Mary's Concord relatives "flout her and contradict her, and compassionate her whims, we all stand in awe of her penetration, her indignant eloquent conscience, her poetic and commanding Reason."

She could be a terror in her determination. She was boarding in Concord in the fall of 1834 while Emerson and his mother were staying at the Manse. One November morning she paid them a call, driving a shabby horse and a decrepit chaise that she had just bullied a fellow townsman into lending her. The amused owner had at first demurred and then consented, telling her not to hurry, and the indefatigable sixty-year-old whipped up the old nag and drove off in triumph. This, thought Emerson, was one example of the "surprizingly good understanding" that she had established among the residents of the village, despite her "transcendental way of living."

He delighted in her one-liners and faithfully recorded them in his journals. "Hurry," she said, "is for slaves," and again: "Whoever wants power must pay for it." "The finest wits have their sediment. . . . I hate to be expecting a cat. . . . Never much good comes of black bead eyes. . . . When people are going to die their faults come out." And with bitter emphasis, "I am tired of fools."

Her idiosyncrasies were legion. She insisted on using her thimble as a seal for letters, liked best those adversaries who argued back, and often took out her teeth in company "to give herself more ease." She could not bear to throw away medicines: if she found in several old bottles a drop or two of laudanum, quinine, or antimony, and a few old pills, she mixed the lot together and drank off the potion. At meals she was always contrary, saying, for example, that she never took tea and preferred cocoa. When given the cocoa, she'd add a spot of tea to make her lively and another of coffee to get rid of the taste. She was vain about her headgear, refusing to buy from the usual shops, and sending her beloved Elizabeth Hoar "from Dan to Beersheba to find a bonnet that does not conform." Of domestic refinements—"of cleaning and painting and little totty ornaments"—she said that they wore on her "lifestrings" and were "only fit for fools and children." If she found that something was "dear and sacred" to others, she instantly attacked it with "broken crockery." She struck her nephew as "a she-Isaiah but alive to the comedy of her pretensions and costume."

Touchy, harsh, splenetic, disputatious, she called tact "only another name for lying" and asserted that "to live to give pain rather than pleasure. . . . seems the spider-like necessity of my being on earth." Margaret Fuller was to find her "valuable as a disturbing force to the lazy." But she recognized a delighted adversary in Emerson's second wife, Lydia. "I remember several set-tos," wrote the Emersons' eldest daughter, Ellen, "Aunt Mary growing more and more violent, and Mother undismayed and laughing at her shafts." In a characteristic switch, she condemned the Transcendentalists for embracing "Humanitarianism" and denying the divinity of Christ. "Your star has wandered fearfully," she wrote Emerson in 1840, when she was sixty-six. Four years earlier, at dinner in Concord with Emerson and his brother Charles, she had launched one of her verbal attacks and been reprimanded for it. "Angry and ashamed," says Ralph L. Rusk, "she vowed she would never again spend an hour in Waldo Emerson's house unless she were brought there on a litter. On second thought she ruled out the litter."

According to her earlier biographer George Tolman, Aunt Mary's diary entries on her religious retreats "alone with God" sometimes read like passages that might have been written by some "sister of Saint Benedict" in her solitary cell. Other entries betray the morbid strain in her nature. Two of her favorite eighteenth-century poems were Robert Blair's *The Grave* and Edward Young's *Night Thoughts on Life, Death, and Immortality*. These and her own imagination provided her with a set of images—coffins, worms, moldy bones, musty grave clothes—that reflected her own preoccupation with death. As early as 1835, when she was past sixty, she wrote, "O dear worms—how they will at some sure time take down this tedious tabernacle . . . by gnawing away the meshes which have chained it."

Shortly before she died in 1863, Emerson summarized this aspect of her character:

> Saladin caused his shroud to be made and carried it to battle as his standard. Aunt Mary has done the like all her life, making up her shroud, and then thinking it pity to let it die idle, wears it as night-gown or day-

gown until it is worn out (for death, when asked, will not come;) then she has another made up, and, I believe, has worn out a great many. And now that her release seems to be really at hand, the event of her death has really something so comic in the eyes of everybody that her friends fear they shall laugh at the funeral.

Her niece Hannah Parsons, who had faithfully cared for her over the years, told Emerson that Aunt Mary had long had her bed made in the form of a coffin, and "delighted in the figure of a coffin made daily on her wall by the shadow of a church."

At the same time he recalled that "no intelligent youth or maiden could have once met her without remembering her with interest, and learning something of value. Scorn trifles, lift your aims: do what you are afraid to do; sublimity of character must come from sublimity of motive." And continued, "Our Delphian was fantastic enough, Heaven knows, yet could always be tamed by large and sincere conversation. Was there thought and eloquence, she would listen like a child." Wonderfully as she had varied and poetically repeated the images of death on every page and nearly every day, she always returned to another favorite theme: "the grandeur of humility and privation." Thus: "The chief witness which I have had of a Godlike principle of action and feeling is in the disinterested joy felt in others' superiority. For the love of superior virtue is mine own gift from God."

Chapter   Three

ISHMAEL ABROAD

WHEN HE SET SAIL FOR MALTA ABOARD THE BRIG *JASPER* ON Christmas Day, 1832, Emerson could look back upon two years in which, however he tried, he had found much to be endured and little to be enjoyed: the death of his spirited young wife, his voluntary resignation as pastor of the Second Church of Boston, the nagging illnesses of three of his four brothers, and a debilitating sickness of his own that had finally decided him to see what an ocean voyage and a prolonged change of scene might do for his enfeebled constitution. But the voyage began inauspiciously. Almost from the beginning, conditions for the development of new friendships with his fellow passengers were strained by creature discomforts. "A long storm," he wrote, "from the second morn of our departure consigned all the five passengers to the irremediable chagrins of the stateroom, to wit, nausea, darkness, unrest, uncleanness, harpy appetite and harpy feeding, the ugly sound of water in mine ears, anticipations of going to the bottom, and the treasures of memory."

The last item on his sorry list was more a consolation than a complaint. Tossing in his bunk, he "remembered up nearly the whole of Lycidas, clause by clause, here a verse and there a word," approximately, he thought, as the fabled Isis had reassembled the broken body of Osiris. Ragged as was this recollection of Milton's poem on the drowning of his friend Edward King, the reconstruction was a stunt that got Emerson successfully through the storm.

"It takes one 'Grand tour' to learn how to travel," he wrote in Naples during the mid-March rainy season. The maritime leg of his journey had covered forty days, and the whole trip would fill up a little more than nine months—figures to conjure with had he been so minded. By ship, coach, muleback, and often on foot he traversed large areas of Malta and Sicily, Italy and France, England and Scotland, before setting sail for home in the autumn of the year. Meditating over all the ruins, exploring the cultural monuments, genuflecting as well as a nominal Unitarian could before all the major Catholic shrines, he swallowed his New England reserve long enough to interview several of the great and near-great among the literati. Goethe had recently died, or the young Bostonian might have included Germany in his itinerary. Keats, Shelley, and Byron were also gone, but he managed to see Landor at Fiesole, Coleridge at Highgate, Wordsworth at Rydal Mount, and Carlyle at Craigenputtock. Though not yet in any sense a literary celebrity, he was in one way a faithful follower of his more eminent English-speaking brethren. Cached in his luggage when he turned homeward was the longhand record of his grand tour, a treasure of some 50,000 words.

Before he set foot on any foreign soil his hopes for new friendships were high. Lying in quarantine in a Maltese harbor in February, he wrote that he wished to discover "new affinities" between his fellow men and himself, and to observe "the affections, weaknesses, surprises, hopes, [and] doubts" that fresh angles of vision might supply. Already he was working up his Italian for forthcoming visits to Sicily and Italy. Ashore at La Valetta, he found himself increasingly eager for new joys. His American eyes might become like "a child's again to these glorious picture books. The chaunting friars, the carved ceilings, the Madonnas and Saints, they are lively oracles, quotidiana et perpetua. Silver gates."

In Syracuse two weeks later the traveler was still enthusiastic. "I have this day drank the waters of the fountain Arethusa and washed my hands in it. I ate the very fragrant Hyblaean honey with my breakfast." All day from the balcony of his *locanda* he could see Mount Etna far off, huge on the horizon, snow-capped, plumed with smoke. Riding northward on muleback, he got a nearer view of all the "Mountainettes like warts" that diversified the great flanks of the volcano. The streets of Catania were "paved with lava." Along the shore, like an etching, white surf was breaking over black boulders. On the way to Messina he was amused by the graffiti on walls and fences, one of which read, "Viva la Divina Providenza." It was a fitting sentiment for any who lived within shooting distance of Etna, to say nothing of a young New Englander on his first voyage of foreign exploration. His Sicilian companions were a priest called Itellario, his nephews Lorenzo and Gaetano, and a tailor named Francesco. "O, che bella veduta!" they would exclaim whenever a turn in the road offered a new vista. On learning that Emerson was a *sacerdote* in his own country, and that he was able to speak in Latin, they kept crying "che bravo Signore!" with praise in their eyes as well as in their voices.

In Palermo, which had looked so good from the water, he was merely depressed when his officious *cicerone* led him through the Spedale dei Pazzi, the city insane asylum, without telling him their destination in advance. To inform himself and improve his German, he had taken to reading Goethe's *Italian Journey*, for Goethe had preceded him by almost fifty years in sailing from Sicily to Naples. Although he knew the famous maxim *Vedi Napoli e poi muori*, he was unwilling to believe it. Nor could he agree with Goethe's view that, having seen Naples, he would never again be wholly unhappy. "If he had said '*happy*,' " wrote Emerson, "there would have been equal reason. You cannot go five yards in any direction without seeing saddest objects and hearing the most piteous wailings. Instead of the gayest of cities, you seem to walk in the wards of a hospital." It was better than the Spedale of Palermo, but not much. Eating his dinner at a trattoria, he was unhappily aware of a ragged beggar who peered hungrily through the window, "watching every mouthful."

For a long time he stood alone in the window of the monastery beside St. Martin's sumptuous church, gazing down upon this lilliputian capital, or so he called it, and listening to the continuous babble of voices that rose like the sound of surf from the lips of nearly half a million souls. He found Virgil's tomb and the Grotto del Cane, made the usual trip to Pompeii and Herculaneum, admired the grand sweep of the bay, climbed the smoking hulk of Vesuvius—"a fearful place"—and in the museums and churches pored patiently over the marbles, bronzes, frescoes, and canvases. Yet everywhere he was besieged not only by the rain but also by the "swarming, faithless, robber population," in whose furtive eyes every foreigner was a potential, often an actual, victim. Twice in one day his pockets were picked.

Although he wrote his brother Charles exuberantly from Rome that he was now in "better health than ever since I was a boy," most of his fellow travelers were a disappointment. "I would give all Rome for one man such as were fit to walk here, and could feel and impart the sentiment of the place." The complaint recurred in a letter to his Aunt Mary. "The wise man—the true friend—the finished character—we seek everywhere and only find in fragments. Yet I cannot persuade myself that all the beautiful souls are fled out of the planet. . . . After being cabined up by sea and by land since I left home with various little people, all better to be sure and much wiser than me but still such as did not help me—I cannot tell you how refreshing it was to fall in with two or three sensible persons with whom I could eat my bread and take my walk and feel myself a freeman once more of Gods Universe. Yet were these last not instructers and I want instructers. God's greatest gift is a Teacher and when will he send me one, full of truth and of boundless benevolence and heroic sentiments?"

One of his "sensible persons" was William Allen Wall, a young painter from New Bedford, Massachusetts. Wall had told his landlady, an Italian Catholic, that Emerson was a "priest" in America. The landlady asked Wall if he now confessed to Emerson. "I told him he must tell her, yes," wrote Emerson. "All friendship is confession. . . . It is not only so but possesses in some sort the power of absolution also."

During Holy Week, Emerson saw Pope Gregory XVI on many public occasions, pleased to learn that he was reputed to be "a good scholar and a worthy man." Given time and proper instructors, he would have liked to stay on in Rome for long enough to study "the theory and order and politics of the Church." But, he said, "the unhappy traveller revolves ever in a little eddy of an orbit through Museums and caffés and the society of his countrymen"—in one day he had counted fifteen people from Boston—with the result that it was impossible to see and understand "the inner Italy." But Florence in May was a revelation. He was there for his thirtieth birthday, staying in a modest *pensione,* rising early to walk out into the Tuscan mornings when all the Florentine towers "rose richly out of the smoky light on the broad green plain." One could live in Florence more comfortably than in Naples or Rome: "Good streets, industrious population, spacious well furnished lodgings, elegant and cheap Caffés, the cathedral and the Campanile, the splended galleries and no beggars—make this city the favorite of strangers." He naively befriended "the fair Erminia," a flower girl who made the rounds of the cafés each morning. "If you will not buy her flowers she gives them to you and with such a superb air."

His birthday happened to coincide with the Feast of San Zenobio, who had been a Florentine bishop before his canonization. In the Duomo Emerson saw a priest bearing a silver bust of the saint, which he briskly placed on the heads of worshipers who knelt at the barrier. It was rumored to provide protection from headaches for the coming year. When he asked his landlady whether or not it worked, she made a matter-of-fact reply: *"Secondo alla fede di ciascuno"*—according to each man's faith. He was happy enough to share his own *festa,* if not precisely his faith, with the gentle spirit of San Zenobio.

For Venice he cared little. It struck him as "a city for beavers" overhung with the "smell of bilgewater." His gloom rose and spread like a high winter tide over the pavement of the Piazza San Marco. He was beginning to entertain serious misgivings about his capacity for friendship, his ineptitude in conversation, his awkwardness in social encounters. "Sometimes I would hide myself in the dens of the hills, in the thickets of an obscure country town. I am so vexed and chagrined with myself,—with my weakness, with my guilt. . . . It seems to me, no boy makes so many blunders or says such awkward, contrary, disagreeable speeches as I do. In the attempt to oblige a person I wound and disgust him. I pity the hapless folks that have to do with me." He ended this complaint with a curious anticipation of the question his future friend Henry Thoreau would ask and answer, "But would it not be cowardly to flee out of society and live in the woods?"

None of his detailed travelogue was in the end so valuable to him as the series of resolutions that he argued out with himself in the pages of his notebooks. He wrote like a man amassing quotidian facts while standing on the verge of great discoveries. For the end of 1832 and the first nine months of 1833 marked a turning point in his career. He was already beginning to put together that body of beliefs and maxims on which he would take his stand in the years ahead. He was in Paris between the fourth and fourteenth of July, two holidays of revolutionary independence that in their respective ways had helped to prepare the ideological path he was going to follow.

"The errors of traditional Christianity as it now exists, the popular faith of many millions," he wrote, "need to be removed to let men see the divine beauty of moral truth. I feel myself pledged . . . to demonstrate that all necessary truth is its own evidence; that no doctrine of God need appeal to a book; that Christianity is wrongly received by all such as take it for a system of doctrines,—its stress being upon moral truth; it is a rule of life[,] not a rule of faith. . . . How men can toil and scratch so hard for things so dry, [and] life-less . . . as these famous dogmas . . . how they can make such a fuss about the case and never open it to see the jewel—is strange, is pitiful."

Through the rest of July and August he was too busy in France, England, and Scotland to carry on with his iconoclastic speculations—except inside his head. At last in September, in the calmer intervals of yet another stormy pas-sage on board the *New York*, homeward bound, he returned to the subject he had broached in Paris. Perhaps the very ship itself was an image for the poles of his thought. What a machine it was, he thought with faint admiration, "changing so fast from the state of a butterfly[,] all wing[,] to the shape of a log—all spar."

Even though he could not follow the conventional usages, like the sacra-ment of the Lord's Supper, which, by his own decision, had cost him his pul-pit at the Second Church of Boston, he could not bring himself to speak lightly of them. To thousands upon thousands even Calvinism might still prove "wholesome." Having not yet reached the point of "pestering others" with what he personally believed, he thought that he left himself open to the name "of a very loose speculator, a faint heartless supporter of a frigid and empty theism," such as he took Unitarianism to be, "a man of no rigor of manners, of no vigor of benevolence." Even though he still felt "no call to ex-pound," his charge was clear enough: "to act faithfully upon my own faith, to live by it myself, and see what a hearty obedience to it will do."

The trouble with the "religionists," as he called them, was that they did not know "the extent or the harmony or the depth of their moral nature." They clung "to little, positive, verbal, formal versions of the moral law," while "the infinite laws, the laws of the Law, the great circling truths" went all unob-served through their myopic vision. Both Calvinism and Unitarianism offered imperfect readings of the moral law. Every form of Christian or pagan faith in the hands of "incapable teachers" was manifestly in error. The true teacher ought to be capable of showing the falsehoods of sectarianism as well as, pos-itively, "the sublimity and the depth of the Original," which could be defined as "the old revelation[,] that perfect beauty is perfect goodness," that "a man contains all that is needful to his government within himself." The highest revelation was "that God is in every man." If he ever got round to proselytiz-ing among his friends, this was the line he would follow.

Sprawled there in his "rain-dripping cabin" while southwesterly gales harassed the waves around the ship, he wrote that all men are believers and un-believers by inmost constitution. He ranked himself among the believers. All his "opinions, affections, whimsies" were "tinged with belief." As yet he felt unable to offer to the doubting Thomases any reason adequate to the force of his own convictions. But that would come. On October 9 he went ashore in New York, found his land legs after more than a month at sea, and left at once for Massachusetts, more certain than ever that the man who had begun his so-cial service as a preacher might be able to continue it in the equally exacting role of teacher.

Home from his travels in the old familiar landscape, he continued his intel-lectual explorations through the fall of the year. "I cannot but think," he wrote, "that Jesus Christ will be better loved by being less adored. He has had an unnatural, an artificial place for ages in human opinions[,] a place too high for love. There is a recoil of the affections from all authority and force. To the barbarous state of society it was thought to add to the dignity of X+ [Christ] to make him king, to make him God. Now that the SS [Sacred Scriptures] are read with purged eyes, it is seen he is only to be loved for so much goodness and wisdom as was in him, which are the only things for which a sound hu-man mind can love any person. As the world waxes wiser . . . he will attract the unfeigned love of all to whom moral nature is dear because he planted himself in the face of the world upon that sole ground, showing that noble confidence in the reality and superiority of spiritual truths, that simplicity . . . and enthusiasm in declaring them which . . . gives confidence to all thinkers that come after."

Christianity offered one such affirmation, but it was not the last. "There shall be," wrote Emerson firmly, "a thousand more." For none knew better than Jesus "that every soul occupies a new position and that if the stars cannot be counted nor the sands of the sea neither can those moral truths be num-bered and ended of which the material creation is only the shadow." Three days later, hunched over a table in a low-ceilinged room of the Ladd Farm at Newton Upper Falls, he concluded that "the teacher of the coming age must occupy himself in the study and explanation of the moral constitution of man more than in the elucidation of difficult texts." To this degree anyone setting up as a teacher must be ipso facto an imitator of Christ.

The teacher of the coming age must also account for the place of nature in the grand scheme. Emerson agreed with Bacon that man is or should be "the

minister and interpreter of nature." For some months now he had been sporadically preparing himself for just such a task. In Paris in July he had been
greatly struck by a visit to the Cabinet of Natural History in the Jardin des
Plantes. "The Universe is a more amazing puzzle than ever as you glance
along this bewildering series of animated forms," he had written, "—the hazy
butterflies, the carved shells, the birds, beasts, fishes, insects, snakes—and the
upheaving principle of life everywhere incipient in the very rock aping organized forms. Not a form so grotesque, so savage, nor so beautiful but is an expression of some property inherent in man the observer,—an occult relation
between the very scorpions and man. I feel the centipede in me—cayman,
carp, eagle, and fox. I am moved by strange sympathies, I say continually 'I
will be a naturalist.' "

Now in the fall of the year he was saying that the morning cloud contained
more beauty than any prism could analyze, including "something in it that resembles the aspects of mortal life[,] its epochs and its fate." No passage in the
human soul, "perhaps not a shade of thought," but had its emblem in nature.
Every law, once interpreted, proved the nature-mind analogy to be "deeper
and more universal" than one had hitherto suspected. This moralistic approach to nature excited his sensibilities. "Let a man under the influence of
strong passion go into the fields," he wrote, "and see how readily every
thought clothes itself with a material garment." Something should be done
"to explain this attractiveness which the face of nature has for us[—]renewed
this 2nd day of November of the 6000th year of the world." For nature was a
language that Emerson was resolved to learn, not merely its vocabulary
but also its inmost syntax. He believed sincerely that "to an instructed eye
the universe is transparent. The light of higher laws than its own shines
through it."

Although he still preached on occasion, he was rapidly beginning to assume the role of teacher with particular reference to the relation of man to nature. In November he spoke before the Boston Society of Natural History on
"The Uses of Natural History," and in January 1834 gave another on "Water" to the Boston Mechanic's Institute. He believed that the "growing taste
for natural science" was a "good symptom" in American society, and set
himself to read "as much geology chemistry and physics" as he could set his
eyes on.

By August he had arrived at a significant new conclusion. "Natural history by itself has no value," he wrote in his journal. "It is like a single sex. But marry it to human history, and it is poetry. Whole Floras, all Linnaeus' and Buffon's volumes contain not one line of poetry, but the meanest natural fact, the habit of a plant, the organs, or work, or noise of an insect applied to the interpretation [of] or even associated [with] a fact in human nature is beauty, is poetry, is truth at once." His perspective on natural history was shifting accordingly, and the ethical poet was beginning to take over. Less than a year later, he wrote his friend Frederic Henry Hedge that by and by he might be putting together a book of essays "chiefly upon Natural Ethics," the intent being to bring "a pebble or two to the edification of the new temple whilst so many wise hands are demolishing the old."

In the spring of 1834 he returned to his attempt at the definition of friendship, this time with a distinction between the two kinds of assistance a friend could offer. He called them commodity aid and spiritual aid. The first involved such matters as domestic hospitality, gifts, and various kinds of sacrifice. The second was "far more precious," providing such opportunities as "social stimulus," confession (he had learned that in Rome), and the mirroring of ourselves in the minds of others. This last, as he had already discovered, explained the fascination of biography, since the reader was always making silent comparisons between his own mind and the "intellectual and moral endowments" that were being portrayed in the lives of others.

When a Noachian April deluge kept him indoors, he made a joke of it: "The good rain like a bad preacher does not know when to leave off." But the confinement turned his thoughts back to the topic of friendship. "I want instructers," he had said in Italy. Now he was beginning to think that "the whole secret of the teacher's force" might lie "in the conviction that men are convertible. And they are. They want awakening." Beside this conviction so precious a discovery that he was going to stake half his whole future on it— was rising up a corollary: "The wise man must be wary of attaching followers. He must feel and teach that the best of wisdom cannot be communicated; must be acquired by every soul for itself." Here once more was the contrast between the social dimension and the solitude in which the best wisdom might be learned.

"Every soul for itself" was not a new doctrine in the Emersonian *Weltanschauung*. As early as the summer of 1831 he had described as "suicidal" the fear of thinking for oneself, "this distrust of reason," or "this doctrine that 'tis pious to believe on others' words[,] impious to trust entirely to yourself." For "to think is to receive. Is a man afraid that the faculties which God made can outsee God—can find more than he made or different—can bring any report hostile to himself? To reflect is to receive truth immediately from God without any medium. That is living faith. To take on trust certain facts is a dead faith—inoperative. A trust in yourself is the height not of pride but of piety, an unwillingness to learn of any but God himself. It will come only to one who feels that he is nothing. It is by yourself without ambassador that God speaks to you. You are one who has a private door that leads him to the King's chamber. You have learned nothing rightly that you have not learned so."

"Trust thyself" was still in 1834 the ruling conviction that he had described in 1831. Recently he had written that "all the mistakes I make arise from forsaking my own station and trying to see the object from another person's point of view." Next day he formulated a more positive statement of the same position: "Absolve yourself to the universe, and, as God liveth, you shall ray out light and heat—absolute good." He had now the leisure and above all the solitude to speculate further on spiritual light and heat. At the invitation of his stepgrandfather, Dr. Ezra Ripley, Emerson and his mother settled in that fall as boarders at the Old Manse in Concord. A month after the move he made a resolute journal entry: "Hail to the quiet fields of my fathers! Not wholly unattended by supernatural friendship and favor let me come hither. . . . Henceforth I design not to utter any speech, poem, or book that is not entirely and peculiarly my work."

Following this edict did not mean spurning the assistance of others. "As soon as I read a wise sentence anywhere," Emerson confessed, "I feel at once the desire of appropriation." Ever since college he had been using his journals for just such a purpose, setting down ideas that were new, at least to himself, or formulations that he had not previously thought of. Often, too, he discovered with delight in the work of someone else confirmation of the very thoughts at which he had independently arrived.

One of those to whom he often turned in the period 1831–34 was Coleridge. Even before his friendly tête-à-tête with the sage at Highgate, he had been a devotee of *Aids to Reflection*, using the book precisely as its title invited readers to do. When the American edition appeared in 1829, edited by the Vermonter James Marsh, Emerson had at once "appropriated" for his journal one of Coleridge's Latin quotations, *"Quantum scimus sumus"*—We are what we know. Repeated allusions to the book occurred in 1830–31 and again in 1834, by which time Emerson had thoroughly familiarized himself with the turbid contents, as well as the Reverend Mr. Marsh's long introductory essay.

It was clearly in part from his meditations over *Aids to Reflection* that Emerson brought his concept of the higher Reason to its fullest fruition. It became not only one of the major keys to his doctrine of friendship but also one of the basic ideas in the development of what came to be called Transcendentalism. His interest in Reason had, however, preceded by at least seven years his acquaintance with Coleridge's book. As early as the fall of 1822 he had affirmed that we are endowed with "an intelligence which reveals to man another condition of existence and a nearer approach to the Supreme Being. This intelligence is *Reason*." A month or so later he added that God's "law is a moral one, addressed to men's reason, and not their sense."

But it was plainly Coleridge's distinction between Reason and Understanding that excited Emerson's enthusiasm in the late spring of 1834. "Let me ask you," he wrote his brother Edward on May 31, "do you draw the distinction of Milton[,] Coleridge and the Germans between Reason and Understanding. I think it a philosophy itself, and like all truth very practical. . . . Reason is the highest faculty of the soul—what we mean often by the soul itself; it never *reasons*, never proves, it simply perceives; it is vision." On the other hand, the Understanding—"that wrinkled calculator"—"compares, contrives, adds, argues. . . . Reason is potentially perfect in every man," whereas Understanding "points at Custom and Interest and persuades one man that the declarations of Reason are false and another that they are at least impracticable. Yet by and by after having denied our Master we come back to see at the end of years or of life that he was the Truth." The New Testament image of "denying the Master," who after all embodied Truth—as Jesus did and as Reason could do—was an arresting clue to Emerson's apotheosis of this supernal power.

He returned to the topic a few weeks later. "Every true man stands on the top of the world. He has a majestic understanding, which is in its right place the servant of the reason, and employed ever to bridge over the gulf between the revelations of his Reason, his Vision, and the facts within in the microscopic optics of the calculators that surround him."

These observations were set down in May and June. In December the idea was still uppermost in his mind. "/Democracy/Freedom/ has its root in the Sacred truth that every man hath in him the divine Reason." Even though "few men since the creation of the world live according to the dictates of Reason, yet all men are created capable of so doing. That is the equality and the only equality of all men. To this truth we look when we say, 'Reverence thyself. Be true to thyself.' Because every man has within him somewhat really divine therefore is slavery the unpardonable outrage it is." Presently he summed up his speculations on Reason in a typical apothegm: "God has made nothing without a crack except Reason."

Chapter Four

LIDIAN

DURING 1834 EMERSON PAID THREE VISITS TO "THE LITTLE pilgrim city" of Plymouth, twice as guest preacher for Dr. Kendall and once to lecture to the townspeople. Among his listeners each time was a tall, slender woman with dark brown hair, a pale face, and wideset, luminous gray eyes. Her outward demeanor was both pensive and serious, though she was known for her quick wit among her friends and neighbors. She lived in a large mansion called Winslow House where she kept a garden and a flock of chickens, and she seemed to be wholly content with her quiet way of life. She had lost both her parents within three months in 1818. Her sister, Lucy, had made an unfortunate marriage in 1820, and her brother, Charles, a geologist, had recently taken a wife. But Lydia Jackson at thirty-two was still unwed, without visible matrimonial prospects.

As lecturer and preacher, Emerson had already developed a notably charismatic platform presence. Less than a year earlier, a Scotsman named Alexander Ireland had heard him speak at the Unitarian chapel in Edinburgh. "The originality of his thoughts," wrote Ireland, "the consummate beauty of the language in which they were clothed, the calm dignity of his bearing, the absence of all oratorical effect, and the singular directness and simplicity of his manner, free from the least shadow of dogmatic assumption, made a deep impression on me. . . . His voice was the sweetest, the most winning and penetrating of any I ever heard."

The impression he gave was rather of spiritual than of physical vigor. Six feet tall, with sloping shoulders, flat chest, and long arms and neck, he looked excessively slender in his dark ministerial garb. His head, though relatively small, was well covered with finely textured brown hair, abundant and thick and sweeping over one side of his high brow. His chin was firm, his mouth "well formed and well closed," with a slightly protruding lower lip, the only mark of aggressiveness in the whole face except for the prominent Indian nose which, as a later observer remarked, cast a broad shadow. It was evidently an inheritance from the Haskins side of the family, since he and his brother William shared such noses with their mother. Those sitting nearest the platform were commonly struck by the bright, intense blue of Emerson's eyes— such eyes, his daughters were to say, as one associated with those of sea captains accustomed to gaze out over huge expanses of sea and sky.

"We seem to see the people turning out into the snow after hearing" his lectures and sermons, "glowing with a finer glow than even the climate could give, and fortified for a struggle with overshoes and the east wind." So wrote Henry James Junior in 1887, and it had been just so at Plymouth fifty-odd years earlier. Like everyone else in town, Lydia Jackson was strongly attracted to the speaker, the timbre of his baritone voice, his alert manner, and the trenchancy of his ideas. He was eight months younger than she, but wiser, she seems to have felt both then and later, by many years. When he preached the second of his sermons, she found herself "so lifted to higher thoughts" by his philosophical idealism that she "hurried out of church . . . and home lest anyone should speak to her" about mere mundane matters. After the lecture in March, she "regarded him with reverence as an angelic being" who, unlike the angels of biblical fable, could hardly be expected to consort with the daughters of men.

But her subconscious mind had begun to follow another tack. Within a few months of their first meeting, she was astonished by two instances of prescience that she never afterward forgot. One afternoon, ascending to the second floor of Winslow House, "she saw a clear image of herself dressed as a bride" and descending that same stairway to be married to Emerson. The vision shocked her. It was a great psychological "impropriety" in a woman who had thought herself innocent of all such presumptuous illusions. She banished the vision as well as she could, only to have it recur in another form on a Sunday evening late in January 1835. Emerson had meantime given another lecture in Plymouth and spoken with her at a social gathering afterward. Now

Lydia Jackson saw a momentary apparition of his face, "very beautiful, close to her." He was gazing into her eyes, as indeed he may have done at the time of their meeting. Next afternoon came a letter in unfamiliar handwriting. It contained Emerson's proposal of marriage, and she afterward thought that her fleeting vision of his face must have occurred just at the time he was composing the letter.

The message was essentially Christopher Marlowe's "Come live with me and be my Love," but the rather stilted and prolix language was that of nineteenth-century New England. Emerson apologized for not having spoken to her directly about the "deep and tender respect" that he felt for her "earnest and noble mind." He thought that she must love the same things he loved, and that she was aware, as he was, of "the everlasting principles." His excuse for having written his proposal instead of speaking it was that in the "gravest acts" of his life he always trusted more to his pen than to his tongue. He was in love with Lydia "in a new and higher way," and hoped that she would reciprocate. "Demand any time for conversation, for consideration," he concluded, "and I will come to Plymouth with a joyful heart."

On the following Friday they met for a long talk in the parlor of Winslow House. Lydia closed her gray eyes while she explained her reluctance to give up the life in Plymouth that she so "thoroughly enjoyed" and felt herself "exactly fitted" for. She shrank, she said, from the "load of care and labor" that she would have to assume as mistress of his house, and "could not undertake it unless he was sure he loved her and needed her." She had many other questions, and he would long remember what he called "that catechism with the closed eyes." But in the end she opened them and said yes.

His letter of proposal had mentioned his loving Lydia "in a new and higher way." Two days afterward, looking back on their conversation in the parlor, he half apologized for not having uttered one "vehement word" or given "one passionate sign." He had been content to surrender himself to the golden hour, finding "a sort of grandeur in the modulated expressions of a love in which the individuals" had steadily subsumed their "reasonable personal expectations" in favor of a higher "regard for truth and the universal love." But Lydia must not therefore think of him as "a metaphysical lover." The physical had been present, but only postponed. "I am a man," he wrote, "and hate and suspect the over refiners, and do sympathize with the homeliest pleasures and attractions by which our good foster mother Nature draws her children to-

gether." This foster-mother imagery was evidently borrowed from Wordsworth's great ode, but what he really meant was sexual attraction. The "most
permanent [spiritual] ties" came first, and had been satisfactorily established
during the colloquy in Winslow House. After these would come "whatever
others human nature" might suggest, including physical love.

Almost at once he renamed his fiancée Lidian. He may have felt that the
name Lydia did not merge euphonically with Emerson, or it may have been
that something in his quiet association with her recalled to his memory Milton's lines from "L'Allegro":

> And ever, against eating cares,
> Lap me in soft Lydian airs,
> Married to immortal verse
> Such as the meeting soul may pierce. . . .
>   (lines 135–38)

He was an habitual inventor of nicknames to betoken character. Soon he was
calling her his Lydian queen, as if in a former incarnation she might have
ruled over the ancient empire in Asia Minor. The term suited her regal stance,
her notably graceful walk, and what he half humorously described as "her air
of lofty abstraction, like Dante." Sometimes, too, later on, he called her "mine
Asia" or "my sybil [sic]," owing perhaps to the sibylline darkness that
seemed to lurk in her gray eyes. Before long, however, he settled on the
diminutive "Queenie," to which she answered, when she answered at all,
through the forty-seven years of their married life.

Emerson presently notified his brother William of his engagement. "I announce this fact in a very different feeling from that with which I entered my
first connexion [with Ellen Tucker]," he wrote. "This is a very sober joy.
This lady is a person of noble character whom to see is to respect. I find in her
a quite unexpected community of sentiment and speculation, and in Plymouth she is dearly prized for her love and good works." Charles Emerson
sent William a somewhat different appraisal. Lydia Jackson was not "beautiful
anywise that I know, so you look at the outside alone," a hint that in his eyes
her beauty lay within, as befitted one who was "a sort of Sybil [sic] for wisdom." Charles was evidently contrasting her with his memories of Ellen

Tucker, of whom he had said that if he were a Platonist he would have taken her to be "one of the Forms of Beauty in the Universal mind."

Edward Emerson never heard of his brother's plans to remarry. Three months before Waldo proposed to Lidian, he had died miserably in San Juan at the age of twenty-nine, victim of the tuberculosis that had plagued him sporadically during so much of his adult life. Waldo did not hear the news for more than two weeks after the event. He and his mother had moved into the Old Manse in Concord on October 9. A week later he left for New York to pay a visit to William and, as he put it, to refresh his ears "with the roar of a metropolis." But his reception there was gloomy, for William had just heard the news of Edward's death. His "fervid heart," wrote Emerson, was now "forever still." One pile more "of hope for this life" had fallen, and he felt "bereaved of a part" of himself. It is possible that his whirlwind courtship of Lydia Jackson in the following January was in some compensatory fashion related to the loss of Edward. William's wife, Susan, was already pregnant when Emerson visited them in New York. Was it too much to hope that he, too, who had so long reveled in brotherhood, might soon, like William, learn the joys of fatherhood, and help to fill the gap that Edward's death had left?

Toward the end of February 1835 Lidian began a two-week visit to Mrs. Elizabeth Bliss, a girlhood friend then living in Boston. One of those who came to meet her was Elizabeth Palmer Peabody, whose judgment ran roughly parallel to Charles Emerson's:

> She looks *very refined* but neither beautiful or elegant—and very frail—and as if her mind wore out her body—she was *unaffected* but *peculiar*. . . . She sat down by me—and we had a beautiful talk about a variety of most intellectual and spiritual things— And I should think she had the rare characteristic of genius—inexhaustible originality . . . We parted to meet again as friends. . . .

They met again at an evening party three days later. This time the description was offered by Sarah Clarke, who thought Lidian "as remarkable among women as [Emerson is] among men":

> She is a singular looking person, and to my thinking, very handsome. Her eyes are somewhat like lamps, and the expression of her face is that

of a beaming soul, shining through. Then, while she talks, she thinks: and you see it. Her movements are free and graceful; she is a soaring transcendentalist; she is full of sensibility, yet as independent in her mind as—who shall I say? Margaret Fuller.

When the conversation turned to religion, Lidian said that she respected Unitarianism, "for without it we should never have had Transcendentalism." Miss Peabody pounced: Unitarianism, she said positively, was *"terra firma."* "And nothing else," rejoined Lidian, "cold and hard, with scarcely a firmament above it." Like her husband-to-be, who would inveigh against "corpse-cold Unitarianism" and fix his eyes on the living firmament, Lidian was already, as Miss Clarke had divined, a "soaring Transcendentalist." But the soaring was not to last.

The appearance of frailty that Elizabeth Peabody noticed in Lidian was a problem of long standing. At age nineteen in 1821 she had a bad attack of scarlet fever. According to her daughter Ellen, she "did not make a very good recovery, her head was hot ever after, and she never was so well in other ways. She read about Napoleon's never sleeping more than four hours," and tried it herself, reading until one and rising at five. She was troubled by chronic dyspepsia, a disorder that often caused severe neuralgic pain in the gastric and epigastric regions. One of her remedies for this affliction, which began in girlhood and was to complicate all her future pregnancies, was a lowered intake of food. Her doctrine was that "the food you don't eat does you more good than the food you do." An early proponent of this theory was Luigi Cornaro, a sixteenth-century Venetian nobleman, whose guide to a long and healthy life was widely reprinted in translation. Lidian owned a copy, and her belief in Cornaro brought her to the verge of anorexia. According to her daughter, "In those years from 18 to 30 she was sometimes called 'the living skeleton.' " She also read her uncle's medical books, from which she derived "a complete theory of health and medicine." For years afterward she depended heavily on dosages of calomel, a mercury compound often prescribed in those days for purgative purposes. Her program likewise called for fresh air, cold water, and loose clothing. "So," said her daughter, "she used a cold bath and slept with open windows and never wore corsets but buttoned her skirts onto a waist." In certain respects, but by no means in all, her views on health were ahead of her times.

Emerson's burgeoning profession as lecturer kept the lovers apart for longer periods than either of them wished. She would have preferred to go on living in Plymouth, but Emerson was firm about moving her to Concord. Plymouth meant streets, he said, whereas he must have a "wide champaign" such as Concord offered. He was probably thinking of her numerous friends at home when he told her that "a sunset, a forest, a snow storm, a certain riverview, are more to me than many friends and do ordinarily divide my day with my books." He jokingly accused her of loving the surly roar of the sea more than a "childish murmuring" of Concord's slow-moving river, the Musketaquid—Indian for "meadow"—which Holmes later compared to "an English river, licking its grassy margin with a sort of bovine placidity and contentment."

The river was frozen and silent under fresh snow that noontime in March when Lidian first saw Concord. She stayed four days at the Manse, the large, weathered, gambrel-roofed farmhouse, built sixty-five years earlier, with its ill-lighted rooms and drafty windows. There she met Emerson's mother, Ruth, and Charles's fiancée, Elizabeth Hoar, a tall woman nearly as thin as Lidian who gazed at the bride-to-be with her great dark eyes and engaged her in a long private conversation. Either then or soon afterward, Lidian discovered that Waldo planned to include both his mother and his brother Charles as tenants of his house, whenever he could find one. If the prospect of two brothers, two brides, and an aging mother-in-law gave Lidian pause, she did not complain. Waldo had promised to assist her in taking care of her sister, Lucy Brown, whose husband, Charles, had deserted, leaving her with two small children.

Suitable housing was hard to locate in Concord in 1835. Emerson jocosely assured Lidian that she must not worry. Had not George Fox, founder of the Quakers, once lived in a tree? It was late July before he found a homestead that approximated his needs. A large white house with green shutters, a substantial ell, a barn, and a doghouse, it had been built seven years earlier by a man named Coolidge and was locally known as Coolidge Castle. Castle it was not, nor was it nearly so grand as Winslow House in Plymouth, which it somewhat resembled. It would clearly require an addition to accommodate Charles and Elizabeth, and would need considerable landscaping, both tree planting and diversified shrubbery, as well as a garden to take the place of the one Lidian was leaving behind in Plymouth. When in the course of time these various plantations had grown up, the name Coolidge Castle was gradually dropped to be superseded by the less ornate name Bush.

The wedding was planned for mid-September, and the hope was that Charles could marry Elizabeth a year later. Emerson's summer was packed with the past, since he had agreed in June to deliver an "historical discourse" to the citizens of Concord on the two-hundredth anniversary of the incorporation of the town. He worked assiduously to meet the deadline, poring over the ancient records of town and church, consulting dozens of books at Harvard and at home, and borrowing the page proofs of Lemuel Shattuck's history of the village. He also interviewed several former minutemen who had fought the Battle of Concord in the field by the river that he could see from the windows of the Old Manse where he was at work. Some of these old men were present in the meetinghouse when he read his lengthy discourse to a packed audience on Saturday, September 12.

The sound of enthusiastic applause was still ringing in his ears on Sunday when he drove the chaise to Boston, completing the trip to Plymouth in Monday's driving rain, and arriving at four o'clock in reasonable time for the wedding at seven-thirty. He and Lidian sat talking for more than two hours in the front parlor of Winslow House. She thought the rain an ill omen, but brightened when the autumnal sun bored through the clouds at the end of the afternoon. "Women have in themselves no measure of time," wrote Emerson in his journal. "There was a clock set in Adam; none in Eve." Lidian was so charmed by the prenuptial conversation that she had to be warned to go and dress for the ceremony. Emerson hastily changed his own clothes and waited for his bride on the stairway landing. When she appeared at last, wearing white muslin with a scoop neck and puffed sleeves, they went down together, in exact fulfillment of Lidian's earlier vision.

Among Emerson's notebook entries are a series about marriage, all of them more realistic than romantic. One of them refers to Byron's comparison: "the process of love to marriage is like that of wine to vinegar." Emerson quotes Thomas Warton on marriage versus hanging: "Hanging is better of the twayne / Sooner done and shorter payne," and Sir Thomas More's opinion that getting married is like putting one's hand into a bag containing "99 snakes and one eel." Here also is an anonymous sage's remark on sexual attraction, "A drop in the ocean seeking another drop"; another's view that "opportunity is the great match-maker"; and finally a pertinent line from one of Terence's comedies: "I came to her at the right moment, which is always half the battle." Emerson's grouping of such observations did not necessarily mean that he shared the views of Terence, Byron, and the rest, but only that he was well aware of this sardonic strain in the Western tradition. His own opinion was perhaps best embodied in two homely self-generated epigrams: "He champed the bit, but, good husband, went the way the bridle drew"; and "A man wants a wife to be silly unto."

The bride and groom spent the night in Winslow House and drove to Concord on Tuesday. Lidian's and Lucy's furniture and carpets had been sent on ahead, though not yet distributed among the rooms, and it needed the better part of a fortnight to gain some semblance of order. Despite the problems of settling in, Lidian was ecstatic over what Byron had called "the homely household savour." A week after the wedding, she wrote her sister, Lucy, that Mr. Emerson (as she always called him) both enjoyed and imparted "all the various charities of social and domestic life." At the same time, Emerson wrote exuberantly to his brother William, "Send any friends now with confidence to me, as at last we have room bread and broad welcome for friends old and new and lie directly on the stage road 2 1/2 hours from Boston."

By November, chiefly for economic reasons, Emerson resumed his preaching and lecturing, taking over, on an ad hoc basis, a small parish in nearby East Lexington, accompanied by Lidian when the weather permitted, and beginning a series of ten lectures on English literature at the Masonic Temple in Boston, repeating them afterward in other lyceums throughout that cold and snowy winter. His brother Edward had once turned aside someone's praise of his own attainments with a statement about Waldo: "Yes, they say much of me, but I tell them that the real lion of the tribe of Judah is at home." Emerson's position as head of the family was much in evidence during the early months of his second marriage. Domestic problems constantly cropped up to postpone completion of his first book, *Nature*, which he had been dreaming over for more than three years. "To write a very little takes a great deal of time," he told his friend Hedge. "So shall a man weary himself . . . in vain attempts to carve Apollos which all turn out scarecrows."

Besides the book, he was preparing lectures on English biography for delivery at Salem, and supervising the construction of the addition to his house for Charles and Elizabeth to occupy after their marriage. Charles had now taken his brother's "bachelor bedstead" in the room over the kitchen. But in the severe winter weather he was "withering" under the onslaught of another of his heavy colds, with a hacking cough and loss of weight and appetite. It was presently determined that he must go into the milder climate of New York to stay with William, or even further south, as in 1831-32. Emerson had just reached Salem to start his lecture series when he learned that Charles was too feeble to travel alone to New York. He postponed the lectures, accompanied his brother to William's house, and had just returned to Salem when news came that Charles was sinking fast. He rushed home to Concord, gathered up Elizabeth Hoar, and set off for New York once again. But they "arrived too late": Charles had collapsed and died on the afternoon of May 9.

These were dark hours, made yet darker by the fact that Bulkeley, the third of the surviving brothers, had once more become unmanageable on the farm in Chelmsford where Israel Putnam was still serving as his custodian. Emerson was obliged to arrange for his readmission to McLean Asylum for what would become a stay of nearly ten months. Lidian was supportive through these harrowing times, doing her best to console her husband and her hitherto prospective sister-in-law. But the blissful commencement of her own marriage was now overlaid with care and sorrow. In addition to everything else, she had begun in January 1836 a first pregnancy, which, though theoretically a blessing, led to extreme and protracted physical discomfort.

Chapter   Five

BRONSON ALCOTT

JUST OVER EMERSON'S EASTERN HORIZON IN THE FALL OF 1834 an idealistic teacher was convening his classes at the Temple School in Boston. Bronson Alcott had so named it because of its location in rooms seven and eight of the Masonic Temple on Tremont Street. Some thirty pupils appeared, most of them under ten years of age and many from the best-known families of the city. They gazed wide-eyed around the high-ceilinged rooms, one of which was lighted by a large Gothic window. The tall, benign figure of the schoolmaster occupied his semicircular desk facing the light. Behind his head stood a bas-relief of Jesus and a bust of Plato. These were the master spirits of his personal theocracy, and their presence added yet another dimension to the name of his school. It was his temple; he had made it; he would lead his pupils toward the light.

During the fall quarter he gathered and installed more equipment: "tasteful furniture, desks, chairs, books, tablets (paper and wood), cubes, cards, clock, 'hour-glass,' mirror, boxes, vases." The four corners were ornamented with busts of Socrates, Shakespeare, Milton, and Sir Walter Scott. Alcott's liking for all things emblematic was elsewhere reflected in his choice of statuary. Under the window he placed an Image of Silence, "done by the Italian in School Street," holding up one admonitory finger. On his desk was a small sculpture of a "child aspiring." At the north end of the room, opposite the entrance, was the table of his assistant and scribe, a thirty-year-old bluestocking named Elizabeth Palmer Peabody, who taught Latin and arithmetic. Close to her elbow stood another figurine: Atlas shouldering the weight of the world.

The master in the midst of all this grandeur was just turning thirty-five, and hoping against hope that some measure of success was at last within his grasp. "The sensation of thrift is to me a delightful one," he wrote, "and the more so from the continuous scuffling with untoward circumstances to which I have been subjected." With a probable net income of $1,800, he thought he could now remove "some impediments to progress in the celestial life." But his sensation of thrift was far weaker than his longing for splendor. On the terrestrial level he had gone heavily into debt furnishing and equipping his schoolrooms.

"Scuffling with untoward circumstances" had so far been the story of his life. Starting from a hardscrabble farm at Spindle Hill near Wolcott, Connecticut, he had set out at nineteen as a traveling salesman, peddling Yankee "notions" along the country roads and among the green plantations of Virginia and the Carolinas. Admitted sometimes to libraries in the great houses, he discovered an interest in books that carried him well beyond his early fascination with the Bible and Bunyan. During a succession of minor teaching jobs in Connecticut, Pennsylvania, and for a time (1828–30) in Boston, he carried on his self-education. Between further classes in Germantown and Philadelphia he developed a taste for Plato and Coleridge, to whose ideologies his own ran roughly parallel. Now back in Boston, he was peddling notions of a spiritual kind among elementary schoolchildren. He had long since dropped his boyhood name of Amos B. Alcox. He was now A. Bronson Alcott, founder of the Temple School.

Soon after the opening of classes in 1834, he advised Miss Peabody that "every book read should be an event for the child." Few modern works survived his careful scrutiny, but he settled on a narrow shelf of old favorites: the Bible, *The Pilgrim's Progress*, *The Faerie Queene*, *Paradise Lost*, some poems by Wordsworth and Coleridge, and the allegory of the cave from Plato's *Republic*. The death of Socrates from the *Phaedo* made some of the children weep, as did the story of the Crucifixion. Apart from these classics, from which he read aloud with many omissions, paraphrasings, and explanatory interpolations, his tastes ran heavily to symbolic and allegorical writings: the *Emblems* of Francis Quarles; the *Parables* of Friedrich Adolph Krummacher, simple anecdotes leading to moralistic conclusions; and *The Story Without an*

End, by Friedrich Carové, with a brief preface by Alcott himself. This last was the first strictly literary publication of his career, a small book in large print with emblematic illustrations, designed, as he said, "to quicken the hearts of the young by displaying to their view, in the significant Imagery of Nature, an Emblem of their spiritual life. . . . It is a revival, in a new form, of the beautiful fable of Psyche."

The fable of Psyche had long fascinated Alcott. Toward the end of his previous teaching stint in Boston he had married Abigail May, daughter of Colonel Joseph May, a man of some means in the city. Their first two daughters, Anna and Louisa May, were born in Pennsylvania. A third child was now on the way. One of Alcott's journal entries in the spring of 1835 referred to the imminent "appearance of the young celestial whom I am soon to know." They named her Elizabeth, though her father soon began to call her Psyche. This became the title of his most ambitious piece of writing, an extended series of reflections on the spiritual growth of his daughters, framed in elegant and somewhat archaic language. Along with his joy in fatherhood went a strong belief in the rightness of his intuitions, a serene and lofty deportment, and a strong infusion of what Emerson later called a "prophet's egotism."

The books he had gathered sometimes served as springboards for his schoolroom conversations, but he leaned more heavily on his personal convictions, aiming to create "from the ideal of my own mind the material for the spiritual nurture of children." He adapted a version of the Socratic method to draw forth the ideas and reactions of his pupils, patiently pausing to explore the actual or symbolic meanings of single words. The word for the morning of February 4, 1835 was "birth." As Miss Peabody recorded it, Alcott began with four lines from Wordsworth's "Ode: Intimations of Immortality":

It is not now as it hath been of yore;
Turn whereso'er I may,
By night or day,
The Things which I have seen I now can see no more.

(lines 6–9)

What was Wordsworth talking about? Had things changed or had he himself changed? Wordsworth had changed, said a ten-year-old. "Have you had any degree of this change?" asked Alcott. "Yes," the boy said, "and more in this last year than in all my life before." Alcott said he himself had known periods when great changes occurred. "How many of you feel that the schoolroom is a different place from what it was the first day?" All hands shot up. "We know more," the children said, "and think more. You know us, you have looked inside us. We behave better." Alcott nodded. "Knowledge is chaff of itself," he told them. "But you have taken the knowledge and used it to govern yourself better. If I have thought I gave you knowledge only, and could not lead you to use it, I would never enter this schoolroom again." Eventually the discussion came to focus on "birth" from Wordsworth's line "Our birth is but a sleep and a forgetting."

After classes closed for the spring quarter, Elizabeth Peabody hurried into print with her *Record of a School*, a detailed account of Alcott's teaching methods along with extensive verbatim quotations from his talks with the children. Alcott encouraged this undertaking in the hope that such dignified advertising might help to spread the Temple School gospel. But it had also the unexpected advantage of calling himself and his work to Emerson's attention. During his previous time in Boston he had twice heard Emerson preach. On January 29, 1835, he wrote in his journal, "I wish to know Mr. R. Emerson and Mr. [Frederic] Hedge."

On the following Fourth of July, when Emerson's friend George Bradford spoke of Alcott as a "consistent spiritualist," Emerson pricked up his ears. He was already on the lookout for "new men" who might independently have arrived at some of the views he was going to espouse in his first book, *Nature*. Perhaps Alcott was one of them. Shortly thereafter the two men met for the first time at an evening gathering in Alcott's rooms in Boston. Presently Emerson read Elizabeth Peabody's *Record of a School*. He not only admired the book but also recommended it to his brother William as good reading for his wife, Susan, who had recently borne their first child. "To the parents of little Willy," wrote Uncle Waldo, "I cannot doubt it will be engaging." So the Schoolmaster and the Lecturer moved one step closer to a friendship that would last more than forty years.

When the Temple School reopened in the fall of 1835, Alcott began a fresh experiment, conducting conversations on the Gospels. He was keeping a promise he had made to his students in the spring. "I shall get people to come and tell you about many outward things, which I do not know much about myself," he had said. "I can teach better about inward things. Next quarter I am going to teach you about inward things, not in yourselves, but in another—a Perfect Being. . . . We will study Jesus Christ. How many of you will be glad to do this?" Most of the children held up their hands, but none of them could foresee that this experiment, so gently broached, would lead to the master's undoing in less than two years' time.

His first real chance to talk with Emerson came one Saturday evening in October when George Bradford took him to Concord. They spent the night of the seventeenth and all day Sunday with Emerson and his brother Charles. Alcott was greatly impressed. He took at once to Lidian, bride of a month, and thought that she and her husband represented "a new idea of life." He found a "striking conformity of taste and opinion" between his views and theirs, although he felt that "Mr. E's fine literary taste is sometimes in the way of the clear and hearty acceptance of the spiritual." Charles Emerson was handsomer than his brother but otherwise much like him. Alcott was ecstatic: "To have a few such friends," he wrote in his journal, "is the joy and content of life." Emerson shared this view. Alcott was "a wise man, simple, superior to display," who in conversation uttered "the best things as quietly as the least. . . . His book is his school in which he writes all his thoughts." Looking back on the visit, Charles remarked "upon the nimbleness and buoyancy which the conversation of a spiritualist awakens," causing the ordinary material world to "dislimn"—that is, to be blotted out and to vanish.

There was another weekend with Emerson six weeks later. This time Frederic Henry Hedge was there, and Alcott was able to fulfill his dream of the previous January in getting to know them both. He called them "the most earnest spiritualists of the time . . . persons whose culture places them on the Mount of Clear Vision." Emerson in turn took notice of Alcott's skill in the analysis of the characters of men like Hedge and Bradford. Despite his persistent otherworldliness, this analytical power was often reflected in his journal entries. It was an aspect of his interest in what he called "inward things," the same power that made his pupils say, "You have looked inside us." As his acquaintance with Emerson ripened, each of them would bring such skills to bear upon the understanding of the other.

Alcott was eager for Emerson's opinion of the manuscript "Psyche, or The Breath of Childhood," in which he was recording impressions of his daughters. "Thou still art, wast ever, and shalt remain, the horologe of time's transit. . . . Thou comest to me as an inhabitant of a country once mine own." In February 1836 Emerson's curiosity got the better of him: he called on Alcott in Boston and took away the manuscript "for criticizing." The upshot was a tactful letter that called the book original, vital, and earnest. Some passages awakened in the reader "the Apprehension of the Absolute," and the prose was almost uniformly elegant, with many beautiful and a few splendid paragraphs. On the other hand, it was "too much the book of *one idea*," and cried out for compression. Emerson listed his favorite sections, advised heavy cutting, and appended a six-page inventory of "verbal inaccuracies."

In June he read Alcott's manuscript diary for the year 1835. The contrast with "Psyche" was marked. The journal was filled with "perfectly simple and elegant utterance," with no inflation or verbal cramp. Alcott's "one idea" on the relationship between Matter and Spirit was clearer there than in "Psyche." This idea was his faith and his study, night and day: "He writes it in the book, he discourses it in the parlor, he instructs it in the school." With such advance preparation he was in a sympathetic frame of mind on June 15 when he sat on the visitors' sofa at Temple School and heard Alcott lead a discussion of the Gospel according to Saint John. Watching "the gradual dawn of a thought" on the children's faces made Emerson reflect that truth knows neither age nor season, since "we are all alike before the great Whole." Reading a transcript of one such conversation some days afterward, he thought that it showed real thinking on the part of the children. While their instrument was simple enough—"a harp of two strings, Matter and Spirit"—the effect was sublime. "That man [Alcott] grows upon me every time I see him," he wrote Hedge. "He is a world builder—forever occupied with one problem—how spirit makes matter or how Be makes Seem. This singleness is his strength and his weakness."

"Like other sovereigns," Alcott lost much by reason of his grandeur, his preoccupation with infinitude. Emerson himself could enjoy the universe not only through nature (Alcott's "Matter") but also "through the powers and organs of a hundred different men"—Shakespeare, Goethe, Swift, Tennyson. To such influences Alcott seemed blind. "The Whole," said Emerson, "Nature proceeding from himself, is what he studies. . . . Particular thoughts, sentences, facts even, cannot interest him except as for a moment they take their place as a ray from his orb."

Whatever his faults, and Emerson discovered others as time went by, Alcott was a kind of genius:

> Each new mind we approach seems to require an abdication of all our past and present empire. A new doctrine seems at first a subversion of all our opinions, tastes, and manner of living. So did Jesus, so did Kant, so did Swedenborg, so did Cousin, so did Alcott seem. Take thankfully and heartily all they can give, exhaust them, leave father and mother and goods, wrestle with them, let them not go until their blessing be won, and after a short season the dismay will be overpast, the excess of influence will be withdrawn, and they will be no longer an alarming meteor but one more bright star shining serenely in your heaven and blending its light with all your day.

This process of acclimatization to Alcott's "newness" had been accelerated in February while Emerson was reading "Psyche." Several passages from the manuscript he transcribed into his journal. "Nothing is complete until it is enacted," Alcott had written. "A fact is spirit having completed its mission, attained its end, fully revealed itself." And again, "The more of the supernatural the religion embodies, the stronger the evidence in its favor, provided there be . . . no surrender of the supernatural to the natural; no trenching of matter on spirit."

In June Emerson mounted a similar raid on Alcott's journal for 1835: "Successful preaching implies . . . the utterance of profoundest truth in simple phrase. . . . Whoso exerteth this power . . . shall find fit hearers. . . . The ear shall hear and the spirit understand those heavenly words in which the soul's meaning is given forth." He must also have noticed two other passages in Alcott's diary that exactly expressed his idealistic position: "Matter is a revelation of Mind" and "I set out from the wide ground of Spirit. This is; all else is its manifestation." For the schoolmaster deeply believed, as one of his biographers would put it, that nature's whole starry universe was "one enormous web that Man has spun, like a huge omnific spider, out of his own vitals."

Throughout his life Alcott reiterated and elaborated his "one idea" in many contexts. Spirit, he held, is "the sublime architect of Nature," Man being "the *chef d'oeuvre* of its art." He suggested that "mettle"—by which he seems to have meant human sperm—"is the Godhead proceeding into the matrix of Nature to organize Man." This was another way of explaining what he had told the schoolchildren in simpler terms. He said that the Soul was "prior to the elements of Nature," and that it was the Soul which had first said, "Let there be light." Thirty-two years after his first meeting with Emerson, he was still harping on the same two strings: "Not the forms merely but the materials of natural things are preconceived . . . in man's mind, and put forth as the nature we see externally. Nature is Mind in solution—the waste or spent man. Without man, matter were not, nor nature."

In the early days of his friendship with Alcott, Emerson was at work on his first book, *Nature*, published anonymously in September 1836 with an epigraph from Plotinus. The precise extent of Alcott's influence on this book is difficult to determine. But Emerson's journals from February through July 1836 contain many entries that would soon be incorporated into the final text of *Nature*, and it may be a sign of his growing interest in Alcott (a "born-again" Neoplatonist) that he frequently reflected on the relations between Spirit and Matter. One clear instance of probable influence passes through stages: (1) copied from "Psyche": "A fact is spirit having completed its mission, attained its end, fully revealed itself" (February); (2) entry in Emerson's journal: "A fact is only a fulcrum of the spirit" (June); (3) passage in the *Nature* essay: "A fact is the end or last issue of spirit. The visible creation is the terminus or the circumference of the invisible world."

When Alcott received and read his gift copy of *Nature*, he was full of admiration, calling it a "harbinger" to the reestablishment of the spiritual, and noticing especially the ways in which Emerson subordinated "the visible and outward to the inward and invisible." The language here was not far from Saint Paul's. But it seemed to Alcott that Emerson had "adverted," however indirectly, to his own "Psyche," a redaction of which he had brought with him to Concord on August 2 for further criticism.

Even though the Spirit-Matter dualism was plainly of interest to Emerson, his journal entries of these months did not always follow Alcott into the glowing zenith of idealistic utterance. "I see with as much pleasure as another a field of corn or a rich pasture," he wrote, "whilst I dispute their absolute being. Their phenomenal being, I no more dispute than I do my own. I do not dispute but point out the just way of viewing them." Again he wrote, "To the rude it seems as if Matter had absolute existence, existed from an intrinsic necessity. The first effect of thought is to make us sensible that Spirit exists from an intrinsic necessity, that Matter has a merely phenomenal or accidental being, being created from Spirit, or being the manifestation of Spirit." This virtually echoes Alcott's assertion, already quoted, "I set out from the wide ground of Spirit. This is. All else is its manifestation."

Another journal passage might be aimed at correcting Alcott's antinaturalistic bias: "It is a small and mean thing to attempt too hardly to disprove the being of Matter. I have no hostility to oxygen or hydrogen, to the sun or the hyacinth that opened this morning his little censer in his beam. This is not for one of my complexion who do expand like a plant in the sunshine, who do really love the warm day like an Indian or a bird. I only aim to speak for the Great Soul; to speak for the sovereignty of Ideas." Children have no question about believing in an external world. "The belief that it *appears* only, is an afterthought but on the human faculties if cultured this will as surely dawn as did the first faith."

Unlike Emerson, who gleaned ideas eclectically from the whole face of the globe, its literature and history, its many religions, its immense diversities of character and belief, Alcott was relatively impervious to "notions" other than those of his own origination. In such passages as those quoted above, Emerson showed his interest in Alcott's manner of thinking but also his unwillingness to accept without qualification Alcott's "one idea." Alcott's admiration for *Nature* is not hard to understand. He must have taken pleasure in a number of Emerson's public affirmations. "There are new lands, new men, new thoughts" could have included the head of the Temple School. His attention must also have been arrested by Emerson's use of the term "apparition" as a synonym for "nature" in the sentence "Let us interrogate the great apparition that shines so peacefully around us," although, as a declared non-Shakespearean, he may well have missed the veiled and perhaps even subconscious reference to Hamlet's interrogation of his father's apparition. When Emerson asked, in a magnificent apostrophe to the visible world that half echoed Hamlet's to Guildenstern: "What angels invented these splendid ornaments, these rich conveniences, this ocean of air above, this ocean of water beneath, this firmament of earth between, this zodiac of lights, this tent of dropping clouds, this striped coat of climates, this fourfold year?"—Alcott would have been ready to respond that Emerson's angels were only another name for the creative noumenal Spirit to which his whole philosophy paid repeated obeisance.

It is impossible to say how closely Alcott read *Nature*. But in light of his predilections, he could only have applauded such statements as the following: that "the presence of a higher, namely, of the spiritual element is essential to [natural beauty's] perfection"; that "beauty in nature is not ultimate" but rather "the herald of inward and eternal beauty"; that "the world is emblematic"; that "Reason transfers all these lessons [learned by the Understanding] into its own world of thought by perceiving the analogy that marries Matter and Mind"; that "a noble doubt perpetually suggests itself . . . whether nature outwardly exists. . . . Whether nature enjoy a substantial existence without, or is only in the apocalypse of the mind." But when Emerson asked what difference is made whether Orion was actually "up there in heaven" or whether some god had painted "the image in the firmament of the soul," Alcott's reply would have been succinct: "All the difference."

Emerson remained dubious about the extreme ideality of Alcott's position. "Idealism," says the seventh chapter of *Nature*,

is a hypothesis to account for nature by other principles than those of carpentry and chemistry. Yet, if it only deny the existence of matter, it does not satisfy the demands of the spirit. It leaves God out of me. It leaves me in the splendid labyrinth of my perceptions, to wander without end. Then the heart resists it, because it balks the affections in denying substantive being to men and women. Nature is so pervaded with human life that there is something of humanity in all and in every particular. But this theory makes nature foreign to me, and does not account for that consanguinity which we acknowledge to it.

Despite these objections he was willing to let idealism stand "as a useful introductory hypothesis, serving to apprize us of the eternal distinction between the soul and the world." We learn, he said,

that the highest is present to the soul of man; that the dread universal essence . . . is that for which all things exist, and that by which they are; that spirit creates; that behind nature, throughout nature, spirit is present. . . . It does not act upon us from without, that is, in space and time, but spiritually, or through ourselves. Therefore that spirit . . . the Supreme Being, does not build up nature around us, but puts it forth through us, as the life of the tree puts forth new branches and leaves through the pores of the old. . . . Who can set bounds to the possibilities of man? Once inhale the upper air, being admitted to behold the absolute natures of justice and truth, and we learn that man has access to the entire mind of the Creator, is himself the creator in the finite.

This last idea, which appears to be an echo of Coleridge's language in defining the primary imagination as "a repetition in the finite mind of the eternal act of creation in the infinite I Am," offers a hint that Emerson, like Alcott and many other American romantics, was already thinking along lines laid down by the author of *Biographia Literaria* and *Aids to Reflection*. Emerson's familiarity with Coleridge's distinction between imagination and fancy was evident as early as the summer of 1835. It was, he said, "a distinction in kind. The Fancy aggregates; the Imagination animates. The Fancy takes the world as it stands and selects pleasing groups by apparent relations. The Imagination is Vision, regards the world as symbolical and pierces the emblem for the real sense, sees all external objects as types." Both Alcott and Emerson ranged themselves upon the side of Imagination.

It is sometimes asserted that Alcott was the real name of that anonymous "certain poet" with whose quoted words Emerson brings to a close his *Nature*. This may be, especially when one remembers that he had called Alcott "a world builder," and that the peroration of Chapter Eight opens with the injunction "Build therefore your own world." Yet it is more likely that the mysterious poet was Emerson himself, and that the kind of world he was engaged in building differed from that of Alcott. All worlds need not be alike. "Every spirit," wrote Emerson, "builds itself a house, and beyond its house a world, and beyond its world a heaven." That did not mean that his house, his world, or his heaven were exact counterparts of those that Alcott was rearing in the supernal ether.

Chapter Six

MARGARET FULLER

🏵 LIVING IN THE VILLAGE OF GROTON, MASSACHUSETTS, IN 1835 was a young woman who had longed to know Emerson for several years. Certain of his observations from various pulpits stood out in her memory like landmarks in her "spiritual history." In October 1834 she had called him "that only clergyman of all possible clergymen who eludes my acquaintance. Mais n'importe! I keep his image bright in my mind." At this time he knew at least something about her abilities, if not yet of her character, having borrowed her manuscript translation of Goethe's *Tasso* from their mutual friend Frederic Hedge. Hedge served as go-between, assuring her in January 1835 of Emerson's interest. "I am flattered," she replied, "that Mr Emerson should wish to know me. I fear it will never be but 'tis pleasant to know that he wished it—I cannot think I should be disappointed in him as I have been in others to whom I had hoped to look up, the sensation one experiences in the atmosphere of his thoughts is too decided and peculiar." Her reaction to the intellectual and spiritual atmosphere that Emerson projected from pulpit and lectern was a virtual duplicate of Lydia Jackson's at Plymouth in 1834.

Their first actual meeting seems to have taken place at a soirée in Cambridge on August 25, 1835. The hostess was Eliza Rotch Farrar, whose husband was a member of the Harvard faculty. The guest of honor was Harriet Martineau, the English Unitarian and social reformer who was now entering the second year of her stay in America. Emerson, who had already met her in

England two years earlier, came with his brother Charles to pay his respects, but was not mightily impressed, calling her "a pleasant unpretending lady whom it would be agreeable to talk with when tired and at ease but she is too weary of society to shine if ever she does." Miss Martineau was very deaf, and Emerson remarked that the problem of speaking into her ear trumpet made him and Charles feel like Chang and Eng, the fabled Siamese twins.

Another of the guests was Mrs. Farrar's protégée, Miss Sarah Margaret Fuller, aged twenty-five. It is doubtful if the degree of her admiration for Emerson got across to him in the social crush of that warm evening. He must have struck her as excessively preoccupied. Only ten days earlier he had bought his house in Concord, and in less than three weeks he would offer his historical discourse at Concord's Bicentennial and would marry Lydia Jackson.

Margaret had heard about the coming marriage. Owing to her interest in Emerson, she had been speculating about his choice of a bride since the spring of the year:

I have heard much of Miss Jackson [she wrote to Hedge] and should think her every-way calculated to make Mr. Emerson happy even on his own principle that it is not the *quantity* but the *quality* of happiness that is to be taken into consideration. How is it that men who marry a second time usually select a wife of character and manners entirely unlike their first[?] This seems the case with Mr E—and I have just heard a similar instance a gentleman in N York married a young girl of my acquaintance, a gentle, fanciful golden-haired blue-eyed maid—Two years she was "crown to his cap and garnish to his dish." She died at the age of 19—two more years pass and here he is engaged to a woman of six and twenty, as ugly, as ungraceful and as simply devoted to duty as possible with a mind, very substantial, indeed, but from which the elegant imaginings de sa premiere could never have elicited a single spark.—This must be on the principle of reaction, or natural desire for balance of character.

So she had amused herself with a nascent theory on second marriages. But it would be nearly a year after the soirée at Mrs. Farrar's before Margaret succeeded, for the first time, in becoming a guest in the Emerson household, and discovering for herself the quantity and quality of domestic happiness to be found there.

In 1851, after her death by drowning, Emerson looked back over Margaret Fuller's career. "I have heard," he wrote, "that from the beginning of her life, she idealized herself as a sovereign. . . . She early saw herself to be intellectually superior to those around her, and . . . for years she dwelt upon the idea, until she believed that she was not her parents' child, but an European princess confided to their care. She remembered that, when a little girl, she was walking one day under the apple trees with such an air and step, that her father [Timothy] pointed her out to her sister [Ellen], saying *Incedit regina*."

This young queen, stepping so lightly and proudly through the orchard behind her birthplace in Cambridgeport, had evidently reminded her father of Virgil's Juno, plotting to delay Aeneas' founding of Rome. Emerson knew the *Aeneid* well enough to recognize the echo, and took up the image in his part of the *Memoirs of Margaret Fuller Ossoli*. She seemed, he said, "like the queen of some parliament of love, who carried the key to all confidences." She chose as her retinue those "marked by fortune, or character, or success," and "addressed them with a hardihood,—almost a haughty assurance—queen-like." She had, he believed, no instinct for humility. He called her "this imperious dame," and quoted one of her letters to her friend Caroline Sturgis: "I take my natural position always, and the more I see, the more I feel that it is regal.—Without throne, sceptre, or guards, still a queen!" Like a queen, too, as Elizabeth Hoar told Emerson, she wore her circle of friends as if they were "a necklace of diamonds about her neck."

One of the most devoted of these friends was Eliza Rotch Farrar, a handsome woman in her forties, second wife of John Farrar, who since 1807 had been Hollis Professor of Mathematics and Natural Philosophy at Harvard. She came of a New Bedford Quaker family, and had spent much of her childhood abroad. Her paternal grandfather, William Rotch, had established a sperm-whale fishery with headquarters at Dunkerque on the French coast and later at Milford Haven in South Wales. Her autobiography, published in her seventy-fifth year, revealed that as a young girl she had known Lord Nelson and Lady Hamilton, Joanna Baillie and Maria Edgeworth, Mrs. Siddons the actress and George Crabbe the poet. She could also boast of having once been present at a salon of the famous beauty, Madame Récamier.

It was Margaret's good fortune in her early twenties to be taken in hand as a protégée by Mrs. Farrar, who set herself, as Emerson wrote, "to put her on the best footing in the agreeable society of Cambridge," and to make her "a second home" in her own household, performing "all the offices of an almost maternal friendship." According to Colonel Higginson, "she undertook to mould [Margaret Fuller] externally, to make her less abrupt, less self-asserting, more *comme il faut* in ideas, manners, and even costume. She . . . reformed her hairdresser, and instructed her dressmaker; took her to make calls, took her on journeys." Altogether, as Emerson said, Mrs. Farrar admired Margaret's genius "and wished that all should admire it."

Margaret's first journey of any considerable length took place in the summer of 1835 under Mrs. Farrar's kindly aegis. The party embarked for New York on July 27. Besides Mrs. Farrar and Margaret, it included Mrs. Augustus Thorndike and a handsome young man named Samuel Gray Ward, who was about to enter his senior year at Harvard. Although Margaret had known and danced with many Harvard students, including Hedge, James Freeman Clarke, and W. H. Channing, her first acquaintance with Sam Ward came, according to Emerson, while the ship cleaved the calm waters of Long Island Sound. "About six," she wrote, "came out, and had a walk and a talk with Mr. Ward: did not like him much."

This first estimate changed rapidly as the party moved up the Hudson or "North River" aboard the steamboat *Erie*, and had become romantically enthusiastic when the travelers reached their destination: an immense new hotel on a mountaintop at Trenton Falls some twelve miles north of Utica in Oneida County. The chief attraction here was the scenic gorge where the West Canada Creek drove through a deep ravine over six cataracts on its way to join the Mohawk River farther south.

Emerson, who knew the whole strange story of Margaret's friendship with Sam Ward, records her memory, set down in June 1844, of a moment years earlier when she and Sam had come upon a clump of snowdrops at the foot of a rock. "It passed quick, as such beautiful moments do," she wrote, "and we never had such another." But there do seem to have been other such moments both then and later. When Ward himself, aged eighty, completed his memoirs, he recalled their first walk together at Trenton Falls: "I soon found that the defensive exterior assumed by a proud and sensitive nature placed at a disadvantage melted away, revealing rare gifts and solid attainments." Although like many other Harvard juniors Ward thought himself well educated, he was astonished by the breadth of Margaret's learning. "Whatever I knew," he wrote, "she knew as thoroughly and from the most modern standpoint."

But Margaret's always-susceptible heart seems to have been more engaged than her brilliant head. Nine months later she wrote to Sam Ward of how she used to love, at Trenton Falls, "to go to that place where the water seemed collecting its energies so quietly, gliding on so stealthily, you could scarcely believe it was firmly resolved to display such vehemence in one more moment of time and rood of space. . . . Perfectly do I comprehend what I have heard of gazers on a river-side being tempted to drown themselves by sight of the water, and all those tales of mermaid enchantments which embody this feeling." She seemed half intent on suggesting that the calm of the waters which quickly turned vehement as they dove through the chasm might apply in some way to her romantic feelings for Sam Ward.

Back in Cambridge she composed some verses about the trip, concluding with a sonnet called "Sunset After Leaving New York," where the "we two . . . together" is clearly a reference to herself and Sam Ward:

Into Night's secret realms speeding afar
And bearing human hearts from us away
Ere flashing sympathies could bid them say
If they like us trim for the evening star.
All this we two could see, together feel;
Since then no more alone at Nature's shrine I kneel.

From Cambridge she sent her parents in Groton an ecstatic account of her adventures on the return trip from Trenton Falls. "We reached N York at sunset, and found Mr. Sigourney Barker [brother of Margaret's friend Anna] waiting on the wharf to conduct [some of us] to his Father's. . . . We were recd most hospitably and fared sumptuously but alas! Anna was at Newport and my disappointment great—but Mr. Ward, (who has been all kindness throughout) offered to stay with me at Newport as long as I pleased. Here the thread of my narration becomes too entangled to be unwound on paper and how I went to and fro, and how Mrs. Thorndike finally took me to Newport . . . and how I missed Anna and did *not* miss her. . . . I can only tell you in person." In short, she was happy to report on "three weeks of such unalloyed pleasure as are seldom allotted to mortals."

Life at the Farrar mansion was sufficiently exciting. A lot of people were coming for the Harvard commencement, including the Englishwoman Harriet Martineau, who was expected to stay with the Farrars beginning Monday, August 17. Her fame had preceded her across the Atlantic. At thirty-three she was already the author of three books on economic subjects. Here, Margaret thought, was a woman who might be willing to serve as her intellectual guide.

But it was Anna Barker whom she really loved. In 1835 this beautiful girl was twenty-two, the eldest daughter and sixth child of Jacob Barker, an eminent financier and businessman who had been born into a Quaker family in the Province of Maine in 1779. He had begun his financial career in a commission house in New York, and during the War of 1812 had corresponded extensively with President James Madison, floating a loan of several million dollars for the relief of the beleaguered national Treasury. Among his more colorful exploits was helping Dolley Madison, after the Battle of Bladensburg, to spirit away from the White House Gilbert Stuart's portrait of General Washington for safekeeping against British depredations. Following a checkered career as a New York banker, he had moved to New Orleans in 1834, and soon became "one of the leading capitalists of the South." It was Anna Barker's next older brother, Andrew Sigourney, who had met Mrs. Farrar's group in New York and seen to their "sumptuous" entertainment in the Barker household there, and it was in search of the divine Anna that Margaret and Mrs. Thorndike had made the detour to Newport.

Some idea of the relationship between Margaret and Anna may be gained from Emerson's report that Margaret had once spent an evening looking at pictures with a friend and had been much struck by a "large engraving of Madame Récamier in her boudoir." She remembered with pleasure the "intimacy" that had prevailed between Récamier and Madame de Staël, and it is clear that during the middle 1830s the beautiful Anna Barker seemed to Margaret the Récamier to her de Staël, an idea that Emerson himself later took up and often echoed.

"She gave herself to her friendships," he wrote in 1851, "with an entireness not possible to any but a woman, with a depth possible to few women. Her friendships, as a girl with girls, as a woman with women, were not unmingled with passion, and had passages of romantic sacrifice and of ecstatic fusion, which I have heard with the ear, but could not trust my profane pen to report." Without giving Anna Barker's name, he did, however, quote Margaret's forthright statement on love among the sexes. "It is so true," she wrote, "that a woman may be in love with a woman, and a man with a man. . . ."

It is the same love which angels feel, where *"Sie fragen nicht nach Mann und Weib"* [they don't distinguish between man and woman]. It is regulated by the same law as that of love between persons of different sexes; only it is purely intellectual and spiritual. Its law is the desire of the spirit to realize a whole, which makes it seek in another being what it finds not in itself. Thus the beautiful seek the strong, and the strong the beautiful. . . . Why did Socrates love Alcibiades? . . . How natural is the love of Wallenstein for Max; that of De Staël for De Récamier; mine for [Anna]. I loved [Anna] for a time, with as much passion as I was then strong enough to feel. Her face was always gleaming before me; her voice was always echoing in my ear; all poetic thoughts clustered round the dear image. This love was a key which unlocked for me many a treasure which I still possess. . . . She loved me, too, though not so much, because her nature was "less high, less grave, less large, less deep." But she loved more tenderly, less passionately. She loved me, for I well remember her suffering when she first could feel my faults, and knew one part of the exquisite veil rent away; how she wished to stay apart, and weep the whole day. . . . I do not love her now with passion, but I still feel towards her as I can to no other woman. I thought of all this as I looked at Madame Récamier.

Her anticipation at the thought of meeting Harriet Martineau was wholly different from her feeling about Anna Barker. Here it was intellectual guidance rather than tenderness that she hoped to gain. Again, however, it was a picture that brought her thoughts into focus. "With what envy," she wrote in her journal,

I looked at Flaxman's picture of Hesiod sitting at the feet of the Muse! How blest would it be to be thus instructed in one's vocation! . . . I have hoped some friend would do,—what none has ever yet done—comprehend me wholly, mentally, and morally, and enable me better to comprehend myself. I have had some hope that Miss Martineau might be this friend, but cannot yet tell. . . . I mused long upon the noble courage with which she stepped forward into life, and the accurate judgment with which she has become acquainted with its practical details, without letting her fine imagination become tamed.

There would, it appeared, be plenty of time for Margaret to sit at Miss Martineau's feet like Hesiod before the Muse. The Englishwoman planned to spend the winter in America, returning home in the summer of 1836 in the company of Professor and Mrs. Farrar, who were going to make an extended tour of England and the Continent. John Farrar was not well and had already notified the Harvard administrators of his intention to resign his professorship at the end of the academic year. Mrs. Farrar had already proposed that Margaret Fuller should make one of the party.

After the halcyon summer of 1835, Margaret suffered a severe letdown when she returned to Groton. She had been home only a few days in September when she fell ill of what was then called brain fever, which confined her to bed, writhing in agony "for nine long days and nights, without intermission." Always subject to severe nervous headaches, which she once compared to the feeling of a "great vulture" fastening "his iron talons on the brain," she found this attack more than normally unendurable. Her mother tended her by day and night "like an angel." Her father, Timothy, who rarely made such pronouncements, stood by her bed one morning and said, "My dear, I have been thinking of you in the night, and I cannot remember that you have any *faults*. You have defects, of course, as all mortals have, but I do not know that you have a single fault." Margaret wept at this. She had been thinking that she might die, and once or twice would have been quite willing to go. But Providence, as she said, was to provide an even "darker dispensation."

Apart from her parents and her younger brothers and her sister, Ellen, Margaret's visitors were few. The most welcome was Anna Barker, whose father had summoned her back to New Orleans after her New England summer. Anna shed tears at having to leave Margaret in such a plight but could not disobey her father's command. As soon as she was gone, Margaret recorded her feelings in another of her autobiographical sonnets:

Upwards I stretch my arms; aloud I cry
In frantic anguish, "Raise me or I die!"
When with soft eyes beaming with love
I see thy dear face, Anna, far above.
By magnet force drawn up to thee I seem
And for the moment is dispelled the fever's dream.

Now came the "darker dispensation" of Providence. She was no sooner up and around again when Timothy Fuller was struck down by cholera. In the afternoon of September 30 he collapsed and had to be carried to his bed. After great suffering he died on October 1, and Margaret, as the eldest daughter, was obliged to take over the management of the family. Her mother was nearly overcome with sorrow and fatigue and all the younger children were sick. "Grant, oh Father," prayed Margaret in her journal, "that neither the joys nor sorrows of this past year shall have visited my heart in vain! Make me wise and strong for the performance of immediate duties. . . . Nothing sustains me now but the thought that God, who saw fit to restore me to life when I was so very willing to leave it . . . must have some good work for me to do."

She turned courageously to the "practical details" of family supervision. Timothy had died intestate and there were the usual legal problems. "I always hated the din of such affairs," she wrote a month after the funeral, "and hoped to find a lifelong refuge from them in the serene world of literature and the arts. But I am now full of desire to learn them, that I may be able to advise and act."

Through the winter her dreams of completing her cultural education with a trip to Europe in the company of the Farrars still possessed her mind. "The prospect is most alluring," she wrote. "A few thousand dollars would make all so easy, so safe. As it is, I cannot tell what is coming to us, for the estate will not be settled when I go." She really meant "*if* I go," for the matter still hung fire. As spring came on in the fatherless household at Groton, a letter from her tough-minded uncle, Abraham Fuller, made it clear that sufficient funds would not be available. On her twenty-sixth birthday, May 23, 1836, she reluctantly accepted Abraham's verdict:

Circumstances have decided that I must not go to Europe, and shut upon me the door, as I think, forever, to the scenes I could have loved.

Let me now try to forget myself, and act for others' sakes. . . . I am now but just recovered from bodily illness, and still heart-brokern by sorrow and disappointment. I may be renewed again, and feel differently. If I do not soon, I will make up my mind to teach. I can thus get money, which I will use for the benefit of my dear, gentle, suffering mother,— my brothers and sister. This will be the greatest consolation to me.

As she wrestled with her disappointment over the failure of her European plans, her incipient romance with young Sam Ward was much in her mind. He was going, she was not, but she could not forget their "intimacy" of the preceding July. On April 20 she had sent him an expressive account of her morning walk among the "dull brown fields" of Groton, where the "life-like tint" of oncoming spring had not yet appeared. She had been fascinated by the "exquisite wavelets" on the surface of a "shallow pool of the clearest amber." She reminded him of the undulatory motion of the waters they had watched together at Trenton Falls. "These undulations I have seen compared in poesy to the heaving of the bosom, and they do create a similar feeling—at least I, when I see this in the human frame, am tempted to draw near with a vague, instinctive anticipation . . . that a heart will leap forth, and I be able to take it in my hand." Even though such comparisons displeased her taste, she said, they did throw "a light on the sympathies between the human mind and nature. I feel as if I should sometime attain a precise notion of the meaning of Nature's most beautiful display, the *undulatory motion*."

She was not perhaps aware of the implicit sexuality of what she had written—the heaving bosom, the holding of a throbbing heart in her hand, the longing to comprehend the undulating motion in nature. She liked to speak of human love in naturalistic images. Her next surviving letter to Ward, composed when she knew that his declared love was cooling, assured him that her "kernel of affection" was the same, though now it lay "dormant in the husk." Would a "second spring bid it put forth leaf and flower?" The answer was no, but she did not know it yet in the spring of 1836.

All this lay behind her as she carefully engineered her first real chance to talk at length with Emerson. During the winter Miss Martineau had "enjoined" him to seek Margaret's acquaintance. Lidian, in the midst of her first pregnancy, was allegedly eager to meet her, and Elizabeth Hoar volunteered to assist in the arrangements. At last, on Bastille Day, Margaret wrote Elizabeth that she would come along a week later "if that will be agreeable to Mrs. Emerson." On the twentieth, Emerson wrote Frederic Henry Hedge that he had never yet "had the pleasure of any conversation" with Miss Fuller, but that she was coming over from Groton next day. A fortnight afterward, he wrote his brother William that "an accomplished lady" had been staying with Lidian, "quite an extraordinary person for her apprehensiveness[,] her acquisitions, and her powers of conversation." It was, he added, "always a great refreshment to see a very intelligent person." It was "like being set in a large place. You stretch your limbs and dilate to your utmost size."

As for Margaret, the visit became in effect her consolation prize for the cancellation of her European plans. She was already a favored occupant of the Emerson household when the Farrars, in the company of Harriet Martineau and Samuel Gray Ward, embarked for England aboard the *Orpheus*. Sam, whose wealthy banker father, Thomas Wren Ward, was at this time serving as treasurer for both the Boston Athenaeum and Harvard College, had just been graduated, and his reward was to be a two-year grand tour. At Harvard he had discovered an interest in art history and classical architecture and even made a start as an amateur draughtsman and painter. His purpose in traveling was to collect reproductions of famous pictures, especially those of Raphael, and to take lessons in drawing and painting in some atelier of Rome or Florence.

Margaret was able to accept Sam's absence with better grace in that she had now achieved her long-sought goal of direct intellectual companionship with Emerson. Though only seven years her senior, he had long stood as a kind of father figure in her ardent imagination. The morning after the Farrars' group sailed from New York, Emerson brought Bronson Alcott out to Concord to meet Miss Fuller, who had mentioned teaching as a possible means of livelihood. Elizabeth Peabody had resigned from Temple School and there was some preliminary talk about Margaret's taking her place, teaching French and Latin and serving as amanuensis for Alcott's continuing conversations on the Gospels.

By this date, August 2, Emerson had begun, though with certain reservations, to succumb to the charm of Margaret's personality as well as the sharpness of her intellect. "She was already rich in friends, rich in experiences, rich in culture," he wrote. "She was well read in French, Italian, and German literature. She had learned Latin and a little Greek." Indeed, as he said, "her talents were so various, and her conversation so rich and entertaining, that one might talk with her many times by the parlor fire, before he discovered the strength which served as foundation to so much accomplishment and eloquence." They found that they could meet on many levels, all the way from their common interest in Goethe to the fact that both Margaret's youngest brother, Lloyd, and Emerson's brother Robert Bulkeley were mentally handicapped and required special care.

Emerson's first reaction had nevertheless been largely negative. "I still remember the first half-hour of Margaret's conversation," he wrote fifteen years afterward. "She was then twenty-six years old. She had a face and frame that would indicate fulness and tenacity of life. She was rather under the middle height; her complexion was fair, with strong fair hair. She was then, as always, carefully and becomingly dressed, and of ladylike self-possession. For the rest, her appearance had nothing prepossessing. Her extreme plainness,—a trick of incessantly opening and shutting her eyelids,—the nasal tone of her voice,—all repelled; and I said to myself, we shall never get far."

But on that late July afternoon he had not yet reckoned with the force of Margaret's personality, or her determination to employ all her talents in the attempt to win his friendship. She had, he said, "stuffed me out as a philosopher," and was "intent on establishing a good footing between us. . . . She studied my tastes, piqued and amusd me, challenged frankness by frankness, and did not conceal the good opinion of me she had brought with her, nor her wish to please. She was curious to know my opinions and experiences. Of course, it was impossible long to hold out against such urgent assault."

Emerson's phrase "urgent assault" suggests an image of a fortress besieged, as was perhaps roughly the case. He thought that "with all her superiority" she was not free from egotism, and something in his nature made him suspicious of her attempts, thus early, to overpersonalize the budding relationship. One of his journal entries reads:

"I know not what you think of me," said my friend. Are you sure? You know all I think of you by those things I say to you. You know all which can be of any use to you. If I, if all your friends should draw your portrait to you—faults and graces, it would mislead you, embarrass you; you must not ask how to please me for curiosity. You must not look in the glass to see how handsome you are but to see if your face is clean.

Certainly I know what impression I made on any man, by remembering what communications he made to me.

So long as Margaret stayed clear of questions such as "What do you really think of me?" she could be a highly amusing companion. "She had an incredible variety of anecdotes, and the readiest wit to give an absurd turn to whatever passed; and the eyes, which were so plain at first, soon swam with fun and drolleries, and the very tides of joy and superabundant life." Her comic badinage made Emerson laugh far more than he liked. For years now he had "tasted the sweets of solitude and stoicism," and now found "something profane in the hours of amusing gossip" into which she drew him. There was a rumor abroad at the time that "she was sneering, scoffing, critical, disdainful of humble people." Yet he soon decided that this was a superficial judgment: "Her satire was only the pastime and necessity of her talent, the play of superabundant animal spirits." Such gifts required gifts in return. He gave her a copy of *Nature* and, oddly enough, an autograph of Jeremy Bentham, the father of Utilitarianism, a souvenir picked up during his visit to London in 1833.

On one of her habits of speech Emerson took issue with Margaret. "I have been making war against the superlative degree in the rhetoric of my fair visiter [sic]," he wrote in December.

She had no positive degree in her description of characters and scenes. You would think she has dwelt in a museum where all things were extremes and extraordinary. Her good people are very good, her naughty so naughty that they cannot be eaten. But beside the superlative of her mind she has a superlative of grammar which is suicidal and defeats its end. Her minds are "most perfect" "most exquisite" and "most masculine." I tell her the positive degree is the sinew of speech, the superlative is the fat. "Surely all that is simple is sufficient for all that is good," said Mme. de Stael. And when at a trattoria at Florence I asked the waiter if the cream was good, the man replied "Yes, sir, stupendous": *Si, signore, stupendo.*

During her visit Margaret had alluded often enough to her friendship with Anna Barker so that on September 20 he suggested that she bring her friend for "a day in our green fens." But Anna could not come. Her father was taking her to New York to say good-bye to her favorite brother, Sigourney, newly appointed to the American consulate in Antwerp. "I grieve," wrote Emerson, "to have lost the sight of your beautiful friend." Owing to Anna's sporadic absences, whether in New Orleans with her father or in Europe in 1837–38 with the Farrars and Sam Ward, Emerson did not meet her until October 1839.

Chapter Seven

FATHER TAYLOR

"MEN ARE CONVERTIBLE," WROTE EMERSON IN 1834. "THEY want awakening. Get the soul out of bed, out of her deep habitual sleep, out into God's universe." In such terms as these, Bronson Alcott looked like a prophet of the second great awakening since the time of Jonathan Edwards. So did Father Edward Thompson Taylor, a preacher rather than a teacher, but equally devoted to blowing reveille in the dormitory of the soul. Among his early advocates were Emerson and his brother Charles.

Shortly before his proposal of marriage to Lydia Jackson, Emerson fulfilled a New Year's resolution to look into what he called "the living church." On the first Sunday afternoon of 1835 he hurried over the wet cobblestones of Ann Street in the North End of Boston, well away from the sedate Sabbath processions on Tremont, to the Seaman's Bethel in North Square. The Port Society had built it two years earlier at a cost of $24,000: a sturdy, three-story edifice with a squat tower where a blue flag bearing the word "Bethel" flapped in the January breeze. The interior was already crowded with the usual mixed congregation—rough sailors in red shirts in the central pews, and at the sides and in the gallery all manner of visitors: women and children, pale young Unitarian ministers, Harvard intellectuals, the seriously devout, and the merely curious, all of them eager for another demonstration of Father Taylor's prowess.

Emerson had listened to him exactly three years earlier, at a time when the money for the Bethel was still being raised, partly through the efforts of the Unitarian merchants of Boston but mainly through Taylor's vigorous preaching. "Friend Taylor of the Zebulon of ships," Emerson had called him then, recalling Genesis and the sixth son of Jacob by Leah, whom Jacob assigned to the shores of the sea. This new Zebulon had "made his plea in behalf of ye sailors last Monday Evg to a crowded congregation at Dr Channing's with most impressive eloquence." Dr. William Ellery Channing had sat there and heard it all. "Glad was I to have ye Dr hear somebody as good as himself do what he could not. Fifteen thousand dollars will be subscribed, 'tis thot, to the Port Soc[iety]."

Now on this other January afternoon he watched Taylor pacing his pulpit platform while the crowd gathered—restive as a racehorse, beckoning tardy sailors to the front pews, imperiously waving at others to move over and make room. At forty-two he looked to be fifty, a wiry, weather-beaten man of middle height, his highly mobile face grooved with deep lines, his graying hair swept back, his Ben Franklin spectacles perched high on his brow, and the worn old Bible cradled in his arms. In due course he came forward to the lectern, "threw back his coat-collar, rolled up his cuffs, ran his fingers backward through his hair," and began to preach.

Behind him as he spoke was the only ornament in the chapel—a large canvas depicting a ship in distress, braving the billows under lowering skies while mariners labored to keep the hulk afloat. It was a symbolic picture and the congregation knew it. Many a time in the heat and fury of his sermon he pointed it out as a graphic representation of the human predicament. He knew instinctively how to use it for maximum effect, owned the maritime experience and the idiomatic vocabulary to describe it, could in a twinkling summon up many a tale of disasters at sea, when the sailors "cried unto the Lord" and were yanked out of the maw of the deep by timely intercession.

Emerson had spent the morning in the chapel of the Swedenborgians, listening to a sermon as simple and severe as a problem in Euclid, "wholly uncoloured and unimpassioned." But this Bethel sermon was "at the opposite pole, say rather in another zone." Taylor began by wishing his sailor "sons a happy New Year, praying God for his servants of the brine," calling down His blessing on "the bleached sail, the white foam," and petitioning the Almighty "to christianize the universe" through extension of maritime commerce. "May every deck be stamped by the hallowed feet of godly captains," he cried, "and the first watch, and the second watch be watchful for the Divine Light."

"And so he went on," wrote Emerson, "this Poet of the Sailor and of Ann Street—fusing all the rude hearts of his auditory with the heat of his own love and making the abstractions of philosophers accessible and effectual to them also." He seemed to have no vanity; fame would never spoil him. He was "a work of the same hand that made Demosthenes and Shakspear and Burns," and was "guided by instincts diviner than rules." His whole sermon that day consisted of "a string of audacious felicities harmonized by a spirit of joyful love." Seeing him in action, one could understand how George Fox, founder of the Society of Friends, George Whitefield, the Methodist missionary, or Father Samuel Moody, Emerson's great-great-grandfather, famous preacher of Mount Agamenticus, Maine, had handled their congregations. Taylor absolutely dominated the assemblage by the "total infusion of his own soul" into their minds and hearts. "How puny, how cowardly other preachers look by the side of this preaching," wrote Emerson. "He shows us what a man can do."

Anecdotes buzzed round him like bees. They told about his interruption of a slow, dry speaker at a prayer meeting: "Lubricate, Lord, lubricate!" Or the words he hurled after the retreating backs of those who left a sermon early. "Light stuff floats quick," he would cry, or "Little barrels are soon filled." They mentioned his cutting off a redundant testimonial with one slash: "Lord, give us a point!" To a drunken sailor loudly praising God: "Shut up, Jack. We know your latitude and longitude." They liked to tell how he had towered in his pulpit one day with widespread fists, advising his auditors to "grasp the poles with both hands and shake the universe." The younger Unitarians giggled when they mentioned Taylor's happy judgment on their sect: "If they go to hell, they'll change the atmosphere." They quoted his plea for continuing support of superannuated preachers: "They were moral giants. When God made them, he rolled up his sleeves to the armpits."

There was also the famous story of Taylor's tangle with a Cape Cod Come-outer who appeared one day in the chapel and rose to be heard. "You can't speak here today," said Taylor. "I must speak," said the Come-outer. "The Holy Ghost sent me here and gave me permission to speak." Taylor fixed him with a steel-gray stare. "Please give my compliments to the Holy Ghost," he roared, "and tell him you can't speak here today. Sit down!"

Certain Sunday meetings took on the dimensions of a spiritual circus. All his parishioners knew that the preacher could coo like a dove or growl like a lion. He gloried in debate, he was never at a loss for a word or a witticism. To express pain he screwed up his seamed face into "indescribable contortions." He was proud of his membership in the Masonic Order, having joined the Blue Lodge in 1820, and he loved to march on St. John's Day with the Knights Templar, resplendent in the regalia of flowing black cape, plumed hat, and silver sword. When anti-Masons attacked the Order, he called for God's assistance: "Make their hearts as soft as their heads!" A popular story told of two semiliterate sailors searching for the Bethel and seeing the flag on the tower. "B-E-T," read one. "That spells BEAT. H-E-L, that's HELL. BEAT HELL. Come on. This must be the place." But hell's enemy had a milder side. People liked to watch him in North Square feeding the pigeons that squabbled and crowded for places on his hands, his arms, his shoulders, even the top of his old beaver hat.

There is some evidence that Emerson served as substitute preacher in Taylor's place at least once in the spring of 1835. He saw him again that fall in Concord. Old Dr. Ezra Ripley took him for a tour of the Revolutionary battlefield beside the Manse. Emerson repeated with amusement the inscription Taylor proposed for the future battle monument: "Here is the place where the Yankees made the British show the back seams of their stockings."

He had fought the British himself. Born in Richmond, Virginia, on Christmas Day, 1793, he arrived too late for the Revolutionary War but in good time for that of 1812, during which he shipped out aboard the privateer *Black Hawk*. Captured by a British man-of-war, he spent some months as a POW in Halifax, where his fellow prisoners soon discovered his skills as preacher and prayer maker. After the war he worked for a junkman in Ann Street, Boston, traveled the state as a peddler-preacher, and for a time helped manage a farm in Saugus for an aging widow, who taught him to read. His formal education was six months at Wesleyan Academy in Newmarket, New Hampshire, his tuition paid by a Boston merchant. Ten years after his conversion to Methodism, the church elders, recognizing his inimitable oratorical powers, admitted him to the New England Conference of Methodist Episcopal Churches. He had acquired a sturdy wife, née Deborah Millett of Marblehead, and for two years preached in a succession of parishes all over Cape Cod and Martha's Vineyard. Brash, confident, demonstrative, leonine, forceful, and fiery, he was widely known as an "old-fashioned, shouting, hallelujah Methodist," a reputation in which he took pardonable pride without visible loss of essential humility.

Emerson had only recently brought out his book *Nature* when he made a journal entry: "Edward Taylor is a noble work of the divine cunning who suggests the wealth of Nature. If he were not so strong, I should call him lovely. What cheerfulness in his genius, and what consciousness of strength." Speaking of his good health, he had proudly told Emerson, "My voice is thunder," and Emerson studied him as he would have studied "a jaguar or an Indian for his untamed physical perfections." The best of it was that he could "transform all those whiskered, shaggy untrim tarpaulins into sons of light and hope, by seeing the man within the sailor."

Yet as Emerson knew, already beginning that process of acute analysis which he brought to bear soon or late on each of his eccentric geniuses, it was no good trying to make Taylor over into something he was not. He was basically "a creature of instinct"—all opaline colors and "doves'-neck-lustres." This was what one saw from a pew at the Bethel. "If you see the ignis fatuus in a swamp, and go to the place, the light vanishes; if you retire to the spot whereon you stood, it reappears. So with Taylor's muse. It is a panorama of images from all nature and art . . . but go up to it and nothing is there." The nucleus of his power was "unconscious instinct." It defied and eluded scientific analysis. The man himself, for all his eccentricity and originality, was chiefly the conduit-cornucopia through which the imagery flowed.

Emerson revised this reductive opinion upward on March 13, 1837, when Taylor came to Concord to lecture on temperance and spent the night at Emerson's house. "Almost . . . a perfect orator," wrote Emerson in his journal. The qualifying adverb was necessary because one soon became aware of a basic problem, not so much with what Taylor said as with "the utter want and loss of all method, the ridicule of all method." Emerson paraphrased *Othello* when he spoke of the "bright chaos come again" of Taylor's "bewildering oratory." It was this, more than anything else, that "bereaved" what he said of at least part of its power. Yet the splendor remained. "What sweetness!" exclaimed Emerson. "What richness what depth! What cheer! How he conciliates, how he humanizes! How he exhilarates and ennobles! Beautiful philanthropist! godly poet! The Shakspear of the sailor and the poor."

That night in Emerson's study Taylor talked about his daily living in Boston where, with his wife and six children, he occupied a large house across the square from the Bethel. He said that he led "a monarch's life." He was his own boss, and his word was law to "all his people and coadjutors." In the chapel it was the same. Rich and poor, scoffer and drunkard, all acknowledged his power. He liked the closeness of it all. "The world is just large enough for the people," he told Emerson. "There is no room for a partition wall." He spoke satirically about the young men coming out of Divinity School—"poor fellows hobbling out of Jerusalem." He described one of his drunken sailors as "hanging like a half-dead bird over a counter." The image was graphic enough to convert a tippler away from the downward path.

The temperance lectures, like his effervescent sermons, were never the same twice, though he often told his listeners that "sailors cut off the bottom of their pockets with a rum-bottle." He ridiculed those defeatist reformers who said that it was hopeless to try to stop the liquor traffic. "Your patriotic fathers," he roared, "could make a cup of tea for His Britannic majesty out of a whole cargo, but you can't cork up a gin-jug." There was no snoozing in the Concord Lyceum while Taylor stood at the lectern. "The wonderful and laughing life of his illustration keeps us broad awake," wrote Emerson. "A string of rockets all night."

Especially in the pulpit but also in less formal situations, Taylor had a way of dominating any company. "I delight in his great personality," Emerson said, "the way and sweep of the man which like a frigate's way takes up for the time the centre of the ocean, paves it with a white street." In his presence other people willingly took "a deferential and apologetic tone." Even his public prayers were like "a winged ship in which all are floated forward." There was a commanding egotism, certainly—Emerson's chosen geniuses always showed it in one form or another—but no suggestion of narcissism. He was thinking of Taylor when he wrote in his essay on "Character" that "some natures are too good to be spoiled by praise. . . . Solemn friends will warn them of the danger of the head's being turned by the flourish of trumpets, but they can afford to smile."

He was also thinking of Taylor when he began organizing his Divinity School Address in 1838. "I ought to sit and think then write a discourse to the American clergy," he wrote in his journal that March, "showing them the ugliness and unprofitableness of theology and churches at this day and the glory and sweetness of the Moral Nature out of whose pale they are almost wholly shut. . . . Tell them that a true preacher can always be known by this, that he deals them out his life, life metamorphosed; as Taylor, Webster, Scott, Carlyle do. . . . A man's sermon should be rammed with life."

Taylor stood at the opposite pole from a preacher like Barzillai Frost, Dr. Ezra Ripley's junior associate. During one snowy Sunday in March Emerson wrote: "At church all day but almost tempted to say I would go no more." Outside it was snowing heavily. "The snowstorm was real[,] the preacher merely spectral. Vast contrast to look at him and then out of the window. Yet no fault in the good man. Evidently he thought himself a faithful searching preacher." But there was no life in his sermonizing. "He had no one word intimating that ever he had laughed or wept, was married or enamoured, had been cheated, or voted for, or chagrined. If he had ever lived or acted we were none the wiser for it."

In the Divinity School Address, Emerson elaborated on his journal entry about that snowy Sunday in March. "Whenever the pulpit is usurped by a formalist, then is the worshipper defrauded and disconsolate. . . . The true preacher can be known by this, that he deals out to the people his life,—life passed through the fire of thought. But of the bad preacher, it could not be told from his sermon what age of the world he fell in; whether he had a father or a child; whether he was a freeholder or a pauper . . . or any other fact of his biography." In the face of such preaching, said Emerson, "I have heard a devout person, who prized the Sabbath, say in bitterness of heart, 'On Sundays, it seems wicked to go to church.' " The devout person was Lidian, who uttered these words on December 3, 1837.

Barzillai Frost, good man though he was, represented *in parvo* the forms and formalisms of historial Christianity against which Emerson inveighed in his speech to the Harvard Divinity School seniors in mid-July 1838. To the considerable outrage of some of his hearers, he had advanced and defended what he called "the intuition of the moral sentiment," which alone could give insight into the perfection of the laws of the soul. To perceive the law of laws—that the world is a product of one will and one mind—awakened the religious sentiment. It was an intuition; it must come directly; it could not be received at secondhand; one must dare to love God without mediator or veil.

Jesus, said Emerson, was unique in all history in his estimate of the greatness of man. He recognized the eternal revelation of the heart, and declared that this was God. Provocation, not instruction, was all that one could receive from another soul, and in this sense, Jesus was the supreme agent provocateur. True Christianity must be a faith like His in the infinitude of man.

Once in a great while, Mr. Frost said something memorable, as in a remark that Emerson recorded two months after the Divinity School Address: "We see God in nature as we see the soul of our friend in his countenance." But this was rare. For the most part, Frost "grinds and grinds in the mill of a truism and nothing comes out but what was put in. But the moment he or I desert the tradition and speak a spontaneous thought, instantly poetry, wit, hope, virtue, learning, anecdote, all flock to our aid."

This was the power that Father Taylor possessed. It was again revealed to Emerson when Taylor "enriched" a meeting of the Transcendental Club at the Reverend Cyrus Bartol's house in Chestnut Street, Boston, in the spring of 1840. Emerson wrote:

I felt in a higher degree the same happiness I have formerly owed to that man's public discourses, the exhilaration and cheer of so much love poured out through so much imagination. For the time his exceeding life throws all other gifts into deep shade . . . yet how willingly every man is willing to be nothing in his presence, to share this suprising emanation and be steeped and ennobled by the new wine of this eloquence. He gives sign every moment of a certain prodigious nature. . . . We are taught that earnest impassioned action is most our own and invited to try the deeps of love and wisdom,—we who have been players and paraders so long. And yet I think I am most struck with the *beauty* of his nature. This hardfeatured, scarred, and wrinkled Methodist whose face is a system of cordage becomes whilst he talks a gentle[,] a lovely creature—the Amore Greco is not more beautiful.

Bartol shared Emerson's admiration for Taylor, calling him the best extant extemporaneous speaker with "more fiery combustion and less watery dilution" than anyone else in sight. As an *improvisator,* he was "the finest specimen ever," and Bartol believed that his powers as a preacher were even greater than those of the renowned Dr. Channing, an opinion that Emerson evidently shared. Bartol had once heard the two men preach on the same day a few hours apart: "It was the difference between reflection and spontaneity." Taylor "preached as the birds sing." Like Emerson, Bartol admired his "idiomatic raciness of language," as when he compared Transcendentalism to a seagull with "long wings, lean body, poor feathers, and miserable meat."

Not all Taylor's contemporaries shared this enthusiasm. That same spring of 1840, Sophia Peabody tried to persuade her lover, Nathaniel Hawthorne, to visit the Seaman's Bethel. Hawthorne refused. "It would not be an auspicious day for me to hear the aforesaid Son of Thunder," he wrote. "Some sunshiny Sunday when I am wide awake and warm and genial, I will go and throw myself open to his blessed influences." Two weeks later he confessed to feeling "somewhat afraid to hear this divine Father Taylor, lest my sympathy with thy admiration for him should be colder and feebler than thou lookest for." But Sophia must not be troubled: Hawthorne called himself "a most unmalleable man," unfitted to endure even for an hour the rhetorical hammer strokes of the Son of Thunder.

But Emerson continued, like Bartol, to admire "the idiomatic raciness" of Taylor's language. Gradually, he came to associate Boston's North End, that thumb of land washed on the west by the waters of the Charles River and diversified on the east by all the teeming life of harbor and bay, with the kind of "poetry" one could hear from Taylor's pulpit. About the time Hawthorne was declining to listen to the Son of Thunder, Emerson wrote, "I confess to some pleasure from the stinging rhetoric of a rattling oath in the mouth of truckmen and teamsters. How laconic and brisk it is by the side of a page of The North American Review." He was thinking of Montaigne's vigorous language when he added, "Cut these words and they would bleed; they are vascular and alive; they walk and run. . . . [Truckmen and teamsters] do not trip in their speech. It is a shower of bullets, whilst Cambridge men and Yale men correct themselves and begin again at every half sentence. . . . Yet always this profane swearing and bar-room wit has salt and fire in it." He felt "no less disgust than any other at the cant of Spiritualism," and had "rather hear a round volley of Ann Street oaths than the affectation of that which is divine on the foolish lips of coxcombs."

As Ann Street was to the ear, so it was to the eye. Emerson never felt more like a painter than when he invaded Father Taylor's domain. "I frequently find," he wrote, "the best part of my ride in the Concord Coach from my house to Winthrop Place to be in Prince Street, Charter Street, Ann Street, and the like places at the North End. . . . The dishabille of both men and women, their unrestrained attitudes and manners[,] make pictures greatly more interesting than the clean shaved and silk robed procession in Washington and Tremont Streets. I often see that the attitudes of both men and women engaged in hard work are more picturesque than any which art and study could contrive, for the Heart is in these first. I say *picturesque;* because when I pass these groups, I instantly know whence all the fine pictures I have seen had their origin; I feel the painter in me; these are traits which make us feel the force and eloquence of *form* and the sting of color. But the painter is only *in* me; it does not come to the fingers' ends. But whilst I see a true painting, I feel how it was made; I feel that genius organizes, or it is lost."

Although Father Taylor's organizational habits were spur-of-the-moment rather than the result of careful and intensive thought, it is easy to see how Emerson came to associate him with picturesqueness of form, unrestrained attitudes and manners, the "sting" of errant color, as well as the graphic language that he heard in passing among the populace of the North End. It was the Ishmael in him that loved the bloody rhetoric, the bullet shower of a lively verbiage of barroom and sidewalk. Although in his youth he had thought it monstrous that some country Methodists in North Carolina could speak of "treeing Jesus" as if He were a possum or a raccoon, he eventually came round, at least partly through the influence of Father Taylor, to a genuine admiration for the power of the vulgate in expression and attitude.

Taylor was the very embodiment of Eloquence. Emerson portrayed him in his essay of that title:

> You may find him in some lowly Bethel, by the sea-side, where a hard-featured, scarred, and wrinkled Methodist becomes the poet of the sailor and the fisherman, whilst he pours out the abundant streams of his thought through a language all glittering and fiery with imagination; a man who never knew the looking-glass or the critic; a man whom college drill or patronage never made, and whom praise cannot spoil—a man who conquers his audience by infusing his soul into them, and speaks by the right of being the person in the assembly who has the most to say, and so makes all other speakers appear little and cowardly before his face.

For all the overt differences among Bronson Alcott, Margaret Fuller, and Father Taylor, they shared in one special endowment: what Yankees still call, not without admiration, "the gift of gab." In any group conversation, even in one-to-one colloquies, Emerson repeatedly found himself tongue-tied, hesitant of participation except by listening, lying in wait for the right word, the telling phrase. It was not that he lacked essential eloquence, but it is a fact that he always "read" his sermons and lectures, using his memorable voice to give living power to the prose he had already set down in the quiet of his study. He trusted his pen far more than his tongue, as he said in his letter of proposal to Lydia Jackson. He was not, in Bartol's word, an *improvisator*. But this was a skill in which Alcott and Fuller and Taylor excelled. "With his admirable voice and enunciation, with the large and various vocabulary" at his instantaneous command, "Bronson Alcott was an inexhaustible fountain of talk. . . . It was one continuous improvisation . . . [with] all the liberty of a wind-blown raindrop." So wrote Alcott's modern biographer, Odell Shepard. Margaret Fuller often astonished Emerson with her eloquence in conversation and, like Alcott, conducted scheduled "Conversations" at various places in Boston. Emerson found her talents so various, her talk so entertaining, her evident culture so rich, her wit so ready, that he fairly reveled in the "tides of . . . superabundant life" that she regularly displayed.

Taylor, said Emerson once, "was like a cannon, better on the Common than in the parlour." Yet the tides of eloquence and of superabundant life ran even more strongly in him than in Alcott and Fuller. In his sermons, as Allan MacDonald wrote, "there was no regular preparation, no carefully dovetailed outline of thought. His recipe was very simple: 'When the liquor begins to swell and steam and groan, and hum and fizz, then pull out the bung!' He was carried away by his own passion. Tears streamed down the wrinkles charactered by wind and sun. He succumbed to his own eloquence, and his audience wept with him."

Chapter Eight

WALDO
AND NELLY

TOWARD THE END OF JANUARY 1836, LIDIAN HAD BEGUN A difficult first pregnancy. Both parents, and especially Emerson, had been eager to start a family. For a time they feared that no children would come. "Strange is this alien despotism of Sleep," wrote Emerson in his journal, "which takes two persons lying in each other's arms and separates them leagues, continents, asunder." But they had been married only five months when Lidian quietly told him of her new condition. He joyfully kissed her and said, "I hail the little new being."

He could not then foresee the troubles ahead, whether for his wife or for Charles and Bulkeley. Complicated by the usual attacks of dyspepsia, the pregnancy made her very ill throughout the spring. Emerson repeatedly advised her to "walk and walk and walk" for her own well-being and that of the child. "Let nothing disturb your peace but go abroad and walk," he wrote her from Salem shortly before Charles's death. Her face had become drawn, pale, and "set" like a mask. In her own phrase, she "looked like death" itself and her husband was worried. It struck him as grossly unfair that the mother should have so much acute discomfort and the father none. But Dr. Bartlett said cheerfully that he had never lost a maternal case, and predicted that "the pleasures of lactation" when the baby arrived would erase all memory of her present suffering.

Lidian seemed to improve in late July and early August during the two-week visit by Margaret Fuller, a new friend of the family. But in mid-September she was again "quite ill with dyspepsia," which, according to Emerson, "all but starved her," despite an eccentric diet of "poppy and oatmeal." Writing Thomas Carlyle, he said flatly, "My wife is now a feeble dyspeptic." In a final draft of the letter he modified the phrasing to "My wife has been lately an invalid." He was still sure that she was taking too much medicine and spending too much time indoors. "My pill is the sun," he had written in February. But Lidian so dreaded the morning sun that she always drew the shutters against it.

The bridal bed was a large four-poster, bought from Lidian's sister, Lucy. As her lying-in approached, she "rigged the bed in all its white magnificence" of white dimity with a ball fringe, and made four sets of window curtains to match. But Emerson, seeing this display, muttered that it was "too much parade," and Lidian took down the hangings and packed them away. She did not seem unduly upset. " 'Husband knows best' was my creed in those days," she said later, "and I really thought he did." Neither Elizabeth Hoar nor Emerson's mother agreed. They held that she should have ignored his objections. In the end he might have come to revel in all that snowy drapery.

The baby arrived an hour short of All Hallows' Eve, 1836. It was a healthy boy whose head was temporarily elongated by its passage through the birth canal, but Emerson "could see only his perfections," calling the child "a lovely wonder which makes the Universe look friendly to me." In a burst of philoprogenitive exuberance, he called himself Pygmalion, although he felt that he had been "merely a brute occasion" of the baby's being, "nowise attaining to the dignity even of a second cause." He said nothing of the fact that the birth had come on a Sabbath Day—always a special time in his weekly calendar. But promptly on "Monday morn" he wrote Elizabeth Hoar, "Pray come down and see my son ten hours old and impatient to see his Aunty." Now and often afterward he was moved by the sight of mother and child together—"its tiny beseeching weakness" being "compensated so perfectly by the happy patronizing look of the mother."

Old Dr. Ripley soon came over from the Manse to see his step-great-grandson. He laid the boy facedown across his bony knees and gently pulled its undershirt away from the shoulder blades. When they asked what was wrong, he answered that he had been told that "the child of this couple would probably have wings" and he was checking to see if they had sprouted. On May 7 he officiated at the christening in the Concord church. Lidian had been planning to call her son Charles after his uncle, so lately dead, but Emerson insisted on Waldo: the eldest son must always be named for its father. Lidian and Aunt Lizzy wept but complied, as she had done about the bed curtains, yet gained a signal victory by dressing the child in the christening robes that Charles had worn nearly thirty years before.

Emerson's grief for Charles was if possible even more intense than his feelings at the loss of Edward eighteen months earlier. Edward had been "far away" on his adopted tropical island, his death unwitnessed by any of his immediate family. But Charles and Waldo had remained close companions as recently as that last sad April journey to New York. A man named Waterston who had stood beside him at the edge of the grave reported that all Emerson's compressed feelings had eventuated in a burst of rueful laughter and a single exclamation, "dear boy!" Writing home to Lidian the day after the funeral, Emerson called Charles "my noble friend who was my ornament my wisdom and my pride." In the hyperbole of his grief he said that the best of his strength lay with Charles, leaving him not only unfastened and adrift but also almost ashamed of living at all. His journal thereafter devoted many pages to broken and brokenhearted memoirs of his brother. Once he alluded to the contrast between the fortunes of Charles and Edward. "Beautiful without any parallel . . . was his life, happiest his death. . . . I read now his pages, I remember all his words and motions without any pang, so healthy and humane a life it was, and not like Edward's, a tragedy of poverty and sickness tearing genius."

Except for the luckless Bulkeley, back now yet again in the Charlestown asylum, only the two eldest of Ruth Emerson's sons had lived beyond the age of thirty. But William and his wife, Susan, and Waldo and his wife, Lidian, were now the parents of a new generation. These infant sons, named for their respective fathers, and soon nicknamed Willie and Wallie, helped to fill the gap occasioned by the tragic early deaths of Edward and Charles.

The child Waldo was three months old when his father made a journal entry that emphasized the rural peace in which his little family dwelt. "Being a lover of solitude I went to live in the country seventeen miles from Boston, and there the northwest wind with all his snows took me in charge and defended me from all company in winter, and the hills and sand-banks that intervened between me and the city, kept guard in summer." But by the time the boy was six months old, another journal entry showed that neither snows nor sandbanks could guarantee solitude. Living in a house along the main artery between Boston and the North Country was like having a box seat at a perpetual (and romantic) entertainment: "I listen by night I gaze by day at the endless procession of wagons loaded with the wealth of all regions of England, of China, of Turkey, of the Indies which from Boston creep by my gate to all the towns of New Hampshire and Vermont. With creaking wheels at midsummer and crunching the snows on huge sledges in January, the train goes forward at all hours, bearing this cargo of inexhaustible comfort and luxury to every cabin in the hills."

These journal entries suggest an essential dichotomy in Emerson's personality that was summarized in the title of one of his later works, *Society and Solitude*. He alternately longed for both and moved back and forth between one and the other through the whole course of his life. The northwest wind and the snowfalls it brought never in fact kept company from his house, nor did the sandhills of summer serve as an insuperable barrier. In solitude one read and wrote and walked the wide champaign. In society one learned from other men and women, availing oneself of the wealth of the Indies in quite another sense than the cargoes in the wagons that passed by Emerson's door. "All are needed by each one," he would write. "Nothing is fair or good alone." This theme of each-and-all was his perpetual study.

So was the child, now growing apace, the center of attraction for both his parents, and a frequent subject of entries in his father's journals and letters. At five months, wrote Emerson, "My baby's lovely drama still goes forward though he catches sad colds, and wheezes, and grieves. We call him little pharisee who when he fasts, sounds a trumpet before him." The boy's worrisome illnesses elicited a paternal prayer: "Ah! my darling boy, so lately received out of heaven leave me not now! Please God, this sweet symbol of love and wisdom may be spared to rejoice, teach, and accompany me."

Lidian said briskly that Waldo believed his father was a horse and his mother a porridge pot. Those who had only seen this baby in prime health knew but half his perfections, how patient and angelic he was in his sicknesses, how contented he could be after feeding, cooing "like a pigeon house." He cheered his father with his "hearty and protracted laugh" like "thunder in the woods." Both parents were at his side when he stood by himself just short of his first birthday and walked alone six weeks later.

At eighteen months he began to interest his father as a boy rather than a baby. The journals for 1838–39 burgeon with his brightness. He invited the birds, the cat, and even the flies to "come see Waddow." Old Ezra Ripley gave him two early apples, one for each hand, and he gnawed them both on the way home from the Manse. Lidian thought that his tooth marks alone made them worth a whole barrel of untouched apples. "With the gravity of Palladio," as his father said, he built a kind of villa on the study rug, and his mother, coming in, found "two spools, a card, an awl-case, and a flourbox top—each perpendicularly balanced on the other." She could hardly believe that her boy had built it, and dropping to her knees in "a fit of affection," "kissed [the structure] down," declaring that "she could possibly stay no longer with papa, but must go off to the nursery and see with eyes the lovely creature."

Emerson delighted to enlarge upon his son's meanings and the "untranslateable Sanscrit" of his utterances. When he asked for a story, his father remarked, "Who will say then that the novel has not a foundation in nature?" When he demanded, "I want something to play with which I never saw before," Emerson found a classical analogue in the lordly Xerxes "advertising a reward for a new pleasure." He made metaphors, as when, watching Lidian's brother smoke a cigar, he said, "See how the cobwebs go up out of the gentleman's mouth." He gravely assured his mother that God said His prayers every night and never behaved naughty, which made Emerson smile at such "jets of Natural theology." As a hand-me-down from his cousin Willie he inherited a red hobbyhorse. "I like my boy with his endless sweet soliloquies and iterations," wrote Emerson, "and his utter inability to conceive why I should not leave all my nonsense, business, and writing to come to tie up his toy horse."

His father thought this blue-eyed boy "as handsome as Walden Pond at sunrise," and the darling of all the children in the small school across the road. But he was not always so angelic as he looked. The "purgatory of teething" assailed him near his second birthday. With a "face all liquid grief," he refused any comfort "less gross" than molasses candy, for which he asked incessantly. "How we covet insensibility," said Lidian. "My boy whines and wails if I wake him. We are Buddhists all." He slept in a trundle bed in a corner of the master bedroom. One hot night in August he rolled off his mattress and under the four-poster, destroying the night with loud cries.

At age four he discovered snobbery, declining to go to church with Mrs. Mumford because her red hands and florid face were not beautiful. On the following Sunday he told Louisa, another of the domestics, that he had prayed for Mrs. Mumford to become beautiful and now she was. Yet real beauty also bothered him. When Margaret Fuller brought Anna Barker to Concord, Emerson told Waldo that a "Beautiful Lady" was coming. But the small boy backed away from Anna's kiss. "I'm afraid of the Beautiful Lady," he told Lidian. "I'm afraid of her curls."

In the spring of 1838, Lidian began her second pregnancy. The coming child gave her nearly as much trouble as Waldo had done in 1836. At Christmas her spirits hit bottom because of severe dyspepsia. But she recovered perceptibly in the new year as her lying-in approached, and on the morning of February 24, 1839, was delivered of a "fair, healthy," and perfectly formed daughter. The delighted father called her "a sparkle of God," who was "worth a household," and at first slept "incessantly—hands up, as for defence." I hope, said Waldo Minor, she will "stay here all the time." Lidian, with what her husband called "magnanimity and ex[ceed]ing kindness," insisted on naming the child Ellen Tucker after the former wife. "Fair fall the name and every be[autiful] vision it recalls on this n[ew] dreamer," wrote Emerson, but he was soon calling her Nelly. She was slower than Waldo had been in standing free and learning to walk, though her "astonishing sagacity" was much admired in the upstairs nursery. During the spring of 1840, Emerson begrudged the length of his stay in the Providence lecture rooms because he missed Lidian, the "eyes and theology" of Waldo, and "little balancing Nelly" learning to walk "with forthspread arms," and smelling, he said, as delicious as a cake pan. Her brother's bright remarks continued to be spread upon the family record. When Lidian took her children to Boston to show them off to Mrs. Abel Adams, Waldo

Minor, gazing round the Victorian parlor, exclaimed, "How glass their Knobs are!"

Emerson greatly revered domestic life and the bright prattling or wise saws of his children. As he wrote in his essay of that title, looking back at the time of his thirty-seventh birthday,

> the household is the home of the *man*, as well as of the child. The events that occur therein are more near and affecting to us than those which are sought in senates and academies. Domestic events are certainly our affair. What are called public events may or may not be ours. If a man wishes to acquaint himself with the real history of the world, with the spirit of the age, he must not go first to the state-house or the court-room. The subtle spirit of life must be sought in facts nearer. It is what is done and suffered in the house . . . in the temperament, in the personal history, that has the profoundest interest for us. . . . The great facts are the near ones.

Yet this rebel philosopher also recognized the dangers inherent in too much domesticity:

> People wish to be settled. It is only as far as they are unsettled that there is nay hope for them. . . . Rest not. In the thought of tomorrow there is power to upheave all thy creed, all the creeds, all the literatures of the nations, and marshal thee to a heaven which no epic dream has yet foreshadowed. . . . We all stand waiting, empty, knowing possibly that we can be full, surrounded by mighty symbols which are not symbols to us, but prose and trivial toys. Then cometh the god and . . . by a flash of his eye burns up the veil which shrouded all things and the meaning of the very furniture, of cup and saucer, of chair and clock and tester. . . . All that we reckoned settled shakes now and rattles, and literature, cities, climates, religions leave their foundations and dance before our eyes.

As for himself: "I am only an experimenter. . . . I unsettle all things. No facts are to me sacred, none are profane; I simply experiment, an endless seeker, with no past at my back." The futurist was writing here, but the past, and he knew it, was always there. So was Emerson, the Ishmaelite, ready to burn up the veil that intervened between the visible world and its hidden significance. "Call me Ishmael," Melville would write. "Strike through the veil," Ahab would cry. In passages like the foregoing, Emerson anticipated them both.

Chapter Nine

ALCOTT

TOWARD THE END OF 1836, ALCOTT BEGAN EDITING THE bulky manuscript of his *Conversations on the Gospels*, hoping that it would "revive in the minds of this age the spirit of unsophisticated Christianity, and unfold the kingdom of Heaven as it is in the heart of childhood." So much the better if its publication at his own expense would enhance the reputation of the Temple School. His preface, read aloud to Emerson in mid-November, described the book as "the Record of an attempt to unfold the Idea of Spirit from the Consciousness of Childhood," presenting the character of Jesus as "the brightest Symbol of Spirit."

Emerson praised the preface, advising Alcott to bring it out separately as a pamphlet. It appeared under the magniloquent title *The Doctrine and Discipline of Human Culture*, followed by volume one of the *Conversations* in time for the Christmas trade and volume two in February 1837. Alcott looked forward to a period of sunshine and roses with so much confidence that he planned a third volume, having resumed in January the transcription of further conversations, this time with his new employee, Margaret Fuller, as recorder. Perhaps these books would earn enough to help pay off his ever accumulating debts.

Emerson had seized the occasion of the preface-reading to admonish Alcott on his exclusive otherworldliness. At a meeting of their new discussion group in October, Alcott had eloquently maintained that "Genius has two faces, one towards the Infinite God, one towards men." Emerson argued later that "the great Man should occupy the whole space between God and the mob." On one side he "must draw from the infinite source," and on the other "penetrate into the heart and mind of the rabble." This, he said, was what Jesus had done, "dwelling in mind with pure God, and dwelling in social position and hearty love with fishers and women." Shakespeare was another example of this two-pronged penetration. Many famous men had been one-sided; thus Plotinus "united with God" but ignored the world; Napoleon, Rothschild, and Falstaff united with the world but had "no communion with the Divine." The implication was that Alcott in his book was emulating Plotinus rather than Jesus or Shakespeare, and that a deeper involvement with the heart and mind of the rabble might enhance his striking power.

Alcott seems to have had this advice in mind when he went to hear Emerson lecture on "Religion" on January 19, 1837. "The speaker," he wrote in his journal,

> always kindles a sublime sentiment when, in those deep and oracular undertones which he knows when and how to use, he speaks of the divine entities of all being. A solemn and supernatural awe creeps over one as the serene pathos of his manner and the unaffected earnestness of his bearing come upon the senses. Here, I think, lies Emerson's power. At long intervals of remark bordering almost on coarseness—now the tones that he weaves into his diction and the picture of vulgar life that he draws with a Shakespearean boldness of delineation depicting farmers, tradesmen, beasts, vermin, the rabid mob, the courtesan, the under as well as the upper vulgar, and now sliding into all that is beautiful, refined, elegant, both in thought, speech, action, and vocation. . . . The burlesque is, in a twinkling, transformed into the serious. . . . His ideas are clothed in bold, sharp, natural images. He states, pictures, sketches, but does not reason. . . . All his ideas come orbed and winged. Footed and creeping things stand in contrast to give them effect; nor do slime and puddles become insignificant or unworthy in his creation. . . . The day shall come when this man's genius shall shine beyond the circle of his own city and nation. . . . Emerson is destined to be the high literary name of this age.

Alcott's great expectations for the success of his book failed to reckon with the Gog and Magog of Mammonism and Philistinism. Prominent among the Philistines were the newspaper editors. Late in March, Nathan Hale, brother-in-law of Governor Everett and editor of the *Boston Daily Advertiser*, attacked the *Conversations* as a mischievous invitation to ignorant children to express their "crude and undigested thoughts" upon "the most solemn of all subjects—the fundamental truths of religion as recorded in the gospels of our Savior." Next morning *The Daily Centinel and Gazette* took notice of the "visionary pedagogue" and "blockhead" who had compiled the volumes. In the following week the *Boston Courier*, under the editorship of Joseph Tinker Buckingham, observed that these conversations, if taken seriously, would undermine the very foundations of religious sentiment throughout the community.

Emerson sprang at once to Alcott's defense. He was in Salem when he read Hale's review and the "miserable paragraph" in the *Centinel*. Next morning in Boston he called twice at Hale's office with a letter of protest that he vainly hoped the paper would print. He was more successful with Buckingham, who wrote that "the truly Christian temper and amiable disposition of the writer of the following communication are so well known to us that it is really a pleasure to gratify him by placing it in our columns." Emerson's letter was forthright: "Mr. Alcott has given proof . . . of a strong mind and pure heart. . . . These Conversations contain abundant evidence of extraordinary thought, either in the teacher or the pupils, or in both. He aims to make children think, and, in every question of a moral nature, to send them back on themselves for an answer . . . to make them really reverent, and to make the New Testament a living book to them. . . . And I ask you, sir, whether it be wise or just to add to the anxieties of his enterprise a public clamor against some detached sentences of a book which, as a whole, is pervaded with original thought and sincere piety."

"I hate to have all the little dogs barking at you," he told Alcott, advising him to forget such beasts and to keep on writing, using his pen as a lever to lift the world. "I do not want these people to hurt the school," he added. Alcott was grateful: "Emerson sees me, knows me, and more than all others helps me. . . . Only men of like vision can apprehend and counsel each other." But the attacks had done their work and, despite the defensive efforts of some of the Unitarian journals and certain loyal parents, threatened the very survival of Alcott's establishment. One target for the infuriated Bostonians was Alcott's gentle explanation of the birth process: when the mother "is going to have a child, she gives up her body to God, and he works upon it, in a mysterious way, and with her aid, brings forth the Child's Spirit in a little Body of its own." Cooler heads might have found the passage sentimental; to the journalists of 1837, it was downright indecent. The *Courier* presently quoted the remark of the eminent Harvard professor, Andrews Norton, that a third of the book was absurd, another third blasphemous, and the rest obscene.

Mammonism had its day in April. The economic slump of the spring was severe—"cold April," wrote Emerson, "hard times; men breaking who ought not to break"—and Alcott's creditors demanded payment of the debts he had incurred in furnishing the Gothic schoolroom. The result was that "the furniture, busts, casts, globes, the bookcase with a hundred and fifty volumes and as many more from his own library all went under the auctioneer's hammer." Alcott took the blow quietly and valiantly, moving for the summer term into cramped quarters in the Temple basement. "My little room," he wrote in May, "with my ten pupils, and some of the remnants of my former magnificent mansion, with which it is a great contrast, gives me unquiet reflections." It might even be, he guessed, "that the speculative more than the practical element preponderates in me." His earnings from the school had now dropped to $549 from an initial high of $1,784 in 1834–35.

His wife was as strongly supportive as Emerson. On April 23, she wrote her brother,

> You have seen how roughly they have handled my husband. He has been a quiet sufferer, but not the less a sufferer because quiet. . . . I rail; he reasons, and consoles me as if I were the injured one. I do not know a more exemplary hero under trials than this same "visionary." . . . His school is very small, or will be at the commencement of another quarter. He will begin with about ten or a dozen here for the summer term. I sometimes think extreme poverty awaits us. . . . His patient endurance often staggers me, and the undaunted manner with which he assumes his burdens and cares, giving up, with cheerful submission, those

things which I know are dear to his heart . . . for the rigors of toil and privation fill me with admiration.

The sympathetic Emerson urged Alcott back to Concord for another visit. "You have had your share in the evil times that have fallen on the country," he wrote on May 10, "and I rejoice to learn have still evinced the wise man's superiority of temper." Perhaps the "green brookside and budding woods" might speak their own calm language into his ears. Emerson twice quoted Wordsworth as an inducement to his friend to "leave the impracticable world" and "sit apart" to write his oracles. Just at the time of Alcott's visit Emerson came down with a bad cold that made him feel "lumpish." But in retrospect he could not help admiring his "most extraordinary" guest: "Wonderful is his vision. The steadiness and scope of his eye at once rebukes all before it, and we little men creep about ashamed." To be sure, Alcott was "monotonous." One tired of his uniformity and his lack of humor. Yet he kept up undaunted his search for spiritual truth.

Back home in Boston, Alcott wrote that he was "waiting for light as this shall be vouchsafed." But his own retrospect upon the visit made him modify some of his former "notions" about Emerson, who, despite his "high and commanding" genius, did not always seem to be "fully in earnest," and often wrote and spoke "for effect":

Fame stands before him as a dazzling award, and he holds himself somewhat too proudly. . . . His life has been one of opportunity, and he has sought to realize in it more of the accomplished scholar than the perfect man.—A great intellect, refined by elegant study, rather than a divine life radiant with the beauty of truth and holiness. He is an eye more than a heart, an intellect more than a soul.

If Emerson's cold in the head was in any way responsible for these adverse judgments, it also spoiled the ensuing weeks. During much of June he was ill with his old nemesis, inflammation of the lungs, so fatigued that he nearly canceled his dedicatory speech for Hiram Fuller's Greene Street School in Providence on June 10, and so much worse after his return from Rhode Island that he felt "sour and savage" whenever he thought back to "the triumphs of the Philistines" over Alcott in the spring. Alcott also fell sick. On July 25 he wrote Emerson that he was "just up from severe indisposition" and still feeling "weak and shiftless."

Emerson at once invited him to recuperate in Concord: "My wife is a capital nurse, and joyfully offers her services. We have no company and Concord is Lethe's fat wharf for lounging. . . . Nobody shall be allowed to annoy you." Despite his recent opinion that Emerson was "an eye more than a heart," he spent four August days in talk with him and with Frederic Hedge. So much palavar made Emerson drowsy even though he enjoyed, as always, "putting together things that belong together." Drowsy he might have been, but he added that he "would rather have a perfect recollection" of all that had been said, and of all that he had "thought and felt in the last week, than any book that can now be published." Two days later, he reflected that "the secret of the scholar or intellectual man is that all nature is only the foliage, the flowering, and the fruit of the Soul and that every part therefore exists as emblem and sign, of some fact in the soul." Even "rags and offal" could be "elevated into hieroglyphics." Facts struck him as loathsome without clues to their meaning. But given the chain that connected them to the "Universal consciousness," he could "enlarge [his] charity one circle more and let them in."

Almost a year earlier, Emerson had written, "When I see a man of genius, he always inspires me with a feeling of boundless confidence in my own powers." At his best, Alcott was such a genius, a kind of liberator, an opener of doors. Emerson's Phi Beta Kappa address at Harvard was delivered on August 31, exactly two weeks after Alcott and Hedge had ended their Concord visit. When they had gone, he set down in his journal the essence of his forthcoming speech, as if his talks with them had spurred him to action:

> The hope to arouse young men at Cambridge to a worthier view of their literary duties prompts me to offer the theory of the Scholar's function . . . to arouse the intellect; to keep it erect and sound; to keep admiration in the hearts of the people; to keep the eye open upon its spiritual aims. How shall he render this service? By being a Soul among those things with which he deals. Let us look at the world as it aids his function. . . . Now the young are oppressed by their instructors. . . . They were born heirs of the dome of God thereunder or therein to move unshackled and unbounded and we would confine them under a coverlet.

Meek young men grow up in colleges and believe it is their duty to accept the views which books have given and grow up slaves. Some good angel in the shape of a turnkey bids them demand a habeas corpus and the moment they come out of durance the heaven opens and the earth smiles.

All this came close to being the Emersonian version of *Prometheus Unbound*. A good angel in the shape of Bronson Alcott had assisted in its formulation. Alcott himself made no such claim. "Now I am visibly idle," he wrote that fall of 1837. "My hand is without service. The age hath no work for me. I stand with folded arms, desirous of doing some service for soul." Eager to rescue him from the slough of poverty into which bad luck, poor timing, and improvidence had cast him, Emerson in February 1838 urged him to move to Concord: "Our little river would run gentlier and our meadows look greener to me, if such a thing could be." But Alcott stubbornly refused to give up his beloved school, and Emerson, still solicitous, refused to give up on his friend. He sometimes agreed with those who said that Alcott was "onetoned and hearkens with no interest to books or conversations out of the scope of his one commanding idea. May be so, but very different is his centralism from that of vulgar monomaniacs. For he looks with wise love at all real facts—at street faces, at the broad-shouldered long haired farmer, at the domestic woman . . . and so on. He can hear the voice which said to George Fox, 'That which others trample on, must be thy food.' " Moreover he was doing his best to fulfill the aim of the true Emersonian teacher, embracing the "doctrine of the perpetual revelation."

Despite his reverses, Alcott was still bent on proving himself as a teacher and, incidentally, as a writer. In June he spent a week in Concord, placing the revised manuscript of his "Psyche" on Emerson's desk for the third time in as many years. Already at work on his Divinity School Address, Emerson found the task of rejudging and reediting irksome in the extreme. But he punctiliously responded with yet another firm and lengthy letter, along with eight pages of suggested emendations. His conclusion was frank: "If the book were mine, I would on no account print it." At the same time, he said that it would be absurd to require Alcott to conform to the Emersonian position: "Here was a new mind and it was welcome to a new style."

"That is criticism," said Alcott, well pleased, and receiving Emerson's opinion as blandly as before. It seemed to confirm his growing resolution to talk things out instead of writing them down. "This," he wrote some months later, "is to be my way . . . of publishing myself." He liked to say that both Socrates and Jesus had been great talkers, and he continued to make entries in his voluminous private journal, which he called his "psychological Diary," wishing that Jesus had found time to keep one, too.

Having in his daydreams compared himself, not unfavorably, with such eminent figures out of the past, he found no difficulty in contrasting his own powers with those of Emerson in the present. "He, faithful to his own Genius, asserts the supremacy of the scholar's pen. I plead the omnipotence of the prophet's spoken over the written word. . . . I am of a temper too earnest and intense to rest in contemplation. . . . I must think, and set my thought in the drapery of action and living speech."

The author of these words had barely managed to keep his shrunken little school going until June 1839, including one final year in his house on Beach Street, Boston. His income had dwindled to $343: "I earn little or nothing in this miserable school nor am I laboring towards any prospective good in it." His family hovered, as usual, on the brink of indigence. Yet he somehow held onto his Micawber-like faith that something would turn up without his having to meddle in what he called "the arithmetic of this matter." He felt assured that "God has some task allotted and waiting for me, and will employ me in his service in his own time, with wages proportionate to my deserts."

One Sunday in church, which he still sometimes attended, Emerson sat in his pew reflecting on human cares and calamities. Lidian had come with him to seek temporary solace after having been wounded by the sharp tongue of an insolent servant. One of the stage drivers with whom Emerson often rode to Boston had developed a severe case of jaundice. Tolman the shoe-maker and his wife were mourning for their daughter "gone mad." And then Alcott: "My friend, whose scholars are all leaving him, and he knows not what to turn his hand to, next."

Emerson's problem was how to provide Alcott with a habeas corpus that would free him from the prison of penury. It would be a suitable payment for the spiritual and psychological gifts that he repeatedly offered. He was, as Emerson wrote in 1839, "the only majestic converser I now meet. He gives me leave to be, more than all others." He concocted an elaborate simile in which he compared himself to a southerner who had wintered in a polar climate until at last the south wind blew around him, relaxing his rigid fibers, expanding his whole frame in welcome heat, producing a "new nimbleness" almost as if he had suddenly sprouted wings. The fact was that Alcott's "sage and gentle spirit" thawed Emerson out.

Chapter Ten

THOREAU

THE DAY HENRY DAVID THOREAU ENTERED HARVARD AS A sixteen-year-old freshman, August 30, 1833, Emerson, aged thirty, was in Liverpool, England, waiting to board the ship that would bring him home after his grand tour of Europe. During Thoreau's collegiate years, Emerson moved to Concord, bought his house, gave his historical discourse on the history of the town, married Lidian, fathered a son, lost two brothers, and completed his first book, *Nature*. But the young man who would teach him more about the living facts of nature than he had managed to embody in that first book was still a virtual stranger to him until the late spring of 1837.

Twice in later years Emerson asserted that his friendship with Thoreau had begun at that time. "He was not quite out of college . . . when I first saw him," he told J. B. Thayer. To F. B. Sanborn he was more explicit: "My first intimacy with Henry began after his graduation. . . . [Lidian's sister, Lucy Brown] then boarded with Mrs. Thoreau and her children in the Parkman house . . . and saw the young people every day. She would bring me verses of Henry's,—the 'Sic Vita,' for instance, which he had thrown into [her] window." The fact that Henry's lines were wrapped and tied around a bunch of violets gathered in the Concord woodlands suggests the month of May, some ninety days before Henry's graduation, as the probable date of Emerson's dawning awareness of Thoreau's existence. In June he helped his young neighbor with a laudatory letter to President Josiah Quincy of Harvard, which eventuated in a grant of twenty-five dollars, no small sum in those days and enough to see Thoreau through the summer of his senior year.

Yet the "intimacy" that Emerson mentioned to Sanborn seems not to have begun until the fall of the year. Throughout the summer, they kept missing connections. On the Fourth of July, at ceremonies commemorating the Battle of Concord, Thoreau was a member of the outdoor choir that sang Emerson's "Concord Hymn," composed for the occasion and first "published" on slips of paper handed round to the audience so that they could join in the singing. But Emerson was not present that day, having gone to Lidian's beloved Plymouth for a week's vacation with her and their infant son.

At the Harvard graduation on August 30, Thoreau, as one of the ranking seniors, delivered a short oration. All men, he said, must "cultivate the moral affections" and "lead manly and independent lives," straightforward assertions that would doubtless have pleased Emerson if he had been among the listeners. But again he was not there, being still engaged with polishing his Phi Beta Kappa oration, "The American Scholar," which he read to a large audience next day. His theme, like Thoreau's, was the value of independence, of self-trust and self-confidence, of steadfast refusal to "defer" to the popular cry. "So much only of life as I know by experience, so much of the wilderness have I vanquished and planted . . . I do not see how any man can afford, for the sake of his nerves and his nap, to spare any action in which he can partake." If the activist Thoreau had been there, he might well have applauded. But now it was he who was absent. With his commencement duties behind him, he had rapidly disappeared, hurrying home to Concord well before the Phi Beta Kappa audience convened in Cambridge.

In the fall of the year the incipient friendship began to ripen. Thoreau had twice borrowed *Nature* from the college library in the preceding March and was already acquainted with this first major formulation of Emerson's thought. It is widely believed that Emerson was the catalyst for Thoreau's decision to keep a journal, which he began on October 22 and continued throughout the remaining quarter century of his life. But apart from the letter to President Quincy, Thoreau did not figure by name in Emerson's own journal or in his letters until February 1838, when the older man recorded his delight in this "young friend" who seemed to have "as free and erect a mind as any I have ever met." During an afternoon walk that day, he was amused by

Thoreau's story about a boy named Wentworth who had been his classmate at Concord Academy ten years earlier. One of the founders of the school was Dr. Abdiel Heywood, a prominent local citizen. The schoolmistress had cautioned the children to bow to Dr. Heywood in token of respect. When Wentworth next saw Heywood, the doctor stopped and stood waiting, clearing his throat to attract the pupil's attention. "You need not hem, Doctor," said Wentworth. "I shan't bow." The inference was that Thoreau shared his classmate's cheeky defiance of authority.

This was one of the qualities in Thoreau that seized Emerson's interest. Another was simplicity, the condition that Henry was to praise so highly in his masterpiece, *Walden*, when it appeared sixteen years later. "How comic is simplicity in this doubledealing quacking world," wrote Emerson on the heels of a winter walk with Thoreau, who had "made this else solitary afternoon sunny with his simplicity and clear perception. . . . Every thing that boy says makes merry with society though nothing can be graver than his meaning." Soon Emerson was writing of his longtime favorite Montaigne, whose essays were "spiced throughout with rebellion as much as Alcott or my young Henry T." A free-ranging mind, straight-backed principles, clear perceptions, existential belief in what eyes can see and muscles feel, defiance of magisterial pompousness, a degree or more of rebelliousness against the social status quo—these were among the Thoreauvian qualities and attitudes that Emerson seems most to have admired in the early months of their friendship.

Another was quietness. Thoreau was by no means tongue-tied, but his habits as a conversationalist were nothing like those of Emerson's other new friends, Father Taylor, Bronson Alcott, and Margaret Fuller. As over against the river-like flow of their talk, his was laconic, biting, laced with ironic humor, the kind that Emerson loved. Years afterward, he appreciatively quoted some two dozen of Thoreau's epigrams pulled from his unpublished journals: "Fire is the most tolerable third party"; "Nothing is so much to be feared as fear"; "The bluebird carries the sky on his back"; "The chub is a soft fish and tastes like boiled brown paper salted." Emerson long remembered that, when asked what dish he preferred for dinner, Thoreau tartly answered, "The nearest." He was temperamentally reticent, knew the values of silence, and, when he spoke, it was often bluntly, curtly, as if he had not many words to spare. Toward the end of April the two men walked to "the Cliff," a low eminence just across Walden Pond from the site where Thoreau would build his cabin in seven years' time. The day was warm and misty. The air echoed softly with the distant cawing of crows, the chirping of smaller birds, the peeping of springtime frogs. This, thought Emerson, was "a new scene, a new experience," quiet, unspectacular. "Ponder it," he told himself, "and not like the foolish world hanker after thunders and multitudes and vast landscapes, the sea or Niagara."

Almost immediately after his graduation from Harvard, Thoreau had taught briefly in the Center School, part of the public school system in Concord, but soon resigned because he did not believe in corporal punishment for the students. When he took off for Maine in May 1838 to scout for another teaching job, he carried a letter from Emerson that said, "I have the highest confidence in Mr. Thoreau's moral character and in his intellectual ability. He is an excellent Scholar, a man of energy and kindness, and I shall esteem the town fortunate that secures his Services." But none of the towns he visited rose to Emerson's bait, and Thoreau, undiscouraged, returned to open a small school of his own in the Parkman house on Main Street, from which he branched out in September by taking over the administration of Concord Academy, where he had been a pupil years before along with the defiant young Wentworth. The school flourished so well under his jurisdiction that he was joined early in 1839 by his brother John in a partnership that lasted nearly three years. As he had done at Alcott's school in Boston, Emerson paid a visit to Thoreau's. On September 1, 1838, he wrote his Aunt Mary that Thoreau had just stopped in, "with whom I have promised to make a visit, a brave fine youth he is."

"Brave" was the adjective that sprang to Emerson's pen whenever he mentioned one of these early encounters with Thoreau. "My brave Henry Thoreau walked with me to Walden this P.M.," he wrote on November 10, "and complained of the proprietors who compelled him . . . to walk in a strip of road and crowded him out of all the rest of God's earth." The owners said in effect that he must not "get over the fence." Thoreau rejected all such admonitions, and continued to cut fishing poles in other people's woods without asking who had "a better title to the wood than he." Emerson argued the point. Property laws represented a scheme "not good but the best that could be hit on for making the woods and waters and fields available to Wit and Worth, and for restraining the bold bad man." Seeing that Thoreau had "this maggot of Freedom and Humanity in his brain," wouldn't it be wise for him "to write it out into good poetry and so clear himself of it?" But Henry argued back: "In doing justice to the thought, the man did not always do justice to himself." Emerson agreed that it was "the tragedy of Art that the Artist was at the expense of the Man," adding that "Bolts and Bars," like the exclusionary fences that Thoreau overleaped, did not strike him as "the most exalted or exalting of our institutions." So the argument, like so many others between Emerson and Thoreau, ended in a draw.

In another exchange soon afterward, Emerson told Thoreau that Goose Pond should be renamed the Drop or God's Pond. "No," cried Henry. "That will shock the people: call it Satan's Pond and they will like it[,] or still better, Tom Wyman's Pond." Emerson's comment seems to have been aimed at Thoreau: "Alas! say I, for the Personality that eats us up." Such contentiousness, such a habit of direct contradiction, with an almost surly delight in taking issue, was the quality in Thoreau that Emerson had in mind later in writing to Margaret Fuller. He was sorry, he said, that she did not like "my brave Henry" as much as he did. "I admire this perennial threatening attitude, just as we like to go under an overhanging precipice. It is wholly his natural relation and no assumption at all."

As Emerson afterward expressed it, there was "something military" in Thoreau's nature, "not to be subdued, always manly and able, but rarely tender, as if he did not feel himself except in opposition. He wanted a fallacy to expose, a blunder to pillory . . . required a little sense of victory, a roll of the drum to call his powers into full exercise." As in the instance of the renaming of the pond, he always said no more easily than yes—a habit that Emerson called "a little chilling to the social affections." On hearing any proposition, "his first instinct . . . was to controvert it," and in a manner "never affectionate but superior, didactic," scornful of the "petty ways" of his interlocutors, like a New England Socrates at his most eristic.

In May 1839, "my brave Henry Thoreau" reappears in Emerson's journals as one who is "content to live now, and feels no shame in not studying any profession, for he does not postpone his life but lives already,—pours out contempt on these crybabies of routine and Boston." The position appealed to Emerson. Walking alone in Walden Woods that Independence Day, he thought that "the doctrine of hatred must be preached as the counteraction of the doctrine of love when that pules and whines. I hate father and mother and wife and brother when my muse calls me and I say to these relatives that if they wish my love they must respect my hatred. . . . I have no duties so peremptory as my intellectual duties." He had often written in a similar vein before this time. "He in whom the love of Truth predominates will keep himself aloof from all moorings and afloat" was only one example from the latter part of 1835. But his present reference to the puling and whining of the doctrinaires of love is not far different from Thoreau's "crybabies of routine."

Among the intellectual duties that Emerson sporadically and delightedly assumed was the close study of his associates. As one who never feared to generalize, who had all his life in sermons and lectures chosen large synoptic subjects on which to expatiate, he yet knew, as Thoreau did, the immense value of particulars. He wrote in his life a considerable number of formal and informal "essays" that could be called "characters," according to that genre which is said to have originated with Aristotle's pupil Theophrastus and to have reached a modern apogee in seventeenth-century England with collections like the *Microcosmographie* of John Earle. But Emerson's "characters" are not types like those of Theophrastus and Earle; what he valued in his friends was not what made them typical but what made them unique. Examples are numerous enough. He did "characters" of his brothers Edward and Charles, of his son, Waldo, of his gloriously eccentric Aunt Mary, of the grand old sachem Ezra Ripley, of Father Taylor, of Samuel Hoar and his daughter Elizabeth, Bronson Alcott, Margaret Fuller, Anna Barker, Jones Very, Nathaniel Hawthorne, and Theodore Parker. One of the best, both descriptively and analytically, is that of Thoreau, and it is replete with particulars.

He tells us, for example, that Thoreau was of "short stature"—some five inches under Emerson's six-foot height—that he was "firmly built, of light complexion, with strong, serious blue eyes, and a grave aspect." Out of doors "he wore a straw hat, stout shoes, strong gray trowsers, to brave scrub oaks and smilax and to climb a tree for a hawk's or a squirrel's nest. He waded into the pool for the water-plants, and his strong legs were no insignificant part of his armor."

He did not say that apart from height and comparative length of limb, he and Thoreau bore certain physical resemblances. Both had brown hair, fine-textured and abundant, though Emerson was considerably less hirsute than

Thoreau, whose arms were thickly matted with fur, like the pelt of an animal. Both their noses were long and broad, but Thoreau's, curving out and down from the bridge with a pronounced hook, somewhat resembled the beak of a predatory bird. Their eyes were blue, but Thoreau's often blazed with an icy grayish light—Emerson mentioned his "terrible eyes"—whereas the characteristic expression of his own was mild and beatific. In the country, they were accustomed to careless dress, with rusty jackets, rumpled pants, and well-worn shoes. On their walks Emerson sometimes carried a cane. Thoreau never would, calling it "too much company." But he often equipped himself with fishing poles, fashioned from young alders or birch saplings, stolen from the woodlots of local farmers.

Emerson liked people who could do things. In these years the active and agile Thoreau earned his admiration many times over. When Henry and his brother John set out on their river trip the last day of August 1839, Emerson wrote a little essay in his journal:

> We are shut up in schools and college recitation rooms for ten or fifteen years and come out at last with a bellyfull of words and do not know a thing. . . . Far better was the Roman rule to teach a boy nothing that he could not learn standing. Now here are my wise young neighbors who instead of getting like wordmen into a railroad-car where they have not even the activity of holding the reins, have got into a boat which they have built with their own hands, with sails which they have contrived to serve as a tent by night, and gone up the river Merrimack to live by their wits on the fish of the stream and the berries of the wood.

The boat, called the *Musketaquid*, was a fifteen-footer of dory design, with a pair of masts, four oars, punting poles, and even a set of wheels for portaging. The boys took along a cargo of new potatoes and homegrown melons to supplement the "fish of the stream and the berries of the wood" on which Emerson had poetically supposed they were going to subsist. They often replenished their stores at various farmhouses along the banks, buying such items as loaves of bread, draughts of milk, an apple pie, and the abundant muskmelons of the season. Six days out, they moored the boat at Hooksett, New Hampshire, and set out by stage for Plymouth, whence they hiked to

Franconia and Crawford Notches, and climbed to the summit of Mount Washington, breathing "the free air of Unappropriated Land," which Henry called by its Indian name, Agiocochook. After the mountaineering, they rapidly retraced their route by land and water back to their own Massachusetts melon patch, and chained their now experienced boat to the trunk of an ancient apple tree on the bank of the Musketaquid River.

They, too, had been shut up for years in classrooms, including those of their own highly successful school in Concord. Yet they had still been capable of fashioning the equipment of adventure and cheerfully "roughing it" in the northern wilderness. The other side of Emerson's laudatory observations on the Thoreau brothers' ingenuity was to emerge some ten years later in Henry's first book, *A Week on the Concord and Merrimack Rivers*, a volume, as Emerson saw, that was as much indebted to Thoreau's wide reading as to his experiential knowledge of the fields and woods and waters of his native New England.

Emerson's praise of the Thoreau brothers was set down after their return, and his admiration for the achievement was apparently contrasted in his mind with his own ten-day vacation among the White Mountains. His trip partly overlapped theirs, since he left before they did and returned while they were still in transit. During much of that summer he had been feeling out of sorts. Half sick when he left with his old friend George Bradford, he was at one time doubtful whether he had the strength to "crawl after" a group of hikers who were climbing "The Flume." His memories of the journey were evidently discolored by his condition. "The dignity of the landscape makes one more sensible of the meanness and Mud of the population at the taverns untempered by so much as a spark of true fire. Fierce vice, all forms of passion, do not assail our faith like this fritter and degradation of man which we see everywhere in the stage coach and bar room."

In his "Ode Inscribed to W. H. Channing," he wrote that "the God who made New Hampshire / Taunted the lofty land with little men." No such animadversion occurs in Thoreau's account of his boat trip with his brother. They seem to have kept clear of taverns and barrooms and, for the most part, of the "fritter and degradation" among the stagecoach passengers whose empty palaver so often offended Emerson's sensibilities.

Except for a sheaf of pages from Margaret Fuller's journal that he took along to read in off-hours, and his sight of the Great Stone Face, "that grave old Sphinx" gazing eastward from Franconia Notch, Emerson's greatest satisfaction on this trip was his second talk with Sam Ward, whom he had met briefly in Margaret's company in Boston in July. Within a month of his return he had the further pleasure of a first meeting with the beautiful Anna Barker, when she came to visit Margaret at Jamaica Plain.

Thoreau and his brother, John, were both handymen in the old New England sense of knowing how to make things. Their boat, the *Musketaquid*, had cost them only "a week's labor" in the spring of 1839, and when they were not teaching, they often turned their hands to the manufacture of useful objects. Emerson long remembered the bluebird house that John had made for the children, and months before the Concord-Merrimack trip he had dropped a note to Henry that said, "If you have any leisure for the Useful Arts, L[idian] E[merson] is very desirous of your aid."

This was not a skill in which Emerson himself excelled. About the time of his first acquaintance with Thoreau, and as a respite from composing his address on "The American Scholar," he had stolen a few hours from his study, "getting my nail box set in the snuggest corner of the barn chamber and well filled with nails and gimlet pincers, screw driver, and chisel." In such an operation he found "an old joy of youth, of childhood which perhaps all domestic children share—the cat-like love of garrets, barns, and corn chambers and of the conventions of long housekeeping." But his satisfaction in the neat storage of his tools was not matched by any skill in their use. Later, when Oliver Wendell Holmes questioned him about his manual dexterity, Emerson ruefully answered that he "could split a shingle four ways" with a single nail. And the child Waldo, supervising his father's hoeing in the family potato patch, issued a polite admonition: "I wish you would not dig your leg."

But it was Thoreau as naturalist rather than as carpenter who captured and longest held Emerson's attention and admiration. Before he knew that Thoreau existed, except possibly as the adolescent son of a neighboring family, Emerson frequently anticipated the kind of joy he would discover in Thoreau's friendship. Coming into the final stages of his first book, *Nature*, he wrote that "in this pleasing contrite wood life which God allows me, let me record day by day my honest thoughts, and the record ought to have the interest to a philosopher which the life of a gymnosophist [i.e., Hindu ascetic] or stylite had. The book should smell of pines and resound with hum of insects."

In the opening chapter of *Nature*, he wrote:

Crossing a bare common, in snow puddles, at twilight, under a clouded sky, without having in my thoughts any occurrence of special good fortune, I have enjoyed a perfect exhilaration. I am glad to the brink of fear. In the woods, too, a man casts off his years, as the snake his slough. . . . In the woods is perpetual youth. . . . The greatest delight which the fields and woods minister is the suggestion of an occult relation between man and the vegetable. I am not alone and unacknowledged. They nod to me, and I to them. . . .

"In my Pantheon," wrote Thoreau in *A Week*, "Pan still reigns in his pristine glory, with his ruddy face, his flowing beard, and his shaggy body . . . for the great God Pan is not dead, as was rumored. Perhaps of all the gods of New England and of ancient Greece, I am most constant at his shrine." Emerson had long been on the same wavelength. "I love the wood god," he had exclaimed in his journal for June 1836. "I love the mighty PAN."

Emerson was fond of seeing Thoreau in the guise of an antique deity. "The good river-god has taken the form of my valiant Henry Thoreau here," he wrote in 1841, "and introduced me to the riches of his shadowy starlit moonlit stream, a lovely new world lying as close and yet as unknown to the vulgar trite one of streets and shops as death to life or poetry to prose." There was a quality in his presence that betokened the aboriginal. Walking with him in November 1839, Emerson found "heroical and stimulating" the appearance of the woodlands. "In a very thick grove . . . H.D.T. showed me the bush of mountain laurel, the first I have seen in Concord, the stems of pine and hemlock and oak almost gleamed like steel upon the excited eye. How old, how aboriginal these trees appear, though not many years older than I. . . . The invitation which these fine savages give as you stand in the hollows of the forest, works strangely on the imagination. . . . Live with us, they say. . . . Here no history or church or state is interpolated on the divine sky and the immortal year."

Thoreau admired Alexander Henry's *Travels and Adventures in Canada and the Indian Territories* (1809), calling it "a sort of classic among books of American travel. . . . The good sense of this author is very conspicuous. He . . . does not exaggerate, but writes for the information of his readers, for science, and for history. . . . What is most interesting and valuable in it" is "not the *annals* of the country, but the natural facts, or *perennials*, which are ever without date. When out of history the truth shall be extracted, it will have shed its dates like withered leaves." Whenever he was not mythologizing "my brave Henry" as a rough deity of woods and waters, Emerson firmly emphasized the value of his zest for knowledge. He "fortified you at all times with an affirmative experience which refused to be set aside." He much preferred to deal with and in "the natural facts, or *perennials*, which are ever without dates." And yet, as Emerson went on to say, "none knew better than he that it is not the fact that imports, but the impression or effect of the fact on your mind. Every fact lay in glory in his mind, a type of the order and beauty of the whole."

Thoreau likewise shared with other men of his "rare class" that "excellent wisdom . . . which showed him the material world as a means and a symbol. This discovery . . . was in him an unsleeping insight; and whatever faults or obstructions of temperament might cloud it, he was not disobedient to the heavenly vision." So the transcendentalist ethic passed back and forth between the two men, each of whom paid particular attention both to natural facts and their symbolic meanings. Although they lived in the same town, it is well to remember that they were not in daily or even weekly communication, even in those years when Thoreau lived in Emerson's house. Yet a kind of rapport can be achieved that does not require the exercise of daily repetition. "We communicate," wrote Thoreau to Emerson when their friendship was five years old, "like the burrows of foxes, in silence and darkness, under ground."

But they communicated overtly, too. Henry must often have heard one of Emerson's favorite stories that told how "a poor woman having covered her children in the winter nights with all the rags and bits of cloth and carpet she could find, was accustomed to lay down over all an old door which had come off its hinges. 'Ah, dear mother,' said her eldest daughter, 'how I pity the poor children that haven't got any *door* to cover them.' " Recalling this story while writing his first book, Thoreau rejected its humorous aspect and gave it his own empirical twist. During one of his hikes he had spent a night at the summit of Hoosack Mountain. Although it was summer, the air grew so cold around midnight that he "encased" himself "completely in boards" from a pile of unused lumber, even contriving to place a board on top with a large stone to keep it steady. "I was reminded," he says, "of the Irish children who inquired what the neighbors did who had no door to put over them in winter nights. . . . But I am convinced that there was nothing very strange in the inquiry. Those who have never tried it can have no idea how far a door, which keeps the single blanket down, may go toward making one comfortable."

So this dogmatist of tested facts enjoyed a small triumph over his friend Emerson, who had merely chuckled over the irony of the Irish child's remark. Thoreau was a master of the art of one-upmanship a century before the term was invented. It was, as Emerson well knew, a prominent element in his personality. The trait may have come from his mother, Cynthia Dunbar Thoreau, who once proudly exclaimed, "How much Mr. Emerson does talk like my Henry." On many occasions in his life, Thoreau unwittingly anticipated Mr. Fidus Neverbend, a character invented by Anthony Trollope, of whom it is said that he "was an absolute dragon of honesty. His integrity was of such an all-pervading nature that he bristled with it as a porcupine does with his quills." Thoreau was a bristler par excellence.

Chapter Eleven

MARGARET
FULLER

MARGARET FULLER'S "TWENTY-FIVE WEEKS OF INCESSANT toil" at Alcott's Temple School in the winter of 1836–37 drained her energies to the dregs. She not only taught languages but also served as scribe for the projected third volume of the *Conversations on the Gospels*. She was often ill and always forlorn and lonely. When the sheriff's auction virtually decimated the school in April, she returned to Groton to rest before taking up her new duties as "Lady Superior" at the Greene Street School in Providence, recently established by Hiram Fuller (no relation) on pedagogical principles derived from Alcott.

Concord, as she now told Emerson, stood out in her mind as "Lethe and Eunoi," meaning that there she could forget her woes among kindly and friendly people. After the winter's "purgatory of distracting, petty tasks," she was certain that Emerson could "purify and strengthen" her to "enter the Paradise of thought once more." Despite her Dantean metaphor, his reply was down to earth: "We are all well and expect a happiness in your visit. Lidian is gone to a party." He picked her up in his chaise at Groton on Saturday, April 29, and next day drove with her on an errand to Watertown. Birds sang, the south wind blew. "It was beauteous," wrote Margaret, "and care and routine fled." She was equally ecstatic at first sight of the baby Waldo, now six months old. She thought him beautiful, like his father, and smiling sweetly on "all hearty, good people."

But her stay lasted only four days. She was unwell, and the "excitement of conversation" gave her insomnia. The visit, she said afterward, was "*satisfactory;* nothing is *satisfying* in this wale [sic] of tears." Emerson felt somewhat the same: "Among many things that make her visit valuable and memorable, this is not the least that she gave me five or six lessons in German pronunciation never by my offer and rather against my will, each time, so that now spite of myself I shall always have to thank her for a great convenience—which she foresaw." He did not think that she had *genius,* though she did have "genius-in-conversation." He was reminded, oddly, of a shabby opera company he had seen in Palermo in 1833. It was a pitiable affair until the "prima donna appeared and spoke. Presently she uttered cries of passion," and at once the "mimic scene" took on reality, becoming "human and heroic."

Early in June, Margaret paid another flying visit to the Emersons. He had expected her on May 30 and was weeding corn when the stagecoach stopped at his door. Dropping his hoe, he hurried to receive her, but was disappointed to get only a packet of books. She had closed her letter of the same day with a postscript: "What do you suppose Goethe and Scougal will say to one another as they are journeying side by side?" Henry Scougal, author of *Life of God in the Soul of Man*, was as dear to Emerson as Goethe was to Margaret. He filed her letter with the annotation "What shocking familiarity!" Clearly their friendship was losing a little of its initial sheen.

Between classes in Providence, Margaret continued to dream of Concord as a "haven of repose where headach [sic]—vertigo—other *sins* that flesh is heir to cannot long pursue." When Emerson gave the dedicatory address at the school on June 10, she was "much cheered and instructed" by his "noble appeal in behalf of the best interests of culture." In July she half apologized for her remark about Goethe: "I should think after hearing me say so much about him, you wld be aware that I do not consider him from that point of view you wish me to take. I do not go to him as a guide or friend but as a great thinker, who makes me think, a wonderful artist who gratifies my tastes— As far as he had religion and morality, I shd say they were expressed in this poem of his 'Eins und Alles' of whh I send you a rude translation."

Although her translation seems not to have been published until 1910, this lyric, composed in 1821, was well chosen for her immediate purpose of proving that Goethe could invoke the *Weltseele* or *Weltgeist* as an aid to human creativity—indeed, that Goethe's position on this point was not far from Emerson's reiterated opinion that "God is, not was." He soon replied rather noncommittally that "if the soul of Goethe shines . . . with unabated light and attraction before you, who is happy but you?" A year later, Margaret apologized once more: "I will try not to be impertinent about philosophers again."

In mid-August 1837 she wrote that she had recently been feeling "a little misanthropic and sceptical about the existence of any real communication between human beings," but was eager to revisit Concord during her approaching school vacation: "I only should like to be with you that I might see you more." Emerson compliantly invited her to hear his Phi Beta Kappa address at Cambridge. Afterward she could return to Concord with Lidian and himself. Next day at Emerson's house there was to be a meeting of the discussion group they were then calling Hedge's Club, where the male members might well "crave the aid of wise and blessed women at their session." While in Concord, Margaret managed to gallop through the first volume of Carlyle's *French Revolution*, which had reached Emerson only ten days earlier. On September 6 she was present, along with Sarah Clarke and Elizabeth Peabody, at a meeting of the Aesthetic Club in Newton.

Her beloved Anna Barker had been abroad since June, when she sailed from New Orleans to join the Farrars and Sam Ward on their continuing foreign tour. Eliza Farrar later wrote in praise of Anna, the "lovely young lady who travelled with me through France, Switzerland, and Italy" and was very clearly the life of the party. "She was spiritually-minded, and so thoroughly imbued with the love of her fellow-beings that it shone through every act, lending a charm to all she did, and said. No one could resist her fascinations and her presence was a talisman that unlocked all doors and propitiated all officials. Often have I seen custom-house officers, addressed by her, forget their duty, and pass our luggage without examination." In the villages, she was the center of attraction to the local children. Sometimes in the rural inns she played her guitar and sang while the natives gawked at her through the curtainless windows. "She had a way of treating every-one," wrote Eliza Farrar, "as if they were of the utmost importance to her." Passersby in the cities pointed her out as "the beautiful American." The expatriate sculptor Hiram Powers, with his great dark eyes, paper cap, and white apron, was so deeply attracted by her looks when the party reached Florence that he urged her to sit then and there for a portrait bust.

From Switzerland in December she had sent Margaret a "delicious letter."

Whether it contained any allusion to young Samuel Ward does not appear. Yet he must have been impressed, as Mrs. Farrar so clearly was, by the grace and beauty of Anna Barker. Some years later, Emerson called her "a Helen grown up unawares in these trivial New Yorks and New Orleanses of ours." Helen or no, this fetching girl with the guitar and the violet eyes could hardly have failed to arouse Ward's interest.

During this winter of 1837–38, the correspondence between Emerson and Margaret seems to have languished. In October he had warned her that if she came to Concord in the next few months she must bring extra blankets and even some pemican, since his furnace was not functioning. In December he thanked her for a "vivacious letter," which, he said, had quickened and sharpened "our country wits." In the new year he was so heavily preoccupied with lecturing in Boston and environs that he gave up his *pro tem* pulpit in East Lexington. At this time Lidian made a two-week visit to the "sandy 'Paradise' " of Plymouth, that "old natal nest and eggshell of us all," as her husband ironically called it in one of the eight letters he sent her, filled with domestic intelligence and detailed accounts of Waldo's endearing antics. "I am weary of living alone," he wrote her at last, "and hope you have ere this overcome some of your implacable aversion to Concord and will consent to return to yours affectionately, R.W.E."

Margaret reopened her Emerson campaign in March 1838, explaining the lengthy lapse in their correspondence. "You have seemed so busy and noble, and I so poor and dissipated that I have not felt worthy to address you." She must now rekindle her torch. "I want to see you and still more to hear you. . . . I dare to say that being lives not who would have received from your lectures as much as I. . . . I have behaved much too well for some time past; it has spoiled my peace. . . . But why do I write thus to you who like nothing but what is good, i.e. cheerfulness and fortitude? It is partly because yours is an image of my oratory. . . . If I do not jest when I write to you I must *pray*. . . . I hear you are to deliver one of your lectures again in Boston. I would have you do it while I am there. . . . Perhaps you will come to see me, fo[r] though I am not as good as I was, yet . . . I am better than most persons *I* see and, I dare say, better than most persons *you* see." She would be staying with the Sturgises, Caroline's parents, and hoped for a visit from this "unsympathizing, unhelpful, wise good man." She closed the letter on a higher note.

"Adieu Sanctissime. Tell Lidian that the thought of her holiness is very fragrant to me. Tell your son that if he has grown less like Raphael's cherubs I will never forgive him."

The allusion to Lidian's holiness was part of a continuing pattern in which she implicitly contrasted herself to Emerson's wife. A year earlier she had closed a letter with "dear love to the sainted Lidian." Now she wanted Emerson to understand that she herself had "behaved much too well for some time," and was presumably ready to kick over a few traces. In the fall of 1837, thinking of women in general, she had exclaimed to him, "Who would be a goody that could be a genius?"—a remark that he set down in his journal at the time, and on which he expatiated some months later, as if Margaret's audacious query had awakened his own Ishmaelitish tendencies:

I hate goodies. I hate goodness that preaches. Goodness that preaches undoes itself. A little electricity of virtue lurks here and there in kitchens and among the obscure—chiefly women, that flashes out occasional light. . . . But one had as lief curse and swear as be guilty of this odious religion that watches the beef and watches the cider in the pitcher at table, that shuts the mouth hard at any remark it cannot twist or wrench into a sermon. . . . Goodies make us very bad. . . . We will almost sin to spite them. Better indulge yourself, feed fat, drink liquors, than go strait laced for such cattle as these.

"I believe I am long ago in your debt for a letter," he wrote in May, "yet I seldom write one unless my belief in immortality is at the moment very strong and so indulges me in a free use of time. . . . My own appetite for letters is capacious as a sea. . . . Lidian and I have heard that sometime soon there was to be a Vacation in Providence. We wish to secure a part of your holidays the most you can give us at Concord and furthermore that you would induce Caroline Sturgis . . . to come with you." She must name a date so that he and Lidian could prepare for "guests so queenly and poetic."

His brother Bulkeley had been there for the past two weeks, recuperating from "a peculiar debility," but well enough to pull young Waldo around in a new go-cart. As usual, there were other guests: the Unitarian clergymen Frederic Hedge and Cyrus Bartol and the music critic J. S. Dwight made brief visits, and Alcott came for a week. Poor Bulkeley's stay ended when he "became suddenly disordered" and had to be sent back to McLean Asylum. Emerson had meanwhile beautified his grounds by planting forty-four pine trees. He had also acquired a pig and a severe case of laryngitis. He was beginning to wrestle with his address for the graduating class at Harvard Divinity School, which he was going to read on July 15, causing such a furor as neither the seniors nor their professors had hitherto known.

Margaret and Caroline stayed at Coolidge Castle for ten days in early June. Emerson took at once to Caroline, a young friend of Mrs. Bliss, with whom Lidian had stayed in Boston the spring before her marriage, and who had once thought of bringing Caroline to board in Concord. Caroline was a "lofty maiden" then aged nineteen, with a long face, steady brown eyes, smooth dark hair, a graceful neck, and olive skin. She was one of the five daughters of Captain William Sturgis, senior partner in the Boston firm of Bryant and Sturgis, which in those years was doing half the trade between the United States and China, and between the eastern seaboard and the California coast. Caroline had some skill in drawing and poetry. Emerson had noticed that she could "sketch with invention; others can draw as well, but cannot design." During her stay, although his talks with her lasted only a couple of hours, she aroused, as he put it, his "cold pedantic self into a fine surprise of thought and hope." This was often his reaction to the young, and Caroline's quick mind, her sardonic wit, and her ironic humor were not lost upon him. He thought her a protestant in the nonreligious sense, meaning that she repudiated the false out of love for the true. If she sometimes spoke extravagantly, as Margaret also did, he thought it a "good token"—"In an Extravagance, there is hope; in Routine, none." Presently he thanked Margaret for having brought her friend to Concord. "For a hermit," said he, "I begin to think I know several very fine people."

This was the summer when Sam Ward returned from his two-year stay in Europe, bringing back a huge portfolio of prints and etchings, including nearly five hundred "designs" by Raphael. Sam became once more an occasional companion to Margaret, as Emerson later wrote, "and, though much younger, her guide in the study of art. With him she examined, leaf by leaf, the designs of Raphael, of Michel Angelo, of Da Vinci, of Guercino, the architecture of the Greeks, the books of Palladio, the Ruins, and Prisons of Piranesi." But her conversations with young Ward, as Emerson divined, were "only veils and occasions to beguile the time, so profound was her interest in the character and fortunes of her friend."

One entry in Emerson's journal while his "fair visitors" were in Concord said simply: "A man must have aunts and cousins, must buy carrots and turnips, must have barn and woodshed, must go to the market and to the blacksmith's shop, must saunter and sleep and be inferior and silly." That was part of living. But he engaged another aspect of life when he examined some of the pictures from Sam Ward's portfolio that Margaret had brought along for his benefit. "It takes me long to know what to think of them, but I think I find out at last," he wrote. "I am quite confident in my criticism upon that infernal architecture of Piranesi and very delicious it is to me to judge them when at last I begin to see."

But he had little leisure for art criticism that summer. A week after the Divinity School Address he went to Hanover, New Hampshire, to speak on "Literary Ethics" to the students at Dartmouth College. On the way he saw "Monadnoc in its glory, and Ascutney in its pride, and Bellows Falls in its fury, and this blessed Connecticutt [sic] River in its lovely intervales." Lidian, who cared little for travel, was not only at home but often confined to her room. Two months into her second pregnancy, she was finding the going as difficult as it had been with Waldo two years earlier.

Emerson had closed his Dartmouth speech with a tribute to the double value of thought and friendship: "Thought is all light, and publishes itself to the universe. It will speak, though you were dumb, by its own miraculous organ. It will flow out of your actions, your manners, and your face. It will bring you friendships." This was a virtual echo of the view he had espoused in the Divinity School Address: "We mark with light in the memory the few interviews we have had, in the dreary years of routine and of sin, with souls that made our souls wiser; that spoke what we thought; that told us what we knew; that gave us leave to be what we inly were."

Thought that would eventuate in friendships, souls that would make one's own soul wiser: this was Emerson's foremost desideratum that summer of 1838. At home in the doldrums of August, he had no special obligations except to the child Waldo, who was cutting teeth, and to Lidian, whose illness, though clearly troublesome, was perhaps natural and normal enough for a pregnant woman in her late thirties. Margaret reappeared on August 15, bringing another sheaf of Sam Ward's pictures, including Raphael's arresting study of the Angel driving out Heliodorus. Emerson was so much taken with this further sample that he wrote Ward on the sixteenth, inviting him to Concord. He did not come, and it was not until eleven months later that the two men first met at an art gallery in Boston. But Emerson was now able to look at Sam's pictures "with leisure and with profit. In the antiques I love that grand style—the first noble remove from the Egyptian block-like images, and before yet freedom had become too free." The face of Raphael's Angel was "an ideal. The purity, the unity of the face is such that it is instantly suggested, *here is a vessel of God.*"

Apart from the pictures, Margaret's two-day visit added little to Emerson's summer. Waldo's "purgatory" of teething problems, Lidian's physical discomforts, and Margaret's "state of weak sensitiveness," for which she afterward apologized in a note to Lidian, did not illuminate the season. There was also some minor verbal altercation between Lidian and Margaret, who wrote, "Fret not that kindest heart because of my evil doing. Your remark was rather the occasion than the cause for any pain I felt." But the nature of the problem remains obscure.

The weather may have contributed. The severe heat of June had been followed by a long drought. Two days after Margaret left for Groton, old Dr. Ripley prayed for rain "with great explicitness," and on the Monday "showers fell." Emerson congratulated him on "the speed with which his prayers were answered," and "the good man looked modest." After his experience in looking at the "infernal architecture of Piranesi" in Sam Ward's dossier, Emerson turned back with relief to Dr. Ripley's church. On August 25 he wrote:

> What is more alive among works of art than our plain old wooden church built a century and a quarter ago with the ancient New England spire? I pass it at night and stand and listen to the beats of the clock like heartbeats; not sounding . . . so much like tickings, as like a step. It is the step of Time. You catch the sound first by looking up at the clock face and then you see this wooden tower rising thus alone, but stable and aged, toward the midnight stars. . . . Not less than the marble

cathedral it had its origin in sublime aspirations, in the august religion of man. Not less than those stars to which it points, it begun [sic] to be *in the soul.*

Emerson returned the Italian pictures to Margaret in September, and in October opened a small campaign to persuade her to live in Concord as soon as she had finished her two-year teaching stint in Providence. He still nourished dreams of a convocation of friendly souls in the village, and in February had raised the same question with Alcott. During the winter of 1838–39 he made repeated inquiries about possible housing for Margaret, undeterred by the safe arrival of his daughter Ellen, born on February 24, as well as Margaret's determination, now that she and her mother had sold the house in Groton, to take another, smaller place called Willowbrook at Jamaica Plain only five miles from Boston, into which they proposed to move early in April. Margaret stayed in Groton from January until the end of March, writing some fifty letters to her friends, sorting through her father's huge accumulation of papers, untouched since his death in 1835, and working on her translation of Eckermann's *Gespräche mit Goethe*, completed in February and published in Boston in May. On March 28, to escape the "dust and Babel" of the Groton household, she began a week's stay with the Emersons, delighted, as always, to return to "this mansion of peace," and enjoying the company of Elizabeth Hoar.

Elizabeth shared Emerson's admiration for Margaret. "Her wit, her insight into characters," she wrote to a friend,

... the rapidity with which she appropriates all knowledge, joined with habits of severe mental discipline ... her passionate love of beauty, her sympathy with all noble effort; then her energy of character and the regal manner in which she takes possession of society wherever she is ... all these things keep me full of admiration ... and inspire me with new life, new confidence in my own power, new desires to fulfill "the possible" in myself. ... But ... you cannot write down Genius. ... Only her presence can give you the meaning of the name Margaret Fuller. ... And her power of bringing out Mr. Emerson has doubled my enjoyment of that blessing to be in one house and room with him.

On the last day of March, Margaret had written to one of her brothers, "I have Elzh Hoar in the room with me, and like it very much, though we talk rather too much for my strength." She had just met Emerson's brother William, who had brought his wife, Susan, for a few days' visit. Margaret found him "as unlike his brother as possible . . . very gentlemanly, very amiable very clear headed, but a mere business man."

It was Emerson himself who stood at the center of Margaret's interest. "In the morng," she told her brother, "I write and read, Mr. E. being engaged in his study till twelve o'clock. Then he reads to me, or we talk the remaining hours." There were also opportunities for "meditation . . . in the tangled wood-walks" of the late afternoons. Above all she valued her conversations with Emerson, "whose serene and elevated nature I never came so near appreciating as now."

Emerson was recalling such visits as this one as he wrote his part of the *Memoirs* twelve years later. "She had so many tasks of her own, that she was a very easy guest to entertain, as she could be left to herself, day after day, without apology. According to our usual habit, we seldom met in the forenoon. After dinner, [about one o'clock] we read something together, or walked, or rode. In the evening, she came to the library, and many and many a conversation was there held, whose details, if they could be preserved, would justify all encomiums. They interested me in every manner;—talent, memory, wit, stern introspection, poetic play, religion, the finest personal feeling, the aspects of the future, each followed each in full activity, and left me, I remember, enriched and sometimes astonished by the gifts of my guest. Her topics were numerous, but the cardinal points of poetry, love, and religion were never far off." By 1839, three years into their friendship, the opulence of Margaret's powers had almost completely overcome Emerson's early prejudice against her.

Chapter Twelve

JONES VERY

"ENTERTAIN EVERY THOUGHT, EVERY CHARACTER THAT goes by, with the hospitality of your soul," wrote Emerson in the fall of 1838. "Give him the freedom of your inner house. He shall make you wise to the extent of his own uttermost receivings." Such a program ought to be followed, he felt, even or perhaps especially in the case of those "monotones (whereof, as my friends think, I have a savage society, like a menagerie of monsters)." Each one of these must be given sympathetic welcome to the sanctum of Coolidge Castle. "For the partial action of his mind in one direction" might serve as a sort of telescope, revealing to the observer something fresh and hitherto unsuspected about the objects or ideas on which it was trained.

The man he had in mind was a young enthusiast named Jones Very, just then a guest in his house. Very was a native of Salem who until recently had been a tutor in Greek at Harvard. Emerson had first heard of him late in 1837 from the energetic teacher Elizabeth Palmer Peabody, Bronson Alcott's quondam assistant and scribe. At the Lyceum in Salem shortly after Christmas she had listened to Very's lecture on "Epic Poetry," finding it so impressive that she moved at once to befriend the speaker.

Very was the eldest of six children of a marriage between cousins. His American ancestry went back to 1648, when one Bridget Very came to Danvers from Salisbury, England. Her great-grandson was a noncommissioned officer in the Revolutionary army; others of her lineage were farmers or sailors. The father and both grandfathers of the boy were shipmasters. At ages ten and eleven, Jones accompanied his father aboard the barque *Aurelia* on two long foreign voyages, but the captain's early death soon after the second trip turned his son's eyes inland toward the Pierian spring forty miles away in Cambridge. As a teenager he worked in a Salem auction room, reading widely in his spare time. In 1834 he matriculated with advanced standing at Harvard, graduating in 1836 second in his class, and happily accepting an appointment as Greek tutor to the freshmen, while continuing his studies at the Divinity School.

He had made few friends as an undergraduate. Excessively shy, devoted to books rather than people, he kept a scrapbook of favorite quotations, revealing strong interest in Coleridge, Wordsworth, and Byron, and began to compose poems for publication in his hometown paper, the *Salem Observer*. Tall and gaunt, with dark hair and eyes, high cheekbones, and a characteristically morose expression, he stalked about the Yard with an air of lonesome dignity, the very antithesis of his handsome, curly-haired classmate, Sam Ward. In his senior year, his discourse on "Epic Poetry" won him a Bowdoin Prize, and the subject of his address at commencement was "Individuality."

Very's speech at the Salem Lyceum took place during the midwinter vacation in his second year of teaching Greek. According to Very's biographer, Edwin Gittleman, Miss Peabody's admiration was so strong that she wrote at once to Emerson, begging him to befriend this youthful scholar: "The introduction of rare strangers to each other was her most extravagant indulgence, certainly her emotional fulfillment, and almost her career." Emerson asked Very to repeat the lecture at the Concord Lyceum on April 4, 1838. He brought along his heavily annotated copy of *Nature*, and Emerson inscribed it with an enigmatic epigraph: "Har[mony] of Man with Nature Must Be Reconciled With God." Next day he thanked Miss Peabody for having discovered so wise a man as Very, and a month later introduced his new disciple to the Transcendental Club at Medford, where the topic for discussion was "Mysticism." Such men, as he wrote in his journal, made him hopeful about the future of the Republic. In his Divinity School Address that summer he might have been addressing Very directly: "Yourself a newborn bard of the Holy Ghost, cast behind you all conformity, and acquaint men at first hand with Deity. . . . We mark with light in the memory the few interviews we have had, in the dreary years of routine and of sin, with souls that made our souls wiser; that spoke what we thought; that told us what we knew; that gave us leave to be what we inly were."

Emerson reiterated his praise in a letter to his lively old Aunt Mary. "There is a young man at Cambridge named Jones Very who I think would interest you. He studies Shakespear [sic] now and will presently finish and probably publish an Essay on S[hakespeare] and from a point of view quite novel and religious. He has been here twice yet be not uneasy on that account for he does not agree to my dogmatism."

The Shakespeare essay was soon done. But the effort involved in setting it down was such that within a week Very began to show signs of serious nervous disorder. "I felt within me a new will . . ." he explained afterward. "It seemed like my old will only it was to do good—it was not a feeling of my own but a sensible will that was not my own. Accompanying this was another feeling . . . a consciousness which seemed to say, 'That which creates you creates only that which you see or him to whom you speak.' . . . These two consciousnesses, as I may call them, continued with me . . . and went as they came impercept[i]bly."

Under the domination of his double consciousness, Very began to speak and act irrationally. One of his most admiring students at Harvard was Samuel Johnson Junior, the son of a Salem physician. On September 14 Johnson wrote home that Very had recently "gained the fame of being cracked (or crazy, if you are not acquainted with Harvard technicalities) among a set of thoughtless and ignorant young fellows" who had been ridiculing him behind his back. Though Johnson stayed loyal to his tutor, the thoughtless undergraduates turned out to be right. On the evening of the thirteenth, unknown to Johnson, Very invaded the study of Henry Ware Junior, professor of pulpit eloquence and pastoral care at Harvard Divinity School, and launched into a wild account of a divine inspiration that he said had enabled him for the first time to understand the meaning of the twenty-fourth chapter of the Gospel according to Matthew. He ended with the astonishing assertion that Christ's second coming was "in him." When Ware took issue with this claim, Very fixed him with a piercing look and said, "I had thought you did the will of the Father, and that I should receive some sympathy from you—But I now find that you are doing your own will, and not the will of your father."

This was too much for the Harvard authorities. Next evening President

Josiah Quincy announced that Very had suffered a "nervous collapse," that he had been relieved of his tutorial duties, and that he must be sent home to Salem in the care of his younger brother, Washington, a Harvard freshman. During the short interval before his departure Very gathered up the sheets of his Shakespeare essay and sent the packet along to Emerson with a covering letter. "My Brother," it began, "I am glad at last to be able to transmit what has been told me of Shakespeare. . . . You hear not mine own words but the teachings of the Holy Spirit." Within the next week or two he was hoping for a day or two of leisure when he could discuss the matter face to face with Emerson in Concord.

But the afflatus that had descended upon him earlier in the week left him no leisure at all. The morning after his return to Salem was a Sunday. He rose early and began knocking at door after door in the neighborhood with the news that the coming of Christ was imminent. Around ten he reached the Peabody house in Charter Street. His champion, Elizabeth, invited him into the parlor, where Very astonished her by placing his hand on her head and announcing in a sepulchral voice that he had come to baptize her with the Holy Ghost and with fire. Then he began a recitative based on the same chapter of Matthew that he had expounded to Henry Ware, and ended by praying over her. Afterward they sat down at some little distance from each other and Very asked how she felt. "I feel no change," she answered. "But you will," said Very. "I am the Second Coming." He called for a Bible and declaimed Christ's prophetic message. Then he spoke of his essay on Shakespeare and his hope of discussing it with Emerson. At last he left the room as suddenly as he had come.

Elizabeth Peabody diagnosed Very's problem as temporary insanity "induced by intense application . . . a passing frenzy caused by overtaxing his brain in the attempt to look from the standpoint of Absolute Spirit." But other Salemites were outraged by Very's Sunday morning visitations. The angriest among them was the Reverend Charles Wentworth Upham, a classmate and former friend of Emerson's who for the past two years had been inveighing against what he called "the infidel tendency" of Transcendentalism. This was the same man who subsequently engineered Nathaniel Hawthorne's dismissal from his post at the Salem customhouse, and the person once described by Senator Charles Sumner as "that smooth, smiling, oily man of God." Upham found no cause to smile over Very's religious delusions. At some time during the night of September 16-17, he invaded the Very household in Federal Street, collared the victim, and carried him off to the McLean Asylum in Charlestown.

Among the other inmates at McLean was Emerson's brother Bulkeley, who had been there since June. Having twice entertained Very at Concord in the spring, Emerson learned of his present predicament with some dismay. "Ha[ve] you heard of the calamity of poor Very, the tutor at Cambridge?" he asked Margaret Fuller. "He is at the Charlestown Asylum and his case tho't a very unpromising one. A fortnight ago tomorrow [c. September 15]—I received from him his Dissertation on Shakespeare. The letter accompanying it betrayed the state of his mind; but the Essay is a noble production; not consecutive, filled with one thought; but that so deep and true and illustrated so happily and even grandly, that I account it an addition to our really scanty stock of adequate criticism on Shakspear[e]. Such a mind cannot be lost." Emerson's long familiarity with the McLean hospital doubtless enhanced his sympathy with the new patient.

During his thirty-one days in the asylum, Very's spiritual excitement gradually simmered down. He wrote to ask for reinstatement in his tutorial position at Harvard, gave moral and religious counsel to some of the other inmates, recited from the Bible, as he had done with Elizabeth Peabody, and began to write an essay on *Hamlet*. Released on October 17, he returned to Salem and on the following Saturday went round to the Peabody house to assure Elizabeth that he was now "sobered" again after a period of having been "intoxicated with the Holy Ghost." He said that he was finishing his *Hamlet* essay and hoped soon to carry it to Concord for a conference with Emerson.

Elizabeth Peabody took it upon herself to warn Emerson about the impending visit, and to advise him about the best method of dealing with Very. "I treat him simply," she confided. "I let him say his say. . . . I give him no false sympathy. . . . But I would not—if I were you—stretch your charity so far as to invite him to stay in the house. . . . Limit your invitation; else you may not easily get rid of him." Emerson, she felt, could assume an authority over his visitor greater than her own. Very's mind was already favorably disposed toward Emerson, who might therefore help him to achieve a greater degree of self-governance.

Emerson ignored Miss Peabody's warning against having Very as a houseguest. The young man had been out of the hospital only a week when he reached Concord and settled in for a Wednesday-to-Monday stay, arriving October 24 and leaving the twenty-ninth. On the whole, as Emerson said, the visit went surprisingly well. At first Very adopted "a certain *violence . . .* of thought and speech," and Emerson had difficulty in adjusting to his high-flown Hebraistic vocabulary. Yet after five days' exposure he judged Very "profoundly sane" and even wished that all the world "were as mad as he." The violence of his language was really "quite superficial": once his mind settled down to a more natural state, few would doubt his sanity. "Talk with him a few hours," Emerson told Margaret Fuller, "and you will think all insane but he. Monomania or monio *Sania* he is a very remarkable person . . . a treasure of a companion, and I had with him most memorable conversations."

These were characteristically generous estimates, for many aspects of the visit could hardly have been anything but trying. Very made no bones about his hatred of the world. During a walk in the October woods, he told Emerson that in such natural surroundings one could forget that "the world was desart [sic] and empty, [and] all the people wicked." In every person he met he could discern an evil element, which he found so repellent that he even shrank a little when shaking hands, as if he might be spiritually tainted by such contact. His hatred, he said, extended into the broader reaches of human society. The cities and institutions that men had strewn across the face of the globe looked to him no better than blots of ink on a formerly virginal surface. Although indisposed to "attack religions and charities" as such, he believed that many or most of them were provably false. Yet he assured Emerson, in an echo of Saint Matthew (12:20), that he wished neither to break the bruised reed nor quench the burning flax. "His position accuses society," wrote Emerson, "as much as society names it false and morbid. And much of his discourse concerning society, the church, and the college was perfectly just."

The key to Very's position was spiritual obedience. "He would obey, obey," wrote Emerson. The power to which he made his genuflections was that of the Holy Spirit. Despite his knowledge of classical languages, pagan philosophers had no place in his scheme. "[I] would as soon embrace a black Egyptian mummy as Socrates," he fiercely cried. Having fixed his faith upon obedience, he took no account of time—always a questionable attitude in a houseguest. "A man who is busy, says, he has no time," he told Emerson, and "a man who is idle, says, that he does not know what to do with his time."

Time, indeed! Very refused to recognize it as a force for good or ill. "Obedience," he remarked sententiously, "is in eternity."

Emerson already knew something about his views on space and time from reading the essay on Shakespeare: "While in the physical world we are waging by our railroads and engines a war of utter extermination against time and space [Very had written], we forget that it is these very things, as motives, that urge us on. . . . While in the physical world we are driving to annihilation of space and time, it is for the very sake of the things of time and sense that we do it. We are therefore excluding ourselves daily from those *many* mansions which Christ has taught are prepared for us."

He sought to convert Emerson to his point of view. "You do not disobey because you do the wrong act," he argued, "but you do the wrong act, because you disobey. And you do not obey because you do the good action, but you do the good action because you first obey." He went on to explain that his hypersensitive state of mind had made him especially accurate in discerning spiritual essences. In the presence of certain people, of whom Emerson was one, he was able to detect an alien element. "He thinks me covetous in my hold of truth," wrote Emerson, "of seeing truth separate and of receiving or taking it instead of merely obeying. The Will is to him all, as to me (after my own showing) Truth." Between host and guest, by Very's reading, there was accordingly a gap or gulf. "I always felt when I heard you speak or read your writings," he later told Emerson, "that you saw the truth better than others, yet I felt that your Spirit was not quite right. It was as if a vein of colder air blew across me." Although Emerson had half affectionately begun to call Very "our brave saint," he kept the cold air turned on: "He seemed to expect from me a full acknowledgment of his mission and a participation of the same. . . . I asked him if he did not see that my thoughts and my position were constitutional, that it would be false and impossible for me to say his things or try to occupy his ground as for him to usurp mine. After some frank and full explanation, he conceded this."

Very excused his proselytizing by saying that it was "the necessity of the Spirit to speak with Authority." Having practiced it himself in all his sermons and lectures, Emerson was ready enough to accept this view. The young man seemed, he thought, echoing a passage from Very's essay on Shakespeare, to have "the manners of a man . . . to whom life was more than meat, the body more than raiment." Such utter sincerity as he displayed was perhaps the highest of compliments: "J[ones] Very charmed us all by telling us he hated us all." Yet this was the same man who asserted, quite seriously, that he felt it an honor to wash his own face, since it was the outward temple of the inward spirit.

For some time in 1837–38, Emerson had served as host at what he called Teachers' Meetings, held at his house on Sunday evenings. One of the high points of Very's visit came at such a gathering on October 28. The guests included Cornelius Felton, Very's erstwhile senior colleague in the Greek department at Harvard, who revered Emerson the stylist but distrusted Transcendentalism; young Henry Thoreau; Rockwood Hoar, Elizabeth's brother; and the Reverend Barzillai Frost, Dr. Ripley's assistant at the First Church of Concord. During the summer Emerson had vastly admired a picture by Raphael based on the original fresco in the Vatican. Its subject was the assault upon Heliodorus, the Syrian statesman, whose attempt to rob the Temple at Jerusalem was interrupted by three angels. As the incident was described in the apocryphal Book of Maccabees, a supernatural horseman in golden armor cast Heliodorus to earth while two other angels scourged him with "many sore stripes."

As the Teachers' Meeting began, the Reverend Mr. Frost made the mistake of sounding off to the company, towering and dogmatizing with many words, like Heliodorus before the Temple. "Instantly," said Emerson, with undisguised glee, "I foresaw that his doom was fixed." Frost had hardly finished speaking when Jones Very wheeled up his howitzers, which "blew away" all the preacher's "words in an instant," and "unhorsed him I may say and tumbled him along the ground in utter dismay, like my Angel of Heliodorus. Never was discomfiture more complete." Emerson remembered enough of this verbal assault to set it down in his journal. The minister must "wonder at the Love," said Very, "which suffered him to speak there in his chair, of things he knew nothing of; one might expect to see the book taken from his hands and him thrust out of the room—and yet he was allowed to sit and talk whilst every word he spoke was a step of departure from the truth."

Very left Concord Monday morning. He was going to Cambridge to try to secure reinstatement as student of theology and teacher of Greek. Emerson gave him a ride as far as Waltham. Watching him as he moved off into the world of ordinary mortals—this tall, slender, twenty-five-year-old, garbed in ministerial black, with that pale dour face and those dark piercing eyes—

Emerson thought that he looked "as solitary as Jesus." He could not help feeling that in saying good-bye to Very on this bright morning he was in effect discharging "an arrow into the heart of society." Wherever this young enthusiast went, he was bound to "astonish and disconcert men by dividing for them the cloud that covers the profound gulf that is in man," much as he had done with the Reverend Mr. Barzillai Frost at the Teachers' Meeting.

Chapter Thirteen

MARGARET FULLER

EXCEPT FOR HIS TRIP TO THE WHITE MOUNTAINS WITH George Bradford and brief visits to Boston, Emerson spent the spring, summer, and fall of 1839 quietly in Concord, rising at six, drinking coffee in his study, working through the "precious and guarded mornings" until noon or one. All was placid. The new baby, Ellen, was a "tranquil little body," and Lidian said that each of her days was "too beautiful to be lost." Waldo, aged three, was full of questions. Emerson and his brother William were still splitting Bulkeley's expenses at Charlestown, where he had been for more than a year.

There were the usual visitors: Thoreau, home again from his Merrimack voyage; Jones Very the sonneteer, whose essays and poems Emerson was editing for September publication; Alcott over from Boston, needing counsel and encouragement. His "usurping conversation" cut heavily into Emerson's working time but did not destroy his liking for Alcott. "I must think very ill of my age and country," he wrote, "if they cannot discover his extraordinary soul."

He was making little headway with his first volume of essays. He read and praised Margaret Fuller's translation of Eckermann's conversations with Goethe. Between April Fool's and Thanksgiving he averaged more than two letters a week to various correspondents. The one that cost him the greatest pains answered a query from young Harrison Blake, one of those who had arranged for the Divinity School Address. Blake was troubled about the duties of a Christian minister. "I infer," wrote Emerson, "that you see light already. That light I am sure is a greater self[-]reliance,—a thing to be spoken solemnly of and waited for as not one thing but all things, as the uprise and revelation of God. . . . All that is alive in the Church is with us. . . . The community will forgive any contradiction of their opinions so that they have a man to their preacher. But he must not be a half-man . . . addicted to dictionaries or pictures or sleep, and bringing them bad sermons half-written. . . . His nerves must tingle first that their nerves shall tingle. . . . The whole of duty seems to consist . . . in obeying the aboriginal truth. . . . The true Fall of man is the disesteem of man; the true Redemption [is] self-trust." This was a summary recapitulation of the ideas espoused in the Divinity School Address, to which Blake had listened; but perhaps the young man was now further reassured.

In the dog days Emerson complained of lethargy: "I can no more write than I can hoe this week," he told Margaret at the end of July. "I lead the life of a blade of grass in mere wind and sun," he added in September, "and have no other events than the weather." In the afternoons he was working faithfully in his half-acre garden, tending corn, melons, and beans, and weeding the hills of potatoes, of which he got so good a crop that he shipped his brother William a full barrel of his own Jacksons and Samuel Hoar's Long Reds in time for Thanksgiving. Waldo, now "more discreet and companionable day by day," helped him in the potato patch, calling his father's digging implement a "hoer"—an inadvertent homonym uttered in perfect innocence—to Emerson's evident amusement.

During all this time, Margaret Fuller had been variously troubled. Early in June, Caroline Sturgis stayed overnight at Willow Brook, went on alone for a week's visit in Concord, gratifying Emerson's wish to know this lofty young woman somewhat better, and then rejoined Margaret for a holiday at Nahant, the peninsula adjoining Lynn. They spent a halcyon afternoon among the tumbled brown rocks, one of them known locally as the Spouting Horn, where centuries of waves had carved a huge fissure. Margaret lolled on a ledge near the slosh and surge of the sea, and Caroline, perched high above in a light green dress, "looked like the nymph of the place."

Such pleasures soon faded when Margaret one day asked Caroline point-blank, "Do you love me?" and Caroline found that she "could not at once say yes." Margaret's wounded pride was not wholly assuaged by Caroline's letters of apology, and they entered a period of silence "by mutal consent." Margaret's emotional life was already in a state of *Stürm und Drang* owing to the imminent failure of her love affair with Sam Ward. Her cousin George Davis had jilted her nine years earlier, and it now seemed that Sam was following suit. "If you love me as I deserve to be loved," she wrote him in July, "you cannot dispense with seeing me. . . . We knew long ago that age, position, and pursuits being so different, nothing but love bound us together, and it must not be *my* love alone that binds us." By September the situation had worsened. "You do not wish to be with me," she complained. "Why try to hide it? . . . You are not interested in any of my interests." Not once since early June had they "seen, felt, admired together." Sam had sometimes called, but often in haste, and always "in the parlor," of all places. He invited her to go to see the work of Michelangelo—by herself! He wrote that he would love her forever. She wanted to believe him, but insisted that she was "entitled to unshrinking frankness."

She closed this letter with an extravagant religious comparison. One of Sam's nicknames for her was "mother," as if he were a kind of Adonais Redivivus in love with Venus Urania, the "mighty Mother" of the celestial realms. But Margaret invoked the New Testament. "You have given me the sacred name of Mother," she wrote, "and I will be so indulgent, as tender, as delicate . . . in my vigilance, as if I had borne you beneath my heart instead of in it. But Oh, it is waiting like the Mother beside the sepulchre for the resurrection, for all I loved in you is at present dead and buried, only a light from the tomb shines now and then in your eyes. But I will wait . . . for thee whom I have loved so well. . . . Only thyself shall have power to divorce my love from its office of ministry." And she signed herself *Isola,* as if to emphasize her aloneness.

This was excess *in extremis,* translating Sam's boyish term of endearment into a metaphorical alliance between herself and the Madonna, waiting at the sepulchre for the Resurrection. Still, the whole letter was distinctly overblown, the complaint of a woman of thirty who saw herself rejected by a youth of twenty-two. Having known her now for three years, Emerson was well acquainted with this aspect of Margaret's character. He had mildly chastised her, though not to her face, in a journal entry of August 1836, for having sought to overpersonalize their developing personal relationship. "How rarely," he wrote, "can a female mind be impersonal." In the *Memoirs* of 1851 he expatiated on the topic: "I had always an impression that her energy was too much a force of blood, and therefore never felt the security for her peace which belongs to more purely intellectual natures. She seemed more vulnerable." Reading through her diaries in preparation for his part of the memoir, he had found that "the unlooked for trait in all these journals to me is the Woman, poor woman: they are all hysterical. She is bewailing her virginity and languishing for a husband." It is possible, even probable, that he had divined this supposed truth as early as 1839.

Whatever Emerson knew of Margaret's unrequited passion for Sam that summer and fall, he had her to thank for an introduction to Ward in Boston. He soon told Margaret of his hope to talk with Ward alone in the relative quiet of Concord. Instead, the two men met again by chance in the White Mountains in August, to Emerson's "great satisfaction." His letter to Margaret about Sam was dated September 3, within a day or two of her "Isola" letter to Ward. It was ironic that the Emerson-Ward friendship was just beginning when Margaret's love affair with Ward was coming to an end.

For several years Emerson had vainly longed to meet another of Margaret's friends. Learning in August that Anna Barker was staying with Margaret at Jamaica Plain, he urged somewhat plaintively that she must allow him to meet the renowned Récamier. But it was not until the end of September that she invited him to drive the nineteen miles that separated his house from hers. He accepted at once and went the distance on October 4 to feast his eyes upon the fabled Anna.

She did not disappoint him. After a couple of days in her company, he called her "a woman singularly healthful and entire":

She had not talents or affections or accomplishments or single features of conspicuous beauty, but was a unit and whole, so that whatsoever she did became her, whether she walked or sat or spoke. She had an instinctive elegance. . . . No princess could surpass her clear and erect demeanour. . . . She is not an intellectual beauty . . . does not resemble the women whom I have most admired and loved. . . . She does not sit at home in her own mind as my angels are wont to do, but instantly goes abroad into the minds of others, takes possession of society and warms it with noble sentiments. . . . Her conversation is the frankest I ever heard. She can afford to be sincere. The wind is not purer than she is.

Aged twenty-six, wealthy and widely traveled, warm and sympathetic, pure of heart, elegant in demeanor, frank in conversation, Anna more than lived up to Emerson's expectations. He wrote his Aunt Mary Moody Emerson about this "vision of grace and beauty—a natural queen—just returned from Europe, where as here she received incense every day, in all places, which she accepts with high glee and straightway forgets from her religious heart."

In October, the birth month of both Sam Ward and Anna Barker, Sam revealed to Margaret that he was in love with this paragon. "My dearest S.," wrote Margaret, "Although I do not feel able at present to return a full answer . . . I will not do myself the injustice of preserving entire silence. . . . I never should make any claim on the heart of any person on the score of past intercourse and those expressions of affection which were the flower and fruitage of its summer day. If autumn has come, let come also chill wind and rain like those of today. But on the *minds* of those who have known me once I always have a claim." Sam had written that "the world has separated us as intimates and may separate us more." Margaret advised him to think no more about her for the present, to give himself up to the "holy hour" that now shone upon him. "Time, distance, different pursuits may hide you from me," she concluded, "yet will I never forget to be your friend or to visit your life with a daily benediction."

There was much more, for Margaret, pen in hand, could rarely curb her volubility, but she added that she was "very busy with affairs" long deferred until she could bend her mind to them. The fact was that she had determined to return to teaching, partly for needed income, and no doubt partly to sublimate her sorrow over Sam's decision. A week later she and Bronson Alcott called on Emerson to discuss another educational plan—the development of a new journal to rival and perhaps to supersede Orestes Brownson's *Boston Quarterly Review*.

Emerson received them kindly. They were "friendly influences." "Cold as I am," he wrote with his usual self-depreciation, "they are almost dear. . . . They brought nothing but good spirits and good tidings with them of new literary plans." Margaret also told him about Sam and Anna—"a chronicle of sweet romance," as he sentimentally called it, "of love and nobleness which have inspired the beautiful and brave." In long retrospect, Emerson was grateful to Margaret for having been his agent of introduction to Caroline

Sturgis, Sam Ward, and Anna Barker. Twenty-four years later, reading Jean-Paul Richter's *Titan: A Romance*, he could forgive its "excessive efflorescence and German superlative" because of its "noble wisdom and insight." Somehow the book restored to him "the golden thoughts that once wreathed round Margaret F[uller] and Caroline [Sturgis Tappan] and S[amuel] G[ray] W[ard] and Anna [Barker Ward]."

Both of Margaret's new teaching plans were admirably suited to her powers. The first was a series of "Conversations," held at Elizabeth Peabody's bookshop on West Street near Boston Common, beginning November 6, 1839. The second was her managing editorship of the new quarterly magazine, which Alcott wanted to call the *Dial*. On New Year's Day 1840 she wrote two of her oldest friends, Frederic Hedge and W. H. Channing, asking for contributions to the first number.

"Margaret's Parlatorio" was Emerson's name for the conversations. Their purpose was to give intelligent women a chance to explore ideas and images through "Socratic" dialogues. The first series examined the Greek and Roman deities "as a good means of opening a vista" into their symbolic meanings. "You joke about my Gods and Goddesses," she wrote her Providence friend, Sarah Whitman, "but really my class in Boston is very pleasant. . . . We have time, patience, mutual reverence and fearlessness eno' to get at one another's thoughts. Of course our treatment of topics is superficial but good, I think so far as it goes." Jupiter embodied creative energy, Apollo stood for genius, Bacchus for geniality, Venus Urania for ideal beauty, and so on.

Her preceptees, ranging in number from twenty-five to forty, included many of the brightest women in Boston and environs, among them Lydia Maria Child, Sarah Clarke, Eliza Farrar, Elizabeth Hoar, Elizabeth and Sophia Peabody, and Caroline Sturgis, as well as Lidian Emerson whenever her health allowed. Her daughter Ellen later recalled that her mother "used to get up before light on those winter mornings, jump into her tub of cold water . . . and be dressed and ready to go" when the stagecoach left Concord at seven.

"M[y] class is singularly prosperous I think," said Margaret. "All seem in a glow and quite as receptive as I wish. . . . The first time, ten took part in the conversation; the last still more." According to Sarah Clarke, Margaret was "the most powerful stimulus, intellectual and moral. It was like the sun shining upon plants and causing buds to open into flowers. This was her gift, and she could no more help exercising it than the sun can help shining. This gift, acting with a powerful understanding and a generous imagination, you can perceive would make an educational force of great power."

With the parlatorio well launched, she returned to the *Dial*. Its prospectus said that it aimed to "furnish a medium for the freest expression of thought on the questions which interest earnest minds in every community," and "to examine the ideas which impel the leading movements of the present day." Contributors would be oriented toward the future rather than the past, trusting in "the living soul more than the dead letter." George Ripley, who wrote the prospectus, was at first the business manager and Margaret, as editor, was promised a salary of $200, though in the end, as in her teaching for Alcott's Temple School, she got nothing at all—except the experience.

Gathering materials for the opening number took much of the winter and spring. She and Caroline Sturgis had mended their differences of the preceding summer. "Only for a moment did I cease to love you," she wrote. Early in the new year she read some of Caroline's poems. They were "almost as good as your best prose. . . . Even where most unmusical and unfinished they have the great beauty of being written to the dictation of Nature." Caroline's married sister, Ellen Hooper, also composed verse—in Margaret's view "sweet though pale buds of daily life." One of her lyrics began, "I slept, and dreamed that life was Beauty; / I woke and found that life was Duty." Margaret planned to print it in the July number and promised to include the work of both sisters in future issues.

It was a strange winter, subzero in January, with false spring a month later. Bluebirds appeared on February 21, moving into the house that John Thoreau had made and nailed to Emerson's barn. Margaret rejoiced in the weather while feeling that she did not deserve it. "I have been so deeply engaged . . . yet there is little outward token. . . . Few can suffer at falling short of the ideal standard so much as I, for few have had occasion to raise it so high." Her correspondence with Emerson had greatly accelerated. Between October 1839 and the same date in 1840 they exchanged at least fifty-five letters, more than one a week.

He was deeply engaged with lectures in Boston, New York, Providence, and Salem. In March he wrote from Rhode Island that his first book of essays must take precedence, "yet I think I will write [for the *Dial*] as many pages as you wish." In the event, his contributions to the first number consisted of a

1,500-word address to readers, and two poems, one of them perhaps about Caroline: "Fair and stately maid, whose eye / Was kindled in the upper sky / At the same tórch that lighted mine," and the other, in characteristic couplets, a rebel poem called "The Problem," which still stands among the best verse he ever wrote. The contents for July drew heavily on the Emerson family, with Edward's poem "The Last Farewell," some "Notes from the Journal of a Scholar," which Emerson had culled from papers left by his brother Charles, and a graceful set of quatrains by Emerson's first wife Ellen. Margaret herself contributed two essays and seven poems and printed eight verses by her close friends Ellen Hooper, Sarah Clarke, and Sam Ward, as well as Thoreau's "Sympathy," which Emerson greatly admired. Ripley reviewed a religious novel by Orestes Brownson; Theodore Parker's "The Divine Presence in Nature and in the Soul" was a vigorous statement of the transcendentalist position on God, nature, and man; and Thoreau did a little essay on the satires of Aulus Persius Flaccus. Both Margaret and Emerson had their doubts about Alcott's "Orphic Sayings," which filled thirteen printed pages with what might have been whipped cream. Most of the other contributions were either anonymous or signed with single initials. But Emerson insisted that Alcott's "Sayings" should bear his full name. His struggling friend needed the encouragement of wider recognition.

Neither his winter's lectures nor *Dial* I wholly satisfied Emerson. "All life is a compromise," he had written. "We are haunted by an ambition of a celestial greatness and baulked of it by all manner of paltry impediments." To his brother he wrote, "Ten decorous speeches and not one extacy [sic], not one rapture, not one thunderbolt." In Providence he had found his youthful audiences eager for "more light." They hoped to see it shining in the coming *Dial*, though Emerson warned them that the contents would be "rather literary than psychological or religious." This did not satisfy them. They were thinking of Emerson as the ace Transcendentalist, and kept asking when he would give them a lecture on the "Great Subject," explaining precisely what it was and how it worked. He heard of one man who defined it as "Operations on the Teeth." Another said that it was "the nickname which those who stayed behind, gave to those who went ahead."

This last was at any rate closer to the mark. Yet even the most progressive audiences had to be handled with care. It was partly a matter of nomenclature. "In all my lectures," wrote Emerson, "I have taught one doctrine, namely, the infinitude of the private man. This the people accept readily enough, and even with loud commendation, as long as I call the lecture, Art; or Politics; or Literature; or The Household; but the moment I call it Religion,—they are shocked, though it be only the application of the same truth."

Soon after his thirty-seventh birthday in May, Emerson took Waldo to see a traveling circus that boasted bareback riders and a horse trained to carry a basket in its teeth and to pick the right card from a group of four. Asked for his reaction, Waldo said, "It makes me want to go home." This exactly hit his father's conception after the long winter of lecturing in alien towns and cities.

Why should I covet a knowledge of new facts and skills, when I know that they are only other illustration of laws playing daily before my eyes? Day and night, garden and house, art and books serve me as illustration just as well as would all trades, all skills. Indeed I am far from having exhausted the significance of the few symbols I use. . . . What is it to be a poet? What are his garland and singing robes? What but a sensibility so keen that the scent of an elderblow [the white blossoms of an elderbush] or the timberyard and corporation works of a nest of pismires is event enough for him. The poet's wreath and robe is to do what he likes; is emancipation from other men's questions and glad study of his own.

Day and night, garden and house, art and books. What else was needful? One answer was friends. The news from Margaret's friends in late May was that Anna Barker had broken her engagement to Sam Ward. He had been planning an artistic career, but Anna insisted he must follow his father and hers into the banking business. Learning of this "new act in the romance," Emerson told Margaret that "the polarities of such agreeable beings cannot be quite sad, only sober geranium-colored to the imagination." When Anna and some of her family came north shortly afterward, she told Emerson her "winsome story" during a ride to and from the village of Newton. Since the details of her revelation were "in great part confidential," he mentioned them to no one, though he did tell Caroline, when she came to Concord early in June, that "Anna and her lover had parted," a fact which, after all, belonged "to the world."

Sam Ward had gone to New Orleans, listened sadly to Anna's negative decision, and come home by steamboat up the Mississippi River, stopping over in northern Illinois to pay an abortive call on his friend and former school-mate, the poet Ellery Channing, who had been living in a log hut on the prairie but was no longer there. When Sam returned to Boston he was visibly the worse for wear. In mid-June he wrote Emerson about his "vain visit" to Channing's "hermitage," adding that he himself was not well. Although Emerson thought the illness was "nothing serious," and may even have suspected that one of its causes was the broken engagement, he discovered in Boston on June 20 that Sam was confined to bed with "fever and ague."

Anna, meantime, was "giving all her time to her favorite brother, Tom." They were "walking and driving and looking on the solemn mountains" that seemed to Anna "most beloved and blessed friends—so calm, so majestic, as if waiting God's word." Margaret, back from a seaside holiday with Caroline at Cohasset, was expecting a visit from Anna at Jamaica Plain. She took the occasion of a letter full of *Dial* business to give Emerson an analysis of Anna's character and to explain the impulse that had made her confide in him during their ride to Newton:

> A[nna]—though frank is not communicative, she has perfect power of keeping a secret. I do not think she would have spoken on the subject [of the broken engagement] to any other than yourself. You gave her the feeling of the holy man, the confessor who should enlighten her at this moment to act in conformity with her purest and highest nature. She felt at once that she was spiritually in relation with you, and spoke as she would in the confessional. . . . I know how to keep relations sacredly separate. I should never have let *you* know any thing about this if we had been intimate forever unless A[nna] had. I never told C[aroline] till the other day as she knew so much I could not bear she should put the vulgar construction on the matter and told her enough to show how true and noble he [Sam] had been.

Margaret had not seen Sam until recently. She was shocked by his appearance. "He is even emaciated," she told Caroline, "and seems scarce able to move. He has lost all his beauty for the present, but was the more dear. I had a most happy hour with him. He was most happy, leaning on his own thoughts, gentle celestial, not hopeful, but faithful. He was delighted to find me in so quiescent a mood. He begged me to stay so, as long as he did. May our relation remain as sweet and untroubled as at present!"

"I give you joy of Ward's returning health," wrote Emerson. Sam was vacationing at Nahant with his younger brothers and finding "miraculous good" in the salt air. Emerson assured Margaret that he felt "no coldness no commonness when any tidings or thoughts of the fair Anna come. You need never fear my desecration of such deodands." His brother Bulkeley was staying with Emerson, "very calm and happy." The garden was rejuvenated after a fourteen-hour rain, and the children were thriving. Emerson was pretending "to write a little from upper [i.e., supernal] dictation," but soon found himself "copying old musty papers," then reading "a little in Plato, a little in the Vedas," until the outdoors called him to pick peas, water his melons, or thin his carrots. After a little walking and talking he found that the "marvellous Day" had "fled forevermore." He was thinking again, as he so often did, in the strain of his poem "Days," although it had not yet seen the light.

Chapter   Fourteen

VERY

THE AUTHORITIES AT HARVARD WOULD NOT CONSIDER readmitting Jones Very. Back in Salem, reflecting on Emerson's praise of his essays, he presently sent along a couple of his latest sonnets. Emerson answered that he "loved" the poems and had been reading them aloud "to all who have ears to hear." The language was as simple as the sentiments were profound. "You will find your audience very large," he wrote, "as soon as the verses first take air and get abroad." He generously volunteered to help Very prepare and publish a collection of his verse and prose.

Very took this generosity as a sign that Emerson was coming round to his own religious position. "I was pleased," he said, "to hear that my stay with you was [spiritually] improving, and that you love that which is spoken by the word. If you love it aright in the spirit of obedience it shall be unto you given to hear and speak of the Father in Christ." Though Emerson was ten years older than he, Very wrote as if to a much younger disciple, advising him to "pass out of that world in which you are, naked (that is, willess) as you came in. Then shall you have a *new* will born of the spirit. . . . Soon may you learn that to obey or disobey the will within is all that we can do."

As to Emerson's proposal to make a book of Very's poetry and prose, Very added that he would welcome the offer of help "whenever it is so ordered for the junking and disposal of that which is placed in my hands," curious language from one who held that the Holy Ghost had directly dictated his sonnets. As soon as Elizabeth Peabody heard about the project, she eagerly asked

Emerson to urge upon Very the idea of writing a "psychological autobiography" as an introduction to the book.

Emerson was in an odd position. Having given Very the freedom of his "inner house," listened for the best part of five days to his exhortations, praised his writings, and suggested publication, he was now bidden to pass naked out of the world and to see God as a spirit. But this unclad acrobatic leap did not tempt Emerson. The side of his mind that admired Yankee practicality and common sense could not agree with any doctrine of will-less separation from the world of action. He was a householder, a husband, and a father. He was already launched on a successful career as writer and lecturer. People constantly came to him for conversation and counsel. A lesser man might have rejected out of hand the imperious injunctions of the young man from Salem.

Yet if Emerson had reread his journals for the past four years, he could have found adumbrations of Veryism in nearly every volume. For example: "To a soul alive to God every moment is a new world"; "And suddenly in any place, in the street, in the chamber will the heaven open and the regions of boundless knowledge be revealed"; "In proportion as your life is spent within,—in that measure are you invulnerable"; "If I could persuade men to listen to their interior convictions, if I could express, embody their interior convictions, that were indeed life"; "What nimbleness and buoyancy the conversation of the spiritualist produces in us. We tread on air[;] the world begins to dislimn"; "The book is always dear which had made us for moments idealists. That which can dissipate this block of earth into shining ether is genius." And yet again: "I suppose there is one spirit, and only one, the self-same which I behold inly when I am overcome by an aweful moral sentiment and He made the world. I do not choose to say this. It is said for me by tyrannical instincts."

The question of Very's sanity was much bruited about in Boston that winter of 1838–39. Between December 5 and the end of February, though harassed by colds and insomnia, Emerson delivered to attentive audiences in the Masonic Temple his series on "Human Life." Very came to town for the opening lecture and took the occasion to pay a three-hour call on the Reverend William Ellery Channing, who said afterward, quite seriously, that the young man had "not lost his *Reason*," but only "his *Senses*." The Reverend James Freeman Clarke, who listened in on the conversation, shared Channing's opinion. One might admit, he said, "a partial derangement of the lower intellectual organs, or perhaps an extravagant pushing of some views to their last results," yet the main thrust of Very's argument was not widely different from that of many other "pure and earnest religionists." Who could doubt the good sense of saying that "all sin consists in self-will" and "all holiness in an unconditional surrender of our own will" to that of God?

After Emerson's lecture, Very went along to Dr. Cyrus Bartol's house for a meeting of the Transcendental Club. Bronson Alcott was there, and Very impressed him much as he had impressed Channing and Clarke. "His language is that of an Oriental," Alcott wrote, "and one might almost fancy himself in the presence of St. John. . . . He is a phenomenon quite remarkable in this age of sensualism and idolatry. . . . A mystic of the most ideal class; a pietist of the transcendental order." But the other side of the coin was considerably darker. Very was "insane with God," thought Alcott, "diswitted in the contemplation of the holiness of Divinity." He distrusted intellect, love of truth, love of rectitude, love of imagination. Nothing must be allowed to break down his internal connections with supernal power.

Emerson later remembered and recorded a further encounter with Very that winter. Very had attended another of Emerson's lectures and came up afterward to discuss it. Learning that he had (typically) made no plans for the night's lodging, Emerson invited him "to go home to Mr. [Abel] Adams's with me and sleep which he did." He was mildly embarrassed next morning when Very appeared at the door of his room just as the gray winter dawn was breaking and insisted on coming in for a talk while Emerson was getting dressed. His October visit to Coolidge Castle was still on his mind. "When I was in Concord," he said, "I tried to say you were also right; but the Spirit said, you were not right. It is just as if I should say, It is not morning; but the Morning says, It is the Morning." When Emerson, still baffled by his prebreakfast visitor, offered some tentative reply, Very firmly summed up his views. "Use what language you will," he said, "you can never say anything but what you are." This was one of the doctrines that Emerson had spoken of during their Concord conversations. Now Very seemed to be claiming it as his own, a not-uncommon phenomenon among Emerson's self-appointed disciples.

During November, in a first flush of enthusiasm, Emerson had predicted a large audience for Very's poems once they were published and disseminated.

In January 1839 Very himself began the process in a small way by sending twenty-seven new sonnets to James Freeman Clarke, editor of the *Western Messenger*, who brought them out in successive numbers during the spring. But the plans for book publication of Very's poems ran into delays. Emerson's "Human Life" lecture series kept him busy and exhausted until late in February. He had no sooner finished the course than his daughter, Ellen, was born. It was not until mid-March that the household settled down enough so that he was able to invite Very to Concord to discuss arrangements for the book. Very, meantime, had been passing through a struggle of his own. Sometime in March he had retired to his room in the house at Salem, writing and reading all day long, and refusing to see anyone except the members of his immediate family.

His main purpose in self-imprisonment, according to his chief modern biographer, was to take time to develop a book that Emerson would approve of. Bearing in mind the psychological autobiography that Elizabeth Peabody had suggested as a preface, he was trying to embody in symbolic verse statements the story of his own search for salvation. Afterward, perhaps, he would attempt to summarize in a prose tract the essence of his strange vision of human life.

It was not until the middle of June that he felt far enough advanced in this work to risk a visit to Emerson. On the way to Concord he stopped in Boston for dinner with Bronson Alcott, who found him "much better both in body and spirit" than at the time of their last meeting. His interest in men and nature appeared to be reviving; there was now a good possibility that he might "regain his human position, and walk about among men as one of them, and not, as heretofore, a spectre." Yet the man who knocked at Emerson's door later that afternoon was still far gone in eccentricity.

What are persons [asked Emerson in his journal] but certain good or evil thoughts masquerading before me in curious frocks of flesh and blood. I were a fool to mind the color or figure of the frock and slight the deep aboriginal thought which so arrays itself. And now in my house as I see them pass or hear their step on the stair, it seems to me the step of Ages and Nations. And truly these walls do not lack variety in the few individuals they hold. Here is Simeon the Stylite, or John of Patmos in the shape of Jones Very, religion for religion's sake, religion divorced, detached from man, from the world, from science and art; grim, unmarried, insulated, accusing; yet true in itself and speaking *things* in every word. The lie is in the detachment; and when he is in the room with other persons, speech stops as if there were a corpse in the apartment.

Even Lidian—"mine Asia," in Emerson's phrase—was "not without a deep tinge . . . of the same old land and exaggerated and detached pietism," a fact that enabled her to serve "as bridge between Very and the Americans."

This visit was far shorter than that of the preceding October. Very arrived late on Friday afternoon and left on Monday morning. Much of the weekend he spent alone, writing poems as he had been doing in his room in Salem. For the rest, he was often in the company of Lidian, who, as Emerson had implied, was a most sympathetic listener, and who happened to be a namesake of Very's mother and his sister. Indeed, had he not been so intent upon converting her to his point of view, one might suppose that Very was half in love with her, like Thoreau later on. When Emerson urged him to linger, he answered that the Holy Spirit would not allow it. Apart from this reference, which suggested that his spiritual enthrallment was continuing, Very had seemed to be "serene, intelligent, and true" whenever they talked, though Emerson admitted that they had spent little time together. "He gives me pleasure and much relief after all that I had heard concerning him," wrote Emerson. "His case is unique. And I have no guess as to its issue, which I trust will be the happiest." One practical result of the visit was Emerson's mid-June resolution to go to Boston to find a publisher for Very's little book.

Emerson was so eager to find evidence of good new young American poets—Thoreau, Very, and Ellery Channing were among his prime examples— that he characteristically overestimated their powers and always did his level best to get them into print. When Elizabeth Peabody made her annual visit to Concord—"the Mount of Transfiguration," she called it because of Emerson's presence—she was eager to interest Emerson in the work of Nathaniel Hawthorne, another of her reclusive Salem neighbors and her brother-in-law-to-be. But Emerson was already deeply involved with his Very project. Elizabeth reminded him of Hawthorne's opinion that Very was "always vain." Emerson agreed that some personal vanity was undoubtedly there "amidst all

[Very's] sublimities." He recorded a remark of Very's to George Bradford, that he "valued his poems not because they were his, but because they were not." This position led to certain editorial problems. Since the sonnets allegedly came directly to him from supernal sources, he insisted that it was wrong to tamper with them in any way. But Emerson told Elizabeth Peabody that he was selecting and combining Very's verses "with sovereign will" and that he hoped in the end to "make out quite a little gem of a volume."

He performed his altruistic task with so much dispatch that by July 9 Messrs. Charles C. Little and James Brown had agreed to bring out the book that fall. Although publication would hardly make Very a rich man, the proposed list price of seventy-five cents a copy could bring him total royalties of $150, which he sorely needed. Emerson whittled down the bulky manuscript of 200 poems to the sixty-six that seemed to him to show "rare merit," and these, together with the essays on epic poetry, Shakespeare, and Hamlet, would make up a neat small volume of 175 pages.

Very complicated the editorial task by mailing Emerson four new poems to be added to the table of contents. "There is more joy and freedom as I advance," he told Emerson in a covering letter, "yet still I long to be clothed upon with my house from heaven. In you too may mo[re] of the old pass away and the new and abiding be more and more felt." Although Emerson was now so fatigued that he was obliged to take a brief vacation in the White Mountains at the end of August, he agreed to print three of the four new pieces, though this meant eliminating some of those that he had previously chosen. He ended with a total of sixty-five poems, all but nine of them sonnets.

Very's notion of ringing out the old and ringing in the new for both Emerson and himself was an echo of the idea that dominated his essay on epic poetry. For the Greeks of Homer's time, he argued, the highest "exemplification of morality was patriotism," and they had seen it as their mission "to make a material impression on the material world." But as the human mind "advanced" [Very's word], the Homeric stress on physical action gave way to an interest in "those mental struggles which precede physical action," and these accordingly became the stuff of dramatic poetry: "The soul of the modern poet, feeling itself contending with motives of godlike powers *within,* must express that conflict in the dramatic form." This, said Very, was the development that differentiated *Paradise Lost* from such a poem as the *Iliad*. "The epic poet of our day" must "possess an introspective mind" so as to give "an inwardness of meaning to his characters" in place of the Homeric stress on outward physical activity.

The second essay was an attempt to account for the special nature of Shakespeare's genius. According to Very, the bard's "childlike love of variety and joyous sympathy with all things" had continued into his maturity. While it could not be said of him "that he conformed to God's will," it was evident that "the Divine will . . . moved his mind as it does the material world. *He* was natural from an unconscious obedience to the will of God" whereas "*we . . .* must become natural by a conscious obedience to it." Very held that to be natural, whether consciously or not, was the only way to become truly great. "To become natural," he wrote, "to find again that Paradise which he has lost, man must be born again; he must learn the true exercise of his own will is only in listening to that voice which is ever walking in the garden, but of which he is afraid and hides himself." Very's peroration was typically noble and moving: "Let us labor then, knowing that the more we can erase from the tablets of our hearts the false fashions and devices which our own perverse wills have written over them, the more will shine forth, with all their original brightness, those ancient primeval characters traced there by the finger of God, until our whole being is full of light."

His interpretation of *Hamlet* centered on the soliloquy beginning "To be or not to be." In the figure of his protagonist, according to Very, Shakespeare set forth his own conviction that "to be or not to be forever" is the supreme question for all men. No matter how strong his "sense of continued life," Shakespeare was never able to attain to "that assurance of eternal existence which Christ alone can give." In Hamlet himself it was precisely the psychomachia between belief and unbelief which gave "that depth and mystery which startle us" as we watch him in action. For this dark prince must struggle "with the mystery of his own being, the root of all other mysteries, until it has become an overmastering element in his own mind," the veritable "hinge on which his every endeavor turns." In Very's arresting phrase, Hamlet had "looked . . . into shape" both his father's ghost and the "dark clouds that hang over the valley of the shadow of death." This was what made him so different from Macbeth. For Macbeth contended "with the realities of this world," whereas it was Hamlet's business to wrestle with "those of the next."

Like most of his fellow Transcendentalists, Emerson included, Very shared with the English romantics a belief that "all things in Nature are beautiful types to the soul that will read them." This was the burden of his sonnet "The Wind-Flower," among those chosen by Emerson for the new volume:

> Thou lookest up with meek, confiding eye
> Upon the clouded smile of April's face,
> Unharmed, though Winter stands uncertain by
> Eyeing with jealous glance each opening grace.
> Thou trustest wisely! In thy faith arrayed,
> More glorious thou than Israel's wisest King.
> Such faith was his, whom men to death betrayed,
> As thine, who hear'st the timid voice of Spring,
> While other flowers still hide them from her call,
> Along the river's brink, and meadow bare;
> Thee will I seek beside the stony wall,
> And in thy trust with childlike heart would share,
> O'erjoyed that in thy early leaves I find
> A lesson taught by Him who loved all human kind.

This is fairly typical of Very's "nature poetry." He follows the Shakespearean rhyme scheme of three quatrains and a couplet. Now and again, as here, he varies the pattern with an Alexandrine in the closing line. Thematically, he liked to assert or at least to hint at the possibility of supernal control over nature and man, and one often discovers biblical echoes like that in line six, which paraphrases from Matthew the words of Jesus about King Solomon and the lilies of the field.

The spring numbers of James Freeman Clarke's *Western Messenger*, which carried more than two dozen of Very's poems, were also the first to publish Emerson's early verses on "The Rhodora." Although Emerson was not a sonneteer, "The Rhodora" followed a presentational strategy not unlike Very's:

> In May, when sea-winds pierced our solitudes,
> I found the fresh Rhodora in the woods,
> Spreading its leafless blooms in a damp nook,

To please the desert and the sluggish brook.
The purple petals, fallen in the pool,
Made the black water with their beauty gay;
Here might the red-bird come his plumes to cool,
And court the flower that cheapens his array.
Rhodora! if the sages ask thee why
This charm is wasted on the earth and sky,
Tell them, dear, that if eyes were made for seeing,
Then Beauty is its own excuse for being:
Why thou wert there, O rival of the rose!
I never thought to ask, I never knew:
But, in my simple ignorance, suppose
The self-same Power that brought me there brought you.

Emerson was to note in this period the "new taste for . . . private and household poetry," and how "every day witnesses new attempts to throw into verse the experiences of private life." In this instance he was thinking of some of the poems of Ellery Channing, which he was reviewing for the *Dial*. But he must have noticed the same tendency in Very's sonnet "The Presence," apparently written in the young bachelor's severely monastic room at home in Salem. It emerged as a quiet attempt to domesticate the Holy Ghost:

I sit within my room, and joy to find
That Thou who always loves art with me here,
That I am never left by Thee behind,
But by Thyself Thou keep'st me ever near;
The fire burns brighter when with Thee I look,
And seems a kinder servant sent to me;
With gladder heart I read Thy holy book,
Because Thou art the eyes by which I see;
This aged chair, that table, watch and door
Around in ready service ever wait;
Nor can I ask of Thee a menial more
To fill the measure of my large estate,
For Thou Thyself, with all a Father's care,
Where'er I turn, art ever with me there.

On a strictly practical plane, Emerson took up the management of Very's first book where the Holy Ghost had left off. When the *Essays and Poems* appeared in September, Very made another trip to Concord, this time to secure a written order from Emerson so that he could stop off on his way home to pick up his author's copies from the publishers. Emerson wrote out and signed the chit and Lidian gave Very some cake. Then the grave young sonneteer set out along the turnpike on the first leg of his long trek home. In due course he gave Emerson's message to someone at the firm of Little and Brown and was handed four copies of his handsome little book, bound in gray covers and stamped with gold. Crossing Chelsea Bridge over the Mystic River on his way back to Salem, he was picked up by a neighbor with a horse and wagon. Before he climbed down again, he had parted with one of his precious copies as a present for the good neighbor's children.

His bread-and-butter letter thanked Lidian for the cake. "My return a few days since from Concord through Watertown, Cambridge and Boston was as pleasant as one but little accustomed to travelling and its fatigues has a right to expect. Your cake was well supplied [supplemented?] by a piece of white bread and a cup of milk and water from a poor yet worthy woman on your turnpike at whose house I rested a little while on my way. Alas, it went to my heart to take it; for I feel I could not as yet give her the true bread in return. I was wearied much by a few days stay at Cambridge, but am now as if with you again and well; waiting for that daily direction which is a path unseen through the world and its visible evils. . . ." Lidian and her sister Lucy Brown recalled this visit with sympathy and amusement. They spoke of his childlike simplicity—"how he sat there with a piece of gingerbread in each hand, so innocent and unconscious! and how beautifully he was talking!"

Part Two

THE

FORTIES

Chapter   Fifteen

ELLERY

CHANNING

EMERSON'S BENEVOLENT EDITORIAL ACTIVITIES CARRIED over into the 1840s. The appearance of the essays and poems of Jones Very seems to have encouraged Sam Ward to call Emerson's attention to the work of another young poet. At intervals, starting in September 1839, Sam sent along some fifty poems by William Ellery Channing. He and Ellery were exact coevals, born in Boston only two months apart, and had first met as pupils at the Round Hill School in Northampton. Early in October, Emerson acknowledged receipt of the first poem, a set of Spenserian stanzas called "Dreaming."

> Certainly your friend in these lines and in the very few others of his that
> I have seen, goes to the very end of poetic license, and defies a little too
> disdainfully his dictionary and logic. Yet his lines betray a highly poeti-
> cal temperament and a sunny sweetness of thought and feeling which
> are high gifts; and the voluminous eloquence of his Spenserian stanza is
> by itself an indication of great skill and cunning. . . . I entreat you not to
> despond of your friend's success because of any temporary inaction[.]
> Wit and imagination, Milton said, are tender maidens.

Emerson was clearly leaning over backward in referring to the "voluminous eloquence" of such Spenserian stanzas as the following:

There was a plain beneath a summer sky,
Stretching away to mountains like blue air,
Whose points, though surely not to heaven nigh,
Did ever a most azure vestment wear,
On whose pure heights man's life became more rare;
So when we meet a soul of great design,
Its noble presence is a weight to bear,
Capped with pure snows, on which the few rays shine
Of this world's gratitude, now in a swift decline.

Channing's "soul of great design" was Emerson, to whom the poem was dedicated. "I was very happy to meet this kindness," Emerson told Ward. "But I know the lines would have pleased me if addressed to a third person." Apart from the evidence that Channing, like Thoreau and Very, thought highly of Emerson, the best that could be said of such a stanza was that it was not bad for a novice of twenty-two. But Emerson was apparently struck by a quality that transcended the actual versification. "In a society as imperfect as ours," he continued, "I think no man can afford to spare from his circle a poet as long as he can offer so indisputable a token as a pure verse of his communion with what is highest in Being. It is possible that my love of these gifts might enable me to be useful to your friend if once I knew him."

Presently he wrote in his journal: "How can the Age be a bad one which conveys to me the joys of literature?" He could "read Plutarch and Augustine, and Beaumont and Fletcher, and Landor's Pericles," and then, "with no very dissimilar feeling the verses of my young contemporaries, T[horeau]. and C[hanning]." Having explored further examples of Channing's work, he found that they conveyed "a certain steady autumnal light," giving him more than they actually contained. "Over every true poem lingers a certain wild beauty immeasureable; a happiness lightsome and delicious fills my heart and brain." His response was considerably more powerful than the poetical stimuli that brought it forth.

Young Ellery was by way of being the black sheep of the numerous Channing tribe. His father, Walter, was a leading obstetrician who had presided at his son's birth on November 29, 1817, and had since become dean of the Harvard medical faculty. The child bore the same name as his famous uncle, William Ellery Channing, Boston's foremost Unitarian preacher—"the Star of the American Church," as Emerson called him. Another uncle, Edward Tyrrell Channing, was Boylston Professor of Rhetoric at Harvard during the undergraduate years of Emerson, Thoreau, Very, and Sam Ward. Ellery's cousin, William Henry Channing, was the clergyman and abolitionalist to whom Emerson was to inscribe the fiercest of his odes. Along with other relatives and friends of the family, these men sought repeatedly to help Ellery through his turbid adolescence and young manhood.

He was a strong-boned boy with sloping shoulders, large brown eyes, and shoulder-length hair. With such a background as his, it was predictable that he should enter Harvard in September 1834, shortly before turning seventeen, and equally probable, given his moody and intractable personality, that he should have left Cambridge after only fourteen weeks. What he had refused to gain from Harvard he soon undertook to discern for himself. Living in his father's house, supported by a small allowance, he began to make use of his father's membership in the Boston Athenaeum, frequenting the library on Pearl Street, acquainting himself with the poetry of Wordsworth, Coleridge, and Byron, and reading in translation some of the lyrics of such German romantics as Goethe and Herder.

In the spring of 1835, five months after leaving Harvard, he began to experiment with writing, choosing the singular nom de plume of Hal Menge, and contributing prose and poetry to the *Mercantile Journal* of Boston. His most notable achievement of that year was "The Spider," which appeared in the *New England Magazine* for October. This may have been one of the "very few others" among his poems that Emerson had read before receiving Sam Ward's sheaf in 1839. Both in form and substance, "The Spider" resembled Herder's little lyric on the dragonfly. There can be little doubt that it lingered on the edge of Emerson's memory when he composed "The Humble-Bee" in 1837–38. If this was so, it helps to explain his critical hospitality toward Channing's other poems when he first saw them in 1839.

Apart from this brief splurge of reading and writing in the middle 1830s, Ellery's future prospects remained indeterminate. He spoke halfheartedly of becoming a surgeon. He thought of devoting his energies to painting, following the lead of Washington Allston, an uncle by marriage. He made short walking trips into New Hampshire and upstate New York. But most of all he courted idleness, as if anticipating by twenty years Walt Whitman's declaration "I loafe and invite my soul, / I lean and loafe at my ease observing a spear of summer grass." Two of his favorite haunts for this purpose were Curzon's Mill, at the confluence of the Merrimack and Artichoke rivers near Newburyport, and Lenox, at the opposite end of Massachusetts among the Berkshire hills.

The first of these, to which Ellery had fled just after leaving Harvard, was a summer refuge for Caroline Sturgis, whose family owned a cottage called Blue Bell in the small compound. The Curzons were a lively family, with three daughters and a son, and rented rooms both in the farmhouse and the gristmill to various Boston visitors. It was the mill itself that most entranced Ellery. "The beams," he later wrote, "coated with dust, glow like dead alabaster, and every spider's web is made of white yarn. Even at noon, the rooms [above the mill] are lit badly, and at twilight, they gloom. . . . When grinding stops, silence hangs over the chambers, tenanted by squab figures, in white clothes, while down stairs the water trickles under the wheel, and the rats play hide-and-go-seek." This was a charming passage, suggesting that Ellery was a better poet in prose than he was in metrical forms, although it was to the latter that he eventually (and mistakenly) devoted his life.

Two of Channing's early poems belong to the Curzon's Mill experience and they suggest why at this time and afterward Caroline thought that she was in love with Ellery. In "The River" (the Artichoke) he wrote:

> Sweet falls the summer air
> Over her form who sails with me;
> Her way, like it, is beautifully free,
> Her nature far more rare;
> And is her constant heart of virgin purity.

In "To Clio" he again addressed Caroline:

> When the sprites outwatch the moon . . .
> Through the shimmering, shadowed dells . . .
> There thou weaves unknown spells. . . .

The magnetic family that drew him to Lenox was that of Charles and Elizabeth Sedgwick. According to Ellery's chief modern biographer,

Charles Sedgwick, clerk of the Berkshire County Court in Pittsfield, presided over the most distinguished household in western Massachusetts—a home in which intellectual brilliance and artistic talent were joined with a heritage of wealth and social position. . . . Charles's sister was Catherine Maria Sedgwick, the novelist, whose books were read even in England. His wife Elizabeth Buckminster Dwight was descended from Jonathan Edwards and belonged to the intellectual peerage of the Connecticut Valley. . . . Their only son, Charles, had by 1839 completed two years at Harvard, leading his class in scholarship. . . . Catherine Maria II, familiarly called Kate, was a musician, already at the age of sixteen giving piano lessons to her neighbors.

Ellery was particularly drawn to the elder Sedgwicks, who were well aware of his temperamental idiosyncrasies, and treated him with the firmness they felt his case required. Elizabeth Sedgwick, who had established a school for girls in her capacious household, was a stickler for polite behavior. Among her boarders in the late 1830s was Ellery's sister Lucy; Emerson's eldest daughter Ellen became an enthusiastic pupil at the school a dozen years later.

Even as Emerson was reading Ellery's poetry in the fall of 1839, Ellery himself was developing plans that would, if successful, give shape and direction to his hitherto rather inchoate career. The immediate catalyst was Charles Sedgwick, who had recently persuaded his wife's brother, Josiah Dwight, to go west and cultivate the virgin land. The experiment was working for Dwight, who had taken up 325 acres of rich prairie in a sparsely settled region some forty miles north of Chicago. His exuberant letters, along with Sedgwick's gentle arguments, were enough to activate Ellery. Leaving Boston in October, he became in November sole owner and occupant of a log cabin and 160 acres in McHenry County, Illinois.

He had been there three months when he received an encouraging letter from Emerson apropos of his verses: "I wish that they should not be shut up any longer in the portfolios of a few friends but should be set free to fly abroad to the ear and heart of all to whom they rightfully belong." He told Ellery about the plans for a new journal with Margaret Fuller as editor, and asked Channing's permission to print some of the poems he had been reading. He would frame them with a running prose commentary to "give them due perspective." Channing's rough-hewn experiments looked like first drafts, yet gave Emerson the feeling of being "present at the secret of creation." His quarrel with most American poets was that they were "secondary and mimetic." Channing, he said, could "thank the god for intuition and experience."

Channing was diffident or lazy or both, whether at farming or letter writing. Twice that spring Emerson complained at having had no word from him. But he was determined to be of use, and went ahead with the piece on Ellery's poetry, taking "a solitary joy" in the "entire absence of all conventional imagery" and in this youth's bold embracement of whatever "the moment's mood had made sacred to him." The opening of one of his Petrarchan sonnets was fairly typical:

> The brook is eddying in the forest dell,
> All full of untaught merriment,—the joy
> Of breathing life is this green wood's employ.
> The wind is feeling through his gentle bell,
> I and my flowers receive the music well.

Emerson took special pleasure in the fifth line. Like the lyrics of Caroline Sturgis, he thought, such poems as this had a certain merit that unfitted them for print. Both Caroline and Ellery offered "manuscript inspirations, honest, great, but crude"; each "had a great meaning too much at heart to stand for trifles" such as careful polishing, and "wrote lordly" for their peers alone. Although he had nearly finished his piece for the *Dial* by the end of April, it was not until June, too late for the first number of the new magazine, that Channing finally agreed to Emerson's proposal. At last, in October, a selection from his verses was set free, in Emerson's words, "to fly abroad" into the hearts of the lucky subscribers.

As with Very's poems, Emerson regarded it as his editorial obligation to make revisions and corrections. He pruned Caroline's "Spartan metres" and joined Margaret Fuller in trying to persuade Thoreau to change the wording in one of his stanzas. But "our tough Yankee" resolutely objected. Somewhat to his surprise, Emerson ran into another stone wall when he sought to make "conjectural emendations" in Ellery's fledgling lines. Sam Ward, as well as Margaret and Caroline and even the gentle Elizabeth Hoar, ganged up against him until he thought that Channing must, like Robin Goodfellow, have anointed their eyes with philtres, leading them to suppose that bad grammar and nonsensical statements were somehow "consecrated by his true *afflatus.*" Was poetic inspiration like amber to "embalm and enhance flies and spiders"?

None of this got into Emerson's article for the *Dial* of October 1840. Forbidden by Channing to identify him by name, he gave the chosen poems a typically generous send-off. His three-page introduction said that the "straitest restrictions" had once governed "the admission of candidates to the Parnassian fraternity," requiring excellence in both workmanship and material. Now "verses of a ruder strain" were admissible. Men of talent could give "that cool and commanding attention to the thing to be done" and guarantee a "just performance." But men of genius were less capable of "that elaborate execution which criticism exacts." They were "humble, self-accusing, moody men," worshiping Ideal Beauty, which "chooses to be courted not so often in perfect hymns, as in wild ear-piercing ejaculations, or in silent musings." This explained why certain manuscript poems, however inept, could be more sustaining and stimulating than many "elaborated and classic productions." He followed up these observations with an anthology of a dozen poems from the "portfolio" of his anonymous poet, closing with the statement that "we have more pages from the same hand . . . marked by the same purity and tenderness and early wisdom as these we have quoted. . . . May this voice of love and harmony teach its songs to the too long silent echoes of the Western Forest."

Margaret Fuller was much less sanguine than Emerson about Ellery's future as a poet. She declined to print anything of his in the *Dial* for January 1841. "Of Ellery's verse I think not much," she confided to Caroline Sturgis. "I am ill at appreciating a nature so noble, yet with no constructiveness and no force of will. Yet I take no vulgar view of him either." One further effusion of Ellery's ("Theme for a World Drama") appeared in April, and in July a sonnet dedicated to Emerson which made him exclaim, "O pudor!"—perhaps because he thought that readers might construe it as a quid pro quo for his October article.

Despite his repeated championship of Channing, Emerson had yet to meet him in person. More than sixty years later, Frank Sanborn said offhandedly that the two men had first met in Concord in December 1840. Nothing in the contemporaneous record confirms this statement. Instead of making a pilgrimage to see his benefactor, Ellery was busily idle elsewhere. A year after buying his Illinois farmstead, he profitably disposed of it in what Robert Hudspeth calls "the one successful business venture in his long life." Then, apparently with some cash in his pockets, he resumed the restless nomadism that had characterized all the years of his youth. Just as Emerson was puffing him in the October *Dial*, he reappeared at his old stand in Lenox, taking a room in the village, and paying warm attention to Kate Sedgwick during the overnight absence of her parents, though in the presence of a chaperone. The upshot of this visit was a desperate letter to Kate which said, inter alia, that "I am worthy of you, the extreme fidelity of my affections is enough." From Lenox he departed for New York, ostensibly bound for Cincinnati, sending Kate an apologetic letter that struck her as "half-crazed," though Ellery's putative insanity may have been only a romantic pose. In choosing Cincinnati, where his maternal uncle, James Perkins, had been variously occupied since 1832, Ellery thought of trying his hand at law or journalism. If not crazed with unrequited love, he was still at loose ends.

In the late summer of 1841, his life turned an unexpected corner. He had been in Cincinnati since April experimenting with paralegal work, writing a little for the *Gazette*, and dabbling in social services. That summer, by a curious train of circumstances, Margaret Fuller's young sister Ellen, after adventures and illnesses in Louisville and New Orleans, drifted into town in August, hoping to teach French and music at a school operated by Ellery's Uncle James. Thereafter matters moved swiftly. On the twentieth, Perkins reported that Ellen was "decidedly impressed" by Ellery. Two weeks later news of their engagement reached Boston and Concord, and on September 24, having known each other for less than six weeks, Ellen and Ellery were married by an Episcopalian rector.

To Margaret Fuller this was a kind of bombshell. "In its suddenness it comes like a blow," she told Emerson. "In what I know of either party I see such perils to the happiness and good of the other, and the connexion has been so precipitately formed that I feel overshadowed by it as by a deep tragedy that I foresee, but, as if in a dream, cannot lift my hand to prevent." Emerson the optimist shared her astonishment but not necessarily her sense of tragedy. The news, he told her, "runs across all my dreams: but since the beginning no two dreamers could dream alike. May a great happiness attend these children."

Other members of Margaret's inner circle took the news with equanimity. Sam Ward called it "an auspicious connection." Caroline Sturgis felt no pain. "For a little time," she told Margaret, "I thought I could love him, but it has past [sic]. . . . I saw from Ellery's letter that he was withdrawing himself from me. It was very sweet, but nothing for me." Her sole objection was that she did not think Ellen "noble enough" to be Ellery's wife!

Once the marriage was accomplished, Margaret's love of making arrangements took over. When and if Ellery should leave Ohio for Massachusetts, he must on no account think of joining Brook Farm. "By and by," she told him prophetically, "you could have a little cottage of your own." A small farm might be best, where he could chop wood and have a garden. But Ellery was not yet ready to move. He had rented a small house in Cincinnati, landed a paying job on the *Gazette*, working with unusual devotion and apparently satisfied with his mode of life on the banks of the Ohio. He kept in touch by mail with Sam Ward, Caroline, and most of all with Margaret, who forwarded a batch of his letters for Emerson's perusal. "I like all these letters of Ellery's," said Emerson. "He should live here [in Concord]; he ought to write every month for the Dial which ought to have fifty thousand subscribers and ought to yield him house, diet, clothes, power, and fame."

Ellen's mother, Mrs. Fuller, joined the bride and groom in April, and seems to have taken at once to her son-in-law. Margaret's dream of a farm for Ellery resurfaced in June. "Now," she told Emerson, "if you would sell us for some two thousand dollars a house and small farm, and promise that a frugal subsistence could there be obtained, my mother Ellen and Ellery might live in Concord, too. They might keep there my goods, my pen and paper, and I might find a home there whenever I could pause from winning lucre. . . . I think, too, I should like to live with Ellery a part of the time, and I now feel confidence in him that if he do not win a foothold on this earth, it will not be that he deprives himself of it, by indulgence in childish freaks."

Another change was imminent. In July, just when Ellery seemed to be winning a foothold in Cincinnati, he suddenly resigned his newspaper job and left alone for Boston. The decision might have been a childish freak: he had followed the promptings of many such in the course of his life. On the other hand, he may at last have succumbed to Margaret's hints, suggestions, and exhortations about the desirability of setting up as a small farmer in or near Concord. He must likewise have known that Emerson had now succeeded Margaret as editor of the *Dial*. The July number contained seven more of his poems, as if to signify that in 1842 as in 1839 he still ranked high in Emerson's estimation.

When Emerson learned in August that Ellery wished to locate a suitable boardinghouse in Concord for himself and Ellen, presumably as a pied-à-terre until more nearly permanent quarters could be found, he rose joyously to the occasion. On August 10 he was in Boston for the funeral of his mother's sister, Aunt Nancy Haskins. Next day he met Ellery, probably for the first time, and brought him back to Coolidge Castle. "I comfort myself with the hope that he will find Concord habitable," wrote Emerson to Margaret, "and we shall have poets and friends of poets and see the golden bees of Pindus swarming on our plain cottages and apple trees." In the following week Margaret herself was coming for a lengthy stay. Henry Thoreau was still living with the Emersons, and Hawthorne and his bride had recently moved into the Manse. Emerson was already attuning his ears to the pleasant hum of all those golden bees.

Chapter   Sixteen

SAM
AND ANNA

BY THE END OF JULY 1840, EMERSON CONCLUDED THAT THE first number of the *Dial* had not been shocking enough. His introduction for it had bravely stated that a new revolution was in progress, a recrudescence of hope, "a greater trust in the nature and resources of man" than had hitherto prevailed. The *Dial*'s purpose was "to give expression to that spirit which lifts men to a higher platform, restores to them the religious sentiment, brings them to worthy aims and pure pleasures, purges the inward eye . . . and reconciles the practical with the speculative powers." In short, this new quarterly aimed to become "one cheerful rational voice amidst the din of mourners and polemics."

To Margaret, who was already at work on *Dial* the second, he said that the first number was a "good book" which the "wise public ought to accept" as such. But he hoped she would agree that future *Dials* must "get to be a little *bad*." The first had not been radical enough "to scare the tenderest bantling of Conformity." He was even having second thoughts about the journal's true raison d'être. "I would not have it too purely literary. I wish we might make a Journal so broad and great in its survey that it should lead the opinion of this generation on every interest and read the law on property, government, education, as well as on art, letters, and religion. . . . So I wish we might court some of the good fanatics and publish chapters on every head in the whole Art of Living."

Now, at the end of June 1840, in the relative privacy of his journal, he set down words of rebellion against the transient population that had been making his house into a virtual hotel, often at his own instigation. It was another example of the constant battle waged in his mind between society and solitude: "I think we must give up this superstition of company to spend weeks and fortnights. Let my friend come and say that [what] he has to say and go his way. Otherwise we live for show. That happens continually in my house that I am expected to play tame lion by readings and talkings to the friends. The rich live for show; I will not."

Tame lion or not, Emerson was not caged. In the hot weather with the windows open, he could sometimes hear one who was. While living in Newton in June 1834, he had recorded a comic invasion of privacy by a noisy neighbor: "Next door to us lives a young man who is learning to drum. He studies hard at his science every night. I should like to reward his music with a wreath of smilax peduncularis," a plant known for its sickening stench. But now in 1840, the sounds that reached his ears were of another order.

> Now for near five years I have been indulged by the gracious Heaven in my long holiday in this goodly house of mine entertaining and entertained by so many worthy and gifted friends and all this time poor Nancy Barron the madwoman has been screaming herself hoarse at the poorhouse across the [Mill] brook and I still hear her whenever I open my window.

Throughout that summer, despite his momentary resolution to the contrary, his worthy and gifted friends continued to visit the most hospitable private house in Concord. Caroline Sturgis spent half a dozen days there in June, delighting in the beauty of the clouds, "the shining people of the sky." "We are beginning to be acquainted," Emerson told Margaret sardonically, "and by the century after next shall be the best friends. Beings so majestic cannot surely take less time to establish a relation."

The astonishing news of August was that the broken engagement of Sam and Anna had been mended: plans were afoot for their marriage that fall. Margaret, who thought that Sam should have stuck to his guns about living a life devoted to art, was wretchedly disappointed. She took out some of her frustration on Emerson himself. In the *Memoirs* he wrote: "At the very time when I, slow and cold, had come fully to admire her genius, and was congratulating myself on the solid good understanding that subsisted between us, I was surprised with hearing it taxed by her with superficiality and halfness. She stigmatized our friendship as commercial."

She launched this accusation on August 14 during a ride with Emerson back to Jamaica Plain. "She taxed me," he wrote, "as often before . . . with inhospitality of soul. She and C[aroline] would gladly be my friends, yet our intercourse is not friendship, but literary gossip. I count and weigh but do not love." A clue to Margaret's intent was offered by her phrasing. Sam Ward, the young apostate from the artistic life, was going into business, much against Margaret's wishes: he would count and weigh, buy and sell. Now she was unfairly tarring Emerson with the same brush.

"I confess to all this charge with humility unfeigned," wrote Emerson. "Yet would nothing be so grateful to me as to melt once for all these icy barriers, and unite with these lovers. But great is the law. I must do nothing to court their love which would lose my own. Unless that which I do to build up myself, endears me to them, our covenant would be injurious. Yet how joyfully would I form permanent relations with the three or four wise and beautiful whom I hold so dear, and dwell under the same roof or in a strict neighborhood."

He tried to explain his position to Caroline. "I confess to the fact of cold and imperfect intercourse, but not to the impeachment of my will, and not to the deficiency of my affection. If I count and weigh, I love also. . . . You give me more joy than I could trust my tongue to tell you. Perhaps it is ungrateful never to testify by word to those whom we love, how much they are our benefactors. . . . Come and live near me whenever it suits your pleasure and if you will confide in me so far I will engage to be as true a brother to you as blood ever made." Although she was his "dear sister," as for years he had called Elizabeth Hoar, he laid no personal claims upon her. "I wish you to go out an adventurous missionary, into all the nations of happy souls, and by all whom you can greatly, and by any whom you can wholly love, I see that I too must be immeasurably enriched. . . . So, dear child, I give you up to all your Gods . . . and you shall not give me so great a joy as by finding yourself a love which shall make mine show cold and feeble—which certainly is not cold or feeble."

Suspecting as he must have done that Margaret's accusations against him were connected in her mind with Sam's coming marriage, he told her that *she* must be generous enough to "resign without a sigh two Friends." The end result for her would be that, like Emerson himself, she could "retreat always upon the Invisible Heart[,] upon the Celestial Love, and that not to be soothed merely but to be replenished,—not to be compensated but to receive power to make all things new."

Four years into their friendship, he well knew, in the words of Paula Blanchard, that Margaret was afflicted "with a variety of 'neurotic' characteristics: the supercharged feelings which found expression in hyperbole; the vehement, occasionally strident assertions of self-confidence; the moods of lassitude . . . which could suddenly flare up into restless high spirits; the quasi-erotic intensity of her friendships with both sexes." To Emerson it seemed that in the summer of 1840 she "passed into certain religious states, which did not impress me as quite healthy, or likely to be permanent." He told her that he did not understand her tone. "It seems exaggerated. You are one who can afford to speak and to hear the truth. Let us hold hard to the common-sense, and let us speak in the positive [rather than the superlative] degree."

He was still critical of her tendency to speak and write in superlatives—a habit born, perhaps, from her constant readings in German romanticism— Goethe, Schiller, Tieck, Novalis, Jean Paul among others. Adjectives like "purest" and "highest" came as naturally to her prose as leaves to a tree, and Emerson adjured her in effect to be content with "pure" and "high." To Caroline, his newly appointed "sister," he wrote, "I believe I hate buskins and heroics, and do value a little commonsense[,] a nod of hearty goodwill, a darning needle and the baking of dough more than all tragedy kings and queens." Margaret was surrendering to "a certain pathos of sentiment" which threatened to plunge her "into the sea of Buddhism and mystical trances." The events of the summer had "combined great happiness and pain for her affections," and driven her into "a sort of ecstatic solitude." Feeling "vexed at the want of sympathy" on Emerson's part, she displayed "a certain restlessness and fever" which he thought dangerous for "a soul which was capable of greatness."

The causes were plain enough. She must endure the forthcoming marriage of two people with both of whom she had been deeply in love, and then to suffer, though to a lesser degree, the partial apostasy of Caroline, recently promoted to the status of Emerson's "sister." Yet it was she who had introduced all three of them to Emerson, and now it seemed that all four were departing from the jurisdiction of her love.

Exactly a week before the marriage of Sam and Anna, she told Caroline of the "mighty changes" in her "spiritual life," which she owed to a new epiphany: "Experiment has given place to certainty, pride to obedience, thought to love, and truth is lost in beauty." Three days closer to the wedding she wrote Emerson that her having stuck with him thus far was "a strong proof that we are to be much to one another." How often had she left him in forlorn despair, saying, "This light will never understand my fire; this clear eye will never discern the law by which I am filling my circle; this simple force will never interpret my need of manifold being." She did not love power except as "every vigorous nature delights to feel itself living." Nor did she have any wish to "violate the sanctity of relations"—by which she evidently meant the relations between Emerson and Lidian. Indeed, if she could capture the highest angel "by a look," she would not do so "unless prompted by true love" on the angel's part. "I am no usurper," she went on. "I ask only mine own inheritance." If she had "mistaken its boundaries," she would at once surrender "to its lawful owner" the "fairest flower-garden," and the "choicest vineyard."

If this was the feverish love letter it seemed to be under all that verbal efflorescence, it prepared the way for the contretemps between Margaret and Emerson in the following month, and it looked back, in a manner of speaking, to her attempted "over-personalization" of their early relationship in the fall of 1836. Another paragraph in her letter of September 29 sought to introduce the religious dimension: "If you have not seen this stair on which God has been so untiringly leading me to himself, you have indeed been wholly ignorant of me. Then indeed, when my soul, in its childish agony of prayer, stretched out its arms to you as a father, did you not see what was meant by this crying for the moon, this sullen rejection of playthings which had become unmeaning? Did you then say [i.e., If you then said] 'I know not what this means; perhaps this will trouble me; the time will come when I shall hide my eyes from this mood,'—then you are not the friend I seek." There was more, as always with Margaret, more extravagance, more high-flown imagery, more evidence of longing for the impossible.

Emerson's evident determination to hold Margaret's emotional advances at arm's length while still maintaining his respect for her intellectual powers gains further emphasis by an anecdote that Lidian afterward told to her daughter Ellen:

> One day when Miss Fuller had been staying with us and departed in the stage Father said to Mother
> "Happy—happier far than thou
> With the laurel on thy brow—
> She who makes the humblest hearth
> Happy but to one on earth. . . ."

The couplets he quoted came from the lyric "To Corinna," by Felicia Hemans. They were all the more apposite because Corinne was one of Margaret's adopted nicknames. Lidian, who added that Emerson's quotation seemed to her "very sweet," clearly recognized the implicit contrast he had intended between herself as keeper of the hearth and Margaret with all her laurels.

After his social splurge of August, Emerson had told Margaret that he needed solitude more than ever. Even his quiet river, the Musketaquid, was not solitary enough for one who wished to be "alone with the Alone." For "a hermit so dangerously favored by the Social Gods," his necessary regimen for weeks and months should be "a barn chamber with a salad or a potato." Yet he continued through September to keep in touch by mail with Margaret and Caroline, Sam and Anna, determined to play his role as spiritual brother to them all. In another chapter of his debate on friendship with Margaret he said, "You and I are not inhabitants of one thought of the Divine Mind, but of two thoughts,"—"we meet and treat like foreign states, one maritime, one inland, whose trade and laws are essentially unlike." He had said that he and Caroline were "brother and sister by divine invisible parentage," and wrote a fervent letter of congratulation to our "radiant" pair of "lovers," Sam and Anna.

On the evening of October 3, Sam and Anna were married at the house of Professor Emeritus and Mrs. John Farrar in Cambridge. It was Sam's twenty-third birthday; Anna's twenty-seventh was only three weeks off. Margaret postponed a serious operation on her brother Arthur's eye in order to attend. According to Emerson, who was also a wedding guest, "She went, from the most joyful of all bridals, to attend a near relative during a formidable surgical operation." In a journal entry Emerson permitted himself a ministerial blessing on the wedded pair: "Peace go with you, beautiful, pure, and happy friends—peace and beauty and power and the perpetuity and the sure unfolding of all the buds of joy that so thickly stud your branches." They were only four days into their three-week honeymoon when he asked Margaret to "give me any tidings you can of the bridegroom and the bride," and they had been married only a little over two weeks when they sent him a joyous letter from Brattleboro, Vermont, promising to see him as soon as they returned from exploring both the Green and the White mountains.

Margaret continued to be the businesslike editor of the *Dial*, a dutiful daughter to her mother, and guardian to her sister, Ellen, and her five brothers. Yet at the same time she was capable of extreme emotional self-dramatization in her letters to Caroline and Emerson. When she visited Concord on October 16 for a talk with Emerson about Brook Farm, she said, "I looked at him with great love." Soon afterward she wrote Caroline that "the life that flows in upon me from so many quarters is too beautiful to be checked. I would not check a single pulsation. It all ought to be;   if caused by any apparition of the Divine in me I could bless myself like the holy Mother. But like her I long to be virgin. I would fly from the land of my birth. I would hide myself in night and poverty. Does a star point out the spot? The gifts I must receive, yet for my child, not me." This extravagant piece of Mariolatry, where she placed herself in the situation of the Holy Virgin before the birth of the Savior, soon shifted over to the opposite end of the New Testament story, and she began to write of the Cross. "Daily, hourly it is laid upon me. Tremulously I feel that a wound is yet to be given. . . . Because I dread it, because my courage is not yet so perfect as my submission, because I might say, Father, if it be thy will let this cup pass, . . . I am not yet purified." The idea of purification suggested the Vestal Virgins of ancient Rome and she wrote, "Let the lonely Vestal watch the fire till it draws her to itself and consumes this mortal part." She closed the long letter with imagery suggestive of the coming winter: "Only one soul is there that can lead me up to womanhood and baptize me to gentlest May. Is it not ready? I have strength to wait as a smooth bare tree forever, but ask no more my friends for leaves and flowers or a bird haunted bower."

She read through Emerson's letter to Caroline that closed with the state-

ment: "I have written you down in my book and in my heart for my sister because you are a user of the positive degree. If you use the superlative you must
explain it to your aff. brother." What was all this talk about the preferability of
the positive over the superlative? "Still this same dull distrust of life!" she exclaimed to Caroline. "The fact on which Waldo ever dwells in the world of
thought . . . is expressed in the world of feeling by use of the superlative. Do
we say dearest, wisest, virtuosest, best—we make no vow, but express that the
object is able to supersede all calculation. O these tedious, tedious attempts to
learn the universe by thought alone. Love, Love, my Father, thou hast given
me. I thank thee for its pains." The trouble with Emerson was that he was
"still only a small and secluded part of Nature, secluded by a doubt, by a
sneer." He called Caroline his sister and his saint yet could not trust her insights. Many beings had reached a height of generosity and freedom far above
him, though none was truer and purer than he. Margaret felt a strong renewal
of her desire to "teach this sage" all he needed "to make him a full-formed Angel." Yet the attempt might not work: she and Emerson were separated by too
wide a gulf.

She tried once more to bridge this chasm between thought and feeling with
a forthright and apparently strongly emotional letter to "the Sage." This document was lost or destroyed and its contents can only be surmised. Yet it is
clear from Emerson's reply that she must have used some such direct query
about their personal relationship as the one with which she had embarrassed
Caroline at Nahant in the summer of 1839: "Do you love me?" Caroline had
found it impossible to say yes. So it was with Emerson sixteen months later.
"I ought never to have suffered you to lead me into any conversation or writing on our relation, a topic from which with all persons my Genius ever
sternly warns me away," he told her. She was a woman of sense and sentiment
with whom he could exchange "reasonable words." Such exchanges gave
"value to thought and the day," and resembled the kind of "robust and total
understanding" which he had enjoyed with his brothers William and Edward
and Charles, who had been "intimate and perfect friends without having ever
spoken of the fact." This was the way it ought to be. Talking about personal
relationships might work for others but would never do for him.

He cited his son, Waldo, as another example. "I see precisely the double of
my state in my little Waldo when in the midst of his dialogue with his hobby

horse in the full tide of his eloquence I should ask him if he loves me?—He is mute and stupid. . . . I talk to my [own] hobby and will join you in harnessing and driving him, and recite to you his virtues all day—but ask me what I think of you and me,—and I am put to confusion. . . . Tell me that I am cold or unkind, and in my most flowing state I become a cake of ice. I can feel the crystals shoot and the drops solidify. . . . Instantly I find myself a solitary unrelated person, destitute not only of all social faculty but of all private substance."

Why did Margaret have to keep pushing, pushing—as with her leading question back there in 1836, "I know not what you think of me?" He tried to explain to her the differences between them:

We use a different rhetoric . . . as if we had been born and bred in different nations. . . . Yet we are all the time a little nearer. I honor you for a brave and beneficent woman and mark with gladness your steadfast good will to me. . . . A vast and beautiful Power to whose counsels our will was never party, has thrown us into strict neighborhood for best and happiest ends. The stars in Orion do not quarrel this night, but shine in peace in their old society. . . . Let us live as we have always done, only ever better, I hope, and richer. Speak to me of every thing but myself and I will endeavor to make an intelligible reply. Allow me to serve you and you will do me a kindness; come and see me and you will recommend my house to me; let me visit you and I shall be cheered as ever by the spectacle of so much genius and character as you have always the gift to draw around you. I see very dimly in writing on this topic. It will not prosper with me. Perhaps all my words are wrong. Do not expect it of me again for a very long time.

So, with kindness and courtesy, but also with firmness, Emerson made his position clear. Margaret got the message. If she answered Emerson in kind, her letter has not survived. The only sign that she had taken up his views was a remark in a letter to W. H. Channing a few days later: "I shall wait for [Waldo] very peaceably, in reverent love as ever; but I cannot see why he should not have the pleasure of knowing now a friend, who has been 'so tender and so true.' " Five long paragraphs later she added: "There is some magic about me which draws other spirits into my circle whether I will or they will or no." The period of *Stürm und Drang* was evidently past or passing, but her pride was still in evidence.

She had recently indulged her love for Caroline and for solitude with a three-day visit to Curzon's Mill, that same magical region to which Ellery Channing had fled after leaving Harvard. The chief distinguishing features of the area were the gristmill that Ellery so greatly loved, and the slow-flowing, soup-green Artichoke, next-to-last tributary of Thoreau's Merrimack River before it reached Plum Island and the ocean seven miles to the east. Margaret was on easy terms with Margaret Curzon, the wife of the miller, but her preference was for the quiet companionship of Caroline. They spent many hours in a small green skiff with orange gunwales, exploring the river reaches with Caroline at the oars. To Margaret then, as earlier on the brown rocks of Nahant, Caroline seemed "the very genius of the place so calm and lofty and so secluded." Over the gristmill, as Ellery had noticed, was a small room with a fireplace, and Margaret dreamed of communing there with Sam and Anna, and perhaps Ellery's cousin William H. Channing, talking politics or social reform undeterred by the rumble of the great millstone downstairs. Like Emerson beside the Musketaquid, she longed to people the banks of the Artichoke with mild-mannered intellectuals, avoiding such "Phalansterian organizations" as Brook Farm. "What a happy place for children to grow up in," cried Margaret, anticipating by sixty years the opinion of John Marquand the novelist, whose ancestors were Curzons, and who spent much of his boyhood at Curzon's Mill.

Margaret and Emerson now returned to business matters and the preparation of the *Dial* for January 1841. The October number had not differed greatly from its predecessor. Margaret had chosen Emerson's "Woodnotes" and some verses by Caroline and her sister, Ellen Hooper. Emerson had contributed heavily, with a lead article on modern literature that included a firm critique of Goethe as "the poet of the Actual, not of the Ideal . . . of limitation, not of possibility." Another of his pieces was devoted to the poems of young Ellery Channing, and he briefly reviewed R. H. Dana's *Two Years Before the Mast* as well as Albert Brisbane's summary of Fourierist doctrine. J. F. Clarke and Margaret both did art criticism, there was another solid religious essay by Theodore Parker, and George Ripley, on the eve of establishing Brook Farm, had written a "Letter to a Theological Student" as well as half a dozen book reviews on religion and philosophy. As before, all the contributors were friends of Margaret and of Emerson, all hierophants of the inner circle of Transcendentalists. "I begin to be more interested in the Dial," Margaret wrote Emerson, "finding it brings meat and drink to sundry famishing men and women at a distance from these tables. Meseems you ought to know with what delight the 'Woodnotes' have been heard!"

Her days now flowed "sweetly on." She had resumed the Wednesday "Conversations" in Boston, with Lidian Emerson as a regular attendant. She told her class of the "great changes" in her mind and "they all with glistening eyes seemed melted into one love." Anna Barker Ward, "all glowing," sat beside Margaret, who recalled her recent evening with the bride and groom, during which Anna had said repeatedly, "I feel as if I had been married twenty years." After two busy December days in Boston she wrote, "I am always most happy to return to my solitude, yet willing to bear the contact of society, with all its low views and rash blame, for I see how the purest ideal natures need it to temper them and keep them large and sure. I will never do as Waldo does, though I marvel not at him."

He came to call on her in mid-December on *Dial* business and they discussed his refusal to join George Ripley's Brook Farm community. Emerson had just seen Sam Ward, whom nothing could induce to leave the "golden routine" of his house in Louisberg Square and the beautiful bride who lived there. "He may certainly stand acquitted in Heavens Chancery for a week or two longer," said Emerson.

Something like a "golden routine" had now settled over his relations with Margaret after the contrarieties of October. "Margaret's wonderful talent[,] her stream of eloquent speech I always recognize," he told Caroline. "Her native nobleness I see also—her capacity for virtue. And now I see with joy a certain progress out of her complex into a simpler life and some of the gorgeous palaces in which she has dwelt are losing their lustre for her. Let us behold with love and hope."

Chapter Seventeen

ALCOTT, ELSSLER,
NEWCOMB

AFTER THE DEBACLE AT TEMPLE SCHOOL, EMERSON HAD rightly seen that Alcott needed a strong infusion of success: If important people "could see him as he is" and say so, as some of his English admirers were beginning to do, "his genius would be exalted." Up to the end of 1839, his career had been overshadowed by injustice and loneliness. For nearly two years Emerson had believed that Alcott ought to shake off the dust of Boston, move to Concord, "work a small farm for his bread, and dictate his gospel" from such green pastures. He was more than pleased in the spring of 1840 when his dream became an actuality and the Alcotts made their move, taking up residence in a small cottage owned by the Hosmer family. It was typical of Emerson that he quietly paid Edmund Hosmer the house rent of $52 per annum.

Emerson was in Providence lecturing when the Alcotts settled in. "I hardly dare hope for him success in an adventure so new and remote from all his habit," he wrote home to Lidian. "Beside that he has not yet brought before himself the naked fact so familiar to every young farmer that he must depend on himself." One of his troubles was that he still looked to others for "all contingent aid." This meant that he could never plan well. Still, thought Emerson, "his project is brave and wise, and will, if he can persist, be an everlasting honor to the man."

Home from Rhode Island on April 3, he found Alcott busily nailing down carpets and buying garden tools. His chief complaint was that his new situation required him to deal with merchants, whom he felt to be his social inferiors. But he soon said cheerfully that he was now in command, and that for the first time in years his wife went singing about the house. They had lost their only son a few hours after his birth in April 1839, but they were expecting another child, born that June at Dove Cottage and named Abby May after her mother. Alcott was now, said Emerson, "to get his living by the help of God and his own spade."

"I must think very ill of my age and country, if they cannot discover his extraordinary soul," was still Emerson's opinion. Continuing his campaign for the establishment of Alcott's reputation, he invited him to contribute to the first number of the *Dial*, the new magazine for which Alcott had provided the name, as well as much excited interest: "We must have a free journal for the soul which awaits its own scribe," he had asserted on learning that the *Dial* was to become a reality. Unwisely, as it turned out, Emerson suggested that "a string of Apothegms" might do for Alcott's opening contribution. Even though they were not so bad as Emerson feared, they still showed Alcott's "inveterate faults" whenever he took up his pen for formal utterance—"cold vague generalities" that did not reflect the man's matchless conversational powers. Margaret Fuller surprised Emerson by saying that some of them struck her as "quite grand, though ofttimes too grandiloquent."

Samples from the fifty "Orphic Sayings" that appeared in July 1840 show Alcott's characteristic manner of thought and expression:

VOCATION: Engage in nothing that cripples or degrades you. Your first duty is self-culture, self-exaltation: you may not violate this high trust.

ASPIRATION: The insatiableness of her desires is the augury of the soul's eternity. . . . She is quivered with heavenly desires; her quarry is above the stars; her arrows are snatched from the armory of heaven.

THEOCRACY: In the theocracy of the soul majorities do not rule. . . . The voice of the private, not popular heart, is alone authentic.

SPEECH: There is magic in free speaking, especially on sacred themes. It is refreshing, amidst the inane commonplaces bandied in pulpits and parlors, to hear a hopeful word from an earnest upright soul. . . . Sweet the sound of one's own bosom thought, as it returns laden with the fragrance of a brother's approval.

People who knew Alcott, thought Emerson, might be able to read such sayings with "his voice in their ear," recognizing as authentic and characteristic the "majestical sound" and the "Zoroastrian style." Yet on the printed page many of them looked abstract, anemic, prettified, even namby-pamby, and gave Emerson more pain than pleasure. Later, he quoted the *Boston Post*: that they "resembled a train of 15 railroad cars with one passenger." Even later, James Russell Lowell in his *Fable for Critics* offered a view of Alcott long familiar to his immediate associates:

> While he talks he is great but goes out like a taper
> If you shut him up closely with pen, ink, and paper . . .

When Alcott, ever hopeful, asked for six copies of the first number of the *Dial* to send his admirers in England, Emerson, ever helpful, gave him a dozen. "Majestic egotist" he might be, but his friends "must show all kindness and countenance to this prophet of the Lord." Moreover, "there could be no more fatal omen to the prosperity of any Dial or literary enterprise than the disapprobation of this cold piece of spiritual chemistry." If not exactly cold, Alcott remained cool when his old enemies, the newspapers, printed parodies of his "Orphic Sayings." No doubt pleased by the attention if not by the criticism, he gathered the clippings and pasted them neatly into his diary.

Emerson's championship of Alcott, which had prevailed through the first five years of their friendship, persisted through the 1840s. Both before and after the failure of Temple School, he had repeatedly offered him vacations in Concord; read, reread, and laboriously criticized the various versions of "Psyche," encouraged him to publish the *Conversations on the Gospels*, publicly defended him when they were attacked, urged him to settle in Concord, and invited him to become a *Dial* contributor with the intent of making his name better known. When William Ellery Channing, the sixty-year-old Unitarian leader, heard that Alcott was supporting his family by chopping wood and plowing fields, he wrote Elizabeth Peabody that such a combination of day labor and high thought made this man "the most interesting object in our

Commonwealth." Channing's heart lay open to the concept of "Orpheus at the plough." Emerson had already located another classical analogue, comparing Alcott to Apollo serving among the herdsmen of Admetus. Remembering also the Athenian custom of entertaining distinguished citizens gratis in a central building, he said that Alcott was valuable enough to be "maintained at the public cost in the Prytaneum."

Shortly before Christmas 1840, having bowed out of participation in Brook Farm in a long, frank, and final letter to George Ripley, Emerson began thinking seriously of establishing a private prytaneum for Alcott and his family at Coolidge Castle. He told Ripley and then William of a couple of experiments he wanted to make in the general spirit of Brook Farm: one was to undertake "manual labor to some considerable extent"; the other, to ameliorate or abolish "the condition of hired menial service" in his house. Beside these rose up a third notion: "Next April we shall make an attempt to find house room for Mr Alcott and his family under our roof; for the wants of the man are extreme as his merits are extraordinary." He and Lidian had already explained to the Alcotts their own "views or dreams respecting labor and plain living"; it would be a kind of Brook Farm *in parvo*, and would avoid the deep inconvenience of pulling up stakes and moving into another milieu whose future was unpredictable.

The upshot of Emerson's triune plan was a triune failure. The winter of 1840–41 gave little opportunity for manual labor except for shoveling snow, even if Emerson had not been embroiled with seeing his first book of essays through the press. When Lidian got round in March to persuade the two domestics, Louisa and Lydia, that it would be both practical and democratic if they were to eat with the family, Louisa was willing but Lydia firmly refused: "A cook," said she, "was never fit to come to table." Next day when Waldo Minor was sent to tell Louisa that breakfast was ready, Louisa had already eaten with Lydia, and the noble plan evaporated. As for the further proposal to keep the Alcotts fed and housed, though Alcott was eager to come, his wife wisely declined, and made financial arrangements with her brother that would see them through another Concord summer.

It was just as well. Lidian was now beginning her third pregnancy with the usual consequences to her health, strength, and spirits. Among nearer relatives, Bulkeley was still at McLean Hospital in "a demented state" and would always remain a care. Aunt Mary had sustained a recent attack of paralysis or apoplexy, which did not greatly inhibit her ability to write inimitable letters. When Emerson asked her to come for a long visit in May, she replied tartly that she had vowed back in 1835 never to set foot in her nephew's house and was not about to change her mind. Dr. Ezra Ripley, approaching his ninetieth birthday, was planning to deliver a "last" sermon in the old meetinghouse (1712) before it was torn down and replaced by a modern structure. The one major change in the Emerson household, after all the backing and filling of the winter, was the arrival of Henry Thoreau to live for a year in the room at the head of the stairs and to perform all such chores as Emerson, Lidian, Waldo, Ellen, Louisa, and Lydia might require.

As always there were visitors. Margaret Fuller spent two weeks in May and Caroline Sturgis a week in June. Mary Russell came over from Plymouth for the summer. Lidian, still a virtual invalid, had planned a recuperative vacation in Plymouth until Elizabeth Hoar announced that she would accompany Lidian to Staten Island to stay with William and Susan. "It is of little use for me to journey with Lidian," Emerson told his brother, "for she carries her home thoughts and histories all with her, and journeying to Andes or Alps, she would not get an inch from home. But going with Elizabeth will be a true diversion," calculated to bring "great exhilaration and pleasure" to a "too pensive careful and melancholy wife." The idea worked. The visit lasted from June 12 to July 1 and Lidian returned visibly improved in mental if not in physical health.

In the following week Emerson went alone to Worrock's Hotel at Nantasket Beach, hoping to complete an oration on "The Method of Nature" for delivery in August to the undergraduate members of the Erosophian Adelphi on their commencement day in Waterville, Maine. "I have walked and ridden and swum and rowed and fished," he reported to Margaret Fuller, "Yea, with these hands I have caught two haddocks, a cod, a pollack, and a flounder. . . . The sea and I shall be good friends all the rest of my life." And to Caroline Sturgis: "You know I was baptised in Walden Pond—here is a better font." But he came home on July 26, having found that he could not write orations "out of any inkstand but [his] own." He took Lidian and the baby Ellen for a week's stay in Plymouth before leaving for Maine with his lecture in his pocket.

Alcott's experiment as husbandman at Dove Cote was not working out. "He has no vocation to labor," said Emerson, "and, although he strenuously preached it for a time, and made some efforts to practise it, he soon found he had no genius for it, and that it was a cruel waste of his time. It depressed his spirits even to tears." What he really loved was conversation, speculation, and was "quite ready at any moment to abandon his present residence and employment, his country, nay, his wife and children, on very short notice, to put any new dream into practice which has bubbled up in the effervescence of discourse."

On Friday, September 17, Dr. Ezra Ripley was felled by a stroke and lay in a coma until his death four mornings later. He had been the oldest active clergyman in Massachusetts, and had last preached on May 1, his ninetieth birthday, in the Concord church before it was demolished. Laid out on the well-worn couch in the parlor at the Manse, he looked to Emerson like "a sachem of the forest fallen." Waldo Minor, taken to see the corpse, evinced "neither repulsion nor surprise but only the quietest curiosity." This "patriarch of the tribe," as Emerson called him, had been just, kind, and companionable, with a character "so thoroughly intelligible that every child could read him." He seemed also the last of the warriors of the Puritan rear guard. "What is this abolition and Nonresistance and Temperance," asked Emerson, "but the continuation of Puritanism, though it operate inevitably [to produce] the destruction of the Church in which it grew, as the new is always making the old superfluous?"

Emerson was in a holiday mood on the evening of October 13 when he watched the ballet *Nathalie* at the Tremont Theater in Boston. The star of the show was the Viennese Fanny Elssler, then halfway through her triumphal tour of the United States and Cuba, with extended engagements in New York and New Orleans. Before crossing the Atlantic, she had appeared to great acclaim in Austria, France, and England, and had made her London debut in 1833, just when Emerson was in the midst of his own far-less-spectacular European tour.

He was anything but an inveterate balletomane. After attending one ballet in Florence at the time of his thirtieth birthday, he had said in his journal that he "could not help feeling . . . that it were better for mankind if there were no such dancers," and when someone told him that all ballerinas were "nearly idiotic," he found the slander easy to believe. But Fräulein Elssler, aged thirty, quickly converted him to another point of view. "Where do you think I went on Wednesday eve last?" he asked his brother William. "Where but to see the dancing Fanny? I killed that lion well: Had a good sight, was much refreshed, and shall know better what people mean when they talk of her. She is not wonderful but she is very good in her art. Is it not strange that power and grace in the carriage of the body should be so rare—rare as genius in any other mode?"

One of Fanny's Parisian admirers was the poet Théophile Gautier, who described her charms in considerable detail. She was tall and supple, with slim wrists, delicate ankles, legs and knees worthy of the goddess Diana, a full bosom, and well-modeled back and shoulders. Her complexion, Gautier suggested, combined Teutonic characteristics with those of the Mediterranean: her white skin, calm brow, and merry mouth betrayed her Viennese origin, but a strain of romantic exoticism was visible in her wide-set luminous dark eyes and the lustrous brown-black hair, which she parted in the middle and drew back above her ears, with a bun at the nape of her graceful neck.

Although Emerson was unaware of Gautier's opinions, he was similarly impressed. "She must show," he wrote, "the whole compass of her instrument," by which he meant her limbs and torso, and her modes of action ranged from "the softest graces of motion" to the "feats of the rope dancer and tumbler." The beauty of the performance was enhanced "by this that is strong and strange," as when she stood "erect on the extremities of her toes," or when, leaping, she attained an altitude seemingly impossible. But her energetic athleticism was of less consequence in his eyes than "the extreme grace of her movement, the variety and nature of her attitude, the winning fun and spirit of all her little coquetries, the beautiful erectness of her body and the freedom and determination" with which she could project across the footlights such an appearance of ease. Equally striking was "the air of perfect sympathy" with her audience, as well as a curious "mixture of deference and conscious superiority" which fitted her so perfectly for her role. When the last curtain came down, she managed such a "sweet and slow and prolonged salam" that she seemed "to have invented new depths of grace," and clearly deserved the profusion of bouquets hurled onstage in tribute. So Emerson the aesthetician, admirer of power and grace, strength and strangeness, freedom and control, all at work in perfect concord with notable beauty of face and body.

Ethics and aesthetics were always closely associated in Emerson's mind. "The basis of this exhibition like that of every human talent is moral," he wrote. It is "the sport and triumph of health or the virtue of organization." Her charm for the audience meant that "she dances for them or they dance in her, not being (fault of some defect in their forms and educations) able to dance themselves. We must be expressed. Hence all the cheer and exhilaration which the spectacle imparts and the intimate property which each beholder feels in the dance, and the joy with which he hears good anecdotes of her spirit and her benevolence. They know that such surpassing grace must rest on some occult foundations of inward harmony."

There were, of course, "incidental vices"—some evidence of false taste and certain "meretricious arts" designed to stir the groundlings. "The immorality the immoral will see, the very immoral will see that only; the pure will not heed it, for it is not obtrusive, perhaps will not see it at all." Young women, accompanied by fathers or brothers, might watch her with impunity. But college boys, like those from Harvard, having left their study of metaphysics or conic sections or Tacitus in order "to see these tripping satin slippers," might find it hard to "forget this graceful silvery swimmer" when they went home to their "baccalaureate cells." Miss Elssler, he thought, could well have inflamed youthful male sensibilities to dangerous levels. He dissociated himself from such younger colleagues by ending on a semi-Platonic note: "It is a great satisfaction to see the best in each kind, and as a student of the world, I desire to let pass nothing that is excellent of its own kind unseen, unheard."

Margaret Fuller shared in the general approbation of Miss Elssler's performances. "How did you like the military spiritual heroico vivacious phoenix of the day?" she asked Emerson in November. "The chronicler said you were delighted." She included a commentary of her own in a piece called "Entertainments of the Past Winter" for the *Dial* of July 1842. In *Nathalie*, Miss Elssler had been perfect. Her charms were of "a naive sportive character . . . the young girl, sparkling with life and joy . . . half coquettish, more than half conscious of her captivations."

Other admirers, including young Longfellow, recognized the sexually seductive aspects of Miss Elssler's presentations. One anecdote was going the rounds in Boston about an incident during her engagement in New Orleans. Emerson repeated it to Alcott, whose customary preoccupation with the spiritual did not prevent his appreciation of the sensual. "Like all virtuous persons," wrote Emerson, "he is destitute of the appearance of virtue, and so shocks all persons of decorum by the imprudence of his behaviour and the enormity of his expressions. When I told him the story of F.E., he said he should like to have been one of the party." This was far from the moral extremism of another friend of Emerson's, the Brook Farm boarder Charles Newcomb, who had begun by calling Fanny a vile creature and then, having seen her dance, enshrined her picture on his wall between engravings of the saints Francis Xavier and Ignatius Loyola.

This Newcomb was another of Margaret Fuller's protégés. Emerson first met him on March 30, 1840, while lecturing in Providence, just as the Alcotts were moving to Concord. A slender dark-haired stripling, aged twenty and of feeble constitution, Charles had lost his father, a distinguished naval lieutenant, in 1825. The boy and his sisters had been raised by Rhoda Marlborough Newcomb, their strong-willed and overprotective mother. A graduate of Brown University in 1837, Charles nurtured his religious interests with a year at the Episcopal Seminary in Alexandria, afterward drifting back to Providence and joining Margaret's retinue in the fall of 1838. Much as she had done with Sam Ward some years before, Margaret corresponded with this youngster, loading her letters with superlatives about gorgeous sunsets and moonlight rambles, and offering her assistance in his growth and education. "My ear and heart will always be open if you desire to call upon me," she assured him in April 1839. Presently she gave signs of an overpossessiveness not unlike that of Charles's mother: "My dear Charles, if you still value my friendship do not rashly lay yourself open to others, I valued your delicacy about intercourse and the sacredness of your life more than almost anything, do not let me suppose it infringed."

In May 1841, Charles signed the register at Brook Farm, where he remained as a part-time boarder for upward of four years, diversifying his stay with frequent trips to the Newcomb family home in Providence, social visits to Boston, Newport, and New York (usually in his mother's company), and once making a tour to Niagara Falls. At first he roomed with Margaret's mentally disturbed brother, Lloyd, nursing him through an attack of measles. At this time he was observed reading Greek in the haymow with Caroline Sturgis during one of her fugitive visits to Brook Farm. His mother, who called him Carolus Rex, sought to encourage his interest in "your *beloved Caroline*," though the affair, such as it was, amounted only to a continuing friendship.

Charles's religious propensities remained paramount. One of Emerson's letters to Margaret wryly hoped that a reading of the *Dial* might help to "cure your young Catholic Fra Carlo." But the Brook Farmers took note of his love of incense and ritual. He decorated his room with ferns, rushes, and pictures of Jesus and selected Catholic saints, and persisted in reading aloud from the church litany at all hours of the night. For reasons that remain obscure he insisted on wearing gloves and a veil as he slept. Shy, solitary, romantic, he seems not to have been universally popular, though some of the more ardent young women found him attractive. One male resident, George Curtis, wrote him off as "slight in person, awkward, and slouchy in gait." His mother, seeking from Providence to control his living habits, urged him to remove his muddy farm boots before entering the kitchen and to clean his fingernails, explaining that "such niceties were among the sacrifices we must make for the sake of our fellows." In 1836 he had begun a voluminous journal in which he scribbled during off-hours and which by the end of his life contained some three million words. For the rest, he rambled through the woods, perched high in the branches of trees, read aloud to the children while they sorted potatoes, and "recruited" his delicate health by working on the farm for two or three hours a day. Occasional reports on Newcomb reached Emerson seventeen miles away in Concord. He was almost ready to believe that Charles might be another youthful genius like Very, Ellery Channing, and Thoreau.

Unlike the relatively affluent Newcombs, the Alcott family had fallen as usual into dire financial straits. Mrs. Alcott's father, Colonel May, had died early in 1841, leaving her $3,000. But this was absorbed at once by creditors in partial settlement of the outstanding Temple School debt. By January 1842, the long-suffering Abba Alcott was seriously concerned over her husband's health: "If his body don't fail his mind will," she wrote her brother. "He experiences at times the most dreadful nervous excitation—his mind distorting every act however simple into the most complicated and adverse form—I am terror stricken at this and feel as if I would rather lay him low than see his once sweet calm, imperturbable spirit experiencing these fluctuations and all the divine aspirations of his pure nature suffering defeat and obloquy."

Emerson, who had long believed that Alcott needed frequent encouragement, began gathering funds to pay his passage to England, where a group of British admirers had already established in Surrey an institution they called Alcott House. Emerson himself subscribed $500—"It will give me great pleasure to be responsible for you to such an amount," he wrote on February 12—and called on various other contributors to swell the sum.

For all his outward air of spiritual superiority, Alcott was deeply touched by Emerson's largess. On a visit to Margaret Fuller in March, he said that the preceding year had been the worst of his life, darkened by "moody musing" and sometimes even reaching "the borders of frenzy." This experience had taught him, he believed, to recognize his own limitations. But the "greatest gain" of his life had come about through Emerson's magnanimity. Thereat, as Margaret reported, he wept a "plenteous shower" of tears. Despite such moments of self-depreciation and self-recognition, Alcott was rarely able to hold himself in low esteem. Six years later he said to Emerson, "You write on the genius of Plato, of Pythagoras, of Jesus, of Swedenborg, why do you not write of me?"

After many delays, Alcott sailed off aboard the *Rosalind* on May 8, carrying a supply of applesauce and potatoes as his vegetarian diet. Emerson was amused to learn that he had also wished to take miniatures of Elizabeth Peabody, Margaret Fuller, and Emerson, benefactors all. It was an appreciable irony of June, after Alcott had reached England, that a Boston lawyer named Manlius Clarke bought up 750 copies of the *Conversations on the Gospels* in sheets, for sale as waste paper to a trunkmaker.

Chapter Eighteen

WALDO MINOR

JANUARY 1842 WAS A TRAGIC TIME FOR TWO PROMINENT families in Concord. On New Year's morning Henry Thoreau's brother, John, cut his finger while stropping his razor and died of lockjaw eleven days later. On Monday night the twenty-fourth, Waldo Emerson fell ill with scarlatina and died of it in the early evening of the twenty-seventh. That midnight in his study, Emerson wrote his brother William, Lidian's sister and brother, and Abel Adams, his old friend and financial adviser. Next day he wrote to five women: Aunt Mary, Elizabeth Hoar, Elizabeth Peabody, Margaret Fuller, and Caroline Sturgis. He did not attempt to conceal his agony. "My boy is gone. . . . The world's wonderful child . . . has fled out of my arms like a dream. He adorned the world for me like a morning star. . . . All his wonderful beauty could not save him. . . . I cannot in a lifetime incur such another loss. . . . Shall I ever dare to love any thing again?"

The Friday morning after Waldo's death he awoke at three to find the whole wintry landscape "dishonored" in his eyes, while all the roosters in the neighborhood crowed lustily in anticipation of a dawn that the boy would never know. "A boy of early wisdom," his father wrote, "of a grave and even majestic deportment, of a perfect gentleness." He had given up his "little innocent breath like a bird," and left a gap in nature. "If I go down to the bottom of the garden[,] it seems as if some one had fallen into the brook." This child had "touched with his lively curiosity . . . all the particulars of daily economy . . . every trivial fact and circumstance in the household—the hard coal and the soft coal which I put into my stove, the wood of which he brought his little quota for grandmother[']s fire, the hammer, the pincers, and file, he was so eager to use; the microscope, the magnet, the little globe, and every trinket and instrument in the study; the loads of gravel on the meadow the nests in the henhouse and many and many a little visit to the doghouse and to the barn,—For every thing he had his own name and way of thinking[,] his own pronunciation and manner. . . . He named the parts of the toy house he was always building . . . by fancy names which had a good sound as 'the Interspeglium' and 'the coridaga' which names he told Margaret 'the children could not understand.' "

Thoreau suffered under his double bereavement. As an adopted member of the family for the past year, he had, as Emerson said, "charmed Waldo by the variety of toys whistles boats popguns and all kinds of instruments which he could make and mend; and possessed [the boy's] love and respect by the gentle firmness with which he always treated him." As spring came on, Henry found some consolation in nature's annual renewal. Waldo had died, he wrote, "as the mist rises from the brook, which the sun will still dart his rays through. Do not the flowers die every autumn? He had not even taken root here, I was not startled to hear that he was dead;—it seemed the most natural event that could happen. His fine organization demanded it, and nature gently yielded its request. It would have been strange if he had lived. Neither will nature manifest any sorrow at his death, but soon the note of the lark will be heard down in the meadow, and fresh dandelions will spring from the old stocks where he plucked them last summer."

Waldo was buried beside old Ezra Ripley, his step-great-grandfather, who had died in the fall. Emerson presently wrote Margaret Fuller that the family was "finding once again our hands and feet after our dull and dreadful dream which does *not* leave us where it found us. . . . Meantime the sun rises and the winds blow[.] Nature seems to have forgotten that she has crushed her sweetest creation." And to Caroline Sturgis next day, "I chiefly grieve that I cannot grieve; that this fact takes no more deep hold than other facts, is as dreamlike as they; a lambent flame that will not burn playing on the surface of my river. Must every experience . . . only kiss my cheek like the wind and pass away?" He thought of Ixion, bound to a wheel that turned forever; of Tantalus, set under fruit-laden trees whose branches eluded his grasp; even of Southey's Kehama, who drank of the cup of immortality only to find in it a draught of punishment and death. This boy had been "too precious and unique a creation to be huddled aside into the waste and prodigality of things." Still emotionally numb, Emerson was groping for the Wordsworthian consolation, "a timely utterance" that might help to make him whole again.

He had at least the solace of work, with lectures to deliver in Providence beginning two weeks to the day after Waldo's death. "Work in every hour," he wrote, in what seemed an echo of Carlyle's *Sartor Resartus*: "paid or unpaid see only that thou work; and thou canst not escape the reward"—in this case the temporary mitigation of pain. At home with her two young daughters, Lidian had only their care to engage her mind. "Have the clouds yet broken, and let in the sunlight?" he asked in a letter. "Alas! Alas! that one of your sorrows, that our one sorrow can never in this world depart from us! . . . Meanwhile Ellen and Edith shall love you well, and fill all your time, and the remembrances of the Angel shall draw you to sublime thoughts." Although the boy was gone, "the far shining stone that made home glitter to me when I was farthest absent. . . . Yet the other children may be good babes yet—I will breathe no despair on their sweet fortunes[.] Nelly is a good little housewife and that Lidianetta may come to great heart and honor in the months and years to come." So he tried to alleviate Lidian's sorrow, who remained inconsolable.

The Providence lectures earned little, the City Bank of Boston skipped an expected dividend of $600, and Emerson was obliged to try his fortunes in New York. From the home base with William on Staten Island he went into the city to dine at Graham's boardinghouse with Horace Greeley and Albert Brisbane. Greeley, with his mane of "white soft hair," was founder and editor of the *New York Tribune*, and Brisbane, an avowed socialist, was an eager student of Fourierist doctrines. Bent on "popular action," they inquired into the possible pertinence of Emerson's social philosophy. "They fasten me in their thought to 'Transcendentalism,' " he wrote home to Lidian, "whereof you know I am wholly guiltless, and which is spoken of as a known and fixed element like salt or meal: So that I have to begin by endless disclaimers and explanations—'I am not the man you take me for.' " If they could only understand the truth: "I am in all my theory, ethics, and politics a poet and of no more use in their New York than a rainbow or a firefly."

Writing of these encounters to Margaret Fuller, he said that Lidian sometimes taxed him at home "with an egotism more virulent than any against which I rail. Perhaps she is right. . . . I must unfold my own thought. Each must build up his own world, though he unbuilt [sic] all other men's, for his materials. So rabid does egotism, when contradicted, run." For all her gentle nature, Emerson's wife could be sharp. He quoted in his journal one of her deflationary apothegms: "Queenie says, 'Save me from magnificent souls. I like a small common sized one.' "

Margaret, too, mourned Waldo's death. "I loved him more than any child I ever knew, as he was of nature more fair and noble," she wrote Elizabeth Peabody. "Five years he was an angel to us, and I know not that any person was ever more the theme of thought to me. . . . He was the only child I ever saw, that I sometimes wished I could have called mine. . . . I saw him but little, and it was well; for it is unwise to bind the heart where there is no claim. But it is all gone, and is another of the lessons brought by each year, that we are to expect suggestions only, and not fulfilments, from each form of beauty."

The major event of March was Margaret's decision to resign the editorship of the *Dial*. "I have tonight your sad and sudden conclusion," wrote Emerson. He was sympathetic: her health was suffering, and she had "never had a penny for all her time and toil." "You have played martyr a little too long alone," he told her, "let there be rotation in martyrdom!" She suggested that Emerson and Theodore Parker might take over. "I had rather undertake it alone," he said. Parker, who had contributed heavily to the April number and was seeing two books through the press, applauded Emerson's decision with the advice that the new editor should write a large part of the July issue. Emerson at once set to work. Through April and May he assiduously sought to line up contributors, including Parker, the Sturgis sisters, Longfellow, Charles King Newcomb, and Henry Thoreau. Henry had been very ill after his brother's death, and even in April was not well enough to work in Emerson's garden. But Emerson thought it might be good therapy for him to undertake a lengthy piece on "The Natural History of Massachusetts."

At Providence in February Emerson had renewed his nascent friendship with Charles Newcomb, home on furlough from Brook Farm, who had conversed intelligently and read aloud to Emerson samples of his fiction. One of these was a strange tale called "The Two Dolons," about another wonderful boy who in some respects bore resemblance to Waldo Minor. Early in March Margaret reported that she and Charles had enjoyed "the divine musical evening together," and that he had promised to submit "Dolon" for the July *Dial*. Emerson welcomed the news of "Dolon":—"I had set my heart on it and fully intended to obtain it." Twice in succeeding weeks he urged Newcomb to come to Concord with the story. But Charles procrastinated. Emerson wrote him twice more in May, promising to publish "the *first* Dolon" in July, and adding that he and his wife were glad to have found a poet who valued Waldo's "precious ashes" and could give "a green leaf and a breath of music" to such a "darling of Nature."

When he received and read the manuscript on June 5, he wrote the author that it had given him "the most joy I have felt for many a day." It was replete with genius, but could be improved by revision. Emerson had devised two ways to conclude the chapter: Newcomb must come to Concord and resolve the editorial dilemma. He must also bring Caroline Sturgis's poems, which had been confided to his care, as well as her pencil-sketch illustrations for "Dolon" and his own essays on *Romeo and Juliet* and the dancer Fanny Ellsler. On June 19 Charles appeared at last, bringing his "Book-Journal" from which he read aloud his critiques of classical and modern writers. During his one-day visit Lidian poured "anecdotes of her sweet Boy" into his friendly and eager ears. Next day, when Charles was back at Brook Farm, Emerson wrote him about various changes that must be made in "Dolon," quoting one passage which unhappily typified the prose style of the narrative: "The thing which is beautiful acts as a thing upon the child, and Being answers Being than looks at each other and feels each other as what they internally are."

Other such syntactic tangles presently caused Emerson to call "Dolon" "the maddest piece" in the July number, and privately to condemn its "odious licences." Yet he found in the tale the "native gold" of consolation. In March he had written of Waldo's absence: "I comprehend nothing of this fact but its bitterness. Explanation I have none, consolation none that rises out of the fact itself; only diversion; only oblivion of this and pursuit of new objects." All the spring he had been trying to forget that death by new undertakings. Now in June he found the account of the boy in the story so reminiscent of Waldo Minor that he was deeply touched. "Charles is a Religious Intellect," he wrote in his journal. "Let it be his praise that when I carried his MS story to the woods, and read it in the armchair of the upturned root of a pine-tree I felt for the first time since Waldo's death some efficient faith again in the repairs of the Universe."

One of Emerson's own contributions to the July number might have been called a chapter in the supernatural history of Massachusetts. It was a semi-satirical piece on the fourth meeting of the Chardon Street Chapel Bible Convention, held at the end of March to discuss the validity of the Scriptures. Emerson attended, along with Father Taylor, Theodore Parker, Jones Very, and "many other persons of a mystical, or sectarian, or philanthropic renown," including Mrs. Abigail Folsom ("the flea of the Conventions," Emerson called her), who was all "too ready with her interminable scroll." Bronson Alcott, at first received with derision, remained to conquer, and emerged as the hero of the day. Otherwise, as Emerson told his brother William, the gathering revealed "fanaticism of all shades and forms . . . mad men and mad women were there, and madly did behave." His *Dial* article listed some of the other participants: "Dunkers, Muggletonians, Come-outers, Groaners, Agrarians, Seventh-day-Baptists, Quakers, Abolitionists, Calvinists, Unitarians, and Philosophers—all came successively to the top, and seized their moment, if not their *hour*," to chide, pray, preach, or protest.

Emerson was still eager to assemble a group of "wise and endeared spirits" to come and live near him in Concord. He and Lidian hoped for a visit from Margaret Fuller in April, though she was too ill to come, and in May, having heard that Samuel Ripley had refurbished the Old Manse for rental, both Frederic Hedge and Nathaniel Hawthorne made inquiries. Hawthorne, like Charles Newcomb, had been a resident of Brook Farm. In urging Newcomb to come and look for a rentable house in Concord, Emerson said, "Those of us who do not believe in [Fourierist] Communities, believe in neighborhoods and that the kingdom of heaven may consist of such." When she saw "our fair prospects for a good neighborhood," he told Margaret, she would not "pitch tent anywhere else for good." With her presence, and Elizabeth Hoar, Hedge and Hawthorne, Newcomb and Thoreau, the nucleus of a lively neighborhood was within reach. But Caroline Sturgis disappointed him when she came in June for a four-day visit. "Tormented with ennui," she spent all her time riding horseback, and left behind only one gloomy quatrain for the July *Dial*.

In the second week of August, Margaret's new brother-in-law, Ellery Channing, was established in one of Emerson's spare rooms. He was something of a disappointment. "All the Channings," said Emerson, were "men of the world" with "a little silex" or flint in their composition, which gave "a good edge" and protected them "like a coat of mail." Ellery himself had "the manners and address of a merchant," though not, presumably, a merchant prince. But the poet was there. His "cool hard sensible behavior" was capable of "melting to emotion." With his "great self-possession, great simplicity and mastery of manner," he seemed to be "very good company to live with." If, much of the time, he was an "unedifying sort of person," he was also a "good vagabond" who knew "how to take a walk," as he did nearly every day with Emerson or Thoreau. And yet, as Emerson told Caroline, "I much doubt his power to do anything good with a farm, and if he must maintain himself, I think he must learn to write. If he could only master his negligent impatient way of writing—this impatience of finishing, his sweet wise vein of thought and music would have no rival. And it seems worth his while to try, as I told him, when he sees that in a million lovers of poetry there shall not be one poet." But Ellery, as his Harvard professors had found, was unteachable.

The child Waldo had been dead for seven months when Margaret Fuller at last took up Emerson's invitation and came to Concord for a visit that lasted forty days. When she arrived "all things looked sad" to her. Despite Emerson's perennial busyness, the household was still in mourning. That first evening she walked out with him beside the quiet river in misty August moonlight. They rehearsed the shape their lives had taken during the past winter and spring—a mere "interchange of facts," as Margaret called it in her journal. They had been in touch by mail often enough, chiefly on matters pertaining to the *Dial*, though on March 8, in a letter that began "Dearest Waldo," she had said, "I have thought of you many times, indeed in all my walks, and in the night, with unspeakable tenderness."

Toward noon next day, Lidian appeared. Her face was swollen from a recent dental operation. She wept when she spoke of her lost child, and Margaret wept also, somewhat relieving the sense of "oppression" that she had felt since she came. Emerson and his wife had been collecting anecdotes about Waldo and showed the packet to Margaret. When they walked together to Walden Pond that afternoon, she thought him a far better companion than formerly. Where once he had talked "obstinately" throughout their walks, he now seemed more willing to be silent, and she, having moderated her expectations, was content to revel in what she called "his beautiful presence."

On the night of the nineteenth they walked again beside the slow river. Emerson's journal entry said that they "saw the moon broken in the water, interrogating[,] interrogating." Margaret, he guessed, wished to "beat with the beating heart of nature," whereas, for himself, "I feel that underneath the greatest life . . . must lie an astonishment that embosoms both action and thought." As Margaret said later, he seemed to have "little sympathy with mere life," caring nothing for facts except insofar as the "immortal essence" could be distilled from them. They were agreed, she thought, that if her god was love, his was truth. They spent the afternoon of August 27 in his study, talking of God and the world. Outside it was raining heavily and the room was so cold that Emerson was wearing his long blue cloak, in which, as she said, he looked like a statue, already immortal.

The "slow fever" from the infection in her jaw had kept Lidian in bed most of the time since Margaret's arrival, and Margaret had left her largely alone. Once when she entered the sickroom, Lidian burst into tears, blaming the influence of the laudanum that she had been taking for pain. But the cause of her tears evidently lay deeper: she half hinted that she thought Emerson and Margaret had been spending all their evenings together. Margaret said quickly that she had been often with Ellery Channing and Thoreau, and that Emerson had been writing alone in his study. This was a half-truth, but surely Lidian must understand, after all these years, that such affection as Emerson felt for his "fair visitor" was based on her skill in quickening his intellect with her high talk.

During the one o'clock dinner on September 1, an embarrassing contretemps arose. Lidian said that she had not been out-of-doors and asked Margaret to accompany her that afternoon. Margaret blurted out that she was engaged to walk with Emerson. She was going to add that she would take Lidian first, but before the words were out Lidian began to cry. Looking as "soft and serene as ever," Emerson said nothing. "My dear Lidian," said Margaret, "certainly I will go with you." Lidian shook her head. "No," she said, "I do not want you to make any sacrifice, but I do feel perfectly desolate, and forlorn, and I thought if I once got out, the fresh air would do me good, and that with you I should have courage. But go with Mr. E[merson]. I will not go."

In the event, Lidian and Margaret did walk together, and Lidian talked "so fully" that her companion felt reassured. At the same time, without using any such term as sexual jealousy, she thought that Lidian must always remain emotionally distraught because of her "lurking hope" that Emerson's character would change, that he would become capable of "an intimate union." In response to all that Lidian was saying, Margaret simply advised her to "take him for what he is." She had supposed that Lidian was glad to have her in the house solely for Emerson's sake. Now it dawned on her, as it ought to have done before, that Lidian's seeming "magnanimity" had been a mask for her true feelings. "Women can't bear to be left out of the question. And they don't see the whole truth about one like me, if they did they would understand why the brow of Muse or Priestess must wear a shade of sadness. . . . They have so much that I have not, I can't conceive of their wishing for what I have." But when Emerson's wife, "the mother of that child that is gone thinks me the most privileged of women . . . it does seem a little too insulting at first blush." And yet, she concluded, not without a hint of her usual queenly self-assurance, there was something to be said for Lidian's view.

The day before on a golden September afternoon, Margaret walked with Emerson as far as "the hemlocks," staying until sunset, and conversing as they often did on man, woman, and marriage. He took his usual position: "Love was only phenomenal, a contrivance of nature. . . . The soul knows nothing of marriage, in the sense of a permanent union between two personal existences. The soul is married to each new thought as it enters into it." What, then, if this thought should take the form of man or woman, "even if the marriage should last for seventy years?" There was but one love, "that for the Soul of all Souls," whatever cunning disguises it might assume. "Ask any woman," said Waldo, "whether her aim in this union is to further the genius of her husband, and she will say yes, but her conduct will always be to claim a devotion day by day that will be injurious to him, if he yields." He glanced at Margaret when he added, "Those who hold their heads highest would do no better, if they were tried." Margaret understood that this satirical jibe was meant for her.

So, at any rate, Margaret reported the conversation. If Emerson's argument on the phenomenality of love was metaphysical, his down-to-earth attitude about marriage was patriarchal, a built-in determination not to yield to the emotional importunities of the women around him, whether the hero worship of a Margaret Fuller or the lachrymosities of his wife, ill though she was in the cruel aftermath of her bereavement, and determined, as perhaps she was, to cultivate invalidism as a spur to her husband's daily devotion.

His views on marriage, as set forth in his journals for 1841–42, bore out Margaret's report to some degree. About a year before the conversation under the hemlocks, he had written that "marriage is not ideal but empirical. It is not in the plan or prospect of the soul, this fast union of one to one[;] the soul is alone and creates these images of itself. . . . Every one of its thoughts it casts into an incarnation which is a man, a woman, exhausts it of its sweetness and wisdom, and passes on to new. To a strong mind therefore the griefs incident to every earthly marriage are the less, because it has the resource of the all-creating[,] all-obliterating spirit; retreating on its grand essence the nearest persons become pictures merely. The Universe is his bride."

Or again: "It will not do to abrogate the laws which make Marriage a relation for life, fit or unfit. Plainly marriage should be a temporary relation, it should have its natural birth, climax, and decay, without any violence of any kind,—violence to bind, or violence to rend. When each of two souls had exhausted the other of that good which each held for the other, they should part in the same peace in which they met, not parting from each other, but drawn to new society. The new love is the balm to prevent a wound from forming where the old love was detached. But now we could not trust even saints and sages with a boundless liberty. For the romance of new love is so delicious, that their unfixed fancies would betray them, and they would allow themselves to confound a whim with an instinct, the pleasure of the fancy with the dictates of the character."

Or yet further: "Permanence is the nobility of human beings. We love that lover whose gayest love song, whose fieriest engagement of romantic devotion is made good by all the days of all the years of strenuous, long-suffering, ever-renewing benefit. The Old Count said to the old Countess of Ilchester, 'I know that wherever thou goest thou wilt both trust and honor me, and thou knowest that wherever I am, I shall honor thee.' " As for English nobility, so for the American aborigines: "The sannup and the Squaw do not get drunk at the same time. They take turns in keeping sober and husband and wife should never be lowspirited at the same time, but each should be able to cheer the other."

Margaret got on well with Lidian and "Mama," as she called Madam Emerson, but her journal makes it clear that her chief interest was in men. She saw a good deal of Ellery Channing, who read her his poems, and talked at length about her sister Ellen, who was soon coming from Cincinnati to join him. She called on the Hawthornes on August 20 and Hawthorne walked her back to the Emerson house in the broken moonlight. The recent bridegroom said, rather oddly, that he would now be much more willing to die than before his marriage, for in the past six weeks "he had had some real possession in life." Next day, a Sunday, he returned a book that she had left at the Manse, only to discover that she was out. On his way home he found her lounging on a tussock in Sleepy Hollow, and sat down beside her for a long talk, which was interrupted by Emerson, who emerged from the woods and joined them.

Almost as if he were tracking a woodland goddess, he appeared again a week later while Margaret and Ellery were enjoying a conversation on the shores of Walden Pond. Ellery had just been daydreaming about building a cottage at Walden to write poetry in when Emerson "dashed through the trees, and came down close to us." He made, said Margaret, "the same lovely apparition, as when he came down the bank where I was sitting with Hawthorne the other day, cleaving the shade like a sunbeam, the same lovely light in his eye and happy smile on his lips."

Her one uninterrupted séance with a gentleman caller took place back in Sleepy Hollow, this time with Sam Ward, her former Platonic lover, who spoke of the "crisis his mind had gone through." Nobody, said he, had fought more pitched battles than he had, but always felt that "this fiend of inheritance and temperament" was not his real self. As with Emerson, Margaret was newly impressed by "the peace and beauty of his countenance," despite the difficulties of which he complained.

While Margaret was conversing with her male friends in the leafy dells, Lidian continued to mourn for her lost child. Hawthorne once told Margaret of his surprise at "having met Lidian out at noon day," adding that it "seemed scarce credible you could meet such a person by the light of sun." Behind his observation was his own taste for the crepuscular and probably the knowledge that Mrs. Emerson seldom went abroad until the afternoon. "She does look very ghostly now as she glides about in her black dress, and long black veil," wrote Margaret Fuller.

The other eve[']g I was out with her about nine o'clock; it was a night of moon struggling with clouds. She asked me to go to the churchyard, and glided before me through the long wet grass, and knelt and leaned her forehead on the tomb. The moon then burst forth, and cast its light on her as she prayed. It seemed like the ghost of a mother's joys, and I have never felt that she possessed the reality. I feel that her child is far more to her in imagination than he ever was in reality. I prayed, too; it was a good moment and will not be fruitless.

Fruitful for whom? Whose good moment? Her remark about the two Waldos, the child that was gone and the other that lived on, as she thought, too powerfully and exclusively in Lidian's imagination, revealed an essential weakness in Margaret's empathetic powers. During one of their talks, Lidian had apparently complained that her husband refused to answer her questions about religious belief in such a way as to meet her needs for consolation. She thought that if Christ were there, His answers would help her more. But Margaret argued that Christ's answers to his disciples were like those of Emerson: "Feed my lambs and nothing more, no explanations, no going out of himself to meet their wants." She thought that Lidian was laying "undue stress on the office of Jesus, and the demands of the heart." As for herself, she wrote in her journal, "Nothing makes me so anti-Christian, and so anti-marriage as these talks with Lidian." The scene in the moonlit churchyard had given evidence to her that Lidian was not only leaning too heavily on Christian doctrine but also protracting unduly the season of mourning for the dead.

Emerson was doing his best to accept the loss of his son. "The Dial is my trial just now," he told his brother William early in September. But he had also begun to compose some lines for "Threnody," the memorial poem for Waldo, and to work on a draft of "Saadi," which would eventuate in nearly a hundred of his favorite tetrameter couplets for publication in the October number of the *Dial*. He and Margaret were continuing to meet sporadically, either in the "red room" which had been assigned to her, or sometimes in his own library.

"I wish it would be so always that I could live in the red room," wrote Margaret, so that her host would "be stimulated by the fine days to write poems and come the rainy days to read them to me."

My time to go to him is late in the evening. Then I go knock at the library door, and we have our long word walk through the growths of things with glimmers of light from the causes of things. Afterward, W. goes out and walks beneath the stars to compose himself for his pillow, and I open the window, and sit in the great red chair to watch them.

She was especially struck by one of the couplets in the "Saadi" poem:

And yet it doth not seem to me
That the high gods love tragedy. . . .

This meant to her that, unlike Lidian, he had "entirely dismissed" the idea of personal tragedy. With his permission she had been reading his journals for 1841–42. Wherever he had written of his "peculiar character and limitations," he had made the marginal notation, *"Accept."* She thought not only that he had "put more of himself into Saadi . . . than in anything" he had written before, but also that the theme of the poem was "one acceptance throughout."

Yet she presently discovered that she herself was by no means impervious to the tragic loss of Waldo. When he read her some lines that he had been adding to the "Saadi" manuscript, she sniffled so loudly that he asked how she had caught such a cold. "I could not but laugh then to see that grief was the *last* thing Saadi ever thought of," she wrote in her journal, "and I told him Lidian had been making me cry. 'What,' said he, 'my boy?' I told him afterward how I was affected for I did not wish him to think it was all for the child's sake, but I don't know that I did well, for Saadi the joygiver walked in deep shadow for one or two days after."

Margaret's forty days in the Concord wilderness were now nearly done. On Saturday the twenty-fourth the Emersons gave a tea in her honor, with Ellen Hooper, Sarah Clarke, Elizabeth Hoar, Sophia Hawthorne and her mother, Margaret's brother Richard, and Ellery Channing and his wife Ellen, who had joined him on September 8. "It was not very pleasant, rather a mob, though of fine people," wrote Margaret. When it was over, Emerson and Margaret accompanied Sophia and Mrs. Peabody back to the Manse, and then took a long moonlight walk. "I can[']t think about what passed all the time," wrote Margaret. "I have only an indefinite recollection of the moonlight and the river. We were more truly together than usual." She spent her final Sunday morning finishing up her reading of Emerson's journal for 1842, "even *intoxicated*" with the quality of his mind. "I am not in full possession of my own," she wrote. "I feel faint in the presence of too strong a fragrance. . . . Farewell, dearest friend, there has been dissonance between us, and may be again, for we do not fully meet, and to me you are too much and too little by turns, yet thanks be to the Parent of Souls, that gave us to be born into the same age and the same country. . . ."

The chief literary result of Margaret's visit was a long, discursive essay-review called "Romaic and Rhine Ballads" based on two recent anthologies of modern Greek folk poetry and German balladry relating to the Rhine. Emerson gave it the place of honor in the October number of the *Dial*, and wrote to thank her for the contribution. "I feel a conviction," she replied, "that I shall be worthy of this friendship. . . . You need not be terrified at this prophecy nor look about for the keys of your cell. . . . [I] feel more and more unfit to be with any body. I shall no more be so ruled by the affectionate expansions of my heart."

She had left behind a key and a penknife—"touching symbols," she called them—but Lidian was in bed again with a "nervous fever," and too ill to wrap and return them. "To be sick and lose this [October] weather of Paradise is sad," wrote Margaret. But the fever lingered through the month and Lidian's gloom remained. "She sends her love to you," wrote Emerson on October 30, "and says that it is Waldo's birthday and that her life is darkened."

Chapter Nineteen

THEODORE
PARKER

ONE MEMBER OF EMERSON'S AUDIENCE WHEN HE DELIVERED his address to the graduating class at Harvard Divinity School on Sunday, July 15, 1838, was Theodore Parker, the twenty-eight-year-old pastor at the Spring Street Church in West Roxbury. Later that day he made a journal entry:

> Proceeded to Cambridge, to hear the valedictory sermon by Mr. Emerson. In this he surpassed himself as much as he surpasses others in the general way. I shall give no abstract. So beautiful, so just, so true, and terribly sublime was his picture of the faults of the Church in its present position. My soul is roused, and this week I shall write the long-meditated sermons on the state of the Church and the duties of these times.

Parker's reaction to the Address was fairly typical of Emerson's catalytic effect upon the men of his age and station among the Unitarians of the late 1830s. A farmer's son from Lexington, the last of eleven children, he could trace his American ancestry back to the Bay Colony 200 years earlier, but he felt closest to his paternal grandfather, Captain John Parker, who had commanded a company of militia on April 19, 1775, at Lexington, and had reputedly uttered the famous words "If they mean to have a war, let it begin here." The Captain's grandson always treasured two muskets, one that had fired endless rounds on the Lexington battlefield, and the other, as he said in his last will and testament, being "the first fire-arm taken from the enemy in the War for Independence." Young Parker's wars, and they were many, were going to be conducted against different foes.

As they used to say in New England, work was his middle name. In 1858, twenty years after the Divinity School Address, Parker looked back to his vigorous youth: "Do you know I could once *carry a barrel of cider* in my hands? I don't mean a glass at a time—I could do that now—but a *barrel* at a time. I have worked (not often, though) at farming *twenty hours* out of the twenty-four for several days together, when I was eighteen or twenty. I have often worked from twelve to seventeen hours a day in my study for a considerable period; and could do that now."

He had easily passed the entrance examinations for Harvard, but could not afford to attend. Like many another poverty-stricken youth in those days, he took up schoolteaching. His immediate mentor was the Reverend Convers Francis of Watertown, a good friend of Emerson's. In the spring of 1832, Parker presided over thirty pupils in Watertown village, met his future wife, Lydia Cabot, at the local boardinghouse, and with what he earned teaching was able to finance two years at the Harvard Divinity School. His work habits accelerated; classmates called him "a prodigious athlete in his studies," while deploring his failure to take regular exercise. But he answered that it was intellectual "planting-time" for him, and that he "relied on his constitution to carry him through." At one point he became convinced that his memory was failing. He posted a huge historical chart on one wall of his room, listing the chief events in human history from Adam on down, and set about memorizing it. His talk, said his friends, was full "of odd learning and scraps of curious information." At the end of 1836 he set down the titles of the 320 volumes he had read in slightly more than a year. Following an apprenticeship at Barnstable on Cape Cod, he accepted the call to West Roxbury, married his Lydia, and was ordained in June 1837.

During the spring of 1838 Parker began to move in Transcendentalist circles. His early champion, Convers Francis, was probably responsible for his attendance at a meeting of the "club of clubs" in Medford on May 20. The topic of the day was "Mysticism," and the other participants included Emerson, Frederic Hedge, George Ripley, Alcott, Jones Very, and Cyrus Bartol. When the first number of the *Dial* reached the planning stage two years later,

Parker stood out among the potential contributors. Volume I, Number 1 contained his essay "The Divine Presence in Nature and the Soul." He held that God perpetually "influences" the outer world of nature, but acts from within upon the souls of men, who perceive divine power intuitively as an "inspiration" according to the relative acuity of their intellects, affections, and religious sensitivities.

Afterward he recalled that his interest in the "metaphysics and psychology of religion" had begun at the Divinity School where, many years before William James, he had undertaken to explore the nature of religious experience. He was convinced that "religious consciousness was universal" in the history of the human race, and sought to discover and identify "the special element which produced religious consciousness" both within himself and in the experience of mankind. "The authority of Bibles and Churches" provided no adequate answer; John Locke and his followers gave little help. Only in the works of Immanuel Kant—"one of the profoundest thinkers in the world, though one of the worst writers, even of Germany"—could Parker discover a method of thought that put him "on the right road." He concluded that among the primal intuitions of human nature a great triad stood out: "the instinctive intuition of the divine, the consciousness that there is a God; the instinctive intuition of the just and right, a consciousness that there is a moral law, independent of our will, which we ought to keep; [and] the instinctive intuition of the immortal, a consciousness that the essential element of man, the principle of individuality, never dies." These together made "the foundation of religion, laid in human nature itself."

The same autobiographical memoir recalled how "the brilliant genius of Emerson rose in the winter nights, and hung over Boston, drawing the eyes of ingenuous young people to look up to that great new star, a beauty and a mystery, which charmed for the moment, while it gave also perennial inspiration, as it led them forward along new paths, and towards new hopes."

Apart from his own contributions, which in the first three years of the *Dial* amounted to a half dozen articles, a dozen long essay-reviews, and a single poem, Parker was critical of the magazine where, as he said, the "wisdom" and the "folly" of the new movement "rode together in the same saddle." His somewhat acerbic nature was evident in his journal entry for August 10, 1840, when he accompanied George Ripley to Emerson's house to evaluate the first number of the magazine. "We saw Emerson, who looked as divine as usual, in his somewhat slovenly attire. . . . He and Ripley had all the talk, which turned entirely upon the *Dial*—its merits and defects, its uses and abuses. Really it was quite too bad. . . . In our walk Emerson expressed to me his admiration for Thoreau and his foolish article on Aulus Persius Flaccus. . . . He said it was full of life. But alas the life is Emerson's, not Thoreau's. . . . I count this evening wasted—so few good things said, by our philosopher and Prophet."

Despite profound differences in personality, which both men frankly recognized in their pronouncements about each other, Parker clearly belonged to the ministerial men of action whose powers Emerson had invoked in the Divinity School sermon. "A son of the energy of New Eng[lan]d," Emerson later called him, "restless, eager, manly, brave, early old, contumacious, clever. Our minds and methods were unlike," and yet, as Emerson added, "I saw with pleasure that men whom I could not approach were drawn through him to the admiration of that which I admire." His chief deficiency was perhaps in the realm of aesthetics. Like a latter-day Othello he might have said, "Rude am I in my speech, and little bless'd with the soft phrase of peace," a habit that Parker himself summed up as "all my directness of homely speech." What he said, Emerson complained, "as mere fact, almost offended you, so bald and detached." Yet in lieu of grace and artifice, Parker's prose revealed intellectual incisiveness and genuinely vast learning.

By the spring of 1841 he was ready to say in public what he had proved to his own satisfaction in private, or fed in smaller doses week by week to his Roxbury congregation. As guest minister at the ordination of a young friend in South Boston, he hauled himself out of sickbed to preach his vigorous "Discourse of the Transient and Permanent in Christianity." The sermon lasted ninety minutes but its echoes reverberated for months afterward. He took as his text a verse from Luke: "Heaven and earth shall pass away; but my words shall not pass away." And they did not, at least among a clear majority of his Unitarian brethren.

The position was that there is and has always been a profound difference between real Christianity, the pure religion that Jesus taught, and "the history of what men call Christianity," that of the pulpit, the forms, the doctrines, the sects, the accessories, the absurdities, and the accidents. One was permanent, the other was transient and kept changing from age to age. This phenomenon was analogous to the difference between "the true system of nature, which exists in the outward facts, whether discovered or not," and a scientific "philosophy of nature," which men advance in a series of hypotheses and "change every month." So it was that "the heresy of one age is the orthodox belief . . . of the next." So it was that from age to age "men are burned for professing what men are burned for denying." Why therefore "need we accept the commandment of men as the dotrine of God?"

"To turn away," said Parker, "from the disputes of the Catholics and the Protestants, the Unitarian and the Trinitarian, of old school and new school, and come to the plain words of Jesus of Nazareth—Christianity is a simple thing, very simple. It is absolute pure morality, absolute pure religion—the love of man; the love of God acting without let or hindrance. The only creed it lays down is the great truth which springs spontaneous in the holy heart: there is a God. Its watchword is: Be perfect as your Father in Heaven." Thus, "though Christianity gives us the largest liberty of the son of God," there is no Christian sect "which does not fetter a man." For "real Christianity gives men new life. . . . It makes us outgrow any form or system of doctrines we have devised. . . . It is not so much by the Christ who lived so blameless and beautiful eighteen centuries ago that we are saved directly, but by the Christ we form in our hearts and live out in our daily life that we save ourselves."

Although Parker had said, far too hopefully as it turned out, that Unitarianism was not yet congealed into a sect, the explosions that followed his ordination sermon seemed to prove otherwise. Those in control of the denomination began to say that he must be silenced; Unitarian periodicals closed their columns to him; secret attempts were made to alienate his little congregation in West Roxbury against him; and his mail was filled with scurrilous threats and objurgations. He complained that in some quarters he was as much feared and avoided as a leper. But he refused to back down. His brilliant and forthright "Discourse of Matters Pertaining to Religion," preached in 1842 at the Masonic Temple in Boston, fearlessly carried on his exposition on the state of religious thought in the nineteenth century. Once again he showed his skill at hacking his way through doctrinal entanglements and arriving at fresh conclusions.

The core of his analysis was a three-part division among the available approaches to the problem of man's relationship with God. What he called "The Rationalistic View, or Naturalism" was essentially the Lockean position. Creation is presided over by a deity "not immanently present and active therein" and having "nothing to do with the world but—to see it go." Man himself has no other means to knowledge than sensation, or perception through the senses. Man's reflection upon the knowledge thus gained can lead him only to the "hypothesis of a God"—a supposititious possibility unsusceptible of proof. "The Anti-Rationalistic View, or Supernaturalism" has the effect of "banishing Reason from the premises," and rests its case upon a belief in revelation by miracles. It holds that God is at least sporadically immanent in Nature and that He occasionally intercedes in human affairs. But its vice, as Parker saw, "is to make God transiently active in man, not immanent in him," and to "restrict the divine presence and action to times, places, and persons" in the remote past rather than to the mass of mankind in any and all ages.

"The Natural-Religious View, or Spiritualism" was the position Parker espoused. "As we have bodily senses to lay hold on matter and supply bodily wants . . . so we have spiritual faculties to lay hold on God, and supply spiritual wants. . . . As we observe the conditions of the body, we have nature on our side; as we observe the Law of the Soul, we have God on our side. He imparts truth to all men who observe these conditions" and "we have direct access to him through Reason, Conscience, and the religious sentiment, just as we have direct access to nature through the eye, the ear, or the hand. Through these channels, and by means of a law, certain, regular, and universal as gravitation, God inspires man." This inspiration, moreover, "is no miracle, but a regular mode of God's action on conscious spirit, as gravitation on unconscious matter. It is not a rare condescension of God, but a universal uplifting of man." As Emerson had told the graduating class at the Divinity School, "God is, not was." In addressing himself to the same problem, the justification of God's ways to man, Parker defined the essential position of the Transcendentalists with a clarity and force that Emerson himself might have envied, although Emerson characteristically presented his own convictions under what Parker not unscornfully called "the veil of poetry."

Meantime he had continued his contributions to the *Dial.* In October 1840 had come his essay on "the Christianity of Christ," which frees men to

obey God's will, since the influence of real Christianity is always "to disen-
thral" the individual rather than to enslave him to formal doctrines within the
church. Far below that of the church lay the Christianity of society, and
Parker took fierce notice of the failures of alleged Christians in their dealings
with the "Red-man" and the "Black-man," an early instance of his sympathy
with downtrodden minorities in American civilization. He contributed also a
short parable called "Truth Against the World," in which Saint Paul is made
to say to an orthodox rabbi: "I am no longer a slave to the old Law of Sin and
Death, but a free man of God, made free by the Law of the Spirit of Life in Jesus Christ." A long essay on "The Pharisees" impugned six subdivisions of
that ubiquitous brotherhood, each of them pursuing various forms of wicked-
ness while failing to understand that "God is never deceived." Yet another article, printed in January 1842, pointed out that true Christianity is based on
two great injunctions: love man and love God. Like the earlier parable, this
essay strongly defended Pauline principles, and stressed the manliness of
Saint Paul's position as over against the frailties of "pale-faced pietism."

All through the year 1842, like friendly duelists, Emerson and Parker kept
in touch, coming together now and again at gatherings of the "club of clubs,"
and exchanging politely wary letters, usually addressed to "My dear sir,"
about the contents of forthcoming *Dial*s. When Margaret Fuller withdrew as
editor, she suggested that Parker and Emerson might team up to run the magazine. But Emerson quickly and firmly declined that gambit and took over on
his own. Parker paid him the compliment of saying that Emerson himself
ought to write most of the next number. Emerson in turn implored Parker to
"fail you me not, but send me something good," and Parker, though nearly
overwhelmed with other duties, including his highly successful "Six Plain
Sermons for the Times," did his level best to comply.

Despite the similarities among their spiritual goals, neither man was temperamentally suited to work arm in arm with the other. "Sympathy is always
partial," Emerson had written. "Two human beings are like globes which can
touch only in one point." Whether in writing or in preaching, Parker's methods were not the same as Emerson's. Two of Emerson's adjectives for his
friend were "contumacious" and "clever." Neither of them could be fairly applied to Emerson himself even when the Ishmaelitish mood was most upon
him. "T.P. has beautiful fangs," wrote Emerson, "and the whole amphi-

theatre delights to see him worry and tear his victims." Neither in public nor usually in private discourse did Emerson customarily bare his fangs, though he once pointed out that "I too like puss have a retractile claw." But the partial sympathies of the early 1840s gradually merged into a larger whole in the following decades. Parker in 1850 and Emerson in 1860 looked back on their association with mutual admiration and respect.

Chapter   Twenty

HAWTHORNE

![O]ONLY TWO DAYS AFTER MARGARET FULLER ENDED HER LONG stay in Concord, Emerson arranged a walking tour with Hawthorne to the Shaker community near the village of Harvard, which lay some twenty miles to the west by a dogleg route through Stow. Hawthorne knew more about the Shakers and their customs than Emerson did. His visit to the Shaker settlement at Canterbury, New Hampshire, in 1831 had eventuated in a story, "The Canterbury Pilgrims," with a bow to Chaucer and another to Mother Ann Lee, the founder of the sect. The similar establishment at Goshen, New Hampshire, became the site of a second and better story, "The Shaker Bridal." He found some of the women attractive, but thought the men "great boobies" as they performed, with the gravest of facial expressions, the "ridiculous capers" required by their ritual dances.

Although Emerson, on this trip, was afflicted with "a disgraceful barking cold," he found it a luxury to walk in the midst of all that "warm and colored light." Red fruit hung like berries on the wild apple trees, and the fields along the road were blue with fringed gentians. Hawthorne would have liked to pluck a bouquet for Sophia, but they were going, not coming back, and Emerson was eager for talk. "We were both old collectors," he wrote afterward, "who had never had opportunity before to show each other our cabinets." They stopped at Stow for dinner and in the afternoon were hailed by a pleasant officious man who recognized Emerson, insisted on giving them a ride in his wagon, and would not leave until they were safely installed in the tavern at Harvard.

Hawthorne also had a cold in the head, which no doubt explained his taciturnity next morning when they were on the road by six-thirty in order to breakfast with the Shakers. Emerson was soon deep in discussion with a couple of the brethren, but Hawthorne stood apart, dignified and aloof. During the inspection of orchards, vineyards, and outbuildings, he tagged along. But it was Emerson, who had declined to join the communal experiment at Brook Farm, rather than Hawthorne, who had lived there, who showed the stronger curiosity about the Shaker organization.

Despite objections that would later appear, Emerson called it a successful "experiment of Socialism" that fell in exactly with the spirit of the age, as well as a going concern that fed, clothed, and sheltered 200 people, and a model farm for neighboring yeomen to study and imitate. The Shakers were famous for their handsome, hand-made garden implements, but Emerson noticed that precise carpentry was not among their virtues. During the tour he picked up a spirit level in the main building. Trying it out on nearby surfaces, he found that the table, the shelf, and the window seat were all out of plumb. But on the whole Emerson was favorably impressed. As he soon reported to Sam Ward, he and Hawthorne had made themselves very much at home in Shaker-land, "conferred with them on their faith and practice, took all reasonable liberties with the brethren, found them less stupid, more honest than we looked for, found even some humour, and had our fill of walking and sunshine."

Their "pedestrian excursion" marked a watershed in the relations between the two men. Hawthorne's journal entries of the later fall displayed none of the churlishness that had crept into his running commentaries on Emerson in August while Margaret Fuller was in Concord. One inference might be that his respect for Emerson had risen as a result of the tour, that he had become a partial convert to the man, if not to his ideas. Emerson seems to have suspected that some inward restraint was holding his friend back from literary fulfillment. Shortly after the Shaker trip he made a journal entry that "a man cannot free himself from self denying ordinances," but "only by the freest activity in the way constitutional to him does an angel seem to arise and lead him out of all wards of the prison." Such statements represented the Ishmaelite side of Emerson's character, as in a journal entry of 1841, which said that it was his custom on Sundays to take walks in the woods, and to read Aristophanes and Rabelais during church hours.

He was still full of praise for the "exhaustive affluence" of Rabelais during a talk with Hawthorne in October. Reading Rabelais, he said, was one of his own "gipsy-making" proclivities: "I told Hawthorne yesterday that I think every young man at some time inclines to make the experiment of a dare-God and daredevil originality like that of Rabelais. He would jump on top of the nearest fence and crow. He makes the experiment, but it proves like the flight of pig-lead into the air which cannot cope [in flying ability] with the poorest hen. Irresistible custom brings him plump down, and he finds himself instead of odes, writing gazettes and leases." In such terms as these, Rabelais could be counted as one of the kings of roosterdom. "His place in Parnassus," said Emerson, "is as firm as Homer's. . . . His wit is universal. . . . His joke will fit any town or community of men. The style at once decides the high quality of the man. It flows like the river Amazon."

How much of this got across to Hawthorne is unclear. He had proved his "gipsy-talent" for walking, but his works, Emerson believed, could have profited by a strong infusion of Rabelaisian "affluence," in place of the costive effects of New England Puritanism. Whatever the final result of Emerson's harangue, it is curious that at twelve noon on October 10 Hawthorne wrote in his journal that he was reading Rabelais. Perhaps he had begun to understand the Ishmaelitish strain in Emerson, and was seeking through Rabelais to discover its source.

The nascent friendship had been long in developing. Although Hawthorne was only a year younger than Emerson, he had entered Bowdoin College as a freshman just as Emerson was being graduated from Harvard. In the twelve years after his own graduation, he had served his writer's apprenticeship with an abortive novel, *Fanshawe*, and some forty-four tales and sketches, which appeared in the *Token*, the *New England Magazine*, and the *American Magazine of Knowledge*. Despite his reclusive life in Salem, he must certainly have heard of Emerson, who often lectured there. But it was not until his courtship of Sophia Peabody in 1838 that he began to hear from her and her bluestocking sister, Elizabeth, a veritable barrage of praise for Emerson. Much given to hyperbole, Sophia was accustomed to speak of his simplicity of manner, his "*diffused* smile; the musical thunder of his voice; [and] his repose, so full of the essence of life." There were even occasions, both early and late, when she seemed to confuse his beatific expression with the splendors of the setting sun. It does not, as a rule, take much of this sort of idolatry to sour the mind of one's swain against the alien object of his lady's worship.

Elizabeth Peabody strove hard to interest Emerson in Hawthorne's early work. During a visit to Concord in June 1838, she persuaded him to read "Footprints on the Seashore," an account of a day's excursion along Salem's beaches that Hawthorne had published in the *Democratic Review* for January. Emerson disappointed her by saying that the piece had "no inside to it." She might have been upset, though probably not discouraged, if she had read his concurrent journal entry, which said that it would take Alcott and Hawthorne together to make a man. Back in Concord for another visit in June 1839, she found Emerson full of praise for Hawthorne's work at the Boston Custom House. George Bancroft had told him that Hawthorne "was the most efficient and best of the Custom House officers," after only six months as weigher of coal and salt at the end of Long Wharf. Since Emerson now seemed "all congenial" about Hawthorne, Miss Peabody seized the occasion "to bring him to his knees," as she put it, by urging him to read the whole volume of *Twice-Told Tales*, published two years earlier. This second try was no better than the first, leading only to another remark in Emerson's journal: "It is no easy matter to write a dialogue. Cooper, Sterling, Dickens, and Hawthorne cannot." At least he had placed the author of the *Tales* in illustrious company.

When Sophia Peabody went to stay with the Emersons in June 1840, Emerson invited Hawthorne to Concord while his fiancée was there. Hawthorne declined: Sophia must tell Emerson that the work at the customhouse had converted him into a mere "business-machine," unsuited for the social amenities. In the fall of 1841, Hawthorne was at West Roxbury, partway through his residency at Brook Farm. On September 27, exactly a year before his hike with Emerson to visit the Shakers, the Brook Farmers held a masquerade picnic, ostensibly to celebrate the sixth birthday of Frank Dana, but also to allow the members of the colony to let off social steam.

In due course this became a memorable episode in *The Blithedale Romance* (1852), where Hawthorne portrayed himself under the fictional mask of Miles Coverdale, who lurked behind a tree, looking on while the Blithedalers made merry in their woodland glade, variously disguised as Indians, witches, devils, and Gypsy fortune-tellers. "The wood," mused Coverdale, "seemed as full of jollity as if Comus and his crew were holding their revels" in the midst of New England on a harvest afternoon.

Although the novel naturally says nothing of it, the day of the picnic may have marked Hawthorne's first meeting with Emerson. In the actual event, the revels had wound down with the sudden appearance of Margaret Fuller and Emerson, who "came forth into the little glade" where the masquers had been dancing. They had reached Brook Farm an hour or two earlier, apparently in time for the midday dinner, and it is likely that Hawthorne had seen them in the refectory. Now, taking his ease, his hat shadowing his sunburned face, he watched pensively as the romping tapered off and the conversation began, probably under Margaret's leadership. "Here followed much talk," he wrote in his journal. He did not feel moved to summarize its substance. Possibly, and if so, characteristically, he did not even bother to listen, preferring his station at the edge of the group, the typical *spectator ab extra* who came forward only to partake of the "cold collation of cakes and fruit" that brought Frank Dana's birthday party to an end.

At this time, Emerson still nourished his latent prejudice against Hawthorne the writer, and hardly knew Hawthorne the man. If Hawthorne had read anything of Emerson's, he gave no sign of interest or approbation, and if he felt any spleen toward Sophia's living idol, he waited until the summer of 1842 to indulge it with satirical remarks about the nebulosity of Emerson's transcendental visions and his habit of collecting eccentric disciples, among whom Hawthorne's fellow townsman, Jones Very, had been a notable example.

For Sophia, as for her sister, Elizabeth, Concord was magnetized by Emerson's presence, and it was only seven months after the sylvan fête at Brook Farm when she and Hawthorne appeared in the village to ask about the possibility of renting the Old Manse. Although the place stood at the opposite end of town from Emerson's, it swarmed with Emersonian ghosts. His grandfather had built it, his father had been born there, and Emerson himself had known it from boyhood, besides having boarded there with his mother and his brother Charles before his marriage to Lidian. He had then called it "this lone parsonage in this thin village." Yet it was there in the study that he composed much of his first book, *Nature*. Vacated after the death of old Ezra Ripley in the fall of 1841, it had been refurbished by Samuel Ripley, the new owner, and now stood, as Emerson said, "all new and bright again as a toy," and solidly planted on the rise above the river.

Whatever he thought of Hawthorne's writing, Emerson was delighted at the prospect of his moving to Concord. "If they shall come to live here I shall be content," he wrote Elizabeth Hoar. "It seems they are sent by you. I like him well." When he met Hawthorne by chance at the Boston Athenaeum later in May, he was able to assure him that, owing to Thoreau's early planting, the vegetable garden that went with the Manse was already flourishing— good news to the impecunious author, who would be needing all the new potatoes and peas he could dig or pluck, to say nothing of the prospective harvest of apples in the orchard behind the house. Late in June, a couple of weeks before Hawthorne's wedding day, Margaret Fuller assured Emerson that the "new colonists" would soon be in residence. He must get to know Hawthorne better: "You will find him more *mellow* than most fruits at your board, and of distinct flavor too."

Nathaniel and Sophia were married on Saturday, July 9, at her father's house in West Street, Boston. Next day they took the coach to Concord, arriving late in the afternoon during a thunderstorm. Elizabeth Hoar had filled the Manse with flowers, and Sophia felt like a phoenix reborn. The Emersons immediately called to greet them. "How do you do, *Mrs. Hawthorne?*" said Emerson, accenting her new name with one of his beatific smiles. When they left, Sophia accompanied them to the door, where the cold rain was still beating. Emerson, aware of her physical frailty, said paternally that she must not come out into the east wind.

The new residents liked to pretend that the Manse was an updated Eden, and saw themselves as Adam and Eve. The bride was exaggerating as usual when she wrote in retrospect that the honeymoon summer was without interruption. She did not count the visits from Elizabeth Hoar, who could "hardly be called an earthly inhabitant," or from Emerson, "whose face pictured the promised land (which we were then enjoying), and intruded no more than a sunset, or a rich warble from a bird." Margaret Fuller was more of a problem. When she arrived in mid-August, she proposed that Ellery Channing and his wife Ellen, her sister and brother-in-law, should move into the Manse as boarders. Hawthorne, whose wildest nightmares could have conceived nothing worse than a *ménage à quatre* at this point in his marriage, nipped her suggestion in the bud, saying that if Adam and Eve had been asked to take in a pair of angels, they would have rejected the notion as summarily as he was now doing.

Thoreau came round to inspect the garden he had planted for the new-comers. Early in August Sophia jubilantly listed the vegetables his foresight had led to: "peas, beans, beets, turnips, parsnips, carrots, cabbages, corn, and tomatoes." Although grateful for this abundance, Hawthorne described "Mr. Thorow" as "ugly as sin," with his long nose, asymmetrical mouth, and "uncouth" rusticity. At this period, the handsome bridegroom tended to overuse such terms as "ugly" and "uncouth." For the time being, he grouped Thoreau with Ellery Channing as among "those queer and clever young men whom Mr. Emerson (that everlasting rejecter of all that is, and seeker for he knows not what) is continually picking up by way of a genius." But he soon found that Thoreau was "a keen and delicate observer of nature" as well as a skillful navigator. After dinner on the last day of August—"at which we cut the first water-melon and musk melon that our garden has ripened"— Thoreau took him for a ride in the *Musketaquid*, the boat in which he and his brother John had made their famous voyage in 1839. In want of cash, he sold it for seven dollars to Hawthorne, who promptly rechristened it the *Pond Lily*.

The acerbic reference to Emerson as collector of odd geniuses resounded several times in Hawthorne's account of his first visit to Walden Pond. George Hillard was the Boston lawyer who had sheltered him during the Custom House period, and in mid-August the Hillards spent a weekend at the Manse. The fourteenth, a Sunday, dawned gray and sullen. Having break-fasted on fresh-caught bream from the river, fresh-picked whortleberries from the meadows, and Sophia's best flapjacks, Hillard and his host left around nine for a Walden ramble. When they stopped at Emerson's to ask the way, Hawthorne was maliciously amused to find that the great man was not plan-ning to attend church, though some "scruple of his external conscience" made him ask his visitors to stay with him out of sight until the townspeople were safely at worship. Then they all set out together, or, as Hawthorne said with a hint of sarcasm, Mr. Emerson "accompanied us in his own illustrious person."

They detoured to Edmund Hosmer's farm, where they found the owner inspecting his fields—a short stalwart man who struck Hawthorne as "somewhat uncouth and ugly to look at," even though his face was shrewd and kindly and his manners courteous. With some prodding from Emerson, Hosmer discoursed on agriculture, business, and the state of the nation. Emerson had recently praised him in the July *Dial*, and Hawthorne, who had read the piece, was inclined to blame the author for having put Hosmer into print. Such publicity had made this guileless man self-conscious and driven him to adopt an "oracular" manner that Hawthorne found mildly offensive. Still, Hosmer was "more natural" than most men, and it was clear that he was "a man of intellectual and moral substance . . . a reality, something to be felt and touched."

These were qualities that Hawthorne admired, and he might have credited Emerson with the same perspicacity. Instead, he amused himself by contrasting Emerson and Hosmer—"the mystic, stretching his hand out of cloudland, in vain search for something real," as over against this plain farmer whose ideas were as sound as the vegetables he raised. Hawthorne admitted that Emerson was "a great searcher for facts," and yet they all seemed "to melt away and become unsubstantial in his grasp." Had either Emerson or Hawthorne recognized it, they were in the midst of a critical contretemps in which each thought the other's work too distant from actuality. To Emerson, Hawthorne's writings were thin and empty; to Hawthorne, Emerson was a mere dreamer in vain search of the actual.

The following Sunday gave him occasion for another mild sneer at Emerson's expense. This was the time when he happened to meet Margaret Fuller basking in the woods at Sleepy Hollow. Their conversation was moving quietly along when they heard footsteps on the high bank behind them and a voice calling Margaret's name. The tall figure that "emerged from the green shade" was Emerson. "In spite of his clerical consecration," wrote Hawthorne derisively, he "had found no better way of spending the Sabbath than to ramble among the woods." Emerson smiled and explained that there were muses in the forest, and "whispers to be heard in the breezes." But the author of "Young Goodman Brown," who had dealt with such phenomena in his own story, pretended to think that this was balderdash. He nodded with an appearance of politeness when Emerson asked him to dinner and also to a Phi Beta Kappa celebration at Mrs. Samuel Ripley's house in Waltham. But he had not the least intention of accepting. Like Keats fending off the kindly ministrations of Shelley, Hawthorne was stubbornly determined not to join

Emerson's flock of wayward geniuses. He could hardly have anticipated the ironic entry that Emerson would presently make in his journal: Hawthorne's "reputation as a writer is a very pleasing fact, because his writing is not good for anything, and this is a tribute to the man."

In the afternoon of August 30, wrote Hawthorne, "Mr. Emerson called, bringing Mr. [Barzillai] Frost, the colleague and successor of Dr. [Ezra] Ripley. He is a good sort of hum-drum parson enough, and well fitted to increase the stock of manuscript sermons, of which there must be a fearful quantity already in the world. I find that my respect for clerical people, as such, and my faith in the utility of their office, decreases daily. We certainly do need a new revelation—a new system—for there seems to be no life in the old one." These remarks could perhaps be construed as another dig at Emerson for having brought the humdrum Frost to call. But the surprising aspect of this notebook entry was that Hawthorne's anticlerical opinions should have led him toward, if not to, the "new revelation" of which Emerson for the past seven years had been so active a champion.

While Hawthorne was listening to Emerson and Frost, Sophia was calling on Lidian. "I went to see her Tuesday afternoon," she wrote her mother. "The house was utterly deserted, all the birds [having] flown to the woods," the birds being Margaret Fuller, Ellery Channing, and Emerson. "Poor Mrs. Emerson" had been "very ill with ague accompanied with fever. She took tons [?] of calomel and now walks abroad but is exceptionally feeble and paler than snow. She has now to recover from the disease of calomel. . . . I found her in the garden superintending Henry Thorow's flower-planting. . . . We soon came into the house, after I had invited Mr. Thorow to dine with us next day." Sophia went back again late in September to return a parasol that Lidian had lent her. "The phoenix," as she called Emerson, had again "flown to the woods, but we found that pale lady abbeys [sic] who was very lovely."

Sophia's second visit took place soon after the walking trip to the Shaker village, and suggests that a genuine thaw in the relationship between Emerson and Hawthorne had finally set in. Whenever Emerson came to call, said Sophia, he always took Hawthorne away "so that no one may interrupt him in his close and deadset attack upon his ear." One day in October when Lidian and Sophia were out walking with their husbands, Emerson soon looked back and said, "You two ladies must find each other agreeable, for I must have Mr. Hawthorne."

Hawthorne now seemed far readier than formerly to accept Emerson's repeated invitations. When Alcott returned to Concord with his English friends, and George Ripley brought a contingent of Brook Farmers to an evening discussion on communal living at Emerson's house on November 19, Hawthorne was there, no doubt listening quietly in a corner, yet present. He put on a clean shirt and took Sophia and Elizabeth Hoar to the Emersons' festival dinner on November 25, the "good Friday" after Thanksgiving. When the river froze solid in December, converting the lower end of the orchard behind the Manse into a private skating rink, Hawthorne asked Emerson and Thoreau to join him for a bout of year-end exercise, while Sophia, who was pregnant, peered at them from an upstairs window. She thought that Thoreau's dizzy turns and "Bacchic leaps" were athletic but ugly to watch. Not so Hawthorne, muffled in his cloak and moving "like a self-impelled Greek statue, stately and grave." As for Emerson, Sophia guessed that he was "evidently too weary to hold himself erect." He leaned awkwardly forward, "half lying on the air." The whole wintry scene was a study in contrasts. When Emerson came stumping into the Manse kitchen to get warm, he told Sophia admiringly that her husband was tireless as a tiger, a bear, a lion, or a satyr, and then added, with that kindly smile that Sophia adored, "Mr. Hawthorne is such an Ajax, who can cope with him!"

Chapter Twenty-one

ALCOTT HOMESTEADING,
1842-47

THE OLD CONFLICT BETWEEN SOCIETY AND SOLITUDE ROSE up once more in Emerson's mind during the fall of 1842. "What obstinate propensity to solitude is this?" said his journal entry. "I fancied that I needed society and that it would help me much if fine persons were near, whom I could see when I would, but now that C[hanning] and H[awthorne] are here, and A[lcott] is returning, I look with a sort of terror at my gate."

Hawthorne was too busy to be troublesome, but Channing and Thoreau were both in residence in Coolidge Castle, Margaret Fuller had just departed after a visit of forty days, and Alcott would soon be coming back from his sojourn in England. The news on October 5 was that he would be accompanied by two "mystics" named Charles Lane and Henry Wright, as well as Lane's nine-year-old son, William, and a boxed library of 1,000 volumes from the estate of James P. Greaves, a disciple of Pestalozzi and a former mentor to Wright and Lane. Lidian, ill and feverish, loudly asserted that this triumvirate-cum-puer had no proper business in Concord. But Emerson helpfully saw the "cabalistic collection" of books through customs in Boston and prepared for the invasion.

At first nothing happened. Alcott kept his charges sequestered in Dove Cottage, where he and Abba and their little women had been subsisting on a "Pythagorean diet"—meatless, eggless, butterless, cheeseless, milkless—with bread and cereals, fruits and vegetables as their daily fare, and well water their only drink. By some socioarchitectural sleight of hand, Alcott's small house managed to accommodate nine people. Wright, who bore a faint resemblance to Lord Byron, soon withdrew and went to Lynn, unable to stand Alcott's despotic diet or, probably, the close quarters. But Lane, a tall, dour-looking ascetic, made himself at home, teaching the Alcott daughters and playing his violin for their amusement. As long as Wright was there, the trio held what Emerson called "perpetual Parliament" by day and by night, thick as thieves in socialistic plans. "Mamma, they have begun again," said one of the Alcott girls.

In November they came to Emerson's house for a conference on "social institutions." George Ripley and his Brook Farmers appeared in strength, and the Brook Farm alumnus Hawthorne was quietly present. Next morning Emerson woke up cantankerous. "Discussions like that . . . invade and injure me," he wrote. "I often have felt emptiness and restlessness and a sort of hatred of the human race after such prating by me and my fellows. . . . Absence from them is better for me." Apparently some of the group had claimed God's imprimatur on their plans. "You may associate on what grounds you like," wrote Emerson disgustedly, "for economy, or for good neighborhood, for a school, or for whatever reason, only do not say that the Divine Spirit enjoins it. The Spirit detaches you from all associations, and makes you to your own astonishment secretly a member of the Universal Association but it descends to no specialties, [and] draws up no Articles of a Society. . . ."

Alcott, Lane, and Wright might well be "admirable instruments for a master's hand," but in the absence of a true leader, they were, said Emerson, "too desultory, ignorant, imperfect, and whimsical to be trusted for any progress." Alcott himself was "a natural Levite . . . whom all good persons would readily combine . . . to maintain as a priest by voluntary contribution. . . . But for a founder of a family or institution, I would as soon exert myself to collect money for a madman." A year later Emerson would add that "Alcott and Lane want feet; they are always feeling of their shoulders to find if their wings are sprouting; but next best to wings are cowhide boots, which society is always advising them to put on."

In the meantime he collared Alcott to learn what his plans were. Alcott observed innocently that "there should be found a farm of a hundred acres in excellent condition with good buildings, a good orchard and grounds . . . and this should be purchased and given" to himself and Lane. This was asking too much, said Emerson. Only that man "will instruct and strengthen me, who, there where he is, unaided, in the midst of poverty, toil, and traffic, extricates himself from the corruptions of the same and builds on his land a house of peace and benefit, good customs, and free thoughts." But, said Alcott, "How is this to be done, how can I do it who have a wife and family to maintain?" Obviously, said Emerson, Alcott was not the person to do it or he would not have asked such a question. The true builder would "not only see the thing to be done, but invent the . . . ways and means of doing it." The champion of self-reliance was speaking here: Alcott had shown too little of that quality.

But the philosophers still dreamed of their hundred-acre farm. Lane had money and was ready to invest it. He and Alcott examined several possible sites. In the middle of April Emerson called in at Dove Cottage to give them a piece of his mind. He told them that he "loved every thing by turns and nothing long"; that he "loved Man", but that men seemed to him "mice and rats"; that he "revered saints" but every day "woke up glad that the dear old Devil kept his state in Boston." He was happy that such men as Lane and Alcott existed, but would not grieve were they living in another town than Concord. If the centers of their lives coincided with "the Centre of Life," he would accept all they said as gospel; yet their centers were off balance, slightly dislocated, eccentric. Having said this, or something like it, Emerson invited them to pound him a little as punishment for his sauciness. But they only looked at him blandly, swallowing any anger they may have felt. "And so," Emerson concluded, "I departed from the divine lotos-eaters."

Late in May, Charles Lane invested $1,800 in a ninety-acre farm near Harvard village, some fourteen miles north of Concord. The site was physically magnificent, with ample pasturage and woodland, and distant views of Wachusett and Monadnoc. On a slope of the wide valley stood an old red farmhouse, considerably dilapidated, which came rent-free for a year with the purchase price. Lane settled Alcott's outstanding debts in Concord, and on June 1 the Lanes and Alcotts moved in, with two young and two middle-aged men to assist in the farming operations. Despite his tough talk of April, Emerson felt "sad at heart" that he could not help them in their great experiment. When he made a visit that summer, all looked serene. The crops were planted—eight acres in grains, two in potatoes, and one in vegetables and melons. "They look well in July," said Emerson skeptically. "We will see them in December."

They named the place Fruitlands. Among the temporary visitors were Isaac Hecker, an erstwhile Brook Farmer, and Jane-Ann Page, who served briefly as tutor for the five children. "Far too much labor devolves on Mrs. Alcott," Lane wrote Thoreau. But Anna and Louisa, aged twelve and eleven, became their mother's chief assistants. "I rose at 5 and had my bath. I love cold water!" wrote Louisa in September. "Then we had our singing-lesson with Mr. Lane. After breakfast I washed dishes, and ran on the hill till nine. . . . We had bread and fruit for dinner. I read and walked and played till supper-time. . . . Mr. Parker Pillsbury came, and we talked about the poor slaves. I had a music lesson with Miss P[age]. I hate her, she is so fussy. I ran in the wind and played be [sic] a horse, and had a lovely time with Anna and Lizzie. . . . It rained when I went to bed, and made a pretty noise on the roof."

By November there were signs of strain. Miss Page had gone, but the work continued unabated. "I rose at five," wrote Louisa. ". . . Father and Mr. L[ane] had a talk, and father asked us if *we* saw any reason for us to separate. Mother wanted to, she is so tired. I like it, but not the school part, or Mr. L[ane]." And in December: "Father read to us in dear Pilgrim's Progress. . . . Mr. L[ane] was in Boston, and we were glad. In the eve father and mother and Anna and I had a long talk. I was very unhappy, and we all cried. Anna and I cried in bed, and I prayed God to keep us all together."

As he had done after the Temple School auction, Alcott now fell ill, this time of a disappointment so profound that he turned his face to the wall, refused to eat, and nearly died of starvation. The breakup was imminent. During the first week of January 1844 Lane and his son joined the Shaker community. A week later the Alcott family moved into three rooms in the house of a farmer named Lovejoy, and afterward into a half house in the impoverished little village of Still River—"a quiet little nook," wrote Mrs. Alcott, "where we will try to vegetate." In April, Alcott planted a small garden, producing, as his wife felt, "rapid and beautiful changes." With the produce of summer, the family survived, but the prospect of another winter drove them in October back to Edmund Hosmer's capacious farmhouse in Concord.

For a time the ever-hopeful Alcott believed that Emerson would build him a house "free of rent and landlords." Instead, early in 1845, with a portion of Mrs. Alcott's patrimony and yet one more substantial grant from Emerson, they bought the old Cogswell place on the Lexington road, half a mile from Coolidge Castle. On April Fool's Day they moved in, calling the house Hillside, since it stood under the brow of Revolutionary Ridge. Alcott, with some enthusiasm, busied himself with its rehabilitation.

Many years afterward Alcott wrote of the abortive Harvard plantation: "Fruitlands was an adventure undertaken in good faith for planting a Family Order here in New England, in hopes of enjoying a pastoral life with a few devoted men and women, smitten with sentiments of the old heroism and love of holiness and humanity. But none of us were prepared to actualize practically the ideal life of which we dreamed. So we fell apart, some returning to the established ways, some soured by the trial, others postponing the fulfilment of his dream to a more propitious future."

Emerson's skepticism about Fruitlands had been well founded. After eight years of friendship, during which he had so often served as Alcott's champion, mentor, psychiatrist, consoler, encourager, and even banker, he was fully aware of his friend's virtues and limitations. Always a curious analyst of those to whom he felt drawn, he repeatedly gave over paragraphs or pages in his journal in attempts to sum them up. On the eve of Alcott's departure for England, he had made an extended try at a "character" of this not very intrepid voyager:

> He delights in speculation . . . and is very well endowed and weaponed for this work with a copious, accurate, and elegant vocabulary . . . so that I know no man who speaks such good English as he. . . . Where he is greeted by loving and intelligent persons, his discourse soars to a wonderful height. . . . He takes such delight in the exercise of this faculty that he will willingly talk the whole of a day, and most part of the night, and then again tomorrow, for days successively, and if I, who am impatient of much speaking, draw him out to walk in the woods or fields, he will stop at the first fence and very soon propose either to sit down or to return.

Alcott believed the colloquy was the perfection of society, and it was speculation he loved, not action. He entertained in his spirit all vast and magnificent problems, Emerson went on, and he seemed often to realize the pictures of the old Alchemists: for he stood brooding on the edge of discovery of the Absolute from month to month, ever and anon affirming that it was within his reach, and nowise discomfited by uniform short-comings. . . . The other tendency of his mind was to realize a reform in the Life of Man. This was . . . the monotonous topic of years of conversation. This drew him to a constant intercourse with the projectors and saints of all shades . . . and non-intercourse with the scholars and men of refinement who are usually found in the ranks of Conservatism. Very soon the Reformers whom he had joined would disappoint him. They were pitiful persons. . . . In these oscillations from the Scholars to the Reformers and back again he spent his days.

His vice, an intellectual vice . . . was that to which almost all spiritualists have been liable—a certain brooding on the private thought which produces monotony in the conversation, and egotism in the character. . . . Unhappily, his conversation never loses sight of his own personality. He never quotes; he never refers; his only illustration is his own biography. His topic yesterday is Alcott on the 17th October; today, Alcott on the 18th October. . . . This noble genius discredits genius to me. I do not want any more such persons to exist.

Emerson was at first wryly dubious about Alcott's success as a Concord homesteader. This talker at the gates of the world had never yet done justice to the merits of labor. Instead of a few fine words, there must be "very many hard strokes every day, to get what even an ascetic wants." But in 1845–46 Alcott surprised his critic. He told Emerson that whatever could be done with the eye he could do, meaning the development of garden plots and the deletion of architectural monstrosities. He rose to the challenge of Hillside House. When he was satisfied with the interior repairs, he built an outdoor bathing pavilion and a rustic arbor partway up the slope. His journal recorded his pleasure in adding something to the landscape. He had no taste for untamed wilderness: even the domestic woodlands were like unkempt savages which must be cropped and combed. A good man always left his image on the land, imparting to it qualities that would remind him of himself. He invested $75 in three more acres and set out apple trees. His joy in the work eventuated in a couplet dated September 18, 1846: "Sweet is the toil and swift the hours glide by / While I my grounds delight to beautify."

His enthusiasm spilled over into Emerson's cornfield. In July 1847, he walked out to Walden with Thoreau and Emerson and felled twenty hemlocks to serve as posts for a summerhouse. Emerson had agreed to pay him $50 for the construction, but Alcott would gladly have done the work for nothing. He was chief architect and Thoreau his practical assistant, who laughingly told Emerson that working with Alcott was like being nowhere, doing nothing. A month later Emerson wrote sardonically that "in spite of their joint activity," the strange edifice had not yet fallen down. The structure was vaguely Gothic, like the great window in Temple School. "I call this my style of building the 'Sylvan,' " wrote Alcott happily. Emerson's quizzical name for it was Tumbledown Hall and Lidian spoke of it as The Ruin. Over the front entrance the builder installed a simulated harp of rough wood, another of his beloved emblems.

Emerson left for England before the summerhouse was done, but Alcott kept on. "I seldom reach home from my work at Emerson's till quite dark . . . ," he wrote in October. "After a supper of cream, honey, and wheaten cakes, with apples and peaches, [I] find myself pursuing my charming occupation to bed and all through the night long, in happy dreams. And when the morning comes it is with an urgency to resume my toil. . . . I am at E[merson]'s field with my hammer and saw again." He continued until the snow flew, good-naturedly recording in his journal the remarks of passersby who variously thought the building odd or strange, a log cabin, even a whirligig.

Emerson was now ready to admit that he had underestimated Alcott's practical powers. "After all his efforts on that most incorrigible of all materials, man," he had found "a real comfort in working on that most corrigible and docile of all pupils, Nature." He surprised Emerson with the remark that gardening was a good refuge for reformers and Abolitionists, enabling them to acquire that realism that people so much approved of in merchants or in Napoleon. On the other hand he was remarkably blind to natural facts. Out walking with Emerson in July, he had suddenly asked, "Why the boys waded in the water after pond lilies?" Emerson answered that they could sell them in town for a cent apiece: people liked to carry them to church for use as pro tem cologne bottles. "What!" cried Alcott. "Have they a perfume? I did not know it."

Amused or bemused by his friend's eccentricities, Emerson resumed his growing "character" of Alcott. When ordinary descriptive terms failed him, he resorted to metaphor: a fluid, a golden ore, a slate pencil with a sponge attached:

> Alcott is a certain fluid in which men of a certain spirit can easily expand themselves and swim at large. . . . There is in California a gold ore in great abundance in which the gold is in combination with such elements that no chemistry has yet been able to separate it without great loss. Alcott is a man of unquestionable genius, yet no doctrine or sentence or word or action of his which is excellent can be detached and quoted. . . . Alcott is "like a slate-pencil" with a wet sponge attached to the other end. . . . He talks high and wide, and expresses himself very happily, and forgets all he has said. If a skilful operator could introduce a lancet and sever the sponge, ABA would be the prince of writers. . . .

If. The small word bulked large in other accounts of Alcott. Thoreau, writing to Emerson in England, said of their mutual friend: "If he would only stand straight and toe the line!—though he were to put off several degrees of largeness—and put on a considerable degree of littleness." But he was still trying to get himself organized, "rallying for another foray with his pen . . . not discouraged by the past—into that crowd of unexpressed ideas of his— that undisciplined Parthian army—which as soon as a Roman soldier would face retreats on all hands—occasionally firing behind—easily routed—not easily subdued—hovering on the skirts of society."

Thoreau's military image was neither better nor worse than those in which Emerson had sought to summarize the oddly recalcitrant quality of Alcott's thought and expression. Both his friends were plainly trying to unscrew the inscrutable with wrenches that did not precisely fit the nut. Both were critical of Alcott's extremisms, his airy amplitudes, his lack of discipline. But there he was, unchanged, unchangeable. After many talks at the Walden hut, Thoreau called him "the best-natured man I ever met. . . . I do not see how he can ever die. Nature cannot spare him. Great Thinker! Great Expecter! to converse with whom was a New England Night's Entertainment." To Emerson, after all the years of association, he was "the magnificent dreamer, brooding as ever on the renewal or reedification of the social fabric after ideal law, heedless that he had been uniformly rejected by every class to whom he has addressed himself and just as sanguine and vast as ever;—the most cogent example of the drop too much which nature adds of each man's peculiarity."

Chapter   Twenty - two

HAWTHORNE
AT THE MANSE

AFTER THE CHRISTMAS SEASON OF 1842, IN SOPHIA'S phrase, "Sirius was not visible to the eye for nearly three months." What she meant was that Emerson was absent from Concord on a long lecture tour. At the same time, Hawthorne was slyly making his first public literary allusion to Emerson in a sketch called "The Hall of Fantasy." Begun in November, it stood complete a week before Christmas. He sent it off to James Russell Lowell's new journal, the *Pioneer*, where it appeared in February 1843 while Emerson was still away from home.

The reference was mild and complimentary, suggesting how far Hawthorne had overcome his anti-Emersonian prejudice of the preceding August, though he still stressed the "mystic" element in Emerson's version of truth:

Mr. Emerson was likewise there [in the Hall of Fantasy], leaning against one of the pillars and surrounded by an admiring crowd of writers and readers of the *Dial*, and all manner of Transcendentalists and disciples of the Newness, most of whom betrayed the power of his intellect by its modifying influence upon their own. He had come into the hall in search, I suppose, either of a fact or a real man; both of which he was as likely to find there as elsewhere. No more earnest seeker after truth than he, and few more successful finders of it; although sometimes the truth assumes a mystic unreality and shadowiness in his grasp.

Emerson had just returned from the lecturing trip when Hawthorne set to work on another sketch, "The Celestial Railroad," far sharper satirically than the other, but more nearly indebted to the allegorical Bunyan than to the affluent Rabelais. Without naming Emerson, he portrayed "the terrible giant Transcendentalist," who had recently taken over a cave once occupied by those hoary troglodytes, Pagan and Pope. Seizing travelers as they passed by the cave mouth, the monster fattened them for his table on a diet of smoke, mist, moonshine, raw potatoes, and sawdust. No one had yet been able to see him clearly enough to describe him except to say that, like Shelley's Demogorgon, he resembled "a heap of fog and duskiness." In the end, Hawthorne had achieved a rough landscape of the cloud-cuckoo-land that he sometimes took to be Emerson's philosophical home, and he sent off the pages to the *Democratic Review* to be published in May.

These and other sketches emanated from the Manse with a regularity that would have been impossible for a writer more socially active than Hawthorne. He stayed home, sat on the seat of his pantaloons, and wrote, with interludes of sawing and splitting wood for fuel and exercise. Once a day, by his account,

I trudge through snow and slosh to the village, look into the Post Office, and spend an hour at the reading-room [of the local Athenaeum]; and then return home, generally without having spoken a word to any human being. My wife is, in the strictest sense, my sole companion; and I need no other—there is no vacancy in my mind, any more than in my heart. In truth, I have spent so many years in total seclusion from all human society, that it is no wonder if I now feel all my desires satisfied by this sole intercourse. But my Dove has come to me from the midst of many friends, and a large circle of acquaintance; yet she lives from day-to-day in this solitude, seeing nobody but myself and our Molly [Bryan], while the snow of our avenue is untrodden for weeks by any footstep save mine; yet she is always cheerful. . . . Thank God that I suffice for her boundless heart.

To this quiet mode of life there were exceptions. About the middle of February Sophia fell on the ice and suffered a miscarriage. "One grief we had," wrote Hawthorne, "all else has been happiness. Nor did the grief penetrate to the reality of our life. We do not feel as if our promised child was taken from us forever." Their current name for the Manse was "the old Abbey," in contrast to the house in Salem where Hawthorne had grown up, which he called "Castle Dismal," inhabited by his mother, his sisters, and innumerable cats. The old Abbey included a single cat named Pigwigger and later a Newfoundland pup called Leo. Husband and wife separated for two weeks in March, Sophia to Boston to stay with her parents, Hawthorne to Salem to check on his family.

Apart from these excursions, Hawthorne stayed in his study, which he called "the most delightful little nook . . . that ever afforded its snug seclusion to a scholar." Although it had been recently refurbished, this was the room where Emerson had composed *Nature*, pausing between paragraphs to gaze through the western windows at the Paphian sunsets, slightly obscured by the branches of a willow. One day in April, Hawthorne borrowed Sophia's ring to etch one of the windows:

Nath Hawthorne
This is his study
1843

Above his name Sophia wrote, "Man's accidents are God's purposes," and signed her name: Sophia A. Hawthorne. Under his inscription appeared a small prose poem: "The smallest twig / Leans clear against the sky"—to which Hawthorne added, "Composed by my wife / and written with her diamond." And Sophia: "Inscribed by my / husband at sunset / April 3d 1843 / In the gold light SAH." Below that was *Sund,* no doubt meant for Sunday, though April 3 fell that year on a Monday. The symbolic value of these inscriptions was to make the Manse and the study more their own than ever, as if they had now permanently superseded Emerson, and even exorcised by such an act the more elderly Emersonian ghosts.

Sophia returned to Boston on April 7 to see her sister Mary, about to be married to Horace Mann and to spend a six-month honeymoon in Europe. Hawthorne split some wood, ate a solitary dinner, and was just recording Sophia's departure in his journal when Thoreau appeared with the news that he would soon be leaving for Staten Island, and that Ellery Channing was coming to live in Concord in the small red farmhouse near Emerson's. Ellery, thought Hawthorne, was "but a poor substitute for Mr. Thoreau." Indeed, Thoreau was one of the few "with whom to hold intercourse is like hearing the wind among the boughs of a forest-tree."

Next day came Emerson for a long talk, one of the best, said Hawthorne, that they had yet enjoyed. As usual, he wore "a sunbeam in his face," and spoke admiringly of Margaret Fuller, Ellery Channing, and Sam Ward—all of them closer associates of his than Hawthorne would ever be. When Thoreau's name was mentioned, Hawthorne caught the implication that Emerson might welcome the end of his long stay at Coolidge Castle: his brusque manner, his argumentativeness over trifles, and his habit of contradicting could sometimes be a little wearing. Hawthorne was ready to admit that "such a sturdy and uncompromising person" was perhaps "fitter to meet occasionally in the open air, than to have as a permanent guest at table and fireside." He also believed that families should live by themselves, as he had firmly told Margaret Fuller in 1842. But in less than a year of sporadic association, he had come to revere Thoreau, especially his love of nature, but also his "high and classic cultivation" under that outward cloak of "wild freedom."

Hawthorne was sporting a black-and-purple eye from a wood-chopping accident when Thoreau reappeared on the eleventh. He wanted to take one last row in the *Pond Lily* (née *Musketaquid*) before leaving Concord. The boat was drawn up at the bottom of the orchard and filled with water. They bailed it out and set sail on the swollen river. Coming back, they boarded a large cake of ice, riding it home with the leaky boat in tow. Hawthorne had just gone out to his woodhouse behind the Manse when Molly Bryan ran out to say that Emerson had come to call. He wanted to read Hawthorne a letter from Ellery Channing, whose first volume of poems would soon be published.

Although the ground was still covered with melting snow, the sudden spate of visitors after the winter solitude gave notice that the season was changing. By the end of the month, robins and swallows were back, a few gulls ventured upriver from the sea, and huge flocks of blackbirds vociferated, said Hawthorne, like a convention of politicians. He bought a load of manure and thought of spading up the garden. "I hate all labor," he wrote, "but less that of the hands than of the head."

By the time of their first wedding anniversary in July, the garden was flourishing "like Eden itself." Hawthorne, who could never write well in summer, spent much of his time outdoors, hoping for renewal of his creative powers in the fall. Dr. Peabody brought Sophia a batch of clay and she set about modeling a bust of her husband. The Hillards came out from Boston for a long weekend. But the most memorable visitor was Sophia's friend Anna Shaw. The Emersons were bidden to dinner with her, but Emerson came alone. Anna was at her best, "in full glory of her golden curls, flowing free over her neck and brows, so that she looked like the goddess Diana, or Aurora." When Emerson arrived, wrote Sophia, he "shone back to the shining Anna. He was truly 'tangled in the meshes of her golden hair,' for he reported in several places how beautiful it was, afterwards. It was very warm, and after Mr. Emerson left us, we went out upon the lawn under the shady trees, and Anna extended herself on the grass, leaning her arms upon a low cricket, and 'Sydnian showers of sweet discourse' distilled upon us."

Sophia's report to her sister Mary on Emerson's response to Anna Shaw was certainly perceptive and possibly guileless. Herself rather plain-featured, she had known him long enough to recognize that his interest perked up in the presence of more beautiful and graceful women than she was. She knew, moreover, of Lidian's persistent illnesses. Early in May, while Hawthorne was burning old leaves and beginning to plant his garden, Sophia had told her mother, "Mr. Emerson is to have no visitors this summer because he wants his wife to rest and have no [care?]. She is very feeble. This is the best thing I know of Mr. Emerson." Some weeks later, Lidian called at the Manse, shocking Sophia by saying that she was going to drown her "homeopathic powders in a tablespoon of heavy molasses." Tall and straight, but noticeably pale and thin, Lidian could not now compare physically with such incipient goddesses as Anna Shaw, and Sophia knew it.

What she could not know was Emerson's speculations on beauty, as when he wrote that "the felicities of design in art or in works of nature are shadows or forerunners of that beauty which reaches its perfection in the human form. All men are its lovers. Wherever it goes it creates joy and hilarity. . . . It reaches its height in woman. 'To Eve,' say the Mahometans, 'God gave two thirds of all beauty.' " Yet he recognized, like Keats before him, the evanescence of that beauty: ". . . the radiance of the human form, though sometimes astonishing, is only a burst of beauty for a few years or a few months at the perfection of youth, and in most rapidly declines," though "we remain lovers of it, only transferring our interest to interior excellences." Watching Anna Shaw at the Hawthornes' dinner party, he might have thought what he later wrote: "A beautiful person among the Greeks was thought to betray by this sign some secret favor of the immortal gods; and we can pardon pride, when a woman possesses such a figure that wherever she stands or moves or leaves a shadow on the wall, or sits for a portrait to the artist, she confers a favor on the world."

Earlier that summer, Emerson wrote to Thoreau in Staten Island of an afternoon's walk with Hawthorne: "Not until after our return did I read his 'Celestial Railroad,' which has a serene strength which one cannot afford not to praise,—in this low life." This seems to have been the first occasion on which he wrote admiringly of any of Hawthorne's prose. In August, he told Margaret Fuller that Hawthorne was "well and quiet in his study," adding, "I have never had a moment[']s regret or uneasiness concerning him, since he was here [in Concord]. Is not that much to say of a neighbor?"

In spite of his liking for "The Celestial Railroad," and his words of praise to Margaret, he could not help adding that neither Elizabeth Hoar nor Ellery Channing was yet sure of Hawthorne's genius. Next day he wrote his former student, Benjamin Hunt, whose "Voyage to Jamaica" had appeared in the *Dial* for July. Emerson said that he had discussed the piece with Hawthorne, who had admired it as "a solitary example of facts which had not lost their vigour by passing through the mind of a thinker." This acute remark, said Emerson, still harping on the old string, proved that Hawthorne was better as a critic than he was as a writer. Previous reservations about Hawthorne had been confided only to his journal or to close friends. Now he had revealed his private opinion to a relative stranger.

Sophia, pregnant for the second time, was now beginning to voice certain reservations about Emerson in letters to her mother. "Waldo Emerson knows not much of love," she wrote in September. "He has never yet said anything to show that he does. He is an isolation. He has never yet known what union meant with any soul." Pleased and proud over her own successful union with Hawthorne, Sophia said that it was not her husband's vocation to be a social visitor and chatting companion. "He is not a talker like Mr. Emerson. . . . Words with him are worlds, suns, and systems, and cannot move easily and rapidly. The light of them radiates from his well-like eyes, and from a smile. . . . Mr. Emerson was always content to talk to those wells of light and receive as response that smile only. And even Mr. E, who is ever searching after a *man,* used always to call him 'the Man.' " Both men were great. "But Mr. E. is not so whole-sided as Mr. Hawthorne. He towers straight up from a deep root. Mr. H. spreads abroad many branches also."

Despite their admiration for each other as people, a curious opposition of attitude toward the past continued to divide the two men. Born only thirteen months and a few miles apart, they both traced their paternal ancestries back to colonial New England of the 1630s. In the years of their maturity, both were aware of the surviving force of Puritanism in the internal lives of the citizens of nineteenth-century Massachusetts. "I acknowledge (with surprise that I could ever forget it,)" wrote Emerson, "the debt of myself and my brothers to that old religion which in those years, still dwelt like a Sabbath peace in the country population of New England, which taught privation, self-denial, and sorrow." When Dr. Ripley died, Emerson had apostrophized the band of "great, grim, earnest men" of whom Ripley was one of the last representatives: "I belong by natural affinity to other thoughts and schools than yours, but my affection hovers respectfully about your retiring footprints, your unpainted churches, street platforms, and sad offices[;] the iron-clad deacon and the wearisome prayer rich with the diction of the ages." This was an influence which he had voluntarily and even decisively shed, having seen it as his task to "invite men drenched in time to recover themselves and come out of time, and taste their native immortal air."

Hawthorne, on the other hand, was not only imaginatively "drenched" in the ancient ways of his Puritan ancestors but also felt a natural affinity for the superannuated. Side by side with the gentle fantasies of his other *Twice-Told Tales* stood the stories that he had dredged up from colonial history: "The Gray Champion," "The Maypole of Merry Mount," "The Gentle Boy," and "Endicott and the Red Cross." Although none of these dealt specifically with his own forebears, he was still haunted, as he wrote in the "Custom House Prologue" of 1849, by the dour figure of Major William Hathorne, who had been "present to [his] boyish imagination" as far back as he could remember. It gave him, he confessed, "a sort of home-feeling with the past" to think upon this "grave, bearded, sable-cloaked, and steeple-crowned progenitor" whose character embodied all the best and worst of Puritanical traits, as well as the Major's son John, who inherited his father's "persecuting spirit" and earned his place in New England history as one of the judges at the Salem witchcraft trials. Hawthorne was submerged in the Gothic aspects of American colonial history as Emerson would never be. He, too, had personally known lengthy services in unpainted and unheated churches, felt the cold that settled first in the flesh and then in the bones as the gray deacons stood with blue and folded hands, and the long-winded preachers harassed their congregations with hours of prayer and sermonizing.

But his invitation to his readers was far different from that of Emerson. He wanted to lead them back into former times in order to give them vicarious experiences of privation, self-denial, and sorrow, to say nothing of sin, expiation, and redemption, by which they could become freshly cognizant of the human predicament in all the ages of man. This was evidently a point of view toward the past that Emerson never completely accepted. His spiritual direction was futuristic rather than retrospective, and although, like Hawthorne, he was continuously conscious of the incursions of the past upon the present, he sought always to show how their adverse effects might be overcome through changes of mind, changes of heart.

Less than two weeks after his first meeting with Hawthorne in the fall of 1841, he defined skepticism in terms that might have been applied to Hawthorne himself: "Skepticism esteems ignorance organic and irremoveable, believes in the existence of pure malignity, believes in a poor decayed God who does what he can to keep down the nuisances, and to keep the world going for our day. It believes the actual to be necessary; it argues habitually from the exception instead of the rule; and if it went to the legitimate extreme, the earth would smell with suicide." Hawthorne did not carry his innate skepticism to its ultimate extremity, any more than Emerson was willing to follow certain of his more enthusiastic followers into the excesses of the Transcendentalist position. Between the two men lay a few rods of common ground, and from time to time they met upon it.

Chapter Twenty-three

CHANNING IN CONCORD,
1843–45

IN THE SPRING OF 1843, EMERSON ASSISTED WITH THE publication of Ellery Channing's first volume of poems, paid for by Sam Ward and brought out in Boston in May. The book contained an elegy called "The Sleeping Child." The subtitle was "Waldo Emerson, Dead," and the closing stanza said:

> Let your tears dissolve in peace!
> For he holds high company;
> And he seeks, with famous men,
> Statelier lines of ancestry;
> He shall shame the wisest ones
> In that palace of the suns.

Among the domestic events of that summer were other quiet reminders of the absent child. During Lidian's Plymouth vacation, Emerson wrote his wife that the baby Edith was "admired of all beholders," who filled her days with caresses, naps, currants, raspberries, and perambulations in the garden. She was cutting teeth, though with less complaint than Waldo had shown some years earlier. He had cried incessantly for molasses candy. Edie was content with custards. Nelly, at four and a half, was far livelier than her sister, "as much in papa's eyes, nose, and mouth as a fly." When she heard that Herr Driesbach's menagerie was coming to town, she gave her father no peace until he agreed to take her. Waldo had fervently disliked a much smaller show with a horse that carried baskets. But Nelly watched entranced when the trainer slapped and kissed a tiger. Afterward she rode the lone elephant's back with joyous aplomb.

Since May 5 Ellery and his wife, Ellen, had been close neighbors in the four-room red farmhouse next below Emerson's on the Turnpike. "Ellery has many values for me," wrote Emerson, "or would have, if I were better and more social. . . . For his sake I wish I were younger and gladder for he is, I think, very susceptible of influence from such as he could love." With his usual blend of hope and generosity, he assured his English friend John Sterling that Channing, though young, was "the best poet we have." In the privacy of his journal he was more circumspect. "When Ellery's muse finds an aim, whether some passion, or some fast faith, any kind of string on which these wild and sometimes brilliant beads can be strung, we shall have a poet." But the problems he had noticed in 1839 were still evident: "He breaks faith continually with the intellect. . . . If only I could confide that he had any steady meaning before him, that he kept faith with himself; but I fear that he has changed his purpose with every verse; was led up and down . . . with the exigences of the rhyme . . . and stopped when he came to the end of the paper." Although Emerson did not say so, some of these tendencies were apparent even in Ellery's little elegy for Waldo.

During Thoreau's absence on Staten Island, Ellery took his place as Emerson's walking companion. Emerson found that he could be very good-natured one minute and in the next could shock his associates with his cold selfishness. Ellery's "freaks" were "entitled to no more charity than the dulness and madness of others which he despises." Elizabeth Hoar, whom he adored and saluted in verse, compared him to the wood elf in the fairy tale with whom a young girl fell in love only to grow uneasy, wishing that he might be baptized. Ellery reminded Margaret Fuller of "a great genius with a little wretched boy trotting beside him." The small boy often predominated. He took a surly pleasure in demeaning the great, as when he said that Wordsworth wrote "like a man who takes snuff." He might have been thinking of himself when he told Emerson that "writers never do anything: they are passive observers." His absent friend Thoreau would never be a writer; he was "as active as a shoemaker."

The two strollers kept watch on the Boston to Fitchburg Railroad as it bored north and west through the pastoral scenery. Every day but Sunday they heard the distant thump of blasting operations. Out at the site in August, Emerson found a gang of forty or fifty Irish laborers sweating with pickaxes and shovels under the cold eye of their job boss. Their jerry-built shanties clustered along the riverbank, and one of the women told Emerson that her man was working long hours at short wages—dark to dark for fifty cents a day. Emerson the moralist reflected that their peaceful shovels were better than the martial pikes they might have been carrying in the Old Country; Emerson the aesthetician thought that a sculptor could have learned much from the postures, dress, and carriage of these husky toilers. Through the winter of 1843–44 the line inched ahead at a cost of $22,000 a mile. Walking in the frozen woods near Lincoln, Emerson saw that the snowbanks were liberally sprinkled with tobacco juice, a sign of the times.

"I know you are not a 'marker of days,' " wrote Margaret Fuller late in January 1844, "yet it seems to me this season can never pass without opening anew the deep wound." She hoped Lidian's current pregnancy would produce another son: "Men do not feel themselves represented to the next generation by *daughters*." She still missed the absent child and believed that he had filled a unique place in his father's life. Emerson's reply on January 30 confirmed this surmise: "When last Saturday night Lidian said, 'It is two years today'—I only heard the bellstroke again." He had lately been reading Ben Jonson's account of his son's death in the London plague. Jonson afterward saw the child in a vision "of a manly shape, and of that growth he thinks he shall be at the resurrection." Emerson sharply recalled how his own "beautiful statue" had assumed "that same preternatural maturity" the day following his death. Ellery's threnody had not been far off the mark:

> Now he roams the sun's dominion,
> Our chill fortunes quite forsaken;
> There his eyes have purer sight
> In that calm, reflected light.

Between February and April, Emerson paid Ellery fifty cents a cord for chopping twenty-five cords of firewood. After such daytime labors, which he seemed to enjoy, Ellery gave his evenings to the rounding out of his epistolary and semiautobiographical "novel," which Emerson was serializing in the *Dial* as "The Youth of the Poet and Painter." Like Emerson, he had a pregnant and ailing wife, but unlike him, an obligation to perform many of the domestic chores in the red farmhouse. But the spring was full of imminent change. The *Dial* and Ellery's "novel" both ended in April. Emerson hailed the demise of his editorial responsibilities while readily assuming such other obligations as helping Margaret with the publication of her travel diary of her western tour of 1843, *Summer on the Lakes*, which appeared in June, the preparation of his address on the anniversary of the emancipation of the Negroes in the British West Indies for delivery on August 1, and the completion of his second volume of essays, which appeared in October.

For the more restive residents of Concord, the great public event of 1844 was the inauguration of passenger service on the new railroad. D-Day was June 17. The ride from Concord depot to Charlestown took less than an hour. "The cars will run regularly four times every day, both ways," wrote Emerson exuberantly. "The reason why I wish to live near Boston, is, because I use Boston." After nine years in the stagecoaches, he would now be nearer than ever to the Athens of America, in time and convenience if not in distance.

The Shaker village in the opposite direction continued to amuse and irritate him. In the middle of June he drove out there with young Isaac Hecker, late of Brook Farm and Fruitlands, and was newly disgusted by the Shakers' shuffling "dunce-dance" in which they held out limp and shaking hands like dog paws, and chanted their monotonous homemade hymns. He was somehow reminded of his visit to the Spedale dei Pazzi at Palermo in the spring of 1833. "These poor countrymen with their nasty religion," he wrote, "fancy themselves *The Church* of the world, and are as arrogant as the poor negroes on the Gambia river." Although they worked hard, they lived for show, "with [their] buildings ostentatiously neat." They were doers, not lovers, so exaggerating the virtue of celibacy that a chance visitor might imagine that he had entered a "hospital ward of invalids afflicted with priapism." Apart from Shaker publications, their only reading was the Bible. In their eyes the capital sin of world history was Adam's impregnation of Eve. One wondered how they explained all the "begats" in the Pentateuch.

Celibacy was not the general custom in Concord. That spring and summer three new babies enlarged the population of the Emerson circle. First prize in the sweepstakes went to Sophia Hawthorne. On March 3 she bore an auburn-haired girl, promptly named Una after Edmund Spenser's heroine in the first book of *The Faerie Queene*. In January Lidian Emerson had called at the Manse to advise Sophia about baby powder. Most mothers used perfumed hair powder, said she, but plain starch was preferable, "made palpable by pounding, grinding, and sifting," and applied with something called a puff.

Ellen Channing was next. On April 11, as her lying-in drew near, she and Ellery moved out of the Red Lodge into a larger house on the Lexington Road. The child, a girl, born May 2, was named for Margaret Fuller, Ellen's sister. Unlike his friend at the Manse, Ellery was an obstreperous father. He ardently disliked the practical nurse, his nerves were set on edge by the infant's caterwauling, and he fled to the White Mountains to regain his composure. Hawthorne disgustedly called him "a gump"—"little better than an idiot"—who ought to have been "whipt often and soundly in his childhood." But Ellery again fled the obligations of fatherhood in July by joining Thoreau in Pittsfield for a walking tour that extended to the Catskills.

Unlike Sophia and Ellen, Lidian Emerson, aged forty-two, was now at the end of her child-bearing years. "Lidian's hour draws near," wrote her husband on June 17, "and between this and the 4 July, she promises me a babe: a work which dear nature in civilized countries seems to take sadly to heart, and one way or another to make us pay high prices for—tears, groans, indispositions, wondrous discomforts and spleens, and very shattered constitutions." The baby appeared a week later than expected. As Margaret Fuller had hoped, it was a boy, born July 10 and named Edward Waldo Emerson. As had happened with all three of her previous pregnancies, Lidian quickly bounced back from the trauma of delivery. Next day, Sophia Hawthorne paid a call at the Emersons' and climbed the stairway to the second floor front. "It is a very red blackhaired baby and quite large," she reported to her mother, "but I could not see well its face. Mrs. E. was sitting up and there seemed to be a mob in the chamber. Mr. Emerson looked taller and more shining than ever."

With a mixture of relief and self-doubt Emerson returned to his literary labors: "I am really trying to end my old endless chapters that they may decently appear in the world, but the stress of my thought too closely resembles our Concord River which is narrow and slow and shallow." Along with work on his essays, he spent many hours in developing his address on the West Indian emancipation. Caroline Sturgis, who was knocking around Massachusetts that summer, wrote from Brook Farm for further particulars. Except for the song of the grasshoppers she knew nothing of what was going on in the world, and she wanted to come to Concord to find out. Were the cars running? Could she come to pass the day? Was Emerson to speak in the morning or the evening? She couldn't come in the evening, for all the spare rooms in the village would certainly be engaged and she was not Indian enough to sleep outdoors. She half apologized for having played a tearful Niobe during her visit to the Emersons in 1843. Now she had renounced Niobe and for the moment was a phoenix lying amid her ashes. But she "most seriously" desired to come to hear Emerson, joining the audience of several hundred antislavery women from Concord and environs whose fair this year commemorated the tenth anniversary of the freeing of the West Indian slaves.

The women in charge of the arrangements set up their tables in the hall of the courthouse, having been refused access to a glade in Sleepy Hollow—not yet a cemetery—and having been obliged by intermittent rain to decline Hawthorne's offer to let them use the grounds of the Manse. The selectmen forbade the sexton to ring the meetinghouse bell to summon the audience. But Henry Thoreau and Ellery Channing had just returned that morning from their Catskill trip, and Henry, defying the authorities, rang the bell "right merrily" to convene the meeting in the Town Hall.

Emerson had long hated slavery. A journal entry of 1835 stated: "Though the voice of society should demand a defense of slavery . . . that service can never be expected from me. . . . I do not wish to live in a nation where slavery exists. . . . In the light of Christianity is no such thing as slavery. The only bondage it recognizes is that of Sin." His essay on "Compensation" elaborated these opinions: "If you put a chain around the neck of a slave, the other end fastens itself around your own." But this day's meeting marked the first occasion on which he chose to explore at length and in public the evils of slavery. His theme was, in essence, "Conscience rolled on its pillow and could not sleep," as if the current antislavery agitation had at last aroused him from broken slumbers to take a public stand.

He celebrated "the bright example that England set on this day ten years ago." It had been "a moral revolution," for "the end was noble and the means were pure." A new element had entered modern politics, "namely, the civilization of the negro." A man had been "added to the human family," and "if you have man, black or white is of no significance. . . . The civility of no race can be perfect while another race is degraded." Emerson went on to summarize the antislavery efforts in England from the middle of the eighteenth century to the abolition of the slave trade in 1807. Yet this was not the end of the age-old curse. In 1821 a quarter million victims were abducted from Africa. In the port of Havana alone, some 30,000 were put ashore. One slave ship, evading a British man-of-war, had thrown 500 blacks into the sea. It was not until 1834 that the British Parliament passed a bill of emancipation and appropriated 20 million pounds sterling for division among its nineteen colonies to pay off slave owners. But neither money nor law destroyed the "habit of oppression," and the same "licentious despotism" continued unabated. Not until the beginning of August 1838 did the shackles drop at last from every slave in England's western colonies.

Emerson pulled no punches. His Massachusetts audience had not personally witnessed the actualities: "men's backs flayed with cowhides . . . runaways hunted with bloodhounds into swamps . . . and, in cases of passion, a planter throwing his negro into a copper of boiling cane-juice." Had they or he seen such horrors, none of them could have endured the sight. "The blood is moral; the blood is anti-slavery: it runs cold in the veins: the stomach rises in disgust and curses slavery."

Thoreau, who had helped to gather the audience that wet day, sent a copy of Emerson's address to N. P. Rogers, editor of the *Herald of Freedom*, an abolitionist paper published in Concord, New Hampshire, which shortly printed the full text. Having read it with admiration, the Quaker poet John Greenleaf Whittier asked Emerson to a meeting of the Middlesex County Freedom Convention held at Acton in September. Emerson declined: he was reading proof on his second book of essays and confessed that he had no skill in debate. He half promised to send Whittier his ideas on "the best way of befriending the slave and ending slavery." But the opposing forces seemed for the time to be ineluctable. "What argument, what eloquence can avail," asked Emerson, "against the power of that one word *niggers*? The man of the world annihilates the whole combined force of all the antislavery societies of the world by pronouncing it."

So saying, he returned to his literary labors. Repeated rereadings of his essays had made him freshly aware of the inherent vices of his prose style and the "tough unalterableness of sentences" that he well knew must be altered. When the proofs were sent in and the book came out, he surprised himself by exuberantly buying fourteen acres of land on the north shore of Walden Pond for $200. This purchase, he told his brother, must be regarded as "the light headed frolics of a hack of a scribe when released at last from months of weary tending on the printers devil!"

The place on Lexington Road held the Channings for a mere seven months. By mid-November, while Ellen was preparing to spend the winter at Dr. Walter Channing's house in Boston, Ellery suddenly departed for New York. It was another instance of that perennial restlessness that had made him pull up stakes in Cincinnati in 1842. He broke the trip with a three-day visit to Margaret and Caroline, who had been vacationing at Fishkill Landing on the Hudson since the first of October, and then moved downriver to his job with Horace Greeley's *Tribune*. "His arrival at N.Y. was unfortunately timed," said Emerson. "Greeley, sick and prostrate, was just leaving the city—he threw to Channing some broadest general directions, and left him to make his own work—the one thing he could not do." Emerson asked his brother to invite him out to Staten Island some Sunday. "He has left his wife and child for the present, here in Concord. Channing is of a very tender and delicate nature as poets are wont to be and though in manner and speech a man of the world, yet as easily disconcerted and disheartened as a child." Most of all he stood "in need of society and affection."

"It is all an experiment," said Emerson, "but he wants work and a living." Like most of Ellery's other experiments, this one failed. Emerson's young friends Giles Waldo and William Tappan each took him in for a time, but their proffered friendship did little to assuage his homesickness for Concord. Emerson missed his presence. "I have my old neighbors still, Hawthorne, Thoreau, and Alcott," he told Sam Ward, "but can ill spare this incomparable companion." Ellery felt much the same. When Emerson wrote him encouragingly in February, he replied by calling himself a child of impulse looking up to his Concord champion, who stood firm, secure, and "cased in triple steel."

As might have been expected, the New York experiment ended in less than four months. "Ellery Channing has been here in our house for a week or two," wrote Emerson on April 5, "exploring Concord again for a farm which he would buy." His wife Ellen had come out from Boston to do some preliminary scouting. In the end they decided to build, rather than renting or buying. Near the end of April they chose a twenty-acre tract on Punkawtasset

Hill, out past the Manse roughly two miles north of the center of the village. Over the summer of 1845 they built a cottage and moved in early in September. Hawthorne, Thoreau, and Emerson once again had their incomparable companion. The only catch was that Hawthorne was planning to leave Concord early in October. It was like the old game of musical chairs.

THOREAU IN
NEW YORK, 1843

BY JANUARY 1843, HENRY THOREAU HAD BEEN OCCUPYING the room at the head of the stairs in Emerson's house for twenty-one months. During Emerson's extended absences from home since the spring of 1841, he had been serving, so far as his health allowed, as majordomo to the household, gardener, carpenter, tree surgeon, companion to the children, and sometime secretary. "I have been your pensioner for nearly two years," he now wrote Emerson at Philadelphia. " . . . It has been as free a gift as the sun or the summer, though I have sometimes molested you with my mean acceptance of it,—I who have failed to render even those slight services of the *hand* which would have been a sign, at least; and, by the fault of my nature, have failed of many better and higher services. But I will not trouble you with this, but for once thank you as well as Heaven."

During February, Thoreau sought to repay Emerson's long hospitality by helping to assemble some of the contents of the forthcoming *Dial*. His own contributions were three original poems; a short account of the Ionian lyricist Anacreon, with eleven sample translations; selections from the "Sayings of Confucius"; and a brief ironic essay on the so-called "Dark Ages." His main editorial task was to procure a long review of Bronson Alcott's works, done by his English friend, Charles Lane, which was to stand first in the table of contents as if to celebrate Alcott's eminence as an educator.

Returning to Concord early in March, Emerson followed up on Henry's preliminary labors. There was reason to think that this might be the final issue of the *Dial*: Elizabeth Peabody, publisher and business manager, pointed out that with only 220 paid subscriptions, the journal was no longer earning expenses. This, said Emerson, borrowing a phrase from Wordsworth's "Resolution and Independence," looked like "a leading from above," a supernal warning that publication ought to stop. But by the end of April, seeing that Alcott, Lane, and others were eager to continue, he resolved to carry on for one more year. The April number contained Charles Emerson's sprightly account of his voyage to Puerto Rico in 1831 and Margaret Fuller's essay on the Italian sculptor Canova. But the most memorable item of all was probably James Freeman Clarke's memoir of George Keats, brother of the poet, late of Louisville, who had preserved John Keats's commentaries on Milton's *Paradise Lost*, which were now printed for the first time.

Emerson undertook other tasks, including arrangements for the American publication of Carlyle's *Past and Present*. With the latest *Dial* behind him, he stole a glorious April day to prune his fruit trees, calling himself "a whittling Yankee." He welcomed Ellery Channing and his bride as immediate neighbors in a cottage named Red Lodge on the Cambridge Turnpike, and accepted Ellery's prose and poetry for the next number of the *Dial*. "Ellery has many values for me," he told Margaret, "or would have, if I were better and more social." Like other close friends of Caroline Sturgis, he knew that she had been in love with Ellery and that she had been disappointed when he married Ellen Fuller. In May, Emerson quietly opened a campaign to make her acquainted, however distantly, with William A. Tappan, an employee in a Wall Street brokerage house—"a lonely beautiful brooding youth" who had mightily impressed him during his recent stay in New York. Tappan, he told Thoreau, spoke seldom but easily and strongly, and "moves like a deer." His only problem was that he did not read enough.

Another offshoot of Emerson's sojourn in New York was an arrangement whereby Thoreau would go to live on Staten Island, serving as tutor to Judge William Emerson's oldest son, Willie. Emerson praised Thoreau in a letter to his brother—"no truer and no purer person lives in wide New York; and he is a bold and a profound thinker"—but also warned that "he may easily chance to pester you with some accidental crotchets and perhaps a village exaggeration of the value of facts." These habits of Henry's were well known among his Concord peers, and would presently become apparent to Judge Emerson. Although Lidian complained that she could not do without Thoreau as general factotum in the Concord household, "the Oneida Chief," as Emerson called him, left for his new job on May 6. He may have been hastened on his way by the horde of invaders .that had begun assembling in the Concord woods as soon as the frost was out of the ground. These were the engineers, surveyors, and subcontractors who were laying out the right-of-way for the extension of the Fitchburg Railroad, which was to pass the western end of Walden Pond. They were soon followed by hundreds of Irish laborers to perform the dogwork of digging and leveling the roadbed. "I hope you will not be washed away by the Irish sea," Thoreau wrote his sister Sophia. He was evidently happy enough to escape the incipient chaos in what once had been his quiet woodland domain.

Thoreau's departure was accomplished at some cost to Lidian, and he, for his part, seems to have felt much the same. "I think of you as some elder sister of mine," he wrote her from Staten Island,

> whom I could not have avoided,—a sort of lunar influence,—only of such age as the moon, whose time is measured by her light. You must know that you represent to me woman . . . I like to deal with you, for I believe you do not lie or steal, and these are very rare virtues. I thank you for your influence for two years. I was fortunate to be subjected to it, and am now to remember it. It is the noblest gift we can make. . . . You have helped to keep my life "on loft," as Chaucer says of Griselda, and in a better sense. You always seemed to look down at me as from some elevation—some of your high humilities—and I was better for having to look up. I felt taxed not to disappoint your expectation; for could there be any accident so sad as to be respected for something better than we are?

Thoreau's allusion to Griselda, the patient and virtuous heroine of "The Clerk's Tale," was neither an extravagant compliment nor yet a full reading of Lidian's character. Back in 1835, during the colloquy that followed Emerson's proposal of marriage, she had said that she shrank from "the load of care and labor" that she would have to carry if she became his wife. This fear was prescient, but she could hardly have known then what she had learned by 1843. Emerson's lecture tours, which often kept him away from home for months at a time, left her to manage the household as well as to dole out piecemeal payments to creditors. Although she commonly had a crew of servants, some of them were of limited usefulness, and the efflux of daily problems was often overwhelming, even with Thoreau's skilled assistance as a troubleshooter.

As Thoreau must have known after two years in the same house, Lidian could not stand to hurry or be hurried, whereas her husband's life was composed of a series of deadlines. Although generally thoughtful of her welfare, he seemed at times remarkably obtuse about leaving her to carry on, even though they both recognized his need of earning lecture money to keep up the establishment. He repeatedly supposed that "a perfect tranquillity" prevailed in his absence. "Lidian dear," he had written from Hanover in 1838, "I trust you have grown stronger each hour, not having the fear of Hurry in the shape of a husband ever at your elbow."

The absent paterfamilias was still trying to salve his conscience with the same supposition early in January 1843. The first anniversary of Waldo's death was approaching, but for consolation there were two small and busy daughters in the house, as well as Emerson's mother, the faithful and energetic servant Louisa, and Henry Thoreau in the room at the top of the stairs. Emerson was "well lodged and well fed" at Barnum's Hotel in Baltimore, which Charles Dickens had called the best hostelry in America. From there he wrote home:

> And so tell me, kind wife, how is all with you at home? those two young things that are left there with you? How walks the gentlest Edie? how goes the affable Nelly? housewifely, talking by night? How fares my gracious mother? And how [Elizabeth] my sister dear? And Henry brave and good? . . . and have the good angels, or that more sombre Spirit that loves you so well, prevailed over your thought by night and by day? The Good Spirit is always nearest do not hearken to that Sad brother. With the good Louisa by your side, and all your helpful company, and the thin critical man removed so far away, I think of you as very placid. . . . You are to send me you know a financial letter reciting all the depths and straits of your beggary and the methods by which you have kept the regiment of creditors at bay, and what truces and treaties you have made and what is the latest day, on which, if succour do not first come, Coolidge Castle must be surrendered and sacked?

The "sombre Spirit" was Lidian's tendency to melancholia—what her daughter Ellen later called "sad thoughts which were the heaviest cloud of all, and made the dungeon in which she suffered for so many years. They were the natural result of her character, her temper, and her principles." Emerson's adjective, "sombre," was exact: Lidian literally preferred deep shade to full sun. According to Ellen, "she always spoke of 'the sun, my enemy.' She said she felt worse and worse every day till noon. About four in the afternoon, relief began to come, when she felt better and better till at midnight she was bright and well." This explains Emerson's comment on little Ellen—the "affable Nelly—housewifely, talking by night." But he knew by long experience that the "Sad brother" of gloom was as close to Lidian as the "thin critical man" when he was at home.

Now, approaching his fortieth birthday, he was determined, as he had written her from the Carlton Hotel in New York, to develop a philosophy of *carpe diem,* forgetting "all the particulars of yesterday and the day before, and all the expectations of tomorrow" in order to "suck the deep life of the present hour." He would have liked to have her follow this same regimen. She had been ill again during his absence, and only recovered a week after his return. But her recoveries were nearly always temporary. His journal for this period contained two pertinent entries within three pages. One was cryptic: "Queenie's epitaph[:] 'Do not wake me.' " The other was apparently a quotation: "Dear husband, I wish I had never been born. I do not see how God can compensate me for the sorrow of existence."

In June he said that she was still "a wreck of dyspepsia and debility." The dyspepsia reappeared in July and was assuaged only by a three-week vacation in her beloved Plymouth. In September she fell ill again with her usual low-grade fever. This time she resorted to homeopathy, seemed to respond favorably, and took another short vacation with her brother's family in Boston. Just before Thanksgiving, Emerson conducted her back to the city, along with Elizabeth Hoar. They met the famous actor-manager William Charles Macready and watched him play *Hamlet* in the first stage production Elizabeth had ever seen. Ten days later Lidian came down with a cold and associated ailments to which, as Emerson said, paraphrasing *Hamlet*, "her flesh [was] much too much heir to." Once more she took to her chamber, though she did come downstairs for the annual "Good Friday" dinner the day after Thanksgiving, and seems to have dined with the family until Christmas. As if she were seeking a new anodyne, she began in December to remodel the dining room. But this burst of energy was atypical. About the time of her second visit to Boston, she had begun her fourth pregnancy and was soon involved with what Emerson later summarized as "tears, groans, indispositions, wondrous discomforts and spleens."

From his new base on Staten Island, Thoreau anxiously followed the reports of Lidian's illnesses through the summer and fall. On reaching New York he was himself confined for a week with a severe cold and bronchitis, but he presently began to revel in the flowering fruit trees and the proximity of the sea. During the first month he made a few trips to the city, finding it "a thousand times meaner" than he had imagined: "The pigs in the street are the most respectable part of the population." But he liked Emerson's young friends, William Tappan and Giles Waldo, who bore him off to dinner at an English ale house near Wall Street. His tutorial duties were not onerous: teaching Latin to Willie from nine until two left him free to wander the fields and beaches in off-hours. In July he wrote his mother about the current plague of seventeen-year locusts that was badly damaging the fruit and forest trees besides assailing all human eardrums with the high-pitched, incessant choral din of the mating season. Soon they would disappear as mysteriously as they had come out of the ground, not to return until 1860.

The plague in Concord was the railroad. Emerson reported that the woods were now swarming with engineers bearing theodolites and red flags, and the streets of the village were teeming with Irish laborers. Margaret Fuller was far away, having undertaken a western tour with Sarah Clarke and (for a time) Caroline Sturgis. The expedition had begun with a "sadly cold and rainy" visit to Niagara where Emerson himself had not yet been. Margaret's journal of the three-month trip would be rewritten and enlarged to become her first major book after the earlier translations from Goethe and *Günderode* and would appear a year hence as *Summer on the Lakes, 1843*. The *Dial* for July opened with her article "The Great Lawsuit," later expanded as *Woman in the Nineteenth Century*. Thoreau sent Emerson an acute appraisal of the *Dial* article, calling it "a noble piece, rich extempore writing—talking with pen in hand—It is too good not to be better even. In writing[,] conversation should be folded many times thick." The same number of the *Dial* closed with an announcement from Alcott and Lane about the establishment of their experimental farm, Fruitlands, near the Shaker settlement at Harvard.

Since the Griselda letter of May, a small correspondence had sprung up between Lidian and Henry. "My very dear Friend," he wrote her on June 20:

> I have only read a page of your letter and have come out to the top of the hill at sunset . . . to read the rest. . . . You seem to me to speak out of a very clear and high heaven. . . . Your voice seems not a voice, but comes as much from the blue heavens, as from the paper. . . . The thought of you will constantly elevate my life . . . as when I look up at the evening star. . . . Sometimes in Concord I found my actions dictated, as it were, by your influence. . . . To hear that you have sad hours is not sad to me. I rather rejoice at the richness of your experience. . . . Our sadness is not sad, but our cheap joys. Let us be sad about all we see and are, for so we demand and pray for better. . . . I could hope that you would get well soon, and have a healthy body for this world, but I know that cannot be—and the Fates, after all, are the accomplishers of our hopes. Yet I do hope you may find it a worthy struggle, and life seems grand still through the clouds. What wealth is it to have such friends that we cannot think of them without elevation. . . . I cannot tell you the joy your letter gives me—which will not quite cease till the latest time. Let me accompany your finest thought. I send my love to my other friend and brother, whose nobleness I slowly recognize.

Thoreau was obviously placing Lidian upon a very high pedestal. His experience with women had not been extensive, and he was so shy in their presence, as Emerson noticed with amusement, that he always blushed when passing through the kitchen where the maid and the cook were at work. It is doubtful if he could have summoned the courage to tell Lidian to her face what he had now written her from his distant hilltop. Yet in this transcendental love letter, blending romantic sentiment with a doctrine of stoical acceptance, he managed to convey the kind of advice she needed if she were ever to overcome her recurrent melancholia. Emerson's future friend Arthur Hugh Clough had not yet written the lyric beginning "Say not the struggle nought availeth," but Emerson's friend Thoreau, young as he was, had embodied its essential preachment in words designed to lift the spirits of Emerson's wife.

For whatever reason, Henry addressed his next letter to both the Emersons. He was nostalgic for Concord. His midnight thoughts reverted to "those dear hills," the river "still drinking its meadows," and half a dozen of the town's inhabitants—Lidian's sister Lucy, Elizabeth Hoar, George Minott and Edmund Hosmer, Hawthorne and Ellery Channing. Along with the Emersons, they were "a rare band" who did not "make half use enough of one another." Then he turned typically contrary: "But know, my friends, that I a good deal hate you all in my most private thoughts—as the substratum of the little love I bear you." Why hate? Why so little love? Was the sentence only meant as a counterpoise to the nostalgic temper of the rest of the letter? Or was it only a joke? He said in closing that he was sorry to learn that Mrs. Emerson's health had not improved. "But let her know that the Fates pay a compliment to those whom they make sick—and they have not to ask what have I done."

Emerson's answer, ignoring the passage on hate, thanked Henry for his "cordial greetings." Lidian, he said, was "at Plymouth to recruit her wasted strength," but had left word with him "to acknowledge and heartily thank" Henry for his most recent letter. So Emerson tactfully indicated that his wife had gladly received the communication from the hilltop but had left to her husband the task of acknowledging it. When Lidian afterward told Henry's family that she had heard from their son and brother, they were eager to see the letters. In those days the sharing of even presumably private letters was a fairly common practice. Lidian reluctantly consented, but warned Mrs. Thoreau that Henry "had exalted her by very undeserved praise." "O yes," said his mother, "Henry is very tolerant." If Henry heard of this incident, as he probably did, it would explain the change of tone in his letters to the Emersons during the late summer and fall. In August, he closed a note to Emerson with a message for Lidian: "Say to Mrs. Emerson that I am glad to remember how she too dwells there in Concord, and shall send her anon some of the thoughts that belong to her." In September, hearing that she was still unwell, he gave his regards to her through Emerson, but it was not until mid-October that he kept his promise to send her some "thoughts." They were nothing like those of the hilltop letter. Instead he asked for news about the annual berrying party, mentioned his current interest in the Elizabethan poet Francis Quarles, expressed his regret at her continuing ill health, and closed with a tenderly jocular allusion to her daughters, Ellen and Edith.

The only real altercation between Emerson and Thoreau came about while Emerson was editing "A Winter Walk" for the October *Dial*. He admired the allusions to the pickerel fisherman and the woodchopper, but took umbrage at Henry's use of oxymoron, the rhetorical linkage of contradictory terms—calling "a cold place sultry, a solitude public, and a wilderness *domestic.*" This struck Emerson as mere eccentric trickery. As usual he made the deletions he thought necessary with sovereign editorial aplomb, expecting no backtalk from the author. Thoreau perkily rejoined with a forthright critique of Emerson's "Ode to Beauty." It was wash day at Judge Emerson's and Henry had been banished from the house. He set down his objections in the middle of a cornfield, using the inkstand that Elizabeth Hoar had given him as a going-away present. He rightly called Emerson's attention to such awkward lines as "Thee knew I of old" and "Remediless thirst," and harangued him for having "sloped" too quickly to his rhymes, as if he had taken a hatchet and "chopped off the verses" as they emerged. "I had rather have the thoughts come ushered with a flourish of oaths and curses," wrote Henry. "Yet I love your poetry as I do little else that is near and recent." This last sentence was doubtless intended as a balm and a bandage for whatever wounds his sharp words might have inflicted. In the event, Emerson published "Ode to Beauty" with no changes at all.

Thoreau's Staten Island experiment may have helped to enlarge his horizons, but that was about all. He had not found William and Susan Emerson to be his "kith and kin in any sense," irreproachable and kindly though they were. Of his Latin pupil Willie he said that "I am not attracted toward him but as to youth generally. He shall frequent me, however, as much as he can, and I'll be I." Emerson came to understand the situation. A long time later he told Frank Sanborn that Judge Emerson and Henry Thoreau "were not men that could get along together.—Each would think whatever the other did was out of place." By the end of October he was already preparing for Thoreau's return. "If as we have heard, you will come home to Thanksgiving, you must bring something that will serve for Lyceum lecture," he wrote and sat back to await results.

Thoreau had assured his mother that he had not been homesick, but added that he would be perfectly content to sit in her backyard under the poplar tree "henceforth forever." Apart from "moping about" the fields and woods of the island until people took him for a surveyor, he had been making further trips into the city, cementing relations with Emerson's friends, the Reverend W. H. Channing and Henry James Senior; getting to know the dynamic editor of the *Tribune*, the tow-headed Horace Greeley, whom he found to be as "hearty [a] New Hampshire boy as one would wish to meet"; talking with Tappan and Giles Waldo in their noisy countinghouse; and reading voraciously in the Mercantile Library. His hope of selling articles to the magazines was largely frustrated until Hawthorne's editor, John L. O'Sullivan, finally bought two of his pieces. One of them, an essay-review of J. A. Etzler's book on the use of technology to harness natural forces for the benefit of mankind, appeared in the *Democratic Review* under Thoreau's witty title "Paradise (To Be) Regained." This sardonic article was in itself enough to justify his seven-month, self-imposed exile from his own native paradise. He came home to Concord, armed with a Lyceum lecture, in ample time for Thanksgiving.

Chapter Twenty-five

MARGARET FULLER IN
NEW YORK, 1844–46

IN THE LATE FALL OF 1844, MARGARET FULLER WAS GRADU-
ated magna cum laude from Boston and environs, from New England
Transcendentalism, from her position as nominal head of the Fuller family,
and from her nine years' fixation on Emerson—this last a slow withdrawal,
never complete but increasingly attenuated by distance and new interests.

During the early summer she had paid a visit to Concord with Caroline
Sturgis and Sarah Clarke. In July she stayed at the Manse with the Hawthornes and later moved to Ellery Channing's farmhouse on the Lexington
Road while Ellen and the new baby were in Boston. When she first reached
Concord the fruit trees were in bloom, but the very effulgence of the season
depressed her: "I cannot help wearying myself of this ugly cumbrous mass of
flesh. When all things are blossoming, it seems so strange not to blossom too;
that the quick thought within cannot remould its tenement. . . . I am such a
shabby plant, of such coarse tissue. I hate not to be beautiful when all around
is so."

On May 23, her thirty-fourth birthday, she set down the final sentence of
Summer on the Lakes. Two days later, Emerson turned forty-one. The seven-
year discrepancy in their ages was never wider than it now seemed to her. She
saw little of him, since Lidian was in the final stages of her fourth pregnancy
and guests at Coolidge Castle would have been an inconvenience. The Sage,
as Margaret called him, was more than usually aloof. "Any relation to him,"
she wrote in her commonplace book, "is deeply tragic on one side . . . but on

the other, how noble, how dear! . . . Let me once know him and I shall not be disappointed. But he is hard to know, the subtle Greek." Their one extended conversation centered on marriage, their old topic of 1841–42. "At present," she wrote, "I am able to take the superior view of life . . . but, I know, the deep yearnings of the heart and the bafflings of time will be felt again, and then I shall long for some dear hand to hold. But I shall never forget that my curse is nothing compared with that of those who have entered into those relations but not made them real; who only *seem* husbands, wives, and friends." Emerson, she added, had said as much only the other evening. She had a long talk with Elizabeth Hoar in Sleepy Hollow on the morning of July 3. "What fine just distinctions she made," wrote Margaret. "Worlds grew clearer." Part of the conversation concerned Elizabeth's eight years of "widowhood" following the death of Charles Emerson. "She said she would have for a motto: 'In Arcady I too was born / Tho' now a maiden all forlorn / I milk the cow with the crumpled horn.' "

But Margaret, also born in Arcady, was now entertaining other plans, specifically an offer from Horace Greeley to come to New York and work as literary critic for his newspaper, the *Tribune*. By the end of September, she had accepted Greeley's proposal. But her first move was a kind of working holiday at Fishkill Landing, New York, on the east bank of the Hudson ten miles south of Poughkeepsie. She gloried in the scenery of river and mountain; composed a snatch of blank verse about a dell where "evergreens and red and golden trees / At varying elevations grouped around"; and expanded her *Dial* article, "The Great Lawsuit," into a pamphlet with the somewhat grander title *Woman in the Nineteenth Century*. Caroline Sturgis was with her there when Ellery Channing passed through on his way to work for Greeley. He was still in New York when Margaret joined the staff, though she saw little of her errant brother-in-law. When he returned homesick to Concord in March, she was already earning her spurs in the fusty third-floor editorial rooms of the *Tribune* building on Nassau Street.

The invitation to join the staff was an indirect result of her "Conversations" in Boston. "My wife," wrote Greeley, "having spent much time in and near Boston, had there made Margaret's acquaintance, attended her conversations, accepted her leading ideas; and, desiring to enjoy her society more intimately and continuously, Mrs. G. planned and partly negotiated an arrangement whereby her monitor and friend became an inmate of our family and a writer for *The Tribune*."

For some thirteen years Greeley had been living and working in downtown New York, half a mile from City Hall. He had begun publication of the *Tribune* in April 1841. When James Polk defeated Henry Clay for the presidency in 1844, Greeley, who had worked hard for the Whig ticket, called himself "the worst beaten man on the continent . . . covered with boils and thoroughly used up." To recuperate, he had acquired a large old farmhouse that faced the East River at Turtle Bay and Forty-ninth Street, roughly opposite Blackwell's Island. Soon after the Greeleys took possession, Margaret joined the family, which then consisted of Mary Cheney Greeley, called Molly, and their eight-month-old son, Arthur, a flaxen-haired baby nicknamed Pickie, for whom Margaret soon developed an affection nearly as strong as the love she had lavished on Emerson's fair haired son Waldo in the years 1837-42.

Her sense of having discovered a *vita nuova* was apparent in a letter to her favorite brother, Richard, early in March 1845:

I have now a position where I can devote myself entirely to use its accessions, a noble career is before me yet. I want to be unimpeded by cares which I cannot, at this distance, attend to properly. I want that my friends should *wish* me now to act in my public career rather than towards them personally. I have given almost all my young energies to personal relations. I no longer feel inclined to this and wish to share and impel the general stream of thought.

Her career had taken a sharp turn since the days of her "Conversations" at Elizabeth Peabody's bookshop and her two-year unpaid editorship of the *Dial*. Apart from the earlier volumes of translation from the German, she had now brought out two books of her own: *Summer on the Lakes*, which appeared in Boston in June 1844 under Emerson's benign aegis; and *Woman in the Nineteenth Century*, finished at Fishkill in mid-November and published in February by Greeley's Tribune Press.

Neither book was faultless. *Summer on the Lakes*, the travelogue of her western tour in 1843 with Caroline Sturgis and the Clarkes, would have been more inchoate than it was but for the thread of chronology. Excessive interpolation of irrelevant matter disguised the fact that when she had something important to reveal—like the unfitness of many pioneer women for their hard lot—or to attack—like the white man's mistreatment of the Indian—she was capable of writing with clarity and force. Emerson called the book "very good and entertaining." To Greeley, as an old newsman, it was "one of the clearest and most graphic delineations . . . of the Great Lakes, of the Prairies, and of the receding barbarism, and the rapidly advancing but rude repulsive semi-civilization, which were contending with most unequal forces for the possession of those rich lands." Pruned of its excesses, as in Bell Gale Chevigny's well-edited version of 1976, it still stands as a worthwhile travel book.

Margaret grappled with a larger subject in *Woman in the Nineteenth Century*, the first long sections of which suggest that she was baffled by the magnitude of her task. Both Emerson and Thoreau knew from experience that her prose lacked the memorable power of expression that distinguished her conversations, whether private or public. At least half the book is nearly unreadable—subjective, diffuse, filled with wasteful similes that change form and meaning as she toys with them. Lydia Maria Child, a good friend and sharp critic, warned her against this tendency in two metaphors of her own: "The stream is abundant and beautiful; but it always seems to be *pumped* rather than to *flow*"; and again, "Your house is too full; there is too much furniture for your rooms." An even closer friend, Caroline Sturgis, who had watched the final struggle with the pamphlet at Fishkill Landing, was also troubled by Margaret's style: "There is a recurrence of comparisons, illustrations, and words, which is not pleasing. . . . It is not a book to take to heart and that is what a book upon woman should be." Edgar Allan Poe condemned her excessive subjectiveness: "She judges woman by the heart and intellect of Miss Fuller, but there are not more than one or two dozen Miss Fullers on the whole face of the earth." Whatever the merits of these caveats, it is only toward the end, in the hortatory pages, that Margaret's trenchant opinions on the predicament and duties of women bring her tract to life.

Back in June, Emerson had advised her not to present copies of *Summer on the Lakes* to her friends: "In this country it is an absurd practice for the author to present his books, it is enough that he writes it, he should not be his own purchaser." But he had regularly sent out dozens of his own books to friends, as well as free tickets to his lectures, and when his second volume of essays appeared in mid-October 1844, he again mailed copies to many people, including Margaret and Caroline. "I have read quite through some of it in the neighborhood of hawks and such like," she wrote him from Fishkill, "but will not mar the effect by a few inadequate words. It will be a companion through my life. In expression it seems far more adequate than the former volume, has more glow, more fusion." She postponed mention of "two or three cavils" until she had reexamined the essays.

Her critical assessment of Emerson's book appeared in the *Tribune* on December 7, shortly after her arrival in New York: His "only aim is the discernment and interpretation of the spiritual laws by which we live. . . . History will inscribe his name as a father of the country, for he is one who pleads her cause against herself." He had prepared the way for such books as this by his great powers as a speaker. His lectures were "didactic poems," and his permanent audience valued his words as the "signets of reality." His books performed the same function, though less powerfully because printed rather than spoken.

She cited the charges against the essays: obscurity, lack of perfect articulation, more use of fancy than of imagination, subtlety at the expense of strength. If a good work were defined as "one where the whole commands more attention than the parts, or if after accumulation of materials there is fire enough to fuse the whole into one new substance," Emerson had "never written one good work." Single passages and sentences engaged the reader's attention too much in proportion. It had been held, by her as it happened, that these essays were like "a string of mosaics or a house built of medals." He was a man of ideas, but one missed "the glow, uniform yet various in tint, which is given to a body by free circulation of the heart's blood." Without naming names, she thought of the giant Antaeus, who gained strength from contact with Gaia, the *Erdmutter*. Emerson had "raised himself too early to the perpendicular and did not lie along the ground long enough to hear the secret whispers of our parent life." One "could wish he might be thrown by conflicts on the lap of mother earth, to see if he would not rise again with added powers." Yet he was among the few in any age who worship the God of Truth. Two important claims could be made for him: first, his sincerity, which uttered his thought "just as it found place in the life of his own soul"; and second, his ability to imprison his hearers only to free them again as "liberating gods." By "making present to us the courses and destinies of nature, he invests himself with her serenity and animates us with her joy."

This was acute criticism, based as it was on close knowledge of Emerson over nearly ten years, and including most of the grounds of their agreements and disagreements in an essay-review that held unrelentingly to its subject without the divagations that often cluttered Margaret's prose. She worked hard at her reviewing, handling upward of eighty books during the first year of her incumbency. Her literary contributions were diversified by accounts of her visits to the penitentiary on Blackwell's Island, just across the river from Greeley's rural retreat, to the Bellevue Alms House, to the so-called Farm School, and to the Asylum for the Insane. She wrote sympathetically about the downtrodden Irish immigrants, fallen women, and the horrors of slavery, and reached out toward the European scene with her own translations of items from the German *Schnellpost*.

Greeley was well pleased with her work: "Her earlier contributions to the Tribune were not her best. . . . She wrote always freshly, vigorously, but not always clearly; for her full and intimate acquaintance with continental litera-ture, especially German, seemed to have marred her felicity and readiness of expression in her mother tongue. While I never met another woman who conversed more freely or lucidly, the attempt to commit her thoughts to paper seemed to induce a singular embarrassment and hesitation." But he presently concluded that her faults "rather dwindled than expanded" the better he got to know her. She emerged in his mind as a "fearless and unselfish champion of Truth and Human Good." Most of her writing was "characterized by a di-rectness, terseness, and practicality" well suited "to win the favor and sway the judgment of the great majority of readers."

As the spring of 1845 moved in, Margaret reveled in the "boskie acres" of Greeley's farmstead, with its tall old trees, a flower garden enhanced by trim boxwood borders, a brook and a small pond, and a view of the handsome sail-boats that seemed "to greet the house" as they swept along the East River channel. "The beauty here, seen by moonlight, is truly transporting," she wrote, "I enjoy it greatly, and the *genius loci* receives me as to a home." When she was not victimized by her always recurrent headaches, which Greeley at-tributed to overdoses of tea and coffee, she did much of her work in her room or on the piazza, though transport downtown by omnibus or horsecar was relatively quick and easy.

Her life was not wholly given to work. During the winter she had heard much music and frequented many soirées in the city. At one of these she happened to meet James Nathan, a gentle, blue-eyed German-Jewish salesman for an importing firm. While Emerson in Concord was helping Margaret's former lover, Sam Ward, to bring out his translation of *Goethe's Essays on Art*, Margaret was entering upon a romantic relationship with Nathan. Except that they were the same age, thirty-four, the affair was almost a repetition of her epistolary courtship of young Sam Ward back in 1835-39. During four shining months they met as frequently as possible, sometimes at the farm, more often in the city. "Almost ever since we first met," she wrote him, "I have felt a strong attraction to you," and she was soon saying that she wanted to furl her tired wings and rest upon his manly bosom.

While he was in New York during that flowering spring, and after he left for Europe in June, she showered him with love letters, sometimes two a day. Like those she had sent to Sam Ward half a dozen years earlier, they were commonly long, verbose, and filled with talk about destiny, rapture, and spiritual intercourse. The experience with Ward had apparently not taught her that it is possible to talk one's lover to death—or to flight. Her ardent missives followed him around Europe until July 1846 on the eve of her own voyage to England, when she was still hoping for a reunion with him somewhere on the continent. Nathan sent her a rose from Shelley's Roman grave, but the blossom fell apart when she took it from the envelope, leaving her with a handful of dry leaves. "Is not that rather sad?" she asked. She was not yet prepared to admit that it was also symbolic.

There is no evidence to show that Margaret revealed to Emerson the secret of her unrequited love affair with Nathan. Had she done so, he might not have been overcome with surprise. He had fended off her repeated attempts to overpersonalize their own relationship, and was well aware, as Hawthorne was, of the exotic and passionate strain in her nature, on which he would expatiate after her death, saying, in effect, that she had longed to lose her virginity and to become a wife and mother. One comment in Greeley's *Recollections of a Busy Life* offers independent support for Emerson's view: "Noble and great as she was, a good husband and two or three bouncing babies would have emancipated her from a good deal of cant and nonsense."

Emerson's summer was relatively quiet until late July, when he spoke at Middlebury College in Vermont. Two weeks later the *Tribune* reported that his address on the functions of the scholar had been received with marked "intensity of interest and pleasure" despite the prejudices entertained in that region against "the peculiar views of the Transcendentalists." It is possible but not certain that Margaret had a hand in this account. He repeated the address at Middletown, Connecticut, on August 6, and left next morning by steamboat for New York, where he visited his brother and family on Staten Island, and on the ninth wrote Lidian that he had just seen Margaret Fuller and that he planned to return home by way of Lenox, where Sam Ward was building a large house. "I have had some congenial hours," Margaret wrote to Nathan on the twelfth, "for Mr. Emerson has been here two days, full of free talk and in serene beauty as ever; he went yesterday."

These few sentences—Emerson to Lidian, Margaret to Nathan—say nothing of Emerson's reaction to Margaret's review of his essays in the preceding December. That he had read the review with attention is fairly certain: a phrase in one of his letters to Caroline in February echoes Margaret's Antaeus image from the review: "I found myself much warped from my own perpendicular." In a letter to Elizabeth Hoar in June, he seemed to be defending himself against Margaret's assertion that he needed contact with Mother Earth: "I truly revolve with humble docility and desire, the world old problems. I worship the real, I hate the critical and athwart the whole skyfull of imperfections can keep some steady sight of the perfect, opening there a new horizon." He had moreover a consistent philosophy about adverse critiques of his writings: "I have long ago settled that it is best not to set up any defence at all, but go on affirming as long as God will let us."

In Margaret's absence, he had continued his friendship with Caroline. After her visit to Concord in late May and early June, he had made a journal entry about her. "Of all the persons I know, this child, called romantic and insane and exaggerating, is the most real. And it is strange that she should not have that which she wants, somewhat to do." Two weeks after his return from New York, he wrote Caroline that Lidian had offered to take her as a boarder. But she refused: "Lidian would find me more trouble than she anticipates, for I am always unpunctual and generally invisible at meal-times and so unsocial at all times that I must give pain even to the most generous."

Margaret, meanwhile, was still at Turtle Bay. "At home the baby is my chief company," she told Nathan. "He grows more and more lovely and begins to talk." Thwarted by circumstance from incipient dreams of motherhood, she often cradled Pickie in her arms as she lay in the hammock on the broad piazza. But she was planning a fall vacation in Massachusetts when the foliage would be at its best. She was much fatigued, and her friendship with Molly Greeley was less firm than formerly. Molly, who had lost two children and suffered two miscarriages before Pickie's birth, was not eager to surrender her only child to "Aunt" Margaret's caresses. During the vacation she paid a visit to Concord and Margaret was deeply disappointed over her talk with Emerson: "Our moods did not match," she wrote Anna Ward. "He was with Plato, I with the instincts."

Back from Massachusetts, she began boarding in town for the winter, first on Warren Street and later in Amity Place near Washington Square. "As I shall find no longer a home in the house of Mr. G[reeley], except for a brief space in the Spring [of 1846]," she wrote Nathan, "I must therefore live at much more expense." The change had become necessary because Molly Greeley was in "a sad state of mind and body," though Pickie was "beautiful . . . the picture of health and gayety."

Margaret was already looking forward to a trip abroad with Marcus and Rebecca Spring, who suggested that she might provide part-time assistance in caring for their son, Eddie, aged twelve. Spring was a successful textile merchant with a wealthy Quaker wife, and could easily have afforded to pay her way, but Margaret insisted on borrowing money to underwrite travel expenses. Her father's untimely death ten years earlier had denied her a similar trip in the company of the Farrars. Nearly all her Massachusetts friends, including Emerson, Alcott, Sam and Anna Ward, and most recently Ellery Channing, had crossed the Atlantic. Now at last she could absorb Old World culture at firsthand.

During April 1846 she was back again at the farm with her beloved Pickie. At the end of the month Molly took the child to Brattleboro, Vermont, for the summer, and Margaret found lodgings in Brooklyn "near the heights" until she left for Boston late in July to say good-bye to her family and friends before sailing aboard the *Cambria* on August 1. Although she was more than ready to go, her stay in New York had been notably productive. Through the spring and early summer she had collected a book of her essays, *Papers on Literature and Art*, published in two volumes by Wiley and Putnam in October 1846. Greeley, who had asked her to serve as foreign correspondent for his paper, saw to it that her final tribute to the city, "Farewell to New York," was prominently displayed in the *Tribune* on the very day the *Cambria* left Boston harbor. She wrote in retrospect that her twenty months with Greeley had given her "a richer and more varied exercise for thought and life" than twenty years could have done elsewhere in the nation, and she concluded: "I go to behold the wonders of art, and the temples of old religion. But I shall see no forms of beauty and majesty beyond what my country is capable of producing in myriad variety, if she has but the soul to will it; no temple to compare with what she might erect in the ages, if the catchword of the time, a sense of *divine order,* should become no more a mere word of form, but a deeply rooted and pregnant idea in her life."

This stirring exhortation to her native land bore at least something of the Emersonian imprint. But Europe was to become her true place of fulfillment. Sixteen months later she was writing to Emerson from Rome: "I find how true was the lure that always drew me towards Europe. It was no false instinct that said I might here find an atmosphere to develop me in ways I need. Had I only come ten years earlier! Now my life must be a failure, so much strength has been wasted on abstractions, which only came because I grew not in the right soil. However, it is a less failure than with most others, and not worth thinking twice about. Heaven has room enough, and good chances in store, and I can live a great deal in the years that remain."

Chapter Twenty-six

THOREAU
AT WALDEN

TALKING WITH MARGARET FULLER BESIDE WALDEN POND IN the summer of 1842, Ellery Channing had voiced his daydream about building a cabin there to compose poetry in. The dream came to little enough for him but would lead to eventual world fame for his friend Thoreau. Writing from New York in March 1845, Ellery told him: "I see nothing for you in this earth but that field which I once christened 'Briars'; go out upon that, build yourself a hut, and there begin the grand process of devouring yourself alive. . . . Concord is just as good a place as any other."

There was no need to tell Thoreau anything about Concord as the great good place. He knew every tree and bush, flower and weed, field and swamp, frog and fish for miles around the village. Building, moreover, was in his blood: he had just finished a new house for his parents near the railroad depot. Now he was resolved to give substance to Ellery's romantic suggestion.

While Channing was negotiating for his tract of land on Punkawtasset Hill, Henry got busy with the construction of a small cabin on Emerson's lately acquired property along the north shore of Walden. A stand of Emerson's white pines fell to Henry's borrowed ax; a railroad laborer named James Collins sold him an abandoned shanty for its well-weathered boards and shingles; the house frame went up in May, and on Independence Day the owner moved in. He had already cleared two acres of the adjoining brier patch for a garden plot, planted five kinds of vegetables—now doing well despite the depredations of a small army of woodchucks—built a woodshed and a privy, and furnished the interior with bed, table, chairs, a small desk and lamp, and assorted cooking utensils. Affixed to one wall was a mirror smaller than a penny postcard. All was not to be vanity in this ascetic *ménage de garçon*.

Two weeks before Thoreau's moving day Father Taylor preached in the First Church to a mixed congregation of Unitarian divines, farmers, and shopkeepers. Prominent in the audience were Emerson, Thoreau, and Channing. Taylor still performed like "mighty nature's child," astonishing his auditors, as Emerson said, with "new and happiest deliverances," perfectly sure of himself and his powers, rolling the world into a ball and carelessly tossing it from hand to hand—touching, plain, grand, and cogent by turns, and disarming criticism and malignity by the straightforward frankness of his presence.

As always, Emerson paid him rapt attention, but now more critically. Instead of checkreining those "grand seahorses . . . with which he caracoles on the waves of the sunny ocean," Taylor gave his steeds their heads to draw him no matter where. His whole system of religion was "a mere confused rigmarole of refuse and leavings of former generations . . . quite accidental and ludicrously copied and caricatured from the old style." He mimicked and exaggerated "the parade of method and logic of text and argument." Evidently "incapable of thought," he seemed unable "to analyse or discriminate." His logical slips would have made him ridiculous but for the dazzling inexhaustibility of his wit. "After much threatening to exterminate all opposition by his syllogisms," wrote Emerson, "he seldom remembers any of the divisions of his plan after the first." Firing off his volleys of imagery and epithets, he repeatedly counted on the luck that often enabled him to hit the bull's-eye. He had "sold his mind for his soul"—but soul defined "in the low semi-animal sense." He was valuable as "a psychologic curiosity"; his powers lay in "a certain mania or low inspiration." And yet, said Emerson, "you feel this inspiration. It clothes him like an atmosphere, and he marches into untried depths with the security of a grenadier. He will weep, and grieve, and pray, and chide in a tempest of passionate speech, and never break the perfect propriety with a single false note; and when all is done, you still ask, or I do, 'What's Hecuba to him?' "

With Thoreau, sitting in the church at Emerson's elbow, such questions were irrelevant. If Henry had his Hecubas, and he owned a few, they were not worth weeping over. They belonged to the past; his business was with the present. Thoreau's conversation, observed Emerson, "consisted of a continual coining of the present moment into a sentence and offering it to me. I compared it to a boy who from the universal snow lying on the earth gathers up a little in his hand, rolls it into a ball, and flings it at me." This snowballing technique was certainly brusque, even impolite. Yet Henry, his friend thought, was "a good substantial childe, not encumbered with himself. He has no troublesome memory, no wake, but lives extempore, and brings today a new proposition as radical and revolutionary as that of yesterday, but different." As "the only man of leisure in the town," he resembled the hero of Carlyle's *Past and Present* (1843), an Abbot Samson, who carried good counsel in his breast. "If I cannot show his performance much more manifest than that of other grand promisers, at least I can see that with his practical faculty, he has declined all the kingdoms of this world. Satan has no bribe for him."

At age twenty-nine, Henry promised more than he had yet delivered. But he excelled in the "vocation of reporting," making sharply limned daguerreotypes of whatever he beheld or experienced. Calling some things indescribable was nonsense, said Emerson. A writer like Thoreau knew better, and "would report God himself or attempt it. . . . In his eyes a man is the faculty of reporting, and the universe is the possibility of being reported."

Ellery's half-jocular name for the new cabin at Walden was "a wooden inkstand." Apart from a good deal more carpentry, masonry, and gardening, Henry's chief occupation for the next two years was writing. This for him always meant a blend of reportorial facts and philosophic meditations, studded with those witty and often ironic apothegms that so delighted Emerson, and indeed almost everyone else. "Proverbs," said Emerson in his essay on "Compensation," "are the sanctuary of the intuitions." Henry's writing at the cabin desk began with a long essay on Carlyle, later boiled down for a lecture at the Concord Lyceum, and afterward revised for magazine publication. He was keeping a careful notebook record of his experiences and expenses at Walden—the total cost of his cabin, for example, was $28.12—as well as of those stratagems by which he resolved daily problems. This record formed the basis for one of the two books that he drafted during his Walden sojourn, though *Walden: Or Life in the Woods* was not to see the light until August 1854. His more immediate plan was to set down the story of the trip he had made with his brother along the Concord and Merrimack rivers in 1839. By the summer of 1846, the first draft was done. Or so, at least, Emerson believed, whose eagerness to see it in print failed to reckon with Thoreau's perfectionism: his dogged determination to load every rift of his manuscript with the best possible blend of reportage and commentary. This process, with many interruptions, required three more years. His residence at Walden was already far behind him when *A Week on the Concord and Merrimack Rivers* finally appeared in May 1849.

Coolidge Castle, with three young children, their parents, their aging grandmother, and a new set of servants—to say nothing of the usual succession of visitors, including Thoreau, who was a frequent dinner guest—was far more crowded than the bachelor cabin in the pine shade beside the former field of briers. Emerson's mother was now recovered from a fall on the stairway caused by horse chestnuts left there by the children, who continued to be the apples of their father's eye. "My little Ellen," he wrote, "is growing up a very intelligent child, a devourer of books with an endless memory for all hymns and juvenile poems. Her vivacity procures her many a chiding from all sides in the house and I doubt not, at school; but she is reasonable and convertible." If Nelly was a handful, "Edith never does wrong, but spends all her soft days in every-body's love." The baby Edward contentedly shook the secondhand rattle inherited, like many another outgrown toy, from his Staten Island cousins. "I spend a great deal of time on my little trinity," said Emerson. He was thankful that no "cruel interferences" had yet marred their happy childhood. Even their Uncle Bulkeley, who came over from Littleton for the Fourth of July and a three-week visit, had been mild and even-tempered, and returned without protest to the farm of Reuben Hoar, his new caretaker. Emerson hoped against hope that the present felicity of his household would not be succeeded by "any dark penumbra."

Although Thoreau's essay on civil disobedience lay well in the future, he stood among those other New England men and women who were already facing up to the "dark penumbra" of slavery. Despite Emerson's own reluctance to become "a mover in politics," he had forthrightly hailed emancipation in the British West Indies, and would gradually become an ever stronger proponent of civil rights for "the colored people" as developing events stirred his anger and his sense of justice.

One such event was the experience of his neighbor Samuel Hoar, Elizabeth's father and a leading resident of Concord. Several maritime cities in the south had been abducting free black sailors and jailing them while their ships remained in port. Whenever a ship captain failed to pay the costs of their detention, the prisoners were sold into slavery. Emerson called this practice a "damnable outrage," and applauded the decision of George Briggs, the Massachusetts governor, to send Mr. Hoar to investigate the situation in Charleston. Elizabeth accompanied her father, and all went well until Monday, December 2, 1844, when a mob threatened to burn their hotel, and Hoar was summarily expelled by action of Governor James Hammond at the instigation of the South Carolina legislature. Back home, Mr. Hoar described his adventure to Emerson, who concluded that he had "behaved with the utmost firmness, and only came away when it would have been the part of a mule not of a man to remain."

Emerson always admired firm adherence to moral principles, no matter how unpopular. The final sentence of "Self-Reliance" had said it well: "Nothing can bring you peace but the triumph of principles." He, too, behaved with "utmost firmness" nearly a year later when the New Bedford Lyceum voted to exclude Negroes from attendance at one of his lectures. "As I think the Lyceum exists for popular education," he wrote the officer in charge, "[and] as I work in it for that, and think it should bribe and importune the humblest and most ignorant to come in, and exclude nobody . . . this vote quite embarrasses me, and . . . in its direct counteraction to the obvious duty and sentiment of New England, and of all freemen in regard to the colored people, the vote appears unkind, and so unlooked for, that I could not come with any pleasure before the Society."

In his new cottage on Punkawtasset Hill, Ellery Channing was already growing restive. Late in September, his brother-in-law Tom Higginson had found him looking extremely seedy, though sporting "bright orange" shoes like a badge of defiance. In October Ellery spent two weeks as Thoreau's houseguest, helping to build the fireplace and chimney, and sleeping on a pallet beside Henry's bed. In November, when Caroline Sturgis rode over to spend an afternoon with Ellery and his family, she found the master of the house "sick and sepulchral," but at least civil. Caroline had once thought Ellen insufficiently noble to be Ellery's wife. Now she suspected that the roles ought to be reversed: "I never saw a prettier external life," she wrote Margaret Fuller, "but pearls are hollow."

Ellen's second pregnancy strengthened her husband's growing determination to go abroad. He broached his plan in February 1846, angering Margaret, who complained to her brother, Richard, about "the unnatural selfishness of a man who, having brought a woman into this situation . . . proposes to leave her without even knowing whether she lives or dies under it." Wild and even ruthless as Ellery's scheme might be, wrote Caroline, Ellen was convinced that her husband had better go: "He cannot keep himself peaceable in the house, even now, when she has a [hired] girl, and it will be worse in the summer."

Once more, as he had done with Alcott in 1842 and Thoreau in 1843, Emerson sprang into the monetary breach. He wrote to various friends, including Sam Ward, Ellery's inveterate benefactor, to gather a purse for the impecunious traveler:

> Ellery Channing has suddenly found out that he must see Europe, that he must see it now,—nay, that it is a matter of life and death that he should set out for Havre and Italy on the first of March. . . . He thinks it indispensable that he should see buildings, and pictures, and mountains, and peasantries, [as] part of his poetic education. . . . He has calculated, Heaven knows how, that he can go for a year to Italy . . . for 250 or at most 300 dollars, including the passage money. . . . It is not desireable . . . that he should have any more than a poor artist[']s provision, for (his wife said this to me) . . . if he has money, he only spends it in idlest indulgences.

The money was soon in hand, with contributions from Ward, Emerson, Caleb Cushing, and Caroline Sturgis, and Ellery sailed from New York on March 3, bound for Genoa and a stay in Rome. Alcott had spent six months basking in the admiration of his British friends. Ellery's hegira took only four: he returned home on July 4, the first anniversary of Thoreau's move to Walden Pond. Thoreau, in situ, had learned and written far more that spring than Channing had in transit. But Ellery had kept a Roman journal that he proposed to submit for publication, and had successfully evaded the domestic upheaval occasioned by the birth of his second daughter, Caroline Sturgis Channing.

Ellery had been home less than a week when a local tragedy agitated the village. A nineteen-year-old schoolteacher named Martha Hunt had been seen pacing the muddy riverbank between five and seven on the morning of

July 9. Later in the day a passerby found her bonnet and shoes on the shore below the north bridge. When Ellery heard of it about nine in the evening, he rushed to the Manse to borrow Hawthorne's boat, and they rowed down to the spot where a crowd gathered carrying lanterns and long poles. Half an hour later a young man in a blue farmer's smock located the body and brought it to the surface. Hawthorne was horrified by the girl's appearance, "stiff as marble" with rigor mortis, her arms bent forward at chest level, her hands clenched in seeming agony. He never forgot the incident, which happened on his third wedding anniversary, and long afterward adapted it for use in describing the climactic drowning of Zenobia in Chapter 27 of *The Blithedale Romance*.

Although Emerson must have known of the death of Martha Hunt, he made no mention of it on July 27 when he wrote Elizabeth Hoar about the recent adventures of Ellery and Henry: "Mr. Channing has returned, after spending 16 days in Rome; Mr. Thoreau has spent a night in Concord jail on his refusal to pay his taxes." Henry's overnight jail term was among the shortest in Middlesex County's penological history. Having come to the village from his Walden hut on an errand one recent afternoon, he had met Sam Staples, tax collector and warden of the county jail. Henry had ignored his poll-tax obligation since 1843. When Sam reminded him of his delinquency, Henry declined to pay up on the grounds that he did not believe in supporting a government of whose actions he disapproved. The upshot of this small debate was Henry's one-night stand behind stone walls and iron bars. When the news of his situation got out around nightfall, someone quietly appeared at Sam's door and paid his daughter the due amount. By the time Sam heard about this settlement, it was too late in the evening to go to the trouble of releasing the prisoner, who was in any case thoroughly enjoying his jailbird's-eye view of the town through the window grating. "I did not for a moment feel confined," he said later in *Civil Disobedience*, "and the walls seemed a great waste of stone and mortar."

Henry's experience was not a Concord first. In January 1843 Alcott had been jailed for the same reason, and released when Squire Hoar paid his tax. The news had delighted Thoreau at the time. He wrote Emerson that when Sam Staples stopped in at the Thoreau household afterward, Helen Thoreau had wondered what Alcott's idea could possibly have been. "I vum," said Sam, "I believe it was nothing but principle, for I never heard a man talk honester."

Henry was free as a bird and back at his Walden hut when Alcott dropped in for a talk with Emerson about the episode. According to Alcott's journal for July 25, 1846, "E[merson] thought it mean and skulking, and in bad taste. I defended it on the grounds of a dignified non-compliance with the injunction of civil powers." This entry has puzzled some of Emerson's biographers, and it is just possible that Alcott could have missed Emerson's point. The quoted adjectives seem much better suited to Sam Staple's action than to Thoreau's. The subject of the Alcott-Emerson conversation was "civil powers and institutions," which Emerson steadily derogated at this period. He may have felt that putting an honest man in jail for a trifling misdemeanor against the state was indeed mean and skulking enough to leave a bad taste in the mouths of Massachusetts citizens.

Emerson's own journal entries for July clearly praise Thoreau for not knuckling under. "Build your prison walls thicker," he cried. "It needs a firmer line of demarcation to denote those within from those without. . . . Is not America more than ever wanting in the male principle? A good many village attorneys we have, saucy village talents . . . but no great captains. . . .O Governor Briggs. Mr. Webster told them how much the [Mexican] war cost, that was his protest, but voted the war, and sends his son to it. They calculated rightly on Mr. Webster. My friend Mr. Thoreau has gone to jail rather than pay his tax. On him they could not calculate. The abolitionists denounce the war and give much time to it, but they pay the tax."

"I had three chairs in my house," wrote Thoreau, "one for solitude, two for friendship, three for society." Sometimes, the house being so small, he had "the difficulty of getting to a sufficient distance" from his guests whenever they "began to utter the big thoughts in big words." During his last year at Walden, Emerson "looked in" at the cabin from time to time, though Thoreau's "solid seasons" with his old friend took place more often at Coolidge Castle. But Henry's closest associates were Alcott and Channing. Neither rain nor snow nor dark of night kept either of them from following the wood path along the north shore of the pond until they saw the light in the cabin window. At this time Hawthorne was already gone to Salem, but he remembered Channing as the prince of idlers: "I do not mean to deny Ellery's ability for any sort of vulgar usefulness," he once wrote, "but he certainly *can* lie in the sun." Thoreau stressed other aspects of Ellery's character. "We made that small house ring with boisterous mirth," he said, "and resound with the murmur of much sober talk, making amends then to Walden vale for the long silences. Broadway was still and deserted in comparison. At suitable intervals there were regular salutes of laughter. . . . We made many a 'bran new' theory of life over a thin dish of gruel, which combined the advantages of conviviality with the clear-headedness which philosophy requires."

The second most welcome visitor was Alcott, who shared many a long winter evening. "I think," wrote Thoreau, "that he must be the man of most faith of any alive. His words and attitude always suppose a better state of things than other men are acquainted with, and he will be the last man to be disappointed as the ages revolve. . . . He is perhaps the sanest man and has the fewest crotchets of any I chance to know; the same yesterday and to-morrow. . . . A blue-robed man, whose fittest roof is the overarching sky which reflects his serenity. I do not see how he can ever die; Nature cannot spare him."

Alcott's admiration for Thoreau was equally strong. "He belongs to the Homeric age," he wrote later. ". . . A sylvan man accomplished in the virtues of an aboriginal civility. . . . He seems alone, of all the men I have known, to be a native New Englander,—as much so as the oak, or granite ledge; and I would rather send him to London or Vienna or Berlin, as a specimen of American genius spontaneous and unmixed, than anyone else. . . . This man is the independent of independents—is, indeed, the sole signer of the Declaration, and a Revolution in himself . . . having got beyond the signing to the doing it out fully. Concord jail could not keep him safely; Justice Hoar paid his tax, too; and was glad to forget thereafter . . . his citizenship, and omit his existence, as a resident, in the poll list."

As if in tribute to such qualities in Thoreau, but also because it was a shady spot with a handsome southward view over the cove in the shoreline of Walden, the taxpaying abolitionists among the women of Concord convened their annual meeting at Henry's now famous hut. The date was August 1, 1846, the second anniversary of Emerson's address to the same group on West Indian emancipation. The program consisted of speeches, followed by a picnic. The speakers included two Unitarian ministers, the Reverend Caleb

Stetson, a Harvard classmate of Emerson's; his close friend, the Reverend William Henry Channing; and Emerson himself. The podium for all three was Henry's front stoop, and the host was among the listeners. It happened to be the very day when Margaret Fuller sailed for Liverpool aboard the *Cambria*, the beginning of her first, and last, foreign tour.

Chapter Twenty-seven

THEODORE PARKER IN BOSTON

THEODORE PARKER WAS THIRTY-FIVE WHEN, BY HIS OWN AC-count, "a few earnest men," fearing that "the great principle of religious freedom was in danger," and seeing that such theological positions as he had outlined were being repudiated, not only by the orthodox but also, and most disturbingly, by liberal Unitarians, invited him to leave West Roxbury and come to Boston. The offer was to take over as leader of the Twenty-eighth Congregational Society at the Melodeon. Much later he recalled that gloomy Sunday, February 16, 1845, when he first mounted his new pulpit. The streets were full of snow and a gray rain was falling. But he had enlisted in what he called another "thirty years' war," and was buoyed up by his belief in the essential unity of human life under all the lively heterogeneity of that "busy bustling town" that was to remain his command post for the remainder of his life.

His congregation saw a plain man, short in stature—as blunt, substantial, and muscular as the prose he wrote and delivered. On the platform, according to H. S. Commager, his manner was "simple, unaffected . . . a little awkward, but never ill at ease, his great Socrates-like head almost bald." At first clean-shaven, he presently grew a fringe of beard, which turned prematurely gray, and in the end a full white beard and mustache. His direct, gray-blue eyes, firm mouth, and snub nose gave his face an expression frank, open, and alive with aggressive energy. "More like a ploughman than priest," wrote

James Russell Lowell in 1848, adding that his prose periods fell upon his listeners "stroke after stroke, / Like the blows of a lumberer felling an oak."

In 1843–44, Parker had enjoyed a year's transatlantic sabbatical, and Emerson had introduced him to Carlyle in a letter that called him "a theologian eminent for his learning and his independence, and for his great power in persuading our people to adopt his opinions." Carlyle took to Parker far more readily than to most of the other American travelers whom Emerson steered in his direction: "a most hardy, compact, clever little fellow, full of decisive utterance, with humour and good-humour, whom I like much."

Parker's "decisive utterance" had been a mainstay of the *Dial*, and he felt its loss when it died. Following his move to Boston, he began to dream of a new quarterly to take its place. In the spring of 1847 he broached his plans to Emerson and others. Emerson cooperated, perhaps a shade diffidently. His two years as editor of the *Dial* had severely drained his time and energy, and he nurtured no wish for further editorial duties. By the fall of the year, owing chiefly to Parker's zeal and resolution, it was clear that the first number of the *Massachusetts Quarterly Review* would be out in time for Christmas.

Zeal and resolution were good words for Parker. He longed for liveliness, and wanted a more forceful dissidence of dissent than the rather pallid esotericism that he had sometimes deplored in the old *Dial*. He agreed with James Martineau's hope for a magazine that would be "a little more acceptable to plebeian apprehensions," and called his new effort "the *Dial* with a beard," though young Tom Higginson afterward complained that it had turned out to be "the beard without the *Dial*." Reading the opening number in England in January 1848, Emerson found that while its spirit was good, the contents lacked intellectual tone and literary skill. Henry Thoreau sourly agreed that the new journal showed "no character," and called it "not so good a book as the Boston Almanack." Emerson urged James Elliot Cabot, Parker's temporary assistant, to line up articles by Thoreau, Alcott, and George P. Bradford, as if an infusion of former *Dial* contributors might lift the level of the *Massachusetts Quarterly*. Twice in August 1848, he even tried to dissuade Parker from going on with the magazine, and scolded him for printing a masthead that named Emerson as an editor when in fact he had hardly "*worked in it*" at all. By the end of September, Emerson had withdrawn entirely. "Parker I prize and respect," he told his brother William. "He is a man of great energy, with a head full of projects, and many chapters lie coiled there, which he is resolved to unfold to the world. . . . He needs an organ, as much as a political chief would do; he fancies himself unpopular, and that his papers would be refused by all journals." As they had done for the *Dial*, Parker and Emerson might both write for the new magazine, but, said Emerson, "I should not be interested in one that was mainly his."

Parker carried on. Lowell wittily told him that his editorial experiences would convert him back to orthodox religious views, since the procrastination of his contributors must convince him of their "total depravity." Parker himself almost never postponed anything. Since his student days he had deeply believed that the way to get something done was to do it, and he had anyway conceived the new journal in part as a lay pulpit for the dissemination of his own sturdy opinions. As Commager points out, every one of the twelve numbers of the *Massachusetts Quarterly Review* carried an article from his pen. He managed also to keep his good humor. In November, undeterred by Emerson's withdrawal, he asked if some of the Emersonian lions had any growling or roaring to do through the throat of the *Quarterly*. Alcott had complained that the Concord circle had not been approached. Would Emerson therefore approach Concord to see if the local lions would favor the *MQR* "with an occasional Roar, or at least a leonine whine?" It would do no harm to twist a few tails.

Parker was still at the helm of his journal when Thoreau's *A Week on the Concord and Merrimack Rivers* finally appeared in May 1849. Asked to review it, Emerson declined on the grounds that he himself belonged to "the same clan and parish." Had he been susceptible to flattery, he might have relented in the face of Parker's opinion that the book was strongly Emersonian in tone and idea, "full of beautiful things, some of them . . . evidently remembered from you," although others were "undoubtedly original" with Thoreau. On the whole, said Parker, the book showed "great merits," a view that Emerson shared and had in fact been trumpeting for many months. This exchange of letters helped to close the gap that had been slowly widening between Emerson and his obstreperous friend.

Shortly before his magazine ceased publication in 1850, Parker went even further, setting himself the task of summing up Emerson's career to midcentury. For fourteen years this "very extraordinary man" had been speaking and writing with a "holy power" such as belonged to no other person then using the English tongue. Many other writers had more readers, were oftener praised in the journals, were never sneered at by respectable men, and exerted greater weight in the pulpits, cabinets, and councils of the nation. But none among them had been working "so powerfully to fashion the character of the coming age."

The source of Emerson's strength was "his intellectual and moral sincerity." Never had he compromised. Never had he sought to "cover up the chasm" which every day grew wider "between Truth and public opinion, between Justice and the State, between Christianity and the Church." Trusting himself, man, and God, he had been able to walk serene and erect through the turmoils of the age. Nothing was allowed to impede his search for the true, the lovely, and the good. Nor had he ever sought after fame. "He takes care of his Being," wrote Parker, "and leaves his seeming to take care of itself. Fame may seek him; he never goes out of his way a single inch for her."

In calling Emerson "the most American" among current writers, Parker meant that his work incorporated "the idea of personal freedom, of the dignity and value of human nature, the superiority of man to the accidents of man." He was also "the most republican of republicans, the most protestant of the dissenters," and looked at "the past and the present, the state and the church, Christianity and the market house in the daylight of the intellect."

The form his writing took was not less American than the man himself. He was plainly an author who lived "in a land with free institutions, with town meetings and ballotboxes; in the vicinity of a decaying church; amongst men whose terrible devils are Poverty and Social Neglect." One could recognize his American origins also by his geographical orientation: "Catskill and the Alleghenies, Monadnock, Wachusett, and the uplands of New Hampshire. . . . Contoocook and Agiocochook are better than the Ilyssus, or Pactolus, or 'smooth-sliding Mincius, crowned with vocal reeds.' New York, Fall River, and Lowell have a place in his writings, where a vulgar Yankee would put Thebes and Paestum."

Finally, his men and women were American—"John and Jane, not Coriolanus and Persephone." He told of "the rhodora, the club-moss, the blooming clover, not of the hibiscus and the asphodel." He knew "the humblebee, the blackbird, the bat, and the wren," and was "not ashamed to say or sing of the things under his own eyes." He "illustrated his high thought by common things out of our plain New England life—the meeting in the church, the Sunday school, the dancing-school, a huckleberry party, the boys and girls hastening home from school . . . the farmers about their work in the fields . . . the voters at a town meeting, the village brawler in a tavern full of tipsy riot, the conservative who thinks the nation is lost if his ticket chance to miscarry, the bigot worshipping the knot hole through which a dusty beam of light has looked in upon his darkness, the radical who declares that nothing is good if established, and the patent reformer who screams in your ears that he can finish the world with a single touch." It was out of all these that Emerson made his poetry and illustrated his philosophy.

He was, in short, a true original. "Eminently a child of Christianity and of the American idea, he is out of the Church and out of the State. In the midst of Calvinistic and Unitarian superstition, he does not fear God, but loves and trusts Him. . . . Reproached as an idler, he is active as the sun, and pours out his radiant truth on Lyceums at Chelmsford, at Waltham, at Lowell, and all over the land. Out of a cold Unitarian Church rose this most lovely light" to shine unclouded over the Tory town of Boston—"graceful as Phoebus-Apollo, fearless and tranquil as the sun he was supposed to guide." Such was the beauty of his speech, "such the majesty of his ideas, such the power of the moral sentiment in men, and such the impression which his whole character makes on them, that they lend him, everywhere, their ears, and thousands bless his manly thoughts."

These were Emerson's virtues. But Parker would not have been Parker had he permitted friendship to hinder him "from speaking of [Emerson's] faults." These included "the want of logic in his method, and his exaggeration of the intuitive powers." Parker found "the unhappy consequences" of these faults among some of Emerson's followers and admirers. They were "more faithful than he to the false principle" that he laid down, thinking themselves wise because they did not study, learned because they were ignorant of books, and inspired because what they said outraged common sense. Although Parker did not name names, he could have had in mind the egregious idiosyncrasies of such an Emersonian as Ellery Channing.

As for Emerson's poetry, said Parker, it often showed a "ruggedness and want of finish" that seemed willful in such a man as he. This fault was very obvious in those pieces he had used as epigraphs to his several essays. Sometimes there was "a seed-corn of thought" in a given stanza, but the rest was "like a pile of rubbish shot out of a cart" that hindered the seed from germinating. One unfortunate result of this careless habit was that "his admirers and imitators" offered up "only the rubbish," and very probably justified themselves "by the example of their master." These defects aside, however, Emerson's works had been an "ennobling influence," had signally helped to "redeem American literature from the reproach of imitation, conformity, meanness of aim, and hostility to the progress of mankind."

In September 1850, when the *Massachusetts Quarterly Review* followed the *Dial* into the limbo of bankrupt magazines, Parker's life accelerated, if that were possible, into a new and final phase. He turned to politics with the same fervor he had brought to the polemics of theology, and his activities might have been described in the terms once applied to English William Hazlitt: "Politics went always at his side like a mastiff, and 'Love me, love my dog' was his maxim." Parker now said that the church had allied itself too closely with the establishment. If it professed Christianity, it should set about reforming the world according to genuine Christian ideals, and reformation of this sort depended above all on practical good works.

This was nothing new for Parker. Ever since moving to Boston, he had met in his crowded study at Exeter Place a continuous flow of assistance seekers. Like Emerson, though more sporadically, he kept a journal, and one typical entry was entitled "Adventures of a Day":

> After attending to numerous little matters, I sat down to complete my sermon; and there came, 1. A black man—a quite worthy one—for some pecuniary aid. 2. An Orthodox minister from Ohio, seeking aid to erect a free church in his State. He wants five thousand dollars. . . . 3. Came a clergyman to talk about the Zoroastrian doctrine of the immortality of the soul, and to get Oporin's *De Immortalitate Mortalium*, which I had imported for him. 4. Silas Lamson, with his full beard and white garments. He has two machines which he wished me to look at. They are to facilitate spading, ploughing, etc. He wants me to get them before the Exhibition in New York. . . .

The black man who had needed money was only one of dozens. It may well have been in honor of such men as he that Parker kept a bronze statue of Spartacus beside his rolltop desk. In one way or another he was associated with almost all the blacks in Boston, whether illustrious or obscure. Frederick Douglass, the "dusky archangel" of abolition, was a close friend, and one of

Parker's own parishioners was the black leader Lewis Hayden, whose house served as a busy way station on the Underground Railroad.

But it was not Parker, or even Parker's good example, that aroused Emerson's anger close to the midpoint of the nineteenth century. It was rather the intransigence of his former idol, Daniel Webster, in a congressional oration on March 7, favoring a complex of separate bills later known as the Compromise of 1850—a speech on which more than 800 Bostonians sent Webster a congratulatory letter hailing the presumptive settlement of the slavery question. Among the provisos of the new legislation was the resurrection of the old fugitive slave ordinance, which became law on September 18. "This filthy enactment," as Emerson called it, was "the most detestable" of statutes. "I will not obey it, by God!"

Early in 1851 he read in a newspaper Webster's open letter invoking the name of liberty. "Pho!" wrote Emerson, "Let Mr Webster for decency's sake shut his lips once and forever on this word." In his mouth "liberty" sounded "like the word *love* in the mouth of a courtezan." It meant the "kidnapping and hunting to death" of black men and women. As for its congressional champion, "morals he has none, but a hole in his head," being unable to "conceive a grand design and put it through." New Hampshire, said Emerson, had "always been distinguished for the servility of its eminent men." Webster had hitherto resisted the habits of his compatriots, but had now miserably succumbed. Living with little people, he showed that he could be too easily led by their limitations.

Chapter Twenty-eight

THE ABSENTEES:
HAWTHORNE

EMERSON'S HOPES FOR A PERMANENT COMMUNITY OF WRITers and thinkers in Concord suffered a series of blows between the fall of 1845 and the summer of 1850. The Hawthornes were the first to leave, after three years and three months at the Old Manse. Emerson's half-uncle, the Reverend Samuel Ripley of Waltham, wished to occupy the house he had inherited in 1841 upon the death of his father, Dr. Ezra Ripley. In anticipation of his move to Concord, Ripley sent round a repair crew of carpenters and painters. They ripped down the woodbine from the southern exterior, made a "tremendous racket among the outbuildings," strewed the lawn with pine shavings and wood chips, and vexed "the whole antiquity of the place with their discordant renovations." Hawthorne found the whole operation comparable to "rouging the venerable cheeks of one's grandmother."

It was obviously time to go. "We gathered up our household goods," he wrote, "drank a farewell cup of tea in our pleasant little breakfast-room . . . and passed forth between the tall stone gateposts" that marked the entrance to the Manse. The irony was that they need not have hurried away after all. Emerson's disappointment showed in a letter to his brother William on October 2: "Mr. Hawthorne leaves Concord today. Mr. Ripley comes not until the spring."

Their destination was the dark and dank old house on Herbert Street in Salem that Hawthorne persistently called Castle Dismal. His mother and his two unmarried sisters, Elizabeth and Louisa, received them cordially enough, but they were barely settled in when Sophia discovered that she was pregnant. "Blessed be the child whom thy heart is brooding over," wrote Hawthorne in November to his wife in Boston, where she and little Una were staying with her sister Mary's family at 77 Carver Street. She would return to Boston at intervals during her pregnancy, feeling safe, as Hawthorne believed, with her sister at her elbow, her mother at arm's length, and her beloved Dr. William Wesselhoeft just around the corner.

Hawthorne himself was intensely busy. Sick of "the anguish of debt" that had sporadically overshadowed the lost paradise in Concord, he was now determined to secure a position that would guarantee him a decent income. Through the fall and winter he pulled all possible political strings to be appointed surveyor at the Salem Custom House. He was also assembling a selection of his stories and sketches for publication under the title *Mosses from an Old Manse*. For many months he had been wrestling with an introductory autobiographical essay that looked back nostalgically upon his life in Concord. On April 15, 1846, it was finished at last and he mailed it off to Evert Duyckinck: "I send you the initial article, promised so many thousand years ago."

The account of Emerson in this essay more than made up for the satirical jibes that had been set down in Hawthorne's notebook in 1842. At the southern end of the village, a brisk fifteen-minute walk from the "serene and sober" Manse, there lived, he wrote, "a great original Thinker"—a "free spirit," whose intellectual fire, like "a beacon burning on a hilltop," had attracted to Concord a veritable host of hobgoblins and night birds. Never, he thought, "was a poor little country village infested with such a variety of queer, strangely dressed, oddly behaved mortals, most of whom took upon themselves to be important agents of the world's destiny, yet were simply bores."

It had not occurred to Hawthorne to ask Emerson for the master word that might have helped him solve the riddle of the universe. He had been content to admire his neighbor "as a poet of deep beauty and austere tenderness" whom it was good to meet in the woodpaths or along the road by the Manse "with that pure intellectual gleam diffused about his presence like the garment of a shining-one; and he so quiet, so simple, so without pretension," as if he always expected "to receive more than he could impart." It was very likely, thought Hawthorne, that many an ordinary man carried in his heart inscriptions that Emerson would not have been able to read. Yet you could not live near him without "inhaling, more or less, the mountain-atmosphere of his lofty thought"—even at the risk of becoming giddy, "new truth being as heady as new wine."

During the first week in April, just as he was polishing up this "character" of Emerson, his political efforts of the fall and winter were rewarded by his appointment as surveyor. On the seventeenth Sophia wrote her father that Hawthorne was starting work immediately, "for the present incumbent is making six dollars a day, which is more than $1,800 a year, and it is a shame that the real surveyor should lose so much." Sophia's computation multiplied $6 times 313 days (Sundays excluded) for a total of $1,878, though the actual salary of the surveyor was roughly $5 a week, or $250 per annum. The port fees more than made up for the niggardly government payments, of which the first, covering the period April 20 to June 30, amounted to only $49.49. On the other hand, the presence of the surveyor was required only three and a half hours per day, and Hawthorne told Duyckinck in mid-April that "my office (the duties of it being chiefly performable by deputy) will allow me as much time for literature as can be profitably applied."

He had recently published an anonymous review of a romance called *Typee* by an obscure young ex-sailor named Melville living in New York. "He has that freedom of view," wrote Hawthorne, "—it would be too harsh to call it laxity of principle—which renders him tolerant of codes of morals that may be little in accordance with our own; a spirit proper enough to a young and adventurous sailor, and which makes his book the more wholesome to our staid landsmen." Hawthorne's *Mosses* had been out four years before Melville discovered and read it, publishing anonymously in the *Literary World* an appreciation that more than repaid Hawthorne for his praises of *Typee*.

Lack of money was a recurrent problem for Hawthorne. In the fall of 1845 he had brought suit against George Ripley and Charles Dana for the repayment of his original investment in Brook Farm. But the Fourierist establishment had fallen upon evil times, including a siege of smallpox and the loss by fire of the New Phalanstery in March 1846. Hawthorne had asked for $800, was awarded about $600, and in the end collected not a penny, owing to a legal stratagem successfully argued by Dana and Ripley, and in the face of persistent rumors that this famous experiment in communal living was on the verge of bankruptcy. "Let it sink," wrote Hawthorne sourly. "It has long since ceased to have any sympathy from me, though individually I wish well to all concerned."

June was a month of new beginnings. On the fifth, a two-volume set of *Mosses from an Old Manse* was deposited for copyright, and Hawthorne soon began to call the book to the attention of various potential reviewers, including Edgar Allan Poe of New York. On the twenty-second he wrote his sister Louisa from Boston about the birth of "a small troglodyte" at 5:50 that morning. The inveterate nicknamer was at work again. The child was not only called a troglodyte, since he had dwelt in a kind of cave for the past nine months, but also "The Black Prince," owing to his dark hair and swarthy complexion, and then, for many weeks thereafter, "Bundlebreech" in apparent allusion to his appearance when diapered. The parents postponed for nearly a year the selection of the boy's name until, having rejected Theodore and Gerald, they fixed at last upon Julian.

During the same period, at home in Concord, Emerson had carried on an epistolary quarrel with Wiley and Putnam, publishers of *Mosses from an Old Manse*, over what he took to be their sharp practice in connection with the American edition of Carlyle's life of Cromwell. The problem first appeared in December 1845, and Emerson was still wrathful about it a year later. As noted earlier, he had meantime declined to lecture at the New Bedford Lyceum as a protest against their exclusion of blacks from the audience. He had revised his will and applied to Harvard College Library for book-borrowing privileges. He had helped gather funds for Ellery Channing's European tour, and said good-bye to Margaret Fuller before she left for England and the Continent. He had welcomed Thoreau back to Walden Pond after his night in jail for nonpayment of taxes. To save the ailing Lidian vexatious problems with servants, he had entered into an agreement with the very capable Mrs. Marston Goodwin to establish a kind of Brook Farm in parvo, whereby the whole Emerson family boarded with her under their own roof.

The rehearsal of all such details seemed to him, as he wrote Elizabeth Hoar in July, like "the very counting of threads in a beggar's coat, to tell the chronicle of nothings into which nevertheless thought and meaning and hope contrive to intervene and it is out of this sad lint and rag fair that the web of lasting life is woven. . . . We should be no better than parsnips, if we could not still look over our shoulders at the Power that drives us, and escape from private insignificance into a faith in the transcendant significance of our doing and being."

When they returned from Boston to Salem in August 1846, the Hawthornes managed to rent one of the stately houses on Chestnut Street. Having now what he called "a moderate share of prosperity," the surveyor of the Port of Salem described himself as "contented and happy." He gave a copy of his *Mosses* to the Athenaean Society and spent an evening out in the company of Emerson, whose first volume of poems was about to be published by James Munroe. In preparing the *Mosses* for publication, Hawthorne had deleted ten paragraphs from "The Hall of Fantasy" sketch, where he had previously alluded semisatirically to some two dozen of the leading literary men of the early 1840s. But the introductory essay had left him open to allegations of overinfluence from the Transcendentalists and the Fourierists. Reviewing the volume, a Unitarian minister named Samuel Dutton blamed the "amiable and highly cultivated, but misty and groping philanthropists of the 'Concord Sect' and the 'Roxbury Phalanx' [at Brook Farm]." On the other hand, Dutton was sufficiently impressed to remark that it was a waste of genius "to shut up Nathaniel Hawthorne in a custom house." Emerson's private criticism, entered in his journal for 1846, was that "Hawthorn [sic] invites his readers too much into his study, opens the process before them. As if the confectioner should say to his customers Now let us make the cake." Hawthorne's encomium in "The Old Manse" essay, while certainly flattering, had not wholly revised Emerson's negative attitude.

Ellery Channing came for a week's visit in March 1847, bringing an enormous appetite—"he eats like an Anaconda," said Hawthorne—and the manuscript of his *Conversations in Rome*, the by-product of his hasty foreign tour of the preceding year. Hawthorne alerted Duyckinck to the existence of the book, but Emerson had interceded with Munroe for the publication of Ellery's poems, second series, which had appeared in January, and subsequently for the *Conversations*, which appeared in Boston that June.

In September 1847 the Hawthorne family located a highly satisfactory house in Mall Street, their third and final Salem address, with room for Hawthorne's mother and sisters, as well as a proper study for the master. But his financial situation was still extremely shaky. When his erstwhile landlord, the Reverend Samuel Ripley, died in November, the surveyor of revenue had to borrow to settle his long-outstanding debt for rental at the Manse.

By this date Emerson was in England, consorting with lords and ladies and the chief literary lights, having persuaded Thoreau to give up his cabin at Walden and to serve again as paterfamilias in the Emerson household. Hawthorne was meanwhile collecting his trifling salary and borrowing from his friends to pay his bills. But in one respect both the Hawthornes adjudged themselves superior to the great man of Concord. Back at the Manse in 1843, Sophia had complained that "Waldo Emerson knows not much of love. . . . He has never yet known what union meant with any soul." Now, nearly five years later, Emerson was writing to Lidian from England that he could not compose the reassuring love letter she had always wanted from him, and acknowledging that the cause was a "poverty" in his nature, a "trick of solitariness" that would never leave him. Now at the same time in Salem, while Sophia was vacationing in West Newton with her sister, Hawthorne repeatedly bemoaned her absence from their "great, lonesome bed . . . the scene of so many blissful interviews." She had lately sent him such a sexy love letter that she begged him to burn two pages of it. "I cannot do it, and will not," said her spouse, "for never was a wife's deep, warm, chaste love so well expressed. . . . I verily believe that no mortals, save ourselves, have ever known what enjoyment was. How wonderful that to the pure in spirit all earthly bliss is given in a measure which the voluptuary never can have dreamed of."

That fall and winter Hawthorne served as program chairman for the Salem Lyceum, extending invitations to a dozen outside lecturers, including Thoreau and Emerson. Thoreau regaled his audiences with preview chapters from his *Walden* manuscript, which would not be published until 1854. The day after one of his lectures, Hawthorne took him to Cambridge to dine with Longfellow, having forewarned their host of Thoreau's "iron-poker-ishness" and "uncompromising stiffness." But Ellery Channing was also there, and Thoreau may have relaxed in the presence of his perennial hiking companion. Emerson, home from his foreign tour, agreed to a lecture on English traits, and stayed overnight in Mall Street with the Hawthornes so that Sophia could show off Una and Julian to the man who loved children.

When Alcott reached Salem in February to conduct one of his "Conversations," he mentioned Thoreau's forthcoming book, *A Week on the Concord and Merrimack Rivers*, due for publication in May after years of postponement. Emerson had been touting it ever since the summer of 1846 when Thoreau had read him extracts from the manuscript in the shade of an oak tree on the Concord riverbank. When Hawthorne wrote to assure Thoreau of his pleasure at the news, Thoreau answered that while writing the book he had thought of Hawthorne as a potential reader of it. He named no particular passages, but in the section called "Friday" he had mentioned the pink flowers of *rhexia Virginica,* which had "almost too gay an appearance for the rest of the landscape, like a pink ribbon on the bonnet of a Puritan woman." The simile was evidently borrowed from Hawthorne's early story "Young Goodman Brown," which had first appeared in 1835 and was now collected in the *Mosses* volume. Brown's pretty Puritan wife proudly sports a cap with pink ribbons that figures prominently and symbolically in the narrative, like the scarlet rosebush beside the gray prison in *The Scarlet Letter.*

Hawthorne rightly foresaw the end of his employment at the customhouse when General Zachary Taylor won the presidency in 1848. The Whigs were in the saddle, riding mankind, and Hawthorne was a Democrat. In March 1849 he heard that a junta had been formed to evict him, and his surmise was confirmed by telegraph on June 8, almost exactly three years after he had taken the oath of office. "I feel pretty well since my head has been chopt off," he told Longfellow. "It is not so essential a part of the human system as a man is apt to think." Later on he would recall that for a week or two after the news broke he had gone "careering through the public prints . . . like Irving's Headless Horseman. . . . Keeping up the metaphor of the political guillotine," said he, his writings might henceforth be called "POSTHUMOUS PAPERS OF A DECAPITATED SURVEYOR."

Insouciant as these words were, it was impossible to shrug off all his troubles. Shortly before his demotion, both his children had come down with scarlet fever—"the little boy . . . in quite an alarming way." Although he did not mention the death of young Waldo Emerson from the same disease in 1842, he was now prepared to understand Emerson's feelings at that time: "I could not have submitted in the least, had it gone ill with [Julian]," he confessed to Longfellow, "but God spared me that trial—and there are no real misfortunes, save such as that. Other troubles may irritate me superficially; nothing else can go near the heart."

One further misfortune was the death of his mother on July 31. After years of hiding away in her chamber at Castle Dismal, she had more recently responded to the presence of Una and Julian in something like a normal grandmotherly fashion. Hawthorne, a faithful if independent son, wept quietly by her deathbed in what he called his darkest hour to date. But the double loss of his job and his closest blood relative had the effect of setting him spiritually free to perform his proper work. Early in September he began to write the book that would establish his reputation as one of the ablest novelists in the Republic. Sophia was almost frightened by the intensity of his effort: "He writes immensely," she told her mother. "But he is well now and looks shining."

As he had done for *Mosses* in 1846, he chose to write an autobiographical preface for his forthcoming novel. He was gently satirical about the elderly hangers-on at the customhouse, and contrasted his new situation in Salem with his old one in Concord:

> After my fellowship of toil and impracticable schemes with the dreamy brethren of Brook Farm; after living for three years within the subtile influence of an intellect like Emerson's; after those wild, free days on the Assabeth, indulging fantastic speculations, beside our fire of fallen boughs, with Ellery Channing; after talking with Thoreau about pine-trees and Indian relics, in his hermitage at Walden . . . it was time, at length, that I should exercise other faculties of my nature, and nourish myself with food for which I had hitherto had little appetite. Even the old Inspector [aged eighty, "and certainly one of the most wonderful specimens of winter-green that you would be likely to discover in a life-time's search"] was desirable, as a change of diet, to a man who had known Alcott. . . .

But he looked even farther back than 1842 for the subject of the novel itself. The ancestress of his heroine, Hester Prynne, had appeared briefly as early as 1838 in the short story "Endicott and the Red Cross," where an un-named young woman is compelled to wear the scarlet letter *A* on the breast of her gray gown to traumatize her for a single act of adultery. Hawthorne had likewise engaged themes like "the unpardonable sin," wherein a man tracks his carbonaceous footprints over the heart of another, as Chillingworth wreaks vengeance upon the Reverend Arthur Dimmesdale; and the theme of *felix culpa,* the fortunate fall by which Hester is enabled to grow stronger and better under her ignominious badge of shame, is foreshadowed in the Red Cross story.

There is, moreover, a curious passage in the twentieth chapter that appears to have been written under what Hawthorne had called "the subtile influence of an intellect like Emerson's," and specifically Emerson the rebel, Emerson the Ishmaelite intent to contravene the polite social restraints of the age. It is toward the end of *The Scarlet Letter*. The minister Dimmesdale is returning from his clandestine tryst with Hester in the forest, charged with unaccustomed physical energy, and conscious of a deep internal "revolution of thought and feeling." As he enters the streets of the town, every step incites him "to do some strange, wild, wicked thing." Meeting one of his deacons, he barely restrains himself from "uttering certain blasphemous suggestions . . . respecting the communion supper." When he encounters a pious old grandam from his congregation, he almost, but not quite, whispers into her ear "a brief, pithy, and unanswerable argument against the immortality of the soul." He overcomes the impulse to teach some very wicked words to a little knot of Puritan children. And when he meets a drunken sailor, he comes close to shaking the blackguard's hand and giving himself the pleasure of uttering "a volley of good, round, solid, satisfactory and heaven-defying oaths."

The man who wrote this memorable scene was the same whom Emerson had once, and probably more than once, urged to read Rabelais, to be a renegade, to defy the prevailing powers. The good round solid volley of oaths that Dimmesdale longs to shout could have found their ancestry in such a passage as the following from Emerson's journals: "I have no less disgust than any other at the cant of Spiritualism. I had rather hear a round volley of Ann Street oaths than the affectation of that which is divine on the foolish lips of coxcombs."

Lidian Emerson

John Murray Forbes,
Ralph Waldo Emerson,
and Ralph Waldo Forbes

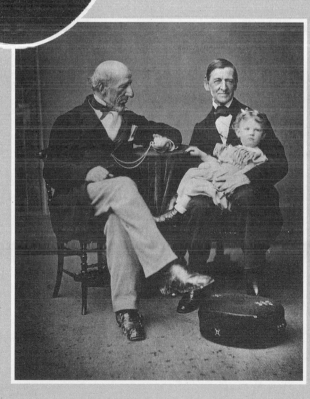

Margaret Fuller

Henry David Thoreau

Nathaniel Hawthorne

Ellery Channing

Bronson Alcott

Louisa May Alcott

*Ralph Waldo and Lidian Emerson
and their descendants*

Ralph Waldo
Emerson

Walt
Whitman

MARGARET FULLER
ABROAD

⊠ ALONG WITH OTHER FRIENDS AND RELATIVES OF MARGARET
Fuller's, Emerson appeared at her mother's house in Cambridgeport
the day before she sailed with the Springs for Liverpool. She had written him
rather plaintively from New York that it had begun to seem "as if you meant
to let me go and make no sign." In fact he had already notified Carlyle of Margaret's imminent departure, asking him to "give a good and faithful interview
to this wise, sincere, accomplished, and most entertaining of women."

Now he handed her a long letter of introduction. It said that he and Margaret had rarely met since her departure for New York in 1844, but that her
performance as literary critic for Greeley's *Tribune* had been entirely "honourable," if not, he had to say, wholly satisfactory as a form of employment.
She deserved better, and he was "heartily glad" of her European plans. Noble
and generous in mind and character, she knew more about Goethe than any
other American, and was well informed in the literatures of France and Italy.
She stood out in New England as an "exotic," like a "foreigner from some
more sultry and expansive climate." In short, said Emerson, "she is our citizen of the world by quite special diploma."

The meeting with Carlyle and his wife, Jane, did not come until October.
In the interim, Margaret and her companions toured the Midlands, the Lake
District, and Scotland. Her adventures included meetings with Wordsworth,
De Quincey, Harriet Martineau, Joanna Baillie, and Alexander Ireland,
Emerson's champion from 1833, as well as a descent into a coal mine in New-

castle and one frigid and dripping night when Margaret got lost on the flanks of Ben Lomond.

The first of three engagements with the Carlyles took place on October 7. Margaret enjoyed "the rich flow of his discourse" while being permitted now and then to talk in her turn—"enough to free my lungs and change my position, so that I did not get tired." Next day Carlyle wrote his brother of this "strange *lilting* lean old maid, not nearly such a bore as I expected," and later sent Emerson a politely tactful account: "a high-soaring, clear, enthusiast soul . . . a sharp subtle intellect too; and less of that shoreless Asiastic [sic] dreaminess than I have sometimes met with in her writings." He picked up Emerson's adjective, "exotic": "Her dialect is very vernacular—extremely exotic in the London climate." But his private note on their third meeting at Lord Ashburton's mansion shortly before the Americans left for Paris was again splenetic: "Last night a weary tea with the American Margt Fuller and Mazzini—not to be repeated!" The presence of Giuseppe Mazzini, a dear friend of his wife's, had led Carlyle to invectives against the "rose-water imbecilities" of all such political idealists. After some efforts to remonstrate, as Margaret reported to Emerson, Mazzini had subsided, looking "very sad."

Then in his early forties, Mazzini was a Genoese who had long before organized the Giovine Italia in Marseilles. Since 1837 he had been living and teaching in exile in London, deluging his native land with pamphlets on the necessity of Italian unity under a republican government. With the thin, bearded face and blazing dark eyes of a revolutionary saint, he soon became the first of the new gods in Margaret's European pantheon: "by far the most beauteous person I have seen," she wrote to Caroline Sturgis. "He is one in whom holiness has purified, but nowhere dwarfed the man." And her estimate of his moral stature steadily advanced the longer she knew him—"a great man," she later asserted, "in mind a great poetic statesman; in heart, a lover; in action, decisive and full of resource as Cesar. Dearly I love Mazzini."

The Americans left for Paris on November 11, 1846, and Margaret's first personal letter to Emerson was sent five days later. She recalled that England had abounded in "devout" admirers of the defunct *Dial* and that people everywhere were reading the second volume of Emerson's essays. Between November and the following June she sent him at least three more letters, to each of which he sympathetically responded. From Naples in mid-March she told him of having met another of his admirers shortly before leaving Paris in

February. This was Adam Mickiewicz, sometime professor of Slavonic literature at the Collège de France. Like Mazzini, he was living in exile because of
earlier revolutionary activities. He was also Poland's leading epic poet, and
when Margaret sent him a copy of Emerson's poems, he came at once to
talk—a large bearded man about the age of Carlyle, but far more winning and
affable. With a sly dig at Emerson's distrust of the passions, Margaret wrote
him that her Polander was just such a man as she had long wished to meet—
one who combined "the intellect and passions in due proportion for a full and
healthy human being, with a soul constantly inspiring." In line with her lifelong policy of keeping secrets secret, she did not tell Emerson of Mickiewicz's
straightforward sexual advice: "You have acquired the right to know and to
maintain the rights and the obligations, the hopes and the exigencies of virginity. For you the first step of your deliverance and the deliverance of your
sex . . . is to know whether you are permitted to remain a virgin." She must
have complained to him of her "ugliness," for he advised her to think of herself as a beauty. She obviously needed the "society of Italians" and the "air of
the South" to refresh and make her bloom.

In Paris she attended lectures at the Academy and visited the picture galleries and the Chamber of Deputies. But what she had really needed there was
someone to show her around the city, "to initiate me into various little secrets
of the place and time." Despite her intimate interview with the famous novelist George Sand and a short private concert by Madame Sand's ailing lover,
Chopin, she always felt pushed for time. It had pained her to have to leave after "having touched only the glass over the picture." Emerson's reply urged
her to conquer the language: it would unlock the "jewelled cabinets" of
French civilization. He added some news from Massachusetts: Thoreau's
two-part article on Carlyle had just appeared in *Graham's Magazine*, and he
had vastly amused a Concord Lyceum audience with a talk on his life at
Walden Pond. Emerson himself had lectured on "Eloquence" in Boston with
a dozen of Margaret's old friends in attendance. According to Caroline Sturgis, they all agreed that his oral essay was too "old." This judgment amused
Emerson, but he was much displeased over the "hateful errata"—in excess of
two dozen—in the British edition of his poems.

Margaret's letter from Naples reached Emerson on April 21, just as he was
plowing his garden plot and planning to set out a small orchard of apples and
pears. He had seen and admired her letter to Elizabeth Hoar on the meeting

with George Sand, and complimented Margaret on having "run out of the coop of our bigoted societies" into a more expansive foreign fellowship. It was just possible that he might be doing the same in the fall. Margaret's meeting in England with Alexander Ireland had apparently stirred Emerson's old friend into action, and arrangements for an English lecture tour had been pending since February.

In May Emerson offered a course of lectures at the Athenaeum in Nantucket. "This island," he wrote his daughter Ellen, aged eight,

is like a ship at sea. . . . All the people here live by killing whales, which in old times used to swim about the island and the men went out in boats and killed them with harpoons; but now they go to the Pacific Ocean for them in great ships. . . . One day [in 1820] when the ship Essex was sailing there, a great sperm whale was seen coming with full speed towards the vessel: in a moment he struck the ship with terrible force, staving in some planks, and causing a leak: then he went off a little way, and came back swiftly, the water all white with his violent motion, and struck the ship a second frightful blow; the crew were obliged instantly to escape in boats, and the ship sunk in a few minutes.

Now in 1847, Captain George Pollard Junior, aged fifty-six, was still living in Nantucket, one of only five survivors of the *Essex* disaster.

In June Emerson resumed his transatlantic correspondence with Margaret, still harping on his former theme of American sterility: "The famine in Europe only affects potatoes, the sterility in America continues in the men." He was "heartily glad" that she had met Sand and Mickiewicz and heard Chopin play, and that she was now in Rome, "which like Nature has that elasticity of application to all measures of spirit," always keeping its old promises. "O Sappho, Sappho, friend of mine!" he exclaimed. "I would fain know the best of your Roman experiences."

But Sappho the secret keeper did not divulge the whole truth about her Roman adventures. It would be a long time before Emerson learned of one crucial meeting that had occurred early in April. Margaret and the Springs had attended vespers at St. Peter's during Easter week. Afterward, temporarily separated from her companions in the evening gloom, she had been at a loss to find her way back to their quarters. A slender stripling with dark eyes and hair, quiet and gentlemanly in deportment, had offered his services, guided her home, and kissed her hand in parting. This was the Marchese Giovanni D'Ossoli, youngest son in a large family of lesser nobility chiefly employed in the court of the new pope, Pius IX. Soon after her encounter with Ossoli, Margaret was attracted to another and even younger man, an American painter named Thomas Hicks, to whom she presently addressed an ardent note beginning "Dear Youth," and including the sentence "I want to know and to love you and to have you love me." This was another version of the old cry "Do you love me?" by which she had variously embarrassed young Sam Ward, young Anna Barker, young Caroline Sturgis, and, in sundry verbal guises, the man she called the Sage of Concord. Hicks answered that there was "but little fire" on his hearth, and seems to have taken prompt evasive action. Although she and he continued on a friendly footing, crowned by his excellent portrait of her, in the end it was Ossoli who was going to change the whole course of Margaret's future life.

But not immediately. Her next extant letter to Emerson was posted from Florence on June 20. She had just left Rome on the first leg of a tour of northern Italy and was soon to revel in her first sight of Venice, where she parted company with the Springs—"high time," she wrote Caroline Sturgis in August, "for I had become quite insupportable. . . . I felt at times a wicked irritation against them for being the persons who took me away from France, which was no fault of theirs." To Emerson she said only that her French was now fluent though not correct, and that she was "sedulously" cultivating her Italian.

Using Goethe's *Italian Journey* as a guidebook, as Emerson had done in 1833, she presently set out alone for Milan and a whole range of other northern cities, as well as the Italian lakes and a corner of Switzerland. She gave herself a two-week holiday in the beautiful village of Bellagio on Lake Como in company with some of the "high society." This group included the Marchesa Costanza Arconati Visconti, whom she had met soon after reaching Rome and who became her closest friend among the women of Italy, and "a fair and brilliant Polish lady, born princess *Radzivill*." In Milan, she consorted with some young radical intellectuals who were working toward the Risorgimento, and spent an afternoon with the white-haired Alessandro Manzoni, known all over Europe for his novel *I Promessi Sposi*. Margaret's letter to Emerson spoke fondly of Manzoni's heroine, Lucia, and the courageous priest Fra' Cristoforo.

Most of September she spent in Florence recovering from the exhaustion of travel in the torrid Italian summer. "For three weeks," she told Caroline, "my life hung upon a thread. The effect of the Italian climate on my health is not favorable." But Rome was like a homecoming. "I am happily settled for the winter," she assured Emerson at the end of October, "quite by myself, in a neat, tranquil apartment in the Corso. . . . I live alone, eat alone, walk alone, and enjoy unspeakably the stillness, after all the rush and excitement of the past year. . . . My time will be like pure gold to me this winter; and, just for happiness, Rome itself is sufficient." All that fall she was doubly intoxicated by the balmy weather and the steady advancement of her love affair with Ossoli. "I have not been so well since I was a child," she wrote her mother in mid-December, "nor so happy ever."

Emerson was now in England. Late in August he had written Margaret about his preparations for travel. "When odd men . . . are to go away from home, it is with them a sort of day of quittance, when all their debts, pecuniary, social, ceremonial . . . must be paid. Garden, orchard, woodlot, peat meadow, all must be remembered, and the exigencies of the next Spring provided for." "This voyage of mine is not much," he told his brother in September. "It would be much if I were ready for it: but I am not. All my life is a sort of College Examination. I shall never graduate. I have always some tormenters ahead."

He had sailed at last on October 5 aboard the packet ship *Washington Irving*. Henry Thoreau, who had terminated his Walden residence after two years, two months, and two days, was back again at Coolidge Castle, watching over Lidian and the children for the duration. He had not been impressed by Emerson's stateroom—"like a carpeted dark closet," six feet by six, "with a large keyhole for a window" and a skylight with the dimensions of a doughnut. But the voyage had gone well enough. Once back on British soil after a lapse of fourteen years, Emerson closed out October with a four-day visit to the Carlyles in London, and gave his first lecture at Manchester on November 2. The torment, such as it was, had begun.

He was a few thousand miles closer to Margaret, but they were in touch only by mail. On December 1 he wrote Lidian: "I have a letter from Margaret

Fuller in Rome who is in a sort of beatitude of rest after years of hurry." He answered it on the fifth: "I rejoice in your beatitude . . . of rest in the old nest of power and fortune. . . . But you must not stay alone long. . . . The function of sibyl is to be sparingly discharged, and always from some domestical basis." But Margaret was not so much alone as she had indicated. "There is a Polish countess here, who likes me much," she told one of her many correspondents. "She has been very handsome, still is, in the style of a full-blown rose. She is a widow, very rich, one of the emancipated women, naturally vivacious, and with talent. This woman *envies* me; she says, 'How happy you are; so free, so serene, so attractive, so self-possessed!' I say not a word, but I do not look on myself as particularly enviable. . . . Had I money now,—could I only remain, take a faithful servant, and live alone, and still see those I love when it is best, that would suit me."

Most of her evenings, she told her mother, were spent in writing and study. She had gathered a small library of books about Italy and Rome. The weather was excellent: "Each day I am out from eleven till five, exploring some new object of interest." These lines were set down on December 16. She did not tell her mother, or anyone else, that many of her exploratory days had been spent in the devoted company of Ossoli, a faithful servant in the special Italian sense of *cavaliere servente*. Soon after her return to Rome in October, they had established a covert sexual relationship.

Thoreau wrote Emerson that he and Lidian were very good housekeepers: "She is a very dear sister to me." He had banked up the new apple and pear trees against winter and mice. He often roughhoused with Eddy, aged three, and gave him rides on his shoulders. "Mr. Thoreau," said the child one day, "will you be my father?" Emerson must certainly hurry home or he would be "superseded." But the boy soon made up for his momentary parental confusion. Thoreau reported: "Eddy climbed up the sofa, the other day, *of his own accord*, and kissed the picture of his father,—'right on his shirt, I did.' "

In England it was raining. "The umbrella," said Emerson, "is as essential as the hat." He could not walk the streets of Manchester without seeing women in rags accompanied by wan little creatures just the age and size of his own Edith. His daughters, as he told Lidian, should thank God that they were born in New England and would never have to "stand barefooted in the mud on a bridge in the rain all day to beg" from passersby. He gave many a coin to these bedraggled waifs, always thinking of Edith and Ellen. Only later, in *English Traits*, did he set down a more cynical judgment: "In cities, the children are trained to beg, until they shall be old enough to rob."

Rain was also falling in Italy. Beginning shortly before Christmas, torrential downpours reduced Rome to a gloomy mudhole for the better part of three months. The arrival of bad weather roughly coincided with Margaret's discovery that she was carrying Ossoli's child. "I have known some blessed, quiet days," she told Emerson on December 20, "when I could yield myself to be soothed and instructed by the great thoughts and memories of the place. But those days are swiftly passing. . . . There is this incubus of the future, and none to help me, if I am not prudent to face it. So ridiculous, too, this mortal coil." She was tired of keeping herself afloat without the strength to swim. "I should like to go to sleep, and be born again into a state where my young life should not be prematurely taxed."

A month later she came nearer to revealing her secret, this time to Caroline Sturgis: "With this year [1848], I enter upon a sphere of my destiny so difficult, that I, at present, see no way out, except through the gate of death. . . . I have no reason to hope I shall not reap what I have sown, and do not. Yet how I shall endure it I cannot guess; it is all a dark, sad enigma. . . . I am all alone; nobody around me sees any of this." Her mother had written about a visit to New York where she had witnessed some of the terrible conflicts between Molly Greeley and little Pickie, and of Molly's doleful remark that no one except Margaret could take proper care of the child. Now that she was to have one of her own, the prospect filled her with foreboding.

Caroline had married William Tappan on December 12, 1847, and might conceivably have understood the implications of Margaret's phrase about reaping what she had sown. Emerson, busy in England, saw the evidences of gloom without suspecting the chief reason for it. On receipt of Margaret's letter of December 20, he wrote a reply that he carried in his pocket for weeks and did not send. Not until March did he explain to Margaret that her complaints had made him wish to say "Come live with me at Concord." In the interim, a disturbing communication from Thoreau had revealed that Lidian had been very ill through most of January and February with an attack of jaundice that kept her constantly nauseated and "yellow as saffron." Emerson had told his wife of his wish to persuade Margaret to live in Concord after her European adventures. But the harassed and exhausted Lidian had responded with such "tragic letters" that he had felt obliged to drop the subject, though he assured Margaret that he still hoped to install her eventually in the small house he had built for Lucy Brown just opposite his front gate. He added that he would be very glad to see her in Paris in May. He presently apologized to Lidian for having upset her with his "plans for Margaret," which must have looked "calamitous enough" to such a "poor invalid" as she.

His homebound letters had been full and frequent, averaging roughly one a week, and Lidian's to him were packed with anecdotes about the children as well as far less welcome news of debts and creditors. But once at least, from the depths of her illness, she sent him a melancholy complaint about his failure to have written the kind of letter she most wanted to receive. His answer could not have done much to relieve her troubled mind:

Ah you still ask me for that unwritten letter always due, it seems, always unwritten, from year to year, by me to you, dear Lidian. . . . I have only to say that I also bemoan myself daily for the same cause—that I cannot write this letter, that I have not stamina and constitution enough to mind the two functions of seraph and cherub, oh no, let me not use such great words—rather say that a photometer [which measures light] cannot be a stove. It must content you for the time, that I truly acknowledge a poverty of nature, and have really no proud defence to set up, but ill-health, puniness, and Stygian limitation. . . . Besides am I not, O best Lidian, a most foolish affectionate goodman and papa with a weak side towards apples and sugar and all domesticities, when I am once in Concord? Answer me that. Well I will come again shortly and behave as best I can[.] Only I foresee plainly that the trick of solitariness never never can leave me.

Now in England his habit of solitude was constantly challenged by the necessity of meeting hundreds of people, both those in his lecture audiences and the many who gave entertainments in his honor or otherwise lionized him. He paid a call on Wordsworth and talked with De Quincey, as Margaret Fuller had done, had his portrait painted by David Scott, dined and breakfasted with lords and ladies and bishops, attended a reception for Chopin, who had come to London to offer a series of *matinées musicales,* spent two days at Oxford, dining at high table with the dons, and even met Byron's daughter Ada. He talked with Dickens about male chastity—"as good as gone in our times," said Dickens—and with the saturnine, pipe-smoking Tennyson—"Take away Hawthorne's bashfulness, and let him talk easily and fast, and you would have a pretty good Tennyson." He conversed with the duke of Argyle, finding it "quite surprising to detect so much good sense in a duke," and attended a soirée given by the marquis of Northampton, where he watched Victoria's Prince Albert "for some minutes across a table as a personage of much historical interest." In April he asked Lidian, "After all the ostentation of my fashionable acquaintance, do you believe that my rusticities are smoothed down, and my bad manners mended? Not in the smallest degree. I have not acquired the least facility, nor can hope to. But I do not decline these opportunities, as they are all valuable to me, who would at least know how that 'other half' of the world lives, though I cannot and would not live with them."

Along with his crowded calendar of social engagements, he accomplished as much sightseeing as time allowed, visiting the House of Lords, the Commons, the British Museum, Kew Gardens, Pope's grotto and Walpole's Strawberry Hill estate at Twickenham, and Gray's country churchyard at Stoke Poges. Late in his stay he met the twenty-nine-year-old novelist-to-be George Eliot, gazed down at the playing fields of Eton (as Gray had done) from the parapets of Windsor Castle, and made a hasty trip with Carlyle to see Stonehenge and Salisbury cathedral.

Each day he read the London *Times*, which he called "the best newspaper of the world," scanning its columns for news of the fall of Louis Philippe in France and the popular uprisings in Sicily, Naples, Milan, and Venice. In Rome, Margaret was steadfastly writing dispatches for Greeley's *Tribune* and enduring the headaches and morning nausea incidental to her developing pregnancy. In mid-March she responded to Emerson's invitation to meet him in Paris by saying that Mickiewicz had recently come to Rome—the one person she would have wished to see if she had returned to Paris—"and [now] I have him much better here." Again she pleaded ill health (she could not leave her fireside or exert herself at all) but without giving the real reasons. Emerson, as always, was touched to learn of her "debility and pain." It was clearly "imprudent" for her to stay on in Italy: "Can you not safely take the first steamer to Marseilles, come to Paris, and go home with me?"

She responded with an even firmer no. She would like to return with him but still had "much to do and learn in Europe." She was deeply interested in the "public drama" of the revolution and wanted to play her part in it, whether as "actor or historian." Her letter reached him while he was in Paris in May. He answered it on the eve of his return to London, where he was scheduled to offer a final series of lectures. Still doggedly persistent, he now urged her to "come to London immediately and sail home" with him.

But she had made up her mind and believed she understood Emerson's position. "I hear often from Waldo," she wrote "Aunt" Mary Rotch. "He sees much, learns much always, but loves not Europe. There is no danger of the idle intimations of other minds altering his course, more than of the moving a star. He knows himself and his vocation." Her own vocation was going to be motherhood and the attempt to summarize recent European history. By the end of May, when Emerson posted his letter from Paris, she had already left for Aquila, a village in the Abruzzi region some sixty miles northeast of Rome. There, and afterward in Rieti, thirty miles west of Aquila, she spent that summer of 1848, trying to get forward with her book on the Italian revolutions and preparing, not without fear, for the arrival of her baby.

She must stay, Emerson would not. In a speech at the annual soirée of the Manchester Athenaeum a month after his arrival in England in 1847, he had predicted that this nation, "Mother of heroes," would survive the current economic depression. If not, said he, "I will go back to the capes of Massachusetts and my own Indian stream, and say to my countrymen, the old race are all gone, and the elasticity and hope of mankind must henceforth remain on the Allegany [sic] ranges, or nowhere." Nine months later, ready for home, he was still of the same opinion: "I told Carlyle on the way to Stonehenge that . . . though I was dazzled by the wealth and power and success everywhere apparent [in England]—yet I knew very well that the moment I returned to America, I should lapse again into the habitual feeling which the vast physical influences of that continent inevitably inspire of confidence that there and there only is the right home and seat of the English race; and this great England will dwindle again to an island which has done well, but has reached its utmost expansion."

In *English Traits* he would put the matter even more bluntly: "England, an old and exhausted island, must one day be contented, like other parents, to be strong only in her children." Although he had congratulated Margaret Fuller on having flown the coop of bigoted American society, he had now arrived, as a result of his English experiences, at a renewed belief in the future of

his homeland. Intimations of this conclusion had been apparent all along. After less than two months in London, he had told Margaret that though the
"book" of British society was "large and voluminous," he was less than eager
to go on with it: "Indeed my interest already flags." She replied from Rome
that she understood his "readiness to close the book of European society."
Yet she continued to be enthralled by the growing conflagration in Italy, by
the news that "Milan, Venice, Modena, and Parma were driving out their
tyrants," by the arrival in Rome of Adam Mickiewicz to mobilize the Polish legion in the republican cause, and by the return of Mazzini, after seventeen
years of exile, "to see what he foresaw" with a vision "far in advance of his
times." The fire that burned in the hearts of such men as these was, she said,
enough to keep her warm.

So they parted who had not been together. Emerson sailed for home from
Liverpool aboard the *Europa* on July 15. Four days earlier, from her "mountain solitude" in Rieti, Margaret had posted a letter that did not reach him until long after his return to Concord. She had recently been brooding upon her
obsessive religious exaltation of the fall of 1840. "Some years ago," she recalled, "I thought you very unjust, because you did not lend full faith to my
spiritual experiences; but I see you were quite right. I thought I had tasted of
the true elixir, and that the want of daily bread, or the pangs of imprisonment,
would never make me a complaining beggar. . . . Those were glorious hours,
and angels certainly visited me; but there must have been too much earth,—
too much taint of weakness and folly, so that baptism did not suffice. I know
now those same things, but at present they are words, not living spells." Although her referents were vague, she seemed to be saying that those hours of
spiritual glory were gone and that the angels had not returned.

She appended an account of her immediate surroundings: the clock that
was striking noon from the bell tower of the Chiesa del Purgatorio, the simple
peasants who tilled the soil, tended the sheep, and slumbered in the shade. "I
am to them a divine visitant,—an instructive Ceres,—telling them wonderful
tales of foreign customs, and even legends of the lives of their own saints.
They are people whom I could love and live with. Bread and grapes among
them would suffice me." Poor Margaret! She would presently discover that
her simple peasants were "the most ferocious and mercenary population of
Italy." They took her for "an ignorant *Inglese*" with untold wealth at her disposal, and assiduously set about plundering her in every way.

Meantime the goddess Ceres, otherwise the generative powers of nature, was steadily employed in Margaret's behalf. Near the end of August, Ossoli temporarily left his duties with the Civic Guard in Rome, came to Rieti on the twenty-seventh, and stayed with his future wife until on September 5, at age thirty-eight, attended by the local midwife, Margaret bore him a son. Whether or not the angels of 1840 had returned, there was no question about the name of this child. They called him Angelo.

Chapter Thirty

THE ABSENTEES:
ALCOTT

AFTER THE DEMISE OF FRUITLANDS AND THE DREARY INTER-
lude in the villages of Harvard and Still River, the Alcotts had taken up
residence at Hillside on the Lexington Road. Now in November 1848, after
three years and eight months of their second stay in Concord, they were
about to move again. One by one, Emerson's good companions were falling
away—Hawthorne to Salem, Margaret Fuller to Rome, and the Alcotts to
Boston. "My friends begin to value each other, now that A[lcott] is to go,"
wrote Emerson in his journal. "Ellery declares 'that he never saw that man
without being cheered,' and Henry says, 'He is the best natured man he ever
met. The rats and mice make their nests in him.' " As a farewell gesture Emerson gave a stag dinner on the afternoon of November 16. Longfellow came
over from Cambridge by train, and the other guests were Alcott's sturdy admirers, Thoreau and Channing.

The Alcotts were following the advice of Mrs. James Savage, who had
helped them through the Temple School debacle, and had recently urged
them to try once again to make their way in the city. Alcott had rebuilt and
considerably beautified Hillside and its environs, to say nothing of the Gothic
summerhouse he had erected in Emerson's yard. His competence as a gardener had kept the vegetarian family fed in the growing seasons, but the long
winters severely taxed their infinitesimal income and brought them repeatedly to the verge of desperation. To Abba Alcott this mode of life seemed
increasingly unendurable. The Emersons, of course, were always there,

watching over the family with neighborly devotion. In the fall of 1847 she had sent a note to Emerson, calling him—doubtless to his embarrassment—"our dearest well-beloved friend . . . invaluable as an influence and a love . . . gracious, generous, [and] good." But there were limits to dependence on one's neighbors, as she had recognized back in 1841 when she had declined Emerson's invitation to move her entire family into his house for an indefinite stay. She could also be acidulous when roused. Concord at large, as she told her brother in January 1848, was "cold, heartless, brainless, soulless," apparently because, as the wife of a known nonachiever, she had not been found socially acceptable. It was her misfortune to revere everything about her husband except his inability to make money. If he could not, she must, and that spring she took the bit in her teeth and went off to work in a private sanitarium in Waterford, Maine. The experiment was not in itself a great success, but it proved to her that she was capable of taking a stand against the always encroaching sea of debts. When she came back to Concord in August, she was determined to carry on, and it was she who finally engineered the move to Boston.

Alcott was ready. During his wife's absence in Maine he had "thought of fixing myself in Boston for more intimate communication with people." In fact he had been dreaming of conducting a series of "Conversations" under the capacious rubric "Man: His History, Resources, and Expectations"—a title that closely and ironically resembled that of David Hartley's century old associationist treatise, *Observations on Man, his Frame, his Duty, and his Expectations* (1749). Once the move was accomplished and the family established in a basement flat in Dedham Street, Alcott rented a room at 12 West Street and launched his project, newly energized by that perennial optimism with which he had started Temple School and Fruitlands.

While Alcott was settling up as a cultural missionary, his wife took on the duties of "Missionary to the Poor," supported by a group of wealthy donors whose aim was to ameliorate living conditions among the paupers of the metropolis. The work was extremely demanding. The city was filled with Irish immigrants, living in filthy slum tenements crammed with exhausted mothers, squalling babies, underpaid and illiterate laborers, drunkenness and disease—the American equivalent of the indigent populace that Emerson had encountered in the British Midlands in 1847. Abba Alcott tramped in all weathers through the streets of Boston, carrying baskets of secondhand clothing and provisions, visiting the sick, whispering words of hope to the hopeless, conferring with the members of her philanthropic board, raising money, handling hundreds of applications for relief, and writing reports on the conditions she encountered, with recommendations for remedial action. These tasks engaged her full attention from January 1849 to April 1850. In August 1850 she established an employment agency, finding domestic jobs for Irish servants.

Alcott, meanwhile, had sat conversing in his shabby West Street quarters, moving out into the hinterlands to gather small groups like the one he addressed in Salem in the winter of 1849. That April he sent his mother a typically bland summary of his recent activities:

I have been much occupied in my *"Conversations,"* both in this city and Salem; and am purposing to give courses in other places during the spring and summer. They interest me, and seem to please and instruct others. I have *"Readings"* also at my Rooms, No. 12 West Street.— Lately I have been interested in getting up a Club, which we call *"The Town and Country Club,"* which is to meet monthly . . . for the discussion of the great questions that now divide the minds of men: and which we hope to see a little more clearly into if we can. Emerson, Channing, Parker, Hawthorne, and others, to the number of 100, or more, of the leading minds of our time, are members, and I am to have charge of the Rooms and act as Secretary of the Club. This will give me a house and home in Boston, and bring most of the active Persons in the Reforms to my doors. It promises well. We shall live during the Summer in Temple Place, near the Masonic Temple where I had my school. . . .

His daughters were doing well—Anna teaching in Roxbury, Louisa living nearby with the family of Samuel Sewell, Elizabeth and Abba at school in Boston. His wife was "City Missionary to the Poor and Perishing in her neighborhood"—"useful to an extent beyond my powers of describing. Her house has been the haunt of hundreds, coming to ask [?] and to leave comforted." Thus, said he, "we pass on and off the stage of existence."

The house in Temple Place, which belonged to the Savage family, adjoined Boston Common, a favorite locale of Alcott's. In this "leafy June," as he recalled it, he strolled out with his family morning and evening. "Our walk before breakfast, and after the bath, is the best meal of the day," he wrote. "Anna and Elizabeth are beginning to taste and find how good it is for mind and body. It was meant that the whole season should be put into us, as it is into a flower; and its virtues should reappear in us, as the sun colours the peach, and mellows the pulp of the plum and apple."

Much as he liked Boston, he was at best a semidetached absentee from former haunts and was never wholly cured of the Concord connection. In July he spent a weekend at Emerson's, managing to sell the hay crop from his fields opposite Hillside in exchange for repairs to the crumbling house, which had now been rented. A month later he was back again, walking with Emerson and talking all day about Goethe, Swedenborg, and Lorenz Oken. "I am afraid," wrote Emerson in his journal, that "Al[cott] can as little as any man separate his drivelling from his divining." He was in fact unwell that summer with another of his physical and emotional relapses. He mentioned "a boding cough," nightmares populated by goblins, and dream sequences in which he seemed to be stumbling over the "plac[es] of the dead." In September he returned to Concord, happily accepting an invitation from Mrs. Edmund Hosmer to board at her house free of charge in order "to recruit a little"—his verb for recovering health. He often passed the Dovecote, where he had lived in 1840. He now called it "my pretty Cottage" and thought that it still showed the marks of his labors nearly a decade before. He spent a day repairing Emerson's gazebo, admiring the view of the front gable from the vantage point of the south door of Emerson's house. The rustic lyre was still in place and he found it and the latticed window "a pleasure to see."

One morning in mid-September he wrote his wife that he was almost himself again. "This last good piece of fortune—restoration from the dead—is likely to prove mine. . . . When you come, lady, we will go see Fruitlands . . . where *A man once lived,* instead of Mt. Auburn [Cemetery] where, perchance the same man, shall find a resting place some half century hence. . . . Come, and leave that Poor Self, and the Poor creatures you enrich, for one clear day, before the winter's campaign opens to us both."

His own winter's campaign consisted of further "Conversations," some of them held at 15 Tremont Row, the headquarters of the Town and Country Club. Emerson came when he could, noticing how each "person who opened his lips seemed in snuffing the air to snuff nitrous oxide, and away he went—a spinning dervish—pleasing himself, annoying the rest. . . . There was much ability and good meaning in the room, but some persons present who should not have been there, and these, like an east wind, checked every growth." Alcott's subject was "The Times," and Emerson was amused that he himself, as well as three or four of his Unitarian minister friends, had all chosen to lecture that winter, midway of the nineteenth century, on the subject of "The Spirit of the Times." Yet he thought that the particular angle of the lecturer's vision was more important than the subject. Alcott, for example, "astonishes by the grandeur of his Angle. I tell him he is the Bonaparte of speculators, born to rout the armies of ghosts, the Austrians of the Soul." If you talked with seers like Alcott, "new eyes bud in your brow, and you see what they see."

Beginning sometime in his forty-ninth year, Alcott had been drifting gradually into a sentimental association with a young woman named Ednah Littlehale, one of the most faithful attendants at his West Street "Conversations." Like Emerson's friend Caroline Sturgis, Ednah was the daughter of a Boston merchant who had accumulated a fortune in foreign trade. Aged twenty-four, five years younger than Caroline, she was so strongly attracted to her mentor that she soon began keeping written records of his talks, reviving an arrangement like those he had maintained in the 1830s with Margaret Fuller and Elizabeth Peabody.

The friendship, which included early morning ambles around Boston Common and a lively if verbose correspondence when she was out of town, seems to have flattered Alcott. One curious entry in his journal early in 1850 linked Ednah and Emerson:

> Miss Littlehale called in the afternoon, and I walked home with her. The company of intellectual women has a certain freshness and zest one seldom tastes from intercourse with cultivated men. Sexual qualities seem as needful to the propagation of thought as of human beings, nor do I like any man who never reminds me of the graces proper to women. It is these qualities that we love in a friend. The best of Emerson's intellect comes out in its feminine traits, and were he not as stimulating to me as a woman, and as racy I should not care to see and know him intimately nor often.

Two later entries elaborate upon his feelings for Ednah:

Now if I covet youth 'tis that I might return the grateful courtesy and almost conjugal confidence with which this young woman approaches me. Nor can I reveal the sentiments that draw me towards one of whom I have known so little, and who in coming as a pupil becomes by some invisible sliding scale of affinities as pleasing as unexpected, a friend and companion, I had almost said mate of a tenderer name. . . . Very pleasant company of a morning is this friend . . . as refreshing as the morning air. So ruddy, so strong and so ideal. A profitable friendship, a culture as well as a pleasure, and fast ripening into confidances [sic] that give lustre to the days and nights. . . .

It is clear that Ednah Littlehale found mature men preferable to more youthful suitors. On vacation in Vermont she presently met, fell in love with, and married a gifted and ailing engraver and artist in crayons who maintained an atelier in Boston. This was Seth Cheney, nearly ten years Alcott's junior, whose first wife had recently died of tuberculosis and who, like Alcott, was strongly attracted to the brown-eyed, dark-haired heiress. The years of their marriage, which took place in 1853, were spent largely abroad. Cheney was only forty-six when he died in 1856, leaving Ednah with their only child, a daughter born in 1855, and a houseful of his artwork, including a handsome bas-relief of Alcott. The widowed Ednah later became the first biographer of Louisa May Alcott, and continued her friendship with the Alcott family as long as any of them lived.

In the spring of 1850 Alcott wrote that he had become "recluse and thoughtful in the extreme. . . . Children were once my companions. Time was when I lived almost exclusively with them, and was privileged beyond most men in being the centre of a lively circle. . . . Those days were golden. But of late I have been drawn aside from this intimacy by pursuits and objects more intellectual and ideal. The diversion has come against my will and wishes, and by the force of circumstances." His continuing preoccupation with intellectual ruminations led to yet another of the family crises which had driven them from pillar to post since 1837. "Further talk with my desponding wife on family affairs," he wrote in April. "Embarrassed on every side, with no possible means of relief. We are spared house rent by the kindness of [Abba's brother] Mr. May, but have no income nor present facilities for earning a support. I am less adapted to existing things than I was when, ten years since, I left this city to seek society and the means of support at Concord and, afterwards, my Paradise at Fruitlands." Six weeks later the situation had grown even worse. "Mrs. A. quite dejected, feeble, weeps from anxiety, is disconsolate, and cannot be comforted."

On top of everything else came the smallpox: Abba had fed an infected family of immigrants in the garden. The daughters came down with light cases, the illness of the parents was far more severe, and Alcott's was the worst of all. "Mine was the old-fashioned small-pox, and kept me in the house a couple of months," he wrote in retrospect. ". . . I could not shave myself for a month, and looked frightful enough—like that wild man, Orson, of the woods, in the story of Valentine and Orson." As late as mid-September he was still "speckled" with slowly eroding pockmarks.

Abba, back at work, was constantly assailed by female gossips, who whispered that her husband allowed her to "delve for the family" while he remained indifferent to its welfare. So, said he, "I must stand for the time as a thriftless if not a heartless and incapable fellow. . . . If I can contest points with the small-pox and come off the victor . . . it will not, methinks, be altogether impossible to hold out sometime longer against the gossip outside, standing fair in my own eyes meanwhile. . . . Had I the available talent, it should supercede [sic] my wife's toils, which yield but a shameful recompense to leave us where we have been left since I was cast out of my proper and chosen employment in the temple [the Temple School] into the oven. I can afford to stand ill in the world, if fair in my own sight."

All this had come about, he thought, "because I had one set of gifts and not the other, and fell so obliquely on my time that none caught my point of view to comprehend the person I was. 'Tis as disastrous to leave body as soul out of our regards. Mind is not always a merchantable commodity." In his youth he had been a peddler of knickknacks and household utensils. Now, here he was, a peddler still, in July 1850, bearing his pack of metaphysic, and "set bodily, mystically, down in the best market in the world. Athenian times, yet without customer for his handsome wares." He deeply believed what he said a year later: "That is failure when a man's idea ruins him, when he is dwarfed and killed by it; but when he is ever growing by it, ever true to it, and does not lose it by any partial or immediate failures—that is success, whatever it seems to the world." It was this attitude that seems all his life to have underlain his incorrigibility.

Alcott's predicament, though bad enough, was not the worst. A week later he set down in his journal the news of Margaret Fuller. "[Horace Greeley's] *Tribune* brings intelligence of the wreck of the ship *Elizabeth* on Friday last, on Fire Island, four miles east of the Long Island Light. On board were Margaret Fuller, her husband, and child, returning from Italy. The noble lady gone down into the sea—fated, as she foresaw, to perish. 'I see nothing but death before me. I shall never reach the shore.' These were her last words, symbolical of the life she had lived of conflict for the truths she saw yet did not quite attain. So near her own friends and country, and yet to go down in sight of them to the silent and insatiate sea! She had been more to many women— and to many men, I may add—than any woman else of these last years; nor is there any to fill and make good her place. How sweetly she rests, now, from all those labours! A memorable life, as it was a memorable end."

Part Three

THE

FIFTIES

Chapter Thirty-one

THE ABSENTEES:
MARGARET FULLER

THE HURRICANE OF JULY 18–19, 1850, THAT SHIPWRECKED and drowned Margaret Fuller Ossoli, her husband, and her infant son roared up the Atlantic coast, caught the bark *Elizabeth* off the New Jersey shore, and some fifteen hours later drove her bow into the shallows of Fire Island, the thirty-mile-long sandbar along the south side of Long Island. Battered by huge combers, the ship broached to, broadside to the beach. In the first gray light of July 19, a Friday, the half dozen passengers abandoned the shattered and roofless cabin and took shelter in the forecastle. Clinging to broken planks, some of the sailors managed to reach land. So did Captain Hasty's indomitable young widow, Catherine, who had tried vainly to persuade Margaret to take the plunge. Horace Sumner, brother of the senator, battled the waves for some minutes before his dark head disappeared in the welter of waters. The ship's steward, Bates, carrying Margaret's child, was washed overboard; both their drowned bodies were cast ashore twenty minutes later. The Ossolis, along with the Italian nurse-girl, Celeste Paolini, had meantime been swept away and were never seen again. People on the beach caught a last sight of Margaret, "seated at the foot of the foremast, still clad in her white night-dress, with her hair fallen loose upon her shoulders," as well it might have been in that fury of wind and driving rain.

News of the wreck reached Emerson at Concord on the night of July 22. He at once asked Thoreau to travel to the scene of the tragedy and to obtain "all the intelligence and, if possible, any fragments of manuscript or other property" that had belonged to the victims. Henry carried a letter to Horace Greeley, whose *Tribune* had printed accounts of the catastrophe, as well as a note to Marcus Spring, with whom Margaret had gone abroad in 1846. Two other close friends of hers, W. H. Channing and Ellery Channing, teamed with Thoreau as investigators.

When William Channing and Thoreau reached the site of the disaster, they learned that Spring and Senator Sumner had been there briefly the day before. The wreck still lay sixty rods offshore, lapped by calm waters and looking not unlike another that Thoreau had seen on Cape Cod a year earlier. Nearby lived the Oakes family, whose house had become headquarters for articles cast up along the strand. The remnants were pitifully few: Margaret's broken desk inside a canvas sack, a black leather trunk containing her letters from Marchesa Visconti, and some two dozen soaked books; a carpetbag of Ossoli's and one of his coats, from which Henry ripped a button to carry away in his pocket. Thoreau talked with Margaret's mother, her brother Arthur, Catherine Hasty, and Mrs. Oakes, who had dried out some of the papers from the trunk. He also paid a visit to the temporary grave of the child Angelino, whose body was presently taken away for burial at Mount Auburn Cemetery in Cambridge. The local pilferers—"pirates," said Thoreau— had been busy for days and nothing valuable remained. To Emerson's disappointment, there was no sign of Margaret's manuscript on the revolutions in Italy.

Mrs. Hasty told William Channing of Margaret's final allusion to the book. The two women were sitting in the forecastle while the intrepid mate, Mr. Davis, made three trips to bring them various items from the wrecked cabin. When he returned for the third time, carrying "a bottle of wine and a drum of figs for their refreshment," Margaret said quietly to Catherine, "There still remains [there in the cabin] what, if I live, will be of more value to me than anything." But she added that it seemed too selfish to ask Davis to risk a fourth trip across the splintered deck.

The book, now lost forever, had been the subject of Emerson's last letter to Margaret, sent to her Florentine address from his Philadelphia hotel on April 11, probably too late to reach her before she sailed for home in the middle of May. He offered to intercede on her behalf with American publishers. So long as his services were available, she must not think of crossing the ocean merely to duplicate what he could do better. Moreover, her continued residence in Italy would doubtless add "solidity" to her reputation as a trustworthy eyewitness. Thus, said he, her "absenteeism" might well be advantageous, though this was certainly an unexpected argument for him to be making—he "who had vainly imagined that one of these days," when she had grown tired of cities, she would be drawn back to "our little Concord" by the united claims of her fast friends there. "You may stay in Italy, for now," he concluded, "but all the more we shall want you and must have you at last. Lidian is never well, but perhaps not much more invalid than you knew her. Mamma is well[—]both are ever your friends, and Ellen, Edith, and Edward I hope will be yet."

His correspondence with Margaret, once so voluminous, had nearly reached the vanishing point by May 1849. Her final year in Italy had found her deeply involved with the revolution. When Emerson wrote, she had just been appointed *regolatrice* of the Ospedale Fate-Bene Fratelli by her friend Cristina, Princess Belgiojoso, as part of Mazzini's newly formed Commission for the Care of the Wounded. Although the republic had been proclaimed in February as a "pure democracy," Rome was now at war. During April and May, Louis Napoleon, the new president of France, had dispatched a substantial expeditionary force to Civitavecchia to obliterate the republican forces and restore Pius IX to the papal throne. Through May and June, having been obliged to leave their infant son with peasant caretakers at Rieti, Margaret and Ossoli were in the thick of the siege of Rome, she at the hospital tending the wounded and he on the walls as a sergeant in the Civic Guard. Emerson's May Day letter reached her on June 10 during a dawn-to-dusk battle, part of which she was able to watch from her balcony overlooking the Piazza Barberini. Most days she carried books and flowers to the mutilated soldiers, sometimes sitting with them in the gardens of the papal palace on the Quirinal with a distant view of the French encampment atop Monte Mario to the north.

Emerson had once ignorantly asked her, "Don't you wish Italy had a great man?" She answered without apparent rancor that the republic had just such a man in Mazzini, who had been "the inspiring soul of his people." On July 8, writing to W. H. Channing, she described a recent encounter with Mazzini, whom the struggle had aged prematurely—"all the vital juices seemed exhausted; his eyes were all bloodshot; his skin orange; flesh he had none; his hair was mixed with white . . . but he had never flinched, never quailed; had protested in the last hour against surrender; sweet and calm, but full of a more fiery purpose than ever."

Mazzini was there, animating and sustaining the popular front. But what of Emerson? In 1848, still then in England, Mazzini had written to Margaret in Rome: "I . . . feel fearful that [Emerson] leads or will lead man to too much contemplation." Such a program might do for America, but "in our own old world we stand in need of one who will . . . inflame us to the Holy Crusade and appeal to the collective influences . . . more than to individual self-improvement." But Margaret, despite her admiration for Mazzini, was not yet ready to disassociate herself entirely from Emersonian ideals. "Love me all you can," she adjured Emerson in June 1849. "Let me feel, that, amid the fearful agitations of the world, there are pure hands, with healthful even pulse, stretched out toward me, if I claim their grasp." Perhaps individual self-improvement was the one attainable goal. No longer, as she had tried to do in 1840, could she take refuge in religious consolations. "You are a Christian," she told Marcus Spring. "You know I never pretended to be, except in dabs and sparkles here and there." Her hopes for the success of Mazzini's holy crusade were fading fast. Garibaldi stopped resistance at the end of June, Mazzini left for Switzerland and eventually returned to England, and the French forces occupied Rome on the fourth of July in an ironic reversal of the American holiday of independence.

Just as the Ossolis were on the point of leaving the capital to retrieve their child in Rieti, a letter from Horace Greeley added fuel to Margaret's miseries: "Ah, Margaret, the world grows dark with us! You grieve, for Rome is fallen;—I mourn, for Pickie is dead." At just the age Waldo Emerson had reached when he died in 1842, Pickie had been "stricken down . . . by the relentless cholera" on July 12, 1849. Margaret shed rivers of tears. "One would think," she told her mother, that "I might have become familiar enough with images of death and destruction; yet somehow the image of Pickie's little dancing figure, lying, stiff and stark, between his parents, has made me weep more than all else. . . . To me he was most dear, and would always have been so. . . . The three children I have seen who were fairest in my eyes, and gave the most promise of the future, were Waldo, Pickie, [and] Hermann Clarke;—all nipped in the bud."

At Rieti in mid-July she discovered that her own Angelino was in danger of sharing the fate of the others. Virtually abandoned by his wet nurse, who had only enough milk for her own baby, he had been subsisting on bread soaked in wine. He lay feeble and torpid on his pallet, his small body "worn to a skeleton." It required six weeks and the services of another wet nurse before he was sufficiently recovered to be taken to Florence, where his parents were going to spend the winter.

By October 1849 they were settled in an apartment overlooking the Piazza Santa Maria Novella, with breathtaking views of the "bridal church" and the more distant Campanile. The city was filled with English and American expatriates, including Robert and Elizabeth Barrett Browning; the sculptors Horatio Greenough, Joseph Mozier, and Hiram Powers; William Wetmore Story and his wife, Emelyn; and Horace Sumner, the senator's younger brother. Except for letters to the members of her family, and such old friends as W. H. Channing and Caroline Sturgis Tappan, Margaret had not hitherto divulged her status as wife and mother. "The American authoress, Miss Fuller . . . has taken us by surprise at Florence, retiring from the Roman field with a husband and child above a year old," wrote Elizabeth Browning. "Nobody had even suspected a word of this underplot, and her American friends stood in mute astonishment before this apparition of them here. The husband is a Roman marquis, appearing amiable and gentlemanly, and having fought well, they say, at the siege, but with no pretension to cope with his wife on any ground appertaining to the intellect." Their other friends in Florence seem to have accepted the assurance that Margaret and Ossoli were married, though there is good reason to believe that the actual ceremony was not performed until the spring of 1850 when they were beginning to lay plans for the long voyage home.

Margaret's final judgment on Emerson came in a letter to William Story, who with his wife, Emelyn, had been steadily helpful. Emerson's English friend Arthur Hugh Clough had sent Margaret his own poems along with those of Thomas Burbidge and Matthew Arnold. She wrote: "They are of the Emersonian kind, entirely out of all rule, not of high power, but genuine though imperfect reflexes of the higher life of their writers." This was a better classification of the poems of Clough, Burbidge, and Arnold than of Emerson's best work, but it indicated the level where she thought Emerson belonged, as well as his limitations as a poet, on which she had expatiated some years earlier.

With her lifelong superstitious belief in "talismans, omens, coincidences," as Emerson phrased it, Margaret was supremely apprehensive about the coming voyage. "I am absurdly fearful," she wrote, "and various omens have combined to give me a dark feeling. . . . Yet my life proceeds as regularly as the fates of a Greek tragedy, and I can but accept the pages as they turn." She scanned the newspapers for news of the recent losses of transatlantic shipping, and found ample evidence that even the safest steam packets were subject to maritime chance and accident. In the end she chose a merchantman, the bark *Elizabeth*, Captain Seth Hasty of Maine, which was then lading in the harbor at Leghorn. Around Easter, the anniversary of her first meeting with Ossoli, she went over to the coast to meet the captain and his young wife, Catherine, finding him to be "one of the best and most high-minded of our American men," and his wife "an excellent woman." The Hastys came to Florence to complete arrangements, and the date of departure was set for May 17. Margaret wrote:

> I shall embark more composedly in my merchant ship, praying indeed fervently that it may not be my lot to lose my babe at sea, either by unsolaced sickness, or amid the howling waves; or, that if I should, it may be brief anguish, and Ossoli, he, and I, go together.

Her premonitions were more than realized. Approaching Gibraltar, the good Captain Hasty sickened and died of confluent smallpox, the same disease that was even then afflicting Bronson Alcott far away in Boston. They buried him at sea, waited out the week of quarantine, and sailed westward on June 9, with Mr. Bangs, the first mate, at the helm. On the eleventh Angelino developed a high fever followed by the facial swelling characteristic of the disease. Margaret and Ossoli gave all their days and nights to save him; in a little more than a week he began to recover, probably because he had already been inoculated by the doctor in Rieti. In a month's time, tacking continuously against prevailing winds from the west, the *Elizabeth* stood off Bermuda, only 600 nautical miles from the final haven of New York.

The rest we know. After it was over, Emerson paid tribute to Margaret in his journals. "To the last her country proves inhospitable to her; brave, eloquent, subtle, accomplished, devoted, constant soul! If nature availed in America to give birth to many such as she, freedom and honour and letters and art too were safe in this new world. She bound in the belt of her sympathy and friendship all whom I know and love, Elizabeth, Caroline, Ward, the Channings, Ellen Hooper, Charles K. N.[Newcomb], Hedge, and Sarah Clarke. She knew more select people than any other person did and her death will interest more. . . . She had a wonderful power of inspiring confidence and drawing out of people their last secret. . . . I have lost in her my audience. . . . There should be a gathering of her friends and some Beethoven should play the dirge. . . . When I heard that a trunk of her correspondence had been found and opened, I felt what a panic would strike all her friends, for it was as if a clever reporter had got underneath a confessional and agreed to report all that transpired."

She had been dead less than two weeks when W. H. Channing came to Concord to urge Emerson to write her biography under the provisional title of *Margaret and Her Friends*. Emerson agreed that it "must be written, but not post haste." He alerted Sam Ward, inviting him to join a committee of three to consider ways and means. Ward was dubious: "How can you describe a Force? How can you write the life of Margaret?" Horace Greeley was already planning "a proper edition of Margaret's works," which he hoped to have published in September or October, "before the interest excited by her sad decease" could fade. As for the memoir, said Horace, everyone thought that Emerson must write it. Margaret's brother Richard agreed: Emerson was clearly her "spiritual representative."

Emerson ranked Sam Ward as the best choice, placing himself second and W. H. Channing third. He was certain that whoever undertook the task must pay the closest attention to the personalities who had surrounded Margaret. "Leave them out," said he, "and you leave out Margaret." Throughout the fall of 1850, he worked to gather materials for the memoir with considerable help from Caroline Sturgis Tappan. Madame Costanza Arconati's letters to Margaret had been in the black trunk that drifted ashore from the wreck. When Sam Ward went to London on banking business in October, he carried a letter from Emerson to Giuseppe Mazzini asking for notes on his friendship with Margaret. Elizabeth Peabody supplied anecdotes. Ward offered an installment, but declined further participation. James Freeman Clarke agreed to serve in his place, and to edit the materials relating to Margaret's life in Cambridge, Groton, and Providence. Emerson and W. H. Channing were to do the rest. Clarke came to Concord early in September and spent a morning in the summerhouse that Alcott had built, reading Margaret's letters from Italy.

All three men spent a week at Emerson's house in editorial conference. Emerson bought a hardcover copybook of some 300 blank pages, supplying a title, *Life and Death of Margaret Fuller Ossoli*, and a Latin tag: "Et quae tanta fuit Romam tibi causa videndi? *Libertas*"—And what was the great occasion of your seeing Rome? Freedom.

He slowly filled the notebook with extracts from letters to, from, and about Margaret, quotations from her journals, a list of several dozen friends of hers, a tentative plan for the chapters of the memoir, and, at the end, a loose chronology from her birth in 1810 to her death forty years later. Along the way he inserted anecdotes and a few longer entries on aspects of her character that eventually appeared in the parts of the history that he himself wrote.

Among many others, Emerson turned for help to Margaret's former protégé, Charles Newcomb, who came to Concord in October. Since leaving Brook Farm in December 1845, he had been living with his mother at home in Providence. In the past two or three years, Emerson's view of his character had suffered a sharp decline. "I grudged him the time I gave him," he wrote in October 1848. "He has become the spoiled child of culture. . . . It was very melancholy to see that what I once esteemed the highest privilege, his conversation, was now sloth and weariness. . . . Farewell my once beautiful genius!" When he returned a year later, he brought a sheaf of his writings, six years old, chiefly soliloquies, witty enough and eloquent but existing, thought Emerson, "to little use." Now in 1850 he accepted Emerson's invitation to submit an account of his friendship with Margaret and to lend the editors a selection of her letters. But when he reappeared in mid-December, he brought only himself. "He wastes my time," wrote Emerson in his journal. "'Tis cruel to think of. Destroyed three good days for me! The Pythagoreans would have built a tomb for him—the unique, inspired, wasted genius." Charles eventually kept his promise to lend the needed letters, but it was not until nine months later, in July 1851, that he mailed his tribute to Margaret. Emerson called it "well weighed . . . minutely true" though disappointingly brief: "I could heartily wish it expanded. . . . Her opulent genius deserves a fluent eulogy."

At first the editors accepted W. H. Channing's title, *Margaret and Her Friends*. But, as Emerson said, "That form proved impossible, and it only remained that the narrative, like a Greek tragedy, should suppose the chorus always on the stage," sympathetically allied to "the queen of the scene." Her friends were "a fair, commanding troop, every one of them adorned by some splendor of beauty, of grace, of talent, or of character." As in Coleridge's account of the Ancient Mariner, "she was the wedding-guest, to whom the long-pent story must be told. . . . She lived in a superior circle; for they suppressed all their common-place in her presence." Wherever she went, she "fused people into society, and a glowing company was the result." "And I, who knew her intimately for ten years,—from July, 1836, till August 1846, when she sailed for Europe—never saw her without surprise at her new powers."

By December, Emerson had amassed an amplitude of unsorted materials and the promise of more, including autobiographical papers in Margaret's holograph, her correspondence with himself and Elizabeth Hoar and Caroline Sturgis Tappan, and a trunkful of memorabilia that she had stored in Paris for safekeeping before she left for Italy. In the new year of 1851 his work was interrupted by a long lecture tour, and he could not take it up again, except sporadically, until May. There were the usual domestic problems: Lidian was still in "the most precarious of female healths"; Bulkeley twice appeared unannounced, "immensely talkative" but otherwise sufficiently "comfortable." In June Emerson's aged mother fell out of bed and broke her hip. Dr. Bartlett, "always an alarmist," predicted that she would never walk again. Her memory, too, was growing dim. But she soon rallied and began to talk feebly of making her will. One day aunts Betsey and Fanny suddenly appeared at the front gate to pay her a call and to stay a few days.

Emerson worked as steadily as such contingencies allowed. On the heels of Theodore Parker's fiery April sermon on the Fugitive Slave Law, he delivered in Concord the first of his addresses on the same subject, afterward returning to "Margaret Fuller's manifold manuscripts [and] letters," as well as "memorials" by her friends. She had been, he said, "a noble brave woman and made others brave and good." Through the summer and fall he stayed "absurdly busy." He had cautioned against "post haste" preparation of the memoirs, but by the end of October 1851, only fifteen months after Margaret's death, the plates had already been cast for Channing's portion of the book. What finally emerged on publication day in February 1852 was a two-volume work of nearly 700 pages, with Clarke and Emerson splitting the contents of volume one at roughly 190 and 150 pages each, and Channing's 340 pages filling volume two. Clarke's contribution dealt with Margaret's youth up to the middle 1830s, Emerson's with her sojourns in Concord and her

"Conversations" in Boston, and Channing's with the last twenty years, including her work for Greeley in New York, her residence in Europe, and her death at sea.

The book had grave faults—loose organization, inevitable temporal overlaps, lack of respect for the integrity of quoted materials, the suppression of the names of people whose feelings or reputations might be harmed, overmuch guesswork on dates and sources—what one of Margaret's twentieth-century biographers has called "literary libertinage . . . a cut-and-paste job, with the scissors acting as censor's shears." Nor did the collaborators choose to include an index. They were following the "unscientific" editorial practices that prevailed among many other nineteenth-century memoirists. Yet Margaret was indubitably there, with all her shortcomings as well as her noteworthy gifts and virtues. The three editors had worked *con amore,* and their love and admiration showed through.

Chapter Thirty-two

THOREAU
AND CHANNING

ONE DAMP MORNING IN MAY 1852, JOHN ALBEE, A NINETEEN-
year-old senior at Phillips Andover Academy, hired a chaise and drove
to Concord to interview Emerson, arriving shortly after noon. Besides his tall
and genial host, another man was there, shorter in stature, with the healthy
complexion of an outdoorsman, and neatly attired in a dark suit. He behaved
like a familiar in the household and his name, which Albee had never heard
before, sounded like Thorough or Thurro.

Albee had come for advice on "how to become educated and where." He
was discontented with Andover and uncertain about going on to college.
Through the afternoon and early evening Emerson did most of the talking
and the other man seemed content to listen. Albee had heard that Emerson always received young people with "unfailing suavity and deference." His manner was mild, he often hesitated over the choice of the right word, and he
seldom looked his visitor squarely in the eye or embarrassed him with direct
questions.

Now and again Emerson glanced at Mr. Thurro as if hoping to elicit a response. When he recommended Harvard College, saying that "most of the
branches were taught there," Mr. Thurro suddenly exploded: "Yes, indeed,
all the branches and none of the roots." At this Emerson laughed heartily, and
it struck Albee that he had not only expected but actually invited the
stranger's "negative and biting criticisms, especially in regard to education."
Around teatime Emerson complained that there was still no real American lit-

erature: what was needed were great poets and orators; some of these would no doubt emerge from the rising generation. Perking up again, Mr. Thurro said he had found one in the woods, "but it had feathers and had not been to Harvard College. Still it had a voice and an aerial inclination."

"Let us cage it," said Emerson.

"That is just the way the world always spoils its poets," said Thurro. This time he joined in the laughter and the trio "went in to tea in right good humor."

Albee set all this down in his diary, and later discovered how to spell Thoreau's name. After tea Thoreau "devoted himself wholly" to the Emerson children, who treated him like a beloved elder brother. Albee long remembered Thoreau leaning over the fireplace, flanked by the Emerson daughters, Ellen and Edith, aged thirteen and ten. They were popping corn, and Thoreau seemed as delighted as they when the "cerealian blossoms expanded."

The little scene by the fire in 1852 was matched by many another through the years. Thoreau's affection for the Emerson children—beginning with Waldo and extending through the early lives of Ellen, Edith, and Edward— was constant and unremitting. Ellen liked to recall the time when Lidian, worried about the miseries of her hens in frosty weather, complained at the injustice and tyranny of keeping them locked up away from her garden. "Mr. Thoreau then made some neat little cowhide shoes for them which fitted well and were tied tight round their slender ancles [sic], so that at least they could promenade about the yard" in the coldest seasons.

In the summer of 1849, when Ellen had gone to her Uncle William's house on Staten Island to recuperate from a severe illness, Thoreau sent her a long letter that said in part: "I can guess pretty well what interests you, and what you think about. Indeed I am interested in pretty much the same things myself. I suppose you think that persons who are as old as your father and myself are always thinking about very grave things, but I know that we are meditating the same old themes that we did when we were ten years old, only we go more gravely about it. . . . [Eddy] tells me that he is five years old. . . . I was present at the celebration of his birthday lately, and supplied the company with onion and squash pipes, and rhubarb whistles, which is the most I can do on such occasions. . . . You must see the sun rise out of the ocean before you come home. I think that Long Island will not be in the way, if you climb to the top of the hill. . . ." And signed himself "Your old acquaintance, Henry Thoreau."

The Emerson children seem to have had no inkling of the gradual estrangement between their father and Uncle Henry that had prevailed for several years and would continue for several more. In the mid-forties, Horace Greeley had urged Thoreau to write up his friendships with Alcott and Emerson. He made a stab at it with a few notes in his journals, but soon gave up the attempt. The version of Emerson that appears there calls him a "critic poet philosopher . . . with talent not so conspicuous—not so adequate to his task . . . not so robust—elastic—practical enough in his own field." He "lives a far more intense life—seeks to realize a divine life—his affections and intellect equally developed . . . faithful a judge of men. . . . More of the divine realized in him than in any. . . . His personal influence upon young persons greater than any man's. In his world every man would be a poet—Love would reign—Beauty would take place—Man and nature would harmonize." At another point he added that Emerson's essays were not poetry "they were not written exactly at the right crisis though inconceivably near it. Poetry is simply a miracle and we only recognize it receding from us not coming toward us."

Some weeks after Albee's visit, Emerson looked back upon his "platoon" of closest friends and the contrasts among them. Besides his brothers, he named Caroline Sturgis Tappan, Margaret Fuller, and Elizabeth Hoar, Alcott and Sam Ward and Jones Very, and those two persistent Concordians, Thoreau and Channing. "Needs all these and many more," he wrote, "to represent my relations." Among the leading Transcendentalists, friendship was a recurrent topic. Drawing in part on his journals, Thoreau wrote an essay on the subject, which he inserted in the manuscript of *A Week on the Concord and Merrimack Rivers* in 1848 while Emerson was still in England. His position was that friendship was not taught by any religion, yet no word was oftener on men's lips. All men dreamed of it. "It is the secret of the Universe. . . . It affects our behavior toward all new men and women and a great many old ones." He cited the opinion of Confucius that one should "never contract Friendship with a man that is not better than thyself," and concluded with a warning: "The only danger in Friendship is that it will end." Implicit among his paragraphs was the notion that his ten-year friendship with Emerson was in some danger. He quoted a poem that almost said so:

Two solitary stars—
Unmeasured systems far
Between us roll,
But by our conscious light we are
Determined to one pole.

If "the only danger in friendship is that it will end," it may be, as Walter Harding says, that Thoreau had grown tired of adverse comparisons between Emerson and himself in which he commonly came out second best. Frank Sanborn later recorded an observation of Alcott's admiring young disciple, Ednah Littlehale, whose first sight of Thoreau came early in 1848 at one of Alcott's "Conversations" in Boston. Like John Albee, she could not spell his name. "Thorault amused me. . . . He is all overlaid by an imitation of Emerson; talks like him . . . brushes his hair in the same way, and is even getting up a caricature nose like Emerson's." Later in the same year Thoreau had to reckon with another reductive comparison in Lowell's *A Fable for Critics*:

How he jumps, how he strains, and gets red in the face
To keep step with the mystagogue's natural pace . . .
Fie, for shame, brother bard; with good fruit of your own,
Can't you let Neighbor Emerson's orchards alone?

But Emerson, at just the time when Lowell's *Fable* appeared, read Henry's "Ascent of Ktaadn" in the *Union Magazine* and said flatly that it was only the second essay in American literature in ten years that he had saved to bind up. When the two men climbed Nagog Hill in the summer of 1849, and looked down on the site of Concord, once the domain of Tahatawan, sachem of Musketaquid, Emerson had no complaint to lodge against his companion. A year later he quoted Thoreau's observation that nature was more interesting than people, adding his own contrary opinion that nature "must always combine with man," since "life is ecstatical, and we radiate joy and honour and gloom on the days and landscapes we converse with."

By the fall of 1850, however, Emerson had become aware of a cosmic drift between Thoreau and himself. He proposed a talk session, "the first for a long time, with malice prepense," to "take the bull by the horns." They quickly disposed of America and England. Emerson argued that Americans didn't ripen soon enough, whereas in England "more calorie was generated, and more completeness obtained." Henry called the English "mere soldiers," whose business was to wind things up while the American pioneers were unwinding their lines. Emerson rejoined that American geography was sublime while the men were not. They did agree that success was defined differently by the two nations. In England, said Thoreau, "their book or man or law [has] no root in nature." "Of course," wrote Emerson wryly, well knowing Thoreau's naturalistic orientation.

So they mildly clashed. Less than a year later, Emerson wrote that "Thoreau wants a little ambition in his mixture. Fault of this, instead of being the head of American Engineers, he is captain of a huckleberry party." Another journal entry said that Henry was a boy and would be an old boy. "Pounding beans is good to the end of pounding Empires but not, if at the end of years, it is only beans. I fancy it an inexcusable fault in him that he is insignificant here in the town. He speaks at Lyceum . . . but somebody else speaks and his speech falls dead and is forgotten. He rails at the town doings and ought to correct and inspire them."

Along with such disparagements, however, should be placed those occasions when Emerson had fair words to say of his younger friend. One of his virtues was his "powerful arithmetic," which enabled him to "pace sixteen rods more accurately than another man can measure it by tape." In June 1852 he quoted with admiration Henry's remark, apropos of lightning rods, that "the only rod of safety was in the vertebrae of his own spine." And presently added: "Thoreau gives me in flesh and blood and pertinacious Saxon belief, my own ethics. He is far more real, and daily practically obeying them, than I; and fortifies my memory at all times with an affirmative experience which refuses to be set aside." Yet underneath the praise there was commonly a note of denigration: "Henry Thoreau seemed stubborn and implacable; always manly and wise, but rarely sweet." The decade of the 1850s was more than half finished when he wrote, once more, of Henry's truculent tendencies: "Must we always talk for victory, and never once for truth, for comfort, and joy? Centrality he has, and penetration, strong understanding, and the higher gifts,—the insight of the real or from the real, and the moral rectitude that belongs to it; but all this and all his resources of wit and invention are lost to me in every experiment, year after year, that I make, to hold intercourse with his mind. Always some weary captious paradox to fight you with, and the time and temper wasted."

Thoreau's journal references to Emerson are rare, considering an association that had lasted so long. But the entry that parallels Emerson's observation of 1856 reveals Henry's disappointment:

> I had two friends. The one offered me friendship on such terms that I could not accept it, without a sense of degradation. He would not meet me on equal terms, but only be to some extent my patron. He would not come to see me, but was hurt if I did not visit him. He would not readily accept a favor, but would gladly confer one.

Such feelings had been festering in Thoreau's mind for more than five years. "I thought that friendship, that love was still possible between [us]," he had written in mid-February 1851. "I thought that we had not withdrawn very far asunder. But now that my friend rashly, thoughtlessly, profanely speaks, *recognizing* the distance between us, that distance seems infinitely increased." That fall he wrote: "Ah, I yearn toward thee, my friend, but I have not confidence in thee. . . . Even when I meet thee unexpectedly, I part from thee with disappointment. Though I enjoy thee more than other men, yet I am more disappointed with thee than with others." Emerson had long since discovered in each of his closest associates an incipient problem. "Nearly all the fine souls have a flaw," he had once told Margaret Fuller, "which defeats every expectation they excite." All through the early 1850s, he and Thoreau had found such flaws in each other, yet both were unwilling to sever the bonds that held them together.

In these years, the party of the third part for both Emerson and Thoreau was Ellery Channing. He and Thoreau took a number of trips together—to the White Mountains in 1848 and to Cape Cod in 1849. In June 1850 Henry traveled alone on a second visit to the Cape, rejoined Ellery at Fire Island after Margaret's death in the wreck, and that fall made an extended journey to Montreal and Quebec, again in Channing's company. From 1848, Thoreau lived with his parents, helped with his father's pencil factory, developed a local reputation as a surveyor, and expanded his schedule of public lectures. In March 1849, Channing gave up his quondam farm on Punkawtasset Hill and moved into an eighteenth-century house on Main Street. The arrival of his and Ellen's third child, Walter, in April did nothing to assuage his discomfort in the presence of children, and kept his wife in bed with a badly inflamed leg for more than a month after her lying-in. When Emerson was in town, they continued their walks and talks together, but Channing's rancor reached out to embrace his benefactor in a letter of the following September that called Emerson "a terrible man to deal with—one has to be armed at all points. He threshes you out very soon; is admirably skillful, able to go anywhere and do anything. Those nearest to him feel him hard and cold; no one knows even what he is doing or studying. . . . Nobody knows what his real philosophy is; his books do not tell it. I have known him for years intimately and I have not found it out. Women do not like him; he cannot establish a personal relation with anyone, yet he can get on agreeably with everyone."

If any of this had its origins in Channing's conversations with Thoreau about their mutual friend, no confirmatory evidence has survived. Nor did Emerson seem to suspect that Channing viewed his character in any such light. During the years around mid-century, he probably saw more of Channing than he did of Thoreau. The two men called themselves the "Saturday afternoon professors," and trudged all over the local terrain, often accompanied by Channing's young dog (fittingly named Professor) who had "a stroke of humor in his eye, as if he enjoyed his master's jokes." Together they gazed down at russet autumnal Massachusetts from the crest of Nobscot, and at the bright foliage reflected in the stillness of Flint's Pond. They crossed Nutmeadow Brook, made the circuit of White Pond, and waded through Ellery's secret garden of wild lupine that stretched like Wordsworth's daffodils over a whole quarter acre. One August day in 1850 they rode a wagon "to Willis's Pond in Sudbury" and took a swim in water that Emerson said was "coloured like sugarbaker's molasses."

"In walking with Ellery," said Emerson, "you shall always see what was never before shown to the eye of man." Although his examples of Ellery's wit and penetration do not wholly bear out this generalization, he could turn a phrase upon occasion. During one winter's walk to Flint's Pond, he squandered his jewels "as if they were icicles." In summer, said he, water comes au naturel, but in winter it's served up as crystal johnnycake. He jocosely complained of Nature's lack of invention: "They had frozen water last year; why should they do it again?" Emerson had long known Ellery's skill at raillery.

As far back as 1847 he had thrown verbal brickbats at Alcott's fancy summer-house on Emerson's lawn, calling it "the eternal pancake which not even the all-powerful rays of the Alcott sun have quite baked . . . the microscopic Cathedral of Cologne . . . this Tom Thumb of a St. Peter's." Now he voiced antifeminist complaints: "Every woman has a design on you—all, all!" He adopted the role of stoic: "Trouble [is] as good as anything else, if you only have enough of it," or turned sardonic: "Life is so short that I should think everybody would steal." He scorned someone's sentimental-poetical refer-ence to affection among birds. All they were was a pair of wings and "a few feathers, with a hole at one end, and a point at the other . . . affection! Why just as much affection as there is in that lump of peat."

In short, as Emerson wrote in the fall of 1850, Ellery was a "perpetual hol-iday" who "ought only to be used like an oroflamme [sic] or a garland for Maydays and Parliaments of wit and love." Yet he must also have noticed, having set down so many examples of Ellery's wit, how often it was mixed with scorn. Once he recorded with evident approval an astute observation of Alcott's: that Ellery had a "keen appetite for society with extreme repulsion, so that it came to a kind of commerce of cats, love and hate, embraces and fighting." Even Ellery's closest friends and walking companions were not ex-empt: "Behold HDT," he wrote in 1853, "he who believed in simplicity, he who has gone steadily along over the rough places and the thorns, in order to crucify and to kill out the human virtues, to render himself a Spartan. Each social faculty in which all others delight, he mortifies. . . . On him neither beauty nor goodness; you have him there, eminently chaste and abstinent, and at the same time dry as husks. His abstinence and chastities have made him only doubly repulsive to his kind. What is his compensation[?] Eternal solitude, and endless blundering. . . . But it may be said, that he went accord-ing to his nature. Well! This is by no means doubtful, but his nature—how tri-fling a space in the great world."

Thoreau's own journal for the spring of 1854 contained what could well have been a response to Channing's animadversions. Channing, he said, "tempts me to certain licenses of speech, i.e., to reckless and sweeping ex-pressions which I am wont to regret that I have used. That is, I find that I have used more harsh, extravagant, and cynical expressions concerning mankind and individuals than I intended. I find it difficult to make to him a sufficiently moderate statement. I think it is because I have not his sympathy in my sober and constant view. He asks for a paradox, an eccentric statement, and too often I give it to him."

Some of the members of Emerson's platoon, their leader included, were clearly rubbing one another's fur the wrong way. Ellery attacked Thoreau for his "abstinence and chastities," Thoreau attacked Ellery for his harsh and cynical language. Emerson was critical of both his younger friends for their respective failures to measure up to his own ideals. Channing held that Emerson could be hard, cold, and secretive, unable to "establish a personal relation with anyone." Thoreau said that he would give greater value to Emerson's praise, which was "always so discriminating, if there were not some alloy of patronage, and hence of flattery about [it]," adding that "Praise should be spoken as simply and naturally as a flower emits its fragrance." And again, following another meeting in May of 1853, when he had vainly tried to talk with Emerson, he said that he had lost his time—nay, almost his identity. "He, assuming a false opposition where there was no difference of opinion, talked to the wind—told me what I knew—and I lost my time trying to imagine myself somebody else to oppose him."

These sad examples go far toward suggesting that Emerson's long dream of a cooperative assemblage of gifted individualists was being rapidly dissipated by their inability to get along with one another. Part of the problem could be laid at Emerson's door. No doubt at times he could be patronizing to his younger brethren, and they both struck back at the master behind the veil of their journals. Yet Emerson continued his Saturday excursions with Channing, and still depended on Thoreau's assistance in domestic affairs and repairs. Under the surface, the town of Concord contained many a hidden discord. On the surface, however, a reasonable serenity seems to have prevailed.

THE LENOX
CONNECTION

BETWEEN 1844 AND 1854 EMERSON DISCOVERED A NEW CEN-
ter of interest in the Berkshire country of western Massachusetts. He
had once planned to settle there while his brother Edward was still alive and
before his marriage to Lidian. Nothing came of that dream, but another gradually took shape in the head of Sam Ward and eventuated in 1844 when he
broke ground for a country villa two miles from Lenox. It was completed in
1845 and named Highwood. Without being robust enough for the ordinary
drudgeries of farming, Sam took pleasure in whatever could be accomplished
with the help of horses, and pride in his gentleman farmer's ability to plow a
straight furrow in the fields adjoining his capacious rural mansion. He
founded a club of neighboring farmers who met alternately in one another's
houses; took long rambles with dog and gun; drove with his wife, Anna, in an
open sleigh among the hills; and regained strength through half a dozen years
of comparative rustication. In the fall of his first year he "harvested a hundred
bushels of excellent potatoes," and spent many hours in his handsome study
translating part of Goethe's autobiography, *Dichtung und Wahrheit.*

Emerson often teased his friend, then still in his late twenties, about his
experiment on the land. "Do the muses speak in these sharp whistling
winds?" he asked. "Are your Berkshire torrents chained up? . . . What a maceration and self-immolation in these children of art and civility to have lent
their grace to those rocks and wildernesses so long! . . . . I long to hear the
tale of your horrible sufferings in savage life."

Soon after the Wards settled in, Ellery and Ellen Channing paid them a visit, and afterward petitioned Anna to let them come to occupy the red farmhouse that adjoined the Highwood estate. Sam opposed the idea, well knowing that Ellery would be "in full sight" each day. "I had other intimate friends," he wrote later on, "and a whole society of excellent people, not one of whom would appreciate him or he them. . . . I had the vision of long winter months on the 'bleak hillside,' . . . and the utter solitude which I knew would be insupportable to him." In the end, Anna Ward sent Ellen Channing a tactful letter against the proposal. The only visible residuum was a sour poem of Ellery's called "Unfaithful Friendship."

Two other families close to Emerson's heart afterward settled in Lenox. When Sam and Anna returned to Boston in 1850, Caroline and William Tappan leased Highwood and moved in. Their first daughter, Ellen Sturgis Tappan, was born in 1849. Caroline "is as much delighted with her baby," wrote a friend, ". . . as she used to be with sky, earth and sea-clouds, birds and flowers." She was already carrying her second daughter, born in February 1851 and named Mary Aspinwall Tappan. In June 1850 she hired Anna, the eldest Alcott daughter, as a nursery helper; but Anna hated the place and was miserably homesick. When Caroline paid her wages, she left the money behind. Caroline sent it to Mrs. Alcott with a note: "I am sorry if I said anything which led Anna to leave the money. I was troubled by her being here—her unhappiness was a weight upon my thoughts and spirits from the first hour she came—indeed it affected everyone in the house."

When Margaret Fuller was drowned a month later, Emerson turned to Caroline for help with the *Memoir*. "Dear Waldo," she answered, "I think nothing can be better now than to write Margaret's life as you propose. No one, except herself, could write a life so multitudinous, but if the three [men] you have mentioned collect her letters from various quarters and hold counsel together, they can select all that is most valuable until the time when she went to N. York. That was an new era. The persons she knew best there were more vehement, adventurous, and various than her friends here; less moral, less poetical, less beautiful than some she had known, but she enjoyed their freedom from the puritanism that had always annoyed her here."

For more than a year Caroline continued to help Emerson with materials for the memoir, urging him to approach Mazzini and the various American and English expatriates whom Margaret had known in Rome and Florence, as well as earlier friends like Hedge, George Davis, Charles Newcomb, and Sarah Clarke. She seems to have heard from James Nathan, Margaret's beau of 1845. "Mr. Nathan, a Jew in N.Y.," she told Emerson, "says you cannot write a biography of Margaret without his letters to her. He wishes to have them himself; then perhaps he would show them to you. . . . Probably you would not like him at first; she thought he would not easily be liked." Besides the letters from Nathan, Caroline lent Emerson her own letters from Margaret, sent him large sections from Margaret's journals, and invited him to Highwood, promising him "a quiet room to write in" as well as an opportunity to discuss Margaret's inmost character, on which she had decided opinions. He paid her one flying visit for a conference on Sunday, June 29.

She was also instrumental in bringing the Hawthornes to Lenox. She had known them for ten years and had stayed with them in the Manse in 1845, helping with the housework and being generally agreeable. When she heard of Hawthorne's loss of the Salem surveyorship in 1849, she urged Sophia to think about moving to the Berkshire country. Wife and husband both made scouting trips to Lenox, Sophia in September and Hawthorne at the end of October. Sam Ward and William Tappan successively conducted him on house-hunting tours. They decided to take the farmhouse down the lane from Highwood—the same place that Ellery had coveted in 1845—"as red as the Scarlet Letter," said Hawthorne, giving it the imprimatur of his first major romance. They arrived in Pittsfield on May 23, 1850, by the Western Railroad from Boston, staying with the Tappans while the farmhouse was readied for their occupancy. Hawthorne planted a vegetable garden, bought some hens and a rooster, and professed himself well pleased with the situation. Una and Julian soon turned "brown as berries," and Sophia took over the interior decoration of La Maison Rouge, as she liked to call it.

They had been there two months when they heard the news of Margaret's death. Caroline brought over clippings from the *New York Tribune* and the Boston papers, and Sophia was overcome with emotion. "Was ever anything so tragical, so dreary, so unspeakably agonizing," she exclaimed, "as the image of Margaret upon that wreck alone, sitting with her hands upon her knees and tempestuous waves breaking over her! But I cannot dwell upon it. . . . I wish at least Angelino could have been saved." Hawthorne's reaction was not recorded in his letters or his notebooks. But he had always been a shade sardonic about Margaret, despite their friendly conclaves in the Old Manse days.

On the other hand, Margaret's brother-in-law, Ellery Channing, told Emerson, who recorded the remark in his journal, that the shipwreck exactly fitted the "life and genius of the person: 'Twas like Socrates' poison, or Christ's cross, or Shelley's death."

The Hawthornes' life in Lenox was a good deal livelier in a social sense than the Salem years had been. "If I had stayed four years longer in the Custom House," said Hawthorne, "I should have rusted utterly away, and never been heard of more." Here, however, he was almost lionized. Early in August he rode over to Stockbridge with his publisher, James T. Fields, who had brought his new wife to see the Berkshires. The immediate occasion was a picnic party of literary people on the slopes of Monument Mountain. The group included Oliver Wendell Holmes, who had been summering in Pittsfield at his mansion called Holmesdale since 1849, and was said to have remarked that "the best of all tonics is the Housatonic"; Evert Duyckinck, editor in chief of the *Literary World*; and Herman Melville, sometimes called "Omoo" after his second adventure novel. Fields presently reported that he had just got back to his desk from the Berkshire hills, where he and his bride had been "tramping over the soil with Hawthorne, dining with Holmes . . . and sitting in all manner of dangerous places with Melville, the author of 'Typee.' "

This day, August 5, 1850, was all the more memorable for marking the first acquaintance between Hawthorne and Melville. "I met Melville, the other day," Hawthorne told his *Fidus Achates*, Horatio Bridge, "and liked him so much that I have asked him to spend a few days with me." The fourday visit was postponed until early September, but in the interim Melville asked Duyckinck to send copies of his own books for the Hawthornes, and in a burst of enthusiasm for his new friend wrote a long anonymous review called "Hawthorne and His Mosses" for Duyckinck's *Literary World*.

"We have been very much interested in Mr Melville's books, and we are very much obliged to you for them," wrote Sophia to Duyckinck. "Mr Hawthorne has read them all on the new hay in the barn, which is a delightful place for the perusal of worthy books." Hawthorne confirmed his wife's statement: "I have read Melville's works with a progressive appreciation of the author. No writer ever put the reality before his reader more unflinchingly than he does in *Redburn* and *Whitejacket*. *Mardi* is a rich book, with depths here and there that compel a man to swim for his life."

At the same time, whether in his snug second-floor study or lolling in the haymow, Hawthorne had read the two-part commentary on his *Mosses from an Old Manse* in Duyckinck's magazine. Unaware of the real identity of the enthusiastic reviewer, who had signed himself only as "a Virginian spending July in Vermont," Hawthorne told Duyckinck of his "very great pleasure" in what was far and away the strongest commendation his *Mosses* had yet received. "The writer," said he, "has a truly generous heart; nor do I think it necessary to appropriate the whole magnificence of his encomium, any more than to devour everything on the table, when a host of noble hospitality spreads a banquet before me. But he is no comman man; and . . . it is good to have beguiled or bewitched such a man into praising me more than I deserve."

Melville plainly looked up to Hawthorne, possibly in part because he was fifteen years younger. When he arrived at the red farmhouse on September 3, Sophia was more than impressed by this tall, straight-backed thirty-one-year-old, with his "free, brave and manly" demeanor, his abundant hair and reddish beard, and the "strange lazy glance" with which he seemed "to take you into himself." One evening near sunset she went with him to pay a call on the Tappans at Highwood. While Caroline was putting her new baby to bed, the visitors sat on the broad porch overlooking the Stockbridge Bowl. Hawthorne, said Melville, combined a "high calm intellect" with a "glowing, deep heart." He added that "Mr. Hawthorne's hospitable silence drew him out—that it was astonishing how *sociable* his silence was." This, said Sophia, was just what Mr. Emerson used to think. The new friendship was off to an excellent start, which was further cemented when the Hawthornes learned that Melville was the author of "Hawthorne and His Mosses" in Duyckinck's journal.

Hawthorne's mornings were given to writing. He had lately begun work on the second of his major romances. "The scene of it," he told his publisher, "is one of those old projecting-storied houses familiar to my eye in Salem; and the story horrible to say, is little less than two hundred years long; though all but thirty or forty pages of it refers to the present time." He was already planning to name it *The House of the Seven Gables*.

While Hawthorne sat in his study spinning out his account of Miss Hepzibah Pyncheon and her poor little cent-shop in Salem, Melville explored the neighborhood. "One morning," as Sophia reported, "he shut himself into the boudoir and read Mr. Emerson's Essays." Although neither of the friends left a record of their conversations during long afternoon walks, it is a reasonable guess that Emerson's name must sometimes have come up. Only nineteen months earlier, on a visit to Boston, Melville had heard Emerson lecture on "Mind and Manners in the Nineteenth Century." Afterward he had told Evert Duyckinck: "Say what they will, he's a great man. . . . I had heard of him as full of transcendentalisms, myths, and oracular gibberish; I had only glanced at a book of his once in Putnam's store—that was all I knew of him, till I heard him lecture. To my surprise, I found him quite intelligible, tho' to say truth, they told me that that night he was unusually plain." A month later, again to Duyckinck, he wrote: "I do not oscillate in Emerson's rainbow. . . . Yet I think Emerson is more than a brilliant fellow. Be his stuff begged, borrowed, or stolen, or of his own domestic manufacture he is an uncommon man. . . . I love all men who *dive*. Any fish can swim near the surface, but it takes a great whale to go down stairs five miles or more. . . . I'm not talking of Mr Emerson now—but of the whole corps of thought-divers, that have been diving and coming up again with blood-shot eyes since the world began."

Melville's image of the great whale came naturally enough to his talk: he was already many fathoms deep in his "thought-diving" masterpiece, *Moby-Dick*. As James Mellow says, "It was after his initial meetings with Hawthorne that Melville decided to rewrite and expand his whaling story. The force of Hawthorne's allegorical style, the seductive persuasiveness of the man himself, seemed to release Melville's own creative energies, opening up new possibilities in his concept of writing." When *Moby-Dick* at last appeared in November 1851, it was dedicated to Hawthorne "in token of my admiration for his genius."

The House of the Seven Gables, finished at the end of January 1851, was published in April, seven months before *Moby-Dick*. When Melville called at La Maison Rouge on April 11, Hawthorne gave him a signed copy of the first edition. Melville responded a day or two later with an informal review of the book in which he said that he had spent "almost an hour in each separate gable," which robbed him of a day but made him "a present of a whole year of thoughtfulness." The novel surpassed Hawthorne's earlier work: "The curtains are more drawn; the sun comes in more, genialities peep out more." At the same time, Hawthorne had managed to embody in his narrative "a certain tragic phase of humanity . . . the tragicalness of human thought in its own unbiassed, native, and profounder workings . . . the visible truth . . . of the absolute condition of present things as they strike the eye of the man who fears them not, though they do their worst to him."

In a letter to Emerson some months earlier, Caroline had reported on Hawthorne's labors: He "writes in red chalk on his own private blackboard. I am afraid the de'il will carry him off if he walks so much in solitary places; but the only choice here is between the village post office and the solitude of mountains. One may [require?] three days for a poem and three weeks for a novel—but he has been three months writing his and I know the hero will prove chicken-hearted for he has seen nothing living except chickens during that time." Caroline was not far wrong. Hepzibah Pyncheon's shadowy brother Clifford is indeed chickenhearted, though not without reason, and Hawthorne's tenth chapter offers a knowledgeable account of the habits of the chickens in the garden of the seven-gabled house.

Caroline herself had often felt the loneliness of the Berkshire hill country: "no one comes to the Western Land and there are so many cows, horses, and baa-ing lambs about us I begin to think we have returned to the Ark and the world is hidden by a flood. Miss [Elizabeth] Peabody flew hither as a messenger dove and I have seized upon her with great vivacity—it is so pleasant to hear anyone talk the human language."

The year 1851 was productive for the Hawthornes. On May 20 their third child was born and given the name Rose, presently expanded to Rosebud. Although "a little worn down with constant work," Hawthorne was already planning a new book of stories based on such classical myths as those of Midas and Pandora. He was going to call it *A Wonder-Book for Boys and Girls* and gave it all his mornings through June and the first two weeks of July. "The pen," he complained, "is so constantly in my fingers that I abominate the sight of it." When he mailed the final batch of manuscript to Fields on July 15, he swore that he was now going to enjoy the Lenox summer, reading "foolish novels," smoking cigars, and thinking "of nothing at all—which is equivalent to thinking of all manner of things."

At the end of the month, Sophia and her sister Elizabeth, who had come to help with the children, took Rose and Una for a three-week visit to their grandparents in West Newton, leaving Hawthorne and Julian in the charge of Mrs. Peters, a kindly but taciturn black cook. Suddenly released from Sophia's prohibitions against disturbing the new baby, Julian "exercised his lungs to his heart's content," and began to harass his father with an "interminable babble" that ceased only when he was put to bed. After five days, wrote Hawthorne, "it really does seem as if he had baited me with more questions, references, and observations, than mortal father ought to be expected to endure . . . never quitting me, and continually thrusting his word between the clauses of every sentence of all my reading, and smashing every attempt at reflection into a thousand fragments." Despite such intrusions, he kept a detailed record of their domestic adventures. Under the title "Twenty Days with Julian and Little Bunny," it amounted in the end to some 18,000 words, many of them warmly affectionate tributes to the boy he had once called Bundlebreech.

Apart from a few brief letters, Hawthorne did no other writing, and precious little reading except for periodicals and newspapers borrowed from Caroline Tappan. The days were given to feeding Julian's pet rabbit, which they tried unsuccessfully to foist off on Caroline's daughter Ellen; harvesting fresh vegetables, going after milk and the mail; fishing and sailing toy boats in Stockbridge Pond, retiring and rising early. Julian whittled toothpicks with his father's jackknife, wet his bed and his pantaloons, stepped in a cowflop, was stung by a wasp, developed a stomachache, and was frightened to tears by Bruin, Caroline's rambunctious dog. Bunny's short life ended on the morning of August 16 when Hawthorne, peering into its box, found the animal stiff and stark, the victim of some nameless disorder. Julian accepted the loss with a five-year-old's aplomb. "Perhaps tomorrow," said he, "there will be a tree of Bunnies, and they will hang all over it by their ears!"

Their days were otherwise diversified by occasional visitors. Caroline kept an eye on the bachelor household, dropping by with newspapers, sending her nursemaid, Deborah, to pick up Julian for a morning visit to Highwood, borrowing eggs, and lending Hawthorne several volumes of Fourier's works, which he wanted to peruse "with a view to my next Romance"—his earliest allusion to the book that would emerge as *Blithedale*. Hawthorne showed her a letter from Ellery Channing which hinted that he would like to revisit his old Berkshire haunts with a stay at Highwood. But Caroline, well aware of Ellery's dislike of small children, suggested rather airily that he ought rather to be put up by Hawthorne.

Melville was another faithful visitor. On August 1 Hawthorne was reading a newspaper in a nearby grove of trees when a horseman approached and greeted him in Spanish. Hawthorne languidly waved back and resumed his reading. It was not until the cavalier spoke again that he did a double take and recognized Melville, who lifted Julian into the saddle, to the child's immense delight, and walked with Hawthorne back to the farmhouse. It was his thirty-second birthday and Melville was so full of talk that he stayed on until midnight discussing books and publishers, time and eternity, and leaving the sitting room blue with cigar smoke.

There was also a morning call from a pretty young Quaker woman from Philadelphia. Elizabeth Lloyd was a close friend of John Greenleaf Whittier's, with whom she shared an interest in Hawthorne's previous work. Julian was particularly pestiferous, squirming in his father's lap and looking askance at the stranger. Afterward he explained that he had not liked the lady's Quaker dress or her conversational "thees and thous." But Hawthorne had liked all three.

A few mornings later Melville drove up in a barouche, accompanied by the Duyckinck brothers, Evert and George. Hawthorne broke out a bottle of champagne and they trotted off for a sandwich-and-gingerbread picnic in a mountain grove. The picnic site was not far from the Shaker village in Hancock. Visiting Shaker settlements in those days was the custom of the country, and Hawthorne had seen at least three, including the one in the town of Harvard to which he had hiked with Emerson in 1842. Then he had been aloof and indifferent; this time he was disgusted, turning up his nose at the "spit-boxes" that lined the corridors in the main building and the sleeping arrangements in which, he was told, two men shared each of the very narrow beds in a proximity that he found contemptible. These, said he, almost echoing Emerson, must be "the most singular and bedevilled set of people that ever existed in a civilized land."

Sophia returned at last on Saturday, August 16. Next day Sam Ward appeared with an excellent picture of Highwood Porch which he had commissioned Burrill Curtis to draw for the forthcoming *Wonder-Book*. Mailing it off to Fields, Hawthorne called it "the porch of Tanglewood," his name for Highwood, which would be perpetuated in his *Tanglewood Tales* of 1853 and, long afterward, as the site of the Berkshire Music Festival. On the Monday Dr. Holmes rode up "to peep at the Lake through the boudoir window." While he was inside, Hawthorne insisted on holding his spirited horse. "Is there another man in all America," said Holmes laughing, "whoever had so great an honor as to have the author of *The Scarlet Letter* hold his horse?" Sophia was impressed by all the social turmoil. "It is very singular," she told her mother, "how much more we are in the centre of society in Lenox than we were in Salem, and all the literary persons seem settling around us. But when they get established here I dare say we shall take flight."

The notion of moving again had been on Hawthorne's mind for months. Although the prospect from his windows was "the most beautiful in Berkshire," he had come to regard the house itself "the most inconvenient and wretched little hovel that I ever put my head in." He thought briefly of accepting the ex-actress Fanny Kemble's offer to rent out her cottage, The Perch, overlooking Stockbridge Bowl, yet he complained that he had never felt quite at home among those hills, and was not nearly so vigorous as he had been on the seacoast.

A small domestic altercation between Caroline and Sophia finally settled the Hawthornes' decision to move. Sophia admired William Tappan, a kindly and courtly man whom she called "The Castilian, with his curls and dark smiling eyes." He had once told her, as Emerson had noticed in England, that Hawthorne's portrait resembled that of Tennyson, an observation that Sophia took as a compliment, not having seen Lord Alfred in the flesh. But after more than a year of life in the "wretched little hovel" down the lane from the great house, Sophia's familiar references to Caroline became less frequent than formerly, and it may be that she privately resented a tendency in Caroline to play the Lady Bountiful. This is only a speculation. The fact is what happened on the afternoon of September 4.

Strolling over from Highwood, Caroline met Mary Beekman, the Hawthornes' hired girl, carrying a basket of apples home to the farmhouse. That evening Caroline sent down a note to Sophia asking whether she would not prefer to receive kindness from the actual owners of the orchard rather than to assume proprietary rights to its contents. Next day Hawthorne, no doubt spurred by his wife's angry tears, took the "diplomatic correspondence" into his own hands with a long letter to "Dear Mrs. Tappan" that spelled out, in his pellucid prose, his opinion that he had "bought" the rights to the fruit when he rented the farmhouse. He closed with a typical flourish: "The recollection of this slight acidity of sentiment, between friends of some years' standing, may impart a pleasant and spirited flavor to the preserves and jams when they come upon your table. At any rate, take what you want, and that speedily, or there will be little else than a parcel of rotten plums to dispute about." An exchange of notes between Tappan and Hawthorne closed the incident. "I freely confess," wrote Hawthorne to his neighbor, "that the world will not deserve to be called a world of bargain and sale so long as it shall include men like yourself."

Sophia summarized her own views in a letter to her sister Elizabeth: "Caroline has made herself strangely disagreeable and crowned her strange behavior with an overt act which I could not have thought possible in a person of good taste, to say nothing of Christian sentiment (but I believe she despises Christ) and decent manners and human friendliness. Mr. Tappan has proved himself most lovely and of the true ideal courtesy and does not share in Caroline's hostility. But of course we could not live in the red house any longer at any rate with Caroline at war."

They maintained the Lenox connection for six weeks more. At the end of October, Ellery Channing arrived for a ten-day visit, staying with the Hawthornes and renewing old associations with the Sedgwick family as well as with Caroline, who wrote Emerson that he was "gossiping and agreeable." One afternoon he walked out with his host through a golden autumnal scene where the local farmers were repairing last year's cider barrels and feeding great heaps of apples into the presses. Next day he wrote his wife in Cincinnati that Hawthorne's personality was "greatly altered"; he looked "rather dry and out of spirits." Since he always seemed to "find fault with the people among whom he settles" he was already talking of returning to Concord and buying a house there. A bad idea, thought Ellery: he would only tire of his purchase and move somewhere else. Nor was Ellery charmed by Sophia and the children. She was "by no means prepossessing." The passage of time had neither "added to her beauty" nor taught her the art of bringing "elegance and refinement" to her living quarters. The children, moreover, had been "brought up in the worst way for visitors." Their manners were execrable and they kept breaking in "when not required." Outwardly the fun-loving rover, Ellery inwardly could be nastily abrasive.

On moving day, November 21, the Hawthornes packed a farm wagon with their chattels and drove off through a snowstorm to the depot in Pittsfield. Their destination was West Newton and a house that belonged to Sophia's sister Mary, who had offered it to them while the Mann family wintered in Washington. Melville's *Moby-Dick* had just appeared with its noble dedication to Hawthorne, and his farewell letter left no doubt of his continuing admiration: "Lord, when shall we be done changing? Ah! it's a long stage, and no inn in sight, and night coming, and the body cold. But with you for a passenger, I am content. . . . I shall leave the world . . . with more satisfaction for having come to know you."

"I have heard nothing from Concord since Ellery was here," wrote Caroline to Emerson in a Christmas letter. "Perhaps you will write to me and tell me what you are doing and going to do. . . . I am going to N.Y. to hear Jenny Lind—I wish I could say to see her too." Whether or not she was still at war with the Hawthornes, her note made no allusion to them. But Ellery, back in Concord, had changed his October tune: "I am glad you have . . . evacuated . . . that ice-plant of Sedgwicks," he wrote Hawthorne. "I know nothing of West Newton, and do not wish to know any more; but it is further south than the other,—a great advantage. . . . I have now a room at your command. . . . Nobody at home but myself. . . . Emerson is gone, and nobody here to bore you. The skating is damned good. . . . Pipes and old tobac no end."

But Hawthorne was not yet ready for Concord. By the close of the year he was already engaged with the third of his American romances. "Community" was his theme and his locale was Brook Farm, though his fictional name for it was going to be Blithedale.

Chapter Thirty-four

HAWTHORNE,
BIRD OF PASSAGE

ON JUNE 5, 1852, THE HAWTHORNES RESETTLED IN CON-
cord after an absence of nearly seven years. When he left the Old Manse
he had been known only as a contributor of sketches and short stories to a
handful of American magazines. In each of the towns he afterward moved
to—Salem, Lenox, and West Newton—he had completed one of his book-
length "romances," and now, on the eve of his forty-eighth birthday, he had
established a solid reputation as a novelist both at home and abroad.

After ten years of marriage he could at last afford to buy instead of renting. His Concord house was two centuries old, and showed it. Abandoned
by the Alcotts in 1848, it stood in such a state of disrepair that the asking
price of $1,500 was no great bargain. "I find myself surrounded with a host
of carpenters, masons, etc.—each presenting a long bill," he wrote W. D.
Ticknor on June 8. "I have compounded with my creditors to pay them
$100 in hand, and the rest at an early date. . . . I should like to have a certifi-
cate of deposit . . . payable at the bank here, for the above sum." Once the
workmen had finished, he was sure that the place would become "a comfortable and sufficiently pleasant home." But he was giving it a new name. "Alcott called it 'Hillside,' as it stands close at the base of a steep ascent; but as it
is also in proximity (too nigh indeed) to the road leading into the village, I
have re-baptized it 'The Wayside'—which seems to me to possess a moral as
well as descriptive propriety. It might have been called 'Woodside'—the

hill being covered with a growth of birch, locust-trees, and various sorts of pine."

One day in July he walked out for a look at the Manse, the old battleground, and the meandering river. Apart from the addition of a large dormer window high above the front door, the house was little altered, but the trees around the battlefield were taller and leafier than formerly, and the "sluggish river, mystically dark . . . seemed to have spent all the seven by-gone years in vainly deliberating which way to flow." The same was true of Hawthorne himself: "I see that the papers announce me as having begun a new work, the day after finishing the Blithedale Romance," he wrote in June. "My poor intellect is not quite so ready and flexible as that. It is now six weeks since I finished the romance; and I have neither written nor thought of the first sentence of another book."

National politics soon changed his mind. The day he moved back to Concord happened to be the very day when General Franklin Pierce, his old chum from college days at Bowdoin, was nominated for the presidency of the United States on the Democratic ticket, opposed by another general, the Whig candidate Winfield Scott, Pierce's commanding officer during the Mexican War. The news did not reach Hawthorne until June 8. Next day he wrote Pierce to offer congratulations and to suggest himself as the possible author of a campaign biography. "Whatever service I can do you . . . ," said he, "would be at your command." His style and qualities as a writer were "certainly not those of the broadest popularity," and someone else might do the job better. Despite Hawthorne's modest protestations, Pierce at once approved the plan and the matter was settled by June 17. "He wishes me to write his biography, and I have consented to do so," Hawthorne told his publisher, James T. Fields, "somewhat reluctantly, however—for Pierce has now reached that altitude when a man, careful of his personal dignity, will begin to think of cutting his acquaintance. But I seek nothing from him, and therefore need not be ashamed to tell the truth of an old friend."

Six weeks later half the truth was told. "I am taking your life as fast as I can—murdering and mangling you," he told Pierce. His swift progress was temporarily halted when his sister Louisa was drowned in a fiery steamboat accident on the Hudson River. But Pierce proved to be fully cooperative, correcting the manuscript and conferring with his biographer throughout the month of August whenever they could get together, and accompanying Hawthorne on a brief postoperative vacation among the Isles of Shoals, wafted from port to port by the mailboat, *Fanny Elssler*, named for Austria's famous ballet dancer.

The biography appeared on September 11, roughly three months from inception to publication. Reviewers in the Boston papers were not greatly impressed: one of them sardonically called the book Hawthorne's "new romance," and another said that it was an honest biography of a man who had never risen above respectable mediocrity. But Hawthorne was not abashed. "I have done the business, greatly to Frank's satisfaction," he told his old friend Bridge in October. "And though I say it myself, it is judiciously done; and, without any sacrifice of truth, it puts him in as good a light as circumstances would admit. . . . I doubt whether any other could have bestowed a better aspect of sincerity and reality on the narrative, and have secured all the credit possible for him, without spoiling all by asserting too much. And though the story is true, yet it took a romancer to do it."

Despite his satisfactions, he recognized that the book was going to cost him "hundreds of friends, here at the north . . . who drop off from me like autumn leaves, in consequence of what I say on the slavery question." What he had said was that "slavery [is] one of those evils which divine Providence does not leave to be remedied by human contrivances, but which, in its own good time, by some means impossible to be anticipated, but of the simplest and easiest operation, when its uses shall have been fulfilled, it causes to vanish like a dream." Neither on November 4, 1852, when Pierce triumphed in an electoral landslide, nor for many years thereafter, would slavery vanish like a dream, and certainly not by "the simplest and easiest operation."

Hawthorne's espousal of Pierce's cause placed a severe strain on his ten-years' friendship with Emerson. That very Fourth of July Emerson had hung a portrait head of George Washington on the wall of his dining room. "I cannot keep my eyes off it," he wrote in his journal:

It has a certain Apalachian [sic] strength, as if it were truly the first fruits of America, and expressed the country. The heavy leaden eyes turn on you, as the eyes of an ox in a pasture. And the mouth has a gravity and depth of quiet, as if this man had absorbed all the serenity of America, and left none for his restless, rickety, hysterical countrymen. Noble aristocratic head, with all kinds of elevation in it, that come out by turns. Such majestical ironies, as he hears the day's politics [discussed] at table. We imagine him hearing . . . the letter of General Scott, the letter of Mr. Pierce . . . the effronteries of Mr. Webster, recited. This man listens like a god to these low conspirators.

Emerson's ruminations before his homemade mural shrine ironically dramatized how far the nation had sunk in the fifty-odd years since General Washington's death. Two latter-day generals were vying for a post that their first predecessor had filled so well and with so much inherent dignity, while the restless and rickety politicians of 1852 were about to elevate one of their number to the throne of power. Little wonder that when Sophia Hawthorne confided to him a "paper" that presumably asked his support for her husband's candidate, Emerson belatedly apologized for having forgotten to reply. His delay, said he, was "all the more inexcusable, as I do not give my name; not having the smallest interest, unless of aversation, to the whole subject, as it now presents itself in our community." His term "aversation" meant a turning away, and the subject in which he had not the smallest interest as of August 4, 1852, was the fact that less than a mile from his front door Hawthorne was embroiled with a laudatory biography of one of the low conspirators.

Emerson softened the end of his otherwise curt note with a word of sympathy for the death of Sophia's sister-in-law, whose funeral in Salem Hawthorne was just then attending. "I heard with pain the dreadful story of the wreck and fire, and hoped, as long as I could, that there was a mistake in the report that your sister[']s name was in the list" of victims. "But who knows which is the shortest and most excellent way out of the calamities of the present world?" If his final rhetorical question was intended for consolation, neither Sophia nor her husband could have missed the cool tenor of the rest of Emerson's missive. His opposition to Pierce remained adamant. Midway of the general's term of office he wrote: "A bad president, like ours today, is a toad in amber."

Through the fall and winter Hawthorne stayed absurdly busy. "I have a hill behind me," he wrote, "whither I can make my escape when the Philistines knock at the front-door. . . . Mr. Emerson lives within a quarter of a mile, and there are two or three other friends in the village, who supply me with about as much society as I need. The river, I am sorry to say, is quite out of my reach, and I have neither paddled a boat nor caught a fish since my residence here." Although he accepted Emerson's invitation to a complimentary dinner for Arthur Hugh Clough on November 20, he declined to meet another visiting Englishman in January: "I enjoy Thackeray's books above all things; but it is quite a non sequitur that I should therefore seek his society." The new year had hardly begun when he had to contend with two further deaths on top of that of his sister. On January 6 the Pierces' only child, Benjamin, was killed in a railroad accident on the way from Concord to Boston, and on the eleventh Sophia's mother died after a long illness. Only a few days earlier Hawthorne had told Lowell that "amidst innumerable interruptions" he was trying to get forward with a new piece of writing. This was a sequel to his money-making *Wonder-Book*, six more classical myths retold for children. Remembering the Ward-Tappan house in Lenox, he called it *Tanglewood Tales*. When he finished his labors on March 9, he said that it might be a worthy successor to *Mother Goose*.

For the rest, his occupations were decidedly political. In October he had told his friend Bridge that he had at first inwardly resolved not to accept any pork-barrel appointment from Pierce. But now his mind was changing. Some of his English admirers had been urging him to come overseas. Pierce, he felt, certainly owed him a quid pro quo, and the remunerative consulship at Liverpool looked like a tempting possibility.

Soon after the biography appeared, various office-seekers began to pester Hawthorne, assuming that he must be the "prime minister" for the Democratic candidate. Pierce had more than 700 appointments to make, and Hawthorne quietly put forward, among others, the names of his close friends Herman Melville, Ellery Channing, and Horatio Bridge. He chose not to attend Pierce's inaugural on March 4, but when the Senate confirmed his Liverpool consulship soon afterward, he bought a new black dress coat and pantaloons to dandify his three-week visit to Washington for conferences with "Emperor Frank" about his foreign service obligations.

When he got there late in April he found the city glorying in the "beautiful and blossoming Spring." But the extended visit left him with decidedly mixed feelings. "Frank was as free and kind, in our personal interviews, as ever he was in our college days," he told Bridge, "but his public attentions to me were few and by no means distinguished. . . . To confess the truth, I did not in the least regret being almost shut out of the White House; for of all dismally dull and heavy domestic circles, poor Frank's is certainly the most intolerable." Still, as he wrote Sophia, it was astonishing how much he had been able to accomplish both for himself and others in various smoke-filled rooms. His days had been filled with more "political intrigue and management" than he had hitherto dreamed of. Prominent among his personal victories was a joint appointment to the consulship at Manchester, which would supplement his income from the Liverpool post by some $3,000.

Back in Concord early in May, he devoted most of his time to preparations for departure. After a mere thirteen months' residence at "The Wayside," the bird of passage was about to take flight once more. He sent Sophia to Boston to book passage on the Cunard steamer *Niagara*, which was scheduled to sail for Liverpool early in July, shortly after his forty-ninth birthday, and completed arrangements with Sophia's brother Nathaniel, who was to occupy the house while the Hawthornes were abroad. Once his quadrennial duties in England were over, he and Sophia were hoping to fulfill their dream of a visit to Italy. Their residence in Concord had followed an absence of seven years, and it would be another seven before they returned for the last time.

Emerson's adventures in Europe were five years behind him and he was glad enough to stay home, "haying and hoeing and reading and writing," fortifying the roof of his house with tin and slate, and laying a bright new carpet in his mother's bed chamber. His only maritime experience was landlocked: a visit to Donald McKay's busy shipyard in East Boston on June 14, where he spent a happy morning clambering over *The Great Republic*, styled "The King of the Clippers." She was more than half finished and stood grandly in her stocks being readied for launching in the fall. That afternoon he attended Longfellow's "very agreeable" farewell dinner for Hawthorne in a company that included Lowell, Clough, Samuel Longfellow, the poet's brother, and young Charles Eliot Norton. Afterward he reported that his house now sported "a stone cap, with a tin visor." The attendant problem was that the painters and masons were due to arrive any day. "There is no peace for the sons of men," he ruefully remarked, adding that "we are losing Hawthorne, who sails on the 6 July." It was close to the third anniversary of the loss of Margaret Fuller on the stormy shores of Fire Island.

Chapter Thirty-five

ELLEN

WHEN THE EMERSONS' FIRST DAUGHTER WAS BORN IN FEB-ruary 1839, Lidian had "magnanimously" insisted on naming her for Emerson's first wife. By 1853, in her fifteenth year, this second Ellen Tucker Emerson was standing on the verge of young womanhood, as healthy and sturdy as her namesake had never been, reveling in the folkways of her native town, and eager for full acceptance as an adult. She referred to her surviving siblings, Edith and Edward, as "the children," supervised their activities, and had already begun to record their adventures and her own in a series of letters that continued all her life and together constitute the most detailed account of the domestic side of the family.

Ellery Channing, who had watched Ellen "grow up from a mite," later told Frank Sanborn that as a small child she had been "awkward and reserved,"— "a 'great plague' to the whole family," who "used to think they could no noth-ing with her." But she had eventually outgrown this early behavior and had become "one of the most pleasing young people we shall either of us be likely to meet."

Owing to his Lenox connection with the Wards and the Tappans, Emer-son had been laying plans for Ellen's adolescent schooling since the fall of 1852, and had sought Caroline's advice about entering his daughter in Mrs. Charles Sedgwick's School for Girls in Lenox village. At first Caroline op-posed the plan: Lenox was too far from Concord; the child might be homesick; the current crop of schoolgirls was older than Ellen, and probably talked of "nothing but parties, dress, etc., as most girls of sixteen do when alone together." But she invited Emerson to bring Ellen over for an initiatory visit at the end of October. "We will try to have sunny weather for you when you come—and nuts to crack—hard-shelled or soft-shelled at your pleasure. . . . If she comes here to school I will do all I can to make it pleasant for her." In the end, Ellen's entry was postponed until the summer term of June 1853.

Like many of her classmates, she was acutely clothes-conscious, always hungry, and jubilant over the boxes of fruit and crackers that her parents sent. She rode horseback, studied assiduously, and threw herself into the life of the rather straitlaced school with evident enthusiasm. In July Caroline went down to see her. "You will like to see how upright and sensible Ellen looks walking among the other girls in the village," she told Emerson. "She looked so glad to see me that I asked her if she felt homesick, and she said, 'Not often, very; but a little all the time.' I told her I should have been to see her before but had been away. She said 'Yes,' and that little yes was very sweet and touching."

Ellen was growing taller, slender like both her parents, weighing only ninety-eight pounds, and wearing her hair in the severe mode of the 1850s, parted in the middle, drawn tightly back behind her ears, and gathered in a bun at the nape of the neck. She was resolved to behave as a grown-up, consoling and "doctoring" her roommate, Ida Wheeler, who had a bad case of homesickness: "She thinks I am very hardhearted not to cry too but I think I should if I did not try not to think of home."

She was schooling herself in observation and her letters of that summer were filled with reportage that delighted her father. Ida's father and brother rented a carryall with a span of dark gray horses and took the girls on a long Sunday drive through the Berkshire hills. "Best of all," wrote Ellen, "was to look off and see the beautiful green valleys with the handsome trees and such lovely little groves and the houses making it look prettier still and the charm of it was the mountains farther off and farther still, growing bluer and bluer. At one place the driver pointed out the Catskill mountains just visible in the distance."

The route they followed took them past the Shaker village near West Pittsfield. The residents were making so much noise in the meetinghouse that

Ellen and the Wheelers paid them a call, sat in the spectators' seats, and watched the strange Shaker dancing, which had so much disgusted Ellen's father some years before. "All the Shakers," wrote Ellen,

> were hopping round and round the room with their hands shaking about in front of them[,] three abreast. The women had on scant, almost straight, white dresses some of them striped blue and white gingham, white neckerchiefs and white caps. Most of them looked near seventy. Their faces were very yellow-looking. It looked like ghosts to see these straight dressed lank looking old ladies hopping and dancing around with solemn faces and eyes almost shut. Five poor little girls all very pale and sad-looking followed in their train. Ever so many little boys came behind the men. In the middle of the room stood an equal number of men and women ranged in a perfect oval who sang. After a while they stopped dancing and stood with their faces toward the middle of the room while they sang a hymn and a little old lady with her arms spread far out on each side and her eyes shut whirled from one end of the room to the other many times so fast that she seemed to have arms on all sides like the spokes of a wheel. Then they began to dance again.

In the fall of 1854 Ellen paid the Shakers another visit, this time at Tyringham. One Sister Desire was selling sugar nuts, for which this colony was famous: meats of shagbark hickory encrusted with maple sugar. All the members of Mrs. Sedgwick's school were there that day, clamoring for sweets. Sister Desire, a neat and pretty little woman, "attended to everything all at once, gave very full measure, [and] made us a present of a whole box of candied flag-root." None of the schoolgirls seems to have been struck by the irony of a celibate Shaker sister with such a name as Desire.

Emerson wrote to his daughter that she must lose no opportunity for outdoor walking and riding, but also that she must learn as rapidly as possible to read Latin and to speak French. Apart from Ellen's education, his own preoccupations were largely domestic. Lidian spent much of her time in her "chamber," from which she habitually sent down messages to her husband's study. To friends of the family he apologized for her "debility" and her continuing difficulty with "a country matron's cares," which in fact had troubled her throughout seventeen years of marriage. Though Ellen repeatedly urged her mother to come and visit in Lenox, Emerson was obliged to tell his daughter that such a trip was unlikely. "You know she is a bad traveller," he wrote. "She will probably go to Plymouth in August, and, after that, will be expecting you home in September." In the end, it was he who went to Lenox, after a quick trip to New York to see his nephew William Emerson Junior graduated from Columbia, staying at Highwood with the Tappans. Ellen and Ida came over on Sunday, and Emerson heard with pleasure that his daughter had never regretted for a single day her time at Mrs. Sedgwick's school.

For the rest of the summer he was mainly at home. He bought a second-hand carriage from Sam Staples the town jailer, a new horse named Dolly for riding and driving, and a new carpet for his mother's room. The roof was leaking badly and much of July and August was given over to costly repairs, unhappily followed by further leakage and the destruction of a brand-new ceiling in the parlor. Through all the hubbub of tinsmiths and roofers and carpenters, he managed to get in his hay crop, weed his garden, and begin the annual harvest of pears, plums, and apples, while trying to move forward with the book that would become *English Traits*. According to his annual custom, Bulkeley came down from Reuben Hoar's farm in Littleton to spend a few days at "Election" time. He needed new overalls and boots, but seemed very well, and even managed to indite a short letter to his brother William.

Early in June, Caroline Tappan's sister Susan Bigelow, a beautiful young matron with whom Emerson had talked at a party two weeks earlier, bought arsenic at a shop and took her life with it. In July, perhaps with this tragedy in the back of his mind, he had written Caroline on the subject of fatalism. He had lectured on "Fate" in December 1851, and in December 1852 finished an essay on the subject that would lead off the *Conduct of Life* volume in 1860. Now in his fifty-first year, he told Caroline that "Fatalism, foolish and flippant, is as bad as Unitarianism or Mormonism. But Fatalism held by an intelligent soul who knows how to humor and obey the infinitesimal pulses of spontaneity, is by much the truest theory in use. All the great could call their thought fatalism, or concede that ninetynine parts are nature, and one part power, tho' that hundredth is elastic, miraculous, and, whenever it is in energy, dissolving all the rest."

For the past several years he had been reflecting on the ancient dualism of necessity and freedom, limits and illimitability. "Cannot we ride the horse that now throws us?" he had asked in his journal for 1851. "The intellect conquers fate,—and it is the property of men of insight to be serene, for their faith in law has become sight. But they who talk much of destiny, their birth star, etc., are on a lower, dangerous, vertiginous plane, and seem to invite the evils they fear." In 1852 he had written: "History tends to make fatalists. What courage does not the opposite opinion show—a little bubble of will to be freely gallantly contending against the universe of chemistry."

In the later essay, he returned to some of these ideas, and added others, writing of Fate as a form of confinement, boundary, or limitation: "something which cannot be talked or voted away—a strap or belt which girds the world":

> Every spirit makes its house; but afterwards the house confines the spirit. . . . Famine, typhus, frost, war, suicide and effete races must be reckoned calculable parts of the system of the world. These are pebbles from the mountain, hints of the terms by which our life is walled up. . . . No picture of life can have any veracity that does not admit the odious facts. A man's power is hooped in by a necessity which, by many experiments, he touches on every side until he learns its arc. The limitations refine as the soul purifies, but the ring of necessity is always perched at the top. . . . Even thought itself is not above Fate; that too must act according to eternal laws, and all that is wilful and fantastic in it is in opposition to its fundamental essence. . . . Thus we trace Fate in mind, matter, and morals. . . . It is everywhere bound and limitation. But Fate has its lord . . . is different seen from above and below, from within and from without. For though Fate is immense, so is Power, which is the other fact in the dual world. . . . If Fate follows and limits Power, Power attends and antagonizes Fate. We must respect Fate as natural history, but there is more than natural history. . . . On one side elemental order, sandstone and granite, rock-ledges, peat-bog, forests, sea and shore; and on the other part thought, the spirit which composes and decomposes nature . . . here they are, side by side . . . riding peacefully together in the eye and brain of every man. . . . Nor can he blink the freewill. . . . Freedom is necessary. If you please to plant yourself on the side of Fate, and say, Fate is all; then we say, a part of Fate is the freedom of man. Forever wells up the impulse of choosing and acting in

the soul. Intellect annuls Fate. So far as a man thinks, he is free. . . . Fate is the name for facts not yet passed under the fire of thought; for causes which are unpenetrated. . . . Every solid in the universe is ready to become fluid on the approach of mind, and the power to flux it is the measure of mind. If the wall remains adamant, it accuses the want of thought.

"Dear Mother," wrote Ellen in September, "You are all so kind to send me such a nice box with apples and pears[,] peaches, plums and raisins, and such pretty undersleeves. I think the calico is a perfect beauty, the handsomest one I have. All the girls think so. There was a general rapture over it at school this morning. . . . I never knew such large handsome Queen apples and plums, unfortunately most of the plums were rotting on one side but there were enough good ones to show what they *all had* been and we eat the good part of all that were begun to decay. . . . Ida and I live very sumptuously. We have a box of Wine-biscuit under the bed and *now* there is the box of fruit in our little room, beside whenever we want we may get pineapples and cocoanuts of the fruit-man. We are going on another afternoon excursion next Saturday, either to Tyringham or Richmond Hill. . . . Now the last four weeks are come but they grow every day heavier and longer. How can I bear them. But I suppose it will pass . . . and I comfort myself that I have four more weeks to learn and improve in. . . . I guess I was homesick a minute ago, but I am cured now. Goodbye my own dear Mother, Ellen"

She came home for vacation on the twenty-eighth. "She looks very well," wrote her father, "and is fatter, and is overjoyed to get home." Edith and Edward took her on a tour of the house and grounds to admire the repairs and restorations of the summer. Emerson described his recent trip to Cape Cod with Uncle William. It was strange, as he said, "how many particulars worth keeping one brings home from so barren a place." In the Yarmouth woods he had found two plants, a deerberry and a golden Chrysopsis, and gleefully boasted that "Henry Thoreau could hardly suppress his indignation that I should bring him a berry he had not seen." Each morning he retired to his study to work on *English Traits* and a set of lectures on the same subject for delivery at Philadelphia in January. Ellen divided her time between her mother and her grandmother. Ruth Haskins Emerson sat quietly in her newly refurbished chamber, "surprisingly bright serene and cheerfully alive," but at eighty-five increasingly forgetful and inclined to what her son called "illogicalities."

Ellen was back in Lenox in mid-October when her great-uncle Thomas Haskins died in his eightieth year. He had long been a victim of advanced senility, and his death was a blessing to all his survivors except his sister, who followed him exactly a month later. Emerson sent the news to Ellen on November 16: "Your grandmother died this morning at 1 o'clock. She has been very ill since Sunday morning, after riding out as usual on Saturday afternoon. Still, I thought she would rally again and be herself, but without pain and very imperceptibly she ceased to breathe. . . . So has died, my dear child, one of the best and most blameless persons on the earth, whom you, having seen only in her old age, can never but half know, but she never had an evil thought or an evil will, so calm so firm so faithful as few could be. I could heartily wish you were at home, but shall not expect you."

"I have just received Father's letter," wrote Ellen next day. "Did you not know Grandma was going to die and were you not in the room? It does seem so sudden and terrible, I cannot realize it. Was she not herself before she died and did she not know how very ill she was? How little we thought when I came away that I had seen her and bade her goodbye for the last time. Please write me all about her[,] dearest Mother[,] as soon as you can."

The answers to Ellen's questions were that only Elizabeth Hoar and Elizabeth Ripley had been at her grandmother's bedside when she died. Lidian was asleep, and Emerson, not thinking that the end was so near, was absent on a speaking engagement in Charlestown. But he quickly arranged for the funeral service on the eighteenth. William could not come from New York, having just dislocated his shoulder in a bad fall while boarding a steamboat, but Bulkeley was there, brought over from Littleton by Henry Thoreau. Since the cemetery in Sleepy Hollow was not yet open, Emerson buried his mother temporarily near little Waldo in the tomb of the Ripley family—the oldest of his blood kin near the youngest. The day after the funeral he wrote to Ellen that "your grandmother's end was so peaceful, and all remembrances of her life in every body's mind so pleasing, that there was no gloom about the event such as usually belongs to it. Only the house has one less home in it, one less to be interested in, and to enjoy what befals you." This was a view of death that Ellen long remembered, and was to repeat when her father died many years afterward.

Her schooling at Lenox continued until the end of September 1854. On New Year's Eve of 1853, she looked back upon the year just past with a new sense of maturity and experience. "This is the last night of 1853," she wrote her mother. "Oh how I wish I were at home. It seems now as if I was old and home and school and the time when I was young were all gone. . . . And when I remember all my life at home and know that that is gone too for we are all older and Grandma is dead. Oh how you must miss her, how I shall miss her when I come home. When I think of going home and not seeing her and that we shall never sit together in her room with her when Father comes home from lecturing. How sad it seems. Oh how I want you all. I am so homesick tonight. . . . They are so good and kind to me here I believe I am as happy here as it is possible to be away from home." She had received her grand-mother's watch as a keepsake. "I enjoy having a watch so much. I only wish it wouldn't look silly to keep pulling it out all the time. Whenever I have a chance I hold it in my hand while I study. I send a Happy New Year! my own best Mother to you and Father, to the dear children. . . . Are you well Mother dear? . . . I hope you will have plenty of health and leisure this year and when I leave here we'll have a happy time."

Lidian forwarded Ellen's letter to Emerson, who was in Philadelphia and New York on the first leg of his annual winter tour. "I send you home Ellen's letter which I was glad to read," he replied, adding that he was "not glad to see its melancholy tone. What business have fourteen years to be melan-choly[?]" But he was not without some melancholy of his own: "It is strange how much I miss Mother in looking homeward, whenever I am travelling." Lidian faithfully sent all his voluminous mail to the various stops on his itiner-ary, which included Detroit, Chicago, and Milwaukee and lasted a month and a half. Despite the help of three servants and an Irish yardman, she found her tasks burdensome in her husband's absence. The family finances were nearly always on the ragged edge, and she was obliged to handle the drafts and checks that he sent home, and to make piecemeal payments to the local tradesmen.

Emerson returned on February 20 in time to dispatch a box to Ellen for her fifteenth birthday—a ring, a fur piece, "waists, muslins, and handkerchiefs," as well as daguerreotypes of Edith and Edward—all ecstatically received in Lenox. The girls at school had presented a play, followed by a feast of ice cream, cake, biscuits, and oysters, and even small glasses of mulled wine. Ellen was a devoted correspondent, averaging a letter a week through the spring term, all of them bursting with detailed accounts of her daily affairs and extramural expeditions. When she came home for spring vacation in April she was eager to begin housekeeping for her parents. But Emerson had wisely decided that she should spend a third term at Lenox, postponing what he called "our fine new housekeeping" until October. Back at school on June 11, she wrote, "I have quite got over the dolefuls and have a very pleasant time." She was doing 120 lines of the *Aeneid* each day, making trips to Roaring Brook and Bashbish Falls near Copake, New York, listening to sermons by Henry Ward Beecher, and meeting his sister, Harriet Beecher Stowe, already famous for *Uncle Tom's Cabin*. One of Ellen's classmates had described Mrs. Stowe as "a hideous woman . . . so ugly we would dream about her," but Ellen found her not "so very ugly, only homely."

The plan to appoint Ellen as housekeeper originated in her own imagination. Emerson's willingness to follow it was just as certainly owing to his worry over Lidian's precarious health. One of his letters in June 1854 alluded to "my poor broken-to-pieces wife," and in August he wrote Ellen, "Your Mother is very feeble; and I doubt much if in October I can spare you to go to school anywhere. I think we shall have to instal you as housekeeper for a time sole and sovereign to make your blunders and correct them yourself, and find out by hitting and missing and hitting again, the true and perfect way. Meantime your Mother will be relieved, which she needs." Presently, in a mood that approached desperation, he told his old friend and financial adviser, Abel Adams, that "if Ellen were not coming home in October, with ambition to keep house for us, I should be seriously tempted to sell mine, so feeble is Lidian, and such is the trial of bad domestics. Happy are you who shall never know these evils!"

Late in August, Emerson delivered the commencement address at Williams College. To relieve Lidian, he took Edith along to stay with the Tappans in Lenox while Ellen accompanied her father to Williamstown. The harassed orator, working feverishly at his hotel, finished his speech with five minutes to spare. Back in Lenox, he learned from Caroline that Edith had fallen ill, doubtless from a combination of excitement, change of diet, and the extreme heat. But she soon recovered, went home with her father, and presently departed with her mother and brother for a vacation in Lidian's beloved Plymouth.

A severe drought prevailed in Concord. Every day the hot dry winds seared the grass and burned up the gardens. The happiest man around town was Henry Thoreau, whose *Walden* had at last appeared. Emerson thought the book "cheerful, sparkling, readable, with all kinds of merits, and rising sometimes to very great heights. . . . We account Henry the undoubted King of all American lions. . . . He is walking up . . . and down Concord, firm-looking, but in a tremble of great expectation." The town began to breathe again on September 1 when rain fell for the first time in six weeks. Lidian came home from Plymouth "very much healed," and Ellen finished her schooldays at Lenox in time to attend the annual cattle show and exhibition— "What fun it was to see the farmers bring the pride and glory of their hearts"—and to commence her long-postponed stint as keeper of the house.

"I haven't fairly begun my housekeeping yet for of course Mother can't at first give up all power, but I am beginning to peep round to examine the treasures of my kingdom and getting one thing after another into my hands so fast that I expect to be fully installed in my office in the course of a fortnight." She thought that her titles ought to be "Pear-Mistress-General and Universal Reader." After breakfast each day she hurried to the pear room, examined the hoard for ripeness and rot, and chose the best for the dinner table.

Some of them had been exhibited at the cattle show. Emerson was becoming nearly as devoted to his orchard as his good neighbor, Ephraim Bull, was to his flourishing vineyard. Storage was always a problem. "They say," wrote Emerson, "a pear is only in perfection for about ten minutes." Pears glowed golden and brown not only in the official pear room but also in bureau drawers and closets, so that the whole interior took on a delicious fragrance of ripening fruit. There were Easter Beurrés, Flemish Beauties, and others with such exotic names as Duchesse d'Angoulême, Louise Bonne de Jerseys, Glout Morceaus, Winter Nelises, York and Roxbury Russets, as well as the more common Seckels and Bartletts.

Ellen's housekeeping soon settled into a kind of pattern. Shortly before Christmas she told her friend Emma Stinson that "I do whatever is to be done about the house (in my province) such as taking care of the pears, looking to see that the rooms are done right, putting away clean clothes, giving out stores, etc., which things usually take my time till . . . someone says at the door, 'Miss Ellen, your Mother's awake.' So then I go to her and read while she dresses and eats her breakfast. Then she always goes downstairs a little while but when she comes up again and goes to work I read again till half past two when the children come home and we have dinner. After dinner we read again for about an hour then I go out doors and play with the children . . . sliding and coasting . . . till half past six when we come in to tea. . . . So you see I seldom have time to write. Now however I have an excellent opportunity, Mother being in Boston to stay a day or two, Father gone lecturing, the children at school, business done."

During Emerson's prolonged absences, Ellen and Lidian shared the task of keeping him au courant with domestic matters: how Charley Coolidge had pelted Dolly, the new mare, with snowballs; how Edith, anticipating a visit to her friend Lotty Cabot, packed up all seventy of her dolls in a dozen boxes— "teasing me," said Ellen, "to work continually that her family may be complete and have plenty of clothes before she takes them to see Lotty"; how Eddy, whom Ellen sometimes called Bruv, had completed a statue of George Washington, one third head, one third torso, and one third legs, which Emerson laughingly praised as a ridiculously exact portrait of its subject. There was also a cat named J. W. von Goethe Hippins, Goethey for short, which developed a penchant for nibbling Ellen's crocus buds.

Ellen sometimes broke the pattern of her housekeeping with trips to Boston, visits to the Athenaeum art gallery, evenings at the opera, sermons by the ever vigorous Henry Ward Beecher. One Sunday she went twice to hear Emerson's old friend Father Taylor at the Seaman's Bethel. "He cries every once in a while, he makes other people too," she wrote. "Yes he brought even this stony heartless creature pretty near to it. . . . I didn't know what to make of it to see him crying . . . though it was plain he couldn't help it." Later she spent two weeks in New York, listening to an antislavery lecture by Theodore Parker, inspecting the American Crystal Palace, and disporting herself at a house party in Brooklyn where she and a bevy of her former Lenox schoolmates "laughed all day long." But her winsome assumption of the role of subhousekeeper was clearly a boon to both her parents. Over the years her responsibilities gradually increased until, by the end of 1857, her further schooling at last behind her, she could say truthfully and with pride that "Father and Mother are glad to have me stay at home for all reasons."

Chapter Thirty-six

WALT
WHITMAN

FOR TWENTY YEARS EMERSON HAD BEEN CALLING FOR A BARD worthy of the native American genius. In 1836 he had voiced regret that "in this Titanic continent, where Nature is so grand, Genius should be so tame." "Ah my country!" he exclaimed in 1838. "In thee is the reasonable hope of mankind not fulfilled. It should be that when all feudal straps and bandages were taken off[,] an unfolding of the Titans had followed and they had laughed and leaped young giants along the continent and ran up the mountains of the West with the errand of Genius and of love." In place of the genteel prose he found in the magazines of 1841, his own *Dial* included, he wanted to read "initiative, spermatic, prophesying, man-making words." He deplored squeamishness as an American fault: "you must on no account say 'stink' or 'damn.' " It was healthy to make experiments. What if they turned out to be "a little coarse "? What if the experimenter's coat was torn and muddy? By 1846 he was distinguishing between two styles, the Periclean and the Slambang. In some of his moods, the Slambang seemed preferable to the Periclean. Reading the translation of Dante by Carlyle's brother John in the summer of 1849, he wrote of Dante the rhetorician: "I find him full of the *nobil volgare eloquenza;* that he knows 'God damn,' and can be rowdy if he please, and he does please." As if to spread the gospel of literary "volgarismo," he sent copies of the translation to Alcott, Channing, Longfellow, Parker, and Thoreau.

Early in July 1855 he picked up a package at the Concord Post Office. Inside was a slender quarto of ninety-five pages called *Leaves of Grass*. It was bound in hunter's green, with a title in golden letters, each of them ornamented with roots and leaves like a stylized extension of nature's own herbage. The writer remained anonymous, but there were clues to the authorship: a frontispiece portrait, a copyright notice by one Walter Whitman, and a short passage midway of the first long poem:

> Walt Whitman, an American, one of the roughs, a kosmos,
> Disorderly fleshy and sensual . . . eating drinking and breeding,
> No sentimentalist . . . no stander above men and women or apart from
>   them. . . .

The frontispiece seemed to confirm this autobiographical description: a portrait of the artist as a young man with a clipped beard, a loose open-necked shirt, workaday pants, and a large, low-crowned slouch hat of the style called "wideawake." The figure's air of carefree independence anticipated a boast in the longest poem in the book: "I cock my hat as I please indoors or out."

Emerson took the book home and read it. The exuberant introduction (twelve double-columned pages) said that of all nationalities "at any time upon this earth" Americans probably had the "fullest poetical nature." Their "ample largeness and stir" made their foreign predecessors seem "tame and orderly." Here were "the roughs and beards and space and ruggedness and nonchalance" that appealed to the soul. The American genius took root "always most in the common people," with "the freshness and candor of their physiognomy," the "picturesque looseness of their carriage," their "deathless attachment to freedom," their "curiosity and welcome of novelty," and "the fluency of their speech."

Such "unrhymed poetry" awaited "the gigantic and generous treatment worthy of it." The American poet must "incarnate" the geography and natural life of his country—the roster of the states, the Great Lakes, "the beautiful masculine Hudson," the immense variety of people and their occupations, the flora and fauna, "the tribes of red aborigines . . . the weatherbeaten vessels . . . making landings on rocky coasts . . . the unsurveyed interior . . . the loghouses and clearings and wild animals and hunters and trappers." This was plainly a writer who gloried in lists, whether in the prose of his preface or the poetry that followed. He called himself "the arbiter of the diverse." His thoughts were "hymns in praise of things." No regulations could stop him: he was "the president of regulation." If he breathed into "any thing that was before thought small," it dilated "with the grandeur and life of the universe." Able to see farther than others, he had "the most faith." Faith was "the antiseptic of the soul," and whatever satisfied the soul was truth.

Here, in fresh context, were many other ideas that Emerson had been repeating for years. Such an inveterate keeper of journals as he must have been struck by Whitman's statement "All that a person thinks or does is of consequence." The champion of the "lingua communis" and of Dantean "volgare eloquenza" could only have applauded Whitman's assertion that the good poet "can make every word he speaks draw blood," for the English language "is brawny enough and limber . . . the dialect of common sense . . . the chosen tongue to express growth faith self-esteem freedom justice equality friendliness amplitude prudence decision and courage." Emerson as poet and theorist of poetry must surely have agreed with Whitman's opinions that "most works are beautiful without ornament," that "nothing is better than simplicity," and that "the cleanest expression is that which finds no sphere worthy of itself and makes one." The lecturer who had repeatedly celebrated "the infinitude of the private man" and the preacher who had long since laid aside his ecclesiastical robes must have taken note of Whitman's prediction:

> There will soon be no more priests. Their work is done. They may wait awhile . . . perhaps a generation or two . . . dropping off by degrees. A superior breed shall take their place. A new order shall arise . . . and every man shall be his own priest. . . . Through the divinity of themselves shall . . . the new breed of poets be interpreters of men and women and of all events and things. . . .

All this and more simmered in Whitman's preface. Of the twelve untitled poems, the first (later named "Song of Myself") was by far the longest and best. In some 1,300 lines Whitman was attempting to get the United States stated in all its vast richness and diversity, with himself at the center like the "transparent eyeball" of Emerson's *Nature*. This was preeminently a poetry of statement, part observation, part imagination, for no man could have been personally present at so many scenes or among so many people and events: the child in the cradle, the suicide on the floor, the quadroon at the slave market, the tanned workers at the hay harvest, the clam diggers on the flats, the harpooneer poised in the prow of a whaleboat, the wild gander honking across the November sky, the drunkard nodding by the barroom stove, the "clean-haired Yankee girl" at the factory loom, the opium eater in his den, the trapper with his Indian bride, the morning glory at the window—whatever had been or still was or yet might be was Walt Whitman's grist.

He continued the method in several of the shorter poems, pieces that in future editions would bear such titles as "The Song of Occupations," "The Sleepers," or "I Sing the Body Electric." Whitman had written, "I resist anything better than my own diversity." It seemed to be so. The only unity in the midst of all this multiplicity was the stalwart figure he called "kosmos," the microcosm of one man observing and recording as much of the American macrocosm as his words and lists and vignettes could catch and hold.

Uncertain of the author's name and mailing address, Emerson did not acknowledge his Fourth of July gift package until he happened to read an advertisement for the book in a newspaper. Next day, in the extreme heat of July 21, he composed a letter designed to fortify and encourage the new poet. It was typical of his generous attitude toward the work of younger men. Years before he had hopefully hailed the fledgling verses of Thoreau, Very, and Ellery Channing, though never with quite this degree of enthusiasm. *Leaves of Grass*, he assured its author, was a worthy and "wonderful gift"—indeed "the most extraordinary piece of wit and wisdom" yet seen in America. It showed "great power" and "large perception." It said "incomparable things . . . incomparably well." The thought behind it was "free and brave"— adjectives that Emerson had often applied to Thoreau. "I wish to see my benefactor," he wrote in closing, "and have felt much like striking my tasks, and visiting New York to pay you my respects."

What Emerson had written was not criticism but homage. He had made no attempt to distinguish between the prose and the poetry, if in fact they were distinguishable in anything but format. He did not say how feeble some of the shorter poems were in comparison with the "Song of Myself." He did not analyze the images, deplore the singsong repetitions, or criticize the loose syntax and punctuation. He took no note of the overexclamatory passages, the pretentious use of loanwords (admirant, savans, ennuyees, accouchement), the reader's frequent sense of overstuffed luggage bursting at the seams and tied up with rope.

He did not single out passages that accorded with his own habits, like the joyous manipulation of American place-names, or the intentional collocations of the vernacular and the oracular. He made no moral judgments about such lines as "I roll myself upon you as upon a bed" ("The Sleepers") or the "limitless limpid jets of love hot and enormous" ("I Sing the Body Electric"). He must surely have recognized how much acute observation had gone into the construction of the lists, how miraculous were the compressions, how well delineated were such historical vignettes as General Washington's farewell to his troops or the fall of the Alamo. What he did see, and unstintingly praise the unknown poet for, was the astonishing success of this first volume of verse, even with all its faults. Nothing quite like it had ever appeared before, in or outside America. It was to Emerson's credit that he was willing to say so.

He was still in the first flush of enthusiasm for the book on July 10 when he wrote Sam Ward about it. It was "so extraordinary for its oriental largeness of generalization, an American Buddh," that he wanted Sam to look it through. Perhaps he hoped for confirmation of his own opinion from a younger man who had once contributed poems to the *Dial*. A week later he wrote to Caroline Sturgis Tappan, who was to leave Lenox in October for an extended stay in Europe: "One strange book you ought to see before you go, or carry with you—a thin quarto called 'Leaves of Grass,' printed at Brooklyn, N.Y., apparently not published and sent to me thro the Post Office. 'Tis the best piece of American <philosophy> Buddhism that anyone has had strength to write, American to the bone and with large discourse before and after, and in spite of some crudeness and strange weary catalogues of things like a warehouse inventory, and in spite of an unpromising portrait on the frontispiece, contains fine strokes of genius and unforgettable things. Brooklyn too and Walter Whitman. Perhaps you know more of it than I do. I have sent mine to Sam Ward."

Soon he was recommending the *Leaves* to another young friend, a twenty-three-year-old Unitarian minister from Virginia, Moncure D. Conway, who was so fired up by Emerson's comments that he bought the book in Boston, read it on the way to New York, and somehow managed to locate the poet himself at Rome's printshop in Brooklyn. On September 17, some time after this encounter with Whitman, Conway reported back to Emerson, confirming the authorship of the volume. Whitman had "seemed very eager to hear from you and about you, and what you thought of his book." Since Emerson had said very clearly what he thought of the book back in July, it seems probable that his highly laudatory letter had not reached Whitman by the time of Conway's visit and that it still lay unclaimed and unread at the address where Emerson had sent it, the offices of Fowler and Wells in New York.

Meantime, still another young man, exactly Whitman's age, had reviewed *Leaves of Grass* in Horace Greeley's *New York Tribune* on July 23. This was Charles A. Dana, Greeley's managing editor, and a former resident of Brook Farm, where he had composed four sonnets that had appeared in Emerson's *Dial*. Dana called Whitman's poetry "uncouth and grotesque," and thought that "scrupulous circles" would be unlikely to give the book "free circulation." Some of Walt's words "might have passed between Adam and Eve in Paradise" before they discovered shame and "the want of fig leaves." Yet Dana praised Walt's "keen appreciation of beauty," his "intimacy with Nature," and his "bold and stirring" assertiveness.

Caroline Tappan wrote from Lenox on September 26 that she had "seen some extracts from your new ascendant but they were not of great magnitude. I wish you had sent us the unforgetable [sic] things to read here, for we shall never be so quiet in Europe. . . . I will leave my three new vols. of Hegel with you if you wish, that you may not forget us, for we may take up an indefinite residence in the Mountains of the Moon." She did not say what a far cry it was from Hegel to Whitman, farther even than the mountains of the moon.

Another friend of Emerson's, Charles Eliot Norton, presently got into the act. Aged twenty-eight, with a slender build, a long face and nose, scholar's hands, and a penchant for colorful bow ties, he was the son of Andrews Norton, once called by Carlyle "the hard-headed Unitarian Pope," the same who had excoriated Emerson's Divinity School Address as "The Latest Form of Infidelity." The son's review of *Leaves of Grass* was in the September *Putnam's*. Norton called it "a curious and lawless collection of poems" which were "neither in rhyme nor blank verse but in a sort of excited prose broken into lines" with no attempt at "measure or regularity." Whitman used terms "never before heard or seen," making a compound of the "New England Transcendentalist and the New York rowdy." Yet both elements fused "with the most perfect harmony." "The vast and vague conceptions of the one" lost "nothing of their quality in passing through the coarse and odd intellectual medium of the other." Moreover, this new poet showed "an original perception of nature, a manly brawn, and an epic directness" such as belonged to "no other adept of the Transcendentalist School."

Norton wrote James Russell Lowell about the book on September 23. Lowell was not interested. (Eight years later, he confessed that he had only skimmed it for long enough to satisfy himself that "it was a solemn humbug.") By mid-September Norton had seen a copy of Emerson's July letter. He was not surprised that Emerson admired Whitman's work, "for Walt has read the *Dial* and *Nature*, and combines the characteristics of a Concord philosopher with those of a New York fireman." The writing was vivid and vigorous, with some "superbly graphic descriptions." But there were likewise "passages of intolerable coarseness—not gross and licentious but simply disgustingly coarse." Perhaps Norton had read Dana's review before composing his own.

Although Emerson never publicly retracted his initial praise of Whitman, he presently began to hedge a little in his private pronouncements. On September 26, for example, he asked young James Elliot Cabot whether he had yet seen "the strange Whitman's" book. "He seems a Mirabeau of a man," wrote Emerson, "with such insight and equal expression, but hurt by hard life and too animal experience." The allusion to Mirabeau suggests a tie in Emerson's mind between Whitman, prophet of democracy, and the count's eloquence as spokesman for the Third Estate in 1789. For many years he had known Carlyle's *French Revolution*, and may have been recalling its admiring portrait of Mirabeau: that "rough figure with black Samson-locks under the slouch hat. . . . A fiery fuliginous mass, which could not be choked and smothered, but would fill all France with smoke and . . . with flame." Cabot returned the book on November 5 with an apology for having kept it so long. His thoughtful covering letter said that Whitman was "more of a philosopher than a poet, and *zwar* [indeed] a Hindoo philosopher . . . a firm believer in Chaos and the Everlasting NO." He thought that Whitman had sometimes echoed Emerson. He liked the preface "best, and very well." The poem itself failed to provide a solution to the problem of indicating "the path between reality and the souls of men."

Only five days after writing Cabot, Emerson asked his old friend, W. H. Furness of Philadelphia, if he had yet come upon *Leaves of Grass*, "that wonderful book—with all its formlessness and faults." But his reservations in the letters to Cabot and Furness were relatively minor modifications of his earlier position. Neither of them meant that he had surrendered his basic belief in Whitman's genius.

Up to this point, the existence of Emerson's original letter to Whitman was apparently known only to a few—Conway and Norton among them—but when Charles Dana learned of it, he persuaded Walt to let him print it in the *Tribune* for October 10. Eager for acceptance and moral support, Walt sent clippings of Dana's piece to various prominent people, and even devised a small broadside for general circulation. When Emerson heard of this *gaucherie* from the Reverend Samuel Longfellow, brother of the poet, he mildly complained of the "strange rude thing" that Whitman had done in allowing Greeley's paper to print "my letter of thanks for his book."

His trip to New York to "pay his respects" to Whitman did not come until late in the year. He was extremely busy running what he called his "Lyceum Express," which had taken him all over New England and upstate New York in the preceding winter, and would require his harassed presence in the Midwest as well as the eastern seaboard in the winter of 1855–56. His schedule was not very effectively organized. He was in Concord during the first week of December, went down to speak at the Brooklyn Athenaeum on the eleventh, lectured in Salem after Christmas, and from there went by train to Chicago at the end of the year. Home again early in February 1856, he took off almost at once for a tour of the towns of Maine.

Besides all this hectic leaping from rostrum to rostrum, he was trying to finish *English Traits* for publication in 1856, writing long letters in an attempt to gather funds for the support of the Alcotts, and trying to help (as Hawthorne had done) with the piecemeal printing of *The Philosophy of the Plays of Shakespeare Unfolded* by the eccentric Ohioan, Delia Salter Bacon, who was rapidly sinking into hopeless insanity, mainly as a consequence of her fanatical attempt to prove that Shakespeare's plays had been written by several hands, including those of her nominal ancestor, Francis Bacon.

His first meeting with Whitman was accordingly a very brief interlude in a hurried life. He left no record of it, though his daughter Ellen, writing from Boston to her cousin Haven Emerson on December 15, said that her father had gone to New York to persuade the William Emerson family to come to Concord for Christmas. Guided by information from Moncure Conway, Emerson found Whitman at home in Brooklyn on December 11. They talked for a couple of hours and then ate together. Many years later Emerson told

Edward Carpenter, "I saw him in New York and asked him to dine at my hotel. He shouted for a 'tin mug' for his beer. Then he had a noisy fire-engine society. And he took me there and was like a boy over it." Whitman's own later reminiscences of that meeting were probably of a piece with his other attempts to elevate his association with Emerson to a level of intimacy that it probably never attained.

Within a month of Emerson's visit to Brooklyn, another of his young friends, Edward Everett Hale, published a laudatory review of the *Leaves* in the *North American Review* for January 1856, using terms like "remarkable power . . . freshness, simplicity, and reality." But Emerson, in the weeks that followed, seemed to be having second thoughts. In his journal for April, he quoted without comment Edwin Percy Whipple's remark that *Leaves of Grass* "had every leaf but the fig leaf." In writing to Carlyle on May 6, he mentioned the "nondescript monster which yet had terrible eyes and buffalo strength, and was indisputably American." He had thought of sending a copy to Carlyle when the book first came out. But it had thriven so badly with the few to whom he showed it, and "wanted good morals so much," that he had not mailed it off to London. Now he thought he would. "After you have looked into it," he told Carlyle, "if you think, as you may, that it is only an auctioneer's inventory of a warehouse, you can light your pipe with it." Many years later Carlyle remarked sourly that it was "as though the town-bull had learned to hold a pen."

During their brief encounter in December 1855, it seems probable that Whitman must personally have thanked Emerson for his help. But his first public expression of gratitude did not come until the summer of 1856 while he was preparing the enlarged second edition. It took the form of a direct address to Emerson: "Here are thirty-two poems, which I send you, dear Friend and Master, not having found how I could satisfy myself with sending any usual acknowledgement of your letter. The first edition, on which you mailed me that till now unanswered letter, was twelve poems—I printed a thousand copies. . . . These thirty-two Poems I stereotype, to print several thousand copies of. . . . The work of my life is making poems. . . . A few years, and the average annual call for my Poems is ten or twenty thousand—more, quite likely. Why should I hurry or compromise? . . . Master, I am a man of perfect faith."

"In fine an egotist," as Bronson Alcott would say that fall when he first met

Whitman. "In fine, egregious," Emerson might have said (but did not) when the second edition appeared that August. For Walt had not only reprinted Emerson's original letter, but had also taken a sentence from it ("I greet you at the beginning of a great career") to ornament in gilt letters the spine of the book. If these, together with the dedicatory "open letter" that embraced him as friend and master, were offensive to Emerson, he made no public complaint, and even presented his copy of this new edition to Josiah Quincy with the remark that "the inside was worthy [of] attention even though it came from one capable of so misusing the cover." Even as he did so, however, Quincy noticed that Emerson looked troubled: "At no other time had I seen a cloud of dissatisfaction darken that serene countenance."

Soon afterward he told Moncure Conway that he would probably have qualified his praise if he had guessed that his private letter would be thus publicized. "Parts of the book," he said, made him hold his nose as he read them, though he had reminded himself that "one must not be too squeamish when a chemist brings him a mass of filth and said, 'See, the great laws are at work here also.' " Despite such qualifications, he stuck to his guns. He had once referred to the "terrible eyes" of the young rebel Thoreau. Now he said that Whitman's were "terrible eyes to walk along Broadway." Still, it was "all there, as if in an auctioneer's catalogue," and he continued to feel that "any man who has eyes in his head" must recognize the "genius" behind *Leaves of Grass*.

THEODORE PARKER,
CRUSADER

THE DILEMMA THAT EMERSON FACED DURING THE ANTI-slavery agitations of the 1840s was another version of the society-versus-solitude syndrome that for years had beset him. "My Genius loudly calls me to stay where I am," he wrote in 1844, " . . . whilst the Universal Genius . . . beckons me to the martyr's and redeemer's office." This was an uncharacteristic overdramatization of his position. He was obviously not cut out for martyrdom, nor did he really believe that he was capable of redeeming the human race from centuries of error. Yet his private "Genius" had long caused him to oppose slavery in fact and in theory without allowing the "Universal Genius" to persuade him into public utterance on the subject.

The turning point, already noted, seems to have come with his historical discourse on "Emancipation in the British West Indies" given at Concord in August 1844, a powerful condemnation of the institution of slavery accomplished through a history of England's repeated attempts to extirpate this dirtiest of human immoralities. Ten years later he told a New York audience that he did not often speak to public questions: it seemed like "meddling," or abandoning one's own work for an alien cause. "I have my own spirits in prison," he added, enigmatically, "spirits in deeper prisons, whom no man visits if I do not." Yet he had now felt compelled by the passage of the Fugitive Slave Law to abandon temporarily his habitual quiet devotion to the welfare of poets, students, and scholars and to speak out strongly against a federal edict that he knew to be morally reprehensible. The solitudinarian was learning the hard way the truth that he would afterward state in his essay on "The Fortune of the Republic"—viz., that it is simply impossible "to extricate yourself from the questions in which your age is involved."

Theodore Parker had never doubted that this was so, but he made a positive virtue of Emerson's negative truism by direct and courageous assault upon all the major social questions of the day. Slavery must be abolished—along with intemperance, poverty, illiteracy, crime, prostitution, and capital punishment. Women's rights must be established and immediate action was necessary in penal reform. But the curse of slavery stood at the top of Parker's list: whatever laws men had made to perpetuate the ownership of one man by another, the supreme law, made by God, forbade the practice, and the law of God must always take precedence over the law of man.

Emerson easily located four heroes in the struggle against slavery. One was his neighbor, Samuel Hoar, who had bravely carried out his assignment to canvass the jails of South Carolina for Massachusetts citizens wrongly detained, and was expelled from the state for his pains. Another was Charles Torrey, abolitionist, who died in the State Prison of Maryland in May 1846 while serving a term for aiding escaped slaves. A third was the Cape Cod sea captain, Jonathan Walker, whose right hand was branded "S.S." (slave stealer) when he was arrested for trying to carry fugitive slaves out of Pensacola, Florida, to safety and freedom in the British West Indies.

Fourth among his heroes was Parker. One of the strongest bonds between them was their fierce opposition to the passage of the various bills that made up the so-called Compromise of 1850, and in particular the Fugitive Slave Law, strengthening the old 1793 act, largely ignored among Northern states until Daniel Webster's famous seventh of March speech restored it to new prominence. What Emerson deplored as a "filthy enactment" soon roused him to public protest, although at first he only watched restively from the sidelines in Concord while Parker prosecuted his war against the slave hunters who slipped into Boston to recapture escapees and return them in chains to the South. In 1850 there was the case of William Craft and his wife, Ellen. On one occasion, while harboring Ellen Craft in his house on Exeter Place, Parker felt obliged to write his forthcoming sermon with a loaded pistol at his elbow. In 1851 came the capture of Frederick Wilkins, called

Shadrach, safely rescued in February; in 1852 there was Thomas Sims, and in 1854 Anthony Burns, whose detention in the Court House kept the city in an uproar at the end of May, and caused Bronson Alcott, still resident in Boston, to mount the steps alone, careless of personal danger, in an attempt to discover the room where Burns was confined. Alcott listened to Parker's speeches in Faneuil Hall, the Music Hall, and the Melodeon, took counsel with the Vigilance Committee, and sadly watched ("ashamed of the Union, of New England, of Boston, almost of myself, too") when the fugitive Burns, surrounded by hundreds of troops, was marched away to a waiting vessel, and carried off to his fate while the church bells of Boston tolled in protest, anger, and sorrow. Throughout these times of trouble, Parker stood in the forefront of the battle, occasionally seconded by Emerson with speeches of his own.

One of Parker's most eloquent sermons was *The Chief Sins of the People*, preached from his pulpit at the Melodeon on April 10, 1851, and published nine days later. Emerson, receiving an early copy, wrote at once to applaud Parker's "brave harangue," and to add that "we all love and honour you, and have come to think every drop of your blood and every moment of your life of a national value." Parker's reply, sent by return mail, was equally generous, and he called Emerson's attention to the fact that it was being written on the seventy-sixth anniversary of the Battle of Lexington, where Captain John Parker, his grandfather, had used one of the muskets that his grandson so much treasured.

Dear Emerson,

The kindliness of your letter which came this morning touches me exceedingly. But alas I do not deserve all the esteem you entertain for me. I wish I was worthy of what you say. But I will take heart from your commendation. . . . I beg you to remember how much I have got from yourself—how many times I have walked fm [sic] West-Roxbury to Boston and back to *hear you*. Much of the little I do now is the result of seed of your own sowing.—Well, these are sad times. It is the 19th of April today—& there hang before me the two Trophies of the Battle of Lexington—which belonged to my grandfather— They and your letter help inspire me with courage and strength.

Whether or not it was Parker's example or his own aroused indignation—or
more likely a combination of the two—Emerson's speech to the citizens of
Concord on the Fugitive Slave Law was delivered two weeks later, May 3,
1851. In a long and powerful address he said in part:

Fellow citizens. . . . The last year has forced us all into politics, and
made it a paramount duty to seek what it is often a duty to shun. We do
not breathe well. There is infamy in the air. . . . I wake in the morning
with a painful sensation, which I carry about all day . . . the odious remembrance of that ignominy which has fallen on Massachusetts. . . .
Every hour brings us from distant quarters of the Union the expression
of mortification at the late events in Massachusetts, and at the behavior
of Boston. . . . The only haste in Boston, after the rescue of Shadrach,
last February, was, who should first put his name on the list of volunteers in aid of the [United States] marshal. . . . one cannot open a newspaper without being disgusted by new records of shame. . . . Just now a
friend came into my house and said, "If this law shall be repealed I shall
be glad that I have lived; if not I shall be sorry that I was born." What
kind of law is that which extorts language like this from the heart of a
free and civilized people? . . .

An immoral law makes it a man's duty to break it. . . . Here is a
statute which enacts the crime of kidnapping,—a crime on one footing
with arson and murder. . . . If our resistance to this law is not right,
there is no right. . . . This is not going crusading into Virginia and
Georgia after slaves, who, it is alleged, are very comfortable where they
are: . . . but this is befriending in our own State, on our own farms,
a man who has taken the risk of being shot, or burned alive, or cast
into the sea, or starved to death, or suffocated in a wooden box, to get
away from his driver: and this man who has run the gauntlet of a thousand miles for his freedom, the statute says, you men of Massachusetts
shall hunt, and catch, and send back again to the dog-hutch he fled
from. . . .

I am a Unionist as we all are, or nearly all, and I strongly share the hope
of mankind in the power, and therefore, in the duties of the
Union. . . . We shall one day bring the States shoulder to shoulder and
the citizens man to man to exterminate slavery. . . . The ancient maxim

still holds that never was any injustice effected except by the help of justice. . . . Let us respect the Union to all honest ends. But also respect an older and wider union, the law of Nature and rectitude. . . . This [Fugitive Slave] law must be made inoperative. It must be abrogated and wiped out of the statute-book; but whilst it stands there, it must be disobeyed.

Forthright as his speech had been, Emerson was inclined to be apologetic. "In the spring," he wrote Carlyle, "the abomination of our Fugitive Slave Bill drove me to some writing and speechmaking, without hope of effect, but to clear my own skirts. I am sorry I did not print, whilst it was yet time. I am told the time will come again, more's the pity." One of his contemporaneous journal entries said that the passage of the Bill had brought down "the free and Christian state of Massachusetts to the cannibal level."

Parker gladly received his compatriot into the fold of activists. When his *Ten Sermons* volume appeared in 1853 it was dedicated to Emerson. "I read the inscription," wrote Emerson, "if with more pride than was becoming, yet not without some terror." Evidently recalling Parker's laudatory comments on his work and character in the *Massachusetts Quarterly* three years earlier, he mildly complained that his friend was "too good-natured by half" in saluting his contemporaries. As if he were echoing Parker's list of Emersonian virtues, he went on to name some of Parker's own qualities: his hardy realism, his persistent courage and vigor, the power of his local and homely illustrations (one of Parker's own points about Emerson), and his "masterly sarcasm—now naked, now veiled." In the end he returned to the martial imagery that the very thought of Parker always summoned to his mind, calling him "the right soldier whom God gave strength and will to fight for Him in the battle of this day."

A year later Emerson spoke again on the Fugitive Slave Law, this time to a far larger audience in New York. In the speech to the citizens of Concord, he had not hesitated to attack Daniel Webster while he was alive. Now that the morose and embittered Webster had died at his farm in Marshfield in October 1852, Emerson attacked him retrospectively, though he was ready enough, as Parker had been in his own "Discourse on Webster," to acknowledge "Great Daniel's" qualities of leadership during what might have been called his prelapsarian career. Gone were the "dismal guaranties" of state sovereignty that had been "infamously made in 1850," said Emerson. "Before the body of Webster is yet crumbled, it is found that they have crumbled. This eternal monument of his fame and of the Union is rotten in four years." Despite the depth of his feelings, Emerson stayed clear of the terrible invective that Parker had unleashed in his own speech on the dead Webster. Nothing in Emerson's New York oration matched his sarcastic journal entries of the spring of 1851, when he had written that "the word *liberty* in the mouth of Mr Webster sounds like the word *love* in the mouth of a courtezan"—or like "*Hail Columbia* when sung at a slave auction." As late as 1859 he bitterly wrote that "Webster had the head of a bull dog, but the heart of a spaniel."

Despite the valiant efforts of Parker, Emerson, and scores of other dedicated men and women, the gravest problems remained unresolved. A week after his speech in New York, Emerson wrote Carlyle that "vicious politicians" in Washington were even then debating the decision on slavery in Kansas and Nebraska. "The fight of slave and freeman drawing nearer," he wrote sardonically, "the question is properly, whether slavery or whether freedom shall be abolished."

This last was the great issue to which Parker was devoting his works and days. It had become his prime vocation, though for Emerson it continued to be rather more of a fierce avocation, since he was steadily occupied with other subjects than politics, including the much-worked-over manuscript that he was going to publish as *English Traits*. Throughout 1855 he was inordinately occupied. "If I live much longer," he wrote to Lidian in February, "I mean the last part of life shall not be spent in a hurry." Two days later he spoke at Philadelphia on "American Slavery," and said that he had found "many crosses, less or larger," during another winter of lecturing, and indeed had come "to nod to them as old or expected acquaintances." He did not get home to Concord until March.

On May 25 he turned fifty-two. "My children," he wrote, "who are dreadful chronometers, have not failed to notify me that this day is one of my anniversaries." As always there were illnesses to contend with. Early in June Lidian took to her bed for three weeks. Henry Thoreau was also languishing: "We have tried to persuade him to come and spend a week with us for a c[h]ange." Alcott spent a weekend with Emerson in May, eager to go back to England, and hinting for Emerson's support. They walked among the stony hillocks of Sleepy Hollow, soon to be dedicated as a cemetery with an address by Emerson. It was Emerson's position that Alcott must not go. "I plant myself . . . mastiff-like to bark against the plan," said he. Instead, he set about raising money to endow the Alcott family with enough to keep them fed: "Though it is a very bad precedent to release a man from the duty of taking care of himself, yet Alcott has unique claims as a natural Capuchin, or abbot of all religious mendicant orders." Ellery Channing was also talking of another voyage, standing, as Emerson said, "tiptoe on the wharf ready to embark." But he too sailed nowhere.

In June Emerson himself managed to get away for a brief visit with Sam Ward at his new summer home in Canton, and in August for another two days with Cyrus Bartol at Pigeon Cove near Gloucester. In the same period he declined several invitations from Theodore Parker, returning apologetic regrets to Parker's proposal to revive the Transcendental Club, moribund these many years; saying that he could not serve as guest preacher in Parker's Music Hall pulpit owing to the pressures of his own affairs; and refusing to accompany Parker on a fishing expedition, explaining that his "tortoise continuance" on various literary projects could not match the "lion leaps" of his friend in Exeter Place. When Parker was finally indicted for his part in the attempt to rescue the captive slave, the twenty-year-old Anthony Burns, he sent Emerson an early copy of his aggressive book on the subject. Once again, Emerson responded with his now customary military image, assuring Parker of his joy and gratitude that "the best soldier fights on our side."

Chapter Thirty-eight

CAPTAIN
JOHN BROWN

OVER THE SIGNATURE OF FRANKLIN PIERCE, PRESIDENT OF the United States, the Kansas-Nebraska Act became law on May 30, 1854. The extension of slavery was left to the vote of the territorial settlers, thus repealing the Missouri Compromise, which would have barred slavery from both territories, and making possible the future existence of a slave state north of the 1820 line. When the Kansas Territory was opened for settlement by national decree, two major factions were soon at literal war in and for Kansas. One of these consisted of Yankee abolitionists, emigrants from New England who came to establish farms and towns like Lawrence and Topeka; the opposition forces were made up largely of residents of Missouri, the bordering state to the east, who wanted Kansas to become a slave state, saw the Yankee emigrant invasion as a threat to their business interests, and were more than ready, as one of them said, to substitute the cartridge box for the ballot box.

Emerson stood with the free-soil Yankee settlers. On September 10, 1856, he spoke before the Kansas Relief meeting in Cambridge, telling his audience that all the right was on one side. "The people of Kansas ask for bread, clothes, arms, and men, to save them alive, and enable them to stand against these enemies of the human race," the slaveholders. Massachusetts citizens had emigrated to national territory under the sanction of every law, only to be set upon by highwaymen, driven from their new homes, pillaged, and numbers of them killed and scalped. This was no accidental brawl, but a systematic "war to the knife." In the past few years the national government had steadily obstructed the common weal, arming and leading the border ruffians against the poor farmers. In the universal cant of the times, terms like "the Union," "representative government," "freedom," "Manifest Destiny," and even "democracy" had lost their rightful meaning and were being used as cover-ups for the ugliest of political machinations. "They call it otto [attar] of rose and lavender," said Emerson. "I call it bilge-water."

Next morning Theodore Parker wrote to a friend, "I went to a Kansas meeting at Cambridge last night. RWE was expected but did not come until near nine; others wasting the time before in idle laughter and jokes. Yet good things were said. E. was not happy, but said many good things as always. . . . The accounts are awful for Kansas. Five persons were shot after they had surrendered. Scalping is as common as with other savages. We are now in a civil war. . . ."

In the following January, Kansas came back to New England in the person of Captain John Brown, a native of Connecticut who had been actively engaged in the territory since 1855. In 1856, President Pierce had warned the Congress of the "treasonable insurrection" being mounted by abolitionists in and around the town of Lawrence. As one of the leaders of this "insurrection" against the marauders from Missouri, Brown had come east on a money-raising expedition with the aim of forming and equipping a guerrilla force, with himself in command and several of his sons as his lieutenants, in order to carry on his holy war against the proslavery depredators who had indeed, as Emerson and Parker said, been killing, maiming, and even scalping those peaceful settlers whom Pierce had called traitors.

When proslavery gangs sacked and burned the town of Lawrence late in May 1856, Brown and his men responded with a vengeance. It took the form of a nocturnal raid along Pottawatomie Creek. Brown and his men summoned five proslavery settlers one by one from their homesteads, hacking them to pieces with heavy razor-edged cutlasses. In a retaliatory action on June 1, some two dozen Missourians under the command of a deputy U.S. marshal named Pate tried to capture Brown and his minions near a watering hole called Black Jack. Brown turned the tables, ambushing the opposing force from a stand of blackjack oaks that had given the area its name, and causing

Pate to surrender his whole group. Unlike the proslavers at Pottawatomie, these men were not murdered on the spot but held for exchange with a like number of free-soil prisoners.

All this lay behind John Brown when he came to Boston in January 1857. His contact man was Franklin B. Sanborn, a Harvard graduate aged twenty-six who had recently established a small school in Concord under Emerson's aegis. Among his political mentors were the radical Unitarian ministers Parker and James Freeman Clarke, both forty-six, and Ellery Channing's brother-in-law, the fiery Thomas Wentworth Higginson, who had appeared in Court Square in Boston with Bronson Alcott in the attempt to rescue Anthony Burns. Higginson at age thirty-two had already resolved to give up his Worcester pastorate in order to devote more time to the antislavery struggle. Brown told Sanborn of his immediate needs—guns, ammunition, and at least $30,000 in cash or pledges, preferably cash: he had been hard up all his life.

Sanborn was impressed. Cleanshaven in the midst of a generation much given to beards and long hair, Brown had the look of an outdoorsman who might have been a farmer, a soldier, or a deacon. At fifty-seven he seemed older than he was; his short-cut hair was already grizzled. He had a high forehead, perfectly horizontal brows, a sharply jutting nose, a determined jaw, and a thin-lipped mouth that closed like a trap. His most memorable feature was undoubtedly his eyes—gray, fearless, but also pitiless. People thought of him as tall, though Emerson would have topped him by three or four inches; he carried himself militarily erect, with none of that forward-leaning shoulder stoop so characteristic of Emerson's stance. His vigor and perseverance impressed others as well. Between money-raising trips all over New England, including an address to the legislature of the Commonwealth in February, he paused long enough to confer with Theodore Parker at his house in Exeter Place, and with such other supporters as George Luther Stearns and Dr. Samuel Gridley Howe, both of Boston and the National Kansas Committee, and sometimes with Gerrit Smith of Peterboro, New York, a wealthy philanthropist, a confirmed abolitionist, and benefactor to the Northern black population.

One day in March Brown came out to Concord to speak at the Town Hall. Sanborn introduced him to Thoreau and Emerson, who were in his audience that evening. He knew exactly what to say, had given the speech many times before, could predict what the questions would be, knew all the answers, and had even brought along two exhibits—a bowie knife that he held up for inspection, and the very trace chain (so he said) that had been used to bind one of his sons arrested by federal troops and forced to make a long march under intolerable conditions.

Emerson thought that he gave a "good account of himself," and took grim satisfaction in Brown's derisive comments on "the folly of the peace party in Kansas, who believed, that their strength lay in the greatness of their wrongs, and so discountenanced resistance" of the kind that Brown represented. Brown said flatly that anyone entering Kansas to interfere in the elective process deserved to be shot, and offered "a circumstantial account" of the battle of Black Jack, of which he seemed pardonably proud. He said nothing of his murderous exploit along the banks of the Pottawatomie, which would not in any case have squared with his statement to the Concordians that only "the right[-thinking] men" could give permanent direction to the fortunes of a new state. When he left Concord, his funds had been enlarged by contributions from Sanborn, Emerson, and Thoreau's aged father, but his greatest triumph during this Eastern trip was a grant of $7,000 from George Stearns, whom Parker called "one of the noblest men in Boston."

Emerson had only recently returned from a month-long lecture tour in the Middle West, followed at home by an attack of measles. On March 4 he served as host to Parker, who spoke at the Concord Lyceum, although his unstinting labors as lecturer for the abolitionist cause and as preacher to his large congregation at the Boston Music Hall had brought him to the verge of physical collapse. Parker resembled John Brown in at least one respect—his willingness (as Emerson put it) "to perish in the using . . . to sacrifice the future to the present . . . to spend and be spent." No record of his talks with Emerson during this visit has apparently survived, but it is clear enough from their other communications that both men were deeply embittered, not only by the financial depression of 1857 but chiefly by the moral deterioration of a nation that Emerson described on March 9 as "poor betrayed imbruted America, infested by rogues and hypocrites."

Parker's illness that spring obliged him to ask Emerson and others to lecture and preach in his place at the Music Hall in Boston. He was so worried over details that Emerson cautioned him to take things easy. "You are magnanimous and maximanimous, but you must lie still and get ready for a journey to the mountains, or a voyage to the islands, as soon as there is fine weather again and not bother yourself about who comes and goes in the interim to the Music Hall, or about our delicate nerves. I mean to try the plunge." Parker writhed in frustration, but refused to stop working. As far back as 1853, he had admitted that his health and vigor were on the wane: "I walk and work now *with a will*," he wrote, rather than "by spontaneous impulse which once required the will to check it." Now in 1857 he said that although he was only forty-seven by his mother's reckoning, he felt inwardly as if the digits had been reversed.

Throughout that parlous year, his admiration for Emerson remained at the highest level. In December he told one of his correspondents that his friend in Concord had had "a more glorious history than any other American of this generation." He had "touched the deepest strings on the human harp," and in a thousand years would still wake the music that he had first waked in the midst of the nineteenth century. Such extravagant statements were perhaps intended to override the minor reservations he had recorded in his critique of Emerson in 1850.

About this time, back in Kansas, Brown was beginning to speak of "troubling Israel," his way of alluding to his plans for a secret infiltration of the Southern states. He held that "God had created him to be the deliverer of the slaves the same as Moses had delivered the children of Israel." Late in January 1858 he stayed with the black leader Frederick Douglass in Rochester, New York, drawing up a provisional constitution for a "new state in the Southern mountains." In March he returned to Boston for conferences with the Secret Six Committee (Parker, Sanborn, Howe, Stearns, Higginson, and Gerrit Smith), to whom he spoke confidently of setting ablaze the "whole country from the Potomac to Savannah." Pierce's successor, Buchanan, had called on the Congress to admit Kansas to the Union as the sixteenth slave state, and Brown had gone to Canada for a gathering of free and fugitive Negroes to lay plans to establish a black state in the southern Appalachians. In Boston late in May, he met again with the Secret Six, who urged him to postpone his attack, wherever it might be, and to return to Kansas to await a more suitable time.

A young Scottish journalist, James Redpath, was at supper in the hotel dining room in Lawrence, Kansas, on June 25, 1858, when "a stately old man, with a flowing white beard" took a seat at the public table. Redpath immediately recognized John Brown, though "many persons who had previously known him did not penetrate his patriarchal disguise." Despite Buchanan's invitation to Congress, the Kansas voters rejected that August the expansion of slavery into their territory, leaving John Brown free to pursue his plan of attack upon the South.

In 1859, operating under at least two aliases, Brown seemed to be everywhere. In December 1858 he had led a raid into Missouri, liberating a dozen slaves and later conducting them to Canada. President Buchanan put a price of $250 on Brown's head, and Brown, with a rare flash of humor, offered $2.50 for Buchanan's. He appeared in Des Moines, Detroit, Chicago, and Cleveland, and in April stopped in Peterboro to obtain further funds from Gerrit Smith. The Secret Six Committee had now been reduced to four. After a violent lung hemorrhage in January, Theodore Parker had sailed for Vera Cruz, and in June would leave for Europe. Higginson, chafing over Brown's long postponement of promised action, refused to join him for conferences in Boston, although he agreed to help whenever the invasion began.

On May 8, the eve of his fifty-ninth birthday, Brown gave another lecture in the Concord Town Hall. Sanborn, Thoreau, and Emerson were all present, as they had been in 1857, though now, with his full white beard and tangled hair, Brown had taken on the look of an Old Testament prophet. Alcott, meeting him for the first time, thought that he had "the port of an apostle," his frame and countenance "charged with power . . . agile and alert, resolute, and ready for any audacity in any crisis." With the possible exception of Higginson and Frank Sanborn, none of his Yankee adherents yet knew for certain where and when he would launch his attempt to incite thousands of slaves to rebellion. But Alcott surmised that it was "his intention to run off as many slaves as he can," and that Brown was "the man to do the deed if it must be done."

Next day Sanborn accompanied Brown to Boston for meetings with the truncated Committee of Six, and various suburban visits with other potential donors to the cause. One of these was Emerson's State Street friend, John Murray Forbes, who invited Brown and Sanborn to tea at his house in Milton. Forbes was a shrewd analyst of men who thought that Brown's "glittering gray-blue eyes" had "a little touch of insanity about them." In June, after a trip to Connecticut in quest of further armaments, Brown went to see his wife and family at North Elba in the Adirondacks, and then moved southward through Ohio and Pennsylvania toward the site he had chosen for the start of his rebellion, arriving on July 3 at Harpers Ferry, Virginia (now West Virginia).

At eight o'clock in the evening of Sunday, October 16, he was at last ready to move. By midnight he had managed to secure the United States Armory and engine house and Hall's Rifle Works. All day Monday the battle raged as the whole countryside rose up to quell the invaders. President Buchanan ordered troops to the Virginia scene, including ninety U.S. Marines from the Washington Barracks under the command of Colonel Robert E. Lee, aged fifty-two, and two younger lieutenants, J. E. B. Stuart and Israel Green. On Tuesday morning, Lee called on Brown to surrender unconditionally. Brown answered that he would comply only if he and his men were permitted to leave unharmed. Green led the storming party that captured and wounded Brown and killed two of his sons, and the long-planned war of liberation was suddenly over. The raiders were carried by train to Charlestown, eight miles away, to be held in the county jail.

Far away in Concord, Frank Sanborn first heard the news in his "quiet schoolrooms" on Tuesday the eighteenth. As a conspirator whose letters were found among Brown's papers, he knew that he was in imminent danger of arrest. He fled to Canada, reaching Quebec on the twenty-first. In a laconic note on the twenty-third Emerson urged him to return "at the first hour wheels or steam will permit." On the same day, Emerson wrote his brother William that all was well in Concord, "in spite of the sad Harpers Ferry business, which interests us all who had Brown for our guest twice. . . . He is a true hero, but lost his head there." Alcott, who had been at Emerson's with Thoreau when the news came through, remembered grasping Brown's hand after his speech in the Town Hall in May, adding that "this deed of his, so surprising, so mixed, so confounding to most persons, will give an impulse to freedom and humanity, whatever becomes of its victim and of the States that howl over it."

Emerson called Brown "a hero of romance" who had made "this fatal blunder only to bring out his virtues." He composed an elaborate letter to Governor Wise of Virginia (evidently not sent) in which he said, "I shall not insult you by referring to a public opinion changing every day, and which has softened every hour its first harsh judgment of him. The man is so transparent that all can see him through, that he had no second thought, but was the rarest of heroes, a pure idealist, with no by-ends of his own. He is therefore precisely what lawyers call crazy, being governed by ideas, and not by external circumstances. He has afforded them the first trait marked in the books as betraying insanity, namely, disproportion between means and ends."

Of all the men of Concord, Thoreau was the most upset, reacting with anger and dismay, filling his journal pages from October 19 to 23 with entries on Brown, roughly 11,000 words in five days—touchingly interspersed with observations on the local landscape, as if to relieve his supercharged mind with reversions to mild Nature. Unlike Emerson, he fumed and fulminated over the widespread allegations of Brown's insanity. "Insane!" he wrote. "A father and seven sons, and several more men besides,—as many, at least as twelve disciples,—all struck with insanity at once; while the sane tyrant holds with a firmer gripe [sic] than ever his four millions of slaves." He was reminded of the Christian parallel: "If Christ should appear on earth he would on all hands be denounced as a mistaken, misguided man, insane and crazed." And again: "Some eighteen hundred years ago Christ was crucified; this morning, perhaps, John Brown was hung. These are two ends of a chain which I rejoice to know is not without its links." Brown belonged, in Henry's opinion, to the Transcendentalist camp—"a Transcendentalist above all, a man of ideals and principles . . . of unwavering purposes, not to be dissuaded but by an experience and wisdom greater than his own."

Such opinions could not be confined to the pages of his journal but must be spread abroad. On October 30, another Sunday two weeks after Brown's attack began, Thoreau spoke to his fellow townsmen on "The character of John Brown, now in the clutches of the slaveholder," repeating the speech in Boston on November 1 and in Worcester on the third. Alcott had scheduled a meeting of his own, and could not attend the Concord gathering, but he recorded that Emerson had been present and that the whole audience had listened to Henry with delight. "Think much of Capt. Brown," he wrote next day, "and read the newspaper reports with an eagerness and sadness unusual. This is too noble a man to be sacrificed so; and yet such as he, and only such, are worthy of the glories of the Cross."

"Brown's trial is over," he continued on November 2. "The jury bring him in guilty, and he is sentenced to be hanged on the second of December. Sanborn takes tea with us and tells us many things about Brown, all to the credit of the man and hero." In these days immediately after the sentencing, the parallel between the cross and Brown's gibbet, to which both Thoreau and Alcott had alluded, was widely echoed among Brown's sympathizers, Emerson included. In the fall of 1857, he had made the acquaintance of Mattie Griffith, whom he described as a "brilliant young lady from Kentucky." Despite her Southern origin, Mattie strongly admired Brown, and now, two years later, while the hero lay wounded in the Charlestown jail awaiting execution, she wrote to Emerson that "if Brown is hung, the gallows will be sacred as the cross." He copied the sentence into his journal and interpolated it into a lecture called "Courage," which he read in Boston on November 7. Here Brown no longer appeared as a romantic hero who had made a fatal blunder, but emerged in Emerson's speech as "that new saint than whom none purer or more brave was ever led by love of men into conflict and death,—the new saint awaiting his martyrdom, and who, if he shall suffer [execution], will make the gallows glorious like the cross." The opposition was quick to condemn this statement as a blasphemy. But Thoreau and Alcott had already in effect agreed with it, and Theodore Parker, writing from Rome on November 24, told a friend that "Brown will die . . . like a martyr and also like a saint. . . . I think there have been few spirits more pure and devoted than John Brown's, and none that gave up their breath in a nobler cause."

In calling Brown both martyr and saint, Parker evidently saw no need to compare the Virginia gallows to the Roman cross. Others had done it for him, and the idea would gain wide acceptance through the stirring stanzas of Julia Ward Howe's "Battle-Hymn of the Republic," composed on or near the second anniversary of Brown's death. She had met and liked him at her home in South Boston in the spring of 1859, and clearly had him and the Christian parallel in mind at the end of her hymn: "As He died to make men holy, let us die to make men free / While God is marching on."

The approaching date of Brown's execution brought Emerson back again to the platform, this time at a meeting in Tremont Temple arranged for the relief of Brown's impoverished family. In his brief speech there on November 18, he stressed the fact that Brown was a lineal descendant of Peter Brown, who had come to Plymouth aboard the *Mayflower* in 1620, and quoted a passage from Brown's speech to the court that had tried him in Virginia: "If I had interfered in behalf of the rich, the powerful, the intelligent, the so-called great . . . it would all have been right. But I believe that to have interfered as I have done, for the despised poor, was not wrong, but right." It was, said Emerson, "the *reductio ad absurdum* of Slavery, when the governor of Virginia [Henry A. Wise] is forced to hang a man whom he declares to be a man of the most integrity, truthfulness, and courage he has ever met. Is that the kind of man the gallows is built for? It were bold to affirm that there is within that broad commonwealth, at this moment, another citizen as worthy to live, and as deserving of all public and private honor, as this poor prisoner."

On November 23 he wrote to Lydia Maria Child that he would not be present at the deathwatch meeting planned for December 2 in Boston, but would attend instead "a little ceremony" in Concord projected for the same day by Thoreau and Alcott. The planners met several times to establish their program. "It is arranged," wrote Alcott on December 1, "that I am to read the Martyr Service, Thoreau selections from the poets, and Emerson from Brown's words. Sanborn has written a dirge . . . and Rev. Mr. Sears from Wayland will offer prayers."

They met at two o'clock in the Town Hall. A substantial crowd had gathered. Thoreau, Emerson, Alcott, and two others offered readings, and Sanborn's dirge was sung by the standing audience. The services, thought Alcott, were "affecting and impressive; distinguished by modesty, simplicity, and earnestness; worthy alike of the occasion and the man." All over the North the church bells were tolling and thousands of people had come together for similar services. In the field at Charlestown the gallows stood empty. John Brown's body, encased in a black walnut coffin, was borne away to Harpers Ferry and placed aboard a train to be taken to Philadelphia, New York, and at last to the farmhouse in North Elba where the funeral services were held on December 8.

Emerson was called on once more for a commemorative meeting in Salem on January 6, 1860. "I have been struck with one fact," he said, "that the best orators who have added their praise to his fame . . . have one rival who comes off a little better, and that is John Brown. Everything that is said of him leaves people a little dissatisfied; but as soon as they read his own speeches and letters they are heartily contented,—such is the singleness of purpose which justifies him to the head and heart of all." He offered a short summary of Brown's life and habits, calling him "a romantic character absolutely without any vulgar trait" whose picture Sir Walter Scott would have been delighted to draw. "Political gentlemen . . . take it upon them to say that there are not a thousand men in the North who sympathize with John Brown. It would be far safer and nearer the truth to say that all people, in proportion to their sensibility and self-respect, sympathize with him. For it is impossible to see courage, and disinterestedness, and the love that casts out fear, without sympathy. . . . Nothing is more absurd than to complain of this sympathy, or to complain of a party of men united in opposition to slavery. As well complain of gravity, or the ebb of the tide. Who makes the abolitionist? The slaveholder. The sentiment of mercy is the natural recoil which the laws of the universe provide to protect mankind from destruction by savage passions. . . . For the arch-abolitionist, older than Brown, and older than the Shenandoah Mountains, is Love, whose other name is Justice, which was before Alfred, before Lycurgus, before slavery, and will be after it."

WHITMAN
IN PERSON

SHORTLY AFTER EMERSON'S SPEECH TO THE KANSAS RELIEF Society in the fall of 1856, two of his closest associates converged upon New York City, and incidentally upon Walt Whitman in person. One was Bronson Alcott, who had come down from Walpole, New Hampshire, in the hope of repairing his ever-languishing fortunes by holding "Conversations" in and around the metropolis. The other was Thoreau, whose temporary center of operations lay thirty miles south of the city at Marcus Spring's Eagleswood Community near Perth Amboy, New Jersey. There Henry took on the job of surveying Spring's extensive acreage and reading three old lectures to the residents.

Alcott met Whitman before Thoreau did, crossing Brooklyn Ferry for a two-hour session on October 4. Walt he found to be "an extraordinary person, full of brute power, certainly of genius and audacity, and likely to make his mark on Young America." Whitman was thirty-seven, Alcott twenty years older. Graying age looked on vigorous youth and set down a vivid impression of the poet—"broad-shouldered, rouge-fleshed, Bacchus-browed, bearded like a satyr, and rank." The rankness exhaled from his "red flannel undershirt, open-breasted, exposing his brawny neck." Over this he wore a striped calico jacket with a "Byroneal" collar. Coarse overalls, cowhide boots, and a slouch hat ("for house and street alike") completed his attire. The eyes were gray, "unimaginative, cautious yet sagacious," and the voice was "deep, sharp, tender sometimes." Walt told Alcott that he had never been sick or taken medicine, nor had he ever sinned, so that he was "quite innocent of repentance and man's fall." Although unmarried, he professed "great respect for women." He gave his visitor a copy of the new edition of the *Leaves*, and asked him to write if he thought of anything more to say "about him or his master, Emerson."

Five weeks later, Alcott returned to Brooklyn, this time bringing Thoreau and Mrs. Tyndall, a buxom lady from Germantown, Pennsylvania. Walt received them in his unkempt attic study, shared with his mentally handicapped brother, Eddy, who was not present. Alcott took note of the unmade bed, the experienced chamber pot, and the pictures on the "rude walls"—a Hercules, a Bacchus, and a satyr. Walt boasted that he bathed every day, though the small house contained no visible facilities, and that he often rode the omnibuses up and down Broadway, "declaiming Homer at the top of his voice" against the cacophony of traffic. Apart from such activities, he "lived to make pomes," as he pronounced the word. Handing Thoreau a copy of the second edition of *Leaves*, he spoke only half apologetically about his public exploitation of Emerson's praise. "He made the printing of E[merson]'s letter seem a simple thing," wrote Thoreau, and indicated that the blame, if any, ought to fall on Emerson himself. When Henry asked if Whitman had read "the Orientals," Walt answered, "No. Tell me about them," hardly a confirmation of Emerson's remark to Caroline Sturgis Tappan and others that Walt wrote like a Buddhist.

For the rest Walt gabbed away about politics, convincing Thoreau that he was "apparently the greatest democrat" the world had ever seen, ready to cast all kings and aristocrats over the side of the ship of state, a position that Henry agreed with. Yet he was baffled by the seeming contradictions in Walt's character: "A remarkably strong though coarse nature" along with "a sweet disposition," and showing the "peculiar and rough" exterior of one who was "essentially a gentleman." Alcott had called him "rouge-fleshed." Thoreau noted independently that Walt's skin was "all over ? red," inserting the question mark to signify his surmise that the hidden portions of the poet were perhaps as red as his face and his undershirt. Alcott, watching narrowly, thought that the man of Concord and the man of Brooklyn surveyed each other nervously, "like two beasts, each wondering what the other would do, whether to snap or run."

The robust and ruddy Whitman continued to fascinate Alcott, who stayed on in New York and environs long after Thoreau had gone home, eager to understand this "savage sovereign of the flesh." On November 20 he had dinner with Walt and a young Scot named Swinton, and on December 12 he dined alone with Whitman at Taylor's Saloon. Walt said flatly that the best thing America had done was "the growing of Emerson," who was "the only man . . . in it"—present company presumably not excepted. He was planning a visit to Washington, to absorb the sights and smells of that town, hoping to show up the pygmy politicians who frequented the marble halls. Alcott nodded approval of the plan: a sojourn in the capital, he thought, might help to cure Walt of his "arrogance." But the poet had shed his aggressive manners when he appeared at the home of Samuel Longfellow on the twenty-eighth, and listened politely to Alcott's "spirited and metaphysical" Conversation. Alcott was amused to see that Walt was wearing "his Bloomers," probably meaning trousers tucked into calf-length boots, a costume ill-fitted for such a genteel company.

Thoreau had returned to Concord in time for Thanksgiving. Early in December he read the second edition of the *Leaves*. It did him "more good than any reading for a long time." His favorites among the poems were "Song of Myself" and "Crossing Brooklyn Ferry." "After whatever deductions," he thought, the whole book was "very brave and American." It induced "a liberal frame of mind," it was like being set "on a hill or in the midst of a plain." People "ought to rejoice greatly" in Walt, for he sometimes suggested "something a little more than human." Though often "rude and sometimes ineffectual," he had achieved "a great primitive poem,—an alarum or trumpet-note ringing through the American camp." Having now seen and talked with him, wrote Henry, "I find that I am not disturbed by any brag or egoism in his book. He may turn out the least of a braggart of all, having a better right to be confident. He is a great fellow . . . awfully good."

Like many previous readers and reviewers, Thoreau found that two or three of the poems were "disagreeable . . . simply sensual," as if beasts were speaking. Yet "even on this side," Whitman had "spoken more truth than any American or modern," and the effect was "exhilirating [sic]." His sensuality might indeed be less sensual than it seemed. Thoreau did not so much wish that those parts were "not written, as that men and women were so pure that they could read them without harm, that is, without understanding them." He liked this last sentence so well that he copied it into his journal, the only allusion to Whitman in all that vast document.

After what he called "a fortnight's bybye" with his family in New Hampshire, Alcott returned to New York in February 1857, hoping to continue with his "Conversations." Emerson was in town, fresh from a speaking tour of the Midwest, including a course of lectures that Moncure Conway had arranged for him in Cincinnati. On the evening of the twelfth he spoke to an audience in New York, and Alcott attended, finding the lecture "sparkling in parts, but more didactic than usual." Emerson was scheduled to lecture in Jersey City on Friday the thirteenth, but he found time for a visit with Alcott, pleased at his old friend's newfound success and prospects. According to Alcott, Emerson had just seen Walt Whitman for the second time, and said that he valued Walt as much as Alcott did.

It was odd. Both as poet and personality, Whitman was a phenomenon almost in the philosophical sense of the term: an object known through the senses rather than through the processes of rational thought. Young Norton had called him "an adept of the Transcendentalist School," and now, despite his foibles, he had managed to convert three of the leading Transcendentalists to his cause in something less than twenty months. Crude, self-serving, egotistical, he cultivated eccentricity as if he had a patent on it, outperforming such notable eccentrics as Thoreau and Alcott because he seemed willing to go to greater extremes in order to gain an audience. Young John Trowbridge, another of Walt's admirers, had told his sister in 1856 that Whitman was "a sort of Emerson run wild." As for Emerson himself, one reviewer had said that his reputation would "dearly pay for the fervid encomium" with which he had introduced Whitman to the American public. If that were so, he was still willing to take his chances and to pay his fines.

The attacks on Whitman's *Leaves of Grass* had not surprised Emerson. He had endured similar contumely in 1838 after his address at Harvard Divinity School, and had responded to it in his contemporaneous journal: "The taunts and cries of hatred and anger, the very epithets you bestow on me are so familiar long ago in my reading that they sound to me ridiculously old and stale. The same thing has happened so many times over, (that is, with the appearance of every original observer) that if people were not very ignorant of literary history, they would be struck with the exact coincidence. And whilst I see . . . that you must have been shocked and must cry out at what I have said . . . I have a great deal more to say that will shock you out of all patience."

Emerson's earliest emissary to Whitman, Moncure Conway, paid the poet a second visit one Sunday morning that summer of 1857. Out behind the small house in Brooklyn he found Walt lying on his back, gazing at the sky from the top of a knoll. He agreed at once to a "ramble" with Conway, and they passed the afternoon loafing along the shores of Staten Island, where there were still solitary beaches fit for nude swimming. "We had a good long bath in the sea," wrote Conway, who was now able to settle Thoreau's question as to whether Walt was red all over. "I perceived," wrote the young minister, "that the reddish tanned face and neck of the poet crowned a body of lily-like whiteness and a shapely form."

As the fall came on, Emerson found himself less sanguine than formerly about the current state of American poetry—or indeed anything else American in that perilous year of 1857. He wrote Caroline Sturgis Tappan, then still in Europe, that men like himself who had dreamed that "the necessities of the New World would presently evoke the mystic Power" and elicit "the Choral Hymns of a new age" were now discovering that American colleges and books remained "cramp and sterile." The Muses were as reticent as October was flamboyant, and "no fireeyed child" had yet been born. Where now was the American equivalent of Robert Browning with his "wise and deep and subtle" mind? Why could not America "breed a lyric man as exquisite as Tennyson?" The sole producers that America had yielded in ten years' time were "our wild Whitman, with real inspiration but choked by Titanic abdomen, and Delia Bacon, with genius, but mad, and clinging like a tortoise to English soil" in her fervid espousal of the Baconian heresy. Emerson still paid "homage to the gods" for his "two gossips," Alcott and Thoreau, but neither Charles Newcomb nor Ellery Channing had lived up to his earlier expectations. Perhaps it did not matter. "Who cares?" he asked. "As soon as we walk out of doors Nature transcends all poets so far, that a little more or less skill in whistling is of no account. Out of doors we lose the lust of performance, and are content to pass silent . . . into the depths of a Universe so resonant and beaming." This last assertion was almost like an echo of *Nature*, where Emerson had written of those artists whose "operations taken together are so insignificant . . . that in an impression so grand as that of the world on the human mind, they do not vary the result."

The first number of the *Atlantic Monthly* appeared in November. It contained four of Emerson's poems, including "Brahma," where the voice that spoke belonged to the creator-god of the Hindu trinity:

> If the red slayer think he slays,
> Or if the slain think he is slain,
> They know not well the subtle ways
> I keep and pass and turn again.
>
> Far and forgot to me is near;
> Shadow and sunlight are the same;
> The vanished gods to me appear;
> And one to me are shame and fame.
>
> They reckon ill who leave me out;
> When me they fly, I am the wings;
> I am the doubter and the doubt,
> And I the hymn the Brahmin sings
>
> The strong gods pine for my abode,
> And pine in vain the sacred Seven;
> But thou, meek lover of the good!
> Find me, and turn thy back on heaven.

These polished quatrains were a far cry from Whitman's loosely woven reflections on the deity in "Song of Myself":

> . . . Be not curious about God
> For I who am curious about each am not curious about God . . .
> I hear and behold God in every object, yet understand God not in the
>   least,
> Nor do I understand who there can be more wonderful than myself . . .
> In the faces of men and women I see God, and in my own face in the
>   glass,
> I find letters from God dropt in the street, and every one is sign'd by
>   God's name,

And I leave them where they are, for I know that whereso'er I go,
Others will punctually come for ever and ever.

Emerson's "Brahma" was like a letter from God "dropt" into Walt's cub-
byhole at the *Brooklyn Daily Times*, where he was now writing editorials. On
November 16, he defended the poem in a short squib that seemed to show
that he had made good use of an encyclopedia or else paid close attention to
Thoreau's exposition of Hindu mythology at their meeting in Brooklyn a year
earlier:

> Some of the papers are poking fun at Emerson on account of the unin-
> telligibility of his little Mystic Song entitled "Brahma" in the new *At-
> lantic Monthly*. The name of the poem is a facile key to it; Brahma, the
> Indian Deity, is the absolute and omnipresent god, besides whom all is
> illusion and fancy, and to whom everything apparent reverts in the end.
> This pantheistic thought Emerson expresses, not only clearly, but with
> remarkable grace and melody.

Although Emerson knew very well the values of grace and melody, he had
often affirmed the worth of the vernacular as a way of strengthening the affec-
tive force of both poetry and prose. In the spring of 1859 he called Robert
Herrick's verse "the most remarkable example of the low style," doubtless
with reference to the collection called *Hesperides*. He was a "good example of
the modernness of an old English writer," who had "discovered his subject
where he stood, between his feet, in his house, pantry, barn, village, and
neighbors, poultry yard, gossip and scandal of his set, their feasts and holidays. Like Montaigne in this . . . he took what he knew, and 'took it easy' as
we say."

In a brilliant lecture called "Art and Criticism," read at the Music Hall on
April 13, 1859, he summarized and profusely illustrated his views on the low
style, naming Walt Whitman as "our American master" of the *lingua communis,* and placing him squarely in the company of those who had espoused the
vernacular mode.

His theme of "speak with the vulgar, think with the wise" took him back to
ancient Athens. How wise Plato had been to introduce the low-born Socrates
into the "exquisite refinement of his Academy." The "perverse talk" of

Socrates was a counterforce to the "purple diction" of the Platonists, melding coarse fiber into "a dish else too luscious." Among his modern favorites stood Goethe, many of whose poems were "so idiomatic, so strongly rooted in the German soil," that they became "the terror of translators." Another recent example was George Borrow, who "mastered the *patois* of the gypsies, called Romany," and used it with memorable effect in fictions like *Lavengro*. Emerson thought that his beloved Rabelais and Montaigne were "masters of this Romany," and that Francis Bacon must have concealed some of it beneath his brocade robes. He quoted Luther: "I preach coarsely; that giveth content to all. Hebrew, Greek, and Latin I spare, until we learned ones come together, and then we make it so curled and finical that God himself wondereth at us." He who would be powerful, said Emerson, "must have the terrible gift of familiarity." He found it among writers like Swift, Defoe, and his old friend Carlyle, and among such orators as Chatham, Fox, Burke, and Patrick Henry. He recalled the shouts of the sansculottes at Versailles: "Let our little Mother Mirabeau speak!" Whitman was "our American master," who had still to get "out of the Fire-Club" and gain "the entrée of the sitting-rooms."

Poets, preachers, and politicians ought to pay attention to the real language of men. "Who has not heard in the street," he asked, "how forcible is bosh, gammon, and gas? The short Saxon words with which people help themselves are better than Latin. The language of the street is always strong. I envy the boys the force of the double negative (no shoes, no money, no nothing) though clean contrary to our grammar rules, and I confess to some titillation of my ears from a rattling oath." What he had once called the "Slambang" style had its perennial uses.

By grouping Whitman with the other "masters of Romany," Emerson was quietly justifying his now well-known enthusiasm for *Leaves of Grass*. What if Walt chose to talk as perversely as Socrates or as coarsely as Luther, to emulate Goethe by idiomatic speech as firmly rooted in his native soil as Herrick's verse was? What if, like certain pages in Rabelais and Montaigne, his poems could not be safely read aloud in mixed company? In 1856, Whitman had addressed Emerson as master. In 1859, Emerson applied the term to Whitman as a living representative of all those men of power who possessed the "terrible gift of familiarity."

Chapter   Forty

THE MAN IN
THE TURRET

❖ "I ABIDE IN MY OLD TURRET . . . COOP OR TUB OF OBSERVA-
tion," wrote Emerson in the winter of 1858. By this time, aged fifty-
five, he was not only a steadfast paterfamilias to his lively trio of teenagers, but
also a revered father figure and sometime spokesman for all of Concord. It
was he, for example, who officially welcomed the Hungarian patriot Lajos
Kossuth during his American tour in the spring of 1852. He composed the
"Fourth of July Ode," sung at the Town Hall in 1857, and at the annual cattle
show in 1858 he gave an address on "The Man with the Hoe." He was also
the chief speaker during the ceremony of consecration at Sleepy Hollow
Cemetery in the fall of 1855.

He took this occasion for some observations on the theme of immortality:
"I have heard that when we pronounce the name of man, we pronounce the
belief in immortality." Yet all people, himself included, were better believers
than they could give rational grounds for. "The real evidence is too subtle, or
is higher than we can write down in propositions. . . . All sound minds rest
on a certain preliminary conviction, namely, that if it be best that conscious
personal life shall continue, it will continue; if not best, then it will not."
Whatever the truth about the life to come, Sleepy Hollow was fitly named:
"In this quiet valley, as in the palm of Nature's hand, we shall sleep well when
we have finished our day."

Seventeen months later, in July 1857, he was back there once again on a private errand. "This morning," he wrote, "I had the remains of my mother and of my son Waldo removed from the tomb of Mrs. Ripley to my lot in 'Sleepy Hollow.' The sun shone brightly on the coffins, of which Waldo's was well preserved—now fifteen years. I ventured to look into the coffin. I gave a few white-oak leaves to each coffin, after they were put in the new vault, and the vault was then covered with two slabs of granite." At home he told his daughter Ellen that he had opened Waldo's coffin. He did not elaborate, although he could hardly have helped recalling the day in 1832 when he had opened the coffin of that other Ellen whose name his eldest daughter bore.

The financial panic of 1857, though less severe than that of 1837, was still a complicating factor in Emerson's domestic bookkeeping. Banks in Boston and New York suspended specie payments in October. "Nobody knows," said Emerson, in distant allusion to the famous South Sea Bubble of 1720, "how far each of these bankers and traders blows up his little airball on what infinitely small supply of soap and water. They all float in the air alike as balloons and planets . . . until they strike one another, or any house. But this panic is a severer examiner than any committee of Bank Commissioners to find out how much specie all this paper represents, and how much real value." One positive note was the publication of *English Traits*, which had come out at last in August 1856. It sold well—1,700 copies in the first four days, 3,000 in the first month, with a further printing of 2,000 in prospect. But his publishers were damnably deliberate with royalty settlements, and his railroad stocks, bought on the advice of his old friend Abel Adams, were paying next to nothing and usually nothing.

He was obliged to abandon his turret each year for the sake of his always dwindling exchequer. In 1856 he read more than seventy lectures all over the Middle West and throughout New England. "The Lyceum," he told Adams, "is a terrible tyrant with long arms that reach from Chicago and Milwaukie [sic] to Concord, and a hundred hands, each of which writes me a letter that I must answer." In 1857, despite a $1,000 windfall from his first wife's estate, he lectured in upward of fifty cities and towns. Similar trips in 1858 netted him approximately $2,000. In 1859 he gave at least fifty talks, each of them a drain on his physical and nervous resources, but also a pacifying influence to the conscience of one who deeply believed that "poverty demoralizes" and that "a man in debt is so far a slave," and who devised a couplet that said:

To barricade the avenues of ill
Pay every debt, as if God wrote the bill.

Ellery Channing, loafing around the vales of Concord and untroubled by
his own perennial indebtedness, chided his mentor, as he had once chided
Thoreau, for being "as busy as a shoemaker." But Emerson also took these
trips as a challenge. "Home from Chicago and Milwaukee," he wrote later.
" 'Twas tedious the obstructions and squalor of travel. The advantage of their
offers at Chicago made it needful to go. It was in short this dragging a decorous old gentleman out of home, and out of position, to this juvenile career
tantamount to this: 'I'll bet you fifty dollars a day for three weeks, that you will
not leave your library and wade and freeze and ride and run, and suffer all
manner of indignities, and stand up for an hour each night reading in a hall,'
and I answer, 'I'll bet I will.' I do it, and win the $900."

Lidian's recurrent illnesses almost inevitably required an ample household
staff. As far back as 1852, William Emerson had remonstrated with his
brother for employing seven domestics. "You shall go harmless for your audacious attack on my housekeeping," Emerson answered, "but the vice of my
economy lies deep, and is not easy to reach, almost hopeless to extirpate."
Part of his problem was that he had to be certain that the family and the house
would function smoothly during his necessary absences as a traveling salesman for ethical ideas, or, as he once said, "a diamond merchant."

Even more important, however, was his determination that his children, as
they grew up, must not feel the bite of penury, as he and his brothers had
done at the same age. He once quietly said as much to his good friend Abel
Adams: "I have tried to protect [Eddy] and his sisters from any feeling of
poverty." This impulsion was evident in his arrangements for their education, as when he sent Ellen to Lenox in 1853–54, and both Ellen and Edith in
tandem to the private school run by the family of Louis Agassiz in their capacious home in Cambridge, and betweentimes to Frank Sanborn's excellent
academy in Concord. Through their associations at school and frequent visits
to Boston and Cambridge, the girls were maturing on roughly equal social
terms with Sedgwicks, Lowells, Higginsons, Parkmans, and Bancrofts, as
well as with such wealthier families as those of Sam and Anna Ward, William
and Caroline Tappan, and John and Sarah Forbes of Milton and Naushon.

By the end of the 1850s, Emerson had known the Wards for twenty years. The beatific bride and groom of 1840 were now middle-aged, with a family of four: Lydia, nicknamed Lilly; Thomas Wren Ward, named for his paternal grandfather; Elizabeth, called Bessie; and Annie, the youngest. Tom was a handsome adolescent who in 1855 had been put to school in Switzerland, partly owing to his deafness, which seems to have been congenital. Throughout the period 1850–59, the once fabulously beautiful Anna Barker Ward was increasingly troubled by severe neuralgia. Other therapies having failed, she tried foreign travel, a widely accepted anodyne of the times. Early in May 1856, she and her youngest daughter sailed from Boston for Liverpool aboard the *Arabia*, beginning a tour that would last for six months.

Emerson could have been thinking of Anna in a somber journal entry of that year: "I know a song which is more hurtful than strychnine or the kiss of the asp. It blasts those who hear it, changes their color and shape, and dissipates their substance. It is called Time." He alerted his English friends, the Carlyles and the poets A. H. Clough and Coventry Patmore, to Anna's imminent arrival in London. She was, he told Jane Carlyle, "the most beloved and valued of all American women. . . . I wish neuralgic pains were not permitted to assail such good nerves." To Carlyle he was more specific. Anna had been,

ten or fifteen years ago, the loveliest of women, and her speech and manners may still give you some report of the same. . . . Her husband is a banker connected in business with your Barings, and is a man of elegant genius and tastes, and his house is a resort for fine people. [Bertel] Thorwaldsen distinguished Anna Ward in Rome, formerly, [in 1838] by his attentions. Powers the Sculptor made an admirable bust of her; Clough and Thackeray will tell you of her. Jenny Lind, like the rest, was captivated by her, and was married in her house [on February 5, 1852].

Despite this buildup, Anna did not meet the Carlyles, notifying them that she was ill and must leave at once for Paris and a visit to her son in Switzerland. After a summer on the Continent, she returned to London late in September, saw Clough briefly, and was shown round the British Museum by Coventry Patmore, an assistant in the printed books department. She praised his recently published poem, "The Espousals," an apotheosis of married love that was to become part of *The Angel in the House*. "One could not talk for an hour with your friend," Patmore reported, "without discovering that there were better reasons than one's idiosyncratic fondness for female commendation to justify pride in *her* approval." The day before she sailed for Boston on October 11, Hawthorne wrote his publisher, Ticknor, that Sophia had gone to London from their seaside villa at Southport to tell Anna good-bye, having never forgotten the beautiful and beautifully dressed woman who had stopped at the Wayside in 1853 before the Hawthornes left for Liverpool.

Anna had been at home only eight months when she left again for Europe, this time for a year and a half. In mid-May 1858, Emerson wrote Clough about the underlying reasons for the second trip: "You will have seen Mrs. S. G. Ward, ere this, and probably also Sam W. too. I grieve that she has flung herself into the Church of Rome, suddenly. She was born for social grace, and that faith makes such carnage of social relations! But I confide that her happy fortunate nature cannot be thwarted by any accidents, and will certainly bring her into harmony quickly again, from whatever extremist notes." Like Emerson, Clough was shocked by this development. He wrote Charles Eliot Norton in June, deploring Anna's change of faith.

Emerson's own position was firmly anti-Catholic. First exposed in his youth to ancient Catholic monuments in Malta and Italy, he had been mildly enthralled by the "grand Gothic perspectives" of the duomo in Milan and the richly ornamented interiors and stained-glass fenestration of many lesser churches. Ten years later he still understood the aesthetic attractions of antique houses of worship and of church music, especially for those girls and women who wished to escape the "icehouse of Unitarianism." Yet in 1849 he spoke of New England Catholics as "disgusting" and deplored the "futile" spread of popery in the United States. In his poem "The Problem," he had confessed his liking for churches and cowls and any legitimate prophet of the soul, while concluding: "Yet not for all his faith can see / Would I that cowled churchman be." In the ode for W. H. Channing, like many another romantic rebel, he had alluded scornfully to the "cant" of priest-talk. About the time of Anna's conversion, he anathematized "this running of the girls into Popery," who knew nothing about religion or "the grounds of the sects" but slid into the Roman Church for no better reason than their liking for the masses of Mozart and Bach. As Sam Ward believed, doubtless on the basis of his wife's experience, Protestant alternatives to the more attractive aspects of Catholic worship were thin or absent. Emerson replied that it was perhaps unfortunate that the science of "pure Ethics" had not yet been consolidated into a "cultus." Still, the Catholic position on morals reflected only an "effete state of formalism," whereas "the eternal offset of the moral sentiment" was always "creating new channels and forms" of its own.

Anna's conversion, as Emerson later recorded, had been instigated by Father Isaac Hecker, a former resident at Brook Farm and Alcott's Fruitlands, and Emerson's companion on a visit to the Harvard Shaker colony in the spring of 1844. By August of that year, Hecker had abandoned his transcendental ethic in favor of the Roman Church. Having failed to persuade Henry Thoreau to accompany him on a European tour, he set out alone, getting as far as Belgium, where he joined the Redemptorist Fathers at Saint-Trond. His name did not surface again in Emerson's journal until 1862, when Hecker proposed to return to Concord to lecture on the Catholic Church. Emerson dissuaded him; nobody would come to hear him, people were turning away from theological questions. They might be ready enough to accept a man's whim of wearing a painted petticoat, but would not talk with him more than once. He found Father Hecker impervious to such arguments: "He converted Mrs. Ward, and, like the lion that has eaten a man, he wants to be at it again."

She had been abroad for a year when Emerson wrote directly to Anna:

What if you go away, and stay away, and try to hide yourself farther away from me in seclusions of opinion—you have ever been to me an endeared and enshrined person, . . . and I must ever hold life richer for you, even when I do not say so. Then here is ever, if you are gone, the admirable Sam Ward, loyal, high-hearted, and sure . . . and we look in his house for you! And here are these dear children. Tom I see almost daily, a boy whose innocence has not left him; I fancy sometimes that his deafness was some angelic guard to defend his ear from vulgarity and vice. He is a darling of the young people, who all prize in him this infantile purity and grace. Ellen, who is no sentimentalist, says he is always picturesque, and the tones and play of his voice give no hint of infirmity. Of Lily, too, I hear frequent praises from Edith and Ellen. They say she has made great steps lately, and is the loveliest guardian to Bessie. I should not think it prudent to let you overhear my children prate about yours, if you were not already setting your face homeward. . . . I grieve whenever I hear that you still suffer— But what an alternative will this coming home be! . . . You have suffered so bravely and so long—that you ought to reckon securely on that self-limiting rule of all distempers. *They* wear out, and usually much faster than we. Home and solitude, husband and children shall heal you, and the silent benedictions of a wide neighborhood of friends shall not be wanting.

Only at the end of his letter did Emerson mention Anna's conversion. "Some day—a good while hence, you will perhaps tell me . . . of these journeys and abidings; possibly, too, of the passages of religious experience, of which I have heard remotely. Yet to me the difference between church and church looks so frivolous, that I cannot easily give the deference which a sympathetic civility holds due to one another. To old eyes, how supremely unimportant the form under which we celebrate the Justice, Love, and Truth—the attributes of the Deity and the Soul!"

In July Sam Ward took his son, Tom, and Emerson's son, Eddy, for a hiking trip in the Adirondacks. Emerson had sprained his foot and could not go. The campers were just home again when Emerson heard from Anna, still abroad, still ailing. "She is always a porphyrogenet [born to the purple] and her handwriting palatial," Emerson told Sam Ward. "She writes with confidence in her physician and his treatment. But for her church, she shares the exaltation . . . which belongs to all new converts in the dogmatic churches, and which gives so much pleasure that it would be cruel to check it if we could—which we cannot. The high way to deal with her is to accept the total pretension of the Roman Church. . . . But who is good enough to deal with converts so? She was born for dignity, but I would not see her an abbess. Her own house, her children, and her husband's claims to daily and lifelong respect and confidence, are the best electuary. But I hope she is already getting well—then she will get well of this also."

Emerson's closing sentence strongly implied what he evidently believed, that Anna's illness had been one of the primary motivating factors in her conversion. When she returned in October, laden with gifts for the elder Emersons and their children, he wrote to thank her for her "power to radiate happiness." His children and Anna's son, Tom, had returned to Concord from Boston with "favorable assurances" that Anna was not only healthy but also buoyed up by "a certain glory or super health." Anna must come to Concord while the autumnal foliage was still at its height. Emerson was eager to comprehend the full meaning of her recovery.

Presently he made a journal entry on the results of one of their conversations. "Anna Ward was at a loss in talking with me, because I had no church whose weakness she could show up, in return for my charges upon hers. I said to her, Do you not see that though I have no eloquence and no flow of thought, yet that I do not stoop to accept any thing less than truth? that I sit here contented with my poverty, mendicity [beggary], and deaf and dumb estate, from year to year, from youth to age, rather than adorn myself with any red rag of false church or false association? My low and lonely sitting here by the wayside, is my homage to truth." Emerson's argument clearly failed to convert Anna to his own position. It is also doubtful that he unleashed upon her the full force of another contiguous journal entry, which said that he could not "suffer a nasty monk to whisper to *me, to whom God has given* such a person as S[amuel] G[ray] W[ard] and such children, for my confessors and absolvers."

No such problem as that of Anna Ward beclouded Emerson's growing friendship with another wealthy family. John Murray Forbes was a businessman some ten years Emerson's junior. Born in Bordeaux, France, in 1813, he began work as an adolescent in the Boston countinghouse of his uncles, who presently sent him as their representative to Canton, China. At age twenty-four he returned to the United States with the nucleus of a considerable fortune. About 1846 he undertook railroad building and management with a group of capitalists who bought the unfinished Michigan Central, and soon extended their holdings with the formation of the Chicago, Burlington, and Quincy Railroad, of which Forbes ultimately became president.

In 1834 he married Sarah Hathaway of New Bedford, who bore him four daughters and two sons. By the mid–1850s his fortune was secure, and he showed a growing interest in intellectual affairs. His sister Margaret, whom Emerson had known and admired since 1840, seems to have urged him to invite Emerson to speak at the Milton Lyceum. His letter of invitation mentioned Margaret's recent illness and her hope of seeing Emerson again. "I heartily wish," Emerson replied, that "I knew how to be a neighbor to a lady so excellent." He spoke at Milton on March 25, 1857, renewing his association with Forbes's sister and beginning a lifelong friendship with Forbes himself.

At first Emerson had grouped his new friend with other Boston capitalists. In talking with men like him, you talked with "all State Street," and your response depended on your susceptibility to that kind of power. Men like Thoreau, Newcomb, and Alcott, however, brought their own "deep force," speaking from the "far wider public . . . of all sane and good men." But Emerson's early skepticism about the wisdom of associating with powerful State Street capitalists was soon dissipated once he got to know Forbes and saw him in action. Both men had turned against Webster after his infamous Seventh of March Address in 1850. Both were free-soil advocates, sympathetic with the plight of Kansas. They deplored the administrations of Pierce and Buchanan and supported John Brown up at least to the attack on Harpers Ferry, though Forbes was more dubious than Emerson about Brown's sanity. Both left nominal Whig Party membership to join the new Republican Party and both were strongly pro-Lincoln in June and November 1860.

Yet it was Forbes's character rather than his politics that most struck Emerson. "It was my fortune not long ago," he wrote, "to fall in with an American to be proud of. I said never was such force, good meaning, good sense, good action, combined with domestic lovely behavior, such modesty and persistent preference for others. Wherever he moved, he was the benefactor." He could "ride well, shoot well, sail well, keep house well, administer affairs well; but he was the best talker, also, in the company; what with a perpetual practical wisdom, with an eye always to the working of the thing, what with the multitude and distinction of his facts . . . and in the temperance with which he parried all offence and opened the eyes of the person he talked with without contradicting him. Yet I said to myself, How little the man suspects, with his sympathy for man and his respect for lettered and scientific people, that he is not likely, in any company, to meet a man superior to himself."

Besides his palatial mansion at Milton, a southern suburb of Boston, Forbes had recently joined his wife's uncle, W. W. Swain, in acquiring the entire island of Naushon, of which Swain had long styled himself the "governor." Control passed to Forbes in the winter of 1856–57, and he summered there for the rest of his life—"the only 'squire' in Massachusetts," as Emerson fondly held, "and no nobleman ever performed his duties better." Seven miles long, the island divides Buzzard's Bay from Vineyard Sound, and still offers an unspoiled diversity of landscape—hills and woods, open downs, freshwater ponds, and a sandy beach along the south shore—"a paradise," Forbes called it, "for children young and old." A corps of attendants kept the great house in order and the kitchen busy. Cows grazed in the meadows, there was a stable of riding horses, and for the children a succession of ponies of which the eldest was Johnny Crapaud, imported from Le Havre in France but now thoroughly Americanized. In the fall there were ducks and plover to shoot, and Forbes held an annual deer hunt, providing haunches of venison for his numerous friends.

He was a slender and ruddy-faced man, prematurely bald with a semicircular fringe of brown hair, a prominent nose, and a firm and humorous mouth. An inveterate host, he had just settled in during the summer of 1857 when he invited the Emersons to Naushon, listing train schedules from Boston to New Bedford and offering passage to the island aboard his yacht, the *Azalea*. In the following summer, Edith and Edward had their first sight of the island in July, and in September the elder Emersons went as well, this time with Ellen, breaking the trip with an overnight stay at the American House in Boston, where Lidian was kept awake by the mewing of a cat that she feared might be hungry. Ellen, in her role as majordomo of the Emerson household, had insisted that her mother must go. The whole family were agreed "that it is *so* good for her to leave her work and the care that oppresses her . . . at home," even though she always complained of the travail of getting ready, and was often too ill to undertake journeys of any kind. Urged on by her eldest daughter, she had gone in June to Lynn, Medford, and Brookline. In July she accompanied Emerson to Newport for a short stay with the Bancrofts. In August Emerson had spent two weeks rusticating with a stag party of cronies, including Louis Agassiz, William Stillman, and J. R. Lowell, at Ampersand, near Follensbee Pond in the Adirondacks. "Newport, Adirondac, Naushon, all in one summer," he told Forbes, "may well turn the brain of a better scholar."

The Forbes family met the ferry from New Bedford and carried the Emersons in two wagons to the great house. Ellen sent her sister an ecstatic account of their adventures: sea bathing on the south shore, horseback riding through fields and woods to a hollow called the Amphitheatre, gathering shells along the beach at Uncatena Bridge, a two-hour sail in Forbes's boat, the *Gipsey*, and Emerson's trip aboard the *Azalea* to shoot plover near Gay Head and Noman's-Land. Emerson had begun a blank-verse history of his

Adirondack sojourn of 1858, and one evening read it aloud to the admiring company. In the so-called *Island Book*, an album kept for visitors, he set down another of his recent poems, "Waldeinsamkeit" (Woodland Solitude), which contained fitting allusions to the forest and the sea.

Emerson had recently grouped Carlyle's *History of Frederick the Great* with the first four of Tennyson's *Idylls* among the major British achievements of 1859. "What a heart-whole race," he exclaimed, "is that which in the same year can turn out two such sovereign productions." He still lacked full historical perspective on that phenomenal year that had likewise produced Darwin's *Origin of Species*, Dickens's *A Tale of Two Cities*, FitzGerald's translation of the *Rubáiyát*, Eliot's *Adam Bede*, Meredith's *Richard Feverel*, and Mill's *On Liberty*.

But this same year was not for him a very fortunate time. Late in May his brother Bulkeley died at the age of fifty-two. He had been ailing since February, cared for by Reuben Hoar and his second wife, who had converted their parlor to a sickroom, and treated their patient with "uniform kindness." His death was not a surprise. Ellen and Eddy had driven over to Littleton on Easter Sunday to find him "pale and thin, looking quite sick." Henry Thoreau took charge of the funeral, conducted from Emerson's house. Bulkeley's face, said his brother, "was not much changed by death, but sadly changed by life from the comely boy I can well remember." Burial was in Emerson's lot at Sleepy Hollow. "It is very sorrowful," he wrote, "but the sorrow is in the life and not in the death." For more than thirty years Bulkeley had been a constant care, at first in and out of the McLean Asylum in Charlestown, and later in charge of farmers in Chelmsford and Littleton. He had often come to stay in Emerson's house on holidays like Thanksgiving, sometimes for the annual cattle show, and nearly always for "Election" time in the spring of the year. Now the original five brothers were reduced to two.

Soon after the funeral, Ellen Emerson broached a plan for a six-week vacation in Maine—to feel, as she said, "entirely disengaged from home and all belonging to it," and to "try a new kind of life, keeping house for ourselves . . . among the mountains, close to the woods." The site she chose was Waterford, which had been for years the chief rural habitat of Aunt Mary Moody Emerson. Emerson himself had always shown a fondness for Maine, even including the snowbank near Berwick into which his sleigh-stage had inadvertently dumped its passengers back in 1842. He had often lectured in the provincial cities and towns, and had once dreamed of establishing a community of scholars near Bangor. His Adirondack expedition had evidently sharpened his longing for the wilderness, or at least for life in a village less populous even than Concord. Perhaps the continuing flow of visitors through his front gate had made him eager for the solitude he always coveted. He had listened avidly to Thoreau's accounts of his ascent of Katahdin in 1846, moose hunting along the Penobscot in 1853, and canoeing with the Indian Joseph Polis on the Allagash in 1857. Now he was ready to indulge his daughter's scheme for a "vacation of independence" that might profit the whole family.

In June he and Ellen set off in the hope of locating suitable housing in Waterford village. A letter of Ellen's summarized the three-day journey and her father's enthusiasm. The region near South Paris reminded him of the Adirondacks. "Let's never go home any more," he exclaimed to his daughter. They found a section of the Waterford River where the stream flowed over bare granite, without mud or sand or dead leaves. "Father kept wanting to camp down and to sell Bush [the Concord house] and buy this brook, and desired that 20 years might be added to his life that he might spend them there." They watched the moon rise over Bear Mountain and went early to bed at the local inn. Next day they looked at several possible houses and caught the stagecoach for the first leg of the journey home.

Then an accident intervened to spoil the Waterford junket. "Just a week before we were to start," wrote Ellen, "Father sprained his ancle [sic] and we have to put it off for another year. . . . Immediately all fell back into the old path." Emerson was contrite—"It looks badly for my Waterford plan," he told Abel Adams on July 15. One wrong step in descending Mount Wachusett had made him an invalid. "I went to the doctors," he wryly reported. "Dr H. Bigelow said, 'A splint and absolute rest'; Dr Russell said, 'Rest, yes, but a splint, no.' Dr Bartlett said, 'Neither splint nor rest, but go and walk.' Dr. Russell said, 'Pour water on the foot, but it must be warm.' Dr. Jackson said, 'stand in a trout brook all day.' " The victim thought that King Lear had never sprained his foot "or he would have thought there were worse evils than unkind daughters. When I see a man unhappy, I ask, has a sprained foot brought him to *this* pass?" By the third week in August he had decided to make the best of it. His pears and apricot plums were beginning to ripen, and he spoke happily of the succulent sweet apple they called Early Bough.

There were further "frets," as he called them. Two of his cows coming back from summer pasture went astray. A line storm stripped his loaded pear trees, leaving the orchard floor almost knee-deep in fallen fruit. His publishers, Phillips and Sampson, declared bankruptcy. His man-of-all-work, James Burke, went on a drinking spree just when the sprain seemed to be mending. And then Emerson, sure that he could walk as before, walked too far and had to return to his chair, where he consoled himself by reading Boswell's *Life of Johnson*.

Lidian's health and spirits had responded so well to the Naushon visit in 1858 that she and Edith returned to "Prospero's Island," as Emerson called it, for another stay in August 1859. "Father and Eddy and I are at home together," wrote Ellen. "Since I was disappointed of Waterford I have been allowed to work at home, and the cook and chambermaid being dismissed I am taking care of the house and family with the help of the seamstress. It is never-ending work, from five till eight. . . . It is wholly absorbing, too." Care of the family included her father's foot, now encased in a bandage impregnated with linseed oil. Eddy diversified his time by camping out at Walden and climbing Mount Wachusett, wearing his new Adirondack shirt and carrying a knapsack loaded with Ellen's gingerbread. Ellen herself managed to read the first four *Idylls* by Tennyson and to bake an apple pudding that her father called "superb."

The family now included a green parrot unoriginally named Polly. She showed a tendency to bite everyone but Alice, the resident seamstress, and "used to sit on the scraper on the stone doorstep most of the time in summer," reassuming her cage at night. Her raucous voice and limited vocabulary displeased Emerson, who persistently referred to Polly as "that green cat." One ironic entry in his journal observed that "a parrot has few duties." This one could not even learn to say "gingerbread," despite the efforts of two Irish maids. According to Emerson's daughters, he cared nothing for household pets "and shrank from touching them, though he admired the beauty and grace of cats." As for dogs, he liked to repeat a *mot* of the Whig wit and divine, the Reverend Sydney Smith. Asked by a lady to provide a motto for the collar of her little dog Spot, Smith suggested the line from *Macbeth*, "Out, damned Spot!" The only domestic animal that Emerson really cared for was Dolly, the little Morgan mare, who served the family for twenty years and was finally taken to Naushon, where she grazed contentedly until her death at age twenty-five.

Emerson's cordial alliances with the rich did nothing to change his attitude toward such old friends and notably impecunious neighbors as Alcott, Channing, and Thoreau. The Alcotts had returned to Concord in 1857 and bought, with Emerson's help, the decrepit farmstead next door to Hawthorne's Wayside. Alcott named it Orchard House and set about its renovation, a process that took many months because his "Conversations" were nowadays embracing ever-wider geographical areas, though without in the least enriching their perpetrator. The year 1858 was darkened for the luckless family by the death of Elizabeth, called Lizzie or Beth, who for more than a year had been wasting gradually away, increasingly sure that she could not recover. "And so," wrote Alcott, "our daughter Elizabeth ascends with transfigured features to the heavenly airs she had sought so long. . . . She lived a short, innocent, and diligent life with us, and has an early translation." Thoreau, Emerson, and Frank Sanborn attended her burial in Sleepy Hollow, as well as John Pratt, who was shortly to become engaged to Anna, the eldest Alcott daughter, whom he married two years later. The fortunes of the family took a turn for the better during 1859. That spring Sanborn asked Alcott to accept a two-year appointment as superintendent of the Concord school system, and in the fall Lowell bought Louisa's story, "Love and Self-Love," for publication in the *Atlantic Monthly*.

Ellery Channing still occupied his house on Main Street. His wife, Ellen, had died of tuberculosis in September 1856, unable to sustain the weight of care that Ellery's familial irresponsibility had forced upon her since their separation in 1853, their reunion in 1855, and the birth of their fifth child in the following year. The children were being raised by relatives, and the widower was again unemployed, though late in his marriage he had worked sporadically for the *New Bedford Mercury*, taking vacations when the spirit moved him, as it often did. Apart from halfhearted journalism, his only profession was versification. The chief product of these years was *Near Home* (1858), which Emerson described as "pictures seen by an instructed eye"—a series "of sketches of natural objects . . . enwreathed by the thoughts they suggest to a contemplative pilgrim," and good enough to "delight the heart of Wordsworth." Ellery was still walking and talking with Emerson and Thoreau, living at ease, as his poem said, in "ragged independence."

Near Home was dedicated to Thoreau, who was restlessly pursuing his own version of ragged independence. Despite a curious circulatory malady in the spring of 1855 that affected his legs and lasted for the better part of two years, he continued his journeyings outward from the hub of Concord, exploring Naushon in 1856 before John Forbes bought the island, mountaineering in Massachusetts, Maine, and New Hampshire, and paying visits to New Bedford, Cape Cod, and Cape Ann. His facial appearance changed twice in this period: in 1855 he grew a set of "Galway whiskers" under his chin, hoping to ward off throat infections, and by September 1857, as if to salute the advent of his fortieth birthday, had cultivated a full beard that Ellery called "terrible to behold." In this hirsute guise, during 1858, he conducted surveying operations for at least twenty local clients, including Emerson, and accelerated his American Indian studies, which eventuated in eleven fact-filled notebooks and a collection of nearly a thousand aboriginal artifacts.

In the winter of 1859, following the death of his father, he took over the management of the family's graphite business. His vigorous defense of John Brown at the time of Harpers Ferry crowned a year of public speaking during which, according to Walter Harding, he gave more lectures than in any other year of his life. He also took time that spring to supervise the planting of 400 pine trees and 100 larches to establish a new grove at Walden. He was always in "great demand" among the Emerson children, to whom he regularly paid avuncular visits, helping Edith with a wildflower garden, and Eddy with the gathering and classification of birds' eggs and plant specimens. When Eddy built an igloo on the front lawn, Uncle Henry stopped by to test the acoustics of voices through snow. He was, as Ellery had said, "busy as a shoemaker."

But he could also sit still. "The charm," said Emerson, "which Henry T. uses for bird and frog and mink, is patience. They will not come to him . . . until he becomes a log among the logs, sitting still for hours in the same place; then they come around him and to him and show themselves at home." *At home* was a magical phrase for the man in the turret. He quizzically told Henry that "if God meant him to live in a swamp, he would have made him a frog." But he did not mean it. Among all his eccentric disciples, and not least the faithful trio of Alcott, Channing, and Thoreau, he respected what he called "the private power of each person,—the door into nature that is opened to him; that which each can, let him do, satisfied with his task and its instructions and its happiness."

Part Four

THE

SIXTIES

Chapter Forty-one

AN EMERSONIAN

CALENDAR, 1860

THE SPIRIT OF JOHN BROWN WAS STILL ABROAD IN JANUARY 1860 when Emerson gave his final commemorative address to the citizens of Salem. Two weeks later, Frank Sanborn, the Concord schoolmaster and erstwhile member of Theodore Parker's Secret Six, was served a subpoena by a stranger who buttonholed him in the Concord Post Office and said that he was required to appear before a committee of the United States Senate in Washington on the twenty-fourth to defend himself against charges that he had conspired with Brown. "Shall I say you will come, sir?" the messenger asked. "You may make what return you please, sir," said Sanborn loftily. But he took the precaution of fleeing to Canada as he had done after the Harpers Ferry attack, and petitioned the Senate in February to withdraw the charges, meantime running his school as if nothing had happened.

It was the second clash with the law among Emerson's younger friends. John Forbes's eldest son, Will, a junior at Harvard, as part of his initiation into the secret society known as Med. Fac., was ordered to break into the New Chapel in Harvard Yard and to place on the lectern a Bible that had been stolen from Yale. In the small hours of January 11, armed with a policeman's billy, he climbed a ladder, broke a window, and squirmed through the aperture only to be confronted by a night watchman named Hilton, who grappled with the interloper and hit him over the head. Will clubbed Hilton, who in turn fired his pistol, at which Will wisely surrendered, and at dawn was taken in handcuffs to the police station, where he spent a day and a night before being released in his father's custody. Expelled by the Harvard authorities, he was subsequently tried and fined $50 and costs. John Forbes found his errant son a clerkship in the Boston offices of the Chicago, Burlington, and Quincy Railroad, and he began, on this low rung, a lifelong career in business.

As the eyes and ears for her temporarily absent father, and gifted, as always, with almost total recall, Ellen Emerson reported in full on both these altercations. Although still studying at Sanborn's school, she went in January for a vacation with the Forbes family in Milton and in February to Boston to visit the Wards. Sam Ward and James Russell Lowell had gone to the Adirondacks equipped with fur-lined sleeping bags. Annie, the youngest Ward daughter, took Ellen to inspect a Catholic hospital and discoursed at length on the Catholic faith. But, said Ellen, "as I had already learned the whole system, I couldn't think of any new questions to ask."

John Brown's daughters were now in Concord to attend the Sanborn School, staying at first with the Emersons. The eldest girl, aged sixteen, had kept house for her father near Harpers Ferry in the summer of 1859 and told Ellen all about it.

"The other side of her is just what I've always wanted to see," wrote Ellen, "a girl brought up in the primitive spinning, weaving, sheep-tending, butter-making, times which she certainly has been, in every particular, even to the Calvinism. She says, 'I've been the mark for all the church-members to shoot their arrows at, always; but they never get into me. I'm a regular tough one. I can't believe in everlasting punishment, and if I've done anything wrong, I'd rather suffer myself than have anyone suffer for me.' " Lidian mothered the Brown girls, and Edith Emerson and Alice the seamstress took pains to make clothes for them "in Boston fashion" so that they would "look like the rest of the world" when they started school at the end of February.

When Walt Whitman showed up in Boston in mid-March, he was in an ebullient mood. Not only had his new publishers, Thayer and Eldridge, urged him to place in their hands the third and much-enlarged edition of the *Leaves*, but Lowell, editor of the *Atlantic*, had also accepted one of Walt's poems for the April number and paid for it in advance. Walt had been in town only two days when Emerson appeared, enjoying a peaceful interval between a long series of lectures in the Middle West and Canada, and another to be given in New York on the twenty-third. He had apparently been alerted to Walt's arrival either by a newspaper notice or by Thayer and Eldridge, or possibly by a note sent to Concord by Whitman himself. "Emerson called on me immediately," wrote Walt two weeks later, "treated me with the greatest courtesy—kept possession of me all day—gave me a bully dinner, etc." Although Emerson did not say so, he might have grouped Walt with the Midwesterners in his audiences during his recent tour, whom he had described to his daughter Edith, without malice, as "rough grisly Esaus, full of dirty strength."

The third meeting of the two poets was the only one that took place largely out of doors. Walt was planning to stay in town until May, and Emerson walked him over to the Athenaeum Library to register his name for guest privileges there. The rest of the time before the "bully dinner" at the American House, Emerson's favorite Boston hotel, was given over to a peripatetic conversation along the wide paths of the Common. Emerson did most of the talking. His position was that Walt might—for the sake of sales—tone down his more forthright passages, or even delete from this edition some of the poems involving sexuality. Although in the end Whitman declined to follow this advice, he never forgot this man-to-man encounter with his Concord champion.

As usual, Emerson seems to have left no record of this meeting, although it is amusing to remember that ten months later he sent Whitman a copy of his *Conduct of Life* essays. But Walt often recalled the occasion in his later talks with Horace Traubel, the Boswell of his Camden years. One of his reports insisted that:

Emerson's objections to the "outcast" passages in *Leaves of Grass* were neither moral nor literary, but were given with an eye to my worldly success. He believed the book would sell—said that the American people should know the book: yes, *would* know it, but for its sex handicap: and he thought he saw the way by which to accomplish what he called "the desirable end." He did not say I should drop a single line. . . . He asked whether I would consent to eliminate certain popularly objectionable poems and passages. Emerson's position has been misunderstood; he offered absolutely no spiritual argument against the book exactly as it stood. Give it a chance to be seen, give the people a chance to see it—that was the gist of his contention. If there was any weakness in his position, it was in his idea that the particular poems could be dropped and the *Leaves* remain the *Leaves* still: he did not see the significance of the sex element as I had put it into the book and resolutely there stuck to it—he did not see that if I had cut sex out I might just as well have cut everything out—the full scheme would no longer exist—it would have been violated in its most sensitive spot.

More than twenty years later Whitman set down another account: "Emerson, then in his prime, keen, physically and morally magnetic, arm'd at every point, and when he chose, wielding the emotional just as well as the intellectual. . . . More precious than gold to me that dissertation. . . . Each point of Emerson's statement unanswerable, no judge's charge ever more complete and convincing . . . and then I felt down in my soul the clear . . . conviction to disobey all, and pursue my own way. . . ." He remembered for Traubel a snatch of that conversation. Assuming such excisions as Emerson had urged, Walt asked if there would be "as good a book left." Emerson "looked grave. . . . Then he smiled at me and said, 'I did not say as good a book—I said a good book.' " In the end, said Walt, "he liked me better for not accepting his advice."

In another of his recollections, Whitman told Traubel that without using the actual verb, Emerson had advised him to "expurgate"—in effect, perhaps, to scatter a few fig leaves over some of the more phallic spires of grass. But Walt inwardly cried, "No, no." When Traubel asked whether the so-called "free love matter" had come up, Walt nodded, quoting Emerson's admonition: "You are in danger of being tangled up in the unfortunate heresy." Was Emerson shocked at the idea of free love, asked Traubel. "Not at all," said Walt. "He was calm, equable, agreeable . . . not a man to be scared or shocked . . . too wholesome, too well-balanced, to be moved by the small-fry moralities, the miniature vices."

It might have profited Walt if he had ever chosen to read among the *Conduct of Life* essays the one called "Culture." Emerson wrote: "Very few of our race can be said to be yet finished men. We still carry sticking to us some remains of the preceding inferior quadruped organization. We call these millions men; but they are not yet men. Half engaged in the soil pawing to get free, man needs all the music that can be brought to disengage him." He repeated the trope of the quadruped when he speculated in 1862 that Henry Thoreau's "fancy for Walt Whitman" perhaps "grew out of his taste for wild nature, for an otter, a wood-chuck, or a loon. He loved sufficiency, hated a sum that would not prove: loved Walt and hated Alcott."

Early in April Eddy Emerson came down with typhoid fever. He was a slender stripling of fifteen, active in athletics, given to cricket matches, boxing with his friend Storrow Higginson, learning to fence with a fearsome cavalry sabre, or in his milder moments tending an aquarium filled with beetles, tadpoles, and salamanders, and acting in amateur theatricals in the Concord Town Hall and at the Forbes mansion in Milton. His mother and sisters tended him assiduously—"he is often out of his head," said Ellen—and he slowly recuperated, helped by a "treasury of gifts" from Sarah Forbes. Having lost Waldo to scarlet fever, his parents were worried, but by May 2 Emerson was able to report that after thirty-two days the boy had "crept . . . into something like safety and good assurance."

Apart from Eddy's illness, the big news of April was the attack on Frank Sanborn, who had been under threat of arrest since January. On the evening of April 3, he was sitting in his study at home when the doorbell rang. Five men barged into his front hall, one of whom, Silas Carleton, seized Frank's arm and placed him under arrest, reading out the senatorial orders. Sarah Sanborn, Frank's sister and housekeeper, ran out to raise the alarm, while the invaders handcuffed their victim and carried him to a waiting hack in the street. The long-legged Sanborn fought back, kicking in the flimsy door of the vehicle. Sarah grabbed the beard of one kidnapper, yanking so hard that her brother was lowered to the ground. The church bells were ringing as for a fire alarm, and a crowd was gathering. One of Ellen Emerson's friends, Grace Mitchell, scampered through the village like a small Paul Revere, ringing doorbells and screaming, "They've arrested Mr. Sanborn—go help him." Sanborn's lawyer quickly arranged with Judge Hoar for a writ of habeas corpus, and some 150 townspeople, including Emerson and some of Sanborn's Irish neighbors, formed a *posse comitatus* to drive the abductors away.

Sanborn spent the rest of the night at the house of George Prescott near the Old Manse. Ephraim Bull, the town magistrate and grape grower, lent him a six-shooter. Next morning in Boston several lawyers collaborated in his defense at the old Court House where the Supreme Judicial Court of Massachusetts was sitting under Chief Justice Lemuel Shaw, Herman Melville's aging father-in-law. Among the spectators were Wendell Phillips and Walt Whitman. Shaw ended the hearing by ordering Sanborn's release. One of the defense lawyers was John A. Andrew, whom Sanborn took pleasure in nominating for governor in the following September.

"Have you ever enjoyed the interest of being waked by alarm bells and joining a streetfight, as most of the ladies and gentlemen of Concord did last night?" wrote Ellen Emerson. "It must have been delightful, we were so sorry to miss it, but we could not leave Edward. However father and the man [James Burke] brought us news occasionally. Only think how well Miss Sanborn must have screamed. . . . I am so glad that such a thing has happened in my day. The town is in a high state of self-complacency, it flatters itself that this is the spirit of '76." One of his neighbors told Emerson that "a house in Concord was worth half as much again as a house in any other town, since the people had shown a good will to defend each other."

On May 23 Emerson interrupted his labors on the *Conduct of Life* collection long enough to take Lidian to the wedding of the Alcotts' daughter Anna to John Pratt. Sanborn, Thoreau, and Ephraim Bull were among the other guests. It was the elder Alcotts' thirtieth wedding anniversary. "Apple blossoms luxuriant," wrote Alcott in his journal, "and a company of true and real persons present to grace the occasion." Louisa's journal said: "We have had a little feast, sent by good Mrs. Judge Shaw; then the old folks danced round the bridal pair on the lawn in the German fashion . . . under our Revolutionary elm. . . . Mr. Emerson kissed her; and I thought the honor would make even matrimony endurable, for he is the god of my idolatry."

Two days after the Alcott wedding, Emerson turned fifty-seven. Under the rubric "Advantages of Old Age," he wrote in his journal that he was easier in his mind than formerly: "I could never give much reality to evil and pain. But now when my wife says, perhaps this tumor on your shoulder is a cancer, I say, what if it is?" In his essay on old age, the husband's answer became, "I am yielding to a surer decomposition." Always the lover of irony, Emerson cited the case of the thief who drank a pot of beer on his way to the gallows, taking care to blow off the foam because he had heard that it was unhealthy.

When Lidian fell ill again a week later, Ellen went to Boston to engage a new cook and a chambermaid. The problem of domestic help was perennial in the family, and the list of hirings and firings over a thirty-year period would, if kept, have filled a thick notebook. One memorable example was the acidulous Nancy Colesworthy, their cook in the 1830s, who had constantly complained that the number of guests for meals and overnight stays made the household into a virtual hotel. Ellen later recalled a shopping trip to Boston when she and Lidian happened to run into Nancy on Washington Street. "I have always regretted your leaving us," said Lidian, politely. "Mrs. Emerson," replied Nancy briskly, "I have never regretted it, not for a moment."

That spring Theodore Parker wrote George Ripley from Italy: "O, George, it is idle to run from Death. I shrank down behind the sugar canes of Santa Cruz, Death was there, too; then I sneaked into a Swiss valley, there he was; and here he is at Rome. I shall come home and meet him on my own dunghill." Instead he died at Florence on May 10 in his fiftieth year. He was buried in the English cemetery, a green and white island in the Piazzale Donatello, where he was to be successively joined by Elizabeth Barrett Browning, Arthur Hugh Clough, Frances Trollope, and Walter Savage Landor.

Back in Boston in June a number of his admirers planned a memorial service and invited Emerson to speak. At first he declined on the grounds that he was seeing his *Conduct of Life* volume through the press and could not spare the time for yet another address. "I have nothing to say of Parker," he told Moncure Conway. "I know well what a calamity is the loss of his courage and patriotism . . . but of his mind and genius, few are less accurately informed than I. It is for you and Sanborn and many excellent young men . . . to weigh and report. I have just written to his Society who have asked me to speak with [Wendell] Phillips, on the funeral occasion, that I must come to hear, not to speak; (though I shall not refuse to say a few words of honor.) My relations to him are quite accidental and our differences of method and working such as really required and honored all his catholicism and magnanimity to forgive in me. So I shall not write you an Essay: nor shall I in this mood, whilst I am hunted by printers . . . hope for reformation."

Their methods had indeed been different. Parker was by training a far better informed theologian than his friend in Concord, though they both began by hacking away at what Commager called "the theological underbrush"— seeking to extirpate the supererogatory growth of forms and doctrines that over the centuries had obscured the clear view of Jesus's moral counsel. But there were methodological oppositions. Parker characteristically wheeled up batteries of heavy artillery, as his biographer said, using his enormous library as his arsenal. Emerson, Zeus-like, loosed epigrammatic bolts of lightning: his literary eclecticism enabled him to select out a series of tropes to light up the sky, where Parker gained ground yard by yard with the grinding power of his logic. They split also on the matter of poetry. Parker had pointed to the "ruggedness" of some of Emerson's verse, its seemingly willful "want of finish"—a point well taken, though subject to debate. Emerson had longed to find in Parker's prose "a little more feeling for the poetic significance of his facts." This also was just. As Parker once told George Ripley, "I had much rather be such a great man like Franklin than a Michael Angelo. If I had a son, I should rather see him a great mechanic like George Stephenson in England than a great painter like Rubens who only copied beauty." But Emerson's pantheon was large enough to include the great writers and artists as well as the men of action: "I like the successes of George Stephenson, and Columbus, well-won, hard-earned, by 50 years of work, a sleepless eye and an invincible will. Do you not know that 'wisdom is not found in the hands of those who live at their ease'?"

In the end, although he did not write an essay on Parker, he delivered a generous estimate of his late friend at the memorial services on June 15. "At the death of a good and admirable person," he began, "we meet to console and animate each other by the recollection of his virtues." Parker's excellence had lain in a "strong understanding, a logical method, a love of facts, a rapid eye for their historical relations, and a skill in stripping them of traditional lustre." He had been "a man of study" who became "a man of the world," taking up his cudgel against all abusers and limiters of thought and action. The rough story of his life and work would leave oncoming generations in no doubt as to where he had stood. He had "decided opinions and plenty of power to state them." He had "made and held a party" in the service of freedom. Owing to his unremitting determination "to speak tart truth," no matter whose teeth might be set on edge, he was at one with Luther, Knox, Latimer, and Girolamo Savonarola. If he had any fault except the absence of a poetic sense, it was a too-generous tendency to overestimate his friends. "I may well say it," Emerson interpolated, remembering Parker's laudatory remarks of 1850.

The one point on which these two leading Transcendentalists saw absolutely eye to eye was Parker's insistence, which Emerson both recognized and shared, "that the essence of Christianity is its practical morals; it is there for use, or it is nothing." In the force with which his friend had espoused this doctrine, said Emerson, Parker had not a single rival among the preachers of his time. It was here that the two thinkers really met and merged, enabling the survivor to say that his friend, though so early dead, would continue to be "a living and enlarging power wherever learning, wit, honest valor, and independence are honored."

On June 28, after an absence of seven years, the Hawthornes returned to Concord in the midst of the first heat wave of the summer. After their grander residences in England and Italy, the Wayside looked small and rundown, and Hawthorne began, almost at once, to lay plans for its rehabilitation, including a tower room at the back of the house that he was going to call his "sky-parlor." On the twenty-ninth, despite a series of severe thundershowers, he and Sophia ate strawberries and cream at an evening party at the Emersons' in company with the Alcotts, Thoreau, Sanborn, and the Concord banker John Milton Cheney. Next day, again at Emerson's invitation, Hawthorne took the cars to Boston for a meeting of the Saturday Club at the Parker House. He found Emerson "unchanged in aspect" except for a "little hoar-frost" on his brown hair. "He has become earthlier during the past seven years," said Hawthorne, "for he puffs cigars like a true Yankee, and drinks wine like an Englishman."

Hawthorne himself had aged far more markedly. By his own account his hair had receded and turned gray, his face was "wrinkled with time and trouble," and in Italy he had raised a thick mustache that Sophia thought made him look like a bandit. Through all that rainy summer he renewed his former habits of seclusion, living what he called "a monotonous life, seldom quitting my own hillside and trying earnestly to take root here." Even at the jovial meetings of the Saturday Club he had little to say. Henry James Senior, father of the novelist-to-be, reported to Emerson on Hawthorne's behavior at one of these Parker House sessions: "He had the look . . . of a rogue who suddenly finds himself in a company of detectives," or perhaps a Concord owl, "expected to wink and be lively" in a day-lit gathering. He was not a "clubbable man," but buried his eyes in his plate, said James, "and ate with such a voracity that no person should dare ask him a question."

Hawthorne could at any rate look back with pride to the publication of his fourth major romance, *The Marble Faun*, both in England, where it was called *Transformation*, and at home, where critics like James Russell Lowell and E. P. Whipple, writing in the *Atlantic Monthly*, had given the book a decent send-off. His old friend Melville, ailing at forty, had sailed from Boston at the end of May aboard a clipper ship bound for San Francisco by way of Cape Horn. In his book bag was *The Marble Faun*, which he read in July while the *Meteor* plowed through wintry seas approaching Tierra del Fuego. He found Chapter 12, "The Emptiness of Picture-Galleries," to be "most original and admirable, and, doubtless, too true."

Henry Thoreau's only romance was with the fauna, flora, and geography of his Concord domain, where he regularly checked on the growth of trees and plants, and almost daily measured the height of the river and recorded the temperatures of every brook and spring. Otherwise he gave public lectures, surveyed Emerson's Walden woodlot, and bought graphite to carry on with the family pencil business. He would probably have scorned the speculation that Hawthorne had distantly portrayed him in Donatello, the faunlike Italian nobleman whose gradual transformation into a true human being was ironically effected by his murder of the malignant persecutor of the artist Miriam. No such Transcendentalist as he could share in Hawthorne's preoccupation with the theme of the Fortunate Fall. He was far more interested in the summit of Mount Monadnock, to which he and Ellery climbed in the rain of early August, and in the skin and skull of a Canadian lynx shot in the neighborhood and handed over to him for study and identification.

Throughout the long absence of the Tappan family in Europe in the late 1850s, Emerson and Caroline had kept in touch by mail. Writing from Rome in May 1857, Caroline said that she and her husband had been reading Emerson's poetry out on the purple Campagna in tune with the music of larks. In Paris and in Florence she had discussed the poems with Robert Browning, who professed great admiration for the "Dirge," the "Threnody," and "The Snow-Storm," among others. Rome itself seemed to Caroline "larger than America, with all its backwoods. And America from here looks sad, so almost lost and dead." She would like to stay on in Italy and "quite forget all the 'great moral questions of the day,' and not care much whether Kansas and Massachusetts are slave states or not." A year later she said, "I wish you had Music and Pictures there [in Concord] too and then I would bring my children there to live." Much of their correspondence during Caroline's absence had in fact involved a running debate in which Caroline asserted the values of Europe and art and Emerson defended America and nature.

In July 1860 she was spending the summer at Cotuit, a small port on the south shore of Cape Cod a few miles east of Falmouth. When she "implored"

Emerson to come down for a visit, he took the train from Concord in the afternoon of August 2, and afterward reported to Abel Adams that he had spent a "pair of beautiful days" in Cotuit, where "their little mimic port looks so like a picture before them, that I fancied it was a drop-scene which could be drawn up and down, and I should see nothing but pine woods again. But it lasted honest sea, whilst I stayed." At home the first pear appeared and, said Ellen, "was pompously eaten," though the chief available fruit was an abundance of huckleberries.

The autumn began pleasantly enough, though incipient tragedy lurked unseen in the background. On September 10 Emerson walked out with Ellery Channing to Estabrook Farm on what he called the finest day of the year, "a cornucopia of golden joys," with all the "crickets in full cry" and clouds of gnats freckling the sunbeams. On the ninth, Sophia Hawthorne had looked in on Edith Emerson's lawn party for the neighborhood children. Edith, now eighteen, had spread a table under the trees with flowers and cakes, and a dozen youngsters screamed and capered around the Emersons' indignant parrot. Lidian was there, pale as milk, flitting into and out of the house in a black silk gown and lacy cap that made her look like a "Lady Abbess," the same phrase that Sophia had applied to her tall neighbor in the 1840s.

Less than two weeks later, the Hawthornes' daughter Una, aged sixteen, came down with a high fever and was soon writhing in delirium. It seemed at first like a recurrence of the disease that had stricken her in November 1858 while her father was struggling with the early draft of *The Marble Faun* and for six months had made a hell of the Roman spring of 1859. During one major crisis that April, when the girl's life was feared for, Elizabeth Browning and Anna Ward had often called to soothe Sophia. Now, in renewed desperation, the Hawthornes summoned a female therapist named Rollins, who came over from Cambridge to administer electric shock treatments. Una's violent writhings stopped at once, no further restraints were needed, and Hawthorne had nothing but astonished praise for the "incantations" of this "electrical witch." The Forbes family in Milton were not so lucky. Just as Hawthorne was reporting to Franklin Pierce that Una was out of danger, the Forbeses' daughter Ellen, twin sister of Alice, fell ill and suddenly died. Emerson, who had known the girl for three years, composed a heartfelt letter of consolation.

Early in October, gale-force winds strewed Emerson's orchard with fallen pears and apples. Henry Thoreau, nosing around to assess the damage, reflected that the Emersonian pears were all named "after emperors and kings and queens and dukes and duchesses." He feared that he would "have to wait till we get to pears with American names, which a republican can swallow." In the same week a twelve-second earthquake rattled the dishes in Emerson's cupboard in the early morning of October 17, which happened to be the first anniversary of John Brown's attack on Harpers Ferry. Emerson's journal called the visitation "Queenie's private earthquake," which by her report took place "*in the afternoon,* and that of the rest of the world at 6 in the morning."

Through all that summer and fall the bitterly contested political campaign had been waged among Abraham Lincoln, Stephen Douglas, and the secessionist candidate, John Breckinridge. On November 6 Lincoln won over Douglas by half a million votes and by a million over Breckinridge. On the seventh Senator Charles Sumner came to Concord to lecture on Lafayette and to celebrate the Republican victory at Emerson's house. Emerson called the news "sublime, the pronunciation of the masses of America against Slavery." A week later he attended the dedication ceremonies of Louis Agassiz's Zoological Museum at Cambridge. His daughters, Ellen and Edith, had been attending the Agassiz family's school, and his admiration for Agassiz was strong, not only because he was a fellow member of the Saturday Club, a friendly and accessible man, but also because his roots were in nature, extending back to prehistoric times, and because he wished to place natural science on a par with religion.

After his day in Cambridge Emerson delightedly watched a stereoscopic exhibition in the Town Hall, where views of London, Paris, Switzerland, Spain, and Egypt were projected on the wall for the benefit of an audience most of whose members had never been outside Massachusetts. Even to Emerson, the far traveler, it seemed "the last and most important application of this wonderful art," and he thought that "the lovely manner in which one picture was changed for another beat the faculty of dreaming." Many residents of Concord were already familiar with the stereoscope on a smaller scale: handheld instruments into which double pictures of the same scene or object could be inserted to provide a single three-dimensional image. During one of Hawthorne's rare evening visits to the Emerson household, when only Edith and Eddy were present to receive him, he covered his shyness by taking up the family's stereoscope and gazing for some minutes at views of Concord's chief landmarks. At last he looked up and asked the younger Emersons where the pictures had been taken. "We told him," wrote Eddy, that he had been seeing photographs of the "Concord Court and Town-houses, the Common and the Mill-dam, on hearing which he expressed some surprise and interest, but evidently was as unfamiliar with the centre of the village where he had lived for years as a deer or a wood-thrush would be. He walked through it often on his way to the cars, but was too shy or too rapt to know what was there."

Emerson was content to be surrounded once more with his crew of associates—Alcott and Hawthorne dwelling side by side half a mile from his front door, Thoreau and Channing available for afternoon walks through the countryside. It was characteristic of him that he thought of them as friends, not as disciples. "This is my boast," he had written in 1859, "that I have no school and no follower." His aim had always been to convert men to themselves, to "create independence" rather than its opposite. What he could not have known at the end of 1860 was how soon two of the four would be lost to him. On December 3, squatting in the snow to count the rings in a sawn-down hickory, Thoreau "took a severe cold," followed by "a kind of bronchitis" that confined him to his house all winter except for a "very few experimental trips" to the post office. The shark's tooth was not yet fully visible in the gray and wrinkled Hawthorne, but it was already there, and the decade of the 1860s was not yet half over when he followed Thoreau.

Chapter Forty-two

IN TIME
OF WAR

"BLESSED BE THE INEVITABILITIES," WROTE EMERSON IN January 1861. The foremost among them was the war, which was widely predicted now that South Carolina had seceded from the Union shortly before Christmas 1860. Emerson thought that both the helpers and the hinderers of slavery had been about equally diligent in hastening its downfall. But he well knew that all the supporters of slavery were not in the South, a position that was dramatized for him when he accepted an invitation from Wendell Phillips to speak at Tremont Temple before a meeting of the Massachusetts Anti-Slavery Society. Sorely against his inclination and habit, but believing that all thinking men must assume the public duty of speaking out in a defense of freedom, he stood up at the rostrum and attempted to read a short prepared statement. But the hall was so packed with antiabolitionists that his words were drowned out: "The mob roared whenever I attempted to speak, and after several beginnings, I withdrew."

The experience disappointed but did not faze him. In the middle of March he attended a party in Concord to honor Alcott for his two-year term as superintendent of schools. For this occasion Alcott's daughter Louisa May had written a song that contained an allusion to John Brown. Some of the townspeople found this offensive and moved to suppress the stanza. But Emerson said, "It must be sung, and not only sung but read [aloud] first, and I will read it."

During most of March and April, Ellen Emerson was away from home, evidently to recover from the fatigue occasioned by her domestic responsibilities. At first with the Forbes family at Milton Hill, then with the Ward family at Louisburg Square in Boston, she went finally to board for a month with Mr. and Mrs. Increase Smith of Dorchester. She was there on April 12 when General Beauregard ordered the predawn bombardment of Fort Sumter in Charleston harbor, the opening engagement of the Civil War. "Alas that Fort Sumter should be lost so easily," she wrote. In church that Sunday the minister quoted the words of Jesus from Matthew 24: "Ye shall hear of wars and rumors of wars; see that ye be not troubled; for all these things must come to pass, but the end is not yet." When Increase Smith remarked to Ellen, "There are some things infinitely worse than war," she answered, "There are some things better than peace." She sent her brother, Eddy, an account of the Federal warships that were being readied for action at the Charlestown Navy Yard: the *Illinois,* the *Powhatan,* the *Minnesota.* "It appears," said she, "that we are actually fighting now," and signed herself, "Your warlike sister."

Her increasingly warlike father agreed. When given a tour of the Navy Yard, he was heard to exclaim that gunpowder could sometimes smell good. He composed a new lecture, "Civilization at a Pinch," for interpolation into a course on "Life and Literature" that he was offering in Boston. It took note of the "whirlwind of patriotism" that had arisen since Lincoln's call for 75,000 volunteers, and was "magnetizing all discordant masses under its terrific unity." He vowed never again to speak lightly of a crowd—even such a crowd as had hooted him down in January. "We are wafted into a revolution which, though at first sight a calamity of the human race, finds all men in good heart, in courage, in a generosity of mutual and patriotic support. . . . Now we have a country again. . . . The nation which the Secessionists hoped to shatter has to thank them for a more sudden and hearty union than the history of parties ever showed."

Concord responded to Lincoln's call with some four dozen volunteers under the command of Lieutenant George Prescott. On April 19 they assembled at noon around the flagstaff, while the church bells rang and the cannon barked. They listened to short speeches by Judge Hoar, Emerson, and Alcott, were prayed over by the Reverend Grindall Reynolds, sang "Hail, Columbia," and marched to the depot to catch the 1:30 train for Boston. The town raised $4,400 to defray their expenses on the way to Washington. Eddy Emerson said that "the 19th of April this year is a day such as Concord hasn't had since the 19th of April 1775."

Eddy was soon practicing close-order drill with other boys his age; his sister Edith began a scrapbook of news clippings about the war; their neighbor Louisa Alcott wrote in her diary that "we all seem like one family in times like these. . . . I long to be a man; but as I can't fight, I will content myself with working for those who can." Feeling lucky that Julian was too young to bear arms, Hawthorne told his publisher that he would himself volunteer except for his age. As the case stood, he resolved to keep quiet until the enemy reached a point a mile from the Wayside. Next door, Alcott chose to cultivate his garden. He had proved his moral and physical courage on other occasions. Now he planted potatoes, beans, sweet corn, and cucumbers and stood back to admire the neat and serried rows.

Ellen accompanied Lidian, who was wearing "rept silk" and a new spring bonnet, to hear Emerson lecture in Boston on "Poetry and Criticism in England and America"—"Father laughs at the long title," said Ellen. He surprised and saddened his daughter by saying that "Tennyson was after all only the sublime of Magazine poets," recommended Byron's *Hebrew Melodies*, called Browning "ingenious," and read passages from Ben Jonson and Sir Walter Scott. But the war was on his mind next morning when he called on Governor Andrew and took away an authorization to procure thirty muskets from the Cambridge Arsenal, returning home triumphantly to tell the Concord drill club that they would soon be able to march with honest-to-God guns.

Thoreau was still fighting to stay alive. Doctors had urged him to try the West Indies, but in his contrary fashion he opted for Minnesota, leaving on May 11 with his young friend and fellow naturalist Horace Mann Junior. The day before he left, Ellen Emerson brought him a map of the Middle West and asked him to dinner. Emerson supplied a letter of introduction with a list of his friends to whom it might be presented, "praying them, from me, not to let you pass by without salutation, and any aid and comfort they can administer to an invalid traveller, one so dear and valued by me and all good Americans."

Except for a long letter to Frank Sanborn from Redwing, Minnesota, at the end of June, Henry kept only a brief journal-record of his abortive journey.

He was plainly the worse for wear when the travelers returned to Concord on July 9. This happened to be the day when Fanny Longfellow, the poet's wife, set her summer dress on fire while sealing a letter with hot wax, and fled screaming to her husband, who tried vainly to extinguish the flames, burning his own face and arms. She was still in a coma when she died next day. Thoreau's own death was longer in coming. "Never deserted by his good genius," as Ellery Channing wrote, "he most bravely . . . passed down the inclined plane of a terrible malady, pulmonary consumption. . . . Having caught the Indian trick of superlative reticence, he calmly bore the fatal torture . . . working steadily at the completion of his papers . . . so long as he could hold a pencil in his trembling fingers." One by one he sent copies of his essays to James Fields for publication in the *Atlantic* and, when he could no longer write, dictated his correspondence to his faithful sister Sophia. At dinner with him that December, Alcott found him "lively and entertaining, though feeble and failing." Emerson said, "I am ever threatened by the decays of Henry T."

Eddy Emerson was eager to enlist, but when Abel Adams offered to put him through Harvard—partly to repair "the losses which his advice on railroad securities" had occasioned to Emerson—the boy took the entrance examinations, relaxing from the ordeal with trips to Monadnock and then to Naushon to see his idol Will Forbes before buckling down to his books. Just at this time, July 21, Union forces suffered a severe defeat at the First Battle of Bull Run. "Everything shines with us but the Washington news," wrote Emerson. Nine days later Company G of the Fifth Massachusetts Regiment returned to Concord. Four local families had lost sons and brothers, but the worn survivors marched from the depot to the Court House elm, listening to a prayer by the Reverend Mr. Reynolds and a greeting from Judge Hoar. Ellen Emerson reported to her uncle that their officer, George Prescott, was now known everywhere as "the model Massachusetts Captain."

That month Caroline Tappan had written from Lenox that "although not the echo of a drum reaches us," she and her husband could only "talk war, think war, dream war, amid our bees and butterflies." It was a shame that "the most enlightened nation in the world" must fight for its beliefs. "One word of justice through the land should be the rallying point. If there were no slave there would be no rebel, and common honesty demands why there should be a slave among us. . . . Of course we must all go by red tape now-a-days, even if we are to bequeath fugitive slave bills to our children, and other meek Christian compromises."

In August Emerson sent his friend Cabot a fuller analysis:

The war,—though from such despicable beginnings, has assumed such huge proportions that it threatens to engulf us all—no preoccupation can exclude it, and no hermitage hide us— And yet, gulf as it is, the war with its defeats and uncertainties is immensely better than what we lately called the integrity of the Republic, as amputation is better than cancer. . . . If the abundance of heaven only sends us a fair share of light and conscience, we shall redeem America for all its sinful years since the century began. At first sight, it looked only as a war of manners, show-ing that the southerner who owes to climate and slavery his suave, cool, and picturesque manners, is so impatient of ours, that he must fight us off. And we all admired them until a long experience . . . has shown us, I think finally, what a noxious reptile the green and gold thing was. . . . Their detestation of Massachusetts is a chemical description of their substance, and if a state more lawful, honest, and cultivated were known to them, they would transfer to it their detestation. . . . Their crimes force us into virtues to antagonize them and we are driven into princi-ples by their abnegation of them. . . . But one thing I hope,—that "scholar" and "hermit" will no longer be exempts, neither by the coun-try's permission nor their own. . . . The good heart and mind, out of all private corners, should speak and save.

Eddy's first try at Harvard ended in October. "Our poor Edward found he had no strength for College," wrote Ellen, "and is at home again trying to get well, but seems to pine more and more, though doing nothing but ride on horseback when he is able, and amuse himself with society and painting or ly-ing down when he isn't, and his papa is brokenhearted that College is lost." Harvard's President Felton had agreed to his return in 1862 without further examinations. But the boy, said Emerson, was full of other schemes, such as joining "the Hudson's Bay Company," or crossing the plains to California, or carrying a chain on a railroad survey, or going to Maine with a lumberers' gang. In the end he went down to Milton Hill, John Forbes having found him a job surveying lots in Mount Auburn Cemetery. Despite the onset of winter, the outdoor life appealed to him, though he could not help envying his friend Will Forbes, who had applied for a commission as second lieutenant in the First Regiment of Cavalry, Massachusetts Volunteers, and was mustered in the day after Christmas. "I believe all wise fathers are coming to feel that they have no right to dissuade their sons from this career," wrote Emerson to John Forbes. But Eddy was neither old enough nor well enough for soldiering, although his father rightly guessed that he was "always dreaming of a commission in the cavalry, since William Forbes went away." At home in Concord, said Emerson, "we are all knitting socks and mittens for soldiers, writing patriotic lectures, and economizing with all our mights."

Emerson gave his second patriotic lecture of the war years at the Smithsonian in Washington on January 31, 1862. "The South calls slavery an institution," he said. "I call it destitution. . . . We have attempted to hold together two states of civilization: a higher state, where labor and the tenure of land and the right of suffrage are democratical; and a lower state in which the old military tenure of prisoners and slaves, and of power and land in a few hands, make an oligarchy. . . . Our whole history appears like a last effort of the Divine Providence in behalf of the human race. . . . Emancipation is the demand of civilization. . . . Whilst Slavery makes and keeps disunion, Emancipation removes the whole objection to union. . . . Why should not America be capable of a second stroke for the well-being of the human race, as eighty or ninety years ago she was for the first? . . . The end of all political struggle is to establish morality as the basis of all legislation. . . . Ideas must work through the brains and arms of good and brave men, or they are no better than dreams."

After his speech Emerson spent a long weekend in Washington. His old friend Senator Sumner took him in hand to meet all the topmost leaders, including President Lincoln, whom he saw twice, once on Saturday, February 1, and again after church on the second. "The President impressed me more favorably than I had hoped," he wrote. "A frank, sincere, well-meaning man, with a lawyer's habit of mind, good clear statement of his fact, correct enough, not vulgar, as described; but with a sort of boyish cheerfulness; or that kind of sincerity and jolly good meaning that our [Harvard] class meetings on Commencement Days show, in telling our old stories over. When he has made his remark, he looks up at you with great satisfaction, and shows all his white teeth, and laughs. . . . When I was introduced to him, he said, 'O, Mr Emerson, I once heard you say in a lecture that a Kentuckian seems to say by his air and manners, *"Here am I; if you don't like me, the worse for you!"* ' " Since Lincoln himself was a native of Kentucky, Emerson's sentence had stuck in his memory.

Guided by Sumner, Emerson called on William H. Seward in his dingy State Department quarters. Waiting in the anteroom were two friends of Emerson's, Governor John A. Andrew of Massachusetts and John Murray Forbes, both of whom had been active in the prosecution of the war. When Sumner brought them in, Seward lighted a large, half-smoked cigar. Forbes spoke up for Nathaniel Gordon of Portland, Maine, who had been accused of slave-trading and would be hanged in New York three weeks later. Seward looked angry and replied with a coarse remark that so disconcerted Forbes that he and Andrew soon took their leave. Seward closed the interview by asking Emerson to church and dinner next day. That evening, Emerson and Sumner dined with the Treasury Secretary, Salmon P. Chase, whose "pretty daughter Kate . . . did the honors of the house." Chase said that he was organizing 12,000 ex-slaves at Port Royal, paying them wages and teaching them to read.

Meeting Seward on Sunday morning, Emerson said that he hoped the secretary "would not demoralize me; I was not much accustomed to churches, but trusted he would carry me to a safe place." The church was St. John's Episcopal. "I had the old wonder come over me," wrote Emerson, "at the Egyptian stationariness of the English church. The hopeless blind antiquity of life and thought . . . was wonderful to see." The Reverend Smith Pyne's sermon "preached Jacobitish passive obedience to powers that be"—a position that seemed to please Seward, though Emerson felt that the good doctor "had not got quite down into these noisy times."

At the White House afterward they found Lincoln's two small sons being dressed and barbered for Sunday. One of them bet Seward a quarter that he could not guess what new pet they had got. Seward suggested a bird or a pig, and paid up when it turned out to be a rabbit. When Lincoln appeared, Seward asked if he had been to church. "No," said the president. He had been reading Senator Sumner's speech on the *Trent* affair, the maritime incident of the preceding November, when a captain in the Federal Navy had boarded the British mail steamer *Trent* and taken off a pair of Confederate emissaries named Mason and Slidell, precipitating an international crisis that was luckily settled by peaceful diplomacy. When Seward summarized Dr. Pyne's sermon, Lincoln said that he "intended to show his respect for him some time by going to hear him."

Emerson rounded out his Sunday by dining with Seward and Kate and afterward with Mrs. Samuel Hooper, an old friend from Massachusetts who had since moved to wartime Washington. That evening he spent at the house of Charles Eames, a retired diplomat, where he met Lincoln's young secretaries, Hay and Nicolay, as well as Lincoln's eldest son, Robert. Returning to his hotel "at a late hour," he suddenly remembered that Edwin M. Stanton, the secretary of war, had invited him to call that same evening. This was vexatious, but at any rate, thanks to Sumner, he had managed to meet the president, whom he ever afterward revered, and enough of the other men in power to learn how they were trying to assist Divine Providence in behalf of the human race.

During Emerson's absence, all the Concord women who could sew held a mass meeting to make clothes for some of Salmon Chase's huge band of black people at Port Royal. Alcott took cider and apples as a gift for Thoreau, who spoke impatiently of the "temporary policy of our rulers" and also blamed the people for their seeming indifference "to the great issues of national honor and justice." He was critical of Seward's handling of the *Trent* affair, which he thought dishonorable and humiliating. About his own condition, however, Henry was notably stoical. He told one of his correspondents that he was "enjoying existence as much as ever." When Parker Pillsbury asked how the farther shore looked to him, he brusquely answered, "One world at a time," and when his Aunt Louisa wondered whether he had made his peace with God he said, "I did not know we had ever quarreled." All his visitors noticed his increasing emaciation and the hoarseness that reduced his once-strong voice to a whisper. On April 2, Emerson told him that Walden Pond was still frozen: he had just walked across it twice. Henry whispered that he had known the ice to hold as late as the eighteenth. He was right as usual: the ice that year finally broke up on the nineteenth.

"It is better," he had told Ellery Channing, "[that] some things should end." They ended very peacefully for him at nine on the morning of May 6. The funeral was held in the First Parish Church on the ninth with a hymn by Channing, prayers and Bible readings by Reynolds, extracts by Alcott from Henry's own writings, and a poignant eulogy by Emerson. The coffin was

placed in the New Burying Ground at the foot of Bedford Street, to be transferred only long afterward to Author's Ridge in Sleepy Hollow a few hundred
yards to the south.

Three days after the funeral, Eddy Emerson fulfilled a six-months' dream
by setting out overland for California. His traveling companion was Cabot
Russel of New York, whom he had befriended at Harvard in 1861. The trip
was undertaken in lieu of military service and in the expectation that it would
benefit the boy's health. Despite the war and occasional Indian raids, long
trains of emigrant wagons were crossing the plains and mountains of the west
heading for the Promised Land. The boys' itinerary took them by rail, stage,
and horseback to Omaha, Forts Kearney and Laramie, Salt Lake, Carson
City, Sacramento, and at last to San Francisco. From there in September
Eddy would sail for Panama, cross the isthmus, and return up the coast to
Boston in time to reenter Harvard in October.

The Emerson daughters, Ellen and Edith, spent most of July at Newport,
staying with the Wards at their house on Ocean Point, but mainly with the
family of Henry James Senior, whom Emerson had known since 1842 and
who had sired a lively brood of four sons and a daughter. The two younger
boys, Wilky and Robbie, had been pupils at the Sanborn School in Concord,
classmates of Eddy Emerson and Julian Hawthorne. Now, with their sister
Alice and the older sons, William and Henry, they were all assembled in joyous turbulence. "We are staying at the Jameses' now," wrote Ellen, "and having the best time in the world, laughing continually, of course, what with Mr
James and all the four boys, and taking walks on the Cliffs, drives on the Avenue, baths on the beach, and going to parties in the evening. But the funniest
thing in the world is to see this delectable family together all talking at once.
Edith and I spend all dinner-time in convulsions." The whole group delighted her—William, the future philosopher, "the happiest, queerest boy in
the world"; Harry, the future novelist, "the most lovely, gentle and good";
Wilky "equally queer and equally good but very different"; and Robby, a
"dear child" who, "by his piquant silence and dancing eyes kept us in a
chronic fever of curiosity."

But there was a more serious side to life in Newport. Ten miles north of
the town was the military hospital at Portsmouth Grove, a tented camp diversified with enormous new sheds where 1,800 casualties from Yorktown and
Williamsburg had been landed from naval transports to recuperate, but also

sometimes to die, in the salubrious summer air of Rhode Island. "There at Portsmouth Grove," wrote Ellen, "I passed the most valuable morning of the year; I was left alone with a hundred convalescent soldiers for two or three hours and asked every question that I had long been wishing to have answered. . . . I returned utterly unable to send anyone to the war with cheerfulness." In marked contrast was the Naval School at Fort Adams on the nearby peninsula. "We walked up on the ramparts and looked down on the long line of Midshipmen drilling, in their blue suits, straw hats, and shining belts." Some of them volunteered to show the girls around and said that they would soon be back aboard the *Constitution,* which was just being repainted. They did not look forward to the close quarters and the frightful monotony of life at sea. "Your report is admirable of your soldiers," wrote Emerson to his daughter, "and tis a strange tragic interlude in a Newport summer. But it being there, I am glad you should meet it."

Back in Concord, Emerson was reading through Henry Thoreau's letters and journals: "Henry T. remains erect, calm, self-subsistent, before me, and I read him not only truly in his journal, but he is not long out of mind when I walk, and, as today, row upon the pond. He chose wisely no doubt for himself to be the bachelor of thought and nature that he was,—how near to the old monks in their ascetic religion! He had no talent for wealth, and knew how to be poor without the least hint of squalor or inelegance. Perhaps he fell, all of us do, into his way of living, without forecasting it much, but approved and confirmed it with later wisdom." Apart from Henry's way of life, Emerson took delight in his skills in gnomic utterance. In his article for the *Atlantic,* he selected out two dozen Thoreauvian epigrams as evidence of his late friend's wit and worth: "Dead trees love the fire. . . . The bluebird carries the sky on his back. . . . No tree has so fair a bole and so handsome an instep as the beech. . . . The chub is a soft fish, and tastes like boiled brown paper salted." At the head of his list was one that he had not truly understood until the always alert Ellen explained it to him: "Some circumstantial evidence is very strong, as when you find a trout in the milk." Lidian thought that the trout could just as well have been a mouse, but Ellen cried no, that was not the point: someone had watered the milk to bring a better sale price. This was a view that her father had not thought of, and he urged Ellen to try the question on her friends at the next party where games were played. She was astonished that he had not seen the point at once, since he was such a great lover of proverbs, and had himself devised many that had already become a part of the language.

"The war drags on and drags us all into it," wrote Emerson to his brother that July, "ourselves, our children, or our friends. . . . The adult generation seems to have for the most part yielded the point that the juniors must on this matter take their own course. And when they prosper in it, how heartily we applaud them!" Yet there was the other side. His daily newspapers told him that juniors from all northern ranks were dying in the south—Richmond, Ball's Bluff, Antietam—whether sons of Boston Brahmins or farmers' boys from Concord: "the children of our public schools, the children of Harvard College, the best blood of our educated counties." One's voice choked to name those already dead: Winthrop, Lowell, Dwight, Shaw, Bowditch. "Will you send them to die?" he asked himself, and answered, "Yes, when I consider what they have sealed and saved, freedom for the world." He quoted the *Iliad*: "One omen is best, to fight for one's country." Perhaps Hawthorne had been right in saying that "Emerson is breathing slaughter like the rest of us." If the means were dark and bloody, the ends were just and honorable.

When Lincoln issued his preliminary Emancipation Proclamation on September 22, Emerson hailed the act before an audience in Boston. "Every step in the history of political liberty," he said, "is a sally of the human mind into an untried future." He admired the "extreme moderation" with which the president was advancing his design: "He has been permitted to do more for America than any other man." It was almost as if "one midsummer day" had repaired the damage of a year of war. On the first day of the new year of 1863 "the hour will strike and all men of African descent who have faculty enough to find their way to our lines are assured of the protection of American law." The proclamation could not "promise the redemption of the black race; that lies not with us; but it relieves it of our opposition." This war had "existed long before the cannonade of Sumter" and now the public distress was about to be relieved. "With this blot removed from our national honor . . . we shall not fear henceforward to show our faces among mankind."

Eddy returned on October 6, tanned from his sea voyage but otherwise worn and wasted. Although he took the earliest opportunity to convince his father that "his sole duty and necessity was to go to the war," he reluctantly agreed to reenter Harvard, this time with the class of 1866. "He is not a soldier as he tho't himself when he left San Francisco," wrote Emerson. "The boy has much fitness for the college and . . . would like to go with his mates who are now there." One of his classmates was Tom Ward, who undertook to watch over him with care, keeping the alarm clock in his own room and letting Eddy sleep until the last minute before classes began, and stealing a roll each morning from Miss Upham's boardinghouse table as a breakfast supplement. "Edward lives in clover," said Ellen. When she asked if his new room was better than his old one in Brattle House, he exclaimed with enthusiasm, "Ain't it!" and read her extracts from his favorite Aristophanes as long as the light lasted. Emancipation was all the talk at home in Concord, and Lidian rejoiced "often and aloud," surprised that the sky looked no different than usual, and looking forward with high expectation to January 1, 1863.

Chapter Forty-three

GRANDEUR
AND DUST

THE NEW YEAR OF 1863 BEGAN AUSPICIOUSLY ENOUGH WITH the salute to Lincoln's Emancipation Proclamation at the Boston Music Hall. Emerson read his occasional poem "Boston Hymn," in which God was made to speak to the American people of His grand design for the rehabilitation of the world through the Angel of Freedom. It was not a great poem, but it contained at least two memorable stanzas that produced a standing ovation and were afterward widely quoted:

> Today unbind the captive,
> So only are ye unbound;
> Lift up a people from the dust,
> Trump of their rescue, sound!
>
> Pay ransom to the owner
> And fill the bag to the brim.
> Who is the owner? The slave is the owner,
> And ever was. Pay him.

At home that morning the Emersons had followed their custom of family gift giving for New Year's Day. "We had the usual solemn breakfast," wrote Ellen to her cousin Haven, "and Father was in his usual haste to see what his presents were, and he had one beauty which the children made, a little white-pine tray with pictures drawn on it by Edward, then blacked by Edith all round the figures, and varnished, and it is to hold his pens. The children wrote amazing poems to go with it and Father was graciously pleased." One new member of the family was Ellen's semiadopted "daughter," Edith Davidson, aged ten, "whose delight was unbounded," particularly with the bowl of sugar plums.

Walt Whitman, who had been quiescent enough since his colloquy with Emerson on Boston Common in 1860, had just written to say that, having wandered through camp and battle scenes, he had recently "fetched up" in Washington. His health was superb but his purse was empty. He wished to approach certain eminent men in the hope of getting employment, and needed letters of introduction. He had drafted a sample "form," and asked Emerson to prepare duplicates of "something like" it, enclosing his recommendations in envelopes directed to Salmon P. Chase, secretary of the Treasury, and William H. Seward, secretary of state. "Answer me by next mail," he urged, "for I am waiting here like ship waiting for the welcome breath of the wind."

This somewhat presumptuous request followed his previous habit with Emerson. As he told Traubel later, "I was pulling eminent wires in those days." His letter reached Emerson at an inconvenient time, just as he was leaving for a lecture tour of Canada and upstate New York. He spent Sunday, January 4, at Niagara Falls and went to bed that night in the American House only to be awakened at three next morning by cries of "Fire." He threw on his clothes, hurried "down stairs through a cloud of smoke and cinders," and found barefoot women swathed in hotel blankets and "great distress everywhere." The hotel was gutted, leaving nothing but the four walls, but Emerson escaped with no losses except some hairbrushes and his railroad tickets from Buffalo to Chicago, and went off to Toronto to talk about "Classes of Men." But he took time on his return to Buffalo to send the recommendations, assuring Chase that Walt Whitman was a man of "marked eccentricities, great powers and valuable traits of character: a self-relying large-hearted man, much beloved by his friends; entirely patriotic and benevolent in his theory, tastes, and practice." If his writings were "in certain points open to criticism," they showed "extraordinary power," and were "more deeply American, democratic, and in the interest of political liberty, than those of any other poet." He would "quickly make himself useful," and the government might well discover that it had "called to its side more valuable aid than it bargained for."

Emerson's letter to Seward made the same points in slightly different language, adding that Whitman was "a child of the people, and their champion." There was another letter to Senator Sumner, who had introduced Emerson to the two cabinet members in 1862, and whose help might now be crucial to Whitman's cause. Even though these letters made it clear that Whitman was "markedly eccentric" and that his *Leaves of Grass* was in some respects "open to criticism," they were hardly less generous than Emerson's original salute to Walt in 1855.

Despite Emerson's generous support, Walt did not approach either Seward or Chase until the following December when young John Trowbridge volunteered to deliver the by now somewhat dog-eared envelope to Chase. But Chase felt that Walt was "decidedly disreputable" and declined to arrange for his appointment into the federal bureaucracy. Walt later told Traubel that the letter to Seward was never delivered. It was not until January 1865, when the war was winding down, that he landed a clerkship in the Department of the Interior. This lasted about six months until Secretary James Harlan, "a grim Iowa Methodist," happened to find a copy of the *Leaves* in Walt's desk drawer, read it with rising indignation, and summarily sacked its author.

Walt's sojourn in Washington in 1862–63 happened to coincide with that of Louisa Alcott, who had come down from Concord as a volunteer nurse, working from noon to midnight in the hellhole of the Union Hotel Hospital. After three weeks of constant labor, she fell ill with typhoid and pneumonia. Heavily dosed with calomel, the old bane of Lidian Emerson's life, she awoke from a troubled sleep on January 16 to find her father at her bedside. He had been summoned from home by a telegram from Louisa's supervisor, the famous Dorothea Dix, and now quickly concluded, "I see not how she is to regain strength by remaining here. Horrid war; and one sees its horrors in hospitals if any-where." When the doctors at last agreed that she could go, Louisa and her father accomplished the horrendous train trip home, reaching Orchard House on the twenty-fourth. The Emersons' Dr. Bartlett confirmed the diagnosis and was encouragingly hopeful. But her recovery was slow, punctuated with high fever, delirium, and hallucinations. The family collaborated in day-and-night nursing, and Lidian Emerson lent them a maid to help in the scullery. Louisa lost a great deal of weight and all her hair. It was a month before she came downstairs for breakfast and another before her father wrote that "Louisa leaves her chamber and begins to clothe herself with flesh after the long waste of fever."

Louisa was still recovering when Lidian complained that she never saw her own busy daughter. So, wrote Ellen to her cousin Haven, "I forsook the housekeeping and gave up two or three regular engagements, and just as I would visit any-one else I am staying with her. Before she wakes in the morning I attend to my affairs, and then I sit with her all day except walking-time, and do things she wants done and read over her old papers and letters to see what shall be burned. In this way we are accomplishing something and having a great deal of comfort. I do not however give up Soldiers' Aid, or Italian with Uncle George [Bradford], or Dante with Aunt Lizzie [Hoar], and I continue faithful to both Bible classes, which grow more and more delightful as we get to know more."

Apart from such activities, Ellen took long rides with Eddy when he was home from Harvard, urging the two family mares, Dolly and Grace, up the hill behind the Alcotts' house, and once riding through Sleepy Hollow Cemetery to debate the question of a suitable family monument. "Our plan," she wrote her cousin, "if our dear docile papa does agree, is that this cube . . . will have five sides . . . one for us, one for you, one for Grandma, Aunt Mary, and Uncle Bulkeley, and Uncle Edward if he should be removed here, and two for future generations. We are in great danger of leaving the affair unattended to, and I mean never to let the question rest till something is done. . . . I hope your household doesn't hate the subject as some people do."

This cemetery visit, though not exactly prescient, was timely enough. On May Day, Emerson's eccentric aunt, Mary Moody Emerson, aged eighty-eight, died at Williamsburg, New York, where she had spent her declining years. Cousin Hannah Parsons, who had watched over her lifelong, brought the body to Concord and the Emerson family and Elizabeth Hoar followed the hearse to a grave beside that of Emerson's mother. "In so many later years," he wrote his brother William, Aunt Mary had been "only a wreck, and in all years could so readily be repulsive . . . [and] her behavior [so] intolerable . . . that few know or care for her genius. . . . Yet . . . her letters and journals charm me still as thirty years ago, and honor the American air."

The exigencies of the war called Emerson away from Concord in June, when he went to West Point Military Academy as a member of the "Board of Visitors" by appointment of the secretary of the war, Edwin M. Stanton. He was agreeably impressed by conditions in the barracks and by the evident devotion of the cadet corps. Discipline was so strict that these "military monks" never trespassed off post and spent their days in classes and in field exercises under simulated battle conditions. The committee was in session for the better part of two weeks, produced a lengthy report, and met, among others, the redoubtable General Winfield Scott, aged seventy-seven, who resembled a huge old lion and was spending the final years of his retirement within eye-shot of the youthful cadets. "He has," wrote Emerson, "the stateliest form in America and his behavior belongs to it." Emerson had admirers of his own, among them young John Burroughs, who at first took him for an "alert, inquisitive farmer . . . all eagerness and attention." Presently, seeing Burroughs and another young man hanging about, he "came over and talked with us, and beamed upon us in that inimitable way" with his "serene unflinching look" and his firmly closed mouth.

Emerson had been home less than two weeks when the newspapers announced the greatest battle of the war at Gettysburg on July 1-3, 1863. The brigade of which Concord's 32nd Regiment was a part fought continuously for all three days and nights. Colonel Prescott, despite wounds, responded to an order to retreat by saying, "I don't want to retire; I am not ready to retire; I can hold this place"—and did. At least two other Concord natives were among the 23,000 Union casualties. When Lee pulled back after having sustained losses estimated at 25,000, the fortunes of the Confederacy began their long decline.

The news of the slaughter at Gettysburg helped to precipitate savage riots against the draft in New York in mid-July. One mob of protesters burned down a police station on 22nd Street in lower Manhattan near William Emerson's new residence, which luckily escaped unscathed. Ellen and Edith Emerson were back in Newport, though their visit was darkened when they heard that young Wilky James, their blithe companion of 1862, had been severely wounded while serving with the 54th Massachusetts Regiment in the assault on Fort Wagner, which dominated the ship channel two miles south of Fort Sumter in Charleston harbor. As at Gettysburg, the butchery in this engagement was horrific. The 54th pulled back after the loss of two thirds of its officers and at least half its men. This was one of the first enlisted black regiments, including a number of former slaves, and commanded by Colonel Robert Gould Shaw, who was killed in action on July 18. Emerson's poem "Voluntaries," sent to Shaw's parents in September, contained a memorial quatrain for the colonel and his fallen comrades that was later incised on the base of the Soldiers' Monument on Concord Green:

> So nigh is grandeur to our dust,
> So near is God to man,
> When Duty whispers low, *Thou must,*
> The youth replies, *I can.*

Among the other casualties of the summer was Cabot Jackson Russel, Eddy Emerson's companion on the western tour of 1862, who had risen to the rank of captain and was killed in action on the same day as Colonel Shaw. In a letter of consolation to yet another set of bereaved parents whose son, Lieutenant Colonel William Rodman, had been killed by a rebel sharpshooter in Louisiana in May, Emerson wrote:

> I think daily that there are crises which demand nations, as well as those which claim the sacrifice of single lives. Ours perhaps is one—and that one whole generation might well consent to perish, if, by their fall, political liberty and clean and just life could be made sure to the generations that follow. As you suffer, all of us may suffer, before we shall have an honest peace.

Emerson's friend John Murray Forbes had been actively engaged behind the scenes for more than two years, persuading Boston merchants to buy ships for naval transport, organizing the Sanitary Commission, the equivalent of the modern Red Cross, and founding the New England Loyal Publication Society, which issued propaganda for the Union cause. He had just returned from a mission in England, "backed by a million pounds of credit," to purchase vessels that might otherwise have been sold to the Confederates. In September, Emerson reluctantly declined Forbes's invitation to visit Naushon, but hoped for a future occasion to "learn the new English traits" that Forbes had gathered among the British shipbuilders.

Forbes's eldest son, Will, was now a major in the 2nd Regiment of Cavalry, Massachusetts Volunteers, stationed just north of Washington. In June he had written his father: "We have been off on one or two small expeditions so far. In one we went up the river . . . in pursuit of some guerrillas who crossed the Potomac and burned a Michigan camp. We pursued them as far as Aldie but were twenty-four hours behind them and of course could do nothing." In July he wrote home about Colonel Shaw's death: "It is given to very few to die as he has in the successful accomplishment of his great work— that of proving to a reluctant and prejudiced people that the Negro is fit to be treated like a man and will fight as bravely for his freedom as his white fellow countrymen. . . . Bob gave his life in taking them in *well* to their first great trial."

Forbes's battalion was sporadically harassed by the Confederate Ranger John Singleton Mosby, aged thirty, who had begun independent guerrilla operations in January 1863 with remarkable brio and continuing success. Shot through the thigh in September, Mosby was soon back in the saddle, conducting raids in Maryland across the Potomac, and seizing horses and mules as well as scores and sometimes hundreds of Union prisoners. During one counterattack by a squadron of Union cavalry, a deserter from Forbes's unit was captured from a detachment of Mosby's raiders. Colonel Charles Lowell, the commandant, ordered a court-martial with Major Forbes presiding, and the deserter was shot beside his coffin. Will afterward called this the "most sickening" incident of his army life.

In mid-November 1863, President Lincoln signalized the Gettysburg engagement at the dedication of the national cemetery on the site with a speech of 271 words. His oration found a ready admirer in Emerson, who called him "the author of a multitude of good sayings," whose words were to be accepted and echoed by millions. "What pregnant definitions; what unerring common sense; what foresight; and, on great occasion, what lofty, and more than national, what humane tone! His brief speech at Gettysburg will not easily be surpassed by words on any recorded occasion. This, and one other American speech, that of John Brown to the court that tried him, and a part of Kossuth's speech at Birmingham, can only be compared with each other, and with no fourth."

Although the Emerson family records for 1861–64 seem to contain no hint of the fact, Will Forbes had been in love with Edith Emerson since their first meeting at Naushon in 1858. He was still a freshman at Harvard when he saw her again at his home in Milton and confided to his mother that he liked her best of all the girls he knew. After his dismissal from college for the chapel prank, he told his mother morosely, "I can never have any hope of Edith Emerson now." Ellen's wartime letters allude to him occasionally, always with admiration but never in connection with Edith. Yet there are some grounds for believing that Edith's illness of late 1863 and early 1864 was caused at least in part by worry over the dangers through which Will Forbes was then passing.

Emerson's account of his daughter's sickness called it "a morbid condition almost epidemic among young women in and about Boston—they call it *weak back*—which . . . both my girls have suffered from in the last two or three years [i.e., since the war began], Ellen less Edith more, and for which the Water cure has been found by some patients salutary." Just before Christmas 1863 he took Edith to New York to stay with William's family and to consult as an out-patient a doctor named Charles Schieferdecker. Edith was rebellious—"such a vixen," her father called her—writing "stormy letters" home and thoroughly abhorring the hydropathic treatments. By the end of January both her father and her Uncle William began to suspect that Schieferdecker was a quack. "She has such exuberant health," wrote William to his brother, "that all his treatment fails to do her much harm." In the end she gave up the exasperating baths, and Eddy went to New York to bring her home. They were both on hand when their cousin, William Emerson Junior, sickened and died at the end of February. He had married Sally Gibbons only fourteen weeks earlier. "It is a loss to them all," wrote Ellen, "which I can hardly realize."

The day young William died in New York, Alcott paid a call on Hawthorne at the Wayside in Concord. Looking gray and tired, Hawthorne complained of his "indisposition to write" and spoke of his need to "recruit" his failing vigor. Despite his fatigue he had managed to finish *Our Old Home*, an account of his consular experiences in England, published by Ticknor and Fields in September and dedicated to his old friend Franklin Pierce. Emerson privately called the book "pellucid but not deep," and found the dedication so intolerable that he tore out the page from his gift copy, still believing that Hawthorne was "unlucky in having for a friend" a man who had been "either the worst . . . or the weakest of all our Presidents." Fields had warned Hawthorne that the dedication might well ruin the sales of his book, but by publication day 5,500 copies were in print and *Our Old Home* was moving briskly. In December, Hawthorne joined Pierce at the funeral of his wife in Concord, New Hampshire, and in the following April undertook his journey of recruitment with Fields's partner, William Ticknor. They had reached Philadelphia when Ticknor fell ill and died, probably of pneumonia, in the hotel room next to Hawthorne's. On his return to Concord, Sophia was shocked by her husband's appearance—"so haggard, so white, so deeply scored with pain and fatigue . . . so much more ill than I ever saw him before." When Emerson dropped in at the Wayside on the evening of April 20, he found Hawthorne as feeble as Thoreau had been two years before.

Emerson's chief occupation of the spring was to organize a festival of the Saturday Club to celebrate the 300th anniversary of Shakespeare's birth. Among the thirty-two members and illustrious guests who gathered at the Parker House on April 23, the notable absentees were Hawthorne, too ill to appear, and Sam Ward, who was in England on business relating to the prosecution of the war. Two weeks after the celebration, Alcott, carrying his year-old grandson, Frederick Pratt, happened to meet Hawthorne at the front gate of Wayside. "He seemed unequal to meeting anyone," he thought, "and I had but a word with him, he asking me if I was well only." Franklin Pierce had recently suggested a journey of "recruitment" to New Hampshire. When Hawthorne agreed, the two old friends set off on May 12 in Pierce's carriage for an unhurried ride through the north country with frequent hotel stops along the way. They reached Plymouth on the evening of the eighteenth. As had happened with Ticknor in Philadelphia in April, the two men occupied adjoining rooms. Hawthorne ate a light supper and fell asleep at dusk. When Pierce looked in some time after midnight, his friend still lay there quietly. Around three in the morning, awakened by a barking dog, Pierce checked again and found that Hawthorne was dead.

Emerson's journal account of May 24 took up the narrative:

Yesterday, 23 May, we buried Hawthorne in Sleepy Hollow, in a pomp of sunshine and verdure, and gentle winds. . . . Longfellow, Lowell, Holmes, Agassiz, Hoar, Dwight, Whipple, Norton, Alcott, Hillard, Fields, Judge Thomas, and I attended the hearse as pall bearers. Franklin Pierce was with the family. The church was copiously decorated with white flowers delicately arranged. The corpse was unwillingly shown,—only a few moments to this company of his friends. But it was noble and serene in its aspect . . . a calm and powerful head. A large company filled the church and the grounds of the cemetery. All was so bright and quiet, that pain or mourning was hardly suggested, and Holmes said to me, that it looked like a happy meeting. . . .

Emerson's commentary continued:

I thought there was a tragic element in the event . . . in the painful solitude of the man, which, I suppose, could not longer be endured, and he died of it. I have found in his death a surprise and disappointment. I thought him a greater man than any of his works betray, that there was still a great deal of work in him, and that he might one day show a purer power. . . . It would have been a happiness, doubtless to both of us, to have come into habits of unreserved intercourse. It was easy to talk with him—there were no barriers;—only, he said so little, that I talked too much. . . . He showed no egotism or self-assertion, rather a humility, and at one time, a fear that he had written himself out.—One day, when I found him on the top of his hill, in the woods, he paced back the path to his house and said, *This path is the only remembrance of me that will remain.* Now it appears that I waited too long. Lately, he had removed himself the more by the indignation his perverse politics and unfortunate friendship for that paltry Franklin Pierce awaked,—though it rather moved pity for Hawthorne, and the assured belief that he would outlive it, and come right at last.

Alcott could have been writing both for himself and for Emerson that same day: "Fair figures one by one are fading from sight. Thoreau, once the central figure in our landscape, has disappeared from it, and Hawthorne no longer traverses his hilltop near my house. Only Emerson and Channing remain of our village circle. I meet the first familiarly, though seldomer that I could wish, but catch no more of the last named than a glance as he passes by my door once in a long while, or crosses my track in the streets. . . . Capricious man that he is, the victim of his moods, whimsical as any spoiled child . . . always walking and talking from behind his mask, and resenting any stroke of candor on your part, as if that were breaking faith with him."

Other fair figures were fading from sight. On June 18 Concord's Colonel Prescott was killed before Petersburg and brought home to be buried by what Ellen Emerson called "a vast concourse of grateful and honoring people. Through every road in town that day came carriages of flowers, children carrying flowers. . . . It was a beautiful day, and a beautiful funeral. But our Colonel is a loss like no other loss." Shaw, Russel, Rodman, and now Prescott—the list grew steadily longer month after month as if the gaping gullet of the war could never be filled.

Yet another victim close to the Emerson family was Will Forbes, aged twenty-four. He was a major in the 2nd Massachusetts Cavalry under Colonel Charles Lowell, who chose the summer of 1864 to rid the Union forces of that elusive warrior, Colonel John Mosby. On July 6, Mosby set up an ambush in a patch of woods at Ball's Mill near Leesburg, Virginia. With some 200 of his Rangers he attacked 156 troopers commanded by Forbes in a nearby field. Forbes was at the center of the action, standing in his stirrups with drawn sabre and fighting desperately. One of Mosby's officers, Captain Richards, rode at Forbes and snapped his pistol in his face. But the weapon misfired and Forbes, hacking at Richards as he passed, had his sabre wrenched from his hand and lost. Mosby himself bore down at full gallop and fired at Forbes, whose horse tossed its head, took the bullet, and fell dead, pinning Will's leg beneath its body. Will had no choice but to surrender, and spent the next five months in as many Confederate prisons under the usual filthy and crowded conditions.

One of Will's closest friends, Lieutenant Goodwin Stone, was not so lucky. Mortally wounded in the same action, Stone galloped thirteen miles to the Union lines. Picked up by an ambulance sent by Colonel Lowell, he lived long enough to be visited by his mother and sister before he died. Forbes was still in prison on October 18 when his commandant, Colonel Lowell, was killed leading a cavalry charge at Cedar Creek. "It is the greatest loss perhaps that Massachusetts has sustained during the War," wrote Ellen Emerson in December. "Forty days after his death came his baby to console poor Effie, but it is a little girl and cannot bear his name. There is also a baby in Concord, Col[onel] Prescott's, born three months after his father's death. But we are all glad that it is a boy, and I hope the town will adopt him."

Released on parole from the Confederate prison in Columbia, South Carolina, Will Forbes, now a lieutenant colonel, reached his Milton home in time for Christmas. According to his biographer, Arthur S. Pier, "his family were shocked by his emaciated appearance. For the first few days he never rose from the table without slipping bits of food into his pockets to forestall any attacks of hunger between meals. Rapidly, however, he regained his strength, and he was soon employing to the best advantage the short interval before he would be eligible to rejoin his regiment."

In January 1865 Emerson departed on another of his long lecture tours, which had continued and even accelerated despite the war. His daughter Edith stayed at home to watch over Lidian while Ellen and Edward went to Milton for a welcoming party with the Forbes family. "Even the ghosts didn't check the strong joyfulness of the occasion," wrote Ellen to Edith. "Mrs. Forbes was extremely happy and twice remarked, 'Oh, this is very different from Columbia prison. It is perfectly delightful to see him [Will] dancing round among all these girls.' And so it was. I give in with all my heart and say Will is if not handsome, at any rate a sight for sair e'en, and seemed as if he could not possibly get his fill of dancing. . . . We were all at it with all our might till half past twelve." Ellen's "giving in" about Will's appearance was clearly an allusion to previous conversations with Edith, whose opinions about Will Forbes were to become public in two months' time.

Chapter   Forty-four

A FUNERAL
AND A WEDDING

SANDWICHED AMONG LECTURE DATES IN EMERSON'S POCKET diary for 1865 was a four-word notation: "[Sat., Mar. 4] Inauguration WHF and E.E." This was shorthand for the great day that celebrated Lincoln's second inaugural, "with malice towards none, with charity for all," and the forthcoming announcement of Edith Emerson's engagement to Colonel Forbes. On Monday Emerson wrote his old friend Abel Adams: "My daughter Edith is engaged to William Hathaway Forbes. I found him here, and both of them arrived at a perfect understanding, on my return home from Boston on Saturday night. He is still here, and threatens, unless over-ruled, to carry her off with him to Washington in a few days, as his furlough is nearly exhausted. I think Edward who is a devoted friend of William F. takes as much joy in the event as the parties themselves."

On the same day Ellen wrote that "Will has always been one of our greatest interests in the army, and at home our example of everything good. I am overjoyed to have such a brother, I would have chosen him out of the whole world. . . . He is not yet exchanged and the proper place for such officers is Annapolis. He has leave of absence from there at present, but doubts very much whether the authorities will extend it. So he and Edith fear that he must go in another week. That would give them in all only 13 days together, and I don't wonder they think it short."

On March 9 Will and Edith took the train for Washington, where the elder Forbeses were spending the winter. Emerson presently wrote John Forbes,

"In a manly character like [Will's], a tenderness so true and lasting tempers the soldier and endears the man. . . . You can judge I am rejoiced to give my little country girl into the hands of this brave protector, and shall rest at peace on her account henceforward. I hope she may know how to deserve her felicity. . . . She does not please in advance as much as she merits, but can sometimes surprise old friends who tho't they knew her well, with deeper and better traits. She is humble, which is the basis of nobility." After three weeks Will brought Edith home on March 31, and left Concord the same day for the front in Virginia. From Washington on April 2 he sent Edith a "very funny letter," which she shared with the family. "Happily when they are just engaged," wrote Ellen, "people are endowed with extraordinary power of bearing sunshine. Under most circumstances such a strong blast of it would hurt anyone, but now it feels like native air."

Richmond fell on April 3 and the rumor was spreading that the war would soon end. While it lasted Will Forbes was in the thick of it. On the fourth he rejoined his old unit, spending thirty-two hours in the saddle on an all-night ride to Jetersville, Virginia. Under the command of General George Armstrong Custer, the 2nd Massachusetts participated in a successful cavalry charge against a foe too weak to sustain it, and then rode off another twenty-five miles to Appomattox on orders from General Phil Sheridan. There on Sunday the ninth occurred the final cease-fire of the war, and Forbes was present when Generals Lee and Grant arranged the terms of surrender. So was the brigade to which the 32nd Regiment of Massachusetts belonged, including many soldiers from Concord. "What a joyful day is this," Emerson told Caroline Tappan. "Mankind has appeared just now in its best attitude around Mr Lincoln . . . and will aid him to use sanely the immense power with which the hour clothes him."

But the national joy was short-lived. Only five days later Lincoln's power was suddenly decimated. "The assassin Booth," wrote Emerson, "is a type man of a large class of the Southern people. By the destruction of Slavery, we destroy the stove in which the cockatrice eggs are hatched." He drew up a bitter bill of particulars against the erstwhile enemy: "Even the poor prisoners that starved and perished in the Libby and Andersonville prisons rendered a vast service to their country and mankind, by drawing out into the daylight the cruelty and malignity of the Southern people, and showing the corruption that Slavery works on the community in which it exists. . . . I charge the

Southerner with starving prisoners of war; with massacring surrendered men . . . with advertising a price for the life of Lincoln, Butler, Garrison, and others; with assassination of the President . . . with attempts to import the yellow fever into New York; with the cutting up the bones of our soldiers to make ornaments, and drinking-cups of their skulls." If some of this was propaganda, enough of it was true to justify his complaint.

Lincoln died on the fifteenth. On the nineteenth, a famous anniversary for the people of Concord, services in his memory were held in the First Church. "Today we kept the funeral of our dear, our good President," wrote Ellen Emerson, "with more real grief than would have seemed possible for a people to feel at a President's loss." Her father was among the speakers:

On Saturday, every one was struck dumb, and saw at first only deep below deep, as he meditated on the ghastly blow. And perhaps, at this hour, when the coffin which contains the dust of the President sets forward on its long march through mourning states, on its way to his home in Illinois, we might well be silent. . . . Yes, but that first despair was brief: the man was not so to be mourned. He was the most active and hopeful of men; and his work had not perished: but acclamations of praise for the task he had accomplished burst out into a song of triumph, which even tears for his death cannot keep down. . . . This man grew according to the need. His mind mastered the problem of the day; and as the problem grew, so did his comprehension of it. Rarely was man so fitted to the event. . . . He is the true history of the American people in his time. . . . Had he not lived long enough to keep the greatest promise that ever man made to his fellow men—the practical abolition of slavery? . . . Only Washington can compare with him in fortune. . . . There is a serene Providence which rules the fate of nations. . . . It makes its own instruments, creates the man for the time, trains him in poverty, inspires his genius, and arms him for his task.

So Lincoln entered Emerson's pantheon of prime movers in human history.

Since 1862 posthumous works by Henry Thoreau had been published by Ticknor and Fields—*Maine Woods*, *Cape Cod*, and *Excursions*. During the first two weeks of May, Emerson completed work on a volume of Thoreau's

Letters to Various Persons, which he had gathered from recipients and printed pretty much "as they stood," along with a selection of Henry's "best verses," which justified his allusion to these "skyborn letters and poems." He dated his editor's notice May 12, but had subsequently to reckon with editorial changes by Henry's sister Sophia. According to Annie Fields, Sophia said that "she was sure Mr. Emerson was not pleased at the restorations she made after his careful work of elimination was finished, but he was too courteous and kind to say much," only remarking, " 'You have spoiled my Greek statue.' "

From this task he turned to the renewal of his acquaintance with Will Forbes, who was mustered out on May 15, reached home on the seventeenth, and stayed with the Emersons until the first of June. "That was the most splendid fortnight," wrote Ellen, "lovely weather almost all the time, and Edith showed off all the pretty places in Concord, and Will made every one like him. . . . His Father has taken him . . . into partnership, so now he is in business and can have no holidays. But he thought he deserved a little vacation."

During Will's visit Emerson celebrated his sixty-second birthday, signalized by a gift from Alcott, a handsome little book called *Emerson*, privately printed at the expense of Mrs. George Stearns, and bound in brown cloth, with a frontispiece bust of the subject and a tailpiece sketch of the summerhouse that Alcott had built for Emerson in 1847. Although the gift was a surprise, Emerson had long known—and feared—that Alcott had been planning an essay about him. Drafted in the spring of 1863 and submitted that fall to James T. Fields for consideration by the *Atlantic*, it had been gently turned down pending Emerson's permission to publish. Alcott, unabashed, made it into a lecture that he twice read to audiences in Concord in January 1865. Emerson was away at the time on his annual tour of the Midwest and was embarrassed when he heard by mail about Alcott's goodwill gestures. "Tis woe to think of poor Concord choked again with 'Mr. Emison,' " he wrote Lidian from Chicago. "I do not know but the boys in the street will give me a tin pan concert when I get home. You should have absolutely forbidden it to Mr. A., and told him how hateful was honeypie to my weak stomach."

But he came to thank Alcott on May 30, praising "the style and elegancy of the type, binding, ornament," though adding that they would have to talk further about the actual contents. The text, as he wrote Mrs. Stearns in July, "was such a Persian superlative on the poor merits of the subject that I had to shade my eyes. . . . I don't know but I suffered more than I enjoyed; but I soon came to admire the lyrical tone. . . . And now I have learned to look at the book with courage."

Originally called "The Rhapsodist" in a phrase from Goethe, the gift book said that Emerson's works abounded in "strong sense, happy humor, keen criticisms, subtile [sic] insights, noble morals, clothed in a chaste and manly diction, and fresh with the breath of health and progress." Although "not a metaphysician," and "rightly discarding any claims to systematic thinking," he was "a poet in spirit, if not always in form . . . the consistent idealist" yet "the realist none the less," who had "come nearest of any to emancipating the mind of his own time from the errors and dreams of past ages." As Emerson told Mrs. Stearns, in the face of such praise he had been obliged to make a covenant with himself, "ignoring the infirm actuality" but "stoutly holding up the ideal outline of the poor man" whom Alcott had apotheosized. One of Alcott's "epigraphs" had quoted Pythagoras: "Frankincense should be offered to the gods, but praise to good men." An odor of frankincense rose up from these laudatory pages.

While Alcott had been working on his Emerson essay, Emerson had been developing a new one of his own called "Character." On May 30 he read it aloud to Alcott, who gave it his "hearty assent." Emerson defined character as "the habit of action from the permanent vision of truth." But his emphasis fell upon what he variously called the moral sentiment or the moral element. It was a replication in depth of the position he had espoused thirty years earlier. Morals, "the science of substances, not of shows," implied "freedom and will." Man "has his life in nature, like a beast: but choice is born in him . . . here is the Declaration of Independence. . . . He chooses—as the rest of the creation does not. . . . Morals is the direction of the will on universal ends. He is immoral who is acting to any private end. He is moral—we say it with Marcus Aurelius and with Kant—whose aim or motive may become a universal rule, binding on all intelligent beings." Emerson found support for his position not only in Kant's categorical imperative but also in Wordsworth's great ode, from which he quoted the famous passage about "truths that wake / To perish never"—"the fountain light of all our day . . . a master light of all our seeing." The moral element thus invited men "to great enlargements."

The excellence in Jesus is that "he affirms the Divinity in him and in us—

not thrusts himself between it and us," and points to "the presence of the Eternal in each perishing man." There was a time, said Emerson, "when Christianity existed in one child. But if the child had been killed by Herod," the element would not have been lost. "God sends his messages, if not by one, then quite as well by another. When the Master of the Universe has ends to fulfil, he impresses his will on the structure of minds." Now and again through the ages "a soul is born which has no weakness of self, which offers no impediment to the Divine Spirit, which comes down into Nature as if only for the benefit of souls, and all its thoughts are perceptions of things as they are, without any infirmity of earth. . . . See how one noble person dwarfs a whole nation of underlings. This steadfastness we indicate when we praise character."

"I consider theology to be the rhetoric of morals," he continued. "The mind of this age has fallen away from theology to morals. I conceive it an advance. . . . The mind of our culture has already left our liturgies behind. . . . The creed, the legend, forms of worship, swiftly decay. Morals is the incorruptible essence. . . . Whoever feels any love or skill for ethical studies may safely lay out all his strength and genius in working in that mine. The pulpit may shake, but this platform will not. All the victories of religion belong to the moral sentiment. . . . It is only yesterday that our American churches, so long silent on Slavery, and notoriously hostile to the Abolitionist, wheeled into line for Emancipation."

So Emerson, in Alcott's words, continued his chosen task of "emancipating the mind of his own time from the errors and dreams of past ages." James T. Fields had agreed to publish "Character" in the August number of the *Atlantic*, but early in July he came out to Concord to tell Emerson that he had changed his mind. The essay was "not suited to the magazine. Ordinary readers would not understand him and would consider it blasphemous." Withdrawn from the *Atlantic*, it appeared some eight months later in the *North American Review*, but without the author's name, as if to shield Emerson from the contumely of orthodox believers. This was the magazine to which Henry James Junior, beginning his long career at age twenty-one, was likewise making anonymous contributions.

On July 21 Emerson was one of the speakers at the Commemoration of the Living and Dead Soldiers of Harvard University. He quoted Heraclitus: "War is the Father of all things." The recent conflict had given back "integrity to this erring and immoral nation." He cited Napoleon's remark that "it is a principle of war that when you can use the thunderbolt you must prefer it to the cannon." In New England, said Emerson, "enthusiasm was the thunderbolt" that "flamed out when the guilty gun was aimed at Sumter." The little state of Massachusetts was larger than anyone had suspected: when her blood was up, she had a fist "big enough to knock down an empire. . . . We shall not again disparage America, now that we have seen what men it will bear. We see . . . a new era, worth to mankind all the treasure and all the lives of all this generation of American men, if they had been demanded."

Much of the summer was given over to plans for the wedding of Edith and Will, which was set for October. In August the lovers climbed Monadnock with Ellen and Eddy and afterward vacationed on the "Happy Island" of Naushon. "The wedding," wrote Ellen, "takes up more and more of our time and thoughts. I am bidding farewell to life, to friends, and correspondence . . . and shall think and breathe nothing but clothes and furniture, paper, carpets, and curtains, last bequests, invitations, journeys to Boston, presents, and bills." She and her father spoke of the wedding as "the Day of Judgement and End of the World."

In September Emerson spoke at the Middlesex Agricultural Exhibition, locally called the Cattle Show, on the governor's proposal to restock the Concord and Merrimack rivers with fish. He also served as judge of pears, including a handsome basket submitted by his neighbor, Judge Hoar. At the next meeting of the Saturday Club, the judge revealed the secret of his success. Emerson had advised him to fertilize his pear trees with iron and animal matter. The judge had planted all his old iron kettles and a cat and a dog at the foot of his tree, and these magnificent pears were the result. He said that he was holding a couple of terriers in reserve.

The wedding took place on October 3, which happened to be the twenty-fifth anniversary of the marriage of Sam and Anna Ward. Will Forbes helped to decorate the parlor with autumn leaves and the dining room with holly while Edith retired to make her bridal wreath of orange blossoms and rosebuds. Her gown was white muslin, like Lidian's in 1835. Ellen, arraying her sister, was struck by the contrast of her snowy veil with her red cheeks and brown hair. Lidian wore black silk with satin polka dots, and Ellen was in white with red ribbons. Emerson's dark garb was accentuated by white gloves.

Half the population of Concord filed through the front gates in a seemingly endless procession. "The whole place," wrote Annie Fields, "was as beautiful as earthly radiance and joy can make a home. Poor Mrs. Hawthorne, laden with her many sorrows, threw off her black robe for that day that she might rejoice with others." The Reverend Mr. Reynolds officiated. After the ceremony, Emerson and Ellen watched Edith sweep down the white marble walk in her brown traveling dress to the gate where Will was waiting with a two-horse buggy. They drove off for a week's honeymoon at Pigeon Cove near Gloucester, followed by a visit to Naushon, where Will was already planning a deer hunt for his closest friends among the retired officers of the 2nd Massachusetts Cavalry.

After the principals had departed, the usual letdown ensued. The family gathered for a supper of oysters and salad. Emerson proposed a toast to the health of Will and Edith. Lidian, ever mindful of the lower orders, fed leftover ice cream to the mare Dolly, and wedding cake to the parrot. Emerson dolefully remarked, "There are several very agreeable circumstances about that child's going away, but there is one sad one and that is that she is gone." Later, when asked if he did not miss her, he answered, "Yes, she was an idle minx, but she has gone and she troubles me." But while her parents mourned the "loss" of their younger daughter, the indefatigable Ellen, assisted by Una Hawthorne and May Alcott, packed up Edith's books and wedding presents and then went down to Milton to prepare the cottage where Will and Edith were going to set up housekeeping.

Chapter Forty-five

TALES OF
A GRANDFATHER

AFTER THE FAILURE OF PHILLIPS, SAMPSON AND COMPANY, Emerson had gone over to Ticknor and Fields. In 1860 the firm had brought out reprints of the first two volumes of his essays as well as *The Conduct of Life*. In March and April 1865 they reprinted 2,500 copies of the poems of 1846–47 and both sets of the essays appeared in a one-volume edition of some 3,000 copies. Besides his own work, Emerson had been serving as intermediary for Sophia Thoreau in the contractual arrangements for her brother's posthumous publications, including the edition of his *Letters to Various Persons* that Emerson himself edited in 1865. Since James T. Fields was also running the *Atlantic Monthly* between 1862 and 1870, Emerson's contacts with him were frequent.

During the war years a close friendship accordingly developed between Emerson and Jamie, as his wife called him, and with Annie Adams Fields. Their house at 37 Charles Street near the river had become a social center for many of the leading intellectuals of Boston and environs. At forty-nine, Jamie was a tall and robust man with a wiry black beard. His second wife, Annie, still in her early thirties, was a quick-witted and charming woman with dark brown eyes and abundant auburn hair, drawn becomingly over her ears on either side of an amiable face. The earliest recorded visit by Emerson and Lidian to the house in Charles Street seems to have come on December 1, 1863, when Emerson lectured in Boston on "The Fortune of the Republic" and brought Lidian and his daughter Edith to tea. Lidian, said

Annie, was "a woman of proud integrity and real sweetness," with such "an awe of words" that her lips did not "unlock save for truth or kindliness or beauty or wisdom."

In the spring of 1866, at Fields's instigation, Emerson gave a private series of six lectures in Boston that attracted excellent audiences and netted him the astonishing total of $947, an unheard-of sum for a lecturer whose usual earnings seldom exceeded $50 and expenses. "I fear," he wrote to Annie Fields, "it is becoming a fixed idea in the minds of you and your husband to do good to me and mine. My wife does not seem to fear being spoiled, delights in your good offices as you do, and, at this particular moment, answers you, that she will come with the greatest pleasure;—though she has been mostly in her chamber for I know not how many weeks."

The whole Emerson family joined the Fieldses for dinner after Emerson's opening address on April 14. Before lecturing in Boston, Emerson sometimes took a room at Parker's Hotel in order to write without interruption. On one such occasion, Lidian came in to join him, and he arranged to have a driver meet her at the station and bring her to the hotel. "But how will the driver know me?" asked Lidian. "I can tell him," said Emerson, "to look for a tall thin lady, dressed in black, with a white face and her eyes fixed on the distant future." Apart from such urban adventures, Lidian did indeed spend most of her days in her capacious chamber. Her bed was draped and skirted with white hangings, the very decorations that Emerson had deplored before the birth of their first child. Her frequent companions were the white cats, Topaz and Milcah, whom she delighted to feed with scraps from her breakfast tray.

In the summer of 1866 her thoughts were often directed toward Milton. Edith's first pregnancy was going to reach full term in July. "I am to keep that month unengaged," wrote Ellen, "so that I may be quite free to go at once [to Milton], to pour out Will's tea, and see as much of Edith as her dragon may choose to allow." But Ellen could hardly have foreseen the complications that July produced. Eddy had earned his A.B. degree at Harvard, but could not wait for commencement because John Forbes had arranged for his employment as a clerk in the offices of the Chicago, Burlington, and Quincy Railroad in Burlington, Iowa. Eddy's twenty-second birthday came on July 10. Lidian had just finished packing his trunk when a telegram from Will Forbes announced another birthday—the arrival of Edith's ten-pound boy. Emerson's voice broke as he read the message aloud, and he hurried upstairs to awaken

Lidian with "Good morning, Grandmother!" Now, in their early sixties, the elder Emersons had entered a new era.

Eddy and Ellen left Concord next morning, he for Iowa and she for Milton. That night Emerson composed a letter to Edith: "Happy wife and mother that you are. . . . Fair fall the little boy—he has come among good people." Lidian enclosed a reference to a Biblical text from Luke 1:60 about the birth of a son to Elizabeth and Zechariah and Elizabeth's insistence on naming the child John. Lidian may have been hinting that the new child should be named for his paternal grandfather. But when Ellen reached Milton, Will handed her a note purportedly from the baby himself. It closed with the statement: "My name is probably Ralph Emerson Forbes." Will had whooping cough and could not go near the nursery, though he went out that night to help the Fire Department extinguish a blaze in the woods behind the Forbes mansion. All this impressed Ellen more than the baby's appearance. He did not seem to "grow in beauty, being all red and yellow and rash."

Emerson and Lidian were just leaving Concord for a first look at their grandson when Emerson learned from a friend that he had been awarded, in absentia, an honorary LL.D. from Harvard, with a citation that proclaimed him "jucundissimum poetam et hominem multarum literarum," thus restoring him, as Annie Fields said, to the "good graces of his Alma Mater" after a thirty-year exile. But the doctor of laws seemed far more interested in the "small red creature" beside its mother on the bed. "He has been lampooned," cried the grandfather. "He is not ugly, he's a nice little fellow!" Lidian took up the child, praised him in baby talk, and laid him down again, saying, "He isn't pretty, but he's a good-looking baby and there's nothing to hinder his growing pretty." In the end she kissed him and said that she had begun at last to feel like a grandmother. Later, when the rash had cleared up, Emerson was heard to murmur, "A baby's skin is a great luxury."

All that summer and fall Lidian was sporadically ill and often confined to her bedroom. Despite trips to Milton, a visit with the Agassiz family at Nahant, and a rainy two-week vacation in her beloved Plymouth, she remained so frail that Ellen sometimes feared for her life. Ellen's letters of the time contained such phrases as "very unwell . . . utterly weak and broken down . . . exhausted . . . and moaning." In mid-October Ellen reported that Lidian had taken "to her bed again as she did last winter," and required her daughter's services every day. She got up long enough to attend a Thanksgiving feast for twenty-two people, and managed also to spend Christmas with the Forbeses in Milton.

One of Ellen's letters in December summarized her mother's condition. "Very little or no better, frightfully weak, confined almost wholly to the bed, but really enjoys life more than usual. Too sick to work, her habits all broken up, she reads and is read to, and when the day is perfectly beautiful walks out for an hour or two in the early afternoon. Arising at 12 [she] often succeeds in going forth at two. All the cares and sorrows have really fallen away now, and relieved from daily pressures she broods less on the past. Father like every one else is frightened about her. Every one sends her broth and jelly. . . . She has every variety of ale, porter, and wine . . . with ceaseless instruction from Aunt Lucy and me that starving is madness[;] she is really learning to eat something, which gives me some hope. . . . This sickness . . . is teaching her to go to bed early (we have twice attained to 10 o'clock), it may teach her to eat, and to walk at noon instead of sunset. . . . That distress in her head seldom comes now, and I hear no more of her 'enemy, the sun.' She says she doesn't think she shall die, for all her thoughts and wishes are toward life."

When Edith brought the baby to Concord, Lidian found her grandchild a "reviving presence." He spent many hours lying on her bed. "When he is tired," wrote Ellen, "she takes him up and plays with him till they both laugh out." Emerson, looking on, was filled with admiration. "I had no idea," he said, "a young child could be so entertaining. I no longer wonder at Alcott's dedication to his grandchild. . . . He always goes about with that baby—I thought it very frivolous; but now I see how it is." He made some journal entries about his grandson, using the boy's nickname, Ras. "In Boston," he wrote, "I pass for a scholar, but to my friend Ras, only in connexion with the cows, and my name is *Moo*." When the child reached the crawling stage, Emerson dreamed up an anticipatory sequence: "Here is Ralph has got a hammer, and is creeping with all his might in a bee-line for the pier-glass." On his annual lecture tour to New York and the Midwest, he faithfully carried an ambrotype of Ras, and often consulted it for rest and recreation.

Urged on by Jamie Fields, Emerson began collecting his "scattered verses" during the fall of 1866. Eleven of them had appeared in the *Atlantic*, but many others had lain unpublished in his desk since the first volume of poems appeared in 1846–47. The new edition was set in type by December 1, but the proofs contained so many errata that he took them with him in his satchel on a trip to Salem on December 19, and afterward to New York, where he spoke to audiences in Harlem and Newark on a quick pre-Christmas tour. His son Eddy met him in New York about December 21. He was on his way home to Concord, having been obliged to give up his clerkship in Iowa because of a touch of malaria and severe problems with his eyesight. "We spent the night together at the St. Denis Hotel," he later wrote, "and as we sat by the fire he read me two or three of his poems for the new May-Day volume." The one that most struck Eddy was called "Terminus," beginning:

> It is time to be old,
> To take in sail:—
> The god of bounds
> Who sets to seas a shore,
> Came to me in his fatal rounds,
> And said: "No more!
> No farther shoot
> Thy broad ambitious branches, and thy root . . .
> Contract thy firmament
> To compass of a tent. . . .

These words, said Eddy, "almost startled me. No thought of his ageing [sic] had ever come to me, and there he sat, with no apparent abatement of bodily vigor, and young in spirit, recognizing with severe acquiescence his failing forces; I think he smiled as he read. He recognized, as none of us did, that his working days were nearly done."

Yet Edward, aged twenty-two, should not have been surprised. Even in the period 1861–64, when his father was in his late fifties and early sixties, Emerson had amused himself with at least two dozen journal entries on old age, some humorous, many ironic, a few acrimonious or simply resigned. Edward quoted one of them from 1864: "Within, I do not find wrinkles and used heart, but unspent youth." Yet close upon this followed another that said: "The grief of old age is, that, now, only in rare moments, and by happiest combinations or consent of the elements can we attain those enlargements and that intellectual *élan*, which were once a daily gift." A fugitive couplet of his, based on a passage from Herman Grimm, said that "The brook sings on, but sings in vain / Wanting the echo in my brain." As recently as October

1866, he had voiced a similar complaint in thanking Fields for having accepted a mediocre poem called "My Garden" for publication in the *Atlantic* in December: "I had been vexed with a belief that what skill I had in whistling was nearly or quite gone, and that I must henceforth content myself with guttural consonants or dissonants, and not attempt warbling." Even the pleasures of grandfatherhood could not wholly compensate for the gradual diminution of his poetical powers.

Emerson had been home from his western tour for only a month when *May-Day* appeared on April 29. Fields sent an advance copy the day before publication. Ellen Emerson admired the binding, stamped in gold with three fern fronds, but was disappointed with the typeface. "After all the fuss," she wrote, "the critical comparing of every sort of type, the visits to Mr Fields, and all the trumpeting I have heard, the type seems to me . . . mean and cold and ugly." If her father shared this opinion, he said nothing of it, and proudly sent out a hundred gift copies to friends and relatives, choosing May Day as the proper date for transmission of a volume of that title. The opening poem, running to more than 500 lines, was a paean to the renovative powers of spring:

Come the tumult whence it will,
Voice of sport, or rush of wings,
It is a sound, it is a token
That the marble sleep is broken,
And a change has passed on things . . .
For thou, O Spring! canst renovate
All that high God did first create.
Be still his arm and architect,
Rebuild the ruin, mend defect . . .
Not less renew the heart and brain,
Scatter the sloth, wash out the stain,
Make the aged eye sun-clear,
To parting soul bring grandeur near . . .
An energy that searches thorough
From Chaos to the dawning morrow;
Into all our human plight,
The soul's pilgrimage and flight;

In city or in solitude,
Step by step, lifts bad to good,
Without halting, without rest,
Lifting Better up to Best. . . .

These excerpts suggest that Emerson, a grandfather of sixty-three, was seeking to reassert his continuing youthfulness of spirit whatever the calendar might say to the contrary. Harvard's citation had called him *poeta jucundissimus*. Here he had gathered up eighty-six poems that might still prove his right to that designation. How better to begin than with a salute to the rejuvenative greening of the spring, even though, in "Terminus," he would have at last to accept the "legacy of ebbing veins" that presaged a coming winter when the Muses might leave him "deaf and dumb."

Apart from such occasional poems as the "Boston Hymn," "Voluntaries," the long blank-verse "Journal" of his sojourn in the Adirondacks in August 1858, and the verse epigraphs written to accompany the individual essays in the series of 1841 and 1844, the majority of the verses in *May-Day* consisted of tetrameter couplets or quatrains, sometimes intermixed. These were seldom less than competent, but they did not offer the best evidence of Emerson's skills as a versifier. Setting aside "Terminus," which stands close to the end of his poetical career, the most rigorous judgment would have to single out five poems, all composed in the 1850s and worthy to be inscribed in letters of gold: "Days," "Two Rivers," "Brahma," "Seashore," and "Waldeinsamkeit."

Of these, the blank-verse lines of "Days" went back farthest in Emerson's personal history. As early as 1843 he had written in his journal: "We never know while the days pass which day is valuable. The surface is vexation but the serene lies underneath." One morning in May four years later he wrote: "The days come and go like muffled and veiled figures sent from a distant friendly party, but they say nothing, and if we do not use the gifts they bring, they carry them silently away." In 1852 he set down a further observation: "I find one state of mind does not remember or conceive of another state. Thus I have written within a twelvemonth verses ('Days') which I do not remember the composition or correction of, and could not write the like today, and have only for proof of their being mine, various external evidences as, the MS. in which I find them, and the circumstance that I have sent copies of them to friends. . . . Well, if they had been better, if it had been a noble poem, perhaps it would have only more entirely taken up the ladder into heaven."

Ladder to heaven or no, "Days" is a noble poem, first published in the *Atlantic* for November 1857, and summarizing a view of the quotidian that had long endured in the poet's mind:

Daughters of Time, the hypocritic Days,
Muffled and dumb like barefoot dervishes,
And marching single in an endless file,
Bring diadems and fagots in their hands.
To each they offer gifts after his will,
Bread, kingdoms, stars, and sky that holds them all.
I, in my pleached garden, watched the pomp,
Forgot my morning wishes, hastily
Took a few herbs and apples, and the Day
Turned and departed silent. I, too late,
Under her solemn fillet saw the scorn.

In mid-July 1856, he set down in prose form (much as he had done with "The Snow-Storm" many years earlier) the essence of another superb poem, "Seashore." He had just returned from a week's visit with his family to Pigeon Cove on Cape Ann at the invitation of his old friend Cyrus Bartol. The "original charm" of the place, he wrote, was its "magnificent seabeach" with ledges of brown rock like "twenty Romes and Ninevehs and Karnacs in ruins together, obelisk and pyramid . . . prostrate or half-piled." And then the sea itself, "the opaline, plentiful and strong, yet beautiful as the rose or the rainbow, full of food, nourisher of men, purger of the world" with its "unchangeable ebb and flow." This sudden lyrical explosion took place soon after the completion of his long labors over *English Traits*, which he had just seen through the press for publication in August, and signified the joy with which he was returning to poetic utterance.

After "Seashore," based on naturalistic observation, he began at once an equally memorable versification of ideas from the *Upanishads*. In the process, he filled two dozen journal pages with extracts from the *Bibliotheca Indica* and set down what amounted to the final version of "Brahma" under the preliminary title "Song of the Soul." This was the lyric that Walt Whitman liked and defended against widespread accusations of obscurity after its first publication in the *Atlantic* in November 1857. Amused by public bafflement over the meaning of the four enigmatic quatrains, Emerson told Ellen, "If you tell them to say Jehovah instead of Brahma they will not feel any perplexity."

A fourth memorable poem, "Two Rivers," seems to have given Emerson more trouble than the other three. He set down trial lines in his journal in April 1856, carried on with it in June, but did not finish it until the fall of 1857 in time for publication in the *Atlantic* in January 1858. One river is the Musketaquid, the subject over which he had ruminated in the descriptive blank-verse poem of that title in 1847. This time he paired the placid stream that moved through Concord Plain with another, the abstract force of the moralistic élan vital that flows always forward "thr[ough] flood and sea and firmament / Thr[ough] light, thr[ough] life," unbounded and perpetual. It is curious that the germ of this dualism between seen and unseen forces for good could be traced back more than a quarter century to a journal entry of 1840 that said simply: "We see the river glide below us but we see not the river that glides over us and envelopes us in its floods."

Literary echoes are unusual in Emerson's poetry, both early and late. Occasional similarities to Milton's "L'Allegro" can be located in *May-Day*, and "Terminus" closes with a seeming glance at the stouthearted conclusion of Tennyson's "Ulysses." But "Waldeinsamkeit," which he began at Naushon in the summer of 1857 and finished in time for publication in the *Atlantic* in October 1858, displayed an unmistakable Wordsworthian influence. Despite a few adverse judgments, Emerson had been a sporadic reader of Wordsworth for more than forty years and was a particular admirer of the great ode and of "Laodamia." Here, however, his audial memory came to focus on the little sequence from *Lyrical Ballads* that includes "Expostulation and Reply," "The Tables Turned," "Lines Written in Early Spring," and "To My Sister."

One of Emerson's stanzas speaks of wandering "on the mountain-crest sublime / Or down the oaken glade" and exclaims, "O what have I to do with time? / For this the day was made." In "To My Sister," Wordsworth asserts that "Some silent laws our hearts will make / Which they shall long obey: /

We for the year to come may take / Our temper from today." The statement in "Lines Written in Early Spring" that " 'Tis my faith that every flower / Enjoys the air it breaths" anticipates Emerson's "Sober on a fund of joy / The woods at heart are glad." From "The Tables Turned" comes the exhortation to leave books in favor of direct observation: "Up! Up! my friend and quit your books . . . / Close up those barren leaves / Come forth, and bring with you a heart / That watches and receives." The Emersonian version reads: "See thou bring not to field or stone / The fancies found in books; / Leave authors' eyes, and fetch your own / To brave the landscape's looks." The closing stanza of Emerson's poem seems to echo "Expostulation and Reply" where Wordsworth says, "Nor less I deem that there are Powers / Which of themselves our minds impress; / That we can feed this mind of ours / In a wise passiveness." And in Emerson: "Oblivion here thy wisdom is, / Thy thrift the sleep of cares; / For a proud idleness like this / Crowns all thy mean affairs." His "proud idleness" comes sufficiently close to Wordsworth's "wise passiveness" and even approaches the "diligent indolence" of John Keats. It is true that Emerson's lines do not always achieve the prosodic polish of Wordsworth's simple but not simplistic phrasings. Yet no one can read "Waldeinsamkeit" without concluding that many quatrains of both poets are virtually interchangeable.

Other poems in *May-Day* succeed in varying degrees. The ode that Emerson wrote for July 4, 1857, opened with the arresting lines "O tenderly the haughty day / Fills his blue urn with fire." The little love lyric called "Una" reads like a distant reminiscence of Emerson's first wife. "The Titmouse" is a joyous tribute to one of Emerson's favorite birds. "The Romany Girl" may have originated in Emerson's enthusiasm for the writings of George Borrow. But few critics have been harder on Emerson's poetry than he was. "I am a bard least of bards," he wrote in 1863. "I cannot, like them, make lofty arguments in stately continuous verse, constraining the rocks, trees, animals, and the periodic stars to say my thoughts,—for that is the gift of great poets; but I am a bard, because I stand near them, and apprehend all they utter, and with pure joy hear that which I also would say, and moreover, I speak interruptedly words and half stanzas which have the like scope and aim." He reiterates this judgment in "The Test": "I hung my verses in the wind / Time and tide their faults may find / All were winnowed through and through / Five lines lasted sound and true . . . / Have you eyes to find the five / Which five hundred did survive?" And one further sentence in the journal for 1866 plaintively recognizes the imminence of decay in all grandfatherly bards: "I find it a great and fatal difference whether I court the Muse, or the Muse courts me: that is the ugly disparity between age and youth."

Chapter   Forty - six

A FORCE
AT WORK

THE EMERSON HOUSEHOLD IN THE LATE 1860s SUPPORTED various gradations of religious belief. When Ellen joined the Unitarian Church in 1867, Lidian was supportive, but could not bring herself to follow suit. Emerson accepted his daughter's decision without protest while holding that to do likewise would make him feel "as if he had abridged his boundless freedom." His speeches to the Free Religious Association in 1867 and 1869 dilated upon his position. Statistics, he said, showed a marked falling-off of church attendance in America, England, and Germany. "Every healthy and thoughtful mind" found itself "checked, cribbed, confined" by the teachings of the church. The old credos were "outgrown" and "a technical theology" could no longer command wide attention. To discover a religion that combined enthusiasm and genuine exaltation, dominating "all social and private action," one had only to recognize "the Divine Presence within his own mind."

He deeply believed that "the author of Nature," activating the "moral sentiment," spoke to every man the law "after which the universe was made"—to wit, that "there is a force always at work to make the best better and the worst good." He cited the conviction of the Quaker George Fox, who said that though he read of Christ and God, he knew them only from the like spirit in his own soul. "The health and integrity of man is self-respect," said Emerson, "self-subsistency, a regard to natural conscience. All education is to accustom him to trust himself, discriminate between his higher and lower thoughts, exert the timid faculties until they are robust, and thus train him to self-help . . . an adult, self-searching soul, brave to assist or resist a world: only humble and docile before the source of wisdom he has discovered within him."

As he had done so often before, Emerson was here enunciating the central principle of his brand of Transcendentalism. Many years later, Dr. Holmes looked back upon the intellectual career of his late friend: "What could we do with this unexpected . . . unclassified, half unwelcome newcomer, who had been for a while potted, as it were, in our Unitarian cold greenhouse, but had taken to growing so fast that he was lifting off its glass roof and letting in the hailstorms? Here was a protest that outflanked the extreme left of liberalism, yet so calm and serene that its radicalism had the accents of the gospel of peace. Here was an iconoclast without a hammer, who took down our idols from their pedestals so tenderly that it seemed like an act of worship."

Holmes was in the audience when Emerson read his Phi Beta Kappa address, "Progress of Culture," at Harvard on July 18, 1867, which offered a further instance of his brand of radicalism. All history, said the lecturer, demonstrated the supreme importance of minorities of one, proving that the human intellect is the perennial revolutionary power. "The foundation of culture, as of character, is at last the moral sentiment." All great men have recognized that the "spiritual is stronger than any material force, that thought rules the world." The moral element in man was the only effective counterpoise to the otherwise dismaying immensity of Nature, bereaving it of terror. When the will "absolutely surrendered to the moral sentiment," that was virtue; when the wit "surrendered to intellectual truth," that was genius. Emerson's peroration quoted, without attribution, a statement from his son-in-law, Will Forbes: "Difficulties exist to be surmounted." Emerson had copied it into his journal in 1866 as an example of "a right heroic creed." Great hearts did not complain of obstructions, but rose to overcome them. Such men were "strong enough to hold up the Republic" and to fulfill the promise of better times to come.

The preparation of this address had apparently given Emerson a good deal of trouble. On the eve of its delivery, he had complained that he "could not get the frame even to stand until a late hour." His difficulties were compounded when he began reading. The lighting was so poor that Edward Everett Hale had to hunt up a cushion to bring the pages nearer to the speaker's eyes. James Russell Lowell, who had invited him to make the address, afterward reported that Emerson had "boggled . . . lost his place . . . had to put on his glasses; but it was as if a creature from some fairer world had lost his way in our fogs, and it was *our* fault, not his." Annie Fields, who with her husband had driven out from Boston for the occasion, recalled that "poor Mr. E's MSS. was in inextricable confusion . . . and the whole matter seemed at first out of joint in the reader's eyes. However that may have been, it was far from out of joint in our eyes, being noble in aim and influence, magnetic, imaginative. I felt grateful that I had lived till that moment and as if I might come home to live and work better. Thank Heaven for such a master!" But Emerson, she added, "was evidently put out and angry with himself for his disorder and, taking Mr. Fields's arm as he came from the assembly, had to be somewhat reassured that it was not an utter failure."

His disappointment was no doubt increased by the fact that this was the thirtieth anniversary of his epoch-making Phi Beta Kappa address on "The American Scholar," and by his hope to match the original performance in eloquence and force. During the postwar years the new Harvard generation had been gradually relaxing the moratorium that had excluded Emerson for so long from the attentions of his Alma Mater. In 1865 he had been invited to pay public tribute to Harvard's living and dead soldiers; in 1866 he had been awarded an honorary degree; and now in 1867 he had just been elected to the Board of Overseers, a position that he was to fill with unrelenting devotion for the next twelve years. Little wonder that he had felt the need of Fields's reassurances after so middling a performance.

Had he chosen to plead extenuating circumstances, he could have found them aplenty in the schedule he had been following since returning in March from a two-month lecture tour in the Midwest. Despite a bout of erysipelas, an acute inflammation of his face that had appeared on April Fool's Day, he had lectured at the Concord Lyceum on the tenth, given a eulogy at the funeral of his friend George L. Stearns on the fourteenth, and on the nineteenth presented a brilliant speech at the dedication of the Soldiers' Monument on Concord Green. In this warm-hearted commentary, he summarized the war record of the 32nd Massachusetts Volunteers, provided a detailed regimental history that showed close knowledge of the whole course of the conflict, brought the campaigns to stirring life, quoted letters from the Concord soldiers, and saluted the memory of their late heroic commander, Colonel Prescott. He had also given much time and effort to raising funds for the construction of Harvard's Memorial Hall.

These public engagements were punctuated by a private and rather touching interlude on the last day of April. Una Hawthorne, aged twenty-three, had fallen ill with yet another recurrence of the fever she had caught in Rome long ago. On Easter Sunday, she had fainted dead away when her friend Storrow Higginson revealed that he had been "hopelessly in love with her" for years. At first she rejected his proposal and then reconsidered. Torn by her girlish dilemma, she sought Ellen Emerson's advice. Perhaps Emerson would be willing to talk in loco parentis. He was "her idol and Storrow's, too," and had always been "fatherly kind" to her since her own father's death. Ellen promised to raise the question when Emerson returned from lecturing in Malone, New York. Despite his fatigue, he at once set down his valise and walked through the April morning to the Wayside. Una gave him breakfast and they spent the whole morning talking in Hawthorne's study in a father-daughter colloquy that presumably lifted Una's flagging spirits.

Ellen continued to be the staff on which Emerson and Lidian steadily leaned. "Mother is in the first place to be considered," she wrote at the time of her own illness in August 1867, "both because she is Mother, because she is sickest, because she suffers so frightfully. No plan that leaves her in the lurch must be entertained for a moment, and any plan that takes me and leaves her at home is of that nature. We must jog on peacefully within our own walls and I must sternly refrain from doing anything or having anything done till a strength that can be relied on grows again."

She did manage occasional vacation trips, one in June 1867 before she fell ill, to visit the Wards in Newport, where she found that Anna, now aged fifty-four, was still "as of old suffering the most intolerable neuralgia," so that her son, Tom, and her daughters, Lily and Bessie, felt obliged to shield her from all company. In September, Ellen and Eddy went to Naushon, where they rode horseback over the grassy downs and pulled up in the ancient grove of beech trees that Emerson had first admired ten years earlier. At home in October Ellen accompanied her parents to the annual Cattle Show, where a horse stamped on the hem of Lidian's best dress, eliciting one of her famous screams, though she cooed at all the cows and "asked if the sun couldn't be screened from the bossy's eyes."

There was another respite when Edith's second child arrived on October 28. Ellen hurried down to Milton to assist, enraptured by Edith Junior's small fists and lady-like ears. "I no longer canter along the ground as in the old days," she cried, "but skip from tree-top to tree-top, and everyone says, 'We understand it: she has a NEPHEW and a NIECE.'" Emerson followed to see his second grandchild, and spoke admiringly of her rosebud mouth. But he was even more impressed by the "size, strength, and furious activity" of the young savage Ras, now aged sixteen months, whose sharp eyes gave him a "semper paratus demeanor." He was vastly amused by Will Forbes's account of Ras's assumption of a "Society-face" whenever he leaned over the cradle to give his newborn sister "a condescending kiss." Said Ellen: "We all think that Father and Mother are happier in these little children than they ever were in anything, even in their own."

When Charles Dickens came to Boston in November, Emerson dined in his company at the Fieldses' house in Charles Street. But he had already left for the Midwest when Dickens read *A Christmas Carol* to an audience of 1,500 in Tremont Temple. The faithful Ellen sent her father two enthusiastic descriptions of the great event. But his own view of Dickens was far less ardent than hers. Dining with him in England in 1848, he had heard the novelist say that "he should be scared if his son were particularly chaste"—a remark that surfaced three times in his contemporaneous journals. A later entry said simply, "I know a man of undoubted faculty who will be the more respected, like Dickens, the more you do not see his person." His own Christmas carolings took place in Chicago and Cleveland, and he got back to Milton only in time for a postponed New Year's celebration on January 2.

Despite frequent allusions to her recurrent illnesses and loss of strength, Ellen continued to run the household. In March 1868 she exclaimed, "Now I am firmly rooted in Concord, and think it beautiful and comfortable, and oh! how happy; and desire nothing better if I live a hundred years." Her letters of the time repeatedly mention her amusement over such matters as the pair of jays named Atrocious and Peter who appeared each morning on the windowsill to peck up the cold hasty pudding that Lidian put out for them. "Why is this girl always so unaccountably cheerful?" wrote Emerson in June. "Only because the due letter was written and posted yesterday, the valise of her brother's clothes went by the express, and he must have received them hours ago, and there is time this forenoon for all that is to be done. So with the weeks and the months. 'Tis her habit, and every day brings the gay acknowl-edgment of these petty fidelities, by letter or by the faces of all whom she meets."

The clothes for Eddy had been sent to Milton where Will Forbes had set up a ten-acre experimental vineyard on a hill in nearby Quincy to grow Concord grapes. By placing Eddy in charge, Will hoped that the boy's precarious health might benefit from outdoor work, as it seems to have done, particularly since he could rest up in Concord on Sundays and enjoy occasional vacations in the slack seasons.

In February, shortly before Eddy began his labors in Quincy, two of his aunts had died in Concord within three days—William Emerson's wife, Susan, of tuberculosis, and Lidian's sister, Lucy Jackson, of an "acute illness" that may have been cancer. Ellen was faithfully attentive to both of them, though troubled that a bad sore throat of her own had prevented her from comforting them in their final extremities. Emerson's erysipelas returned in March and again in July, but in the interim he took Ellen to New York, where they dined with the Ward family, who now divided their time between winters in their house at 89 Madison Avenue and summers at their "noble house" on Ocean Point in Newport. Ellen and her father also happened to catch a glimpse of General Grant, now a presidential candidate, but arrayed that day in an old Army hat and notably shabby clothing.

Illnesses of various degrees continued to dog the Emerson family. In New York, Emerson's throat had to be packed and massaged before his lectures; in Concord, Eddy came home from his vineyard with a cold that kept him in bed for three weeks in May, and his Uncle William, nursed by Lidian and Ellen, fought off a kind of pleurisy that had troubled him since his wife's death, and was still "very pale and feeble" when all three of the Emerson children joined him in New York for the wedding of his son Haven to Susan Tompkins on June 2.

The rest of the summer was full of arrivals and departures. In July Emerson and Lidian spent four days at Newport with Sarah Clarke and paid several visits to the Wards. An "odious carbuncle" vexed Emerson's face on the twenty-third, but he bore it off to Cambridge for a meeting of the Harvard Overseers and his forty-seventh class reunion. Defying Dr. Bartlett's orders, Ellen camped out with Eddy and several friends on their beloved Mount Monadnock, and in August took Lidian to Princeton, under the brow of

Mount Wachusett, for a rainy vacation that lasted a week before she joined her father on a trip to Middlebury, Vermont, where he spoke before a college convocation, afterward climbing Mount Mansfield with his indefatigable daughter.

All that summer William Emerson lay ill in New York, cared for by his sons, Haven and Charles. Late in August Haven wrote Ellen that his father's condition was steadily worsening. "Send me I pray you better news of your nights and days," wrote Emerson. "When we are old we do not expect the health of youth, but must come as near as we can to the average health of age." William's answer on September 4 said that he was still feeling poorly: for two days he had not even been able to go downstairs. After more than half a century this was the final exchange of letters between the last two of the five Emerson brothers. A week later Emerson left for New York. Haven and his bride, Susan, were at breakfast when he arrived, and Charles was watching at his father's bedside. Emerson found William "much altered in face and in speech," but they reminisced together for half an hour. When Emerson went upstairs again in mid-morning, William was asleep and by one o'clock he was dead.

"It was all a sad surprise to me," Emerson wrote to Lidian. "I am glad to have come, if it was the last day. He did not expect to see me. The boys have been excellent sons, and I tell Charles that he can never reproach himself." Since William had wished to be buried in Concord, they arranged to have the body sealed in a lead coffin, saw it aboard the eight o'clock train on the morning of the fourteenth, and walked behind the hearse that carried it to Sleepy Hollow at noon next day.

In little more than a year, death had struck down five of Emerson's oldest friends: in July 1867 his benefactor Abel Adams, who had left generous legacies to Emerson and his three children, and then the wise and learned Sarah Alden Ripley, who had once told him that "the farmers like to be complimented with thought"; in February 1868, Susan Emerson and Lucy Jackson; and now in September his only remaining brother. Yet it was always his habit to look forward rather than back. Despite such necessary subtractions, the force for good was still at work, and good people were behind it. "The few stout and sincere persons whom each one of us knows," he wrote in his journals, "recommend the country and the planet to us. 'Tis not a bad world this, as long as I know that J[ohn] M[urray] F[orbes], and W[illiam] H[athaway]

F[orbes], and Judge Hoar, and Agassiz, and my three children, and twenty other shining creatures whose faces I see looming through the mist, are walking in it. Is it the thirty millions of America, or is it your ten or twelve units that encourage your heart from day to day?"

Such recognitions as this kept Emerson's face alight and apparently untroubled, as when he and John Murray Forbes, two proud grandfathers, had their photograph taken with their grandson in the fall of 1868. Ras the invincible is sprawled in Emerson's lap while Forbes holds out his gold watch and chain to catch the child's attention. It is curious that Emerson, half smiling at the camera, his still dark hair neatly combed, looks ten years younger than the bald and wrinkled Forbes, though in fact he was ten years older.

It is true that in the same year Emerson had written, "I am the worst speaker known to the platforms and ever deteriorating," and "My pen of late creeps slow and slower," and that when he began a new course of lectures at the Meionaon in Boston on October 12 with a discourse on "Nature and Art," the young Englishman, Leslie Stephen, thought his remarks "rambling and incoherent." Not so Annie Fields, who gave a supper party after the lecture and called Emerson "alive and alert on all topics." His son Edward was "full of his grape culture at Milton," his daughter Ellen "full of good works," and his wife Lidian full of heat against the late W. T. G. Morton, who in 1846 had stolen credit from Lidian's brother, Charles T. Jackson, for the discovery of the anesthetic uses of sulfuric ether that Jackson had made in 1842. As for Emerson, wrote Annie Fields, "it is a pure benediction to see him and I honor and love him." She found his second lecture on "Poetry and Criticism" filled with "touches of light which dropped from him, to us . . . and made us burn as with a kind of sudden inspiration of truth."

"The Hawthornes are breaking up housekeeping this week," wrote Ellen on October 7. Sophia had sold the Wayside and the whole family sailed for Germany on the twenty-second. Julian had been dismissed from Harvard in 1866 and spent the intervening years in desultory attendance at a scientific school in Cambridge. Now he wished to study engineering at the Realschule in Dresden while Una and Rose could take lessons in the arts. Their departure left yet another vacancy in the Emersons' neighborhood. Of the original band only Alcott and Channing remained. Ellery had sold his house on Main Street in 1864 and bought another on Middle Street where he was going to spend much of the final quarter century of his increasingly eremitical life. The

Alcotts were still at Orchard House, buoyed up by Alcott's growing reputation as a lecturer, and most by the successful writing career of Louisa May, now aged thirty-six, the first part of whose *Little Women* had just been published on September 30.

Another departure of even greater consequence to the Emersons was now imminent. This was Ellen's, whose too frenetic activities, including constant attention to her parents' welfare, had at last caught up with her after nearly two years of dwindling strength. On the Saturday morning of October 17, as she told her Cousin Haven, "a bolt fell from a clear sky, and tore me up by the roots. My family told me to pack my trunks, settle my affairs, make my will, and go to Fayal . . . to stay until June. Everything seems to lie about me in a snarl which I ought to unravel before Wednesday [the twenty-eighth] and cannot hope to."

Her destination was one of a small group of islands in the Azores, a Portuguese dependency some 900 miles west of Lisbon in the stormy Atlantic. The choice of Fayal seems to have been based on the recommendation of John Murray Forbes, who was a friend of the American consul, Charles W. Dabney, a Bostonian and the father of a close-knit and musical family of sons and daughters. If that was so, it was yet another instance—like Eddy's vineyard on Quincy Hill—of the Forbes's steady devotion to the Emerson family. Ellen's passage was booked aboard the bark *Fredonia*, with an announced sailing date of October 30, but the captain waited for a favoring wind until November 4, when the ship weighed anchor and left Boston harbor. The delay enabled Ellen to attend her father's fourth lecture at the Meionaon, a much-reworked and tattered version of his theories on "Leasts and Mosts," which she found very funny and a sufficient reward for her detention ashore.

She was still so weak when the twelve-day voyage began that she spent three-quarters of her time in her cabin, emerging only belatedly to see her "longed-for world of pure sea and sky." But her usual exuberance soon returned. She found Fayal "an earthly Paradise," reveling in the abundance of tropical fruits that graced the Dabneys' table at Thanksgiving and Christmas, walking twice daily up and down the steep hills, riding the small plodding donkeys, admiring a smoking volcano called Pico on a neighboring island, and befriending the impoverished natives. She watched the loading of the *Fredonia* with 5,000 cases of green oranges for the Boston market, and recorded the arrivals of the dozens of merchantmen and whalers that put in for repairs after the howling gales of the mid-Atlantic. In February she received and read a copy of *Little Women*, which she promptly lent to the younger Dabney girls. "Louisa," she wrote, "has always been the most lively and original girl, and her three sisters were all bright and able to help in all her schemes," though nowadays she was "always busy writing." The exploits of the March sisters forcibly reminded her of former times with the Alcott family when "to spend a day at their house was a rapturous event."

Caroline Tappan wrote from Lenox that she would be wintering at 9 Louisburg Square and hoped to reach Boston in time to hear Emerson's final lecture at the Meionaon. Ellen's sojourn in the Azores must be delightful for her but rather sad for the elder Emersons. She wondered whether Emerson would take off again "upon the buffalo trail." George Curtis had described the typical lecture tour as "a tough beefsteak before daylight," and Caroline hoped that Emerson was "not still to be a martyr to that stake." Although Emerson obviously missed his "invalided daughter," who sent home "oranges and paradisiacal details of the Azores," he continued his Boston lectures under the astute management of James T. Fields, and in the new year of 1869, at Will Forbes's instigation, began a series of "readings" at Chickering Hall. These required less formal preparation than regular lectures, and permitted such off-the-cuff comments as one on Milton's *Comus*, which he termed "the noblest praise of chastity ever written."

The readings were sandwiched in among some forty lectures at various other nearby cities, as well as a two-week tour on the "buffalo trail" in upstate New York at the end of January. Lidian's view of her husband's repeated absences had once been quoted by Ellen: "Mother says every day, 'Oh if he only would get home and never go away again.' " But the lectures and readings in Boston were producing substantial income. His net receipts for the Meionaon series were in excess of $1,600—"much the largest sum," as he told Jamie Fields, "I ever received for work of this kind." When Will Forbes sent him an advance payment of $600 for the Chickering Hall readings, he called the gesture "a fine piece of knightly courtesy and daring," adding that he had lately been paying off all his debts and might even be induced to make a bid on the Boston State House if it should ever come up for sale.

Part Five

THE

SEVENTIES

THE HIGH MUSE
COMES AND GOES

ELLEN RETURNED FROM FAYAL ON MAY 27, 1869, AFTER SIX months of semivoluntary exile that had more or less restored her health and now enabled her to reassume the multiple duties of housekeeping. These were diversified with trips to Milton and Naushon, which had become second homes to all the Emersons. Her "one hold on health," as she wrote after a visit to New York in September, was going to bed each night at eight and walking out for two hours every day. She spent most of October at Milton, where Edith was just beginning her third pregnancy and where Edith Junior, nicknamed Violet, was sitting (and squirming) for a bust by a black sculptor, a Miss Lewis. Eddy was also there, and presented his sister with a cluster of Concord grapes from the vineyard on Quincy Hill. But he had just changed course again. Having recently determined to follow his cousins, Haven and Charles, into the study of medicine, he was now registered at Harvard Medical School. At home in December he practiced anatomy by "slaying and dissecting one of the large stray cats" that frequented Emerson's barn.

Among the social interludes before Christmas was what Ellen called a "letter dinner party." Henry James Senior and his daughter, Alice, came to Concord on December 10, bringing a sheaf of his son Henry's foreign letters. Henry was spending a year in Europe, and had sent his father an account of his first meeting with George Eliot, whom he called "magnificently ugly—deliciously hideous," yet in whose "vast ugliness" resided such a "powerful beauty" that he ended by falling in love with her. Soon afterward he wrote

from Rome to his brother William: "I am extremely glad you like my letters—
and terrifically agitated by the thought that Emerson likes them."

Emerson had been inordinately busy. In the summer of 1869 he complained that he had "never had so many tasks as in the last twelvemonth," a
problem with which he continued to wrestle for two more years. His recent
assignments had included revision and correction of all six of his prose works
for a two-volume edition to be published in October by the newly constituted
firm of Fields, Osgood; gathering up a dozen essays for a seventh book of
prose—*Society and Solitude*—that appeared in February 1870; serving as
agent for the Class of 1821 in money-raising for Harvard under its brave new
president, Charles W. Eliot; and accepting Eliot's invitation to become a
"University Lecturer" during the spring of 1870.

At the end of May, just as Ellen was coming home from the Azores, he allied himself with the New England Woman Suffrage Association, offering a
"remarkably friendly speech" that eventuated in his election as one of their
vice presidents. At the same time he was conducting an extensive correspondence with Emma Lazarus, a pleasantly aggressive young poet whom he had
met at Sam Ward's house in New York in 1868, and continued thereafter to
advise and encourage for more than three years, much as he had done with
Thoreau, Channing, and other youthful aspirants in the far-off days of the
Dial. On September 14 he was one of the speakers at the centennial celebration of the birth of Alexander von Humboldt, who had been among his gods
for more than thirty years. He called the baron that "wonderful Humboldt,
with his solid centre and expanded wings" who "marches like an army, gathering all things as he goes." He began his sixty-seventh year with no apparent
diminution in his capacity for work.

His New Year's gifts for 1870 reflected the family's continuing care for
their breadwinner. "Father is pompous in his study," wrote Ellen, "with his
new taper and quill pens and his bookrack and blotter." He felt obliged to cut
back on his usual schedule owing to the Harvard commitment, which was
going to require no fewer than sixteen lectures on "The Natural History of
the Intellect." Apart from four short trips in February and a speech to the
New England Women's Club in March, he spent most of the winter at work
on the Harvard series, which began late in April and ended in early June.
"Mother very feeble but gets out on pleasant days," wrote Ellen in May.
"She said lately she thought Father was getting through his lectures wonder-

fully. I think he thinks so. He has given the tenth today, and he never speaks despairingly lately as he did at first; he rather enjoys his class and feels at liberty to favour and help himself with reading, or give a lecture of only half an hour sometimes." Yet his preparations for these appearances were nevertheless time-consuming, and he apologized to Caroline Tappan on May 9: "It has been and is a great grief to me that you should have been all winter in Cambridge and I should not once have found your house—but it could not be helped . . . and I never expect to be such a slave to my tasks hereafter as I have been and am in these weeks and months."

Edith Forbes greeted his sixty-seventh birthday with a new grandson named Cameron. "We are rejoiced in the good tidings you send us," he wrote hastily on the twenty-third, "and send all blessings to the boy." Despite a recent bout with whooping cough, Ellen hurried to Milton to see her second nephew, afterward reporting that the child was large and handsome, with "a spacious rubicund face and very good features situated near the centre," although his voice was so hoarse that he "quacked like a duck."

A couple of weeks earlier, young Henry James had returned to Cambridge from his year abroad. Recalling the "letter dinner party" of the preceding December, the Emersons asked him to Concord. He appeared on July 1, accompanied by three Englishmen. In anticipation of the visit, Lidian had been "very sick and anxious" all morning, but in the evening, which was still her favorite time, "exulted in the pleasures of eager serious general conversation." Everyone, said Ellen, "talked fast all the time" on such topics as the relative beauties of English and American landscapes. Henry remarked that on coming home he had been painfully struck by the meagerness of American grass. The complaint did not apparently fit Concord in midsummer, and he promised himself that he would come there again to "tramp it all over from boundary to boundary." But in a letter to Grace Norton he said only that his days in Concord had passed "pleasantly, but with slender profit."

Another large task now confronted Emerson. All that summer he gave his days and nights to the study of his old friend Plutarch, whose *Lives* and *Morals* had never failed to engage him since the late 1820s. He had agreed to prepare an introduction to a new edition of the *Morals* by the Harvard professor William W. Goodwin. It was set for publication in December, and time, as always with Emerson, moved faster than he was able to. He filled many pages of his journal with Plutarchian notations, compared Goodwin's version with the old translation by "Many Hands" of 1718 and with the Greek of the Tauchnitz edition, and, as Ellen said, "collected all the authors who have written about Plutarch," giving himself "a really delightful time" in rereading their commentaries. On August 10 he complained of the "heavy weight" of his task and of his slow progress. The preliminaries took so long that he had not yet dared to begin writing. He allowed himself only two short vacations, one with Ellen to Nantasket in July and the other with Eddy to Maine and New Hampshire in September, during which they climbed the "great hill" of Mount Washington.

In the end he came up with an essay of 6,000 words that began, as Ellen had predicted, with a brief history of Plutarch's continuing popularity among modern nations. He quoted with relish a statement of Montaigne's from 1589: "We dunces had been lost, had not this book raised us out of the dirt." He thought that Plutarch "perpetually suggests Montaigne, who was the best reader he has ever found, though Montaigne excelled his master in the point and surprise of his sentences. Plutarch had a religion which Montaigne wanted, and which defends him from wantonness; and though Plutarch is plain-spoken, his moral sentiment is always pure." Both these favorites were notably humane, with such a taste for the quotidian that their pages, in Ben Jonson's phrase, were "rammed with life." In reading Plutarch, said Emerson, "I confess that . . . I embrace the particulars. . . . His style is realistic, picturesque and varied; his sharp objective eyes seeing everything that moves, shines or threatens in nature or art, or thought and dreams."

He believed that Plutarch stood as one "chief example of the illumination of the intellect by the force of morals":

We are always interested in the man who treats the intellect well. We expect it from the philosopher . . . but we know that metaphysical studies in any but minds of large horizon and incessant inspiration have their dangers. One asks sometimes whether a metaphysician can treat the intellect well. The central fact is the superhuman intelligence, pouring into us from its unknown fountain, to be received with religious awe, and defended from any mixture of our will. But this high Muse comes and goes; and the danger is that, when the Muse is wanting, the student is prone to supply its place with microscopic studies and logomachy. . . . Whilst we expect this awe and reverence of the spiritual power from the philosopher in his closet, we praise it in the man of the world—the man who lives on quiet terms with existing institutions, yet indicates his perception of these high oracles, as do Plutarch, Montaigne, Hume, and Goethe. Perhaps they sometimes compromise . . . but they keep open the source of wisdom and health. Plutarch is uniformly true to this centre. He had not lost his wonder. He is a pronounced idealist.

Never a dogmatist, always "impatient of sophistry," Plutarch was that kind of Stoic who fought the good fight against "Fortune, vices, effeminacy, and indolence." If his was "not a profound mind," yet he was "a man of rare gifts," and the "most amiable of boon companions." For these reasons, said Emerson, his *Moralia* would be "perpetually rediscovered from time to time as long as books last."

So Emerson placed his subject among those writers of the Western tradition who were at the same time men of the world *and* idealists, in touch with the "moral sentiment" as a prime source of wisdom and intellectual health. In his admirable book, *Emerson's Plutarch*, Edmund G. Berry calls this essay "a readable, useful introduction" to the work at hand, and a "final effective piece of evidence of his devotion to the *Moralia*." He finds some errors of carelessness and mistaken attribution, points out that much of the content is "a string of quotations, many of which he had noted and used many years before," and concludes that the piece "has little of the inspiration and none of the vigor which we associate with the younger Emerson."

With Plutarch behind him, Emerson returned to the podium, delivering some fifteen lectures between December 1870 and March 1871, besides repeating (with some changes) his Harvard course on "The Natural History of the Intellect" during seventeen further appearances. When he finished in early April, showing signs of fatigue, John Murray Forbes came forward with a proposal for a trip by rail to California. "At first more shocked than allured," Emerson was persuaded to accept by his family and his doctor. Ellen was more explicit: "I am helping Edith off to California. All the Forbeses, Mr and Mrs. Forbes Alice, Sara, Will and Edith, are going next week. Mr Forbes has invited Father and Mr Thayer. . . . Father is going, Mr. T hasn't decided.

Wilky James too and Mrs. George Russell and Annie Anthony. . . . The three young Forbeses, Ralph, Edith, and Cameron are coming to Concord to stay meanwhile."

The Boston contingent, including Will and Edith, Emerson and Thayer, entrained on the afternoon of April 11. James B. Thayer was a lawyer who had been helping the Emersons with financial affairs. In 1861 he had married Sophia, daughter of Emerson's half uncle Samuel Ripley, and was thus a relative by marriage. His record of the trip, published in 1884, provided information that would otherwise have been lost, including many of Emerson's obiter dicta along the way. Emerson's satchel, of an astonishing purple shade, contained half a dozen elderly lectures for delivery if called for in California, and a batch of manuscript sheets for his anthology, *Parnassus*, long in preparation and based on his wish to have "a volume on my own table that shall hold the best poems of all my Poets." His chief collaborator in this enterprise was his daughter Edith, now in the midst of her fourth pregnancy and eager to assist with the pleasant duties of selecting and copying out the poems.

Except for John Forbes, who joined them in Iowa, the whole party of twelve convened at Chicago, where they got aboard a well-stocked private Pullman car, the *Huron*, secured by the old railroader Forbes from his friend George Mortimer Pullman, the inventor, a thickset man of forty, who was there to see them off. By April 17 they were crossing the sagebrush plains near Laramie, sighting the shy swift antelopes that fled as the train roared past, but only a single captive representative of the once vast herds of buffalo, long since decimated by wasteful overhunting. Indians appeared at every stop, "the squaws and papooses begging, the 'bucks' as they wickedly call them, lounging." At Ogden, Utah Territory, they detoured south to Salt Lake City and the signs of springtime civilization: men were plowing the fat fields, cherry and peach trees were in bloom.

The main purpose of the stopover was to see Brigham Young, the Mormon president. In 1863 Emerson had written, under the rubric "Good out of evil," that Young's genius must be thanked "for the creation of Salt Lake City . . . an efficient example to all men in the vast desart [sic], teaching how to subdue and turn it to a habitable garden," an operation that had now been going on for nearly a quarter century. The women in the Forbes party declined to visit Young, who was reputed to have sixteen wives. The men found him dressed for a drive in a long cloak and broad-brimmed hat. He received them with stolid dignity—a man of medium height, aged seventy, his auburn beard tinged with gray. He gave no sign of having heard of Emerson, though his pallid young male secretary professed to have read "a great many" of Emerson's books. The talk was desultory and the callers soon took leave. Afterward they located a copy of the *Deseret News* containing one of Young's recent sermons. Apart from "much homely good advice," it struck Thayer as a "revolting mixture of religious fanaticism and vulgar dishonesty." Emerson thought that Mormonism was a latter-day echo of Puritan bibliolatry—an "after-clap of Puritanism"—and now called Young "a sufficient ruler, and perhaps civilizer of his kingdom of blockheads."

Two mornings later the travelers awoke in California. The weather was so Junelike that Thayer recalled the opening of Emerson's "Divinity School Address": "In this refulgent summer, it has been a luxury to draw the breath of life." Emerson himself was struck by the "florescent landscape" and the constant sunshine. By nightfall they were registered at the Occidental Hotel in San Francisco—an address soon located by Dr. Horatio Stebbins, a renowned Unitarian preacher who lost no time in signing up the famous visitor to speak from his pulpit four times between April 23 and the first of May. He took Emerson, Edith, and Thayer on a sightseeing tour that embraced Chinatown and the Cliff House Hotel, where they watched a herd of sea lions disporting themselves among the surges and uttering their hoarse cries, an adventure that Emerson described in a charming letter to his grandson Ras in far-off Concord. He was notably relaxed, his spirits were excellent, and he laughingly boasted that his weight now stood at 140.5: "That *half* I prize; it's an indication of better things!"

The lectures were raptly received. On the second occasion he "accidentally overturned a vase in the pulpit, then descended, gathered up the flowers, and replaced them while the audience applauded." It was the only sign of awkwardness. One reporter described him as "tall, straight, well formed, with a head constructed on the utility rather than the ornamental principle," but "refreshing to look upon." The pages he read from were worn and familiar. The unfamiliar was still to come. Three and a half days to the east lay the great natural showplaces of California—the valley of the Yosemite and the groves of giant sequoias, hundreds of years old, hundreds of feet tall. On May 2 the Forbes party set off to cover the distance by train, wagon, and horseback. At their overnight stops they always seemed to run into transplanted New Englanders. One was a Bostonian named Roberts who ran the ferry across the Tuolumne River and operated a small inn where his wife dished up a dinner of pork, liver, and hot saleratus biscuits, washed down with native wine. After such entertainment, Emerson often smoked with chosen male companions. He had once called tobacco "the scatterbrain," and quoted his Irish yardman, John Clahan, who said that "he was lonesome without tobacco." Now, sitting outdoors with Will Forbes and Jim Thayer, a shawl around his shoulders in the cool dry evening air, listening to the chirp of crickets, he said that he found his cigar "a singular comfort."

On May 4 the covered wagons climbed for twenty miles through virgin timber. At Hazel Green the riders transferred to horseback. Emerson's steed was a mottled mustang. All afternoon they moved through a forest of pines and firs, thick in girth and often more than 200 feet in height. After a rainy night in a shanty at Crane Flat, they rode eighteen miles to the Yosemite and its natural wonders: Bridal Veil Falls, the beetling cliff, El Capitan, the torrential falls of the Yosemite River, and finally Mirror Lake and the Half-Dome. On the sixth Emerson and young Wilkie James measured a prostrate sugar pine and computed its former height at 210 feet. "This valley," said he, "is the only place that comes up to the brag about it and exceeds it." He recalled another traveler's ground rule: "Take notes on the spot; a note is worth a cartload of recollections."

But he left note taking largely to James Thayer. Day after day he chose rather to talk, cheerfully advancing a wide variety of opinions on Goethe, Mirabeau, Boccaccio; Coleridge, Wordsworth, Keats, and Byron; Swedenborg and Linnaeus, and even Machiavelli, who "wrote like the Devil," propounding hellish views with cool sweetness. When queried on his recent course at Harvard, he said that he had not intended to provide a systematic natural history of the intellect, nor had he been concerned with metaphysics, for which he cared little. His only plan had been to explore certain facets of the human mind—memory, for example: "What a range memory gives to a man,—so small a creature!" Luckily for his auditors, his own memorial powers had not yet begun to decay.

The party stayed at Leidig's, the best of the three hotels in the valley. On the eighth Emerson received a letter from a young Scot named John Muir, an amateur naturalist and thoroughgoing Emersonian, who was tending a small sawmill nearby. Thayer and Emerson rode over, climbed the "henladder" to

Muir's "study" in the mill gable, and spent several hours inspecting his collection of dried plants and pencil sketches. Emerson asked many questions, "pumping unconscionably," as Muir said, and ended by asking the blue-eyed, black-bearded youngster to accompany the cavalcade to the Mariposa grove of giant sequoias. The day they left there was a pie on the morning table. Emerson offered slices all round without finding takers. At last he "remonstrated, with humorous emphasis, thrusting the knife under a piece of the pie, and putting the entire weight of his character into his manner—'But Mr.—, *what is pie for?*' "

The twenty-five-mile ride to the Mariposa was rough and consummately beautiful. "He kept me talking all the time," said Muir, "but said little himself." At the lunch stop he called on members of the group to tell stories or recite poems, and lay back on the pine-needle carpet, reminiscing about his days at Harvard fifty years ago. Thayer and others were newly impressed by Emerson's behavior under difficult conditions: "He was always accessible, cheerful, sympathetic, considerate, tolerant," showing "respectful interest in those with whom he talked . . . which raised them in their own estimation." The sequoias they had come to see did not at first look very large since there were no ordinary trees for contrast. But when Thayer rode past a fallen bole, discovering that it stood higher than his head as he sat on horseback, he began to feel like Gulliver among the Brobdingnagians. Emerson "sauntered about as if under a spell," and quoted the famous verse from Genesis, "There were giants in the earth in those days." Galen Clarke, the forester in charge, a native of New Hampshire, invited Emerson to select and name a tree. He chose a vigorous giant and called it Samoset after the seventeenth-century sachem of Lidian's beloved Plymouth. Muir stayed behind when the Easterners mounted and rode away. That night he sat alone by his camp fire. "Emerson," he wrote afterward, "was with me in spirit, though I never again saw him in the flesh."

Only a week remained when they returned to San Francisco on May 15. Emerson completed his lecture engagements by reading "Chivalry," extemporized from fragmentary notes without benefit of his higher Muse, and "Hospitality," given on the eighteenth to an audience in Oakland. He had met a girl from Concord, a professional skater locally billed as "the Skatorial Queen." They happily exchanged complimentary tickets to their respective performances, but seem not to have used them. On the nineteenth, Emerson and most of the others left San Francisco for Truckee and a carriage ride to Lake Tahoe, entraining for Ogden on the twenty-second when the *Huron* caught up with them.

So ended Emerson's first and last visit to California. It had opened his Yankee eyes to the glories of a region that he had hitherto known only from reading and from the reports of his son Edward in 1862. The one major flaw in the western adventure was a telegram from Will Forbes's brother Malcolm that said, "Edward is better." Emerson complained to Lidian that he had not even heard that Edward was sick. In fact the boy had come home from medical school in Boston on April 15, believing at first that his ailment was a return of the old malaria. Six days later the telltale pox of varioloid appeared. The household was quarantined, the small children were vaccinated, while Ellen and Lidian managed to combine housekeeping, nursing, and the care of the three little Forbeses. "The town," wrote Ellen, "was quite alarmed. It was the only case . . . within its borders for fifty years at least. We became as separate from the world as if we had gone to a desert island, except that Aunt Lizzy [Hoar] and Annie Keyes came every day to visit us in the yard. . . . Our kind friends sent baskets of food to the gate . . . a great mercy, as our cook had taken to her bed in terror. . . . Finally . . . the house was fumigated and the happy day came when Will and Edith and Father drove up to the gate. To my surprise there wasn't a ray of gladness in Father's face. I drew Edith off and asked her if anything was the matter." Edith said, "Why Ellen! . . . Edward looks as if he were going to die. Of course Father is miserable." Since the quarantine was still in force, Emerson slept at the Manse as guest of Elizabeth Ripley. It was not, strictly speaking, the happiest of homecomings.

A month later Emerson sent Carlyle an etching of Brigham Young with a covering letter. His trip had ended "in many distractions" at home owing to the smallpox "which my son had ignorantly [i.e., unknowingly] brought home from his Medical Hospital," so that Emerson "could only talk with wife, son, and daughter, from the yard." Even now, late in June, Edward was "not quite healed of the *Sequelae*." The aftereffects included recurrent abscesses that pressed on the boy's lungs, and were successfully though painfully lanced by two of the Forbeses' doctors.

Despite the harrowing circumstances of his return, Emerson managed to celebrate the fiftieth anniversary of his graduation from Harvard and talked happily of his experiences in California. "We must not visit San Francisco too young," he told Jamie Fields, "or we shall never wish to come away. It is called the 'Golden Gate,' not because of its gold, but because of the lovely golden flowers which at this season cover the whole face of the country. . . ." He "smiled at the namby-pamby travelers" who refused to expose themselves to the "discomforts of the trip into the valley of the Yosemite." Annie Fields thought that his chief regret about the whole journey was that it obliged him to miss at least two meetings of the Saturday Club.

Chapter Forty - eight

THE SLOPES
OF PARNASSUS

ANNIE FIELDS'S COMMENT ON EMERSON THE CLUBMAN WAS reasonably exact. "Ah Solidarity! ah Comitatus!" he had exclaimed in 1852. "Yet I cannot coax my mates into any clubs." His problem was resolved early in 1856 by the formation of the Saturday Club, which met for monthly dinners from three to nine, usually at the Parker House in Boston. Beginning with a dozen charter members, the group gradually expanded to nineteen or twenty, along with occasional invited guests. "Is the Club exclusive?" wrote Emerson fifteen years later. " 'Tis made close to give value to your election. There are men who can afford to wait." Through all this time he had been a faithful attendant, and some of his fastest friends could always be found at the meetings: Agassiz, Judge Rockwood Hoar, J. R. Lowell, Sam Ward, Henry James Senior, Longfellow, Dr. Holmes, John Murray Forbes, Jamie Fields, C. E. Norton, Tom Appleton, James Elliot Cabot, and Hawthorne in his last years. Agassiz's word for the association was "a society of friends." Emerson quoted Thomas Hobbes: "For want of good conversation, one's understanding and invention grow mouldy." He enjoyed the "large, discursive, happy talk" where "truths detach themselves as thoughts, spars flake off from the eternal wall, and not only the company enjoy them, but the scholar most of all; he takes possession of them, and uses them henceforward as powers."

As far back as 1856 he had said that "among the good subjects for lectures is the Club." His own lecture on the subject was given at the Concord

Lyceum in March 1860 and published as an essay in *Society and Solitude* ten years later. "Of all the cordials known to us," said he, "the best, safest, and most exhilarating . . . is society; and every healthy and efficient mind passes a large part of life in the company most easy to him." Like Hobbes, he felt that "we lose our days and are barren of thought for want of some person to talk with." After many years in which, to get his work done, he had championed solitude, he now extolled the values of social intercourse. Men of "convivial talent" could "kindle each other" as they sat together around a table over a good supper. He praised Dr. Johnson's prandial conversations and called Coleridge's *Table Talk* "one of the best remains of his genius."

He still believed that the best talk took place in a company of two: "When a man meets his accurate mate, then life is delicious." For this reason, even at the club, he always tried to secure a place beside a valued friend. If this "sometimes too visible" selectivity offended others, he had heard no complaints. On occasion he resisted introductions, having once told Elizabeth Hoar, "Whom God hath put asunder why should man join together?" Yet, as Dr. Holmes said, he did not commonly hold himself apart, was neither shy nor taciturn, and displayed a "spontaneous hospitality of mind." Much as James Thayer had noted during their days in California, he paid other speakers the closest attention, head forward, "shoulders raised," eyes trained on center as if "watching the flight of the thought" that was being uttered. According to Holmes, he was "sparing of words," using them "with great precision and nicety. . . . To hear him talk was like watching one crossing a brook on stepping stones. His noun had to wait for its verb or its adjective until he was ready; then his speech would come down on the word he wanted."

Some few of the meetings saluted birthdays, as for Agassiz's fiftieth in 1857 and Holmes's in 1859. The most elaborate of these was that of April 1864 for Shakespeare's 300th, held at the Revere House. Yet oddly, having been a public speaker all his life, Emerson "rarely attempted the smallest speech impromptu," and, said Cabot, "never with success." At the Shakespeare show, for example, despite his lifelong admiration for the plays, and the trouble he had gone to in organizing the meeting, he got to his feet, looked "about him tranquilly for a minute or two," and then sat down, "serene and unabashed, but unable to say a word." As he had told Lidian in his letter proposing marriage, it was his habit on crucial occasions to prefer the written to the spoken word.

In the summer of 1871, the Club took second place to Emerson's other preoccupations. Chief among these was Eddy's recovery and his newfound plan to pursue his medical studies in Berlin, Germany, with funds provided by Will Forbes. "How dared you carry your kindness to Edward to such a point of romance?" wrote Emerson to his son-in-law. "I have read the like in novels, but do not look for it in houses. How dared you too interfere with my cautious and stingy ciphering, which was to carry the boy through . . . by the blessed force of poverty and perseverance? Well, I hope you will be forgiven for this extravagance, and that the boy will not be spoiled. He is happy in your alliance as is his sister."

As always in the face of his recurrent illnesses, Eddy was showing both remarkable powers of recuperation and a courageous habit of looking to the future rather than the past. He believed, with his father, that the best medicines all began with the letter *W*: "warmth, water, wild air, and walking." His sister Ellen reported in August that he was "pretty nearly well, that is he can shout and sing and walk and ride, lift a mattress or a small trunk, and row a little, but his wounds are not healed and he mustn't do anything violent." The main reason for his exuberance was the announcement of his engagement to Annie Shepard Keyes, one of Ellen's best friends in Concord. Before Eddy sailed for Liverpool aboard the *Malta* on September 5, he and Annie vacationed briefly at Naushon, Ellen and Annie packed his trunks, and Emerson provided him with letters of introduction to various English friends, including Carlyle and John Forster.

In the interim came Will and Edith's fourth child, born at Naushon on August 27 and named John Murray Forbes after his grandfather. "Ellen and Edward agree for once," wrote his other grandfather, "in their testimony to his excellent physique." In the later stages of her pregnancy, Edith had been helping Emerson by copying out materials for the *Parnassus* anthology, especially with passages from Shakespeare and George Herbert. Now she was obliged to give full attention to the exigencies of quadruple motherhood.

Emerson had already resumed speech making with a short address on Sir Walter Scott at the mid-August meeting of the Massachusetts Historical Society, to which he had been elected in June. It was the centennial of Scott's birth, and Emerson recalled the joy with which he and his schoolmates had responded to the metrical romances and above all the Waverley novels, "full of life and reality" like Plutarch's *Morals*, and crammed with fictional portraits of the small farmers and tradesmen, fishermen and Gypsies whom Scott had known. At the end of the month came a concert in the Town Hall in honor of Ephraim Bull Junior, the horticulturalist who had developed the now famous Concord grape, and whose son had lost his right arm on the Fourth of July while loading the village cannon. Emerson spoke again at the dinner that ended the annual Cattle Show, where his daughter proudly exhibited thirteen varieties of pears.

In the fall of 1871, Fields and Osgood urged Emerson to postpone the publication of *Parnassus* until certain revisions could be undertaken. Instead of reading proof on his anthology he turned out a preface for Ellery Channing's new blank-verse poem, *The Wanderer*. During one of their talks in California, he had discussed Channing with James Thayer: "The trouble with him is that you can't get him to make necessary changes and corrections. . . . I and one or two others regard him as a poet; but we are the only ones that do." Now, assuming the role of Horatio as an act of friendship, Emerson called his old walking companion a "Hamlet in the fields, with never a thought to waste on Horatio's opinion of his sallies." His personality was still invincible: with or without readers he would go on writing. If he neglected "conventional ornament and correct finish," some of his lines recalled "the great masters." "We have not been considered in their composition," said Emerson, "but either defied or forgotten; and therefore we consult them as freely as a photograph." William Dean Howells, reviewing the poem and the preface in the *Atlantic*, took both poet and critic to task in a notice that Emerson called "shabby." Somewhat to his surprise, most of the small edition was soon exhausted, and Caroline Tappan, who had once believed herself to be in love with Ellery, was among those who took pleasure in his latest effort.

Ellery was still resident in Concord, a threadbare recluse "frugally supported" by a modest income inherited from his father, subsisting on one meal a day in his bachelor quarters. Frank Sanborn had arranged the publication with funds supplied by Emerson. As Sanborn well knew, Ellery "did not spare his friends in his grotesque observations." One of these got into print when Sanborn edited Channing's life of Thoreau. "Emerson," Channing had written, "was never in the least contented. This made walking or company to him a penance. The Future,—that was the terrible Gorgon face that turned the Present into 'a thousand belly-aches.' 'When shall I be perfect; when shall I be moral? When shall I be this and that? When will the really good rhyme get written?' Here is the Emerson colic. Thoreau had a like disease. Men are said never to be satisfied." Channing might have found Emerson's rejoinder in his lecture on "Boston" in 1861: "There is no strong performance without a little fanaticism in the performer. It is the men who are never contented who carry their point."

When Lidian turned sixty-nine in September, Ellen took her to consult a Boston doctor. They walked across the Public Gardens and met Dr. Edward Clarke in his waiting room, where Lidian rehearsed her medical history: her father's early decline and death, her youthful thinness, the attack of scarlet fever, the rush of blood to her head, the persistent dyspepsia. She spoke of odd sensations in her chest. "There are several organs I haven't interrogated yet," the doctor said. He prescribed phosphate of soda to be mixed with Lidian's food, and said that in due course he would look for a possible "functional difficulty of the nervous system." Three times more that fall and winter, Ellen inveigled her recalcitrant mother into further consultations. Meantime she had sent her brother Eddy in England their father's diagnosis of Lidian's problems: "The Lord made her curiously. She is so sharp and dignified with her morale, and keen as a mathematician on some points—and yet she has many holes in her mind." In the end Ellen conceded temporary defeat, only urging her mother to take the pills, lead a regular life, walk outdoors each day, and overcome her bad habits of introversion. They were back about where they had started on or about Lidian's sixty-ninth birthday.

Despite recurrent "feebleness" Lidian sometimes descended from her chamber for such social occasions as Bret Harte's visit in October. Harte had come from San Francisco on a triumphal tour that embraced his birthplace, Albany, New York, and Boston, where he was working out an arrangement with the *Atlantic* to publish his stories and sketches. At thirty-two he was already nationally known for *The Luck of Roaring Camp*, as well as a magazine piece, "Plain Language from Truthful James," a comic ballad widely quoted and pirated as "The Heathen Chinee," in which a wily Asian outwitted a pair of American sharpers in a card game. Harte's eyes were blue, his nose long, his black hair touched with premature gray, and his face pitted with the old pockmarks of varioloid. Emerson and Lidian thought him "an easy, kindly, well-behaved man," and he aroused Lidian's ready sympathies with an account of his wife, Anna, "a despairing invalid." In one of his essays in *Society and Solitude* Emerson had said, " 'Tis wonderful how soon a piano gets into a log hut on the frontier." Harte pointed out that it was the gamblers who brought the music to California, and the prostitutes who introduced New York fashions to the West Coast.

Ellen was at Naushon the first time Harte appeared, but both she and her sister Edith were there when he returned on November 6. His habit of steady smoking irritated Ellen, but Lidian was charmed. She asked if he had really witnessed the behavior of the rough characters in his sketches or only knew that such people existed. Harte said that he was following nature exactly, but Ellen believed that he had made up his tales out of whole cloth.

Emerson rounded out 1871 with a two-week trip to the Midwest, carrying four well-thumbed and dog-eared lecture manuscripts for delivery in four cities, including Chicago, where he viewed the ruins of the great fire of October 8 that had devastated three square miles of the city—an area, as one eyewitness had reported, equivalent to a whole mile-wide stretch between Lexington and Concord. Back home by December 10, he reported to his son, Eddy, who had kept his own Thanksgiving in Berlin, that the western tour had obliged him to miss the Thanksgiving feast in Concord for the first time in his life. After so many years of successful lecturing to large audiences all along the eastern seaboard, throughout the Midwest, and lately in California, he was finding it hard to recognize that he was, so to speak, over the hill as a public speaker. Both now and in the ensuing years, he had not only to contend with his failing memory but also made the mistake of depending on relatively superannuated lectures, many of which struck his latter-day audiences as old-fashioned and outgrown.

This was part of his problem when he went to Baltimore in January 1872 to offer a four-lecture course at the Peabody Institute. On the way south he forgot the name of his hotel, and told Lidian that he had to ask the conductor on the train which were the "good houses" in the hope that his memory might be jogged by one name or another. The matter was settled when the provost from the Institute met him at the depot and conducted him to Barnum's Hotel, where he had stayed twice in previous years. Just before his second lecture, "Walt Whitman presented his picturesque person." Walt's companion was John Burroughs, the young author who had first met Emerson at West Point during the war. They caught up with him in the vestibule of the lecture hall and moved into a nearby reception room for a short colloquy, chiefly about Thoreau, now ten years dead.

Both Whitman and Burroughs were disappointed with Emerson's talk on "Resources and Inspiration"—"not interesting to me at all," wrote Whitman to his mother next day. He was soon complaining to Edward Dowden that Emerson had maintained the same attitude and drawn on the same themes as he had done a quarter century ago. "It all seems to me quite attenuated," said Walt. One could enjoy "the *first* drawing of a good pot of tea . . . and Emerson's was the heavenly herb itself—but what must one say to a *second,* and even a *third* or *fourth* infusion?" Burroughs agreed: "Emerson's lectures were full of idealism, but they seemed unsuited to our needs. In a book they would have been like a star, but on a lecture platform they were rather ineffectual. But they were all right in a way,—Emerson couldn't unhitch his wagon from a star to drag our little burdens to market."

Whitman's reputation had been spreading gradually in the years since his talk with Emerson on the Boston Common in 1860, chiefly through a growing corps of young admirers. He had acquired a lasting sobriquet when William D. O'Connor brought out *The Good Gray Poet* in 1865. Two years later Burroughs had published *Notes on Walt Whitman as Poet and Person.* Walt's *Drum-Taps* and its sequel had appeared in 1865, including the memorable tribute to Lincoln, "When Lilacs Last in the Dooryard Bloom'd." The fourth and fifth editions of the *Leaves* emerged in 1867 and 1871, and the *Galaxy* printed the prose tracts on "Democracy" and "Personalism," which were merged in 1871 as *Democratic Vistas.*

During these years Walt's only contact with Concord was by letter. Emerson sent him a copy of *May-Day* and helpfully responded to Walt's request to get his "Proud Music of the Storm" into the *Atlantic* for February 1869. Yet as early as 1865, Walt had begun to feel that his erstwhile champion was turning against him. John Trowbridge, another young admirer, told him in September that Emerson, in a lecture about "the very few who write English greatly," had said, "There is also Walt Whitman, but he belongs yet to the fire clubs, and has not got into the parlors." This distant echo of Emerson's "Art and Criticism" lecture, wrenched thus from its context, had the air of an insult, and Walt touchily concluded, "It is plain that Mr. E. has quite thoroughly shifted his position" from that of 1855, "and makes the largest qualifications."

Whitman had delivered a message from Senator Charles Sumner inviting Emerson to Washington. In partial replication of his visit ten years earlier, he was wined and dined, taken sightseeing, and introduced to many eminent people. Somewhat to his discomfiture, he was "compelled by an artifice" to speak to the law students at General Howard's Freedmen's Institute, "an important college for the colored men" that later became Howard University. His topic, "What Books to Read," enabled him to comment seriatim on some of his favorite works, thus avoiding the necessity of a full-fledged lecture. Back in Baltimore for a final speech on "Art and Nature," he obeyed an urgent request from Tom Ward to pay a call on his fiancée, Sophia Howard, a handsome girl who listened eagerly to Emerson's praise of Tom, and shyly mentioned a letter from Tom's father, Samuel Gray Ward, who said that "he had lost his heart to her before Tom had."

Emerson ran into John Burroughs at the Washington depot. "I drew him out on Walt," said Burroughs, "and found out what was the matter. He thought Walt's friends ought to quarrel a little more with him, and insist on his being a little more tame and orderly—more mindful of the requirements of beauty, of art, of culture, etc.—all of which was very pitiful to me, and I wanted to tell him so. But the train started just then and I got off." Reports of this encounter and advice seemed to have trickled back to Whitman, whose wounded feelings were exacerbated in 1874 when Emerson's *Parnassus* anthology appeared without so much as a single line from Walt's work, as if American grass had no business growing on the slopes of Parnassus.

Whitman turned the tables on Emerson late in 1874 with a newspaper piece called "A Christmas Garland." He thought that Emerson's basic fault was perhaps "too great prudence, too rigid a caution." Maybe this was wrong; indeed, he added, "I have generally felt that Emerson was altogether adjusted to himself, in every attribute, as he should be (as a pine tree is a pine tree, not a quince or a rose bush). But upon the whole, and notwithstanding the many unsurpassed beauties of his poetry first, and prose only second to it, I am disposed to think (picking out spots against the sun) that his constitutional distrust and doubt—almost finical in their nicety—have been too much for him—have not perhaps stopped him short of first-class genius, but have veiled it—have finally clipped and pruned that free luxuriance of it which only satisfies the soul at last." The very prolixity of such paragraphs showed Walt's determination to retain in his own prose that "free luxuriance" which he thought Emerson had denied himself through prudence and caution.

A week after Emerson's return from the trip south, Will and Edith, with their four children and a nurse, sailed for Liverpool, beginning a journey that would take them from England through France, Switzerland, Germany, and Italy and would last until the middle of August. Ellen went to Milton to help with the packing, and Emerson arrived breakfastless and breathless to add his own farewell. Lidian said that she "could never understand how anyone dared to cross the sea," and feared that they would all be "drowned like a batch of kittens."

Apart from missing his son, Edward, and the whole young Forbes family, Emerson's problem in the spring of 1872 was failing memory. In the preceding September he had spoken to Ellen of the "holes" in Lidian's mind. Meantime he had been discovering some in his own—deep cavities into which fell the names and words he wished to recall. When he read his old lecture on "Books" to a Boston audience in April, Ellen wrote, "Well, I sat at the lecture in about as great a fear as I was able to bear, lest there should be some terrific crash, for I hadn't heard it beforehand as I ought, and his memory is entirely gone, so that he blithely read the same page twice over, and I mourn for you [she was writing to Eddy] more than I can tell, for you are the only person in creation who could lay out the course for him and help him through. Father has just come home and I have scolded and mourned to him about it and he thinks we shan't have the same trouble again, doesn't feel half as badly about it as I." The good news was that the sale of tickets had already brought in $1,300. "That," said Ellen, "makes Father very happy, and all of us."

Vexed but also amused by his problem, Emerson took pains to develop a form of metonymy in which he groped for the approximate word or phrase he wanted—as, for example, "that bearded young man in California" for John Muir, or for the word "umbrella": "I can't tell its name, but I can tell its history. Strangers take it away." His future biographer, James Elliot Cabot, dated the onset of the difficulty from the summer of 1871, about the beginning of his sixty-ninth year. In June 1872 Ellen wrote, "He forgets names of people and things, and the exercise of his favorite metonymy is on these occasions so witty that I wish it could be recorded. . . . I never tell him what he is trying for, that I may prolong the entertainment." This was all well enough—and even funny—in the domestic circle, but could be an embarrassment both to speaker and audience when it took place in public. Emerson ruefully began to call himself "a man who had lost his wits," while asserting that he was still able "to read with intelligence." But it was not very long after this, in Cabot's phrase, that the "decay of some of the vital machinery" would lead to "insuperable difficulty in a continuous effort of attention." One might have echoed Ophelia's sorrowful lamentation over Hamlet: "O, what a noble mind is here o'erthrown!" But Emerson refused to give up. A journal entry for the first day of his seventieth year stated, "If I should live another year, I think I shall cite still the last stanza of my own poem, 'The World-Soul.' " The words he had in mind were these:

Spring still makes spring in the mind
When sixty years are told;
Love wakes anew this throbbing heart,
And we are never old;
Over the winter glaciers
I see the summer glow,
And through the wild-piled snow-drift
The warm rosebuds below.

Chapter Forty-nine

AMONG
THE RUINS

WHEN THE FIRE BROKE OUT THAT RAINY MORNING OF July 24, 1872, Lidian and her husband seem to have been alone in the Concord house. The family was widely distributed—Ellen visiting at Beverly Farms on the North Shore, Edith and Will and their children in England, and Edward, with his "heart of oak," just recovering from surgery in London. About five-thirty Emerson came awake to the smell of smoke and an ominous crackle of burning wood inside a second-floor closet. He roused Lidian, asleep downstairs in the Red Room, and ran to the front gate in his nightshirt. His cries brought two close neighbors, Staples and Whitcomb, who summoned the Fire Department and began at once to clear the first-floor rooms of furniture, pictures, mirrors, rugs, and curtains.

At least ten others soon appeared, among them George Heywood, Arthur Gray, John Clahan, and Ned Bartlett. Ephraim Bull's son and namesake bestrode the rooftree between the two chimneys, plying the hose with his one remaining arm. The garret was burning briskly under his feet and the smoke was voluminous. During the second hour the slate roof fell in upon the upstairs chambers, and this, together with the continuing drizzle, helped the fire fighters to bring the flames under control by roughly nine o'clock.

In Beverly, Major Higginson, father of Ellen's friend Ida Higginson, "pale with fright," handed Ellen the Boston *Transcript* with its paragraph about the fire, quickly assuring her that her mother and father had escaped injury.

Ellen caught the morning train on the twenty-fifth, ran into Annie Keyes near the Concord depot, and drove with her out to the Manse, where Emerson met them at the door. After breakfast, he and Ellen walked down to see the ruin. The walls of the main house still stood, and the screening trees had luckily escaped damage. Inside, the front stairway had somehow survived, but the floor of the Red Room was a pond, and the ceilings in the parlor and the dining room were hanging and dripping. Most of the interior, in Ellen's phrase, was "an abomination of desolation," blackened with soot, smelling sourly of wet ashes and charred debris.

Ellen checked the houses and barns of the neighborhood where the rescued furnishings—silver, glassware, crockery, books, and blankets, "stacks of pictures and mountains of clothes"—had been stored on the fateful morning. The Alcott sisters, Louisa and May, had salvaged and dried many manuscripts. In the Gregorys' parlor stood Ellen's piano, "looking bright and cool." All was not lost, she thought, and the dirt and waste, once cleared away, would not return. Nina Lowell told her of Lidian's sentimental concern for the rats that had lived in the house and had gone streaming across the fields like the Pied Piper's brood. "They're sure to find a home somewhere," said Lidian happily. Nina was shocked.

In the wake of the destruction, Lidian took to bed for three days at the Manse. Emerson's health appeared to be sound, despite what he was calling "a rude experience to an old housekeeper." He thanked the Fire Department for prompt action and quickly accepted Judge Hoar's offer of a large room in the disused Court House. "Every day he went there, both morning and afternoon," wrote Ellen. "I went to help him set up the book-cases, but everything, books and cases, were so dirty with rain and smoke and sand, besides the dust that was on them before the fire, that cleaning was the first necessity. . . . Mother used also to come in. These weeks at the Manse were a pleasant holiday to her. . . . she often looked back afterwards to that time as a sunny interval."

Three weeks later, Will and Edith brought their family home after nearly seven months abroad. A memorable sequel to the trip was the news that at the recent Harvard commencement, Will Forbes, war hero, businessman, and father of four, had been belatedly awarded his A.B. degree, honoris causa. Ellen, who sharply recalled Will's chapel escapade of 1860 that had caused his expulsion from college, hailed Harvard's gesture and Will's response: "We are all so interested that he found he cared. It is always such a delightful discovery that we do care about anything more than we supposed."

Emerson's feverish reaction to the blows of July came in August. Ellen hurried him off on a week's trip to Rye Beach, New Hampshire, and Portland and Waterford, Maine. The change seemed profitable, though he wryly described himself as "an imbecile most of the time . . . distracted with the multiplicity of nothings I am pretending to do." His prime object was to rebuild his "charred and broken house." An architect relative, William Ralph Emerson, volunteered his services, and John Keyes, father of Edward's fiancée, undertook the role of supervisor. By the middle of September, the rubble had been carted away, the slate roof replaced, and new lumber was stacked in the yard.

Worried over the condition of her father's mind, Ellen composed a letter to Edward Clarke, Lidian's Boston doctor in 1869-70. She dated the loss of memory as early as 1867; since then deterioration had been gradual until the sharp downturn occasioned by the fire. Such tasks as proofreading were no longer feasible. In the spring he had still managed, but now his grip on language was gone or going. It was, he told his daughter, "a triumph to remember any word." The best synonym he could think of in trying to refer to his dressing gown was "the red chandelier."

His friends met the situation with notable generosity. "This late calamity," he wrote, "however rude and devastating, soon began to look more wonderful in its salvages than in its ruins." The salvages took the form of quiet and often anonymous contributions from dozens of admirers. His Harvard classmate Francis Cabot Lowell sent a check for $5,000 gathered from various sources, and his old friend Dr. Le Baron Russell another for $10,000 from many contributors. These sums were presently supplemented by $1,600 more from Russell and yet another thousand from the historian George Bancroft. Caroline Tappan's offer of $5,000 was apparently not taken up, but even without it, Emerson was richer than before the fire by nearly $18,000.

Since rebuilding would require only a fraction of this astonishing total, Emerson and Ellen began to think of a vacation trip to Europe. Eddy was still studying medicine in London; they could join him and plan from there a more extended itinerary. Emerson was even nurturing a "rainbow" hope of traveling as far as Greece and Egypt, as Mark Twain's party of "innocents" had so recently done. Ellen happily served as catalyst and arranger. At age thirty-three she was the only one of the Emerson siblings who had not yet seen Europe, though her stay in the Azores had given her a foretaste. She seems to have believed that a visit to the sites of his foreign adventures in 1833 and 1848 might help to restore her father's enfeebled memory. Moreover, this trip was affordable: Emerson would not need to borrow from the bank as in 1847, nor would he have to earn passage money through lecturing. Finally, he would be seventy in nine months' time. Now, if ever, was the time to go. While the ruins in Concord were being repaired, their owner could find rest and refreshment among far more ancient ruins, whether in Europe, the Peloponnesus, or North Africa.

In September the Emersons converged upon Naushon. After a week in bed, Lidian, according to Ellen, began talking and eating once more as a Christian should. Emerson was losing his hair in patches, and was obliged to have three of his upper front teeth extracted and replaced. Ellen hobbled about with a badly sprained ankle, and Eddy reported from London that another abscess had formed on his shoulder. The good news was that work on the Concord house was moving well. The garret was fully restored and a "beautiful den" had already been built.

Urged on by his daughters and helped by his son-in-law, Emerson booked passage aboard the steamship *Wyoming*, leaving New York October 23. Lidian planned to stay at the Manse until Thanksgiving and to spend the remaining months with the Forbes family in Milton. By November 4, reunited with Eddy, Emerson and Ellen were taking tea with Bishop William Jacobson in Chester, a few miles south of Liverpool. On the sixth, the day they entrained for London, they joined the bishop for a breakfast that included Devonshire cream and raspberry jam. Emerson wore a velvet cap of Edith's to conceal his bald scalp. He had profited, as always, from his time at sea. In spite of rough weather, the *Wyoming* had averaged 270 nautical miles a day. When the ocean was calm the men played shuffleboard on deck. One evening, Emerson was persuaded to read a few of his poems, among them "The Titmouse." Most of the company were hymn-singing missionaries, bound for India. Emerson told Lidian that his "well known orthodoxy" had not been endangered, since the "liberal ocean" sang even more loudly than the Christian choristers. She replied, also ironically, that he must have been happy to escape with his well-known Transcendentalism unimpaired.

Ellen thought that her brother looked rather gaunt, no doubt owing to late study hours in his room at St. Thomas's Hospital. But Emerson praised Eddy's skills as guide around London, and leaned on him in other ways. "When I am fumbling for the name of my wife," he said, "he can remember it for me." Having spoken briefly and badly at a testimonial banquet for James Anthony Froude in New York before sailing, Emerson surprised his children with a graceful extempore speech before the Archaeologic, Architectural and Historic Society meeting. Otherwise he seemed content at first to sleep, eat, or sit with folded hands in his boardinghouse room at Number 11, Down Street.

His American and English friends were unwilling to indulge his appetite for laziness. As in California, invitations poured in and callers abounded. Father and daughter were virtually adopted by Charles Eliot Norton, whose wife had died in Dresden in February. W. H. Channing and Moncure D. Conway came to talk and reminisce. Another devotee was Charles King Newcomb, the reputed genius from Providence, ex-disciple of Margaret Fuller's, and sporadic boarder at Brook Farm. He had stayed with his mother from 1845 until 1862 when he joined the 10th Rhode Island Volunteers in the defense of Washington. After his mother's death in 1865 he had been a virtual recluse for five years in a boardinghouse at 1183 Pine Street, Philadelphia. In 1871 he had become a permanent expatriate, living on a substantial income at the Glendower Hotel in Great Portland Street. When news of the houseburning reached him there, he had offered Emerson a gift or loan of money for rebuilding. Emerson's reply from Naushon had apparently hinted at his disappointment over Charles's failure to live up to his early promise, although, as recently as 1868, he had singled out Newcomb as "one of the subtlest minds . . . I ever met." They saw each other twice in 1872–73, once on November 11 and again in April after Emerson's return from Egypt. This was evidently their final meeting. Newcomb continued to live in England and France until his death in Paris in 1894.

Another permanent expatriate was Una Hawthorne, who was doing settlement work in the city of London. Before Eddy embarked for home on November 12, he and Ellen went to see their childhood friend. Julian and Rose had both married and left England—Rose to the journalist George Parsons Lathrop, and Julian to Minne Amelung, an American he had met in Dresden. Since the fall of 1870 Julian had been working as a hydrographic engineer for the New York Dock Department under the command of the Civil War general George McClellan. Sophia Hawthorne, who had never fully recovered from her husband's death, had died of pneumonia in February 1871. Afterward, with help from Robert Browning, Una had brought out her father's abortive romance, *Septimius Felton*, to very minor acclaim. She was still subject to breakdowns like those she had endured in Concord, and was to die, still alone, in 1877, and to be buried beside her mother in Kensal Green Cemetery.

The truly obligatory event during Emerson's fortnight in London was his reunion with Carlyle, his friend of forty years, whose wife, Jane, had been dead since the spring of 1866. The tall old Scot greeted Emerson with a bear hug and they spent two hours exchanging information on "persons, events, and opinions" that had not got into their now-less-than-lively correspondence. At seventy-seven, Carlyle looked his age and more, but his memory was as sharp as Emerson's was dulled. Will and Edith Forbes had called on him during their recent stay in England, and the famous old man, bearded and grizzled, with deeply sunken eyes, had posed for a picture with Emerson's grandson Ras—a perfect epitome of crabbed age and untried youth.

When the Emersons boarded the ferry at Dover on November 16, they were accompanied by one Curnex, a courier hired for them by Lady Augusta Stanley. Awaiting their arrival in Paris were James Russell Lowell, his wife, and John Holmes, brother of the Autocrat of the Breakfast Table. They were full of the news of the great fire in Boston that had recently devastated the region around Summer Street and Chauncy Place where Emerson had been born and raised, the part of the city where he had trundled hoops as a child and the very region he had revisited by chance on his sixty-ninth birthday. The fire may well have been a conversation piece between Emerson and the young novelist-to-be Henry James when he came to the hotel to conduct Emerson through the Louvre. Another visitor was Emerson's nephew Charles with his new wife, Therchi. But the stay in the City of Light, though warmed by such friendly attentions, was all too brief. Their zigzag journey to Cairo was to begin November 21. "I hate Egypt," wrote Ellen. "It won't let us stop anywhere." In fact the ensuing month was replete with stopovers, first at Marseilles, then at Nice, where Emerson strolled with Curnex along the Promenade des Anglais, then Genoa and Leghorn, then Florence and Rome.

They had just settled into a *pensione* beside the Spanish Steps when they were whisked away to the Villa Celimontana, the "mountain fastness" outside Rome where Sam Ward's eldest daughter, Lily, now the Baroness von Hoffmann, was in residence with her handsome and courtly husband, Richard, and her small son, Ferdy. The baron was so helpful and attentive that Emerson called him a knight of King Arthur's Round Table. Lily's father and mother, Sam and Anna, and her youngest sister, Bessie, had only recently left for Egypt, where they were going to explore the Nile in the company of the Harvard historian Henry Adams and his recent bride, Clover (née Marian Hooper), whom Emerson had known through most of her twenty-eight years. In spite of Emerson's wishes to the contrary, he and Ellen were never able to catch up with the Wards and the Adamses, although a letter from Sam Ward in Siout in December offered an anticipation of the wonders of North Africa: "Cairo and the Pyramids, Beni Hassan, and the Nile, amply repays the voyage to Egypt. . . . The eye never wearies in following and making pictures [of the people] with their background of mosques and palms and camels and donkeys: and their eye for color, which makes them all dress as for a *tableau vivant*. . . . The pictures in Beni Hassan are said to be four hundred years older than Sinai—a thousand years older than Homer. . . . But Homer and Moses remain obstinately my standard of antiquity."

The only flaw in the Roman visit was a curious affliction of Emerson's that might have been a series of small strokes. "The feeling," said Ellen, "is very alarming to him when it comes. He says he never felt anything like it, can't describe it. It comes suddenly in a carriage, in company, at the table, in his bedchamber, walking in the street, without cause and without consequence. When it is over—it lasts a minute or two—he feels perfectly well. He said he remembered Grandma's sometimes saying, 'The water comes into my mouth,' and looking very doleful when she said it, and he thought perhaps she felt this feeling."

The problem, which did not recur for several months, had vanished by Christmas Day when they reached Alexandria. Before the old year ended they were registered at Shepheard's Hotel in Cairo in the chivalrous company of George Bancroft, the small alert historian from Worcester, Massachusetts, who was in the midst of an appointment as American minister to Berlin. Cofounder of the Round Hill School in Northampton, where Sam Ward and Ellery Channing had been pupils, Bancroft had known and liked Emerson for thirty-five years, and had been among his benefactors at the time of the fire. At noon on the twenty-eighth he escorted Emerson to breakfast with the khedive of Egypt before sailing off to Naples in a ship provided by his host. Emerson missed Bancroft, complained that the temperature in Cairo was too chilly for his aging bones, and returned weary and disgusted from a performance by a company of whirling dervishes.

But he enjoyed the distant view of the pyramids through the boughs of a banyan tree outside his hotel window, and presently rode a donkey on an extended circuit of the vast pharaonic tombs and his old poetical friend, the Sphinx. At Thebes he was to ride in splendor on a richly caparisoned Arabian horse lent him by Mustapha Agar, the English consul. But for ordinary purposes he was not at all averse to what Ellen called "donkestrian exercise," the delights of which she had first experienced in Fayal. Emerson liked the names of the rocking-horse-sized beasts they rode, and "laughed very much" over one called Bulbul, Persian for Nightingale. His favorite at Dendera was Abou Keefir, described by its owner as a "very clevery donkey drink birra, drink Hasheesh."

On January 7 they boarded the dahabeah *Aurora* for a thirty-eight-day cruise along the Nile as far south as the first cataract at Assouan. So many British and Americans were doing the same thing that it was almost like joining an English-speaking flotilla. One Saturday late in the month Ellen counted seventeen dahabeahs like their own, and social intercourse among the voyagers was frequent. Ellen was in her element as leader and adventurer, "the only traveller on the Nile," wrote Emerson, "who clung strictly to her own personality and régime, and made some heroic attempts to save other souls." With other passengers she went ashore nearly every day to climb among the ruins. She was apparently thinking of her favorite campsite on Monadnock when she wrote that "a ruin offers as good climbing as a mountain." Once she said that the opaline blue above the desert dunes resembled the sky over Gay Head as seen from Naushon Island. When the temperature warmed to seventy degrees, Emerson was out all day on the sheltered boat deck, and slept a solid ten hours each night, but did not fully share his daughter's lively interest in the scenery and the ruins, and made only a dozen entries in his journal. One sign of his imminent homesickness for Concord, thought Ellen, was his decision to cancel the tentative plans for Greece.

Ellen's eye for detail was as good as Sam Ward's, and her journal letters to friends and relatives contain the fullest record of the Egyptian journey. Their last social engagement before taking the train for Cairo was a luncheon with the Roosevelt family of New York aboard their dahabeah. Of the four Roosevelt children, one was named Theodore, a lad of fifteen with red cheeks, brilliant teeth, and the blazing blue eyes of a chronic asthmatic. Teddy and his father had been shooting birds along the Nile, and his diary recorded a recent game bag that included "a peewit, ziczac, two snipes, and eleven pigions." But the future twenty-sixth president of the United States made no mention of the distinguished guests from Concord whom he ferried across for lunch on February 12.

Their gradual return homeward duplicated in reverse the journey south. Ellen celebrated her thirty-fourth birthday as their ship passed through the Straits of Messina into the warm Tyrrhenian Sea. Sicily and Calabria were all abloom with returning spring. In Rome in early March they rode horseback among the daisies in the Campagna. As he had been in Paris in the fall, young Henry James was a "true comfort" to Emerson—"a sort of son," said Ellen, guiding his elderly companion through the museums. Lily von Hoffman (née Ward) shyly attempted to persuade Ellen into the Catholic faith as she had once sought to do years earlier in Boston. She gave Ellen a ring and promised to pray for her conversion. As before, Ellen sat "motionless under my shield in an attitude that seemed heartless." Aunt Lizzie Hoar and Sarah Clarke greeted the returning voyagers. After seven months of patchy baldness Emerson's hair was growing back, and Sarah thought that he was "wonderfully improved," a view that Ellen could not share, though others were saying much the same thing. During a visit in Florence with Herman and Gisela Grimm, Grimm praised Emerson's "fine sharp manly face" and the bright coloring of his cheeks, an opinion that Lowell echoed when they reached Paris in mid-March. But Ellen said flatly that she could see no improvement whatsoever: his hands were cold and numb, his memory was no better, and he seemed unable to write the smallest note.

Emerson confessed as much in a letter to Lidian that he had started and then abandoned in Thebes, taking it up again in England in May:

Alas, dear Lidian, since the above lines were scratched, a long idleness—say incapacity to write anything has held me;—not a line in my diary, nor any syllable that I remember unless a word or two to the bankers, or unavoidable billets in reply to notes of invitation here or

there has been written. You have been good and forgiving, and have
sent me welcome letters, and must try to believe that this rest or absolute indolence was unavoidable and medicinal. Ellen has been a good
angel here as always, and so acknowledged and received wherever we
have gone—Skilful in business, perfect in temper, a welcome guest in
every house we have entered, so that I have not needed to put off my
solitary and silent ways. Then she has written letters by day and by
night in steamboats and in trains so that there was no need for me to
fight my dumb daemon.

The wonder was that his limitations had been so well concealed from others during the weeks in Italy and France. In Paris in March he had been delighted by a performance of Molière's *Malade Imaginaire*, accompanied Ellen
to the Louvre, and repeatedly visited the Jardin des Plantes, his old haunt in
1833. He had dined with Hippolyte Taine and Ivan Turgenev and talked at
length with Ernest Renan. Back in London in April, where everyone said that
he was "another man from what he was in November," he boldly accepted innumerable social engagements despite a recurrence of the strange malady that
had frightened him in Rome in December. Ellen summoned a doctor who diagnosed indigestion, to which Emerson indignantly replied that his digestion
had always been perfect. If so, it was given dozens of tests during the ensuing
weeks: at breakfast with Gladstone and the duke of Argyll, at lunch with
Thomas Huxley and John Tyndall, at tea with Browning at Lady Amberley's
where they disagreed about the worth of Shelley's poetry, and at visits with
such old friends as W. H. Channing, Charles Newcomb, Alexander Ireland,
Charles Eliot Norton, and of course Carlyle, from whom he was growing
markedly apart. At Oxford in May he and Ellen strolled in Christchurch
Meadows, visited Max Müller, and heard John Ruskin lecture on art. They
managed a trip to Edinburgh, as well as sightseeing that embraced Tintern
Abbey, Eton, and Windsor, a walk-through at Warwick Castle, and a visit to
Shakespeare's tomb in Stratford, where Emerson paused to speculate on exactly how his late correspondent, the obsessed Baconian Delia Salter Bacon,
might have "planned to disturb those mysterious bones."

When Emerson got aboard the steamship *Olympus* at Liverpool on
May 15, his chief companion was Charles Eliot Norton, aged forty-five, returning from a long sojourn in Europe to become professor of the history of

art at Harvard. A close friend of Ruskin, Burne-Jones, Leslie Stephen, and Carlyle, Norton recalled an April afternoon's discussion in Carlyle's study on the character of Emerson. "It's a verra strikin' and curious spectacle," the old man had said, "to behold a man so confidently cheerful as Emerson." This was a theme that Norton pursued at length in his journal during the eleven-day voyage to Boston, while the two men smoked cigars on deck or talked out the evenings in the ship's saloon.

"His serene sweetness . . . the reflection of his soul in his face," wrote Norton, "were never more apparent to me; but never before . . . had I been so impressed with the limits of his mind." The problem was that "his optimistic philosophy" had "hardened into a creed . . . closing the avenues of truth. He can accept nothing as fact that tells against his dogma. . . . To him this is the best of all possible worlds. . . . He refuses to believe in disorder or evil. Order is the absolute law; disorder is but a phenomenon; good is absolute, evil but good in the making." When Norton offered examples of misery and crime in society or the "apparent ruthlessness and disorder in nature," Emerson only shook his head: "His faith was superior to any exceptions."

One stormy day they spoke of the boldness of such early voyagers as Columbus. It was no great wonder, said Emerson: "He had his compass and that was enough for such a soul as his." The miracle of the magnetic needle bore witness to the "Divine spirit in nature." Emerson drew out a small compass from his pocket, saying that he always carried it. "I like," he added with a smile, "to hold the visible god in my hand."

One day out from Boston Emerson turned seventy. When Norton offered congratulations, his friend half humorously dissented: it was a "melancholy anniversary" because it marked for him "the close of youth." Norton was touched and amused. Apart from occasional lapses of memory, he had detected few signs of Emerson's advancing age, and thought that his youthful spirit was perennial. It would last as long as he lived because of his continuing fidelity to his early ideals. When Emerson reached Boston next day, he was still carrying in his pocket the small compass that symbolized for him the foremost of those early ideals—the instant availability of supernal power to the questing human mind.

EPILOGUE

ON MAY 27, AT HALF PAST THREE IN THE AFTERNOON, EMERson, surprised, was met at the Concord depot by a welcoming committee and attendant crowds. (What did the gathering mean, he asked; "Was it a public day?") A hired band marched toward his house, with townspeople and schoolchildren following. At the gate to his house a triumphal arch had been built; children sang "Home, Sweet Home" as the barouche carrying him and other family members arrived. Bronson Alcott, in his journal, described the public honor given to a scholar as "a novelty in the history of this our historic revolutionary village." Emerson, with characteristic modesty, made scant mention of it in his journal; "Arrived home at Concord, with Ellen & most kindly received by our townsmen & brought home to our rebuilt house."

Bush, the house in which Emerson had lived for thirty-eight years, had been carefully restored. The rescued books and manuscripts, the pictures, his writing desk, had been returned to his first-floor study. But its principal tenant was now in inexorable decline. On board the *Olympus*, Charles Eliot Norton had decided that Emerson's optimism had hardened into a creed, "with the usual effects of a creed in closing the avenues of truth." Cynicism had not even begun to rust Emerson's innocence, it seemed. Norton found it inexplicable that Emerson would not entertain "instances of misery, of crime, in society."

But one cannot take the measure of a man from disjunctive episodes lifted from his youth or old age; biography is the study of the whole man in the context of time. Emerson on the *Olympus* was not the younger man, comfortably settled into his residency at Bush in June 1840, who had written the following entry in his journal:

> Now for near five years I have been indulged by the gracious Heaven in my long holiday in this goodly house of mine, entertaining and entertained by so many worthy and gifted friends, and all this time poor Nancy Barron, the mad-woman, has been screaming herself hoarse at the Poor-house across the brook and I still hear her whenever I open my window.

On his seventieth birthday, that recollection must have been long past remembrance—though safeguarded in his journals.

After the fire his memory lapses became more pronounced, and the erosion deepened in the years left to him. Bush became a palace of forgetting. "Alone with us," Ellen noted, "he plays with it and is very witty in his stumbles. Sometimes, having got through a short sentence straight, tho' evidently jumping in the dark for his words, he laughs and says 'It is a triumph to remember any word.' " He searched in vain for the names of common objects like a chair or his dressing gown and came up with a twisted identification for an umbrella: "I can't tell its name, but I can tell its history. Strangers take it away." Norton would vividly remember one of the last, painful remarks Emerson ever made to him: "Strange that the kind Heavens should keep us on earth after they have destroyed our connection with things."

His writing also suffered. A sentence might be repeated four times with only minor variations within a twenty-seven-page manuscript, and another was repeated twice, word for word. Emerson now thought it better to decline invitations, asked friends to visit him instead. But, writing to the poet Emma Lazarus, he confessed that "an old man fears most his best friends. It is not them that he is willing to distress with his perpetual forgetfulness of the right word for the name of book or fact or person he is eager to recall, but which refuses to come. I have grown silent to my own household under this vexation, & cannot afflict dear friends with my tied tongue." Reading, he said, was still an "unbroken pleasure." More and more the study at Bush became his retreat. He clung to the comforting routine of solitude, reading in his study till noon and returning again in the afternoon until it was time for his walk. Gradually he lost his recollection of his own writings, was delighted at rediscovering his own essays: "Why these things are really very good," he told his daughter.

He was well beyond the stage of keeping up his strenuous lecture tours, though he could be persuaded to speak or give a reading for special occasions. Ellen accompanied him on most of those excursions. There were few new lectures; mostly she helped him recycle earlier addresses, some of them written thirty years before. Often she sewed the manuscript pages together so that he wouldn't absentmindedly shuffle the pages and lose his place. On April 19, 1875, at the dedication of the Minute Man Statue near the North Bridge, he was one of the luminaries, along with President Grant and various cabinet members. It was a raw day with intermittent rain, and he gave only a brief talk marking the occasion of the battles of Concord and Lexington. It was one of the last addresses he would write and one of his last successes.

His once-resonant voice had begun to fail along with his memory, and there were the inevitable public embarrassments. On June 28, 1876, during commencement week at the University of Virginia, he spoke on "The Natural and Permanent Functions of the Scholar." But the crowd was huge and young and noisy and mostly paid scant attention. He could be heard only within the front several rows. Sensing his failure, he brought an early end to his speech. The local newspapers made malicious complaints about the Yankee speaker leaving with his carpetbag in hand, his speech to be published later, earning him "a more substantial return" than the expense-paid hospitality he had been given in the South.

Still, he kept on like an old horse in harness. On one occasion when, ironically, he delivered a lecture on "Memory," Ellen had had to stand near him so that he wouldn't read the same page twice. (He had had to read her lips to know where to begin again.) February 1880, he gave his one hundredth lecture at the Concord Lyceum. The subject was "Historic Notes of Life and Letters in Massachusetts." (The lecture had been written thirteen years earlier.) A year later, at the Massachusetts Historical Society, commemorating his old friend Carlyle, he had been unable to write an address; instead, he read some related pages from his journal and a letter he had written Carlyle years earlier.

More as a diversion than as a commitment, he began attending Sunday services. Conservative ministers spread the rumor that he had renounced his earlier heretical religious views. But as his son Edward explained in his memoir, *Emerson in Concord*, it was because he now had nothing better to do: "The instinct had been always there, but he had felt that he could use his time to better purpose."

His friendship with Longfellow had never been deep, but when he attended Longfellow's funeral service on March 27, 1882, he was perplexed, stared into the open casket once, and went back again to settle his mind until he was obliged to ask, "Where are we? What house? And who is the sleeper?" He still took his afternoon walks. But neighbors were alerted to direct him home if he became bewildered and lost his way. It was on one of those afternoons in the cold spring that he walked out in the rain, having forgotten to wear his overcoat. He caught cold but refused to remain in bed. "Sickness," he once maintained, "is a cannibal which eats up all the life and youth it can lay hold of." Edward noted: "He did not know how to be sick and desired to be dressed and sit in his study, and as we had found that any attempt to regulate his actions lately was very annoying to him, and he could not be made to understand the reasons for our doing so in his condition, I determined that it would not be worth while to trouble and restrain him."

It was only on the last day, April 27, 1882, that Emerson remained in bed, fretful about his loss of words but seeing friends and family, communicating as best he could. He died, peacefully, that evening at nine. The church bells rang for each of the seventy-nine years of his life. Three days later, on a Sunday, he was buried in Sleepy Hollow, not far from the graves of Hawthorne and Thoreau. It had been the early haunt of Emerson's walks. There once, forty years before, he had stumbled on Hawthorne and Margaret Fuller deep in conversation and joined them. Hawthorne in his journal noted that, despite Emerson's "clerical consecration," he had found no better way of spending the Sabbath than to ramble in the woods, and gave an account of Emerson's conversation: "He said there were Muses in the woods to-day, and whispers to be heard in the breezes."

Emerson's son Edward, giving his account of the funeral and obsequies in his memoir, thought it appropriate to repeat an entry from the journals, the fund of Emerson's thoughts and days. It was an early premonition of death and of the solace of nature when, after a restless night, Emerson saw the dawn rising outside his window.

I said when I awoke, After some more sleepings and wakings I shall lie on this mattress sick; then dead; and through my gay entry they will carry these bones. Where shall I be then? I lifted my head and beheld the spotless orange light of the morning beaming up from the dark hills into the wide universe.

It was typical of Emerson's optimistic view that he would greet death as another enlightening experience, a new morning.

NOTES

Abbreviations

Abbreviations used in the notes are listed below. Short forms of major sources of information are included in the list as well. Short forms of titles with authors' names are used in the notes, with full citations in the bibliography. When a standard reference for a primary source (letters, journals) has been published since Carlos Baker completed this manuscript, it is noted under the rubric "See now . . ." Texts quoted follow original except that "and" is substituted for the ampersand.

ABA	Amos Bronson Alcott
LMA	Louisa May Alcott
CHB	Carlos Heard Baker
AB(W)	Anna Barker (Ward)
WEC	William Ellery Channing II [Ellery]
CCE	Charles Chauncy Emerson
EE(F)	Edith Emerson (Forbes)
EBE	Edward Bliss Emerson
ETE	Ellen Tucker Emerson (RWE's daughter)
EWE	Edward Waldo Emerson
LJE	Lidian Jackson Emerson
MME	Mary Moody Emerson
RBE	Robert Bulkeley Emerson

RHE   Ruth Haskins Emerson
RWE   Ralph Waldo Emerson
WE   William Emerson
MF(O)   Margaret Fuller (Ossoli)
NH   Nathaniel Hawthorne
SPH   Sophia Peabody Hawthorne
FHH   Frederic Henry Hedge
HM   Herman Melville
CKN   Charles King Newcomb
TP   Theodore Parker
EPP   Elizabeth Palmer Peabody
CS(T)   Caroline Sturgis (Tappan)
ET   Edward Taylor
HDT   Henry David Thoreau
JV   Jones Very
SGW   Samuel Gray Ward
WW   Walt Whitman

ABA Letters   *The Letters of A. Bronson Alcott*
ABA Jrnls   *The Journals of Bronson Alcott*
C-E-C   *The Correspondence of Emerson and Carlyle*
LMA Jrnls   *The Journals of Louisa May Alcott*
ETE Letters   *The Letters of Ellen Tucker Emerson*
Life of Lidian   *The Life of Lidian Jackson Emerson*
Letters of Lidian   *The Selected Letters of Lidian Jackson Emerson*
Letters of MME   *Selected Letters of Mary Moody Emerson*
E Works   *The Complete Works of Ralph Waldo Emerson*
    [Centenary Edition]
JMN   *The Journals and Miscellaneous Notebooks of Ralph*
    Waldo Emerson
L   *The Letters of Ralph Waldo Emerson*
MF Letters   *The Letters of Margaret Fuller*
NH Letters   *The Letters, vols. 15–18 of The Centenary Edition of*
    the Works of Nathaniel Hawthorne
Newcomb Jrnls   *The Journals of Charles King Newcomb*

Mem MFO	*Memoirs of Margaret Fuller Ossoli*
HDT Corres	*The Correspondence of Henry David Thoreau*
HDT Jrnl	*The Journal of Henry David Thoreau*
	[old style]
Am Lit	*American Literature*
DAB	*Dictionary of American Biography*
HLB	*Harvard Library Bulletin*
NH Journal	*Nathaniel Hawthorne Journal*
NAR	*North American Review*
NEQ	*New England Quarterly*
SAR	*Studies in the American Renaissance*

Introduction

xi   "the embattled farmers stood": RWE,
       "Concord Hymn," lines 3–4.
       "I have the feeling": Holmes, *Ralph
       Waldo Emerson*, 1.

xii   "His ideas of friendship": Ibid., 368.
       "Love was only phenomenal": Joel
       Myerson, "MF's 1842 Jnl," *HLB* 21
       (July 1973): 331–32. See Baker,
       Emerson Among the Eccentrics,
       "Waldo Minor," ch. 18, 193.
       "To write what will amount": Baker
       notes, "The Intent."

xiii "aim and hope": Ibid.

xiv   "for ever a sort of beautiful enemy":
       Mumford, ed., *Ralph Waldo
       Emerson: Essays and Journals*, 170.
       "devastators of the day": Holmes,
       Ralph Waldo Emerson, 408.
       "A barn chamber": quoted in Baker,
       notes for "Philosopher of
       Friendship," see *L* 2:329, RWE to
       MF, 6 Sept. 1840.
       "To live in a field of pumpkins": Baker
       notes "Philosopher of Friendship,"
       see *JMN* 4:53, 19–27 Oct.1832.

Chapter 1:
THE BROTHERS

3   "She kept her family together":
       L 4:408.
       "the assistance of some excellent
       friends": Ibid.
       "Her children as they grew up": Ibid.

4   Doctors had urged Edward: *L* 1:117.
       "I did not know where I was going":
       JMN 4:139.
       "have seen enough": Ibid.
       "Bulkeley is perfectly deranged":
       L 1:164.

5   notably garrulous: *L* 4:116.
       In the spring of 1827 he escaped:
       L 1:202.
       in garret rooms upstairs: Ibid., 227
       n. 14.

       "How dare you work so hard": Ibid.,
       233. Cf. *Hamlet* 5. 1.
       fair-haired, blue-eyed Edward:
       L 1:177 n. 33, 210.
       Edward was seized with fainting fits:
       Ibid., 235 n. 47.
       "violently" deranged: Ibid., 236.
       But Edward was obliged: Ibid., 238.
       "the constitutional calamity of my
       family": *JMN* 3:137.

6   "We are devising how": *L* 1:251–52.
       "military carriage": G. W. Cooke, *An
       Historical* 2:8.
       "I do not know that there is any
       chance": *L* 1:259, 28 Jan. 1829.
       Along with Charles, he was present:
       Ibid., 265 and n. 19.
       in October he was admitted: Ibid., 285
       n. 88.
       "taking a chair": Ibid.
       in November he joined William: Ibid.,
       286 n. 101.
       "with lounging moderation": Ibid.,
       289.
       to keep Edward's purse from
       becoming "windy": Ibid.
       Except for a brief holiday: Ibid.,
       307–8.
       On the twelfth he took ship: Ibid.,
       313; G.W. Cooke, *An Historical*
       2:8.
       the "theolog brother": *L* 1:158 n. 1
       (1825).
       Bulkeley had reentered McLean: Ibid.,
       310.
       "a longer illness": Ibid., 321, 323.

7   "Edward writes always sadly": Ibid.,
       320.
       "she should do me more good": *JMN*
       3:226–28.
       "O willingly, my wife": Ibid., 228.
       "the common things go on and she is
       not here": *L* 1:319.
       "walked out regularly": Haskins,
       RWE, 45.
       "pleasanter to me": *L* 1:319.
       "to her beautiful character": Ibid., 321
       and n. 20.
       "do not return": *JMN* 3:244.

8

of "little worth": *L* 1:321.
"I shall go to her": Ibid., 321 and
n. 22.
"slowly disclosed": Ibid., 330.
"every star that sinks": Ibid.
"High over all calamities": Ibid., 331.
"this sickening planet": Ibid., 313,
Dec. 1830.
His "bitter sweet" memories: Ibid.,
325.
"sad recreation": Ibid., 324.
"nowhere and yet everywhere": *JMN*
3:257.
"O pleasant pleasant": Ibid., 230.
"I do not fear death": Ibid., 312.
Back in Boston: *L* 1:326.

9

"We must never be sanguine": Ibid.,
325.
"keep your tranquil temper": Ibid.,
324–25.
"And as the delicate Snow": *JMN*
3:290, 6 July 1831.
"When I think of you": Ibid., 275,
21 July 1831.
"I rejoice to hear": *L* 1:324.
William had been appointed: Ibid.,
337 n. 81.
"happy and happy making line": Ibid.,
332.
"She is not flattered": Ibid., 342.
Edward's limited earning power
continued to harass his conscience.
After his death Emerson exclaimed,
"O what a wailing tragedy is this
world considered in reference to
money-matters." Read EBE's letter
of 6 July 1833 and the other to his
mother, *JMN* 4:344, ca. 26 Nov.
1834.
"honey catcher of pleasure": *L* 1:227.
"I wish Charles was stouter": Ibid.,
332.

10

Presently he came down: Ibid., 334–35.
"Who would have thot": Ibid., 336.
"Every morning I am up": *JMN* 4:14.
Quotations from *JMN* 4:14 and
from "A Leaf from 'A Voyage to
Porto Rico,' " by Charles Emerson,
which appeared in the *Dial* 3 (April

1843): 522–26. He had left New
York City on Dec. 7 and reached
San Juan on the twenty-second.
"battening (would I might say
fattening)": *L* 1:339 n. 91. RWE's
memories of St. Augustine are in his
letter to William: Ibid., 189.
his collection of tropical seashells:
JMN 4:14.
"turning merchant in earnest":
L 1:339 n. 91.
"more good by going": *JMN* 3:228.

11

"It seems that Ellen": *L* 1:323.
"I may have legal rights": Ibid., 327.
"living monument": Ibid., 332.
"refused all compromise": Ibid., 349.
"certainly had opportunity": Ibid. See
also Pommer, *Emerson's First
Marriage*, 02.
"I visited Ellen's tomb": *JMN* 4:7,
29 March 1832.

12

"working in your calling": Ibid., 10
and n. 19, 16–17 and n. 49.
"It is the best part": *JMN* 3:318–19,
10 Jan. 1832.
"a week of moral excitement": *JMN*
4:27.
"I think Jesus did not mean": Ibid.,
30.
The communication was noted:
Listed, *L* 1:351. See now
L 7:207–8, 211–13 and notes for
other letters written on the issue.
"Here among the mountains": *JMN*
4:27–29.

13

"God is, and we in him.": Ibid., 29.
"There is a god within us": Ovid,
Fasti 6:5: *Est deus in nobis agitante
calescimus ille*: *JMN* 4:29; *JMN*
3:12, 139.
"I can only do my work": *L* 1:354.
"The true doctrine": *JMN* 4:40.
a "perpetual celebration": Ibid., 30.
"prepared to eat or drink religiously":
L 1:354.
the closely reasoned sermon was
"noble": Ibid., 355 n. 44.
to grant his "dismission": Ibid., 356
n. 45.

"Waldo looks very sad": Ibid.

"hour of decision": Noted in *L* 1:353
  n. 37. For MME's reaction to his
  dilemma, see now *Letters of MME*,
  313–15.

On his return from New Hampshire:
  L 1:353 n. 37.

"A stomach ache will make": *JMN*
  4:33–34.

to celebrate his engagement: *L* 1:355.

the arrival of Edward: Ibid., 355 and
  n. 41.

14 "fine spirits": Ibid., 355.

"A Last Farewell": printed in the *Dial*
  1 (July 1840): 47; *C-E-C*, 273,
  RWE to Carlyle, 30 June 1840, says
  it was written "when last he left his
  home." For the date 6 Oct. 1832,
  see *L* 1:355 n. 41.

"tedious complaint": Ibid., 357 n. 47.

"Why must I obey Christ?": *JMN*
  4:45.

"I will not see with others' eyes": Ibid.
  47–48.

15 "the severing of our strained cord":
  L 1:357–58.

"Farewell to thee": *JMN* 4:60.

"I have wiredrawn": *L* 1:357.

"Waldo is sick again": Ibid., 357
  n. 47.

"I proposed to make": Ibid., 359.

"A wasted peevish invalid.": Ibid.,
  375.

Luckily, he still had his brothers. See,
  for example, Ibid., 218, 264, 316,
  329, 333, 345.

16 "Give me my household gods": Ibid.,
  358.

"We may break up": Ibid., 357 n. 47.

the dispersal was complete: Ibid., 359.

"to the four winds": Ibid., 361.

Chapter 2: AUNT MARY

17 praised the Arabian "Bedoween":
  JMN 1:328.

the yoke of men's opinions:
  L 1:354.

"the wild freedom of MME's genius":
  JMN 12:513.

"the fire of her piety": *E Works*
  10:594.

"unsparing criticism": Ibid.

"the kind aunt whose cares": *JMN*
  2:316; Tolman, *MME*, 1–5. See
  now *The Selected Letters of MME*,
  edited by Nancy Craig Simmons,
  xxvii–xliii and chapter essays on
  MME's life and work.

"Never any gave higher counsels":
  JMN 8:391.

18 "The Nun's Aspiration": *E Works*
  9:253–54.

"I tire of shams": Ibid., 254.

"Oh Ruthy, may you have grace":
  JMN 9:239, 10:385, 16:189;
  Tolman, *MME*, 13. See now *Letters
  of MME*, 74, dated 12 May 1813.

"like Cicero perhaps": *JMN* 2:373 n.
  67, 26 June 1822. See now *Letters
  of MME*, 155.

"What has done the most": Tolman,
  MME, 21–22.

"prophetic and apocalyptic
  ejaculations": *E Works* 10:599.

"imbuing all her genius": Ibid.

"the relation between you and your
  Creator": Tolman, *MME*, 23. See
  now *Letters of MME*, 314.

"the divine personal agency": Ibid.

human beings could "reach
  perfection": Tolman, *MME*, 6. See
  now *Letters of MME*, 314.

Emerson's limited view: Tolman,
  MME, 8. See now *Letters of MME*,
  333–36.

"I had too proud a spirit": *JMN*
  16:89.

"No aristocrat, no porphyrogenet":
  Ibid.

19 "no fixed faith in a personal God":
  Tolman, *MME*, 24, MME to CCE,

8 Jan. 1833. See now *Letters of
MME*, 330.

"confused and dark": Ibid.

"Aunt Mary wished everybody": *JMN*
15:152.

"the conflict of the new and the old":
JMN 7:446, 6 May 1841; *E Works*
10:596.

Their correspondence continued:
L 1:49 n. 52.

"sneaky short letters": Ibid., 122. See
now *Letters of MME*, 161, 19 July
[1822].

"weird-women": *L* 1:197 and n. 45,
15 May 1827. See now *L* 7: passim
for additional letters of RWE to
MME.

"Pardon the whim": Tolman, *MME*, 19.

But he had already made: *L* 1:300.

an eye like a needle: *JMN* 4:53.

20 "she knew them too well": Ibid.

she was offended "by the irritating
phlegm": *JMN* 8:69.

"She could keep step": "Mary Moody
Emerson," *E Works* 10:407.

"I have from lonely youth": *JMN* 9:97.

Aunt Mary's Concord relatives "flout
her": *L* 1:444 and n. 48.

She was boarding in Concord: Ibid.,
423, 23 Nov. 1834.

she paid them a call: Ibid.

one example of the "surprizingly good
understanding": Ibid.

"Hurry," she said: *JMN* 7:476 and
n. 558.

"Whoever wants power": *JMN*
12:560.

"The finest wits": *JMN* 5:52.

"I hate to be expecting a cat": Ibid.,
419.

"Never much good comes": Ibid., 89.

"When people are going to die": *JMN*
7:312.

"I am tired of fools": Ibid., 30.

Her idiosyncrasies were legion: *E
Works* 10:594.

thimble as a seal for letters: *JMN* 3:98.

"to give herself more ease": *JMN*
15:462.

She could not bear: *JMN* 11:161–62.

"from Dan to Beersheba": *JMN* 14:67.

"of cleaning and painting": Tolman,
MME, 18.

21 "dear and sacred" to others: *JMN*
11:259.

"a she-Isaiah but alive": *L* 1:242.

"only another name for lying":
Tolman, *MME*, 6.

"to live to give pain": ": "Mary Moody
Emerson," *E Works* 10:409.

"valuable as a disturbing force": *MF
Ltrs* 2:246, Oct. 1841; *JMN*
11:493–94.

"I remember several set-tos": ETE,
Life of Lidian, 73. For LJE early
impressions of MME, see now
Letters of Lidian, 25, 27, 39.

for embracing "Humanitarianism":
Rusk, *RWE*, 229–30.

"Your star has wandered fearfully":
Tolman, *MME*, 25. See now *Letters
of MME*, 423, 5 Nov. 1840.

"Angry and ashamed": Rusk, *RWE*,
229, MME to RWE, c. 31 Mar.
1836; *L* 2:397 n. 92, summary of
MME to RWE, 15 May 1841. See
now *Letters of MME*, 367–68 and
428–29 for complete texts

Aunt Mary's diary entries: Tolman,
MME, 7.

Two of her favorite: See now *Letters of
MME*, 251.

As early as 1835: *E Works* 10:429.

"Saladin caused his shroud": *JMN*
15:343.

22 "delighted in the figure": Ibid. For her
death see *JMN* 15:345–46 and
L 5:325–26.

"no intelligent youth": "Mary Moody
Emerson," *E Works* 10:406.

"Our Delphian was fantastic enough":
Ibid., 408.

"The chief witness which I have":
Ibid., 404–5.

Chapter 3:
ISHMAEL ABROAD

23 set sail for Malta aboard the brig
     Jasper: *JMN* 4:102, 2 Jan. 1833.
     he had found much to be endured:
     L 1:318–61 passim, 8 Feb. 1831–14
     Dec. 1832.
     " A long storm": *JMN* 4:102.
     he "remembered up nearly the whole":
     Ibid., 103.
     "It takes one 'Grand tour' ": Ibid., 145.
24 his hopes for new friendships: Ibid.,
     68.
     to discover "new affinities": Ibid.
     "the affections, weaknesses,
     surprises": Ibid.
     Ashore at La Valetta: Ibid., 116.
     "a child's again to these glorious":
     Ibid., 84.
     "I have this day": Ibid., 122.
     he could see Mount Etna: Ibid., 125.
     "Mountainettes like warts": Ibid., 129.
     were "paved with lava": Ibid., 130.
     graffiti on walls and fences: Ibid.,
     132–33.
25 His Sicilian companions: Ibid., 133.
     his officious *cicerone*: Ibid., 139,
     7 Mar. 1833. *JMN* 4:139 n. 12
     wrongly identifies the "sad
     malady" as tuberculosis, but
     Spedale dei Pazzi means insane
     asylum. See Emerson's complaint
     about "the constitutional calamity
     of my family" in *JMN* 3:137, July
     1828.
     To inform himself: *JMN* 4:142.
     Nor could he agree: Ibid., 145.
     "If he had said '*happy*' ": Ibid.
     "watching every mouthful": Ibid.
     For a long time he stood alone: Ibid.,
     141.
     He found Virgil's tomb: Ibid., 142 and
     141–48, for sights seen in Naples,
     12–23 March 1833.
     "swarming, faithless, robber
     population": Ibid., 143.
     Twice in one day: *L* 1:367.
     "better health than ever": Ibid., 373.

     "I would give all Rome": Ibid.,
     374.
26 "The wise man—the true friend":
     Ibid., 375–76.
     One of his "sensible persons": Ibid.,
     378.
     During Holy Week: Ibid., 381.
     "the theory and order and politics":
     Ibid.
     "the unhappy traveller": Ibid.
     "the inner Italy": Ibid.
     But Florence in May: *JMN* 4:167–68.
     "rose richly out of the smoky": Ibid.,
     177.
     "Good streets, industrious
     population": Ibid.,167–68.
     "the fair Erminia": Ibid., 175.
     "If you will not buy": Ibid., 176.
27 His birthday happened to coincide:
     Ibid., 178, 25 May 1833. Cf.
     L 1:385 and n. 80, 28 May 1833.
     "a city for beavers": *JMN* 4:186, ca. 1
     June 1833.
     "Sometimes I would hide myself":
     Ibid., 74, 2 June 1833.
     "But would it not be cowardly": Ibid.,
     74.
     "The errors of traditional
     Christianity": Ibid., 77, ca. 11 July
     1833.
28 "changing so fast from the state":
     Ibid., 240, ca. 13 Sept. 1833.
     even Calvinism might still prove
     "wholesome": Ibid., 80.
     not yet reached the point of "pestering
     others": Ibid., 81.
     "no call to expound": Ibid., 83.
     The trouble with the "religionists":
     Ibid.
     they did not know "the extent": Ibid.
     "the old revelation": Ibid., 84.
     "a man contains all that": Ibid.
     his "rain-dripping cabin": Ibid., 87.
29 all men are believers and unbelievers:
     Ibid., 88
     "opinions, affections, whimsies": Ibid.
     "I cannot but think": Ibid., 92.
     "To the barbarous state of society":
     Ibid., 93.

"There shall be": Ibid., ca. 21 Oct. 1833.

"that every soul occupies": Ibid., 93.

The teacher of the coming age: Ibid., 93–94.

30   "the minister and interpreter": Ibid., 95.

"The Universe is a more amazing": Ibid., 199–200, 13 July 1833. On shipboard, coming home, he had written, "I like my book about nature and wish I knew where and how I ought to live. God will show me.": Ibid., 237, 6 Sept. 1833.

the morning cloud contained: Ibid., 95.

"something in it that resembles": Ibid.

"Let a man under the influence": Ibid.

"to an instructed eye": Ibid., 96, 2 Nov. 1833.

In November he spoke: *L* 1:397 n. 118.

in January 1834 gave another: Ibid., 402 n. 131.

"growing taste for natural science": Ibid., 404, 18 Jan. 1834.

"Natural history by itself": *JMN* 4:311, 15 Aug. 1834.

31   "chiefly upon Natural Ethics": *L* 1:447, 25 June 1835.

"a pebble or two": Ibid. For a valuable census of the steps by which Emerson came to write his first book, see "The Emergence of Nature" in *Emerson's Nature: Origins, Growth, Meaning*, ed. M. M. Sealts Jr. and A. R. Ferguson (New York, 1969), 38–45.

he returned to his attempt: *JMN* 4:270.

"far more precious". . . "social stimulus": Ibid., 23 Mar. 1834.

"intellectual and moral endowments": Ibid., 256, 19 Jan. 1834.

"The good rain like a bad": Ibid., 281.

"I want instructers": Ibid.,

"the whole secret": Ibid., 278.

"in the conviction": Ibid.

"The wise man must be wary": Ibid., 279.

"Every soul for itself": Ibid.

he had described as "suicidal": *JMN* 3:279, 29 July 1831.

"this distrust of reason". . . "this doctrine": Ibid.

32   "to think is to receive": Ibid.

"Trust thyself": "Self-Reliance," *E Works* 2:47.

"all the mistakes": *JMN* 4:274.

"Absolve yourself to the universe": Ibid., 275.

At the invitation of his stepgrand-father: Ibid., 384 n. 376.

"Hail to the quiet fields": Ibid., 335, 5 Nov. 1834.

"As soon as I read": Ibid., 336.

Often, too, he discovered: Ibid., 337.

Even before his friendly: *JMN* 3:164 and n. 3 give Emerson's change from Coleridge's "*Quantum sumus, scimus.*" *JMN* 4:407–12, Aug. 1833, give Emerson's account of the meeting with Coleridge. His allusions to *Aids to Reflection*, 1829–34, are indexed in *JMN* 3:384 and *JMN* 4:452.

33   we are endowed with "an intelligence": *JMN* 2:14, 8 Sept. 1822.

God's "law is a moral one": Ibid., 38, 2 Nov. 1822.

"Let me ask you": *L* 1:412, 31 May 1834 to EBE.

"Reason is the highest faculty": Ibid.

"that wrinkled calculator": Ibid., 413.

"Every true man stands": *JMN* 4:297–98, June 1834. According to Professor Robert E. Spiller, coeditor, vol. 1, *The Collected Works of RWE* (Cambridge, 1971), intro., xxiii, this passage represents Emerson's "first full acceptance of 'Reason' as a higher moral faculty." But the letter to EBE cited above is not only a few weeks earlier, but also clearer and more extensive.

34   "/Democracy/Freedom/": *JMN* 4:357.

"God has made nothing without a crack": Ibid., 362, Dec. 1834.

Chapter 4: LIDIAN

35 During 1834 Emerson paid:
F. B. Sanborn, *Recollections*
2:318–19; ETE, *Life of Lidian*, 47.
"The originality of his thoughts":
O. W. Holmes, *RWE*, 65.

36 "well formed and well closed": Ibid.,
360–61.
"We seem to see the people": Henry
James Jr. reviewed Cabot's memoir
of Emerson in *Macmillan's
Magazine* in 1887 and in 1888
collected it with other essays in
Partial Portraits. The quotation
given here is from the London
edition, 1899, 11.
"so lifted to higher thoughts": ETE,
Life of Lidian, 47.
she "regarded him with reverence":
Ibid.
"she saw a clear image": Ibid.
"impropriety" in a woman: Ibid.

37 "very beautiful, close to her": Ibid.
It contained Emerson's proposal:
Ibid., 48. See now *L* 7:232–33 for
text.
"deep and tender respect": Printed in
G. W. Allen, *Waldo Emerson*,
239–40. See now *L* 7:232–33,
24 Jan. 1835.
she so "thoroughly enjoyed": ETE,
Life of Lidian, 48.
"that catechism with the closed eyes":
Ibid. See now *L* 7:234–35, 8 Feb.
1835, "that catechism of thine with
shut eyes."
"in a new and higher way": *L* 7:232.
"vehement word" or given "one
passionate": *L* 1:434. See now
L 7:232 and other courtship letters,
L 7:232–37.

38 Almost at once he renamed: ETE, *Life
of Lidian*, 51, 68–69, 87, 224 n. 15.
Eleanor M. Tilton in *L* 7:233 n. 4
says the letter shows the name did
not come about for purposes of
euphony and cites Feb. 1 as the first
date of his use of "Lydian."
his Lydian queen: *L* 1:434–35.

Emerson's Aunt Mary often
addressed her favorite nieces as
"Queenie." Waldo had called his
first wife "the Queen," and her
nicknames for him were "the King"
and sometimes "Grandpa."
"her air of lofty abstraction": ETE,
Life of Lidian, 51.
"mine Asia": ETE, *Life of Lidian*,
68–69 and 224 n. 157. Cf. *C-E-C*,
184.
"I announce this fact": *L* 1:436.
"beautiful anywise that I know": Ibid.,
436 n. 21.

39 "one of the Forms of Beauty": Henry
F. Pommer, *Emerson's First
Marriage*, 9.
"with the roar of a metropolis":
L 1:421.
"fervid heart". . . "forever still": *JMN*
4:326.
"of hope for this life": Ibid., 325.
"She looks *very refined*": *L* 1:439
n. 33.
"as remarkable among women": ETE,
Life of Lidian, 49.
"She is a singular looking person":
Ibid.

40 "for without it we should never":
quoted in ETE, *Life of Lidian*, 49.
"did not make a very good": Ibid., 31.
"the food you don't eat": Ibid., 31–32.
An early proponent of this theory:
Ibid., 31–32 and 216 n. 72. Lidian's
copy of Cornaro was an
abridgment by Herman Daggett
(Andover, Mass.: Mark Newman,
1824). The comment on food intake
was on p. 15.
"In those years from 18 to 30": ETE,
Life of Lidian, 37.
"So . . . she used a cold bath": Ibid.,
32.

41 "wide champaign": *L* 1:435, 1 Feb.
1835.
"a sunset, a forest": Ibid.
"childish murmuring": Ibid., 440, ca.
4 Mar. 1835. See also ETE, *Life of
Lidian*, 51.

"an English river, licking": O. W.
   Holmes, *RWE* (Boston, 1890), p. 70.
when Lidian first saw Concord: ETE,
   Life of Lidian, 51.
Coolidge Castle: Ibid., 52. See now
   L 7:242.

42 The wedding was planned: ETE, *Life
   of Lidian*, 52.
arriving at four o'clock: Ibid., 55.
He and Lidian sat talking: Ibid.
"Women have in themselves: *JMN*
   6:228. Cf. *JMN* 5:119.
she had to be warned: ETE, *Life of
   Lidian*, 56.
wearing white muslin: Ibid., 54.
in exact fulfillment: Ibid., 56.
"the process of love to marriage":
   JMN 6:154, from *Don Juan* 3.5.
"Hanging is better": *JMN* 5:85,
   4 Aug. 1835.
"99 snakes and one eel": *JMN* 6:154
   and n. 92.
"A drop in the ocean": Ibid., 154.

43 "I came to her": Ibid., 155 and
   n. 193.
"He champed the bit": Ibid., 155.
"A man wants a wife": Ibid., 188.
"all the various charities": Allen,
   Waldo Emerson, 251, LJE to Lucy
   Jackson Brown, 22 Sept. 1835. See
   now *L* 7:247, where the letter is
   noted, and *Letters of Lidian*, 34–37,
   for the full text which has "various,"
   rather than "warmer" charities
   (Allen, 251).
"Send any friends": *L* 1:454, 21 Sept.
   1835.
"Yes, they say much": Cooke, *An
   Historical* 2:9.
"To write a very little": *L* 2:7, 14 Mar.
   1836.
he was preparing: Ibid., 9 and n. 19.
   See now *L* 7:258 and n. 9.

44 "withering": *L* 2:13.
too feeble to travel: Ibid., 10.
Charles was sinking: Ibid., 18; ETE,
   Life of Lidian, 65.
"arrived too late": *L* 2:18. See now
   L 7:259.

Lidian was supportive: See *Letters of
   Lidian*, 44–49 for Lidian's letters to
   RWE and EPP at this time.

Chapter 5:
BRONSON ALCOTT

45 "tasteful furniture, desks": Sanborn-
   Harris, *ABA* 1:177.
"done by the Italian": Ibid., 184.
At the north end: EPP, *Record of a
   School*, 3rd ed. (1874), 13–14.

46 "The sensation of thrift": Sanborn-
   Harris, *ABA* 1:178.
"some impediments": Ibid.
Starting from a hardscrabble: Shepard,
   Pedlar's Progress, chs. 1–4;
   Sanborn-Harris, *ABA*, chs. 1–4;
   McCuskey, *Bronson Alcott, Teacher*,
   chs. 1–4.
"every book read": EPP, *Record of a
   School*, 3rd ed. (1874), 28–30, ABA
   to EPP 23 Oct. 1834.
he settled on a narrow: Sanborn-
   Harris, *ABA* 1:181; McCuskey,
   Bronson Alcott, Teacher, 104–05,
   197.

47 with a brief preface: Carové, *The Story
   Without an End* (Boston, 1836),
   iii–iv. The preface does not appear
   in the 1899 edition listed in the
   bibliography.
"appearance of the young celestial":
   ABA Jrnls 1:56.
"prophet's egotism": *C-E-C*, 331.
As Miss Peabody recorded: EPP,
   Record of a School, 3rd ed. (1874),
   142–49.

48 Alcott encouraged this: *ABA Jrnls*
   1:12.
he had twice heard: Ibid., 23.
"I wish to know": Ibid., 56.
"consistent spiritualist": *JMN* 5:57.
on the lookout for "new men": Ibid.
Shortly thereafter: *ABA Jrnls* 1:55–58;
   JMN 8:210, Mar. 1842.

Presently Emerson read:
JMN 5:634.

"To the parents of": *L* 1:447–48.

"I shall get people": EPP, *Record of a
School*, 3rd ed. (1874), 235.

49   Bradford took him to Concord: *ABA
Jrnls* 1:68.

"a new idea of life": Ibid., 68–69.

"a wise man, simple": *JMN* 5:98–99.

"upon the nimbleness": Ibid.

"the most earnest spiritualists": *ABA
Jrnls* 1:70.

Emerson in turn took: *JMN* 5:111.

"Thou still art": Sanborn-Harris, *ABA*
1:258–59.

50   took away the manuscript: *JMN* 5:122
n. 379.

"the Apprehension of the Absolute":
L 2:4.

"too much the book": Ibid., 5.

"verbal inaccuracies": Ibid., 6.

"perfectly simple and elegant": *JMN*
5:170.

"the gradual dawn of a thought": Ibid.,
175.

"a harp of two strings": Ibid., 182.

"That man [Alcott]": *L* 2:29.

"Like other sovereigns": *JMN* 5:178.

51   "Each new mind": Ibid., 178–79.

Several passages from the manuscript:
Quoted in *JMN* 5:122, Feb.–Mar.
1836.

"Successful preaching implies": Ibid.,
167–68.

"Matter is a revelation": *ABA Jrnls* 1:65.

"I set out from the wide": Ibid., 73.

"one enormous web": Shepard,
Pedlar's Progress, 457.

Throughout his life: see *ABA Jrnls*
1:77, 121, 124–25, 209 and 388 for
the quotations in this paragraph.

52   But Emerson's journals: *JMN* 5:122.

"A fact is only": Ibid., 177.

"A fact is the end": *Nature, E Works*
1:34–35.

calling it a "harbinger": *ABA Jrnls*
1:78.

he had brought with him: *L* 2:32 and
n. 98.

"I see with as much": *JMN* 5:124; Cf.
Nature, E Works 1:59.

"To the rude it seems": *JMN* 5:125;
Cf. *Nature, E Works* 1:38–39.

53   "It is a small and mean": *JMN* 5:146.

"The belief that it *appears*": Ibid., 172.

"Let us interrogate the great": *Nature*,
E Works 1:4. Cf. *Hamlet* 1.5.

"What angels invented": *Nature, E
Works* 1:12–13. Cf. *Hamlet* 2.2.

54   "the presence of a higher": *Nature, E
Works* 1:19.

"beauty in nature is not ultimate":
Ibid., 24.

"the world is emblematic": Ibid., 32.

"Reason transfers all these lessons":
Ibid., 36.

"a noble doubt": Ibid., 47–48.

"Idealism," says the seventh chapter:
Ibid., 62–63.

"as a useful introductory hypothesis":
Ibid., 63.

"that the highest is present": Ibid.,
63–64.

55   "a repetition in the finite mind":
S. T. Coleridge, *Biographia
Literaria*, ed. J. Shawcross
(London, Oxford, 1907), 1:202,
ch. 13. See also Emerson's remark
about the relationship of Coleridge's churchmanship and his
criticism at *JMN* 5:252, 25 Nov.
1836 after the publication of
Nature.

he had called Alcott: *JMN* 5:76.

"Build therefore your own world":
Nature, E Works 1:76.

"Every spirit": Ibid.

Chapter 6:
MARGARET FULLER

56   "spiritual history": *Mem MFO*
1:194–95.

"that only clergyman": *MF Letters*
1:210.

having borrowed her manuscript
translation: Ibid., 212 and n. 6, 213.
"I am flattered": Ibid., 224.
Emerson, who had already: *L* 1:393.

57 "a pleasant unpretending lady": *JMN*
5:86, 25 Aug. 1835. Cf. *JMN* 6:261.
"I have heard much": *MF Letters*
1:225, MF to FHH, 6 Mar. 1835.

58 "I have heard . . . that from the
beginning": *Mem MFO* 1:235.
had evidently reminded her father:
Virgil, *Aeneid* 1. 46: *Ast ego, quae
divum incedo regina* (Yet I, who
move as queen of the gods . . .).
Reference comes from MF's journal
of May 1844 and is quoted in *JMN*
11:463 and n. 33.
Emerson knew the *Aeneid*: RWE
elaborates the queen image in *Mem
MFO* 1:213, 237.
"like the queen of some parliament":
Ibid., 213.
"I take my natural position always":
MF Letters 1:332, 17 Apr. 1838.
"a necklace of diamonds": *JMN*
11:259 and n. 295.
Eliza Rotch Farrar: For Eliza Farrar's
background see Farrar, *Recollections
of Seventy Years* and *DAB* entry on
William Rotch (1734–1828).

59 "to put her on the best footing": *Mem
MFO* 1:299–300.
"she undertook to mould": Higginson,
MFO, 35–36.
"and wished that all": *Mem MFO*
1:230.
"About six . . . came out": *JMN* 11:184.
as the party moved up: *MF Letters*
1:232–33.
Trip to Trenton Falls: *JMN* 11:505.
First talk with SGW: *JMN* 11:502.
Data on Trenton Falls furnished by
Col. Lawrence Spellman, 1/3/79.
See picture of the Falls in *MF
Letters* 1:234.
a clump of snowdrops:
JMN 11:502.
"I soon found": Chipperfield, *In Quest
of Love*, 113–14.

60 "to go to that place": *MF Letters*
1:249, MF to SGW, 20 Apr. 1836.
Quoted in Higginson, *MFO*, 57.
concluding with a sonnet: Quoted in
Chipperfield, *In Quest of Love*, 114.
"We reached N York": *MF Letters*
1:232–33. Chipperfield, *In Quest of
Love*, 114–15, quotes the letter
inexactly.

61 Jacob Barker: See *DAB* entry on Jacob
Barker; Newhall, *The Barker
Family*, 36–37.
Among his more colorful: *Incidents in
the Life of Jacob Barker*
(Washington, 1855); Anthony,
Dolly Madison, 225, 395–96
(23 Aug. 1814).
"large engraving of Madame
Récamier": *Mem MFO* 1:283.
"She gave herself to her friendships":
Ibid., 281–84.

62 "It is the same love": Ibid.
"With what envy": Ibid., 153.

63 returning home in the summer: *MF
Letters* 1:243, 30 Jan. 1836; see also
Mem MFO 1:159.
then called brain fever: *Mem MFO*
1:154–55.
"great vulture": *Mem MFO* 2:135.

64 "Upwards I stretch": Quoted in
Chipperfield, *In Quest of Love*,
117–18.
Timothy Fuller was struck: *Mem MFO*
1:155–57.
"Grant, oh Father": Ibid. See *MF
Letters* 1:236 n. 1.
"practical details": *MF Letters* 1:237.
"I always hated": Ibid.; *Mem MFO*
1:157, 3 Nov. 1835.
"The prospect is most alluring": *MF
Letters* 1:243; *Mem MFO* 1:159, to
Eugene Fuller, 30 Jan. 1836.
She really meant "*if* I go": *MF Letters*
1:247, 17 April 1836, to Eliza
Rotch Farrar.
"Circumstances have decided": Ibid.,
254, 23 May 1836; *Mem MFO*
1:159–61. Abraham Fuller's
discouraging letter to MF, May

1836, printed in Sanborn,
Recollections 2:406–7 n.

65 "dull brown fields": *MF Letters*
1:249–50, 20 Apr. 1836,
to SGW.
"kernel of affection": *MF Letters*
2:80–81, July 1839.
Miss Martineau had "enjoined" him:
Mem MFO 1:201.
Margaret wrote Elizabeth: *MF Letters*
1:255, MF to Elizabeth Hoar, 14
July 1836; *JMN* 11:479. She named
Friday the 22nd as the date, but
RWE to FHH, 20 July 1836,
L 2:30, said that she was due on the
21st. See also *MF Letters* 1:255,
n. 1.

66 he wrote his brother William: *L* 2:32,
8 Aug. 1836.
when the Farrars: Farrar, *Recollections
of Seventy Years*, 257–58. See also
Cooke, *An Historical* 2:36–39.
Emerson brought Bronson Alcott:
Higginson, *MFO*, 75 for ABA visit
of 2 Aug. 1836.
"She was already rich in friends": *Mem
MFO* 1:204, 216.

67 Margaret's youngest brother,
Lloyd: James Lloyd Fuller
(1826–1891) "was either
emotionally disturbed or mentally
retarded.": *MF Letters* 1:194 n. 1,
by Robert N. Hudspeth.
"I still remember the first half-hour":
Mem MFO 1:202–3.
"stuffed me out as a philosopher":
Ibid.
"I know not what you think": *JMN*
5:187, 190.

68 "She had an incredible variety": *Mem
MFO* 1:202–3.
He gave her a copy: *MF Letters*
1:261–62, 21 Sept. 1837.
an autograph of Jeremy Bentham: *MF
Letters* 1:268 and 270 n. 2, 11 Apr.
1837.
"I have been making war": *JMN*
5:262, 3 Dec. 1836.

69 "a day in our green fens": *L* 2:37.

Her father was taking her: *MF Letters*
1:261.
"I grieve," wrote Emerson: *L* 2:38.

Chapter 7:
FATHER TAYLOR

70 "Men are convertible": *JMN* 4:278.
Among his early advocates: *JMN*
4:381; 5:255; 6:23 and n. 28.
On the first Sunday: *L* 1:430, 7 Jan.
1835.

71 "Friend Taylor of the Zebulon": Ibid.,
344–45 and nn. 5, 6.
"threw back his coat-collar": Haven-
Russell, *Father Taylor*, 260.
"wholly uncoloured": *JMN* 5:4–5.

72 "And so he went on": Ibid.
Anecdotes buzzed round him: See
Haven-Russell, *Father Taylor*, 131,
159, 162, 210, 324 for the
quotations in this paragraph.
There was also the famous story: Ibid.,
126, 132, 203 as above.

73 There is some evidence: *L* 1:430 and
n. 6.
"Here is the place": *JMN* 5:87.

74 an "old-fashioned, shouting": Allan
MacDonald, "A Sailor Among the
Transcendentalists," *NEQ* 8 (Sept.
1935): 307–19; Haven-Russell,
Father Taylor, 136.
"Edward Taylor is a noble work":
JMN 5:255, ca. 28 Nov. 1836.
"a creature of instinct": Ibid.
"Almost . . . a perfect orator": Ibid.,
287 and n. 34; Cf. *Othello* 3.3., 92.

75 He said that he led: Haven-Russell,
Father Taylor, 133.
"Your patriotic fathers": Ibid.,
258–59.
"The wonderful and laughing life":
JMN 5:287.
"some natures are too good":
"Character," *E Works* 3:106–7.
"I ought to sit": *JMN* 5:464–65.

76 "At church all day": Ibid., 463.
"Whenever the pulpit": "Divinity
School Address," *E Works*
1:137–38.
In the face of such preaching: Ibid.,
143; *JMN* 5:442.

77 "We see God in nature": *JMN* 7:73,
16 Sept. 1838.
Frost "grinds and grinds": *JMN*
5:481, 30 Apr. 1838.
"I felt in a higher degree": *JMN*
7:359–60, 28 May 1840.
"more fiery combustion": Haven-
Russell, *Father Taylor*, 427–29.

78 "It would not be an auspicious": NH,
Love Letters 1:147–48, 15 Mar.
1840.
"somewhat afraid to hear": Ibid.,
158–59, 30 Mar. 1840.
"I confess to some pleasure": *JMN*
7:374, June 1840.
He felt "no less disgust": Ibid.,
440–41, Apr. 1841.

79 could speak of "treeing Jesus": *JMN*
3:115, 1 Mar. 1827.
"You may find him": "Eloquence," *E
Works* 8:114.

80 "With his admirable voice": Shepard,
Pedlar's Progress, 228–29.
Taylor, said Emerson once:
MacDonald, "A Sailor Among the
Transcendentalists,"
314–15.

Chapter 8:
WALDO AND NELLY

81 "Strange is this alien": *JMN* 5:119–20,
Jan. 1836.
"I hail the little": ETE, *Life of Lidian*,
65.
"walk and walk and walk": *L* 2:10.
"Let nothing disturb": *L* 2:18.
shortly before Charles's death: Ibid.,
9–19, on the illness and death of
CCE.

drawn, pale, and "set": ETE, *Life of
Lidian*, 67.
"looked like death": Ibid.
"the pleasures of lactation": Ibid.
during the two-week visit: *L* 2:30, 32.

82 "quite ill with dyspepsia": Ibid., 35.
diet of "poppy and oatmeal": Ibid., 37.
"My wife is now a feeble dyspeptic":
C-E-C, 148 and n. 4.
"My pill is the sun": *JMN* 5:119.
she "rigged the bed": ETE, *Life of
Lidian*, 69.
" 'Husband knows best' ": Ibid.
Emerson "could see only": Ibid., 70;
L 2:44.
"a lovely wonder": *JMN* 5:234.
"merely a brute occasion": Ibid.
"Pray come down": *L* 2:44.
"its tiny beseeching": *JMN* 5:235.

83 "the child of this couple": ETE, *Life of
Lidian*, 70; *JMN* 5:234.
A man named Waterston: *L* 2:19,
n. 58.
"my noble friend": Ibid., 20.
"Beautiful without any parallel": *JMN*
5:151, 16 May 1836.
soon nicknamed Willie and Wallie:
L 2:51, RWE to WE, 16 Dec. 1836.
"Being a lover of solitude": *JMN*
5:283, 22 Jan. 1837.

84 "I listen by night": Ibid., 296–97, mid-
Apr. 1837.
"My baby's lovely drama": *JMN*
5:292–93.
Lidian said briskly: Ibid., 327.

85 "like a pigeon house": Ibid., 343.
"hearty and protracted laugh": Ibid.,
371.
Both parents were at his side: Ibid.,
397, 442.
The journals for 1838–39: *JMN*
7:42–43.
"With the gravity of Palladio": *JMN*
5:481. The Palladio reference is in
RWE's essay, "Domestic Life," *E
Works* 7:104.
"untranslateable Sanscrit":
L 2:116.
"Who will say then": *JMN* 7:113.

"I want something to play with": Ibid., 169.

"See how the cobwebs": Ibid., 343.

"jets of Natural theology": Ibid., 346; *L* 2:268.

"I like my boy": *JMN* 7:228; *L* 2:125.

"as handsome as Walden Pond": Ibid., 135.

86   "purgatory of teething": *JMN* 7:22; *L* 2:154–55.

"less gross" than: Ibid., 155.

"How we covet insensibility": *JMN* 7:270.

One hot night in August: Ibid., 390.

"I'm afraid of": Ibid., 541, Dec. 1840; ETE, *Life of Lidian*, 83.

At Christmas her spirits: *L* 2:177, 25 Dec. 1838.

"fair, healthy," and perfectly formed: Ibid., 184.

"a sparkle of God": Ibid., 195, 229, 189.

she will "stay here": Ibid., 185, 189, 256.

the "eyes and theology": Ibid., 264; *JMN* 7:399.

87   "How glass their Knobs are": ETE, *Life of Lidian*, 85.

"the household is the home": "Domestic Life," *E Works* 7:107–8.

"People wish to be settled": *JMN* 7:354, 360, 395.

Chapter 9: ALCOTT

89   "revive in the minds": Sanborn and Harris, *ABA* 1:187.

publication at his own expense: *ABA Jrnls* 1:102.

"the Record of an attempt": Sanborn-Harris *ABA* 1:187.

Emerson praised the preface: *ABA Jrnls* 1:79.

It appeared under: Sanborn-Harris, *ABA* 1:212; *JMN* 5:248–49.

this time with his new: Higginson, *MFO*, 75–76.

"Genius has two faces": *JMN* 5:218, entry of 6 Oct. 1836, reporting on the meeting of the Club at ABA's house in Boston on 3 Oct.

90   "the great Man should": Ibid., 249–50, Nov. 1836.

"The speaker," he wrote: *ABA Jrnls* 1:81–82, Jan. 1837.

91   "crude and undigested": Hale, *Boston Daily Advertiser*, 21 Mar. 1837.

"visionary pedagogue": *The Daily Centinel and Gazette*, 22 Mar. 1837.

observed that these conversations: *Boston Courier*, 29 Mar. 1837; McCuskey, *Bronson Alcott, Teacher*, 102–4.

"miserable paragraph": *L* 2:61.

he called twice: Ibid., 60–61.

"the truly Christian temper": Sanborn-Harris, *ABA* 1:218–19.

"I hate to have all": *L* 2:61–62.

"Emerson sees me, knows me": Sanborn-Harris, *ABA* 1:263.

92   "is going to have a child": McCuskey, *Bronson Alcott, Teacher*, 102; Sanborn-Harris, *ABA* 1:216.

"cold April," wrote Emerson: *JMN* 5:304.

"the furniture, busts, casts": McCuskey, *Bronson Alcott, Teacher*, 108–9.

"My little room": Ibid.

"that the speculative": *ABA Jrnls* 1:90, May 1837.

"You have seen how roughly": Sanborn-Harris, *ABA* 1:231–32, 234.

93   "You have had your share": *L* 2:74–75.

"most extraordinary" guest: *JMN* 5:328.

"waiting for light": Ibid., 335 and n. 172, ABA to RWE, 24 May 1837.

"high and commanding": *ABA Jrnls* 1:91.

During much of June he was ill: *L* 2:80–81, 84. See now *L* 7:281 on illness.

94 Alcott also fell sick: *ABA Letters*, 34.
    "My wife is a capital nurse": Sanborn-
        Harris, *ABA* 1:229; listed in *L* 2:91.
        See now *L* 7:285 for text, RWE to
        ABA, 27 July 1837.
    "putting together things": *JMN*
        5:362–63.
    "the secret of the scholar": Ibid., 366.
    "When I see a man of genius": Ibid.,
        222, 18 Oct. 1836.
    Emerson's Phi Beta Kappa address:
        L 2:94 and n. 150, 17 Aug. 1837.
    "The hope to arouse young men":
        JMN 5:364–65, 18 Aug. 1837.
95 "Now I am visibly idle": *ABA Jrnls*
        1:96.
    "Our little river": *L* 2:116.
    "onetoned and hearkens": *JMN*
        5:457, Mar. 1838.
    "doctrine of the perpetual revelation":
        JMN 7:111, Oct. 1838.
    revised manuscript of his "Psyche":
        ABA Jrnls 1:102 and n. 4.
    Emerson found the task: *L* 2:138–41
        and n. 148. Cf. RWE to MF,
        L 2:142.
    "If the book were mine": Ibid., 138.
    "Here was a new mind": *JMN* 5:506,
        6 June 1838.
96 "to be my way": *ABA Jrnls* 1:103.
    "psychological Diary": Ibid., 132,
        135.
    contrasting his own powers: Ibid.,
        128.
    "He, faithful to his own Genius":
        Ibid., 134, 5 Aug. 1839.
    "I am of a temper": Ibid., 128, 13 May
        1839.
    The author of these words:
        McCuskey, *Bronson Alcott, Teacher*,
        111.
    "I earn little or nothing": Journal
        entry, quoted by Higginson, *MFO*,
        79, 23 Apr. 1839.
    "the arithmetic of this matter": *ABA
        Jrnls* 1:125, 23 Apr. 1839.
    "God has some task": Letter of 28
        Dec. 1839, quoted in Sanborn-
        Harris, *ABA* 1:299.

"My friend, whose scholars": *JMN*
    7:197.
"the only majestic converser": Ibid.,
    176–77, Mar. 1839.

Chapter 10: THOREAU

98 "He was not quite": *L* 5:424, RWE to
        J. B. Thayer, 25 Aug. 1865;
        Sanborn, *Life of HDT*, 128–29.
99 a member of the outdoor choir: *L* 2:85
        and n. 121, 3 July 1837.
    "cultivate the moral affections":
        Harding, *Days of HT*, 50.
    "So much only of life": "The
        American Scholar," *E Works* 1:95.
    With his commencement duties:
        Harding, *Days of HT*, 51.
    Thoreau had twice: Cameron, *The
        Transcendentalists and Minerva*
        1:86. Cited in Harding, *Days of
        HT*, 60.
    Emerson was the catalyst: Ibid., 71.
    "young friend" who seemed: *JMN*
        5:452, 11 Feb. 1838.
100 "You need not hem, Doctor": Ibid.,
        452.
    "How comic is simplicity": Ibid.,
        453–54, 17 Feb. 1838.
    "spiced throughout with rebellion":
        Ibid., 460.
101 "a new scene, a new experience": Ibid,
        480.
    but soon resigned because: Harding,
        Days of HT, 52–54.
    "I have the highest confidence":
        L 2:154 n. 193. See now *L* 7:307,
        for text, and n. 38. *HDT Corres*, 20,
        HDT to Orestes Brownson, 30
        Dec. 1837, mentions RWE, Samuel
        Hoar, and Dr. Ezra Ripley as
        "referees" for his character and
        attainments.
    Thoreau, undiscouraged, returned:
        Harding, *Days of HT*, 75–76.
    "with whom I have promised":
        L 2:154.

"My brave Henry Thoreau": *JMN*
7:143–44.

102 Goose Pond should be renamed: Ibid.,
165, 12 Jan. 1839.

she did not like "my brave Henry":
L 3:75, 19 July 1842.

there was "something military": RWE,
"Thoreau," *Atlantic Monthly* 10:58
(Aug. 1862): 239–49.

"my brave Henry Thoreau": *JMN*
7:201–2.

"the doctrine of hatred": Ibid.,
224.

103 "He in whom the love of Truth": *JMN*
5:112, 26 Dec. 1835.

He tells us, for example: WEC,
Thoreau: the Poet-Naturalist, 32.

104 "We are shut up in schools": *JMN*
7:238, 14 Sept. 1839.

"fish of the stream": HDT, *A Week on
the Concord and Merrimack Rivers*,
Saturday, Wednesday, Thursday.
See also Harding, *Days of HT*,
88–93.

105 he had the strength to "crawl after":
L 2:220–21.

"the God who made New
Hampshire": Robert Frost quoted
this in his poem, "New Hampshire"
(1923), lines 218–19.

106 his second talk with Sam Ward:
L 2:220–21; *JMN* 7:221.

he had the further pleasure: *L* 2:226
and n. 182.

the bluebird house: Engels, *I
Remember the Emersons*, 90.

"If you have any leisure": *L* 2:183,
mid-Feb. 1839.

"getting my nail box set": *JMN* 5:367,
Aug. 1837.

he "could split a shingle": Holmes,
RWE, 364.

"I wish you would not": *JMN* 7:505,
1840.

"in this pleasing contrite wood life":
JMN 5:183–84, June 1836.

107 "Crossing a bare common": *Nature*,
E Works 1:9–10, adapted from *JMN*
5:179.

"In my Pantheon": HDT, *A Week*,
Sunday.

"I love the wood god": *JMN* 5:179.

"The good river-god": *JMN* 7:454.

"heroical and stimulating": Ibid., 313,
20 Nov. 1839.

108 "a sort of classic among books": HDT,
A Week, Tuesday.

"fortified you at all times": "Life and
Letters in New England," *E Works*
10:356.

"none knew better than he":
"Thoreau," *E Works* 10:471.

of his "rare class": Ibid., 464.

"We communicate": *HDT Corres*, 87.

"a poor woman": *JMN* 5:282, Jan.
1837.

During one of his hikes: HDT, *A
Week*, Tuesday, 178–85.

109 "How much Mr. Emerson does talk":
Harding, *Days of HT*, 66.

"was an absolute dragon of honesty":
Anthony Trollope, *The Three
Clerks* (London, 1858), ch. 7.

Chapter 11:
MARGARET FULLER

110 "twenty-five weeks": *MF Letters*
1:278.

her new duties: Ibid., 267 n. 1.

"Lethe and Eunoi": Ibid., 268,
supplied by Professor Janet Martin,
2 Aug. 1983.

"purgatory of distracting": Ibid.,
268–69.

"We are all well": *L* 2:73. See now
L 7:281 for dating problem.

"It was beauteous": *MF Letters* 1:272.

111 "*satisfactory; nothing is satisfying*":
Ibid., 273.

"Among many things": *JMN* 5:319.

she did have "genius-in-conversation":
Ibid., 320.

"What do you suppose Goethe": *MF
Letters* 1:277, 30 May 1837;
L 2:77–78.

"What shocking familiarity": *MF Letters* 1:277, editor's note.

"haven of repose": Ibid., 283, 6 June 1837.

"much cheered and instructed": Ibid., 286.

In July she half apologized: Ibid., 288–89.

Although her translation: Ibid., 282 n. 4.

112 "if the soul of Goethe": See Zeydel, ed., *Goethe, the Lyrist*, 166–69; *L* 2:88.

"I will try not to be": *MF Letters* 1:337.

"a little misanthropic": Ibid., 294–95.

"crave the aid of wise and blessed": *L* 2:94–95.

Margaret managed to gallop: *MF Letters* 1:300 and n. 1.

On September 6 she was present: *JMN* 5:375.

"lovely young lady who travelled": Farrar, *Recollections of Seventy Years*, 273–74.

The expatriate sculptor Hiram Powers: Julian Hawthorne, *Nathaniel Hawthorne and His Wife* 2:192.

she had sent Margaret: *MF Letters* 1:323.

113 "a Helen grown up": *JMN* 8:176. For W. H. Channing's view of Anna, see *Mem MFO* 2:8.

In October he had warned her: *L* 2:98.

for a "vivacious letter": Ibid., 104, 2 Dec. 1837.

visit to the "sandy 'Paradise' ": Ibid., 114.

one of the eight letters he sent her: Ibid., 109–18.

"I am weary of living alone": Ibid., 118. See now *L* 7:298 and n. 15.

"You have seemed so busy": *MF Letters* 1:327–28, 1 Mar. 1838.

114 "dear love to the sainted Lidian": Ibid., 269, 11 Apr. 1837.

"Who would be a goody": *JMN* 5:407.

"I hate goodies": *JMN* 7:31, 23 June 1838.

"I believe I am long ago": *L* 2:128–29, 4 May 1838.

His brother Bulkeley: Ibid., 130–37.

115 a young friend of Mrs. Bliss: Ibid., 10, 10 Apr. 1836.

Caroline was a "lofty maiden": *JMN* 5:288, 19 Mar. 1837.

although his talks with her lasted: *L* 2:143, 28 June 1838.

his "cold pedantic self": *JMN* 7:15, 12 June 1838.

a "good token": Ibid., 23, 18 June 1838.

"For a hermit": *L* 2:143.

"and, though much younger, her guide": *Mem MFO* 1:208–9.

116 "A man must have aunts": *JMN* 7:6–7, 8 June 1838.

"Monadnoc in its glory": *L* 2:144.

Lidian, who cared little for travel: Ibid., 145. Lidian's second pregnancy seems to have begun about the end of the third week of May. The second child, Ellen, was born 24 Feb. 1839. On 2 Aug. 1838, Emerson wrote his brother William that Lidian had been "feeble lately and sometimes confined to her room.": *L* 2:151. See now *Letters of Lidian*, 81, to Lucy Jackson Brown, late 1838, for LJE's description of RWE's delight at the prospect of the second child and his solicitude toward LJE.

"Thought is all light": "Literary Ethics," *E Works* 1:187.

"We mark with light": "Divinity School Address," *E Works* 1:147.

117 Margaret reappeared on August 15: *MF Letters* 1:340 and n. 1.

he wrote Ward on the sixteenth: RWE, *Letters from RWE to a Friend*, 1, 16 Aug. 1838.

to look at Sam's pictures: *JMN* 7:46–47, 17 Aug. 1838, on SGW's portfolio.

Waldo's "purgatory" of teething
  problems: *L* 2:155.
Margaret's "state of weak
  sensitiveness": *MF Letters* 1:340,
  19 Aug. 1838.
"Fret not that kindest heart": Ibid.
old Dr. Ripley prayed for rain: *JMN*
  7:49.
"What is more alive": Ibid., 55,
  25 Aug. 1838.
118 to live in Concord: *L* 2:169.
  During the winter of 1838–39: Ibid.,
    181–84.
  to take another, smaller place: *MF
    Letters* 2:50 and 62, 21 Feb. and
    31 Mar. 1839.
  writing some fifty letters: Ibid., 59.
  to escape the "dust and Babel": Ibid.,
    62.
  "Her wit, her insight": Higginson,
    MFO, 64–65.
119 "I have Elzh Hoar in the room": *MF
    Letters* 2:62.
  "as unlike his brother as possible":
    Ibid., 62–63, 31 Mar. 1839.
  "meditation . . . in the tangled wood-
    walks": Ibid., 64, 18 Apr. 1839.
  "She had so many tasks of her own":
    Mem MFO 1:217–18.

Chapter 12: *JONES VERY*

120 "Entertain every thought": *JMN*
    7:117.
  The man he had in mind: Gittleman,
    Jones Very, 96–97.
121 the subject of his address: Ibid., 97.
  "The introduction of rare strangers":
    Ibid., 158–60. See also Lathrop,
    Memories of Hawthorne, 183, RWE
    to SPH, 20 Jan. 1838. See now
    L 7:294–95 for text and n. 1.
  "Har[mony] of Man with Nature":
    Gittleman, *Jones Very*, 163–64.
  Next day he thanked Miss Peabody:
    Listed in *L* 2:124. See now *L* 7:302

and n. 26. For Lidian's reaction, see
  ibid. and LJE, *Letters of Lidian*, 73.
and a month later: Gittleman, *Jones
  Very*, 167.
Such men, as he wrote in his journal:
  JMN 5:475.
"Yourself a newborn bard": *E Works*
  1:146.
122 "There is a young man at Cambridge":
    L 2:154 and n. 192. Very's two
    visits were those of 4 Apr. and
    20 May 1838, *JMN* 5:502.
  "I felt within me a new will":
    Gittleman, *Jones Very*, 187.
  "gained the fame of being cracked":
    Ibid., 186.
  Very invaded the study of Henry
    Ware, Junior: Ibid., 188.
  "I had thought you did the will": Ibid.,
    189.
123 Very had suffered a "nervous
    collapse": Ibid., 191.
  Very gathered up the sheets: Ibid.,
    193.
  "My Brother," it began: Ibid., 194.
  He rose early: Ibid., 215–18.
  "induced by intense application":
    Ibid., 218; Lathrop, *Memories of
    Hawthorne*, 101, 108.
124 he invaded the Very household:
    Gittleman, *Jones Very*,
    223.
  "Ha[ve] you heard of the calamity": *L*
    2:164–65, 29 Sept. 1838. See now
    L 7:319 and n. 82, RWE to William
    Henry Furness, 20 Sept. 1838.
  During his thirty-one days in the
    asylum: Gittleman, *Jones Very*,
    232–36.
  "I treat him simply": Ibid., 236.
125 Very adopted "a certain *violence*": *L*
    2:170–71, 30 Oct. 1838, RWE to
    EPP, now printed in full *L*
    7:324–35. See also *JMN* 7:116–17,
    122–23, 127–28 for Very's first visit
    to the Emersons, noted in *L* 7:325,
    n. 98.
  "Talk with him a few hours": *L* 2:173,
    RWE to MF, 9 Nov. 1838.

"the world was desart [sic] and empty": *JMN* 7:154.

indisposed to "attack religions and charities": Ibid., 122, 28 Oct. 1838.

"His position accuses society": Ibid., 117, 26 Oct. 1838.

"He would obey, obey": Ibid., 122.

"A man who is busy": Ibid., 123.

126 "While in the physical world": Quoted in Gittleman, *Jones Very*, 206.

"You do not disobey": *JMN* 7:123.

"He thinks me covetous": Ibid., 122–23.

"I always felt when I heard you": *JMN* 8:148.

"our brave saint": *JMN* 7:127 and n. 370.

"the necessity of the Spirit": *JMN* 7:123.

"the manners of a man": Ibid. and n. 356; *Matt.* 6:25.

127 "J[ones] Very charmed us all": *JMN* 7:124, 29 Oct. 1838.

he felt it an honor: Ibid., 123.

One of the high points of Very's visit: Ibid., 127–28 and n. 379. See now *L* 7:324–25 and n. 97.

Its subject was the assault upon Heliodorus: *Macc.* 2.3; *JMN* 7:47. For a discussion of the fresco in the Stanza d'Eliodoro and its iconography, see James H. Beck, *Raphael* (New York: Abrams, 1976), 138 and plate 30.

"Instantly," said Emerson: *JMN* 7:127–28, ca. 30 Oct. 1838.

128 "as solitary as Jesus": Ibid., 123; Gittleman, *Jones Very*, 257.

Chapter 13:
MARGARET FULLER

129 "precious and guarded mornings": *L* 2:195–96, 203.

Emerson and his brother William: Ibid., 218.

His "usurping conversation": Ibid., 198.

He read and praised Margaret Fuller's translation: Ibid., 201–3, RWE to MF, 7 June 1839.

130 "I infer," wrote Emerson: Ibid., 212–13, 1 Aug. 1839. See now *L* 7:351–53 and n. 76.

"I can no more write": *L* 2:211.

"I lead the life": Ibid., 222.

Early in June, Caroline Sturgis stayed: Dimock, *Caroline Sturgis Tappan and the Grand Tour*, 47–48.

one of them known locally: *MF Letters* 2:77.

"Do you love me?": Ibid., 92. For the letters of CS(T) to MF, see now Dedmond, "The Letters of Caroline Sturgis to Margaret Fuller," *SAR 1988*, 201–51.

Margaret's wounded pride: *MF Letters* 2:76–77, 79–82, 94.

131 "If you love me as I deserve": Ibid., 80–81.

"You do not wish to be with me": Ibid., 90–91.

for having sought to overpersonalize: *JMN* 5:187.

"How rarely," he wrote: Ibid., 190.

132 "I had always an impression": *Mem MFO* 1:228.

"the unlooked for trait": *JMN* 11:500.

he had her to thank: *L* 2:208.

to Emerson's "great satisfaction": Ibid., 220.

Learning in August that Anna Barker: *L* 2:215, 14 Aug. 1839.

He accepted at once: Ibid., 226.

She did not disappoint him: Ibid., 228.

"a woman singularly healthful": *JMN* 7:259–60.

133 "vision of grace and beauty": *L* 2:244, 22 Dec. 1839.

"My dearest S.": *MF Letters* 2:95–96.

They were "friendly influences": *JMN* 7:273 and n. 23, 21 Oct. 1839.

134 "excessive efflorescence": *JMN* 15:128, 26 Jan. 1863.

she wrote two of her oldest friends: *MF Letters* 2:111, 113.

"as a good means of opening a vista": Ibid., 118–19.

"used to get up before light": ETE, *Life of Lidian*, 92.

"M[y] class is singularly prosperous": *MF Letters* 2:101, 25 Nov. 1839.

"the most powerful stimulus": Quoted in Higginson, *MFO*, 118.

135 to "furnish a medium for the freest expression": ABA, MS diary, Higginson, *MFO*, 151–52.

was promised a salary: Higginson, *MFO*, 167.

"Only for a moment did I cease": *MF Letters* 2:93, 7 Oct. 1839.

"almost as good as your best prose": Ibid., 106–7.

"sweet though pale buds": Ibid., 120–21.

Bluebirds appeared on February 21: *L* 2:254.

"I have been so deeply engaged": *MF Letters* 2:123, 24 Feb. 1840.

"yet I think I will write": *L* 2:271. For the contents of the July *Dial* see Meyerson, *The New England Transcendentalists and the* Dial, 289–90.

136 "All life is a compromise": *JMN* 7:330, 25 Dec. 1839.

"Ten decorous speeches": *L* 2:256, 25 Feb. 1840. See also *JMN* 7:338–39.

he had found his youthful audiences eager: Ibid., 341–42.

a lecture on the "Great Subject": *L* 2:266, 28 Mar. 1840.

"In all my lectures": *JMN* 7:342, ca. 7 Apr. 1840.

137 "It makes me want to go home": Ibid., 358.

"Why should I covet a knowledge": Ibid., 373, ca. 24 June 1840.

"new act in the romance": *L* 2:298.

she told Emerson her "winsome story": Ibid., 313, 8 July 1840.

138 stopping over in northern Illinois:

McGill, *Channing of Concord*, 33–35; Hudspeth, *Ellery Channing*, 20–21.

his "vain visit": *JMN* 7:496.

with "fever and ague": *L* 2:306, 21 June 1840.

"giving all her time": *MF Letters* 2:150, AB(W) to MF.

"A[nna]—though frank": Ibid., 147, 5 July 1840.

"He is even emaciated": Ibid., 150.

139 "I give you joy": *L* 2:314.

"miraculous good" in the salt air: *MF Letters* 2:154, 24 July 1840.

"no coldness no commonness": *L* 2:319.

"very calm and happy": Ibid., 321, 29 July 1840.

"copying old musty papers": Ibid., 320, 27 July 1840.

Chapter 14: VERY

140 he "loved" the poems: RWE to JV, 18 Nov. 1838, Gittleman, *Jones Very*, 258–60. Listed in *L* 2:174. See now *L* 7:326–27 for full text. For JV's poetry, see now JV, *Jones Very: The Complete Poems*, ed. Helen R. Deese (Atlanta, Ga., 1993).

"I was pleased": Gittleman, *Jones Very*, 262–65, JV to RWE, 30 Nov. 1838.

"whenever it is so ordered": Ibid., 265.

141 "psychological autobiography": Ibid., 267.

"To a soul alive to God": *JMN* 4:266, 22 Feb. 1834.

"And suddenly in any place": Ibid., 274, 12 Apr. 1834.

"In proportion as your life": Ibid., 278–79, 20 Apr. 1834.

"If I could persuade men": Ibid., 346, Dec. 1834.

"What nimbleness and buoyancy": *JMN* 5:124, Feb. 1836.

"The book is always dear": Ibid., 123.

"I suppose there is one spirit": Ibid., 219–20.

the young man had "not lost his *Reason*": Gittleman, *Jones Very*, 268–72.

142 "a partial derangement": Ibid., 270.

"His language is that of an Oriental": Ibid., 271.

Very was "insane with God": Ibid., 277.

"to go home to Mr. [Abel] Adams's": *JMN* 8:148.

143 Very himself began the process: Gittleman, *Jones Very*, 312–23.

Bearing in mind the psychological autobiography: Ibid., 324.

"much better both in body and spirit": Ibid., 334.

"What are persons": *JMN* 7:212–13, 16 June 1839.

144 "not without a deep tinge": Ibid., 213.

Very had seemed to be "serene, intelligent, and true": *L* 2:204–5, RWE to EPP, 17 June 1839. See now *L* 7:346 for slightly different wording from another copy.

Hawthorne's opinion that Very was "always vain": Lathrop, *Memories of Hawthorne*, 28–30.

145 "valued his poems not because": *JMN* 8:52, Sept. 1841.

he insisted that it was wrong: *L* 2:331, 12 Sept. 1840.

"with sovereign will": EPP to SPH, 23 June 1839, in Lathrop, *Memories of Hawthorne*, 29. See now EPP, *Letters of Elizabeth Palmer Peabody*, ed. Bruce A. Randa (Middletown, Conn., 1984), 225–26.

to show "rare merit": *L* 2:209 and n. 109, 9 July 1839.

"There is more joy and freedom": Gittleman, *Jones Very*, 350, JV to RWE, 13 Aug. 1839.

his essay on epic poetry: JV, *Poems and Essays by Jones Very*, 3–26.

146 The second essay was an attempt: Ibid., 27–52.

His interpretation of *Hamlet*: Ibid., 53–57.

147 "Thou lookest up with meek": JV, *Jones Very: The Complete Poems*, 59 (Poem #684).

"In May, when sea-winds": *E Works* 9:37–38.

148 "new taste for . . . private and household": Review of Ellery Channing, *Dial* 1 (Oct. 1840): 222.

"I sit within my room": JV, *Jones Very: The Complete Poems*, 78 (Poem #269).

149 to secure a written order: Gittleman, *Jones Very*, 359.

Before he climbed down again: Ibid.

"My return a few days since": Ibid.

"how he sat there": ETE, *Life of Lidian*, 78.

Chapter 15:
ELLERY CHANNING

153 "Certainly your friend": *L* 2:226–27.

154 "There was a plain beneath": WEC, *The Collected Poems of William Ellery Channing*, 15–16.

"I was very happy to meet this kindness": *L* 2:227.

"In a society as imperfect as ours": Ibid., 227–28.

"How can the Age": *JMN* 7:266.

"a certain steady autumnal light": Ibid., 276–77.

"Over every true poem": Ibid., 277.

"the Star of the American Church": Ibid., 470.

155 His most notable achievement: McGill, *Channing of Concord*, 24 and note.

when he composed "The Humble-Bee": *L* 2:78 and n. 94. Listed in *L* 2:176. See now *L* 7:327–28 and n. 108.

"I loafe and invite my soul": WW,

"Song of Myself," section 1, *Leaves of Grass*, 28.

156 "The beams," he later wrote: *Dial* 4 (July 1843): 49–50.

"Sweet falls the summer air": WEC, *Poems of Sixty-five Years*, 20.

"When the sprites outwatch the moon": Ibid., 24.

157 "Charles Sedgwick, clerk of the Berkshire": McGill, *Channing of Concord*, 30–31.

The immediate catalyst was Charles Sedgwick: Ibid., 32–35.

"I wish that they should not": *L* 2:252–53.

to "give them due perspective": Ibid., 253.

158 Twice that spring: Ibid., 271–76.

went ahead with the piece: Ibid., 288 and n. 180.

"a solitary joy": *JMN* 7:359.

"The brook is eddying": WEC, "Sonnet V," *The Collected Poems of WEC*, 145.

"manuscript inspirations, honest, great": *JMN* 7:372.

"to fly abroad": *L* 2:253.

Caroline's "Spartan metres": Ibid., 306.

"our tough Yankee": Ibid., 322.

"conjectural emendations": Ibid., 331, and RWE to CS(T), 13 Sept. 1840, quoted in McGill, *Channing of Concord*, 44–45. See now *L* 7:406–8 and notes.

159 "straitest restrictions": *Dial* 1 (Oct. 1840): 220–32.

She declined to print: *MF Letters* 2:189.

"Of Ellery's verse I think not much": Ibid., 107.

"O pudor!": *L* 2:413.

Frank Sanborn said offhandedly: F. B. Sanborn, "Address," *Hawthorne Centenary Celebration* (Boston, 1905), 183.

160 "the one successful business venture": Hudspeth, *Ellery Channing*, 21.

"I am worthy of you": Quoted in McGill, *Channing of Concord*, 37–38.

In the late summer of 1841: Ibid., 355–63.

"In its suddenness it comes": *MF Letters* 2:230.

"In what I know of either party": Ibid., 232. See also *L* 2:446, 450.

"runs across all my dreams": *L* 2:447, 13 Sept. 1841.

161 "an auspicious connection": *MF Letters* 2:230. See also *L* 2:446.

"For a little time": Dedmond, "The Letters of Caroline Sturgis to Margaret Fuller," *SAR 1988*, 218–19, CS(T) to MF, 9 Sept. 1841.

"By and by," she told him: *MF Letters* 2:239–40, MF to WEC, 3 Oct. 1841. See also *MF Letters* 2:256, MF to SGW, 6 Dec. 1841.

He had rented a small house: McGill, *Channing of Concord*, 65–67.

"I like all these letters of Ellery's": *L* 3:33, ca. 18 Mar. 1842.

"Now," she told Emerson: *MF Letters* 3:69–71. See also *L* 3:72–73 n. 277.

he suddenly resigned: McGill, *Channing of Concord*, 68.

162 "I comfort myself": *L* 3:81.

Chapter 16:
SAM AND ANNA

163 "a greater trust in the nature": *Dial* 1 (July 1840): 1–4.

the first number was a "good book": *L* 2:311.

must "get to be a little *bad*": Ibid., 316, 25 July 1840.

"I would not have it": Ibid., 322, 4 Aug. 1840.

164 "I think we must give up": *JMN* 7:379.

"Next door to us lives": *JMN* 4:300.

"Now for near five years": *JMN* 7:376
and n. 293.

"the shining people of the sky": Ibid.,
391.

"We are beginning to be acquainted":
L 2:304, 7 June 1840.

"At the very time when I": *Mem MFO*
1:288.

165 "She taxed me": *JMN* 7:509, 16 Aug.
1840; *L* 2:325.

"I confess to all this charge": *JMN*
7:509-10.

"I confess to the fact": *L* 2:325.

"dear sister": Ibid., 326, n. 333.

"I wish you to go out": Ibid.,
326-27.

"resign without a sigh two Friends":
Ibid., 327-28, 29 Aug. 1840.

166 "with a variety of 'neurotic'
characteristics": Blanchard,
Margaret Fuller, 137.

"passed into certain religious states":
Mem MFO 1:289.

"It seems exaggerated": Ibid.

"I believe I hate buskins": *L* 2:343.
See now *L* 7:413-14 and n. 151.

"a certain pathos of sentiment": *Mem
MFO* 1:308-9.

167 of the "mighty changes": *MF Letters*
2:158 and 159 n. 2.

"a strong proof that we are": Ibid.,
159-60.

to her attempted "over-
personalization": *JMN* 5:187.

"If you have not seen this stair": *MF
Letters* 2:159.

168 "One day when Miss Fuller": FTE,
Life of Lidian, 84 and 228 n. 187.
Quoted by RWE in *JMN* 4:300 and
n. 145.

"alone with the Alone": *L* 2:328.

"a hermit so dangerously favored":
Ibid., 329.

"You and I are not inhabitants": Ibid.,
336, 25 Sept. 1840.

"brother and sister by divine": Ibid.,
332, 13 Sept. 1840.

our "radiant" pair of "lovers": Ibid.,
338-39.

"She went, from the most joyful": *Mem
MFO* 1:301.

169 "Peace go with you": *JMN* 7:404.

"give me any tidings you can": *L*
2:344.

they sent him a joyous letter: Ibid.,
349, 20 Oct. 1840; *MF Letters*
2:163.

"I looked at him with great love":
Ibid., 18 Oct. 1840.

"the life that flows in": Ibid., 167-69.

170 "I have written you down": *L* 2:347,
18 Oct. 1840.

"Still this same dull distrust": *MF
Letters* 2:170, ca. 25 Oct. 1840.

"I ought never to have suffered": *L*
2:352-53, 24 Oct. 1840.

171 "I shall wait for [Waldo]": *MF Letters*
2:171, 25 and 28 Oct. 1840.

172 "the very genius of the place": Ibid.,
179-80.

the opinion of John Marquand:
Millicent Bell, *Marquand: An
American Life* (Boston: Little
Brown, 1979), ch. 1: "Curzon's
Mill."

"the poet of the Actual": Originally in
JMN 7:365, June 1840.

173 "I begin to be more interested": *MF
Letters* 2:181, 7 Nov. 1840.

resumed the Wednesday
"Conversations": *L* 2:365.

"great changes" in her mind: *MF
Letters* 2:183, to W. H. Channing,
10 Dec. 1840.

"I am always most happy": Ibid.,
191-92, to W. H. Channing, 10
Dec. 1840.

they discussed his refusal: Ibid., 194,
13 Dec. 1840. See also RWE to
George Ripley, *L* 2:368-71,
15 Dec.1840.

to leave the "golden routine": Ibid.,
368.

"Margaret's wonderful talent": Ibid.,
373-74.

Chapter 17: ALCOTT, ELSSLER, NEWCOMB

174 "could see him as he is": *JMN* 7:298,
Nov. 1839; *L* 2:231.
"work a small farm for his bread":
Ibid., 216, 14 Aug. 1839.
It was typical of Emerson: Sanborn,
Recollections of Seventy Years 2:339.
"I hardly dare hope for him": *L* 2:265.
he found Alcott busily nailing: Ibid.,
273.

175 his wife went singing: Ibid., 281.
"to get his living by the help": *C-E-C*,
269, 21 Apr. 1840.
"I must think very ill of my age": *L*
2:198, 1 May 1839.
the new magazine for which Alcott:
Shepard, *Pedlar's Progress*, 279.
"We must have a free journal":
Higginson, *MFO*, 146; *ABA Jrnls*
1:135 n. 21.
"a string of Apothegms": *L* 2:276.
Alcott's "inveterate faults": Ibid., 291.
"cold vague generalities": Ibid., 294.
"quite grand, though ofttimes": *MF
Letters* 2:135 and *L* 2:297, n. 215,
MF to RWE, 31 May 1840.

176 with "his voice in their ear": *L* 2:294.
"resembled a train of 15 railroad cars":
JMN 8:211, Mar. 1842.
"While he talks he is great": Lowell,
Fable for Critics, 43.
Emerson, ever helpful, gave him: *L*
2:310.
"Majestic egotist": Ibid., 344.
he gathered the clippings: Higginson,
MFO, 159.
"the most interesting object":
W. H. Channing to EPP, Oct. 1840,
in Shepard, *Pedlar's Progress*, 294.

177 comparing Alcott to Apollo: RWE to
W. H. Furness, 24 Oct. 1837,
described by Rusk, *L* 2:100 and
quoted in Sanborn-Harris, *ABA*
1:242–43. See now *L* 7:287–89 and
n. 50 for full text.
"maintained at the public cost":
L 2:372, 21 Dec. 1840.

"manual labor to some considerable
extent": Ibid., 371.
"the condition of hired menial
service": Ibid., 370.
"Next April we shall make": Ibid.,
371.
"views or dreams": Ibid., 372.
"A cook," said she: Ibid., 389.
with the usual consequences: Ibid.,
387, 393.
Aunt Mary had sustained a recent
attack: Ibid., 383.

178 When Emerson asked her to come:
Ibid., 396–98 and n. 92. For
MME's 15 May response, see now
Letters of MME, 428–31.
was planning to deliver a "last"
sermon: *L* 2:394.
the arrival of Henry Thoreau: Ibid.,
402.
"It is of little use for me": Ibid.
"I have walked and ridden": Ibid.,
422–23.
"You know I was baptised": Ibid.,
423. See now *L* 7:464–64 and n. 73
for full text.
"out of any inkstand": *L* 2:434.
"He has no vocation to labor": *JMN*
8:212–13.

179 Dr. Ezra Ripley was felled: *L*
2:450–51.
had last preached on May 1: Ibid., 452
and n. 326.
"a sachem of the forest fallen": Ibid.,
453.
"What is this abolition": Ibid., 451.
"could not help feeling": *JMN* 4:171,
11 May 1833.
"Where do you think I went": *L*
2:460.

180 One of Fanny's Parisian admirers:
Guest, *Fanny Elssler*, 17–18,
72–75, 85–86, 88, 128–85 passim.
"She must show": *JMN* 8:109–10.
"The basis of this exhibition": Ibid.,
110–11.

181 "How did you like the military-
spiritual": *MF Letters* 2:251 and
n. 3, 9 Nov. 1841.

"a naive sportive character": *Dial* 3 (July 1842): 65–67.

"Like all virtuous persons": *JMN* 8:142, 213–14.

182 the Brook Farm boarder Charles Newcomb: Commager, *Theodore Parker*, 52; *Newcomb Jrnls*, introd., 27.

Charles had lost his father: Ibid., 3–15.

"My ear and heart": *MF Letters* 2:64–65.

"My dear Charles, if you still": Ibid., 100–1.

Charles signed the register: *Newcomb Jrnls*, 17–18, 20; *L* 3:81–82.

Margaret's mentally disturbed brother: *MF Letters* 2:212, June 1841.

reading Greek in the haymow: *Newcomb Jrnls*, 19 and n. 3.

who called him Carolus Rex: Ibid., 17–19; *L* 3:74.

183 "cure your young Catholic Fra Carlo": *L* 2:319.

But the Brook Farmers took note: *Newcomb Jrnls*, 18–19, 27.

"slight in person": *MF Letters* 1:342 n. 4.

"such niceties were among the sacrifices": *Newcomb Jrnls*, 19.

In 1836 he had begun: Ibid., 18, 27, 48.

"If his body don't fail": Saxton, *Louisa May*, 127.

"It will give me great pleasure": Listed in *L* 3:12. See now *L* 7:486–87 and n. 7. Text is in Sanborn Harris, *ABA* 1:328–29, with differences. Quoted in Shepard, *Pedlar's Progress*, 300.

184 darkened by "moody musing": *MF Letters* 3:49–50.

"You write on the genius of Plato": *JMN* 10:326, in year 1848.

Alcott sailed off aboard: Saxton, *Louisa May*, 128; *JMN* 8:181, 267.

Chapter 18:
WALDO MINOR

185 "My boy is gone": *L* 3:6–9.

whole wintry landscape "dishonored": In *Nature* he had said, in reference to his brother Charles, "There is a kind of contempt of the landscape felt by him who has just lost by death a dear friend." *E Works* 1:11.

"A boy of early wisdom": *JMN* 8:163–65.

186 "charmed Waldo by the variety": Ibid., 165.

"as the mist rises": *HDT Corres*, 63, HDT to Lucy Brown, 2 Mar. 1842.

Waldo was buried: *L* 3:9–10.

"finding once again our hands": Ibid.

187 "Work in every hour": *JMN* 8:193.

"Have the clouds yet broken": *L* 3:11–13.

"white soft hair": Ibid., 17–20.

"with an egotism more virulent": Ibid., 20.

188 "Queenie says, 'Save me' ": *JMN* 8:242.

"I loved him more": *Mem MFO* 2:62–63, 28 Jan. 1842. See now *MF Letters* 3:42–43, where the letter is dated Feb. 1842 and W. H. Channing is proposed as the recipient.

Margaret's decision to resign: *L* 3:33 and n. 128. See now *MF Letters* 3:53–54 and notes.

"never had a penny": *L* 3:36.

"You have played martyr": Ibid., 35.

"I had rather undertake it": Ibid.

Parker, who had contributed: Ibid., 43 n. 166.

sought to line up contributors: Ibid., 40–55.

to undertake a lengthy piece: Ibid., 47 and n. 177.

One of these was a strange tale: *JMN* 8:201.

"the divine musical evening": *L* 3:28–29 n. 104. See now *MF Letters* 3:49–52 and notes.

189 "I had set my heart on it":
    L 3:30.
    Twice in succeeding weeks: Ibid.,
        34–35, 44–45.
    "the *first* Dolon": Ibid., 51, 7 May
        1842.
    "precious ashes": Ibid., 55 and n. 207,
        22 May 1842.
    "the most joy I have felt": Ibid., 61.
    "anecdotes of her sweet Boy": Ibid.,
        66–67.
    "the maddest piece": Ibid., 71, 74.
    "I comprehend nothing": *JMN* 8:205.
    "Charles is a Religious Intellect":
        Ibid., 178–79.
190 "many other persons": *Dial* 3 (July
        1842): 101. See also *JMN* 8:220
        and n. 62.
    "fanaticism of all shades": *L* 3:41 and
        n. 156.
    His *Dial* article: *Dial* 3 (July 1842):
        101.
    "wise and endeared spirits": *L* 3:47.
    He and Lidian hoped: Ibid., 43.
    both Frederic Hedge and Nathaniel
        Hawthorne: Ibid., 50.
    "Those of us who do not believe":
        Ibid., 51.
    "our fair prospects": Ibid., 53.
    "Tormented with ennui": Ibid., 63.
    "All the Channings": *JMN* 8:319.
191 "cool hard sensible behavior": *JMN*
        7:469.
    a "good vagabond": *JMN* 8:289.
    "I much doubt his power": *L* 3:84.
        See now *L* 7:505–7 and n. 65.
    "all things looked sad": Meyerson,
        "MF's 1842 Journal," 322.
    "I have thought of you many times": *L*
        3:28–29 n. 104. See now *MF Letters*
        3:49.
    Her face was swollen: *L* 3:82, 22 Aug.
        1842.
    relieving the sense of "oppression":
        Meyerson, "MF's 1842 Journal,"
        322–23, 326.
    "saw the moon broken": *JMN*
        8:195–96.
192 "little sympathy with mere life":

Meyerson, "MF's 1842 Journal,"
    324, 328, 330.
But the cause of her tears: Ibid., 331.
Looking as "soft and serene": Ibid.,
    331–32.
193 "Love was only phenomenal": Ibid.,
    330–31.
194 "marriage is not ideal": *JMN* 8:34,
    Aug. 1841.
    "It will not do to abrogate": Ibid.,
    95.
    "Permanence is the nobility": Ibid.,
    134.
    "The sannup and the Squaw": Ibid.,
    286.
    her journal makes it clear: Meyerson,
    "MF's 1842 Journal," 324–25, 332,
    334.
195 he found her lounging: NH, *The
    American Notebooks*, 342–43.
    "having met Lidian out": Meyerson,
    "MF's 1842 Journal," 339.
196 "Feed my lambs and nothing more":
    Ibid., 338.
    "The Dial is my trial": *L* 3:85.
    But he had also begun: *JMN* 8:451–56
    and 508–14.
    "I wish it would be so always":
    Meyerson, "MF's 1842 Journal,"
    338.
197 "put more of himself into Saadi":
    Ibid., 338–39.
    the Emersons gave a tea: *L* 3:86.
    "It was not very pleasant": Meyerson,
    "MF's 1842 Journal," 339–40.
198 "I feel a conviction": *L* 3:89–90 and
    88 n. 333. See now *MF Letters*
    3:96–98, 16 Oct. 1842.
    "She sends her love": *L* 3:95.

Chapter 19:
THEODORE PARKER
199 "Proceeded to Cambridge": Weiss,
    *Life and Correspondence of Theodore
    Parker* 1:113.

he could trace his American ancestry:
Commager, *Theodore Parker*, 4.

200 "the first fire-arm taken": Weiss, *Life
and Corres of TP* 2:443.

"Do you know I could once":
Chadwick, *Theodore Parker*, 346.

"a prodigious athlete in his studies":
Weiss, *Life and Corres of TP* 1:65.

"of odd learning and scraps":
Ibid., 95.

201 "metaphysics and psychology of
religion": Miller, ed., *The
Transcendentalists*, 485.

"one of the profoundest thinkers":
Ibid.

"the instinctive intuition of the
divine": Ibid., 485–86.

"the brilliant genius of Emerson":
Ibid., 487.

the "wisdom" and the "folly": Ibid.,
489.

202 "We saw Emerson": Weiss, *Life and
Corres of TP* 1:125.

"A son of the energy": *JMN*
14:352–53.

Like a latter-day Othello: Ibid., 354;
Othello 1.3.

By the spring of 1841:*Discourse of the
Transient and Permanent in
Christianity*: (Boston: The Author,
1841). Rpt. in *Three Prophets of
Religious Liberalism*, ed. Conrad
Wright, 113–49; *Luke* 21.33.

203 the explosions that followed: Miller,
ed., *The Transcendentalists*, 490.

204 "The Rationalistic View": Ibid.,
316–34.

he had continued his contributions: *L*
3:35.

205 All through the year 1842: Ibid.,
43–44, 54–55, 68–71, 94.

"Sympathy is always partial": *JMN*
7:467.

Two of Emerson's adjectives: *JMN*
8:262.

"T.P. has beautiful fangs": *JMN*
14:352.

206 "I too like puss": *JMN* 7:306.

Chapter 20:
HAWTHORNE

207 thought the men "great boobies": NH
to his sister Louisa, 17 Aug. 1831.
See Mellow, *Nathaniel Hawthorne*,
48–50, 67–68.

"a disgraceful barking cold": *JMN*
8:271–74.

Hawthorne would have liked to pluck:
NH, *American Notebooks*, 361–62.

208 they were on the road by six-thirty:
SPH to her mother, 29 Sept. 1842,
Berg Collection.

a successful "experiment of
Socialism": *JMN* 8:274. Cf. RWE
to SGW, 30 Sept. 1842, *Letters to a
Friend*, 53. See now *L* 7:512 and
notes 92, 93.

he found that the table, the shelf: *JMN*
8:278–79.

"conferred with them on their faith":
Listed *L* 3:87. See now
L 7:512.

"a man cannot free himself": *JMN*
8:282.

209 it was his custom on Sundays: Ibid.,
116.

"I told Hawthorne yesterday": Ibid.,
289–90.

Hawthorne wrote in his journal: NH,
American Notebooks, 363.

his "*diffused* smile": SPH to EPP, ca.
May 1836, Lathrop, *Memories of
Hawthorne*, 16.

210 she seemed to confuse his beatific:
Ibid., 190.

the piece had "no inside to it": *JMN*
7:21.

it would take Alcott and Hawthorne
together: Ibid.

Since Emerson now seemed "all
congenial": Lathrop, *Memories of
Hawthorne*, 29.

"It is no easy matter": *JMN* 7:242,
Sept. 1839.

a mere "business-machine": NH, *Love
Letters of NH* 1:212, 22 Jan. 1840.

211 "The wood," mused Coverdale: NH,

The Blithedale Romance, Cent. Ed.,
209.
"Here followed much talk": NH,
American Notebooks, 201–2.
"this lone parsonage in this thin
village": *JMN* 4:342.
212 "all new and bright again": *L* 3:68.
"If they shall come": Ibid., 50, 7 May
1842.
When he met Hawthorne by chance:
NH Letters 15:626; NH, *Love
Letters of NH* 2:92, 27 May 1842.
the "new colonists": *L* 3:72–73 n. 277,
MF to RWE, 23 June 1842. See
now *MF Letters* 3:70.
Nathaniel and Sophia were married:
Julian Hawthorne, *NH and His
Wife* 1:242.
"How do you do, *Mrs. Hawthorne*":
SPH to her mother, 10 July and 15
July 1842, Berg Collection.
who could "hardly be called":
Lathrop, *Memories of Hawthorne*,
51.
213 if Adam and Eve had been asked:
Julian Hawthorne, *NH and His
Wife* 1:253.
"peas, beans, beets": NH, *American
Notebooks*, 353–57, 31 Aug. and
2 Sept. 1842.
"scruple of his external conscience":
Ibid., 334–35.
214 "somewhat uncouth and ugly": Ibid.,
335–36. See RWE, "Agriculture of
Massachusetts," *Dial* 3 (July 1842):
123–26.
"the mystic, stretching his hand": NH,
American Notebooks, 336.
"emerged from the green shade":
Ibid., 342–43.
215 "reputation as a writer": *JMN* 7:465,
ca. 4 Sept. 1842.
"Mr. Emerson called": NH, *American
Notebooks*, 351–52, 30 Aug. 1842.
"I went to see her Tuesday": SPH to
her mother, Thurs., 1 Sept. and
Fri., 2 Sept. 1842, Berg Collection.
"The phoenix," as she called
Emerson: Ibid., 29 Sept. 1842.

"so that no one may interrupt": Ibid.
"You two ladies must find": Ibid.,
9–10 Oct. 1842.
216 Hawthorne was there: *NH Letters*
15:660.
She thought that Thoreau's dizzy
turns: Ibid., 666–67, SPH to Louisa
Hawthorne, 4 Jan. 1843; Lathrop,
Memories of Hawthorne, 52–53,
where date is given as 30 Dec.
1842.

Chapter 21: ALCOTT HOMESTEADING, 1842–47

217 "What obstinate propensity": *JMN*
8:261, Sept. 1840.
The news on October 5: *L* 3:88,
5 Oct. 1842.
from the estate of James P. Greaves:
Ibid., 96.
Alcott's small house managed to
accommodate: Ibid., 98 and n. 370.
218 "Mamma, they have begun again":
JMN 10:142 and n. 72.
"Discussions like that": *JMN*
8:253–54, 11 Nov. 1842.
"admirable instruments for a master's
hand": Ibid., 300–1.
"Alcott and Lane want feet": *JMN*
9:54, Nov. 1843.
"there should be found a farm": *JMN*
8:310, ca. 19 Nov. 1842.
219 he "loved every thing by turns": Ibid.,
386–87.
on June 1 the Lanes and Alcotts
moved in: Sanborn, *Bronson Alcott
at Alcott House*, 54, 57; Bedell, *The
Alcotts*, 205–8.
Emerson felt "sad at heart": *JMN*
8:403–4.
"They look well in July": Ibid., 433.
220 "I rose at 5": See now *LMA Jrnls* 1:45.
By November there were signs of

strain: Sanborn, *Bronson Alcott at Alcott House*, 63–66; *HDT Corres*, 115.

"I rose at five": See now *LMA Jrnls* 1:47.

A week later the Alcott family: Bedell, *The Alcotts*, 233.

"free of rent and landlords": Shepard, *Pedlar's Progress*, 388–89. Cf. *JMN* 8:310.

221   they bought the old Cogswell place: Ibid., 388–92; *ABA Jrnls* 1:157; Bedell, *The Alcotts*, 235; *L* 3:235–45, 263 and n. 85.

"Fruitlands was an adventure": ABA, *Concord Days*, 79.

"He delights in speculation": *JMN* 8:210–15.

222   "very many hard strokes every day": *JMN* 9:145.

He told Emerson that whatever: Ibid., 429.

He rose to the challenge: Shepard, *Pedlar's Progress*, 392–95.

"Sweet is the toil": *ABA Jrnls* 1:185.

223   Thoreau his practical assistant: *JMN* 10:347.

"I call this my style of building": Shepard, *Pedlar's Progress*, 414; see plate opposite 414.

Emerson's quizzical name for it: *L* 3:411, 413; *JMN* 10:116; Shepard, *Pedlar's Progress*, 413–14; Bedell, *The Alcotts*, 261.

"I seldom reach home": Shepard, *Pedlar's Progress*, 415; *ABA Jrnls* 1:197.

"After all his efforts": *JMN* 10:142, 110.

gardening was a good refuge: *ABA Jrnls* 1:197.

"Why the boys waded": *JMN* 10:113, 25 July 1847.

224   "Alcott is a certain fluid": *JMN* 11:19.

"Alcott is 'like a slate-pencil' ": Ibid., 187.

"If he would only stand": *HDT Corres*, 200, 208.

Both his friends were plainly: Shepard, *Pedlar's Progress*, 298, 401–3.

"the magnificent dreamer": *JMN* 9:50.

Chapter 22:
HAWTHORNE AT THE MANSE

226   "Sirius was not visible": McDonald, "The Old Manse Period Canon," *NH Journal* 1972: 23, 25.

Hawthorne was slyly making: Lathrop, *Memories of Hawthorne*, 57.

"Mr. Emerson was likewise": "The Hall of Fantasy," *Pioneer* 1 (Feb. 1843): 49–55.

227   another sketch, "The Celestial Railroad": *United States Magazine, and Democratic Review* 12 (May 1843): 515–23.

"I trudge through snow and slosh": NH, *American Notebooks*, 367, 31 Mar. 1843.

Sophia fell on the ice: Ibid., 645 n. 366. 25–27.

"One grief we had": Ibid., 366.

228   Their current name for the Manse. NH, *Love Letters of NH* 2:105, 115, 136, 158–60.

Sophia to Boston: Ibid., 105–12.

"The smallest twig": Partly described in *NH Writings* (1900 edition) 1:xiii; Facsimile in McDonald, "The Old Manse Period Canon," *NH Journal* 1972:16; *Mosses from an Old Manse* (1900 edition), 4–5.

229   "but a poor substitute for Mr. Thoreau": NH, *American Notebooks*, 368–69, 7 Apr. 1843.

he wore "a sunbeam in his face": Ibid., 369.

"high and classic cultivation": Ibid., 371–72.

He wanted to take one last row: Ibid., 378–86.

230 flourishing "like Eden itself": Ibid., 390.
  "in full glory of her golden curls":
  Lathrop, *Memories of Hawthorne*,
  59, Aug. 1843.
  "Mr. Emerson is to have": SPH to her
  mother, 5 May 1843 [misdated 5
  April, CHB], Berg Collection.
  "homeopathic powders in a
  tablespoon": SPH to her mother, 30
  May 1843, Berg Collection.
  "the felicities of design": RWE,
  "Beauty," *Conduct of Life*, *E Works*
  6:296–302.
231 "Not until after our return": *HDT
  Corres*, 118, RWE to HDT, 10 June
  1843. See now *L* 7:545–47 and nn.
  120, 128.
  "well and quiet in his study": *L* 3:198,
  RWE to MF, 7 Aug. 1843.
  "a solitary example of facts": Ibid.,
  198–99, 8 Aug. 1843.
  "Waldo Emerson knows not much":
  SPH to her mother, 3 Sept. 1843,
  Berg Collection.
232 "I acknowledge (with surprise": *JMN*
  7:444.
  "great, grim, earnest men": *JMN* 8:53.
  "invite men drenched in time": *JMN*
  7:271.
  "present to [his] boyish imagination":
  NH, *Scarlet Letter* (Custom House
  Prologue), Cent. Ed., 1:9.
233 "Skepticism esteems ignorance": *JMN*
  8:62.

Chapter 23: CHANNING IN CONCORD, 1843–45

234 "Let your tears dissolve": WEC, "The
  Sleeping Child," *The Collected
  Poems of WEC*, 964.
  During Lidian's Plymouth vacation,
  Emerson wrote: *L* 3:189–92.
235 Since May 5 Ellery and his wife: SPH
  to her mother, 5 May 1843

[misdated 5 April, CHB], Berg
  Collection; *L* 3:174 n. 251.
  "Ellery has many values for me": Ibid.,
  174.
  "the best poet we have": Listed *L*
  3:181. See now *L* 7:548–50 and n.
  141, RWE to John Sterling, 30 June
  1843.
  "When Ellery's muse": *JMN*
  8:351–52.
  Ellery took his place: *L* 3:179.
  could shock his associates: *JMN*
  9:120.
  "entitled to no more charity": *JMN*
  8:352.
  "like a man who takes snuff": *JMN*
  9:41.
  "writers never do anything": Ibid., 45.
  The two strollers kept watch: Ibid., 7,
  13, 23, 68, 119.
236 "I know you are not a 'marker of
  days' ": *L* 3:235–38. See now *MF
  Letters* 3:175–80 for full text of MF
  to RWE, 28 Jan. 1844.
  "When last Saturday night": *L*
  3:238–39.
  "Now he roams the sun's dominion":
  WEC, *Poems of Sixty-five Years*, 54.
  Emerson paid Ellery fifty cents:
  McGill, *Channing of Concord*, 80.
237 Like Emerson, he had a pregnant and
  ailing wife: *L* 3:257.
  "The cars will run regularly": *JMN*
  9:301.
  "These poor countrymen with their
  nasty religion": Ibid., 84, 114,
  162–63, 197–98, 201, 349, 401. Cf.
  NH, *American Notebooks*,
  361–62.
  three new babies enlarged the
  population: SPH to her mother, 9
  Jan. 1844 and Mar. 1844, Berg
  Collection.
238 moved out of the Red Lodge: *L* 3:247.
  The child, a girl, born May 2: McGill,
  Channing of Concord, 82.
  called him "a gump": NH, *Love Letters
  of NH* 2:141.
  by joining Thoreau in Pittsfield:

Harding, *Days of Henry Thoreau*,
172.

"Lidian's hour draws near": *L* 3:257.

"It is a very red blackhaired baby":
SPH to her mother, July 1844, Berg
Collection.

"I am really trying to end": *L* 3:252.

239 wrote from Brook Farm: CS(T) to
RWE, 18 July 1844, Tappan
Papers, Smith College Archives.
For RWE's response see now *L*
7:605–6 and n. 83, 20 July 1844.

Henry, defying the authorities: Glick,
"Thoreau and the 'Herald of
Freedom,' " *NEQ* 22 (June 1949):
200–1; *JMN* 15:342–43.

"Though the voice of society": *JMN*
5:15, 2 Feb. 1835.

His essay on "Compensation": *E
Works* 2:109.

240 editor of the *Herald of Freedom*:
Harding, *Days of Henry Thoreau*,
175; Glick, "Thoreau and the
'Herald of Freedom,' " *NEQ* 22
(June 1949): 201.

John Greenleaf Whittier asked
Emerson: *L* 3:260 n. 76.

Emerson declined: Ibid., 260–61.

"What argument, what eloquence":
JMN 9:195.

"tough unalterableness of sentences":
L 3:259.

241 "the light headed frolics of a hack":
Ibid., 263.

"His arrival at N.Y. was unfortunately
timed": Ibid., 268–69. See also *L*
3:269–70 n. 108 for MF to RWE,
17 Nov. 1844, from Fishkill
Landing. See now *MF Letters*
3:243–45 and notes for the same
letter.

"It is all an experiment": *L* 3:268.

"I have my old neighbors still": Ibid.,
267.

"cased in triple steel": Listed *L* 3:276.

"Ellery Channing has been here":
Ibid., 281.

Near the end of April: McGill,
Channing of Concord, 86.

242 Hawthorne was planning to leave: *L*
3:305.

Chapter 24: THOREAU IN NEW YORK, 1843

243 "I have been your pensioner": *HDT
Corres*, 78.

by helping to assemble: *L* 3:154.

There was reason to think: Ibid.,
157–65.

244 Charles Emerson's sprightly account:
Dial 3 (Apr. 1843): 500–4 and
522–26.

John Keats's commentaries: See *The
Keats Circle: Letters and Papers
1816–1878*, ed. by Hyder E.
Rollins (Cambridge, Mass.:
Harvard University Press, 1948),
2:140 and n. 4.

arrangements for the American
publication: *L* 3:166–67 and
n. 226, 168 and n. 232.

"a whittling Yankee": Ibid.,
171.

"Ellery has many values for me": Ibid.,
174.

"a lonely beautiful brooding youth":
Ibid., 149.

"moves like a deer": *HDT Corres*,
149.

"no truer and no purer person":
L 3:172.

245 "the Oneida Chief": Ibid., 168.

"I hope you will not be washed away":
HDT Corres, 106.

He was evidently happy enough:
L 3:158–59, 168 and n. 230.

"I think of you as some elder sister":
HDT Corres, 103.

246 "I trust you have grown stronger":
L 2:145.

"well lodged and well fed": *L* 3:117
and n. 35.

"And so tell me, kind wife": Ibid.,
118–19, 8 Jan. 1843.

247 "sad thoughts which were": ETE, *Life of Lidian*, 128.

"she always spoke of 'the sun, my enemy' ": Ibid., 127.

forgetting "all the particulars": *L* 3:156.

She had been ill again: Ibid., 154, 158.

"Queenie's epitaph": *JMN* 8:363.

"Dear husband, I wish": Ibid., 365.

"a wreck of dyspepsia": *L* 3:181.

The dyspepsia reappeared: Ibid., 184, 193.

This time she resorted to homeopathy: Ibid., 205, 208, 213, 219, 223.

as Emerson said, paraphrasing *Hamlet*: Ibid., 226; *Hamlet* 3.1.

she did come downstairs: *L* 3:227.

248 she began in December to remodel: Ibid., 229.

"tears, groans, indispositions": Ibid., 257.

"a thousand times meaner": *HDT Corres*, 105, 107, 111–12, 114, 121–22.

Margaret Fuller was far away: *L* 3:176–80 and 177–78 n. 259. See now *MF Letters* 3:129–32 for MF to RWE, 16 June 1843.

"a noble piece": *HDT Corres*, 117–18, 125.

249 "My very dear Friend": Ibid., 119–20.

he always blushed when passing: *JMN* 8:375, 400.

Henry addressed his next letter: *HDT Corres*, 123–25.

250 "cordial greetings": Listed *L* 3:187. See now *L* 7:551–52 and n. 152, RWE to HDT, 20 July 1843.

Henry "had exalted her": Rusk, *Life of RWE*, 290–91.

"Say to Mrs. Emerson": *HDT Corres*, 134–39, 143–44.

251 "a cold place sultry": Ibid., 137.

"Thee knew I of old": Ibid., 145–46.

"kith and kin in any sense": Ibid., 112, 114.

"were not men that could get along": Quoted in Harding, *Days of Henry Thoreau*, 155.

"If as we have heard": *HDT Corres*, 149.

under the poplar tree "henceforth forever": Ibid., 128, 130–33. See note p. 131: Etzler's book was entitled *The Paradise Within the Reach of All Men*.

Chapter 25: MARGARET FULLER IN NEW YORK, 1844–46

253 In July she stayed at the Manse: *NH Letters* 16:58–60.

"I cannot help wearying": *JMN* 11:498 and n. 172.

she set down the final sentence: Ibid., 507.

"Any relation to him": Blanchard, *Margaret Fuller*, 209–10.

254 "I am able to take": *JMN* 11:463.

"What fine just distinctions she made": Ibid., 501–2 and n. 189 for lines from Schiller.

"evergreens and red and golden trees": Blank verse sent to James Nathan, 23 May 1845, *Love Letters of MF*, 87. See now *MF Letters* 4:104–7 for text.

"My wife," wrote Greeley: Greeley, *Recollections of a Busy Life*, 176.

255 "the worst beaten man on the continent": Ibid., 177–78.

"I have now a position": Chevigny, *Woman and the Myth*, 135, letter dated 2 Mar. 1845, Houghton MS. See now *MF Letters* 4:53–54 for full text.

Summer on the Lakes, which appeared: *L* 3:252 and n. 61.

and *Woman in the Nineteenth Century*, finished: Ibid., 269 n. 108; Miller, ed., *Margaret Fuller: American Romantic*, 136. See now *MF Letters* 4:48 n. 1.

256 "very good and entertaining":
L 3:255, 7 June 1844.
"one of the clearest and most graphic":
Mem MFO 2:152.
it still stands as a worthwhile: Chevigny,
Woman and the Myth, 316–34.
"The stream is abundant and
beautiful": Quoted in Chevigny,
Woman and the Myth, 232–33. For
CS(T) to MF, 4 Mar. 1845, see now
Dedmond, "The Letters of Caroline
Sturgis to Margaret Fuller," *SAR
1988*, 239–40 and notes.
"In this country it is an absurd
practice": *L* 3:252.

257 "I have read quite through": Ibid.,
269–70 n. 108. See now *MF Letters*
3:243–45.
"only aim is the discernment": New
York *Tribune*, 7 Dec. 1844. See
also *L* 2:455 n. 334.

258 She worked hard at her reviewing: See
bibliography in *Writings of
Margaret Fuller*, ed. Mason Wade,
596–600. See now Myerson, *MF: A
Descriptive Bibliography* and
Myerson, *MF: An Annotated
Secondary Bibliography*.
"Her earlier contributions to the
Tribune": *Mem MFO* 2:154,
156–58.
"boskie acres" of Greeley's farmstead:
Ibid., 151, 153–54.

259 While Emerson in Concord was
helping: *L* 3:278–79, 285–86 and
n. 25.
"Almost ever since we first met": *Love
Letters of MF*, 44, 178. See now
MF Letters 4:324 for index entry on
letters to Nathan.
"Noble and great as she was": Greeley,
Recollections of a Busy Life, 178.
"intensity of interest and pleasure":
L 3:294 and n. 67.

260 wrote Lidian that he had just seen:
Ibid., 295.
"I have had some congenial hours":
Love Letters of MF, 147. See now
MF Letters 4:148.

"I found myself much warped": *L*
3:290. See now *L* 8:10–11 and
nn. 26, 27 for corrected version.
"I truly revolve": *L* 3:290.
"I have long ago settled": Ibid., 288.
"Of all the persons I know": *JMN*
9:222, after 7 June 1845.
"Lidian would find me more trouble":
Allen, *Waldo Emerson*, 450.
Source: Houghton Library.
"At home the baby is my chief
company": *Love Letters of MF*,
158–64. See now *MF Letters*
4:153–57, 161–63, 5 Sept. and 29
Sept. 1845, to James Nathan.

261 "Our moods did not match":
Blanchard, *Margaret Fuller*, 236,
letter of 16 Nov. 1845. See now *MF
Letters* 4:167–69.
"As I shall find no longer a home":
Love Letters of MF, 168, 171–72,
175. See now *MF Letters* 4:177–80
with corrections.
Margaret insisted on borrowing
money: Blanchard, *Margaret Fuller*,
243.
Now at last she could absorb: *Love
Letters of MF*, 176. See now *MF
Letters* 4:189–91.
lodgings in Brooklyn "near the
heights": *Love Letters of MF*, 182,
186. See now *MF Letters* 4:204–6,
218–19.

262 "a richer and more varied exercise":
Miller, ed., *Margaret Fuller:
American Romantic*, 251–52.
"I find how true was the lure": *Mem
MFO* 2:224–25. See now *MF Letters*
4:314–15, 20 Dec. 1847.

Chapter 26: THOREAU AT WALDEN

263 "I see nothing for you": McGill,
Channing of Concord, 85; *HDT
Corres*, 161.

While Channing was negotiating: Harding, *Days of HT*, 179–85.

264 performed likc "mighty nature's child": *JMN* 9:233–39, 259; *Hamlet* 2.2. 585.

"consisted of a continual coining": *JMN* 9:101–02.

265 "a good substantial childe": Ibid., 103 and n. 30. Partly used in "Historic Notes of Life and Letters in New England," *E Works* 10:356–57.

"vocation of reporting": *JMN* 9:121.

"a wooden inkstand": Harding, *Days of HT*, 182.

Henry's chief occupation for the next two years: Howarth, *Book of Concord*, 38–40.

the total cost of his cabin: Harding, *Days of HT*, 182.

This record formed the basis: Ibid., 188.

266 "My little Ellen," he wrote: *L* 3:277.

"I spend a great deal of time": Ibid., 281.

Even their Uncle Bulkeley: Ibid., 291–93.

the experience of his neighbor Samuel Hoar: Ibid., 272 and n. 119; Allen, *Waldo Emerson*, 429–30.

267 "As I think the Lyceum exists": Listed *L* 3:312. See now *L* 8:61–62 and n. 213 for full text.

though sporting "bright orange" shoes: McGill, *Channing of Concord*, 86.

sleeping on a pallet beside Henry's bed: Harding, *Days of HT*, 182.

"sick and sepulchral": Dedmond, "The Letters of Caroline Sturgis to Margaret Fuller," *SAR 1988*, 247, Thanksgiving, 1845.

"the unnatural selfishness of a man": McGill, *Channing of Concord*, 88.

268 "He cannot keep himself peaceable": Dedmond, "The Letters of Caroline Sturgis to Margaret Fuller," *SAR 1988*, 249.

"Ellery Channing has suddenly found out": *L* 3:326–27.

Ellery sailed from New York: McGill, *Channing of Concord*, 89.

a local tragedy agitated the village: NH, *American Notebooks*, 261–67, 604, 620.

269 "Mr. Channing has returned": *L* 3:340.

Having come to the village: Harding, *Days of HT*, 202–5; HDT, *Walden and Civil Disobedience*, 236.

"I vum," said Sam: *HDT Corres*, 77, HDT to RWE, 24 Jan. 1843.

270 "E[merson] thought it mean and skulking": *ABA Jrnls* 1:183 and n. 184.

"Build your prison walls thicker": *JMN* 9:444–45.

"I had three chairs in my house": HDT, *Walden*, ch. 6, "Visitors," 140.

Emerson "looked in" at the cabin: Ibid., ch. 14, "Former Inhabitants and Winter Visitors," 270.

"I do not mean to deny Ellery's ability": *NH Letters* 15:672, 1843.

271 "We made that small house": HDT, *Walden*, ch. 14, "Former Inhabitants and Winter Visitors," 268.

"I think," wrote Thoreau: Ibid., 268–69.

"He belongs to the Homeric age": *ABA Jrnls* 1:238–39, 1851.

the taxpaying abolitionists: Harding, *Days of HT*, 195.

272 It happened to be the very day: *L* 3:341 and n. 68.

Chapter 27: THEODORE PARKER IN BOSTON

273 "a few earnest men": Miller, ed., *The Transcendentalists*, 491–92.

his manner was "simple, unaffected": Commager, *Theodore Parker*, 117–18.

274 "a theologian eminent": *C-E-C*, 340.

"a most hardy, compact": Ibid., 350.

Emerson cooperated: *L* 3:391, 394, 397, 401, 414.

"a little more acceptable to plebeian": Commager, *Theodore Parker*, 130–34.

while its spirit was good: *L* 4:4.

the new journal showed "no character": Ibid., 81–82 n. 292.

Emerson urged James Elliot Cabot: Ibid., 60.

he had hardly *"worked in it"*: Ibid., 106–7, 108–9.

"Parker I prize and respect": Ibid., 113–14.

275 convince him of their "total depravity": Commager, *Theodore Parker*, 133.

"with an occasional Roar": *L* 4:123–24 n. 434.

to "the same clan and parish": Ibid., 151 and n. 88.

this "very extraordinary man": Miller, ed., *The Transcendentalists*, 415–21. Entire essay is printed in Collins, *Theodore Parker: American Transcendentalist*, 170 ff.

278 into the limbo of bankrupt magazines: *L* 4:218 n. 176 for reference to TP to RWE, 8 July 1850.

the church had allied itself too closely: Commager, *Theodore Parker*, 165–67.

"After attending to numerous": Ibid., 113.

he was associated with almost all the blacks: Ibid., 214.

279 "This filthy enactment": *JMN* 11:412. See also Ibid., 249 and n. 201, 352, 360–61, 410–11.

"Pho!" wrote Emerson: Ibid., 345–48.

"morals he has none": Ibid., 345, 405, 409.

Chapter 28:
THE ABSENTEES:
HAWTHORNE

280 "We gathered up our household goods": NH, *Mosses from an Old Manse*, Cent. Ed. 10:33.

"Mr. Hawthorne leaves Concord today": *L* 3:305.

281 "Blessed be the child": *NH Letters* 16:130 and n. 1.

feeling safe, as Hawthorne believed: Ibid., 133–35, 156.

Sick of "the anguish of debt": Ibid., 125.

a selection of his stories and sketches: Ibid., 146.

"I send you the initial article": Ibid., 152.

"serene and sober" Manse: NH, *Mosses from an Old Manse*, Cent. Ed. 10:30–31.

282 "for the present incumbent": *NH Letters* 16:157, n. 2. (MS, Berg).

Sophia's computation multiplied: Ibid., 154, n. 3.

only three and a half hours per day: NH, *Scarlet Letter* (Custom House Prologue), Cent. Ed. 1:35.

"my office (the duties of it)": *NH Letters* 16:153.

"He has that freedom of view": Leyda, *The Melville Log* 1:207–8; *NH Letters* 16:154.

Melville discovered and read it: Leyda, *The Melville Log* 1:378–81, 387–91.

owing to a legal stratagem: Metzdorf, "Hawthorne's Suit Against Ripley and Dana," *Am Lit* 12 (May 1940): 235–41.

"Let it sink," wrote Hawthorne: *NH Letters* 16:144.

283 a two-volume set: NH, *Mosses from an Old Manse*, Cent. Ed. 10:520; *NH Letters* 16:165–70.

for many weeks thereafter, "Bundlebreech": Ibid., 173–74, 192–93, 201–2, 206, 212–13, 224, 227, 231, 233, 238.

they fixed at last upon Julian: Ibid.,
201–02, 235.

the American edition of Carlyle's life of
Cromwell: *L* 3:311–12, 316 and
n. 139, 317–20, 324–26, 331–32.

he had meantime declined to lecture:
Cited above, 267.

for book-borrowing privileges: *L*
3:335–36.

He had helped gather funds: Ibid.,
326–27.

said good-bye to Margaret Fuller:
Ibid., 339.

He had welcomed Thoreau back:
Ibid., 340.

vexatious problems with servants:
Ibid., 331.

"the very counting of threads": Ibid.,
340–41.

284 "a moderate share of prosperity": *NH
Letters* 16:188, 193.

He gave a copy of his *Mosses*: Ibid.,
178.

in the company of Emerson: Mellow,
Nathaniel Hawthorne, 274–75.

Hawthorne had deleted: NH, *Mosses
from an Old Manse*, Cent. Ed.
10:635–38.

"amiable and highly cultivated":
Mellow, *Nathaniel Hawthorne*,
277.

"Hawthorn [sic] invites his readers":
JMN 9:405.

"he eats like an Anaconda": *NH
Letters* 16:199–201; Mellow,
Nathaniel Hawthorne, 287.

the manuscript of his *Conversations in
Rome*: This was Channing's
*Conversations in Rome: Between an
Artist, a Catholic and a Critic*
(Boston: William Crosby and H. P.
Nichols, 1847).

Hawthorne alerted Duyckinck:
Mellow, *Nathaniel Hawthorne*,
287.

Emerson had interceded with Munroe:
L 3:362–66, 403, 413.

the surveyor of revenue had to borrow:
NH Letters 16:217–18.

285 "Waldo Emerson knows not much of
love": SPH to her mother, 3 Sept.
1843, Berg Collection.

the cause was a "poverty": *L* 4:32–33.

from their "great, lonesome bed": *NH
Letters* 16:226, 235, 240.

Thoreau's "iron-poker-ishness": Ibid.,
248.

so that Sophia could show off: Ibid.,
259.

he mentioned Thoreau's forthcoming
book: Ibid., 261–62.

Thoreau had read him extracts: *L*
3:338.

286 "almost too gay an appearance":
HDT, *A Week*, 358.

Hawthorne rightly foresaw: *NH
Letters* 16:154, 263–64, 273.

"I feel pretty well": Ibid., 283;
Mellow, *Nathaniel Hawthorne*,
297.

"careering through the public prints":
NH, *Scarlet Letter* (Custom House
Prologue), Cent. Ed. 1:42–43.

"the little boy": *NH Letters* 16:271.

287 in what he called his darkest hour:
Ibid., 295; Mellow, *Nathaniel
Hawthorne*, 297–99.

"He writes immensely": SPH to her
mother, 29 Sept. 1849, Berg
Collection. See Mellow, *Nathaniel
Hawthorne*, 302–3.

"After my fellowship of toil": NH,
Scarlet Letter (Custom House
Prologue), Cent. Ed. 1:16, 25.

288 "I have no less disgust":
JMN 7:161.

*Chapter 29: MARGARET
FULLER ABROAD*

289 "as if you meant to let me go": *L* 3:339
and n. 59. See now *MF Letters*
4:220, 15 July 1846.

"give a good and faithful interview":
C-E-C, 403–4.

had been entirely "honourable": Ibid., 407–8.

290 "the rich flow of his discourse": *Mem MFO* 2:185. See now *MF Letters* 4:245–50 for full text and notes.

"a high-soaring, clear, enthusiast": *C-E-C*, 408–10 and n. 6.

After some efforts to remonstrate: *Mem MFO* 2:186–88. See now *MF Letters* 4:248.

"by far the most beauteous": *Mem MFO* 2:173. See now *MF Letters* 4:239–42 and notes. Quote, on p. 240, has "nowhere" for "somewhat" in the memoirs.

"a great man": *Mem MFO* 2:263–67. See now *MF Letters* 5:207–11, 16 Mar. 1849. Quote on p. 210.

Margaret's first personal letter: One earlier letter to RWE, London, 30 Oct. 1846 (*L* 3:381) was merely a letter of introduction for Harro Harring. See now *MF Letters* 4:237 and note. *Mem MFO* 2:184–88.

England had abounded in "devout" admirers: *Mem MFO* 2:207.

she sent him at least three more: See now *MF Letters* 4:245–50, 261–62 and notes.

291 "You have acquired the right to know": Blanchard, *Margaret Fuller*, 261–63; Chevigny, *Woman and the Myth*, 299–300, 374; Wellisz, *The Friendship of Margaret Fuller D'Ossoli and Adam Mickiewicz*, 13, 17–18.

"to initiate me into various": *Mem MFO* 2:201–2.

it would unlock the "jewelled cabinets": *L* 3:376–78.

essay was too "old": Ibid., 377–78; *C-E-C*, 413–15; *JMN* 10:127. See now *MF Letters* 4:258–59, to RWE, 18 Jan. 1847.

her letter to Elizabeth Hoar: From Paris, 18 Jan. 1847, *Mem MFO* 2:193–99. See now *MF Letters* 4:256, 258.

292 "run out of the coop": *L* 3:393–95.

stirred Emerson's old friend into action: Ibid., 379–81.

"This island," he wrote: Ibid., 398–99 and nn. 111, 112; *JMN* 10:63.

"The famine in Europe": *L* 3:400–1.

293 Meetings with Giovanni D'Ossoli and Thomas Hicks: Chevigny, *Woman and the Myth*, 372–73, 423–25. See now *MF Letters* 4:269, 270 and notes.

"high time," she wrote Caroline Sturgis: Chevigny, *Woman and the Myth*, 428–30, MF to CS(T). See now *MF Letters* 4:290–92, 26 Aug. 1847.

she was "sedulously" cultivating: *Mem MFO* 2:210, MF to RWE. See now *MF Letters* 4:275–76, 20 June 1847.

some of the "high society": Chevigny, *Woman and the Myth*, 371, 429, 440–41. See now *MF Letters* 4:290–92 to CS(T), 22 Aug. 1847 and *MF Letters* 5:41–45 to CS(T), 11–12 Jan. 1848.

294 Margaret's letter to Emerson: *Mem MFO* 2:213. Cf. MF(O), *At Home and Abroad*, 234. See now *MF Letters* 4:287–88 and notes, 10 Aug. 1847.

"For three weeks": Chevigny, *Woman and the Myth*, 441. See now *MF Letters* 5:43.

"I am happily settled": *Mem MFO* 2:220. See now *MF Letters* 4:308–9.

"I have not been so well": *Mem MFO* 2:223. See now *MF Letters* 4:312–13.

"When odd men": *L* 3:412.

"This voyage of mine": Ibid., 416–17.

"like a carpeted dark closet": *HDT Corres*, 187.

a four-day visit to the Carlyles: *L* 3:422–30 and n. 185.

"I have a letter from Margaret Fuller": Ibid., 444; *Mem MFO* 2:220–21.

295 "I rejoice in your beatitude": *L* 3:447.

"There is a Polish countess here":

Mem *MFO* 2:222–23. See now *MF Letters* 4:310–11.

"Each day I am out": Mem *MFO* 2:224. See now *MF Letters* 4:312–13.

"She is a very dear sister": *HDT Corres*, 188–89, 204.

"The umbrella," said Emerson: *L* 3:438, 442–43.

296 "In cities, the children are trained": *English Traits, E Works* 5:300.

torrential downpours reduced Rome: Mem *MFO* 2:231.

"I have known some blessed, quiet days": Ibid., 224. See now *MF Letters* 4:314–15.

"With this year [1848]": Mem *MFO* 2:332–33. See now *MF Letters* 5:41–45, quote on p. 43.

Now that she was to have: Deiss, *Roman Years of Margaret Fuller*, 82.

"Come live with me at Concord": *L* 4:27–28 and n. 98.

a disturbing communication from Thoreau: *HDT Corres*, 207, 23 Feb. 1848.

297 with his "plans for Margaret": *L* 4:32.

"Ah you still ask me": Ibid., 33.

his habit of solitude was constantly challenged: *JMN* 10:550, 537.

298 "quite surprising to detect": *L* 4:94.

"for some minutes across a table": Ibid., 46.

"After all the ostentation": Ibid., 48–49.

as much sightseeing as time allowed: *JMN* 10:528–29, 281 n. 299.

made a hasty trip with Carlyle: *L* 4:96–97.

"the best newspaper of the world": Ibid., 39; *JMN* 10:211–12.

"and [now] I have him much better here": Mem *MFO* 2:233–34. See now *MF Letters* 5:55.

learn of her "debility and pain": *L* 4:61.

"much to do and learn in Europe":

Mem *MFO* 2:239. See now *MF Letter* 5:66–67.

299 "come to London immediately": *L* 4:79.

"I hear often from Waldo": Deiss, *Roman Years of MF*, 141. See now *MF Letters* 5:70–71.

"Mother of heroes": *JMN* 10:504–6; *English Traits, E Works* 5:309–14.

"I told Carlyle on the way to Stonehenge": *JMN* 10:335–36; *English Traits, E Works* 5:275–76.

"England, an old and exhausted island": Ibid.

300 the "book" of British society: *L* 4:62, 25 Apr. 1848.

"readiness to close the book": Mem *MFO* 2:233–36, 238–39. See now *MF Letters* 5:66.

"Some years ago," she recalled: Mem *MFO* 2:243–44. See now *MF Letters* 5:85–86.

"the most ferocious and mercenary": Mem *MFO* 2:280–81.

301 on September 5, at age thirty-eight: Deiss, *Roman Years of MF*, 164–65.

Chapter 30:
THE ABSENTEES:
ALCOTT

302 "My friends begin to value each other": *JMN* 11:51.

Emerson gave a stag dinner: *L* 4:122 and n. 432.

following the advice of Mrs. James Savage: Bedell, *The Alcotts*, 271.

this mode of life: Ibid., 268.

303 "our dearest well-beloved friend": Abigail Alcott to RWE, 4 Oct. 1847, Alcott Pratt Collection, Houghton Library.

"cold, heartless, brainless": Abigail Alcott to Samuel J. May, 10 Jan. 1848, Alcott Pratt Collection,

Houghton Library; Bedell, *The Alcotts*, 268.

"thought of fixing myself": ABA Jrnl MS, 29 July 1848, Alcott Pratt Collection, Houghton Library.

he had been dreaming of conducting: Bedell, *The Alcotts*, 272, 302.

his wife took on the duties: Ibid., 271–84.

304 to gather small groups: *NH Letters* 16:261.

"I have been much occupied": *ABA Letters*, 149–50.

In this "leafy June": Ibid., 151, 17 June 1849; Bedell, *The Alcotts*, 286.

305 In July he spent a weekend: Bedell, *The Alcotts*, 271, 383; *ABA Jrnls* 1:210.

talking all day about Goethe: *ABA Jrnls* 1:211.

"I am afraid," wrote Emerson: *JMN* 11:130.

He mentioned "a boding cough": *ABA Jrnls* 1:212–16; *ABA Letters*, 152.

"a pleasure to see": *ABA Jrnls* 1:215–16.

"This last good piece of fortune": *ABA Letters*, 152–53, 17 Sept. 1849.

"person who opened his lips": *JMN* 11:215.

306 the subject of "The Spirit of the Times": Ibid., 228.

"astonishes by the grandeur": Ibid., 423.

"new eyes bud in your brow": Ibid., 172.

Alcott had been drifting: Bedell, *The Alcotts*, 302–4.

"Miss Littlehale called in the afternoon": *ABA Jrnls* 1:221.

307 "Now if I covet youth": Bedell, *The Alcotts*, 305–6.

The widowed Ednah later became: Ednah D. L. Cheney, *Reminiscences of Ednah Dow Cheney* (Boston: Lee and Shepard, 1902); *Louisa May Alcott: Her Life, Letters, and Journals* (Boston: Roberts, 1889).

"recluse and thoughtful in the extreme": *ABA Jrnls* 1:229.

"Further talk with my desponding wife": Ibid., 230–31.

308 "Mine was the old-fashioned small-pox": *ABA Letters*, 159.

"I must stand for the time": *ABA Jrnls* 1:231–32; Bedell, *The Alcotts*, 311.

"because I had one set of gifts": *ABA Jrnls* 1:232.

"That is failure when a man's idea": Sanborn-Harris, *Life of ABA* 2:388.

309 "[Horace Greeley's] *Tribune* brings intelligence": *ABA Jrnls* 1:232, 21 July 1850.

Chapter 31:
THE ABSENTEES:
MARGARET FULLER

313 "seated at the foot of the foremast": *Mem MFO* 2:341–49; Blanchard, *Margaret Fuller*, 333–37.

"all the intelligence and, if possible": *L* 4:219–20 and n. 178.

314 containing her letters from Marchesa Visconti: Ibid., 296–97, 12 June 1852.

Thoreau talked with Margaret's mother: *HDT Corres*, 262–65; *JMN* 11:256.

"a bottle of wine": *Mem MFO* 2:345.

the subject of Emerson's last letter: *L* 4:198–99 and n. 114.

315 Her final year in Italy: *Mem MFO* 2:263–67. See now *MF Letters* 5:239–40 and notes.

"Don't you wish Italy": *Mem MFO* 2:266, 268. See now *MF Letters* 5:246–48.

316 "feel fearful that [Emerson]": Deiss, *Roman Years of MF*, 107.

"Love me all you can": *Mem MFO* 2:266. See now *MF Letters* 5:240.

"You are a Christian": Wade, *Writings of MF*, 589.

a letter from Horace Greeley: *Mem MFO* 2:272–73. See now *MF Letters* 5:255–57 for MF's letter of sympathy to Horace Greeley, 25 Aug. 1849 and ibid., 259–62 for her letter to her mother.

317 his small body "worn to a skeleton": Blanchard, *Margaret Fuller*, 320. On Angelino's illness, see now *MF Letters* 5:249, 254, MF to Lewis Cass Jr., the American chargé d'affaires in Rome.

the assurance that Margaret and Ossoli were married: Deiss, *Roman Years of MF*, 291–92; Blanchard, *Margaret Fuller*, 328. See now *MF Letters* 5:301–7, to CST; ibid., 249–50, 269–70, to Arconati; ibid., 259–62, to her mother, Margaret C. Fuller.

"They are of the Emersonian kind": Wade, *The Writings of MF*, 585. See now *MF Letters* 5:286–88.

"talismans, omens, coincidences": *JMN* 11:457.

318 "I am absurdly fearful": *Mem MFO* 2:337.

"one of the best and most high-minded": Chevigny, *Woman and the Myth*, 496.

"I shall embark": Blanchard, *Margaret Fuller*, 329, from Higginson, *MFO*, 275; *JMN* 11:458.

Her premonitions were more than realized: Blanchard, *Margaret Fuller*, 332–33.

"To the last her country proves": *JMN* 11:256–58.

319 it "must be written": Ibid., 258.

inviting him to join a committee: *L* 4:222 and n. 189.

"How can you describe a Force": *JMN* 11:488.

"a proper edition of Margaret's works": *L* 4:225 n. 198.

Emerson was clearly her "spiritual representative": Ibid., 227 n. 200.

"Leave them out": Ibid., 229, 231.

he worked to gather materials: Ibid.,

296–97. See now *L* 8:258–59, 262–67, for additional letters from RWE to CST, and nn. 126, 135.

a letter from Emerson to Giuseppe Mazzini: *L* 4:232–33. See now *L* 8:284–85 and nn. 58, 59 for second letter to Mazzini, listed *L* 4:255.

Elizabeth Peabody supplied anecdotes: *JMN* 9:431; *L* 4:255 and n. 53. See now *L* 8:286 for refs. to EPP.

Ward offered an installment: *L* 4:255 and n. 52.

declined further participation: See *HDT Jrnl* [old style] 8:249–50.

James Freeman Clarke agreed to serve: *L* 4:257 and nn. 58, 65.

320 All three men spent a week: Ibid., 257–58.

supplying a title, *Life and Death of Margaret Fuller Ossoli*: *JMN* 11:456. Quote is from Virgil, *Ecl* 1, 26–27, Loeb trans.

He slowly filled the notebook: See *JMN* 11:455–509 (MFO Notebook).

to Margaret's former protégé: *L* 4:235.

"I grudged him the time": *JMN* 11:10.

existing, thought Emerson, "to little use": Ibid., 170.

"He wastes my time": Ibid., 316.

called it "well weighed": *L* 4:253–54, 23 July 1851. Cf. Ibid., 294–95 and n. 88.

"That form proved impossible": *Mem MFO* 1:205–6.

321 "she was the wedding-guest": *JMN* 11:449; *Mem MFO* 1:214–15.

Emerson had amassed: *L* 4:237.

"the most precarious of female healths": Ibid., 244.

"immensely talkative": Ibid., 248, 260.

Dr. Bartlett, "always an alarmist": Ibid., 252–53, 264.

he delivered in Concord: noted *L* 4:245. See now *L* 8:273–74 and nn. 5, 7.

"Margaret Fuller's manifold manuscripts": *L* 4:251.

the plates had already been cast: Ibid.,
261–62. See now *L* 8:294–95 and
n. 90.

322 "literary libertinage": Deiss, *Roman
Years of MF*, viii.

Chapter 32: THOREAU
AND CHANNING

323 John Albee, a nineteen-year-old senior:
Albee, *Remembrances of Emerson*,
16.
another man was there: Ibid., 18.
"how to become educated": Ibid.,
16.
"unfailing suavity and deference":
Ibid., 57.
he often hesitated: Ibid., 21.
"most of the branches": Ibid., 22.
"Yes, indeed, all the branches": Ibid.
"negative and biting criticisms": Ibid.,
19.
Around teatime Emerson complained:
Ibid., 31.

324 "but it had feathers": Ibid., 32.
"devoted himself wholly": Ibid., 19.
"cercalian blossoms expanded": Ibid.,
20.
"Mr. Thoreau then made": ETE, *Life
of Lidian*, 68.
"I can guess pretty well": *HDT Corres*,
245–46.

325 "critic poet philosopher": HDT, *The
Writings of HDT, Journal*, vol.
2:*1842–48*, 223–24.
"they were not written": Ibid.,
355–56.
"Needs all these and many more":
JMN 13:28. Edward Everett was
also listed.
Thoreau wrote an essay: Harding,
Days of HT, 245.
"It is the secret of the Universe":
HDT, *A Week*, intro. by N. H. Dole
(New York, 1900), 266–91. See
especially 266, 278, 289.

326 Thoreau had grown tired: Harding,
Days of HT, 299.
Frank Sanborn later recorded: Ibid.
"How he jumps, how he strains":
Quoted Ibid.
said flatly that it was only: *JMN* 11:20
and n. 63.
When the two men climbed Nagog
Hill: Ibid., 145 and n. 236, 146.
nature "must always combine": Ibid.,
265–66.
"the first for a long time": Ibid.,
283–86.

327 "Thoreau wants a little ambition":
Ibid., 400.
"Pounding beans is good": Ibid., 404.
his "powerful arithmetic": Ibid., 438.
"the only rod of safety": *JMN* 13:63.
"Thoreau gives me in flesh and
blood": Ibid., 66.
"Henry Thoreau seemed stubborn":
Ibid., 183, early 1853.
"Must we always talk for victory":
Ibid., 54, ca. 1856.

328 "I had two friends": *HDT Jrnl* [old
style] 8:199, 4 Mar. 1856.
"I thought that friendship": *HDT Jrnl*
[old style] 2:161–62.
"Ah, I yearn toward thee": *HDT Jrnl*
[old style] 3:61. This quotation and
the previous one cited by Harding,
Days of HT, 300.
"Nearly all the fine souls": *L* 2:447,
13 Sept. 1841.

329 The arrival of his and Ellen's third
child: McGill, *Channing of
Concord*, 103.
"a terrible man to deal with": Sanborn,
Recollections of Seventy Years
2:349–50.
"Saturday afternoon professors":
JMN 11:36–38, 56, 265; *JMN*
13:59–62, 176–77.
"In walking with Ellery": *JMN* 11:38.
"as if they were icicles": Ibid., 193.
"They had frozen water": Ibid., 185.

330 "the eternal pancake": WEC, *Poems of
Sixty-five Years*, intro. by F. B.
Sanborn, xxxi.

"Every woman has a design on you":
JMN 11:21.

"Trouble [is] as good": *JMN* 13:178.

"Life is so short": *JMN* 11:283.

"a few feathers, with a hole": *JMN*
13:127–28.

Ellery was a "perpetual holiday": *JMN*
11:277.

"keen appetite for society": Ibid., 433.

"Behold HDT": WEC, Jrnl, 17 Apr.
1853, Houghton Library. Quoted
by Harding, *Days of HT*, 306;
McGill, *Channing of Concord*, 123.

"tempts me to certain licenses of
speech": McGill, *Channing of
Concord*, 121–22.

331 "always so discriminating": *HDT Jrnl*
[old style] 3:256, 31 Jan. 1852.

"He, assuming a false opposition":
HDT Jrnl [old style] 5:188,
24 May 1853.

*Chapter 33: THE LENOX
CONNECTION*

332 the Berkshire country: Birdsall,
Berkshire County, 326–27.

"Do the muses speak": Listed *L* 3:273.
See now *L* 7:621 and n. 131 for full
text of RWE to SGW, 17 Dec.
1844.

"What a maceration": See now *L*
8:2–3 and n. 7 for full text of RWE
to SGW, 31 Jan. 1845.

333 "I had other intimate friends": SGW
to F. B. Sanborn, 9 June 1902, in
Sanborn, *Recollections of Seventy
Years* 2:574–77.

The only visible residuum: WEC,
Poems of Sixty-five Years, 118.

Caroline "is as much delighted":
Dimock, *CST and the Grand Tour*,
72, 19 Aug. 1849, Prout Collection.

"I am sorry if I said anything": CST to
Abigail Alcott, summer 1850,
Boston Public Library. Quoted in

Saxton, *Louisa May*, 184. For
LMA's ref. to Anna's employment,
see now *LMA Jrnls*, 64.

"Dear Waldo," she answered: CST to
RWE, 7 Aug. 1850, Smith College
Archives. See now *L* 8:256–57 for
RWE to CST, 3 Aug. 1850 and 256
n. 95 for a partial quotation of her
letter of 7 Aug.

334 "Mr. Nathan, a Jew in N.Y.": Letters
of CST to RWE: Nov. 1850, 19
Jan. 1851, 17 June 1851, Smith
College Archives. See now *L* 8:265
n. 135; Ibid., 271; Ibid., 280 n. 35.

He paid her one flying visit: *L* 4:253.
See also *ABA Jrnls* 1:250–51.

stayed with them in the Manse: *NH
Letters* 16:98–99 and n. 2.

urged Sophia to think: Lathrop,
Memories of Hawthorne, 122–23.

both made scouting trips: Mellow,
Nathaniel Hawthorne, 317; NH,
American Notebooks, 293.

"as red as the Scarlet Letter": *NH
Letters* 16:340, 9 June 1850.

soon turned "brown as berries": Ibid.,
340, 349.

"Was ever anything so tragical":
Mellow, *Nathaniel Hawthorne*,
329, SPH to her mother, 1 Aug.
1850, Berg Collection.

335 fitted the "life and genius": *JMN*
11:384, ca. May 1851.

"If I had stayed four years longer": *NH
Letters* 16:345.

"the best of all tonics": Birdsall,
Berkshire County, 340.

"tramping over the soil": Mellow,
Nathaniel Hawthorne, 332.

"I met Melville": *NH Letters* 16:355.

"We have been very much interested":
Ibid., 361–62, 363 n. 3.

"I have read Melville's works": Ibid.,
362, 29 Aug. 1850.

336 Hawthorne told Duyckinck: Ibid.,
362.

"free, brave and manly" demeanor:
Mellow, *Nathaniel Hawthorne*,
342–44.

"The scene of it": *NH Letters* 16:369, 1 Oct. 1850.

"One morning," as Sophia reported: Mellow, *Nathaniel Hawthorne*, 343.

337 "Say what they will": Leyda, *Melville Log* 1:287.

"I do not oscillate": Ibid., 292.

"It was after his initial meetings": Mellow, *Nathaniel Hawthorne*, 335–36.

Hawthorne gave him a signed copy: Ibid., 369–70.

"almost an hour": Ibid., 370.

338 "writes in red chalk": CST to RWE, Nov. 1850, Smith College Archives. See now *L* 8:265 n. 135 for excerpts from her letter.

"a little worn down": *NH Letters* 16:434, 436–37.

gave it all his mornings: Ibid., 437, 443, 453.

reading "foolish novels": Ibid., 460.

"exercised his lungs": NH, *American Notebooks*, 436.

339 "it really does seem": Ibid., 454.

he kept a detailed record: Ibid., 436–86.

"Perhaps tomorrow": Ibid., 485.

"with a view to my next Romance": Ibid., 477–78.

340 and recognized Melville: Ibid., 447–48.

There was also a morning call: Ibid., 456–57, 482.

turning up his nose at the "spit-boxes": Ibid., 463–67. Cf. *JMN* 9:114.

"the porch of Tanglewood": *NH Letters* 16:475.

"to peep at the Lake": Lathrop, *Memories of Hawthorne*, 162.

341 "It is very singular": Ibid., 170.

"the most beautiful in Berkshire": *NH Letters* 16:454, 465, 10 and 24 July 1851.

Kemble's offer to rent out: Birdsall, *Berkshire County*, 333.

"The Castilian, with his curls":

Lathrop, *Memories of Hawthorne*, 171.

He had once told her: Ibid., 145.

"Dear Mrs. Tappan": *NH Letters* 16:481–85.

342 "I freely confess": Ibid., 485.

"Caroline has made herself": SPH to EPP, 2 Oct. 1851, Berg Collection; Mellow, *Nathaniel Hawthorne*, 639, note for p. 380.

"gossiping and agreeable": CST to RWE, 18 Dec. 1851, Smith College Archives.

he walked out with his host: NH, *American Notebooks*, 312.

Hawthorne's personality was "greatly altered": McGill, *Channing of Concord*, 108–9, 30 Oct. 1851.

343 "Lord, when shall we be done": Melville, *The Letters of Herman Melville*, 143. See now Melville, *Correspondence*, vol. 14 of *The Writings of Herman Melville*, 213.

"I have heard nothing from Concord": CST to RWE, 18 Dec. 1851, Smith College Archives.

"I am glad you have": Julian Hawthorne, *NH and His Wife* 1:432–33.

he was already engaged: *NH Letters* 16:465.

Chapter 34:
HAWTHORNE, BIRD OF PASSAGE

344 "I find myself surrounded": *NH Letters* 16:544.

"a comfortable and sufficiently pleasant": Ibid., 548, to Duyckinck, 15 June 1852.

345 "sluggish river, mystically dark": Ibid., 573.

"I see that the papers": Ibid., 548–49, 15 June 1852.

"Whatever service I can do for you":
Ibid., 545–46, 9 June 1852.

"He wishes me to write": Ibid.,
550–51, 17 June 1852.

"I am taking your life": Ibid., 584;
NH, *American Notebooks*, 517 et
seq.

346 Reviewers in the Boston papers: *NH
Letters* 16:595 n. 2, 597, 598 n. 2,
608 n. 6.

"I have done the business": Ibid., 605,
13 Oct. 1852.

cost him "hundreds of friends": Ibid.,
605.

"slavery [is] one of those evils": Ibid.,
608 n. 9, which cites Cent. Ed. of
NH Works 12:417.

"I cannot keep my eyes off it": *JMN*
13:63.

347 "all the more inexcusable": *L* 4:301
and nn. 116, 117.

"A bad president": *JMN* 13:369, Oct.
1854.

"I have a hill behind me": *NH Letters*
16:636–37, 7 Feb. 1853.

348 a complimentary dinner for Arthur
Hugh Clough: *L* 4:322. See now *L*
8:347 and n. 170, 348, 350.

"I enjoy Thackeray's books": *NH
Letters* 16:627.

On January 6 the Pierces' only child:
Mellow, *Nathaniel Hawthorne*,
419; *NH Letters* 16:635, addendum
to letter in SPH's hand.

"amidst innumerable interruptions":
Ibid., 627.

he called it *Tanglewood Tales*: NH,
American Notebooks, 551; *NH
Letters* 16:636, 647–49.

Pierce, he felt, certainly owed him:
Ibid., 605, 13 Oct. 1852.

the "prime minister": Ibid., 639–40.

Hawthorne quietly put forward: Ibid.,
634, 639–40 and notes, 669, 684.
See also Mellow, *Nathaniel
Hawthorne*, 420–22.

his three-week visit to Washington:
NH Letters 16:658.

"beautiful and blossoming Spring":

Ibid., 679. Cf. NH, *American
Notebooks*, 552.

"Frank was as free and kind": NH to
Horatio Bridge, 21 Dec. 1854,
quoted by Mellow, *Nathaniel
Hawthorne*, 428.

349 "political intrigue and management":
Ibid., 427–28; *NH Letters* 16:679
and notes.

He sent Sophia to Boston: Ibid., 693,
699.

"haying and hoeing": *L* 4:368–69.

a visit to Donald McKay's: Ibid.,
366–67 and n. 110.

Longfellow's "very agreeable"
farewell: Ibid., 366.

"a stone cap, with a tin visor": Ibid.,
370–71.

Chapter 35: ELLEN

350 "magnanimously" insisted on naming
her: *JMN* 7:170.

in a series of letters: See *ETE Letters*.

"awkward and reserved": Sanborn,
Recollections of Seventy Years
2:330–32, WEC to
F. B. Sanborn, 15 Mar. 1859.

Emerson had been laying plans: See
now *L* 8:337 nn. 127–133.

351 "nothing but parties, dress, etc.": CST
to RWE, 5 Oct. 1852, Smith
College Archives.

"We will try to have sunny weather":
CST to RWE, 21 Oct. 1852, Smith
College Archives.

"You will like to see how upright":
CST to RWE, 13 July 1853, Smith
College Archives. See now *L* 8:373
and nn. 44, 47 for CST's visits with
Ellen.

"She thinks I am very hardhearted":
ETE Letters 1:16, 4 June 1853.

"Best of all," wrote Ellen: Ibid., 19,
12 June 1853.

352 "All the Shakers": Ibid., 19–20.

"attended to everything": Ibid., 74,
7 Sept. 1854.

she must lose no opportunity: *L*
4:364.

"a country matron's cares": Ibid., 360.

353 "You know she is a bad traveller":
Ibid., 374.

his daughter had never regretted:
Ibid., 378.

The roof was leaking badly: Ibid.

Bulkeley came down from Reuben
Hoar's farm: Ibid., 361, 386.

Caroline Tappan's sister Susan
Bigelow: Ibid., 366, 372–73 and n.
142.

he had written Caroline on the subject
of fatalism: Allen, *Waldo Emerson*,
566. See now *L* 8:374–75 and nn.
48, 49 for full text of RWE to CST,
22 July 1853.

"Fatalism, foolish and flippant": *L*
4:376–77 and n. 154, partial text,
22 July 1853. See now *L* 8:374–75
for full text.

"Cannot we ride the horse": *JMN*
11:416, 388.

354 "History tends to make fatalists": *JMN*
13:110–11, Oct. 1852.

"something which cannot be talked":
"Fate," *Conduct of Life, E Works*
6:5.

"Every spirit makes its house": Ibid.,
1–49

355 "You are all so kind": *ETE Letters*
1:35–36.

"She looks very well": *L* 4:388.

"Henry Thoreau could hardly
suppress": Ibid., 388 and n. 204.

"surprisingly bright serene": Ibid.,
392.

356 Thomas Haskins died: Ibid., 392–93.

who followed him exactly a month
later: Ibid., 397–98.

"Your grandmother died this
morning": Ibid., 398.

"I have just received Father's letter":
ETE Letters 1:42.

was absent on a speaking engagement:
L 4:400–4.

"your grandmother's end was so
peaceful": Ibid., 399–400.

357 when her father died: *ETE Letters*
2:463, 13 May 1882.

"This is the last night of 1853": *ETE
Letters* 1:50–51.

"I send you home Ellen's letter": *L*
4:414.

"It is strange how much I miss": Ibid.,
419.

358 "our fine new housekeeping": Ibid.,
434.

"I have quite got over": *ETE Letters*
1:64.

making trips to Roaring Brook: RWE
mentions [Bhaspish] Falls in a letter
to Charles K. Newcomb, 23 July
1851. See *L* 4:254, and n. 48 for
usual spelling of Bash-Bish.

not "so very ugly, only homely": *ETE
Letters* 1:73.

"my poor broken-to-pieces wife": *L*
4:449.

"Your Mother is very feeble": Ibid.,
454.

"if Ellen were not coming home":
Ibid., 455.

he took Edith along: Ibid., 456–57.

359 "cheerful, sparkling, readable": Ibid.,
459–60, with order of the quote
changed by CHB.

"What fun it was": *ETE Letters* 1:79.

"I haven't fairly begun": Ibid., 79–80.

"a pear is only in perfection": *JMN*
13:98.

the whole interior took on: *ETE
Letters* 1:79, 107, 134, 138, 149
(1855–57).

"I do whatever is to be done": Ibid.,
80–82.

360 "teasing me," said Ellen: Ibid., 85, 87,
90.

"He cries every once in a while": Ibid.,
84, 87–88.

"Father and Mother are glad": Ibid.,
137.

Chapter 36:
WALT WHITMAN

361 "in this Titanic continent": *JMN*
5:195.

"Ah my country": *JMN* 7:24.

"initiative, spermatic, prophesying":
JMN 8:148.

"you must on no account say": *JMN*
7:22.

turned out to be "a little coarse": *JMN*
8:255–56.

By 1846 he was distinguishing: *JMN*
9:442.

"I find him full of": *JMN* 11:134.

he sent copies of the translation: Ibid.,
134–35.

362 a slender quarto of ninety-five pages:
Allen, *Waldo Emerson*, 581–82.

364 Next day, in the extreme heat: RWE to
WW, 21 July 1855, listed
L 4:520–21. See now *L* 8:446 and
n. 89 for full text.

365 "so extraordinary for its oriental":
Rusk, *Life of RWE*, 372. See now
L 8:442–43 and n. 74, RWE to
SGW, 10 July 1855, for full text.

"One strange book": RWE to CST, 17
July 1855, MS Sophia Smith
Collection, Smith College Archives.
See now *L* 8:444–45 and n. 83 for
full text.

"seemed very eager to hear from you":
Conway, *Autobiography* 1:189–91.
See also Loving, *Emerson,
Whitman and the American Muse*,
90–91.

366 "uncouth and grotesque": Review
reprinted in *New York Dissected*, ed.
Holloway and Adimari, 154–61.
Quotes on 157, 161.

"seen some extracts": CST to RWE,
26 Sept. 1855, MS Sophia Smith
Collection, Smith College Archives.

"a curious and lawless collection":
Review reprinted in Norton, *A Leaf
of Grass from Shady Hill*,
27–31.

367 Lowell was not interested: Lowell,

Letters 1:242, Lowell to Norton, 12
Oct. 1855.

"it was a solemn humbug": Lowell,
New Letters of James Russell Lowell,
ed. M. A. DeWolfe Howe (New
York: Harper's, 1932), 115, Lowell
to W. L. Gage, 7 Dec. 1863.

"for Walt has read": Norton, *Letters of
Charles Eliot Norton* 1:135.

"the strange Whitman's" book: *L*
4:531.

"rough figure with black Samson-
locks": Carlyle, *The French
Revolution*, vol. 1, bk. 4, ch. 4,
"The Procession."

"more of a philosopher than a poet":
Tilton, "*Leaves of Grass*: Four
Letters to Emerson," *HLB* 27 (July
1979), 339.

"that wonderful book": Furness,
Records of a Lifelong Friendship,
106–7, RWE to Furness, 1 Oct.
1855. Listed *L* 4:531. See now *L*
8:453 and nn. 110, 111 for full text.

368 when Charles Dana learned of it:
Traubel, *With Walt Whitman in
Camden* 3:124–25.

"strange rude thing": Rusk, *Life of
RWE*, 373, 539, note, RWE to
Samuel Longfellow, 24 Oct. 1855.
See now *L* 8:458 and n. 132 for full
text.

called his "Lyceum Express": *L* 4:131.

trying to help (as Hawthorne had
done): *L* 4:521–23 and nn. 151–55.
For additional letters to Delia Salter
Bacon see now *L* 8:447–48 and nn.
92–94, 465–68 and nn. 157–61.

Ellen, writing from Boston: *ETE
Letters* 1:105–6.

369 "I saw him in New York": Carpenter,
Days with Walt Whitman, 166–67.

Whitman's own later reminiscences:
Traubel, *With Walt Whitman in
Camden*, vol. 5:119, 238.

"remarkable power": Kaplan, *Walt
Whitman*, 204.

"had every leaf but the fig leaf": *JMN*
14:74.

"nondescript monster which yet":
C-E-C, 509.

"as though the town-bull": Wilson,
MacArthur, *Carlyle in Old Age*, 261.

"Here are thirty-two poems": Kaplan,
Walt Whitman, 207–8.

"In fine an egotist": Quoted in Saxton,
Louisa May, 232, from ABA
Journal, Oct. and Nov. 1856,
Houghton MS.; Loving, *Emerson,
Whitman and the American Muse*,
97.

370 taken a sentence from it: Perry, *Walt
Whitman*, 114–15 and plate
opposite 114.

"Parts of the book": Conway,
Autobiography 1:190–91.

Chapter 37: THEODORE PARKER, CRUSADER

371 "My Genius loudly calls me": *JMN*
9:61–62.

it seemed like "meddling": "The
Fugitive Slave Law," *E Works*
11:217.

372 "to extricate yourself": "The Fortune
of the Republic," *E Works*
11:539.

Emerson easily located four heroes:
JMN 9:382 n. 87, 411 n. 173.

while Parker prosecuted his war:
Commager, *Theodore Parker*,
214–47.

373 and caused Bronson Alcott: *ABA Jrnls*
1:272–74.

"ashamed of the Union": Ibid., 273,
445–46.

to applaud Parker's "brave harangue":
L 4:249–50 and nn. 33–36.

Parker's reply: Ibid., 250, n. 37.

374 "Fellow citizens": "The Fugitive Slave
Law," *E Works* 11:179–82, 186–88,
206–8, 211–12.

375 "In the spring," he wrote Carlyle:
C-E-C, 470, 28 July 1851.

"the free and Christian state": *JMN*
11:355.

"I read the inscription": *L* 4:346–47
and nn. 25–26, 19 Mar. 1853.

in his own "Discourse on Webster":
Chadwick, *Theodore Parker*,
258–59.

376 "the word *liberty* in the mouth of Mr
Webster": *JMN* 11:345–46.

"Webster had the head of a bull dog":
JMN 14:276.

"vicious politicians" in Washington:
C-E-C, 499, 11 Mar. 1854.

"If I live much longer": *L* 4:490–91.

"many crosses, less or larger": Ibid.,
496.

He did not get home: Ibid., 498.

"My children," he wrote: Ibid., 510.

"We have tried to persuade him":
Ibid., 512.

Alcott spent a weekend with Emerson:
ABA Jrnls 2:276.

the stony hillocks of Sleepy Hollow: *L*
4:530.

"I plant myself": Ibid., 504.

377 "Though it is a very bad precedent":
Ibid., 514, 29 June 1855, 504 n.
105.

"tiptoe on the wharf": Ibid., 505.

two days with Cyrus Bartol: Ibid.,
524.

he declined several invitations: Ibid.,
517, 534.

"the best soldier fights": Ibid., 536.

Chapter 38: CAPTAIN JOHN BROWN

378 "The people of Kansas ask for bread":
"Affairs in Kansas," *E Works*
11:257–59. Cf. *JMN* 14:54.

379 "I went to a Kansas meeting":
Frothingham, *Theodore Parker*,
437.

Brown had come east: Oates, *To Purge
This Land*, 114–15.

a nocturnal raid along Pottawatomie
Creek: Ibid., 133–37, 152–54;
McDonald, "Emerson and John
Brown," *NEQ* 44 (Sept. 1971):
378–79; Forbes, *Letters and
Recollections* 1:181–82.

380 when he came to Boston: Oates, *To
Purge This Land*, 181–84.

Between money-raising trips: Ibid.,
65, 181–91. He also spoke to the
legislature of the Commonwealth on
18 Feb: Redpath, *The Public Life of
Capt. John Brown*, 176–80.

Brown came out to Concord:
Commager, *Theodore Parker*,
251–52.

381 gave a "good account of himself":
JMN 14:125.

"to perish in the using": Ibid., 353.

"poor betrayed imbruted America": *L*
5:67.

"You are magnanimous": Ibid., 72.

382 "I walk and work now": Frothingham,
Theodore Parker, 481.

as if the digits had been reversed:
Commager, *Theodore Parker*, 273.

"a more glorious history":
Frothingham, *Theodore Parker*,
441–42.

to speak of "troubling Israel": Oates,
To Purge This Land, 221–22.

for a "new state in the Southern
mountains": Ibid., 224–28.

the "whole country from the
Potomac": Ibid., 233–34.

Brown had gone to Canada: Ibid.,
236–37, 243–44.

he met again with the Secret Six: Ibid.,
224–29, 233–38, 243–44,
249–51.

"a stately old man": Redpath, *The
Public Life of Capt. John Brown*,
199.

383 leaving John Brown free: Oates, *To
Purge This Land*, 256–57.

Brown seemed to be everywhere:
Ibid., 262, 264, 267, 269–70.

"the port of an apostle": *ABA Jrnls*
2:315–16.

"glittering gray-blue eyes": Forbes,
Letters and Recollections 1:179–82.

after a trip to Connecticut: Oates, *To
Purge This Land*, 269–75.

384 he was at last ready to move: Ibid.,
290–301.

in his "quiet schoolrooms": Sanborn,
Recollections of Seventy Years
1:187–96. For the Sanborn-RWE
interchange see listing in *L* 5:279
and n. 203, and see now *L* 8:642
and n. 182 for other references.

"this deed of his": *ABA Jrnls* 2:320.

"a hero of romance": *L* 5:179–80.

"I shall not insult you": *JMN* 14:334.

385 filling his journal pages from October
19 to 23: *HDT Jrnl* [old style]
12:406–7, 411, 420. See also
400–39 passim.

Thoreau spoke to his fellow
townsmen: *HDT Corres*, 563, HDT
to H. G. O. Blake, 31 Oct. 1859.

"Think much of Capt. Brown": *ABA
Jrnls* 2:320, 30 and 31 Oct. 1859.

"Brown's trial is over": Ibid., 321.

386 "brilliant young lady from Kentucky":
L 5:83. See now *L* 8:532 for RWE
to Mattie Griffith, 22 Sept. 1857,
and *L* 8:590 n. 155.

"if Brown is hung": *JMN* 14:333.

"that new saint": Allen, *Waldo
Emerson*, 591; McDonald,
"Emerson and John Brown," *NEQ*
44 (Sept. 1971): 386.

"Brown will die": Weiss, *Life and
Correspondence of Theodore Parker*
2:178, TP to Francis Jackson.

She had met and liked him: Oates, *To
Purge This Land*, 271.

In his brief speech: "John Brown," *E
Works* 11:267–73.

387 "a little ceremony": *L* 5:182.

"It is arranged": *ABA Jrnls* 2:322–23.
See also *HDT Jrnl* [old style]
12:457.

John Brown's body: Oates, *To Purge
This Land*, 353–58.

"I have been struck": "John Brown,"
E Works 11:277–81.

Chapter 39:
WHITMAN IN PERSON

389 "an extraordinary person": *ABA Jrnls* 2:286–87.

390 this time bringing Thoreau and Mrs. Tyndall: Ibid., 289–91.

"declaiming Homer": *HDT Corres*, 441–42, 444–45.

"apparently the greatest democrat": Ibid., 441–42.

"like two beasts, each wondering": *ABA Jrnls* 2:290.

391 "the growing of Emerson": Ibid., 293.

"spirited and metaphysical" Conversation: Ibid., 293–94.

"more good than any reading": *HDT Corres*, 444–45, HDT to H. G. O. Blake, 6–7 Dec. 1856; *HDT Jrnl* [old style] 9:149, 2 Dec. 1856, slightly altered.

392 "a fortnight's bybye": *ABA Letters*, 230.

According to Alcott, Emerson had just seen: Ibid. For a detailed account of this second meeting, see WW to H. Traubel, *With Walt Whitman in Camden* 2:504, 19 Oct. 1888.

"an adept of the Transcendentalist School": Norton, *The Letters of Charles Eliot Norton*, 1:195.

"a sort of Emerson run wild": WW, *The Correspondence* 1:190 n. 79.

"dearly pay for the fervid encomium": Review reprinted in *New York Dissected*, ed. Holloway and Adimari, 174.

"The taunts and cries": *JMN* 7:105.

393 a "ramble" with Conway: Conway, *Autobiography* 1:191–92.

"the necessities of the New World": *L* 5:86–87, RWE to CST, 13 Oct. 1857.

394 "If the red slayer": RWE, "Brahma," *Atlantic Monthly* 1 (Nov. 1857):48.

"Be not curious about God": WW, "Song of Myself," section 48, *Leaves of Grass*, 86.

395 "Some of the papers": WW, *Complete Poetry and Prose*, 613.

"the most remarkable example": *JMN* 14:281.

he summarized and profusely illustrated: RWE, "Art and Criticism," *E Works* 12:283–305, 462. For date and place of lecture see *L* 5:139 n. 51.

Chapter 40: THE MAN IN THE TURRET

397 "I abide in my old turret": *L* 5:99.

welcomed the Hungarian patriot Lajos Kossuth: "Address to Kossuth," *E Works* 11:395.

composed the "Fourth of July Ode": "Ode," *E Works* 9:199–200.

"The Man with the Hoe": von Frank, *An Emerson Chronology*, 334. See also *JMN* 14:xxiii, 423–28.

the chief speaker during the ceremony: *E Works* 11:429–36.

"I have heard that when we pronounce": Ibid. See also RWE's remark on immortality to Fredrika Bremer, *The Homes of the New World* 1:221–22, Jan. 1850. Bremer was in Concord from the seventeenth to the twenty-first: "The resurrection, the continuation of our being is granted, we carry the pledge of this in our own breast." See *L* 4:176–77 and nn. 10, 11, 13 and 16 for Bremer's visit.

398 "I had the remains of my mother": *JMN* 14:154, 8 July 1857. See also *JMN* 4:7 and ETE, *Life of Lidian*, 90, 229.

"Nobody knows," said Emerson: *JMN* 14:138, 141.

the publication of *English Traits*: *L* 5:29–30, 34 and nn. 106, 107, 109.

"The Lyceum," he told Adams: Ibid., 47.

despite a $1,000 windfall: ETE, *Life of Lidian*, 127.

"poverty demoralizes": *JMN* 14:324–25. See also "Wealth," *Conduct of Life*, *E Works* 6:90.

399   chided his mentor: For RWE's lecture schedule see *JMN* 14:xxii–xxiv.

"as busy as a shoemaker": *JMN* 9:45, 1843; *L* 5:92, 30 Dec. 1857.

"Home from Chicago and Milwaukee": *JMN* 15:457.

"You shall go harmless": *L* 4:288 and n. 66.

"a diamond merchant": *JMN* 15:127.

"I have tried to protect [Eddy]": *L* 5:250.

400   "I know a song which": *JMN* 14:74.

"the most beloved and valued": *C-E-C*, 508 and n. 2, 5 May 1856.

"ten or fifteen years ago": Ibid., 509–10.

saw Clough briefly: *Emerson-Clough Letters*, #28, RWE to A. H. Clough, 5 May 1856. See now *L* 8:485 and nn. 53–55 for full text. See also *Emerson-Clough Letters*, #30, A. H. Clough to RWE, 10 Oct. 1856.

was shown round the British Museum: *L* 5:20–21, Patmore to RWE, 30 Sept. 1856. For RWE's letter to Patmore, 5 May 1856, concerning ABW, see now *L* 8:485–86 and nn. 53–60.

401   Hawthorne wrote his publisher: *Letters of NH to William Ticknor* 2:28, 10 Oct. 1856.

Anna had been at home: *ETE Letters* 1:144, 31 May 1858.

"You will have seen Mrs. S. G. Ward": *Emerson-Clough Letters*, #31 and note, RWE to A. H. Clough, 17 May 1858. See now *L* 8:562–64 and nn. 54–57 for full text. In n. 54 the letter is wrongly cited as #28.

"grand Gothic perspectives": *JMN* 4:117, 189–90, Feb. and June 1833.

"icehouse of Unitarianism": *JMN* 8:181–82, June-July 1849.

"this running of the girls into Popery": *JMN* 14:129, ca. Mar. 1857.

402   the science of "pure Ethics": *JMN* 15:336–37, Apr. 1863.

Emerson's companion on a visit: *JMN* 9:114 and n. 70.

failed to persuade Henry Thoreau: *HDT Corres*, 154, 158–59, 161.

Emerson dissuaded him: *JMN* 15:303 and n. 198. See also Elliott, *The Life of Father Hecker*. Isaac T. Hecker founded the Paulist Fathers.

"What if you go away": *L* 5:142–44.

403   Sam Ward took his son: Ibid., 163, 20 July 1859.

"she is always a prophyrogenet": Ibid., 169, ca. 10 Aug. 1859.

"power to radiate happiness": Ibid., 176, 4 Oct. 1859.

404   "Anna Ward was at a loss": *JMN* 14:330–31.

John Murray Forbes was a businessman: *DAB* (Henry G. Pearson), 3:507–8.

His letter of invitation: *L* 5:44 n. 148.

"I heartily wish": Ibid., 44–45.

beginning a lifelong friendship: Ibid., 65–67.

405   talked with "all State Street": *JMN* 14:45.

once he got to know Forbes: Forbes, *Letters and Recollections* 1:171–72, 179–80, 183–84; *JMN* 14:363.

"It was my fortune not long ago": Forbes, *Letters and Recollections* 2:111–12, 12 Oct. 1864. Printed in *Letters and Social Aims*, *E Works* 8:103. Cf. *JMN* 15:446, 448.

acquiring the entire island of Naushon: Forbes, *Letters and Recollections* 1:16–27, 107, 159–60; 2:111.

406   he invited the Emersons to Naushon: *L* 5:80–81 n. 130.

"that it is *so* good for her": *ETE Letters* 1:144–47.

she had gone in June to Lynn: *L* 5:111, 114, 116–17.

Ellen sent her sister: *ETE Letters*
1:147–49.

Emerson had begun a blank-verse
history: *L* 5:118–19 and nn. 104–5;
JMN 14:186–87 and notes show
that RWE was working on
"Waldeinsamkeit" in Sept. 1857.

407 "What a heart-hole race": *JMN*
14:288.

"pale and thin, looking quite sick":
ETE Letters 1:183.

"was not much changed by death": *L*
5:148–50.

"entirely disengaged from home":
ETE Letters 1:188.

including the snowbank near Berwick:
L 3:104.

408 He had listened avidly: Harding, *Days
of HT*, 208–10, 309–12, 385–90.

A letter of Ellen's summarized: *ETE
Letters* 1:185–88.

"Just a week before we were to start":
Ibid., 188.

"It looks badly for my Waterford
plan": *L* 5:161.

"I went to the doctors": *JMN*
14:311–12.

There were further "frets": Ibid.,
317–19, 326; *L* 5:172–73 and
n. 173, RWE to WE, 6 Sept. 1859.

409 she and Edith returned to "Prospero's
Island": Ibid., 168.

"Father and Eddy and I": *ETE Letters*
1:190–93.

"a parrot has few duties": *JMN*
14:244, 259, 307.

"and shrank from touching them":
ETE Letters 1:192, July 1857; *JMN*
14:244, 259; Gregg, "Emerson and
His Children," *HLB*, 420–21. See
also *The Wit and Wisdom of the
Reverend Sydney Smith* (New York,
1858), noted in *JMN* 14:432
n. 3.

Dolly, the little Morgan mare: *L* 4:314,
350.

410 The Alcotts had returned to Concord:
ABA Jrnls 2:302, 307, 315.

the death of Elizabeth, called Lizzie:

Saxton, *Louisa May*, 238–39, 257.
See now *LMA Jrnls* 2:88–89 and
LMA, *The Selected Letters*, 32–33.

"pictures seen by an instructed eye":
JMN 14:246–47.

as his poem said, in "ragged
independence": McGill, *Channing
of Concord*, 148–53; Hudspeth,
Ellery Channing, 103–6.

411 he continued his journeyings outward:
Harding, *Days of HT*, 357–402
passim.

a set of "Galway whiskers": Ibid., 367.

"terrible to behold": Ibid., 380.

he conducted surveying operations:
Ibid., 381.

accelerated his American Indian
studies: Ibid., 426–28.

he took over the management: Ibid.,
408–9.

he gave more lectures: Ibid., 412.

in "great demand" among the
Emerson children: *ETE Letters*
1:127–28, 142–44, 174.

classification of birds' eggs: Harding,
Days of HT, 406.

"The charm," said Emerson, "which
Henry T. uses": *JMN* 14:203.

"if God meant him to live in a swamp":
Ibid., 265.

Chapter 41:
AN EMERSONIAN
CALENDAR, 1860

415 Two weeks later, Frank Sanborn:
Sanborn, *Recollections of Seventy
Years* 1:222–23.

"You may make what return": *ETE
Letters* 1:201, 209. Cf. *L* 5:193–94
and n. 34, F.B. Sanborn to RWE,
from Montreal, 24 Jan. 1860.

John Forbes's eldest son Will: Pier,
Forbes: Telephone Pioneer, 12–17;
ETE Letters 1:202–6.

416 "as I had already learned": *ETE Letters* 1:210.
"The other side of her": Ibid., 211.

417 "Emerson called on me": WW, *The Correspondence* 1:47–49.
"rough grisly Esaus": *L* 5:200 and n. 65.
he sent Whitman a copy: *JMN* 14:367.
"Emerson's objections to the 'outcast' ": Traubel, *With Walt Whitman in Camden* 1:50–51. Cf. 2:15–16, 3:321.

418 "Emerson, then in his prime": WW, *Prose Works 1892* 1:281, dated 10–13 Oct. 1881.
"as good a book left": Traubel, *With Walt Whitman in Camden* 3:439–40.
In another of his recollections: Ibid.
"Very few of our race": "Culture," *Conduct of Life, E Works* 6:165.
Thoreau's "fancy for Walt Whitman": *JMN* 15:238.

419 He was a slender stripling: *ETE Letters* 1:212, 214, 219.
a "treasury of gifts": *L* 5:210.
"crept . . . into something like safety": Ibid., 214. Cf. 209, 211–14.
the attack on Frank Sanborn: Sanborn, *Recollections of Seventy Years* 1:208–18, 222. See also *L* 5:210 and n. 119.

420 "Have you ever enjoyed": *ETE Letters* 1:212–13.
"a house in Concord was worth": *JMN* 14:350.
"Apple blossoms luxuriant": *ABA Jrnls* 2:326–27 and n. 2. See now *LMA Jrnls*, 99, 23 May 1860.
"I could never give much reality": *JMN* 14:355–56.
"I am yielding to a surer decomposition": "Old Age," *Society and Solitude, E Works* 7:323.
The problem of domestic help: *ETE Letters* 1:213–14.

421 "I have always regretted your leaving us": ETE, *Life of Lidian*, 72.

"O, George, it is idle": Quoted in Saxton, *Louisa May*, 254.
"I have nothing to say of Parker": *L* 5:220–21, 6 June 1860.
"the theological underbrush": Commager, *Theodore Parker*, 285.

422 "I like the successes of George Stephenson": *JMN* 14:175 and n. 146.
"At the death of a good": "Theodore Parker," *E Works* 11:286–87, 289–90, 293.

423 "unchanged in aspect": NH to Henry Arthur Bright, 17 Dec. 1860, quoted in Mellow, *Nathaniel Hawthorne*, 539. See also *L* 5:222 and *ABA Jrnls* 2:328–29. See now *L* 9:19–20 and n. 53.
"wrinkled with time and trouble": Mellow, *Nathaniel Hawthorne*, 516.
"a monotonous life": Ibid., 539.
"He had the look": Ibid., 540–41. See now *L* 9:41–42 and nn. 29–32, for RWE's response to Henry James Sr., 29 Mar. 1861.
the publication of his fourth major romance: Mellow, *Nathaniel Hawthorne*, 525–27.

424 "most original and admirable": Leyda, *Melville Log* 2:617, 621.
geography of his Concord domain: *HDT Jrnl* [old style] 20:3–68 passim; *HDT Corres*, 567, 576–77, 583–84, 586, 591.
he and Ellery climbed in the rain: *HDT Jrnl* [old style] 20:78–86; *HDT Corres*, 591–92.
Emerson and Caroline had kept in touch: Dimock, *CST and the Grand Tour*, 65–67.
Much of their correspondence: See, for example, *L* 5:87.

425 a "pair of beautiful days": *L* 5:223–24. See now *L* 9:20 and n. 54.
"was pompously eaten": *ETE Letters* 1:216.
"a cornucopia of golden joys": *JMN* 14:357.

Edith Emerson's lawn party: Lathrop,
Memories of Hawthorne, 428.

like a recurrence of the disease:
Mellow, *Nathaniel Hawthorne*,
510–11.

summoned a female therapist: Ibid.,
537.

Emerson, who had known the girl:
Listed in *L* 5:226–27.

426 "after emperors and kings and
queens": *HDT Jrnl* [old style]
20:114.

"Queenie's private earthquake": *JMN*
14:335.

"sublime, the pronunciation of the
masses": Ibid., 363.

his admiration for Agassiz: *JMN*
15:237, 251, 281, 351–52, 437,
440.

"the last and most important": *JMN*
14:363.

427 "Concord Court and Town-houses":
EWE, *Emerson in Concord*, 109–10
n. 1.

"This is my boast": *JMN* 14:258.

Thoreau "took a severe cold": *HDT
Corres*, 609, HDT to Daniel
Ricketson, 22 Mar. 1861.

Chapter 42:
IN TIME OF WAR

428 "Blessed be the inevitabilities": *JMN*
15:91.

"The mob roared": Ibid., 111.

"It must be sung": Saxton, *Louisa
May*, 268. See now *LMA Jrnls*, 104
for other version of RWE's words
and *The Selected Letters of LMA*,
62–63 for her account of the
event.

429 "Alas that Fort Sumter": *ETE Letters*
1:228–32, 238–44.

He composed a new lecture,
"Civilization at a Pinch": Cabot,
Memoir of RWE 2:600–1.

On April 19 they assembled at noon:
L 5:246.

They listened to short speeches: *ABA
Jrnls* 2:338–39.

430 "the 19th of April this year": *ETE
Letters* 1:244.

Eddy was soon practicing: Ibid.,
250–51.

"we all seem like one family": Saxton,
Louisa May, 269. See now *LMA
Jrnls*, 105. See also Mellow,
Nathaniel Hawthorne, 542.

Hawthorne told his publisher: Ibid.,
542–43.

Alcott chose to cultivate his garden:
ABA Jrnls 2:339.

to hear Emerson lecture in Boston:
ETE Letters 1:247–49.

Ellen Emerson brought him a map:
Ibid., 250.

"praying them, from me": *HDT
Corres*, 616. See now *L* 9:47.

Except for a long letter: *HDT Corres*,
618–22.

431 "Never deserted by his good genius":
Channing, *Thoreau, the Poet
Naturalist*, 336, 339–40.

dictated his correspondence: *HDT
Corres*, 636–40, 645.

"lively and entertaining": *ABA Jrnls*
2:341.

"I am ever threatened": *JMN* 15:165.

"the losses which his advice": *L* 5:250
n. 63.

"Everything shines with us": Ibid.,
250–51.

"the model Massachusetts Captain":
ETE Letters 1:252–55.

"although not the echo": CST to
RWE, 2 July 1861, Smith College
Archives.

432 "The war,—though from such
despicable": *L* 5:252–53, 4 Aug.
1861.

"Our poor Edward": *ETE Letters*
1:262.

"the Hudson's Bay Company": *L*
5:256–57.

433 "I believe all wise fathers": Ibid., 258.

"always dreaming of a commission":
    Ibid., 263.
"we are all knitting socks": Ibid., 259.
"The South calls slavery":
    "Nationality," *E Works*
    11:297–300, 307–10.
"The President impressed me": *JMN*
    15:187.
434 Emerson called on William H.
    Seward: Ibid., 188–89.
"pretty daughter Kate": Ibid., 191.
"would not demoralize me": Ibid.,
    193–95.
He had been reading Senator
    Sumner's speech: Ibid., 194, 190
    n. 77.
435 "intended to show his respect": Ibid.,
    195.
to his hotel "at a late hour": Ibid.,
    195–99.
all the Concord women: *ETE Letters*
    1:266–67.
Alcott took cider and apples: *ABA
    Jrnls* 2:343. See also Harding, *Days
    of HT*, 456.
"enjoying existence as much as ever":
    Quoted in Harding, *Days of HT*,
    457.
All his visitors noticed: Ibid., 456–66
    passim.
Walden Pond was still frozen: *JMN*
    15:249.
"It is better": Quoted in Harding,
    Days of HT, 462.
on the morning of May 6: Ibid.,
    466–68. See also Lathrop,
    Memories of Hawthorne, 431 for
    SPH's entry on the funeral.
436 by setting out overland for California:
    L 5:263, 271–91 passim; *JMN*
    15:251–52, 256.
spent most of July at Newport: *L*
    5:282–85.
a lively brood: Edel, *Henry James: The
    Untried Years*, 40, 170.
"We are staying at the Jameses' now":
    ETE Letters 1:291–92, 297.
437 "There at Portsmouth Grove": Ibid.,
    275–84, 288–91, 295–97.

"We walked up on the ramparts":
    Ibid., 284–86.
"Your report is admirable": *L* 5:281.
"Henry T. remains erect": *JMN*
    15:261–62.
In his article for the *Atlantic*: RWE,
    "Thoreau," *Atlantic Monthly* 10
    (Aug. 1862): 239–40, 249.
Ellen explained it to him: *ETE Letters*
    1:274.
438 "The war drags on": *L* 5:280.
"the children of our public schools":
    JMN 15:211 and n. 120.
"Will you send them to die": Ibid., 334.
"One omen is best": *JMN* 15:171 and
    n. 9. RWE quotes the *Iliad*, 12,
    243, in Greek, but it is translated
    here, in n. 9, as it appears in *E
    Works* 8:33 and 10:13.
"Emerson is breathing slaughter":
    Mellow, *Nathaniel Hawthorne*,
    544.
"Every step in the history": "Address
    on the Emancipation
    Proclamation," *E Works* 11:315,
    319–21.
"his sole duty and necessity": *L* 5:291.
"He is not a soldier": Ibid., 290.
439 "The boy has much fitness": Ibid.,
    292.
"Edward lives in clover": *ETE Letters*
    1:301.
"often and aloud": Ibid., 300.

Chapter 43:
GRANDEUR AND DUST

440 "Today unbind the captive": "Boston
    Hymn," *E Works* 9:201–4. Cf.
    Fields, *Authors and Friends*, 95 for
    her recollection of the event.
"We had the usual solemn breakfast":
    ETE Letters 1:306–7.
441 Ellen's semiadopted "daughter": ETE,
    Life of Lidian, 145.
he had recently "fetched up": WW,

The Correspondence 1:61; *L* 5:302, WW to RWE, 29 Dec. 1862.

"I was pulling eminent wires": Traubel, *With Walt Whitman in Camden* 2:414–15.

He spent Sunday January 4: *L* 5:304–5 and nn. 3, 8.

"marked eccentricities": WW, *The Correspondence* 1:64–65, WW to Salmon P. Chase; Kaplan, *Walt Whitman*, 273–75. RWE's letter to Chase listed *L* 5:302. See now *L* 9:93 and n. 2 for full text.

442 "a child of the people": WW, *The Correspondence* 1:65–66, WW to William H. Seward. RWE's letter to Seward listed *L* 5:303. See now *L* 9:92–93 and n. 1 for full text and *L* 9:94, RWE to WW, 12 Jan. 1863, and listing of RWE to Charles Sumner. Cf. *JMN* 15:379.

"decidedly disreputable": Trowbridge, *My Own Story*, 377–81.

he landed a clerkship: Kaplan, *Walt Whitman*, 303–6.

she fell ill with typhoid: Saxton, *Louisa May*, 255–56.

"I see not how": *ABA Jrnls* 2:353–55. See now *LMA Jrnls*, 115–17.

443 "I forsook the housekeeping": *ETE Letters* 1:307–8.

"In so many later years": *L* 5:325–26 and nn. 102, 103. Order of quoted material slightly altered by CHB. Cf. *ETE Letters* 1:310.

444 as a member of the "Board of Visitors": *L* 5:329–31 and nn. 114, 127.

these "military monks": *JMN* 15:215–18 for RWE's visit to West Point.

an "alert, inquisitive farmer": Cabot, *A Memoir of RWE* 2:613.

Colonel Prescott, despite wounds: "Dedication of Soldiers' Monument in Concord," *E Works* 11:370.

savage riots against the draft: *L* 5:333 and n. 136.

near William Emerson's new residence: Ibid., 326 n. 104.

heard that young Wilky James: Ibid., 335 and n. 147; *ETE Letters* 1:311; Edel, *Henry James: A Life*, 61–62.

445 "Voluntaries," sent to Shaw's parents: Noted *L* 5:336. See now *L* 9:113–14 and n. 64 for full text of letter.

"So nigh is grandeur to our dust": "Voluntaries," *E Works* 9:207, 470.

Among the other casualties: *L* 5:277 n. 56.

"I think daily": Ibid., 331–32 and n. 129.

Forbes had been actively engaged: Pier, *Forbes: Telephone Pioneer*, 18–20; *L* 5:337 and n. 156.

"backed by a million pounds of credit": Ibid., 337 n. 154; Forbes, *Letters and Recollections* 2:5–48.

446 "We have been off": Pier, *Forbes: Telephone Pioneer*, 37–40.

Will afterward called this: Ibid., 41–42.

"the author of a multitude": "Lincoln," *E Works* 11:333–34.

447 "I can never have any hope": Pier, *Forbes: Telephone Pioneer*, 8, 15.

Ellen's wartime letters: *ETE Letters* 1:313–14.

"a morbid condition almost epidemic": *L* 5:352.

a doctor named Charles Schieferdecker: Ibid., 343 n. 178, 346 and n. 2, 348, 351 and n. 23. See now *L* 9:126.

"such a vixen": *L* 5:340.

"She has such exuberant health": Ibid., 351 n. 23.

she gave up the exasperating baths: Ibid., 348, 351–53.

"It is a loss to them all": *ETE Letters* 1:313–14.

"indisposition to write": *ABA Jrnls* 2:362.

"pellucid but not deep": Fields, *Authors and Friends*, 72. Cf. Howe, *Memories of a Hostess*, 15 for

RWE's phrase as quoted in Annie
Fields' diary.
"unlucky in having for a friend": *JMN*
15:361.
448   Hawthorne joined Pierce: Mellow,
Nathaniel Hawthorne, 570–71.
"so haggard, so white": Ibid., 575–76.
he found Hawthorne as feeble: *L*
5:373.
"He seemed unequal to meeting
anyone": *ABA Jrnls* 2:363–64.
found that Hawthorne was dead:
Mellow, *Nathaniel Hawthorne*,
577.
"Yesterday, 23 May, we buried
Hawthorne": *JMN* 15:59–60. Cf.
Lathrop *Memories of Hawthorne*,
455–56, RWE to SPH, 11 July
1864. See now *L* 9:147–48 and nn.
73–76 for full text.
449   "Fair figures one by one": *ABA Jrnls*
2:364.
450   "a vast concourse of grateful": *ETE
Letters* 1:314.
Forbes was at the center of the action:
Pier, *Forbes: Telephone Pioneer*,
44–46, 51–56.
"It is the greatest loss": *ETE Letters*
1:314, 317.
451   "his family were shocked": Pier,
Forbes: Telephone Pioneer, 56.
"Even the ghosts didn't check": *ETE
Letters* 1:324.

Chapter 44: A FUNERAL
AND A WEDDING

452   "[Sat., Mar. 4] Inauguration WHF and
E.E.": *JMN* 15:527.
"My daughter Edith is engaged": *L*
5:407–8. See now *L* 9:173–74,
176–77 and nn. 25, 26, 34 for other
letters reporting Edith's
engagement.
"Will has always been": *ETE Letters*
1:334.

453   "In a manly character": *L* 5:410.
a "very funny letter": *ETE Letters*
1:339–40, 342.
the 2nd Massachusetts participated:
Pier, *Forbes: Telephone Pioneer*,
57–61.
the 32nd Regiment of Massachusetts:
"Dedication of Soldiers' Monument
in Concord," *E Works* 11:374.
"What a joyful day": *L* 5:412.
"The assassin Booth":
JMN 15:460.
"Even the poor prisoners": *JMN*
15:458, 471–72.
454   "Today we kept the funeral": *ETE
Letters* 1:342.
"On Saturday, every one was struck":
"Abraham Lincoln," *E Works*
11:329–38.
a volume of Thoreau's: HDT, *Letters
to Various Persons* (Boston: Ticknor
and Fields, 1865). For the dates, see
L 5:413 and nn. 57, 58.
455   "she was sure Mr. Emerson": Fields,
Authors and Friends, 68–69.
"That was the most splendid
fortnight": *ETE Letters* 1:343.
a handsome little book called *Emerson*:
ABA, *Emerson* (Cambridge;
Privately Printed, 1865). The
volume was published in 1882 as
*Ralph Waldo Emerson: An Estimate
of His Character and Genius in
Prose and Verse* and was reprinted
in 1888.
"Tis woe to think of poor Concord":
L 5:406 and n. 32; *ETE Letters*
1:329.
"the style and elegancy": *ABA Jrnls*
2:372.
456   "was such a Persian superlative":
RWE to Mary Preston Stearns, 5
July 1865, later printed as a preface
to ABA's *Ralph Waldo Emerson:
Philosopher and Seer* (Boston:
Cupples and Hurd, 1882), 2nd
edition, 1888, pp. v–vi. Listed *L*
5:421. See now *L* 9:190 and nn. 82,
83 for text.

"strong sense, happy humor": ABA, *Emerson*, 22, 31–32.

"ignoring the infirm actuality": *L* 9:190.

"Frankincense should be offered": For the Pythagoras "epigraph" see the 1968 reprint of the 1882 edition of the essay where it appears opposite the frontispiece.

gave it his "hearty assent": *ABA Jrnls* 2:370–72.

"the habit of action": "Character," *E Works* 10:120.

"the science of substances": Ibid., 91–92.

"truths that wake": "Ode: Intimations of Immortality from Recollections of Early Childhood," lines 156–57, 153–54.

"he affirms the Divinity in him": "Character," *E Works* 10:97–102.

457 "I consider theology": Ibid., 108, 112–14.

"emancipating the mind": ABA, *Emerson*, 32.

"not suited to the magazine": Howe, *Memories of a Hostess*, 67. See now *L* 9:186–89 and nn. 73, 78 on this issue.

it appeared some eight months later: *NAR* 102 (Apr. 1866): 356–73. Cf. *ABA Jrnls* 2:374.

making anonymous contributions: Edel, *Henry James: The Untried Years*, 200, 206–9, 245–46, 269 for references to these works.

Emerson was one of the speakers: "Harvard Commemoration Speech," *E Works* 11:341–45.

458 "The wedding," wrote Ellen: *ETE Letters* 1:345–46.

locally called the Cattle Show: *L* 5:425–26 and n. 106.

The wedding took place: *L* 5:426–27 and n. 111. See now *L* 9:197 and nn. 108–10.

459 "The whole place": Howe, ed., *Memories of a Hostess*, 91.

Lidian, ever mindful: ETE, *Life of Lidian*, 150.

"There are several very agreeable": *ETE Letters* 1:346–53; *L* 5:429–30 and n. 117.

Chapter 45: TALES OF A GRANDFATHER

460 Emerson had gone over to Ticknor and Fields: *JMN* 14:343; *L* 5:167, n. 137, 178, 190, 233, 336, 376–77 and nn. 126 and 128, 413, 415, 421. See now *L* 9:113 n. 62.

on "The Fortune of the Republic": *JMN* 15:xxii. See now von Frank, *An Emerson Chronology*, 390. "The Fortune of the Republic," *E Works* 11:509–44.

461 "a woman of proud integrity": Howe, ed., *Memories of a Hostess*, 89.

"I fear," he wrote to Annie: *L* 5:460.

The whole Emerson family: Ibid., 460 n. 79. See now *L* 9:219.

Emerson sometimes took a room: ETE, *Life of Lidian*, 145–48, 247 n. 302.

"I am to keep that month unengaged": *ETE Letters* 1:379.

the arrival of Edith's ten-pound boy: *L* 5:471–72 and n. 115.

462 "Good morning, Grandmother": *ETE Letters* 1:385–91.

with a citation that proclaimed him: *L* 5:470 n. 112.

"good graces of his Alma Mater": Howe, ed., *Memories of a Hostess*, 91.

the "small red creature": *ETE Letters* 1:389–90, 409.

Ellen sometimes feared for her life: ETE, *Life of Lidian*, 151.

"very unwell . . . utterly weak": *ETE Letters* 1:395–98, 406, 409, 412–15.

463 "Very little or no better": Ibid.,
   416–17.
   a "reviving presence": Ibid., 417.
   "In Boston," he wrote: *JMN* 16:76.
   "Here is Ralph": Ibid., 12.
   he faithfully carried an ambrotype: *L*
   5:544 and n. 266.
   "scattered verses": *L* 5:506–7.
   proofs contained so many errata: Ibid.,
   505–6.

464 and afterward to New York: *JMN*
   16:xxi.
   "We spent the night together": *E
   Works* 9:489–90.
   "It is time to be old": "Terminus," *E
   Works* 9:251–52.
   "Within, I do not find wrinkles": *JMN*
   15:416.
   "The grief of old age": Ibid., 422.
   "The brook sings on": "Fragments on
   the Poet and the Poetic Gift," *E
   Works* 9:332. Cf. *JMN* 15:135 and
   n. 147.

465 "I had been vexed": *L* 5:479–80 and
   n. 155.
   "After all the fuss": *ETE Letters* 1:438.
   sent out a hundred gift copies: *JMN*
   16:56–61.
   "Come the tumult whence it will":
   May-Day, E Works 9:164, 181.

466 "We never know": *JMN* 9:347.
   "The days come and go": *JMN* 10:61,
   24 May 1847. Cf. *JMN* 10:104;
   JMN 11:21; *JMN* 13:348.
   "I find one state of mind": *JMN* 13:10.

467 "Daughters of Time": "Days," *E
   Works* 9:228.
   visit with his family to Pigeon Cove:
   JMN 14:100–1.
   an equally memorable versification:
   Ibid., 65–67, 94, 140–41.

468 A fourth memorable poem: "Two
   Rivers," *E Works* 9:248.
   "thr[ough] flood and sea": *JMN*
   14:140–41.
   "We see the river glide":
   JMN 7:499.
   displayed an unmistakable Wordsworthian influence: "Waldein-

samkeit," *E Works* 9:249–51. Cf.
   JMN 14:145–46, 161–62, 181–87.

469 "I am a bard least of bards": *JMN*
   15:308.

470 "I find it a great and fatal difference:
   JMN 16:25.

Chapter 46:
A FORCE AT WORK

471 When Ellen joined the Unitarian
   Church: *ETE Letters* 1:245.
   speeches to the Free Religious
   Association: "Free Religious
   Association," *E Works* 11:477–81.
   "the author of Nature": Ibid., 485–91.
   Cf. *JMN* 16:151–52.

472 "What could we do": *E Works* 11:640.
   "The foundation of culture":
   "Progress of Culture," *E Works*
   8:205–34.
   "Difficulties exist to be surmounted":
   JMN 16:34.
   "could not get the frame": *L* 5:522
   and n. 164. See now *L* 9:277–78
   and nn. 61, 62.

473 "boggled . . . lost his place": Lowell,
   Letters, 393–94, Lowell to Charles
   Eliot Norton, 18 July 1867.
   "poor Mr. E's MSS.": Howe, ed.,
   Memories of a Hostess, 92–93.
   elected to the Board of Overseers:
   JMN 16:xxii.
   Despite a bout of erysipelas: *L* 5:511.
   presented a brilliant speech: *JMN*
   16:xxi.
   In this warm-hearted commentary:
   "Dedication of Soldiers' Monument
   in Concord," *E Works* 11:349–79.

474 time and effort to raising funds: *L*
   6:71–72. See now *L* 9:342–43 and
   n. 18 for original version.
   "her idol and Storrow's, too": *ETE
   Letters* 1:439–40.
   "Mother is in the first place": Ibid.,
   444–45.

"as of old suffering": Ibid., 442, 28 June 1867.

Ellen and Eddy went to Naushon: Ibid., 446, 19 Sept. 1867; *JMN* 16:xxii.

"asked if the sun": *ETE Letters* 1:447–48, 5 Oct. 1867.

475 "I no longer canter": Ibid., 449.

the "size, strength, and furious activity": Ibid., 461.

assumption of a "Society-face": *JMN* 16:77.

The faithful Ellen sent her father: *ETE Letters* 1:452–54.

"he should be scared": *JMN* 10:255, 333, 550–51.

"I know a man": *JMN* 16:116.

"Now I am firmly rooted": *ETE Letters* 1:466–71.

"Why is this girl": *JMN* 16:116.

476 Will Forbes had set up: *ETE Letters* 1:461; Pier, *Forbes: Telephone Pioneer*, 70–79.

Ellen was faithfully attentive: *ETE Letters* 1:472, 476–77.

he took Ellen to New York: *L* 6:12. See now *L* 9:309 for New York visit.

Illnesses of various degrees: *L* 6:13, 15, 17, 20.

the summer was full of arrivals and departures: *L* 6:25–27, 30–31. See now *L* 9:314–15 and n. 46.

Defying Dr. Bartlett's orders: *ETE Letters* 1:475–78, 483–85, 488–500.

477 on a trip to Middlebury, Vermont: *JMN* 16:119–22.

Haven wrote Ellen: *ETE Letters* 1:506.

"Send me I pray you": *L* 6:31.

William's answer on September 4: Ibid., n. 128.

"much altered in face and in speech": Ibid., 33.

wished to be buried in Concord: Ibid., 33–35 and n. 138. See now *L* 9:318–19.

his benefactor Abel Adams: *L* 5:528–29 and n. 195.

the wise and learned Sarah Alden Ripley: Ibid., 523 and n. 165.

"The few stout and sincere persons": *JMN* 16:142.

478 Ras the invincible: *ETE Letters* 1:487 and plate opposite.

"I am the worst speaker known": *L* 6:17.

"My pen of late creeps": Ibid., 37–38.

"rambling and incoherent": Ibid., 35 n. 144.

"alive and alert": Howe, ed., *Memories of a Hostess*, 94–95.

against the late W. T. G. Morton: On Jackson-Morton controversy, see *L* 4:57 and n. 206, and *L* 5:57, 317, 367–68.

"it is a pure benediction": Howe, ed., *Memories of a Hostess*, 94–95.

"touches of light which dropped": Fields, *Authors and Friends*, 78.

"The Hawthornes are breaking up housekeeping": *ETE Letters* 1:508.

Sophia had sold the Wayside: Mellow, *Nathaniel Hawthorne*, 585–86.

Ellery had sold his house: McGill, *Channing of Concord*, 160–61.

479 writing career of Louisa May: Saxton, *Louisa May*, 326. See now *LMA Jrnls* 1:118.

"a bolt fell from a clear sky": *ETE Letters* 1:509–10.

The delay enabled Ellen: Ibid., 510–11.

She found Fayal "an earthly Paradise": Ibid., 511–23.

480 Caroline Tappan wrote from Lenox: CST to RWE, 8 Nov. 1868, Smith College Archives.

missed his "invalided daughter": *L* 6:45, 63.

a series of "readings" at Chickering Hall: Ibid., 52 and n. 2.

"Mother says every day": *ETE Letters* 1:434.

"much the largest sum": *L* 6:55.

sent him an advance payment: Ibid., 48. See also *L* 6:45–46, 52–53, 55, 58.

Chapter 47: THE HIGH MUSE COMES AND GOES

483 "one hold on health": *ETE Letters* 1:530.

Eddy was also there: Ibid., 533–35, 537.

"letter dinner party": Ibid., 537.

"magnificently ugly": James, *Letters of Henry James* 1:116, 10 May [1869].

484 "I am extremely glad": Ibid., 179, 27 Dec. 1869.

"never had so many tasks": *L* 6:75.

for a two-volume edition: Ibid., 78 and n. 112.

for a seventh book of prose: *JMN* 16:147 n. 117, 148–50.

serving as agent for the Class of 1821: *L* 6:69, 71–74, and see now *L* 9:345 and n. 29 for RWE to John Boynton Hill, 25 June 1869.

a "University Lecturer" during the spring of 1870: *JMN* 16:394–95.

a "remarkably friendly speech": *L* 6:78 n. 110.

an extensive correspondence with Emma Lazarus: *L* 6:6–144 passim.

celebration of the birth of Alexander von Humboldt: *L* 6:86 n. 135; *E Works* 11:457–59.

"Father is pompous in his study": *ETE Letters* 1:538.

"Mother very feeble": Ibid., 554.

485 "It has been and is": *L* 6:116.

"We are rejoiced": Ibid., 117.

"a spacious rubicund face": *ETE Letters* 1:556.

"very sick and anxious": Ibid., 560–61.

Henry remarked that on coming home: Edel, *Henry James: A Life*, 112, 120–21.

"pleasantly, but with slender profit": James, *Partial Portraits*, Greenwood reprint, 1970, p. 9.

a new edition of the *Morals: L* 6:128 and n. 136; *JMN* 16:101–226 passim, indexed at 567.

486 "collected all the authors": *ETE Letters* 1:568.

"great hill" of Mount Washington: *L* 6:131.

with an essay of 6,000 words: "Plutarch," *E Works* 10:293–322.

"We are always interested": Ibid., 298, 306–7.

487 "a readable, useful introduction": Berry, *Emerson's Plutarch*, 48–54.

"At first more shocked": *L* 6:147.

"I am helping Edith off": *ETE Letters* 1:583.

488 James B. Thayer was a lawyer: For references to James B. Thayer, see *L* 5:394, 400, 425–26, 466; *L* 6:43, 53, 166, 169, 212–13, 255–56.

His record of the trip: Thayer, *A Western Journey*, 14–15.

"a volume on my own table": *JMN* 16:224.

the whole party of twelve: Thayer, *A Western Journey*, 10, 24, 28–29.

"the squaws and papooses begging": *C-E-C*, 578–82.

under the rubric "Good out of evil": *JMN* 15:379.

He received them with stolid dignity: Thayer, *A Western Journey*, 33–39.

489 "after-clap of Puritanism": *C-E-C*, 582.

Thayer recalled the opening: Thayer, *A Western Journey*, 48.

He took Emerson, Edith, and Thayer: *L* 6:152–53, 159–60.

"accidentally overturned a vase": Ibid., 152 n. 30.

to cover the distance by train, wagon: Thayer, *A Western Journey*, 53–58.

490 a Bostonian named Roberts: *JMN* 16:410.

"he was lonesome without tobacco": *JMN* 16:20.

his cigar "a singular comfort": Thayer, *A Western Journey*, 61, 66.

the riders transferred to horseback: Ibid., 68–83.

prostrate sugar pine: *JMN* 16:409.

"This valley," said he: Thayer, *A Western Journey*, 76, 83.

But he left note taking: Ibid., 15–88
  passim.
received a letter from a young Scot: *L*
  6:154–55 for John Muir to RWE, 8
  May 1871. See also *L* 6:155–57 for
  Muir to RWE after his visit to
  Yosemite.
Thayer and Emerson rode over: Ibid.,
  88–95.

491 "pumping unconscionably": Badè,
  Life and Letters of John Muir
  1:252–55.
"He kept me talking all the time":
  Ibid., 255.
"He was always accessible": Thayer, *A
  Western Journey*, 96–109.
"Emerson," he wrote afterward: Badè,
  Life and Letters of John Muir
  1:255–57.
Emerson and most of the others:
  Thayer, *A Western Journey*,
  120–22; *JMN* 16:408–11.

492 "Edward is better": *L* 6:153.
"The town," wrote Ellen: *ETE Letters*
  1:585–93; ETE, *Life of Lidian*,
  156–57.
Emerson slept at the Manse: *JMN*
  16:411.
"in many distractions": *C-E-C*,
  581–82.
"We must not visit San Francisco":
  Fields, *Authors and Friends*, 101–2.

*Chapter 18: THE SLOPES
OF PARNASSUS*

494 "Ah Solidarity! ah Comitatus!": *JMN*
  13:95.
"Is the Club exclusive": *JMN* 16:244.
"a society of friends": *JMN* 15:51.
Emerson quoted Thomas Hobbes:
  JMN 13:89–90.
"large, discursive, happy talk": *JMN*
  15:304–5.
"among the good subjects": *JMN*
  14:110, 478.

495 "Of all the cordials known to us":
  "Clubs," *Society and Solitude*, E
  Works 7:225–37.
"When a man meets his accurate
  mate": *JMN* 15:42.
If this "sometimes too visible": *JMN*
  16:158.
once told Elizabeth Hoar: Cabot, *A
  Memoir of RWE* 2:623.
"spontaneous hospitality of mind":
  Ibid.
"shoulders raised": Ibid., 620.
for Shakespeare's 300th: *JMN* 15:40,
  49–50.
"rarely attempted the smallest speech":
  Cabot, *A Memoir of RWE* 2:621.
it was his habit: See now *L* 7:232–33.
  See also EWE, *The Early Years of
  the Saturday Club*, 342 and
  n. 1.

496 "How dared you carry": *L* 6:176,
  6 Sept. 1871.
"warmth, water, wild air": EWE,
  Emerson in Concord, 166.
"pretty nearly well": *ETE Letters*
  1:598.
the announcement of his engagement:
  Ibid., 602, 606.
vacationed briefly at Naushon: *L*
  6:178.
with letters of introduction: Ibid.,
  174–75, 189; *C-E-C*, 584.
Will and Edith's fourth child: *ETE
  Letters* 1:601–2.
"Ellen and Edward agree": *L* 6:176.
Edith had been helping: Ibid., 164,
  174–77.
short address on Sir Walter Scott:
  "Walter Scott," *E Works*
  11:463–67.

497 whose son had lost his right arm: *JMN*
  16:240 and n. 84.
his daughter proudly exhibited: *ETE
  Letters* 1:604, 608.
to postpone the publication: *L*
  6:177–79.
a preface for Ellery Channing's new
  blank-verse poem: Ibid., 188 and
  n. 182.

"The trouble with him": Thayer, *A Western Journey*, 117.

"We have not been considered": *JMN* 16:246. See also Sanborn, introd. to WEC, *Poems of Sixty-five Years*, xxvi; McGill, *Channing of Concord*, 165–66; *ETE Letters* 1:608.

reviewing the poem and the preface: *L* 6:188 n. 183.

"frugally supported": Sanborn, introd. to WEC, *Poems of Sixty-five Years*, xxx, xliii.

"was never in the least contented": Channing, *Thoreau: The Poet-Naturalist*, 132 and note.

498 "There is no strong performance": Cabot, *A Memoir of RWE* 2:779.

Ellen took her to consult: *ETE Letters* 1:606–7, 610–11, 615, 620, 622–23, 629, 636–38, 647.

Bret Harte's visit in October: *L* 6:183 and n. 153.

" 'Tis wonderful how soon a piano": "Civilization," *Society and Solitude*, *E Works* 7:21.

499 it was the gamblers: *JMN* 16:247.

she and her sister Edith were there: *ETE Letters* 1:612–13, 619.

with a two-week trip to the Midwest: *L* 6:187 and n. 171.

he reported to his son, Eddy: Ibid., 188.

he forgot the name of his hotel: Ibid., 193 and n. 1.

"Walt Whitman presented his picturesque person": Ibid., 193 and n. 3.

500 "not interesting to me at all": WW, *The Correspondence* 2:150.

"It all seems to me quite attenuated": Ibid., 155.

"Emerson's lectures were full of idealism": Barrus, *Whitman and Burroughs, Comrades*, 66. See also *L* 6:193 n. 3 where Rusk corrects Barrus's error from 1871 to 1872.

Emerson sent him a copy of *May-Day*: *JMN* 16:59.

John Trowbridge, another young

admirer: WW, *Leaves of Grass*, Nonesuch Edition, ed. Holloway, 1938, p. 657. WW repeated this information to Horace Traubel, 1888. See Traubel, *With Walt Whitman in Camden* 1:101–2.

a message from Senator Charles Sumner: *L* 6:194.

501 "compelled by an artifice": Ibid., 195.

"What Books to Read": Ibid., 195 and n. 16.

Back in Baltimore: Ibid., 196 and n. 20.

to pay a call on his fiancée: Ibid., 196–97 and n. 22–23.

"I drew him out on Walt": Barrus, *Whitman and Burroughs, Comrades*, 63.

whose wounded feelings were exacerbated: Kaplan, *Walt Whitman*, 353–58.

"too great prudence": WW, "A Christmas Garland, in Prose and Verse," *New York Daily Graphic*, 25 Dec. 1874, reprinted in *Prose Works*, ed. Stovall, 1964, 2:258–59.

Will and Edith, with their four children: ETE, *Life of Lidian*, 157–59; *ETE Letters* 1:631–33.

502 "Well, I sat at the lecture": Ibid., 658.

"I can't tell its name": Cabot, *A Memoir of RWE* 2:652.

dated the onset of the difficulty: Ibid., 648–49.

"He forgets names of people": *ETE Letters* 1:666.

"a man who had lost his wits": Cabot, *A Memoir of RWE* 2:652.

"to read with intelligence": Ibid.

503 "decay of some of the vital machinery": Ibid., 651.

"insuperable difficulty": Ibid., 655.

sorrowful lamentation: *Hamlet* 3.1.

"If I should live another year": *JMN* 16:274.

"Spring still makes spring": "The World-Soul," *E Works* 9:19.

Chapter 49:
AMONG THE RUINS

504   with his "heart of oak": *ETE Letters*
1:670.

Emerson came awake to the smell of
smoke: Ibid., 676–82 passim;
Cabot, *A Memoir of RWE* 2:653–55;
ETE, *Life of Lidian*, 159–60; *L*
6:214 n. 86.

505   Lidian took to bed: *ETE Letters* 1:682.

"rude experience to an old
housekeeper": *L* 6:214–15.

He thanked the Fire Department:
Ibid., 215.

accepted Judge Hoar's offer: Ibid.;
Cabot, *A Memoir of RWE* 2:655;
ETE, *Life of Lidian*, 160.

"Every day he went there": Ibid. Cf.
LJE to Annie Fields, 31 July 1872
in Howe, ed., *Memories of a Hostess*,
88.

Will Forbes, war hero, businessman:
Pier, *Forbes: Telephone Pioneer*, 96.

506   "We are all so interested": *ETE Letters*
1:670.

Ellen hurried him off: Ibid., 685–92; *L*
6:217 and nn. 93, 95.

"an imbecile most of the time": Cabot,
A Memoir of RWE 2:708.

"charred and broken house": *L* 6:216.

An architect relative: ETE, *Life of
Lidian*, 161; *L* 6:218 and n. 101;
JMN 16:278 and n. 176.

Ellen composed a letter: *ETE Letters*
2:75–76, 1:691; Rusk, *Life of RWE*,
455–56.

"This late calamity": Cabot, *A Memoir
of RWE* 2:706.

contributions from dozens of admirers:
Ibid., 654, 705–8; *L* 6:220.

Eddy was still studying: See now LJE,
Letters of Lidian, 285–86.

a "rainbow" hope: *L* 6:225.

507   the Emersons converged upon
Naushon: *ETE Letters* 1:693–701;
L 6:220–21.

Emerson booked passage: Ibid.,
224–25; *ETE Letters* 2:4–10.

his "well known orthodoxy": *L* 6:225.

She replied, also ironically: Ibid., 225
n. 126. See now LJE, *Letters of
Lidian*, 285–86.

508   Ellen thought that her brother: *ETE
Letters* 2:12–14.

at a testimonial banquet:
L 6:222.

a graceful extempore speech: Ibid.,
226 n. 130.

room at Number 11, Down Street:
Ibid., 226 n. 130 and 227 n. 132.

invitations poured in and callers
abounded: Ibid., 226 and n. 130;
ETE Letters 2:74–77.

Another devotee was Charles King
Newcomb: *Newcomb Jrnls*, introd.
30–34.

at the Glendower Hotel:
JMN 16:274.

he had offered Emerson a gift: Listed
L 6:220 and see *L* 6:226
n. 130.

Charles's failure to live up to his early
promise: Sherman Paul, *Emerson's
Angle of Vision*, 252 n. 33.

"one of the subtlest minds": *JMN*
16:94.

Another permanent expatriate:
Mellow, *Nathaniel Hawthorne*,
585–86.

he and Ellen went to see: *ETE Letters*
2:16–17.

509   his reunion with Carlyle: *C-E-C*, 549
and plate 7.

"persons, events, and opinions": *L*
6:226–27.

Awaiting their arrival in Paris: *JMN*
16:435, 289 n. 194.

the very region he had revisited: Ibid.,
274.

"I hate Egypt": *ETE Letters*
2:18–21.

the ensuing month was replete: *L*
6:227–29 and n. 134.

510   they were whisked away: *ETE Letters*
2:24–30.

in the company of the Harvard
historian: Adams, *Letters of Henry*

Adams 1:229–40 for account of travels.

never able to catch up with the Wards: *L* 6:235–36.

"Cairo and the Pyramids": *JMN* 16:294–95.

"The feeling," said Ellen: *ETE Letters* 2:75–76.

in the chivalrous company of George Bancroft: *L* 6:230–32.

511   the boughs of a banyan tree: *JMN* 16:285.

they boarded the dahabeah *Aurora:* Ibid., 286.

"the only traveller on the Nile": *L* 6:235.

she went ashore nearly every day: *ETE Letters* 2:30–38, 49, 52, 56.

512   Their last social engagement: Ibid., 56–57.

one was named Theodore: Roosevelt, *Diaries of Boyhood and Youth* (New York, 1928), p. 309.

Their gradual return homeward: *ETE Letters* 2:58–60, 62–64, 166–68.

"Alas, dear Lidian": *L* 6:234.

513   The wonder was: *ETE Letters* 2:75–87.

his chief companion was Charles Eliot Norton: Norton, *The Letters of Charles Eliot Norton* 1:484, 501–14 passim.

Epilogue

515   "Was it a public day": Rusk, *Ralph Waldo Emerson*, 480.

"a novelty in the history": Ibid.

"Arrived home at Concord": *L* 6:243.

"with the usual effects": McAleer, *Ralph Waldo Emerson*, 620–21.

516   "Now for near five years": RWE, *Heart of Emerson's Journals*, ed. Perry, 154–55.

"Alone with us": Rusk, *Ralph Waldo Emerson*, 456.

"I can't tell its name": McAleer, *Ralph Waldo Emerson*, 628; Baker, *Emerson Among the Eccentrics*, 502.

"Strange that the kind Heavens": McAleer, Ralph Waldo Emerson, 630.

"an old man fears most": *L* 6:296.

517   "Why these things are really very good": McAleer, *Ralph Waldo Emerson*, 630.

"a more substantial return": Ibid., 638.

518   "The instinct had been always there": EWE, *Emerson in Concord*, 191.

"Where are we?": Allen, *Waldo Emerson: A Biography*, 668.

"Sickness . . . is a cannibal": McAleer, *Ralph Waldo Emerson*, 658.

"He did not know how to be sick": EWE, *Emerson in Concord*, 194.

"clerical consecration": Mellow, *Nathaniel Hawthorne*, 213.

519   "I said when I awoke": EWE, *Emerson in Concord*, 195–96.

BIBLIOGRAPHY

Adams, Henry. *Letters of Henry Adams.* 2 vols. Edited by W. C. Ford. Boston, New York: Houghton Mifflin, 1930, 1938.

Albee, John. *Remembrances of Emerson.* New York: Grafton Press, 1901. Rpt., Folcroft, Pa.: Folcroft Library Editions, 1973.

Alcott, Amos Bronson. *Concord Days.* Boston: Roberts Brothers, 1872.

———. *The Journals of Bronson Alcott.* Selected and edited by Odell Shepard. 2 vols. Boston: Little, Brown, 1938.

———. *The Letters of A. Bronson Alcott.* Edited by Richard L. Herrnstadt. Ames, Iowa: Iowa State University Press, 1969.

———. *Ralph Waldo Emerson: An Estimate of His Character and Genius in Prose and Verse.* Cambridge: privately printed, 1865.

———. *Ralph Waldo Emerson: Philosopher and Seer.* Boston: Cupples and Hurd, 1882. 2nd ed. 1888.

Alcott, Louisa May. *The Journals of Louisa May Alcott.* Edited by Joel Myerson and Daniel Shealy. Introduction by Madeleine B. Stern. 2 vols. Boston: Little, Brown, 1989.

———. *Louisa May Alcott: Her Life, Letters, and Journals.* Edited by Ednah D. Cheney. Boston: Roberts Brothers, 1889; Boston: Little, Brown, 1924.

———. *The Selected Letters of Louisa May Alcott.* Edited by Joel Myerson and Daniel Shealy. Introduction by Madeleine B. Stern. Boston: Little, Brown, 1987.

Alcott-Pratt Collection, Houghton Library, Cambridge, Mass.

Allen, Gay Wilson. *Waldo Emerson: A Biography.* New York: Viking Press, 1981.

Anthony, Katharine S. *Dolly Madison: Her Life and Times.* Garden City, N.Y.: Doubleday, 1949.

Badè, William Frederic. *Life and Letters of John Muir.* 2 vols. Boston, New York: Houghton Mifflin, 1924.

Baker, Carlos H. "Emerson and Jones Very." *New England Quarterly* 7 (March 1934): 90–99.

Baldwin, David. "The Emerson-Ward Friendship: Ideals and Realities." *Studies in the American Renaissance 1984.* Edited by Joel Meyerson. Charlottesville, Va.: University Press of Virginia, 299–324.

Barker, Jacob. *Incidents in the Life of Jacob Barker of New Orleans, Louisiana; With Historical Facts; His financial transactions with the Government and His Course on Important Political Questions from 1800-1855*. Freeport, N.Y.: Books for Libraries Press, 1970. Reprint of 1855 ed.

Barrus, Clara. *Whitman and Burroughs: Comrades*. Boston, New York: Houghton Mifflin, 1931.

Bartlett, William Irving. *Jones Very, Emerson's "Brave Saint."* Durham, N.C.: Duke University Press, 1942.

Bedell, Madelon. *The Alcotts: Biography of a Family*. New York: C. N. Potter, Crown Publishers, 1980.

Berg Collection: New York Public Library. New York, N.Y.

Berry, Edmund Grindlay. *Emerson's Plutarch*. Cambridge, Mass.: Harvard University Press, 1961.

Birdsall, Richard D. *Berkshire County: A Cultural History*. New Haven: Yale University Press, 1959.

Blanchard, Paula. *Margaret Fuller: From Transcendentalism to Revolution*. New York: Delacorte, 1978.

Borst, Raymond R. *The Thoreau Log: A Documentary Life of Henry David Thoreau 1817-1862*. New York: G. K. Hall, 1992.

Bremer, Fredrika. *The Homes of the New World: Impressions of America*. Translated by Mary Howitt. 2 vols. New York: Harpers, 1853; London: A. Hall, Virtue, 1853.

Burkholder, Robert E., and Joel Myerson. *Emerson: An Annotated Secondary Bibliography*. Pittsburgh, Pa.: University of Pittsburgh Press, 1985.

Cabot, James Elliot. *A Memoir of Ralph Waldo Emerson*. 2 vols. Boston: Houghton, Mifflin, 1887.

Cameron, Kenneth Walter. *The Transcendentalists and Minerva: Cultural Backgrounds of the American Renaissance with Fresh Discoveries in the Intellectual Climate of Emerson, Alcott, Thoreau*. 3 vols. Hartford, Conn.: Transcendental Books, 1958.

Capper, Charles. *Margaret Fuller: An American Romantic Life*, vol. 1: *The Private Years*. New York; Oxford: Oxford University Press, 1992.

Carlyle, Thomas. *The French Revolution: A History*. 3 vols. London: Chapman and Hall, 1870.

Carové, Friedrich Wilhelm. *The Story Without an End [Marchen Ohne Ende]*. Translated by Sarah Austin. Boston [1836]; Boston: D. Estes, 1899.

Carpenter, Edward. *Days with Walt Whitman*. London: G. Allen, 1906.

Chadwick, John White. *Theodore Parker: Preacher and Reformer*. Boston: Houghton, Mifflin, 1900.

Channing, William Ellery II. *The Collected Poems of William Ellery Channing the Younger, 1817-1901*. Edited by Walter Harding. Gainesville, Fla.: Scholars' Facsimiles and Reprints, 1967.

———. *Poems of Sixty-five Years*. Edited by F. B. Sanborn. Philadelphia and Concord, Mass.: James H. Bentley, 1902.

———. *Thoreau, the Poet Naturalist; With Memorial Verses*. Boston: Roberts, 1873. Enl. ed. edited by F. B. Sanborn. Boston: Charles E. Goodspeed, 1902.

Charvat, William. *Emerson's American Lecture Engagements: A Chronological List*. New York: New York Public Library, 1961.

Chevigny, Bell Gale, ed. *The Woman and the Myth: Margaret Fuller's Life and Writings*. Old Westbury, N.Y.: Feminist Press, 1976.

Chipperfield, Faith. *In Quest of Love: The Life and Death of Margaret Fuller.* New York: Coward-McCann, 1957.

Clarke, James Freeman. *Autobiography, Diary and Correspondence.* Edited by Edward Everett Hale. Boston: Houghton, Mifflin, 1891.

Collins, Robert E. *Theodore Parker: American Transcendentalist; A Critical Essay and a Collection of His Writings.* Metuchen, N.J.: Scarecrow Press, 1973.

Commager, Henry Steele. *Theodore Parker.* Boston: Little, Brown, 1936. Boston: Beacon Press, 1960 [with a new introduction].

Conway, Moncure Daniel. *Autobiography, Memories and Experiences of Moncure Daniel Conway.* 2 vols. Boston: Houghton, Mifflin, 1904; London: Cassell and Company, 1904.

———. *Emerson at Home and Abroad.* Boston: Houghton, Mifflin, 1883.

———. *Life of Nathaniel Hawthorne.* London: Walter Scott, 1890.

Cooke, George Willis. *An Historical and Biographical Introduction to Accompany the Dial.* 2 vols. Cleveland, Ohio: Rowfant Club, 1902.

Dahlstrand, Frederick C. *Amos Bronson Alcott: An Intellectual Biography.* Rutherford, N.J.: Fairleigh Dickinson University Press, 1982.

Dedmond, Francis B. "The Letters of Caroline Sturgis to Margaret Fuller." *Studies in the American Renaissance 1988.* Edited by Joel Meyerson. Charlottesville, Va.: University Press of Virginia, 201–51.

Deiss, Joseph Jay. *The Roman Years of Margaret Fuller: A Biography.* New York: Thomas Y. Crowell, 1969.

Dimock, George. *Caroline Sturgis Tappan and the Grand Tour: A Collection of 19th Century Photographs.* Catalogue of Lenox Library Association exhibition, July 10–September 11, 1982. Lenox, Mass.: Lenox Library Associates, 1982.

Edel, Leon. *Henry James: A Life.* New York: Harper and Row, 1985.

———. *Henry James: The Untried Years.* Philadelphia: Lippincott, 1953.

Elliott, Walter. *The Life of Father Hecker.* New York: Columbus Press, 1891.

Emerson, Edward Waldo. *The Early Years of the Saturday Club: 1855–1870.* Boston: Houghton Mifflin, 1918.

———. *Emerson in Concord: A Memoir.* Boston: Houghton, Mifflin, 1889.

Emerson, Ellen Tucker. *The Letters of Ellen Tucker Emerson.* Edited by Edith E. W. Gregg. 2 vols. Kent, Ohio: Kent State University Press, 1982.

———. *The Life of Lidian Jackson Emerson.* Edited by Delores Bird Carpenter. Boston: Twayne Publishers, 1980.

Emerson, Lydia Jackson. *The Selected Letters of Lidian Jackson Emerson.* Edited with an introduction by Delores Bird Carpenter. Columbia, Mo.: University of Missouri Press, 1987.

Emerson, Mary Moody. *The Selected Letters of Mary Moody Emerson.* Edited by Nancy Craig Simmons. Athens, Ga.: The University of Georgia Press, 1993.

Emerson, Ralph Waldo. *The Collected Works of Ralph Waldo Emerson.* Edited by Alfred E. Ferguson, Joseph Slater et al. 5 vols. to date. Cambridge, Mass.: Harvard University Press, 1971–.

———. *The Complete Sermons of Ralph Waldo Emerson.* Edited by Albert J. von Frank et al. 4 vols. Columbia, Mo.: University of Missouri Press, 1989–92.

———. *The Complete Works of Ralph Waldo Emerson* [Centenary Edition]. Edited by Edward Waldo Emerson and James Elliot Cabot. 12 vols. Boston: Houghton, Mifflin, 1903–4.

———. *The Early Lectures of Ralph Waldo Emerson.* Edited by Robert E. Spiller, Stephen E. Whicher, and Wallace E. Williams. 3 vols. Cambridge, Mass.: Belknap Press of Harvard University Press, 1959–72.

——. *Emerson in His Journals.* Selected and edited by Joel Porte. Cambridge, Mass.: Belknap Press of Harvard University Press, 1982.

——. *Essays and Journals.* Edited by Lewis Mumford. New York: Doubleday & Co., 1968.

——.*The Heart of Emerson's Journals.* Edited by Bliss Perry. Boston: Houghton Mifflin, 1926.

——. *The Journals and Miscellaneous Notebooks of Ralph Waldo Emerson.* Edited by William H. Gilman et al. 16 vols. Cambridge, Mass.: Harvard University Press, 1960–82.

——. *Journals of Ralph Waldo Emerson.* Edited by Edward Waldo Emerson and Waldo Emerson Forbes. 10 vols. Boston: Houghton, Mifflin, 1909–14.

——. *Letters from Ralph Waldo Emerson to a Friend, 1838–1853.* Edited by Charles Eliot Norton. Boston: Houghton, Mifflin, 1899.

——. *The Letters of Ralph Waldo Emerson.* Vols. 1–6, edited by Ralph L. Rusk; vols. 7–9, edited by Eleanor M. Tilton. New York: Columbia University Press, 1939; 1990–93.

——. *The Topical Notebooks of Ralph Waldo Emerson.* Edited by Susan Sutton Smith. 3 vols. Columbia, Mo.: University of Missouri Press, 1990.

——, and Thomas Carlyle. *The Correspondence of Emerson and Carlyle.* Edited by Joseph Slater. New York: Columbia University Press, 1964.

——, and Arthur Hugh Clough. *Emerson–Clough Letters.* Edited by Howard F. Lowry and Ralph Leslie Rusk. Cleveland, Ohio: Rowfant Club, 1934.

Engel, Mary Miller. *I Remember the Emersons.* Los Angeles: Times-Mirror, 1941.

Farrar, Eliza Rotch. *Recollections of Seventy Years.* Boston: Ticknor and Fields, 1866.

Fields, Annie Adams. *Authors and Friends.* Boston: Harper and Brothers, 1893.

Forbes, John Murray. *Letters and Recollections of John Murray Forbes.* Edited by Sarah Forbes Hughes. 2 vols. Boston: Houghton, Mifflin, 1899.

Frothingham, Octavius B. *Theodore Parker: A Biography.* Boston: James R. Osgood, 1874.

Fuller, [Sarah] Margaret. *The Letters of Margaret Fuller.* Edited by Robert N. Hudspeth. 5 vols. to date. Ithaca, N.Y.: Cornell University Press, 1983–.

——. *Love-Letters of Margaret Fuller 1845–1846.* Introduction by Julia Ward Howe. New York: B. Appleton, 1903.

——. *Margaret Fuller: American Romantic, A Selection from Her Writings and Correspondence.* Edited by Perry Miller. Garden City, N.Y.: Doubleday, 1963.

——. *Papers on Literature and Art.* New York: Wiley and Putnam, 1846.

——. *Summer on the Lakes, in 1843.* Boston: Charles C. Little and James Brown, 1844.

——. *Woman in the Nineteenth Century.* New York: Greeley and McElrath, 1845.

——. *The Writings of Margaret Fuller.* Selected and edited by Mason Wade. New York: Viking Press, 1941.

Furness, William Henry. *Records of a Lifelong Friendship, 1807–1882: Ralph Waldo Emerson and William Henry Furness.* Edited by Horace Howard Furness. Boston: Houghton Mifflin, 1910.

Gittleman, Edwin. *Jones Very: The Effective Years, 1833–1840.* New York: Columbia University Press, 1967.

Glick, Wendell P. "Thoreau and the 'Herald of Freedom.' " *New England Quarterly* 22 (June 1949): 193–204.

Gonnaud, Maurice. *An Uneasy Solitude: Individual and Society in the Work of Ralph Waldo Emerson.* Princeton: Princeton University Press, 1987.

Greeley, Horace. *Recollections of a Busy Life.* Boston: H. Brown, 1868.

Gregg, Edith E. W. "Emerson and His Children: Their Childhood Memories." *Harvard Library Bulletin* 28 (October 1980): 407–30.

Guest, Ivor Forbes. *Fanny Elssler*. Middletown, Conn.: Wesleyan Univesity Press, 1970.

Harding, Walter. *The Days of Henry Thoreau: A Biography*. New York: Knopf, 1965. Enl. ed., New York: Dover, 1982.

Haskins, David Greene. *Ralph Waldo Emerson: His Maternal Ancestors with Some Reminiscences of Him*. Boston: Cupples, Upham, 1886.

Haven, Gilbert. *Father Taylor, the Sailor Preacher*. Boston: B. B. Russell, 1872.

Hawthorne, Julian. *Nathaniel Hawthorne and His Wife*. 2 vols. Boston: James R. Osgood, 1884.

Hawthorne, Nathaniel. *The American Notebooks*. Edited by Claude M. Simpson. Columbus, Ohio: Ohio State University Press, 1972.

———. *The Centenary Edition of the Works of Nathaniel Hawthorne*. Edited by William Charvat et al. 20 vols. to date. Columbus, Ohio: Ohio State University Press, 1962–88.

———. *The Letters, 1813-1843* and *The Letters, 1843-1853*. Edited by Thomas Woodson, L. Neal Smith, Norman Holmes Pearson. Vols. 15–16 of *The Centenary Edition of the Works of Nathaniel Hawthorne*. Columbus, Ohio: Ohio State University Press, 1984–85.

———. *Letters of [Nathaniel] Hawthorne to William D. Ticknor, 1851-1864*. 2 vols. Newark, N.J.: Carteret Book Club, 1910.

———. *Love Letters of Nathaniel Hawthorne: 1839-1841*. 2 vols. Chicago: Society of the Dofobs, 1907.

Higginson, Thomas Wentworth. *Margaret Fuller Ossoli*. Boston: Houghton, Mifflin, 1884.

Holmes, Oliver Wendell. *Ralph Waldo Emerson*. Boston: Houghton, Mifflin, 1884.

Howarth, William L. *The Book of Concord: Thoreau's Life as a Writer*. New York: Viking, 1982.

Howe, M. A. DeWolfe, ed. *Memories of a Hostess: A Chronicle of Eminent Friendships Drawn Chiefly from the Diaries of Mrs. James T. Fields*. Boston: The Atlantic Monthly Press, 1922.

Hudspeth, Robert N. *Ellery Channing*. New York: Twayne Publishers, 1973.

James, Henry. *The Letters of Henry James*. Edited by Leon Edel. 4 vols. Cambridge: Belknap Press of Harvard University Press, 1974-84.

———. *Partial Portraits* (1888). London: Macmillan, 1905.

———. *Hawthorne*. London: Macmillan, 1879.

Kaplan, Justin. *Walt Whitman: A Life*. New York: Simon and Schuster, 1980.

Lathrop, Rose Hawthorne. *Memories of Hawthorne*. Boston: Houghton, Mifflin, 1897.

Lauter, Paul. "Emerson's Revisions of *Essays: First Series*." *American Literature* 33 (May 1961): 143–58.

Leyda, Jay. *The Melville Log: A Documentary Life of Herman Melville*. 2 vols. New York: Harcourt, Brace, 1951. Enp. ed., New York: Gordian Press, 1969.

Loving, Jerome. *Emerson, Whitman and the American Muse*. Chapel Hill, N.C.: University of North Carolina Press, 1982.

Lowell, James Russell. *A Fable for Critics*. New York: George P. Putnam, 1848.

———. *Letters of James Russell Lowell*. Edited by Charles Eliot Norton. 2 vols. New York: Harper's, 1894.

———. *My Study Windows*. Boston: J. R. Osgood, 1871.

———. *New Letters of James Russell Lowell*. Edited by M. A. DeWolfe Howe. New York: Harper and Brothers, 1932.

MacDonald, Allan. "A Sailor Among the Transcendentalists." *New England Quarterly* 8 (Sept. 1935): 307–19.

McAleer, John. *Ralph Waldo Emerson: Days of Encounter*. Boston: Little, Brown, 1984.

McCuskey, Dorothy. *Bronson Alcott, Teacher.* New York: Macmillan, 1940.

McDonald, John J. "Emerson and John Brown." *New England Quarterly* 44 (Summer 1971): 377–96.

———. "The Old Manse Period Canon." *Nathaniel Hawthorne Journal* (1972): 13–39.

McGill, Frederick T. Jr. *Channing of Concord: A Life of William Ellery Channing II.* New Brunswick, N.J.: Rutgers University Press, 1967.

Mellow, James R. *Nathaniel Hawthorne in His Times.* Boston: Houghton Mifflin, 1980.

Melville, Herman. *Correspondence.* Vol. 14 of *The Writings of Herman Melville.* Edited by Lynn Horth. Evanston, Chicago: Northwestern University Press and Newberry Library, 1993.

———. *The Letters of Herman Melville.* Edited by Merrell R. Davis and William H. Gilman. New Haven: Yale University Press, 1960.

Metzdorf, Robert F. "Hawthorne's Suit Against Ripley and Dana." *American Literature* 12 (1940): 235–41.

Miller, Edwin Haviland. *Salem Is My Dwelling Place: A Life of Nathaniel Hawthorne.* Iowa City: University of Iowa Press, 1991.

Miller, Perry, ed. *The American Transcendentalists: Their Prose and Poetry.* Garden City, N.Y.: Doubleday, 1957.

———. *Margaret Fuller: American Romantic.* Garden City, N.Y.: Doubleday, 1963.

———. *The Transcendentalists: An Anthology.* Cambridge, Mass.: Harvard University Press, 1950.

Myerson, Joel. *Margaret Fuller: A Descriptive Bibliography.* Pittsburgh, Pa.: University of Pittsburgh Press, 1978.

———. *Margaret Fuller: An Annotated Secondary Bibliography.* New York: Burt Franklin, 1977.

———. "Margaret Fuller's 1842 Journal: At Concord with the Emersons." *Harvard Library Bulletin* 21 (July 1973): 320–40.

———. *The New England Transcendentalists and the* Dial: *A History of the Magazine and Its Contributors.* Rutherford, N.J.: Fairleigh Dickinson University Press, 1980.

———. *Ralph Waldo Emerson: A Descriptive Bibliography.* Pittsburgh, Pa.: University of Pittsburgh Press, 1982.

———, ed. *The Transcendentalists: A Review of Research and Criticism.* New York: Modern Language Association, 1984.

Newcomb, Charles King. *The Journals of Charles King Newcomb.* Edited, with a biographical and critical introduction, by Judith Kennedy Johnson. Providence, R.I.: Brown University Press, 1946.

Newhall, Barker. *The Barker Family of Plymouth Colony and County.* Cleveland, Ohio: 1900.

Norton, Charles Eliot. *The Letters of Charles Eliot Norton.* Edited by Sara Norton and M. A. DeWolfe Howe. 2 vols. Boston: Houghton Mifflin, 1913.

———. "Walt Whitman's *Leaves of Grass.*" *Putnam's Monthly Magazine* 6 (Sept. 1855): 321–23. Rpt. in *A Leaf of Grass from Shady Hill, with a Review of Walt Whitman's "Leaves of Grass."* Edited with an introduction by Kenneth B. Murdock. Cambridge, Mass.: Harvard University Press, 1928, 27–31.

Oates, Stephen B. *To Purge This Land with Blood: A Biography of John Brown.* New York: Harper and Row, 1970. 2nd ed., Amherst, Mass.: University of Massachusetts Press, 1984.

Ossoli, Margaret Fuller. *At Home and Abroad: or, Things and Thoughts in America and Europe.* Edited by Arthur B. Fuller. Boston: Crosby, Nichols, 1856.

———. *Memoirs of Margaret Fuller Ossoli*. Edited by R. W. Emerson, W. H. Channing, and J. F. Clarke. 2 vols. Boston: Phillips, Samson, 1852.

Parker, Theodore. *Theodore Parker: An Anthology*. Edited by Henry Steele Commager. Boston: Beacon, 1960.

Paul, Sherman. *Emerson's Angle of Vision: Man and Nature in American Experience*. Cambridge, Mass.: Harvard University Press, 1952.

Peabody, Elizabeth Palmer. *Letters of Elizabeth Palmer Peabody: American Renaissance Woman*. Edited with an introduction by Bruce A. Ronda. Middletown, Conn.: Wesleyan University Press, 1984.

———. *Record of a School*. Boston: James Munroe, 1835.

Perry, Bliss. *Walt Whitman: His Life and Work*. Boston: Houghton Mifflin, 1906.

Pier, Arthur S. *Forbes: Telephone Pioneer*. New York: Dodd Mead, 1953.

Pommer, Henry F. *Emerson's First Marriage*. Carbondale, Ill.: Southern Illinois University Press, 1967.

Porte, Joel. *Representative Man: Ralph Waldo Emerson in His Time*. New York: Oxford University Press, 1979.

Redpath, James. *The Public Life of Capt. John Brown*. Boston: Thayer and Eldridge, 1860.

Richardson, Robert D. Jr. *Henry David Thoreau: A Life of the Mind*. Berkeley and Los Angeles: University of California Press, 1986.

Roosevelt, Theodore. *Theodore Roosevelt's Diaries of Boyhood and Youth*. New York: Charles Scribner's Sons, 1928.

Rusk, Ralph L. *The Life of Ralph Waldo Emerson*. New York: Charles Scribner's Sons, 1949.

Sanborn, Franklin B. *Bronson Alcott: At Alcott House, England and Fruitlands, New England (1842–1844)*. Cedar Rapids, Iowa: Torch Press, 1908.

———. *The Life and Letters of John Brown*. Boston: Roberts, 1885.

———. *The Life of Henry David Thoreau*. Boston: Houghton Mifflin, 1917.

———. *Recollections of Seventy Years*. 2 vols. Boston: Richard G. Badger, 1909.

———, ed. *The Genius and Character of Emerson*. Boston: James R. Osgood, 1885.

Sanborn, Franklin, B., and William T. Harris. *A. Bronson Alcott: His Life and Philosophy*. 2 vols. Boston: Roberts Brothers, 1893.

Saxton, Martha. *Louisa May: A Modern Biography of Louisa May Alcott*. Boston: Houghton Mifflin, 1977.

Sealts, Merton M. Jr., and Alfred R. Ferguson, eds. *Emerson's Nature: Origins, Growth, Meaning*. New York: Dodd Mead, 1969.

Shepard, Odell. *Pedlar's Progress: The Life of Bronson Alcott*. Boston: Little, Brown, 1937.

Smith, Sydney. *Wit and Wisdom of the Reverend Sydney Smith: With a Biographical Memoir and Notes by Evert A. Duyckinck* (1858). New York: A. C. Armstrong and Son, 1876, c. 1879.

Sophia Smith Collection, Tappan papers, Smith College, Northhampton, Mass.

Stern, Madeleine B. *The Life of Margaret Fuller*. New York: Dutton, 1942. 2nd ed., New York: Greenwood, 1991.

Thayer, James B. *A Western Journey with Mr. Emerson*. Boston: Little, Brown, 1884. Rpt. Port Washington, N.Y.: Kennikat Press, 1971.

Thoreau, Henry David. *The Correspondence of Henry David Thoreau*. Edited by Walter Harding and Carl Bode. New York: New York University Press, 1958.

———. *The Journal of Henry David Thoreau*. Edited by Bradford Torrey and Francis H. Allen. 14 vols. Boston: Houghton Mifflin, 1906.

———. *Letters to Various Persons*. Edited by R. W. Emerson. Boston: Ticknor and Fields, 1865.

———. *Walden*. Edited by J. Lyndon Shanley. Princeton, N.J.: Princeton University Press, 1971.

———. *A Week on the Concord and Merrimack Rivers*. Edited by Carl F. Hovde et al. Princeton, N.J.: Princeton University Press, 1980.

———. *The Writings of Henry D. Thoreau*. Edited by John C. Broderick, Elizabeth Hall Witherell et al. 7 vols. to date. Princeton, N.J.: Princeton University Press, 1971–84.

Tilton, Eleanor M. "*Leaves of Grass*: Four Letters to Emerson." *Harvard Library Bulletin* 27 (July 1979): 336–41.

———. "The True Romance of Anna Hazard Barker and Samuel Gray Ward." *Studies in the American Renaissance 1987*. Edited by Joel Myerson. Charlottesville, Va.: University Press of Virginia, 53–72.

Tolman, George. *Mary Moody Emerson*. Cambridge, Mass.: privately printed by Edward Waldo Forbes, 1929.

Traubel, Horace. *With Walt Whitman in Camden*. 6 vols. Vol. 1, Boston: Small, Maynard, 1906; vol. 2, New York: D. Appleton, 1908; vol. 3, New York: Mitchell, Kennerley, 1914; vol. 4, edited by Sculley Bradley, vol. 5, edited by Gertrude Traubel, vol. 6, edited by Gertrude Traubel and William White, Carbondale, Ill.: Southern Illinois University Press, 1953, 1964, 1982.

Trowbridge, John Townsend. *My Own Story, with Recollections of Noted Persons*. Boston and New York: Houghton, Mifflin, 1903.

Turner, Arlin. *Nathaniel Hawthorne: A Biography*. New York: Oxford University Press, 1980.

Very, Jones. *Jones Very: The Complete Poems*. Edited by Helen R. Deese. Athens, Ga.: University of Georgia Press, 1993.

———. *Essays and Poems by Jones Very*. [Edited by Ralph Waldo Emerson]. Boston: Charles C. Little and James C. Brown, 1839.

———. *Poems and Essays by Jones Very: Complete and Revised Edition*. Edited by J. F. Clarke and C. A. Bartol. New York and Boston: Houghton, Mifflin, 1886.

von Frank, Albert J. *An Emerson Chronology*. New York: G. K. Hall, 1994.

Wade, Mason. *Margaret Fuller: Whetstone of Genius*. New York: Viking, 1940.

Weiss, John. *Life and Correspondence of Theodore Parker*. 2 vols. New York: D. Appleton, 1864.

Wellisz, Leopold. *The Friendship of Margaret Fuller D'Ossoli and Adam Mickiewicz*. New York: Polish Book Importing, 1947.

Whicher, Stephen E. *Freedom and Fate: An Inner Life of Ralph Waldo Emerson*. Philadelphia: University of Pennsylvania Press, 1953.

Whitman, Walt. *Complete Poetry and Prose, and Letters*. Edited by Emory Holloway. London: Nonesuch, 1938.

———. *The Correspondence*. Edited by Edwin Haviland Miller. 6 vols. New York: New York University Press, 1961–77.

———. *Leaves of Grass: Comprehensive Reader's Edition*. Edited by Harold W. Blodgett and Sculley Bradley. New York: New York University Press, 1965.

———. *New York Dissected: A Sheaf of Recently Discovered Newspaper Articles by the Author of "Leaves of Grass."* Introduction and notes by Emory Holloway and Ralph Adimari. New York: R. R. Wilson, 1936.

———. *Prose Works 1892*. Edited by Floyd Stovall. 2 vols. New York: New York University Press, 1963–64.

Wilson, David Alec, and David Wilson MacArthur. *Carlyle in Old Age (1865–1881)*. New York: Dutton, 1927; London: K. Paul, Trench, Trubner, 1934.

Wright, Conrad, ed. *Three Prophets of Religious Liberalism: Channing, Emerson, Parker*. Boston: Beacon Press, 1961.

Zeydel, Edwin H. *Goethe, the Lyrist*. Chapel Hill, N.C.: University of North Carolina Press, 1955.

———. *Poems of Goethe: A Sequel to Goethe, the Lyrist*. New York: AMS Press, 1966.

INDEX

Grateful acknowledgment is made to the following for permission to reprint excerpts from these works:

Ralph Waldo Emerson Memorial Association for *The Letters of Ralph Waldo Emerson*, volumes 1–6, edited by Ralph L. Rusk, and volumes 7–10, edited by Eleanor M. Tilton; *The Life of Lidian Jackson Emerson* by Ellen T. Emerson; and *The Letters of Ellen Tucker Emerson*, edited by Edith E. Gregg.

Harvard University Press for *The Journals and Miscellaneous Notebooks of Ralph Waldo Emerson*, volumes 1–16, edited by William H. Gilman et al. Copyright © 1960, 1961, 1963, 1964, 1965, 1966, 1969, 1970, 1971, 1973, 1975, 1976, 1982 by the President and Fellows of Harvard College.

Trustees of the Boston Public Library for letters of Margaret Fuller.

Margaret Fuller Collection, Clifton Waller Barrett Library, Special Collections Department, University of Virginia Library, and Willard P. Fuller, Jr., for a letter of Margaret Fuller.

Collection of G. W. Haight for a letter from Margaret Fuller to Caroline Sturgis, November 16(?), 1846, appearing in *The Letters of Margaret Fuller*, edited by Robert N. Hudspeth, Cornell University Press.

The Houghton Library, Harvard University, for Margaret Fuller letters in its collection.

Manuscript Collection, The Rhode Island Historical Society, for a letter from Margaret Fuller to Sarah Helen Whitman, January 21, 1840.

Ohio State University Press for *The American Notebooks*, volume 8 of the *Centenary Edition of the Works of Nathaniel Hawthorne*, edited by Claude M. Simpson, 1972, and *The Letters, 1813–1843* and *The Letters, 1843–1853*, volumes 15 and 16 of the *Centenary Edition of the Works of Nathaniel Hawthorne*, edited by Thomas Woodson et al., 1984, 1985.

Columbia University Press for *Jones Very: The Effective Years, 1833–1840* by Edwin Gittleman. Copyright © 1967 by Columbia University Press.

Rutgers University Press for *Channing of Concord* by Frederick T. McGill, Jr. Copyright © 1967 by Rutgers, The State University.

Houghton Mifflin Company for *Nathaniel Hawthorne in His Times* by James R. Mellow. Copyright © 1980 by James R. Mellow. All rights reserved.

Georges Borchardt, Inc., for *Louisa May: A Modern Biography of Louisa May Alcott* by Martha Saxton, 1977.

Theresa W. Pratt Trust for *The Journals of Bronson Alcott*, edited by Odell Shepard, Little, Brown, 1938.

Iowa State University Press for *The Letters of A. Bronson Alcott*, edited by Richard L. Herrnstadt, 1969.

New York University Press for *The Correspondence of Henry David Thoreau*, edited by Walter Harding and Carl Bode. Copyright © 1958 by New York University.

Dover Publications, Inc., for *The Days of Henry Thoreau: A Biography* by Walter Harding, 1982.

Harvard Library Bulletin and The Houghton Library, Harvard University, for "Margaret Fuller's 1842 Journal: A Concord with the Emersons" by Joel Myerson, *Harvard Library Bulletin* 21 (July 1973).

Henry W. and Albert A. Berg Collection, The New York Public Library, Astor, Lenox, and Tilden Foundations, for letters of Sophia Peabody Hawthorne.

The Houghton Library, Harvard University, and the literary heirs of Abigail Alcott and A. Bronson Alcott for a letter from Abigail Alcott to Samuel J. May (*59M-305 [25]) and a journal of A. Bronson Alcott (*59M-308 [17]).

Ralph Waldo Emerson Memorial Association, The Houghton Library, Harvard University, and the literary heirs of Abigail Alcott for a letter from Abigail Alcott to Ralph Waldo Emerson (bMS Am 1280 [75]).

Caroline Sturgis Tappan Papers, Sophia Smith Collection, Smith College, Northampton, MA, for a letter from Caroline Sturgis Tappan to Ralph Waldo Emerson and a letter from Ralph Waldo Emerson to Caroline Sturgis Tappan.

Jones Very Collection, Clifton Waller Barrett Library, Special Collections Department, University of Virginia Library, for "The Wind-Flower" by Jones Very.

Portrait of Nathaniel Hawthorne on page four (top) of photo insert courtesy of Peabody Essex Museum, Salem, MA. All other photographs courtesy of Concord Free Public Library.

FOR THE BEST IN PAPERBACKS, LOOK FOR THE

In every corner of the world, on every subject under the sun, Penguin represents quality and variety—the very best in publishing today.

For complete information about books available from Penguin—including Puffins, Penguin Classics, and Arkana—and how to order them, write to us at the appropriate address below. Please note that for copyright reasons the selection of books varies from country to country.

In the United Kingdom: Please write to *Dept. JC, Penguin Books Ltd, FREEPOST, West Drayton, Middlesex UB7 0BR.*

If you have any difficulty in obtaining a title, please send your order with the correct money, plus ten percent for postage and packaging, to *P.O. Box No. 11, West Drayton, Middlesex UB7 0BR*

In the United States: Please write to *Consumer Sales, Penguin USA, P.O. Box 999, Dept. 17109, Bergenfield, New Jersey 07621-0120.* VISA and MasterCard holders call 1-800-253-6476 to order all Penguin titles

In Canada: Please write to *Penguin Books Canada Ltd, 10 Alcorn Avenue, Suite 300, Toronto, Ontario M4V 3B2*

In Australia: Please write to *Penguin Books Australia Ltd, P.O. Box 257, Ringwood, Victoria 3134*

In New Zealand: Please write to *Penguin Books (NZ) Ltd, Private Bag 102902, North Shore Mail Centre, Auckland 10*

In India: Please write to *Penguin Books India Pvt Ltd, 706 Eros Apartments, 56 Nehru Place, New Delhi 110 019*

In the Netherlands: Please write to *Penguin Books Netherlands bv, Postbus 3507, NL-1001 AH Amsterdam*

In Germany: Please write to *Penguin Books Deutschland GmbH, Metzlerstrasse 26, 60594 Frankfurt am Main*

In Spain: Please write to *Penguin Books S.A., Bravo Murillo 19, 1° B, 28015 Madrid*

In Italy: Please write to *Penguin Italia s.r.l., Via Felice Casati 20, I-20124 Milano*

In France: Please write to *Penguin France S.A., 17 rue Lejeune, F–31000 Toulouse*

In Japan: Please write to *Penguin Books Japan, Ishikiribashi Building, 2-5-4, Suido, Bunkyo-ku, Tokyo 112*

In Greece: Please write to *Penguin Hellas Ltd, Dimocritou 3, GR–106 71 Athens*

In South Africa: Please write to *Longman Penguin Southern Africa (Pty) Ltd, Private Bag X08, Bertsham 2013*